Chris Livesey

Cambridge International AS and A Level

Sociology

Coursebook

CAMBRIDGE
UNIVERSITY PRESS

CAMBRIDGE
UNIVERSITY PRESS

University Printing House, Cambridge CB2 8BS, United Kingdom

Cambridge University Press is part of the University of Cambridge.

It furthers the University's mission by disseminating knowledge in the pursuit of education, learning and research at the highest international levels of excellence.

www.cambridge.org

First published 2014

Printed in the United Kingdom by Latimer Trend

A catalogue record for this publication is available from the British Library

ISBN 978-1-107-67339-7 Paperback

The publisher would like to thank Mike Kirby for his expertise and invaluable contribution to the production of this book.

Contents

Introduction

Cambridge International AS and A Level Sociology has been designed and written to reflect the changes to the Cambridge International Syllabus (9699) introduced in 2013 for first examination in June and November 2014. In this respect, the text has two broad aims:

1 To help you understand exactly what is required by the structure of the new syllabus in terms of content and skills.

2 To provide content clearly focused on this structure; a central feature of the text is complete coverage of the AS and A Level syllabus.

This book aims to provide you with the knowledge and understanding required to succeed at both AS and A Level. To this end, the text can be used both for individual work or if you are part of a larger teaching group.

Content

With one or two minor exceptions, the structure of each chapter reflects the order of information as it appears in the syllabus. This allows you to track your progress through the syllabus in a logical way. Slight adjustments have been made in the order of the AS chapter 'Methods of research' and the A Level chapter 'Global development' to provide a more logical teaching and learning flow. However, the syllabus is still fully covered in these sections.

Although the chapter structures follow that of the syllabus, you may find that the units are taught in a different order. Unit 2 ('Theory and methods') provides a basic grounding in sociology that is useful for students who are new to the subject. It introduces a range of perspectives and concepts that can be helpful in understanding other parts of the syllabus. For this reason, coverage of Unit 2 appears first in this book.

AS Level consists of two compulsory units:

Unit 1: The family (Chapter 5). Here, the content focuses on three related areas: the family and wider social change; changing family roles and relationships; and the social construction of age.

Unit 2: Theory and methods (Chapters 1–4). For convenience, this unit has been divided into four chapters. Together, these cover the syllabus requirements for the complete unit and are examined in a single paper.

A Level consists of four optional units. You must study at least three of these:

Unit 3: Education (Chapter 6). First, this unit looks at education systems as part of wider social, economic and political contexts (for example, this section explains how education is linked to the economy and the state). The second part of this unit looks at what happens inside schools – the structures and processes that shape education itself and individuals within the education system.

Unit 4: Global development (Chapter 7). This unit investigates how and why societies around the world develop at different rates. In addition, the chapter examines different forms of inequality, based on concepts of class, age, gender and ethnicity. It also looks at the role of transnational organisations in cultural systems, and issues such as poverty and population growth.

Unit 5: Media (Chapter 8). This unit examines the development and role of both old and new media, from newspapers, through television and film to social networking. The chapter focuses on the significance of changing trends in ownership and control. It also looks at how different media represent social groups and the effect these media might have on personal and social behaviour.

Unit 6: Religion (Chapter 9). This unit studies religion in a social context, investigating different perspectives on religion and its relationship to social change. A range of religious organisations, from churches through new religious movements to new age and fundamentalist movements, are also examined. The chapter also includes an overview of secularisation and the debates that surround it.

Chapter 10 offers tips and techniques for exam preparation. These range from basic revision through assessment techniques, to exam structure, timing and planning. The chapter also identifies some common errors and suggests how to avoid them.

Features

In addition to providing complete coverage of the 9699 syllabus, this book includes a range of features designed to enhance your understanding of the subject. These include:

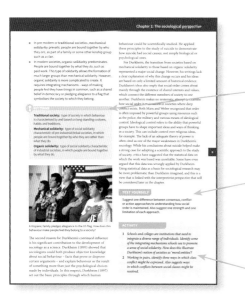

- Key terms: key concepts for the Cambridge syllabus are highlighted in green when they first appear in the text. Definitions of these terms are provided in boxes throughout the book.

- 'Test yourself' questions are short comprehension questions designed to consolidate your understanding of the topic. They could also be used as revision aids. If you are not sure of the answer, you could look back through the text, discuss with a classmate or ask your teacher for support.

- Activities appear at the end of each section within a chapter. They are mainly intended to be group exercises to encourage discussion, apply learning to specific problems and introduce different forms of learning, such as visual memory techniques.

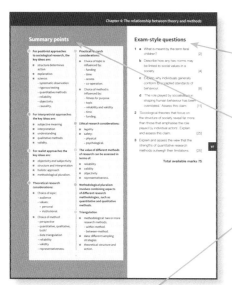

- Exam-style questions also appear at the end of each chapter. You can use these to familiarise yourself with the new exam format and to check your overall understanding and progress.

- Summary points are listed at the end of every chapter as a reminder of the key concepts that have been covered and a useful guide to revision topics.

- Bibliography: an extensive bibliography covering all the references in the text is included to enable you to explore studies in more depth.

Chapter 1:
The sociological perspective

Learning objectives

The objectives of this chapter involve understanding:

- the origins of sociology as a reasoned and rigorous study of social life
- sociology as the scientific study of social behaviour
- the uses of sociological knowledge; the role of values in sociology
- the meaning of science and different sociological approaches, positivist and interpretivist, to generating knowledge about the social world
- the difference between social and sociological problems
- the relationship between sociology and social policy
- the diversity of people's behaviour within and between societies
- different sociological explanations of social order, social control and social change.

Introduction

This chapter focuses on the idea of sociology as the study of social order, from its origins in the works of Comte, Marx, Durkheim and Weber to modern, often competing, sociological perspectives. These writers take as their starting point different conceptions of the relationship between the individual and society. The chapter also introduces ideas about cultural similarities and differences within and across societies. It explores how the research process can broaden our knowledge and understanding of the social world. This section leads to a consideration of the different uses of sociological knowledge, with a particular emphasis on the relationship between sociology and social policy.

Sociology as a reasoned and rigorous study of social life

Sociology is the study of how membership of social groups, from families through schools to workplaces, influences people's behaviour. Sociologists create factual knowledge about how and why people behave in particular ways. Facts are true, regardless of whether we believe them to be true; opinions, however, may or may not be true. The crucial difference is that factual knowledge is supported by evidence that has been systematically created and tested.

Sociologists are not interested in facts for their own sake. They are interested in how facts are:

- created: how to produce knowledge that is superior to simple opinion
- linked: how one fact connects to another to create an overall picture of 'social reality'.

This involves developing theories that explain how and why things are connected. We can only explain facts by constructing possible explanations (theories) and then testing those theories against *known* facts.

Origins

The end of the 17th century was notable in Europe for great **cultural** upheavals. At this time, intellectuals and scientists such as Sir Isaac Newton (1643–1727) began to question the prevailing view of the world, which was based on religious faith, magical superstition, custom and tradition. This period is called 'The Enlightenment' and it marked the first attempt to challenge traditional **beliefs** through reason and science. Enlightenment thinkers believed that scientific knowledge could help society develop from its superstitious past to a reasoned future. Alongside these cultural challenges to the established religious and academic order, the French Revolution (1789) provided a strong political challenge. The monarchy and the aristocracy that ruled one of the most powerful nations in the world were overthrown by republican forces.

A third source of disruption was the economic changes introduced by the Industrial Revolution. These changes included the development of factories and machine-based production processes that began around the middle of the 18th century in Britain and parts of Europe.

Comte

It was against this background of change that the French philosopher and mathematician Auguste Comte (1798–1857) raised the question of how **social order** was created and maintained. Comte argued the case for a **scientific method (positivism)** through which the 'laws of social development' could be discovered.

KEY TERMS

Culture: the 'way of life' of a particular group. This is normally defined in terms of material culture, or the objects people produce, and non-material culture – the ideas and beliefs they create.

Beliefs: ideas that are accepted as true, whether or not they are supported by evidence.

Social order: the behavioural patterns and regularities established by societies that make social action possible.

Scientific method: a way of generating knowledge about the world through objective, systematic and controlled research. The hypothetico-deductive model is an example of a scientific method.

Positivism: a methodology based on the principle that *it is possible* and *desirable* to study the social world in broadly the same way that natural scientists study the natural world.

In this respect, Comte (1830) argued that all human societies passed through three stages:

1 the theological, where order was based on religious beliefs and controls
2 the metaphysical, a 'transition phase' characterised by upheaval and disorder, where the old religious order was challenged by the emergence of science

3 the positive, where science and reason revealed the nature of the social world and replaced religion as the basis of social order.

Auguste Comte (1798–1857)

Comte stated that the scientific basis of social order could be revealed through a new science of social development called *La Sociologie* (sociology). Similar 'positivist' principles had been successfully applied in the natural sciences, such as physics and chemistry, to understand development in the natural world.

Marx

Comte adopted a 'consensus' perspective, which stressed that social order was created and maintained through co-operation. However, Comte's contemporary, the German philosopher and economist Karl Marx (1818–83), had a different perspective on the question of social order. For Marx, order was created and maintained by conflict, not co-operation. He argued that social development had passed through four epochs or time periods:

- primitive communism
- ancient society
- feudal, or pre-industrial society
- capitalist or industrial society.

Each time period was characterised by a different type of economic relationship. In feudal society the relationship was between lord and peasant, while under **capitalism** it

 KEY TERM

Capitalism: an economic system based on the pursuit of private profit. Capitalism's defining relationship is between employer and employee (owner and non-owner).

was between owner/employer and non-owner/employee. These relationships were always characterised by conflict because they were based on the domination of one group over another. In capitalist societies, for example, the dominant group was the bourgeoisie – those who owned the means of economic production, such as land, factories and machines. The proletariat, the vast majority, owned nothing but their ability to work (their labour power), which they exchanged for money.

TEST YOURSELF

Suggest one way people co-operate to create order in your society.

The class conflict between the bourgeoisie and the proletariat was one of many ideas that Marx introduced that remains significant in sociology today. Marx also believed that social order is maintained through a mixture of force and persuasion. For example, people can be controlled through violence and the threat of imprisonment or even death. People can also be persuaded to behave in an orderly way through, for example, religious teachings that encourage belief in a higher power and an individual's predetermined place in the world.

Another significant idea that flows from class conflict is class inequality. This is the idea that in capitalist societies one small group owns most of the wealth, while the vast majority owns little or nothing. The idea of class inequality re-emerged recently in the various Occupy movements around the world, where the wealth and power of the 'top 1 per cent' was contrasted with that of the 'bottom 99 per cent'. The Occupy movements involved protests against social and economic inequality in countries around the globe, from the USA to China, Mexico and Nigeria, and sought to distribute power and wealth more evenly.

Marx believed that inequality was inextricably linked to stratification – the ranking of different social classes in order of their wealth, power and influence. In this respect, power is a significant sociological concept. For Marx, power came primarily from economic ownership. Those who controlled economic resources were also powerful across all areas of society, from politics to religion to the media.

One strength of Marx's work is the contribution it makes to understanding the role of conflict in bringing about social change. Marx also showed how competition for scarce economic resources can have a significant influence on the way societies are organised. However, Marx has been criticised for placing too great an emphasis on the role of economic factors in shaping social institutions and the way people behave. Writing primarily about class conflict, Marx fails to recognise the importance of other forms of conflict that may divide a society and lead to social change, such as conflict between religious groups and between the sexes. Marx's ideas can also be seen as 'deterministic'. The behaviour of the individual is explained in terms of the impact of wider social forces and Marx gives little consideration to the idea that the individual might choose to act in ways that are different to those directed by the economic structure of society.

Weber

A third major theorist is the German sociologist Max Weber (1864–1920), who was concerned with **social change** in the form of how societies modernised. For example, **Weberian theory** examined how and why pre-industrial societies based on agricultural production, powerful feudal lords and a relatively powerless peasantry developed into industrial societies based on manufacturing and various forms of political democracy.

KEY TERMS

Social change: on a macro level, social change involves a major shift in the political, economic or cultural order (such as the change from feudalism to capitalism or pre-modern to modern society). On a micro level it can refer to everyday changes in political, economic or cultural relationships.

Weberian theory: a sociological perspective, deriving from the work of Max Weber, focused on understanding and explaining social action. Contemporary forms of Weberian sociology are usually expressed as interactionist sociology.

Weber (1905) argued that social development, once started, followed a process of modernisation. Features of this process included:

- industrialisation
- urbanisation
- rationalisation: behaviour and social organisation based on bureaucratic scientific principles.

Weber's theory of social action (1922) stated that social change is the result of individuals and groups acting purposefully. For example, change could be brought about by the behaviour of charismatic leaders, such as Jesus Christ (Christianity) or Mohammad (Islam), who influence others through the strength of their personality. In a wider context, Weber (1905) argued that modernisation in Europe was fuelled by the ideas and principles of the Calvinist (Protestant) religion.

Weber's ideas can be seen as a useful counter to the economic determinism in Marx's work. Whereas Marx felt that social change was driven primarily by economic forces, Weber stated that other factors also contributed. For example, political struggles, ideas and belief systems, demographic changes, and developments in science and forms of government could all have an influence in transforming society. Weber argued that each social change has to be analysed separately in order to identify its causes; he rejected the idea that economic forces are always the most significant factor in social change. Like Marx, Weber saw that conflict is of great importance in understanding how societies are organised and operate. He believed that social class is often a source of conflict – particularly in capitalist societies – but that economic relations are not the *only* source of conflict in society.

Durkheim

The French sociologist Emile Durkheim (1857–1917) followed in the general consensus tradition established by Comte. Durkheim's ideas remain influential in the theory and practice of sociology to this day, for two reasons.

Firstly, Durkheim argued that societies could only be fully understood in terms of the relationship between their various institutions. These institutions are patterns of shared behaviour that persist over time, such as families, the workplace, religion, education and politics. Understanding the relationship between institutions might, for example, involve looking at how and why the family is connected to the workplace. Durkheim felt that all forms of sociological analysis faced a fundamental problem: understanding what holds a mass of individuals together as a society. His solution was to regard social systems as 'moral entities' – something to which people feel they belong and to which they owe allegiance.

In Durkheim's view, society is an entity that exists in its own right, beyond the ideas, hopes and desires of its individual members. Order is based on common agreement about the things a society, and by extension every individual in that society, thinks are important. (Later functionalist sociologists called this type of agreement 'value consensus'.) For Durkheim (1895), therefore, societies did not just 'exist'; people had to develop social solidarity, a belief they belonged to a larger group:

KEY TERM

Value consensus: agreement about the things a society, and by extension individuals within that society, thinks are important.

- In pre-modern or **traditional societies**, **mechanical solidarity** prevails: people are bound together by who they *are*, as part of a family or some other kinship group such as a clan.
- In modern societies, **organic solidarity** predominates. People are bound together by what they *do*, such as paid work. This type of solidarity allows the formation of much larger groups than mechanical solidarity. However, organic solidarity is more complicated to create. It requires integrating mechanisms – ways of making people feel they have things in common, such as a shared belief in democracy or pledging allegiance to a flag that symbolises the society to which they belong.

KEY TERMS

Traditional society: type of society in which behaviour is characterised by and based on long-standing customs, habits and traditions.

Mechanical solidarity: type of social solidarity characteristic of pre-industrial/tribal societies, in which people are bound together by who they are rather than what they do.

Organic solidarity: type of social solidarity characteristic of industrial societies, in which people are bound together by what they do.

A Hispanic family pledges allegiance to the US flag. How does this behaviour make people feel they belong to a society?

The second reason for Durkheim's continued influence is his significant contribution to the development of sociology as a science. Durkheim (1895) showed that sociologists could both produce objective knowledge about social behaviour – facts that prove or disprove certain arguments – and explain behaviour as the result of something more than just the psychological choices made by individuals. In this respect, Durkheim (1897) set out the basic principles through which human

behaviour could be scientifically studied. He applied these principles to the study of suicide to demonstrate how suicide had social causes, not simply biological or psychological ones.

For Durkheim, the transition from societies based on mechanical solidarity to those based on organic solidarity represented a major social change. However, his writings lack a clear explanation of why this change occurs and his ideas are based on only a limited amount of historical evidence. Durkheim's ideas also imply that social order comes about mainly through the existence of shared interests and values, which connect the different members of society to one another. Durkheim makes no systematic attempt to examine how social order is maintained in societies where deep conflict exists. Both Marx and Weber recognised that order is often imposed by powerful groups using resources such as the police, the military and various means of ideological control. Ideological control refers to the ability that powerful groups have to shape important ideas and ways of thinking in a society. This can include control over religious ideas, for example. The lack of an adequate theory of power is often cited as one of the major weaknesses in Durkheim's sociology. While his conclusions about suicide helped make a strong case for adopting a scientific approach to the study of society, critics have suggested that the statistical data on which the work was based was unreliable. Some have even argued that this data was wrongly applied by Durkheim. Using statistical data as a basis for sociological research may be more problematic than Durkheim imagined, and this is a view that is linked with the interpretivist perspective that will be considered later in the chapter.

TEST YOURSELF

Suggest one difference between consensus, conflict or action approaches to understanding how social order is maintained. Also suggest one strength and one limitation of each approach.

ACTIVITY

1. Schools and colleges are institutions that need to integrate a diverse range of individuals. Identify some of the integrating mechanisms schools use to promote a sense of social solidarity. How does this illustrate Durkheim's notion of societies as 'moral entities'?

2. Working in pairs, identify three ways in which class conflict might be expressed. Also suggests ways in which conflicts between social classes might be resolved.

Sociology as a science: positivist, interpretivist and postmodernist perspectives

One way in which sociologists try to develop factual information is to adopt a scientific approach to evidence (*data*) collection, testing and analysis. This section outlines three perspectives relating to sociology as a science, but before looking at these perspectives, it is important to understand what we mean by 'science' in this context.

Defining science

Science is a way of producing a particular kind of knowledge, one that is factual and objective rather than based on opinion, guesswork or faith. Popper (1934), for example, argues that science 'involves identifying a problem to study, collecting information about it and offering an explanation for it. All this is done as systematically as possible.' Science, therefore, is a methodology – a way of producing knowledge that has two main qualities:

1 It is reliable. This refers to the idea that it is possible to check the accuracy of a piece of research by repeating (*replicating*) it to see if we get the same, or very similar, results.

2 It is valid. Data is only useful if it actually measures or describes what it claims to measure or describe. It is possible to measure the extent of crime using government crime statistics. However, the validity of these statistics may be limited if they only record crimes that are reported to the police because many crimes go unreported.

So, a scientific methodology encompasses certain procedural and ethical rules that should be followed in order to 'do science'.

Procedural rules

Scientific knowledge is created by following a set of *procedures*, agreed by the scientific community, that govern how data can be collected and analysed. Popper's (1934) **hypothetico-deductive method** is a standard example of a scientific procedure. A scientific procedure generally begins with a **hypothesis** or research question. This question must be tested or answered by the systematic

> **KEY TERMS**
>
> **Hypothetico-deductive method:** positivist research design based on the development and systematic testing of hypotheses.
>
> **Hypothesis:** statement or question that can be systematically tested.

collection, presentation and analysis of data. A crucial idea here is that any conclusions drawn from scientific research have not been disproven or shown to be false in the course of testing them against the available evidence. This procedure gives scientific knowledge greater plausibility because it is based on tested facts rather than untested opinions. It also gives this knowledge a crucial quality: the ability to make predictive statements. Scientific knowledge means we can say with a level of certainty that something will happen in the future.

> **TEST YOURSELF**
>
> Suggest one reason why testing is important for the generation of scientific knowledge.

Ethical rules (a scientific ethos)

To ensure that scientists follow the procedures outlined above, rather than making up their results, Merton (1942) argued that a scientific ethos is required. There must be rules governing the general conditions that research must satisfy in order to both attain and maintain scientific status. Science has to be:

1 Universal: knowledge is evaluated using objective, universally agreed, criteria. Personal values play no part in this process and criticism of a scientist's work should focus on the **falsification** of their conclusions or identifying weaknesses in the research process.

> **KEY TERM**
>
> **Falsification:** the principle that scientific theories should be framed in such a way that they can be disproved (falsified).

2 Communal: scientific knowledge is 'public knowledge' that must be freely shared within the scientific community. Scientists must, for example, be able to build on the work done by other scientists. This inspires scientists to develop new ideas based on those of other scientists, causing scientific understanding to advance on a *cumulative* basis. By making their work available for peer review, scientists also accept that scientific knowledge cannot be taken 'on trust'. Other scientists must be free to replicate their work, which requires detailed knowledge of the original research.

3 Disinterested: the main responsibility of the scientist is the pursuit of knowledge. While scientists should be recognised for their achievements and rewarded for their efforts, they should not have a personal stake,

6

financial or otherwise, in the outcome of their research. If the researcher was not disinterested, there would be a risk of **researcher bias**, calling the validity of the research into question.

4   Sceptical: nothing is beyond criticism. The scientific community must continually evaluate knowledge because this questioning process contributes to the development of human understanding. For Merton, this 'sceptical attitude' represented the main way in which scientific knowledge differed from other forms of knowledge, such as religious faith. Science is 'true' only because it has not yet been disproved. Faith, however, is considered by believers to be self-evidently true; it cannot be disproved.

We can develop these general ideas about how sociologists produce scientific knowledge by outlining two different perspectives: positivism and **interpretivism**.

> **KEY TERMS**
>
> **Researcher bias:** condition in which the presence or behaviour of the researcher introduces uncontrolled variables into the research, making it unreliable or invalid.
>
> **Interpretivism:** methodology based on the principle that social behaviour can only be understood subjectively, by understanding how people interpret situations and, by so doing, give them meaning. Participant observation is a classic interpretivist method.

How is scientific knowledge different from non-scientific knowledge?

Positivism

Positivism is based on the idea that it is both *possible* and *desirable* to study the social world in broadly the same way that natural scientists study the natural world. Positivist methodology (the rules governing how we should study social behaviour) has a number of features.

Knowledge is created by constructing and testing hypotheses, which are broadly defined as questions to which answers are required. Such questions take the form of a testable relationship between two or more things. A simple example is the question; 'Does poverty cause crime?' Testing is crucial because the objective is to *disprove* a hypothesis ('poverty *does not* cause crime'), because if a hypothesis cannot be falsified, it might be true.

The purpose of science is to discover objective knowledge, so sociologists must be personally objective. The research process must not be influenced by the researcher's values, beliefs, opinions or prejudices. This is the idea of **value-freedom**. To avoid biasing the data-collection process, the scientist should not participate in the behaviour being studied but merely observe it.

> **KEY TERM**
>
> **Value-freedom:** general principle that the conduct and findings of the research process should not be influenced by the values of the researcher.

In general, the positivist approach involves the ability to quantify (express in numerical/statistical form) and measure behaviour. Therefore, scientific knowledge is:

- factual
- objective
- evidence-based
- testable.

Non-scientific knowledge is based on:

- opinion
- guesswork
- untested assumptions
- faith.

Interpretivism

Interpretivism is sometimes called 'anti-positivism' because it involves a different approach to research. Interpretivists argue that different people in different situations understand, or 'interpret', the social world in different ways. As a result, sociologists can only describe reality from the viewpoint of those who create and define it.

Harris (2005a) captures the difference between the two methodologies when he notes that positivists use terms such as 'cause', 'law' or 'fact' to convey the idea that human behaviour is governed by forces that the individual social actor is powerless to resist.

7

Interpretivists, however, argue that people are different from inanimate objects because they have consciousness – an awareness of both themselves and the world in which they live. The ability to think, reflect and act, rather than simply *react*, makes people very different from inanimate objects. This means that people cannot be studied in the same way we study plants or rocks. The scientific study of living, thinking beings, therefore, requires a more subtle and flexible approach, in which social behaviour is described in terms of the meanings and interpretations people give to behaviour.

Essentially, positivism explains people's behaviour 'from without' (not interacting with the people and behaviour being studied). In contrast, interpretivist explanations are developed 'from within' (how people understand the behaviour in which they are involved). Interpretivism suggests that sociologists should take advantage of the human ability to empathise – to 'take the role of the other' and experience the world in the way it is experienced by those being researched. For example, to truly understand what it means to be homeless, the researcher should become homeless. This practice allows sociologists to gain a vital insight into why people behave as they do.

Interpretivists argue that sociology cannot predict the behaviour of conscious human beings in the same way that physics can predict the changes that affect inanimate objects. Interpetivism states that the behavioural rules in a society are determined by context – they change depending on the situation in which people find themselves. For example, if a teacher tells a student to 'be quiet', the student's response will vary depending on whether the instruction was given in the classroom or in the street. How people react to the behaviour of others depends, therefore, on their understanding of the social context in which that behaviour takes place.

Interpretivism focuses on the collection of qualitative data – information that tells the researcher something about the experiences and feelings of the people being studied. Qualitative research is less reliable than its quantitative counterpart, because it is impossible to replicate accurately. However, it has potentially much greater validity because it can reveal much more about how and why people live their lives in particular ways.

For these reasons, interpretivist research follows a different set of methodological rules than positivist research. It uses what Oberg (1999) characterises as an 'emergent research design' built around four ideas.

1 Planning: a research issue is identified and a 'research question' takes shape.

2a Data collection: this research design is non-linear; it does not begin with a hypothesis and end with confirmation or rejection. The researcher is not looking for definitive answers, so a research question is explored from different perspectives, such as those of the people being researched or of the researcher themselves. If, as Firestone (1987) suggests, 'reality is socially constructed through individual or collective definitions of the situation', the researcher must use a research design that offers the greatest opportunities to capture this 'subjective sense of reality'.

Where positivist research is 'goal-based' – the objective being to test whether a hypothesis is true or false – Lindauer (2005) argues that interpretivist research is 'goal-free'. The researcher can explore whatever they or the people they are studying feel is important or interesting. In this respect, interpretivist research is emergent: it 'takes shape as data collection and analysis proceed'. Positivist research design is rigid, strong and directs the researcher through every stage of the process. In contrast, the exploratory framework is flexible, weak and bends to take account of new research ideas and developments.

Emergent (exploratory) research model

2b Data analysis: while attempts may be made to categorise data or sort it into a logical, descriptive story (*narrative*), Schultz et al. (1996) argue that data analysis actually takes place *throughout* the research process, rather than *after* data has been collected. This involves a 'feedback loop', where the analysis of collected data is used to inform *further* data collection, which in turn informs *further* analysis. Where there is no requirement to collect data to test a hypothesis, analysis is both descriptive and seen from the viewpoint of both researcher and researched.

3 Evaluation: where positivist research involves the researcher making judgements about what data to collect and drawing conclusions about whether a

hypothesis is true or false, interpretivist research is generally non-judgemental. The reader is left to draw their own conclusions. As Firestone (1987) suggests, the main objective is to 'help the reader understand' how people *see* their world and situation, or, as Schwandt (2002) puts it, social research involves not so much a 'problem to be solved … as a dilemma or mystery that requires interpretation and self-understanding'.

Identify two differences between positivist and interpretivist approaches. Also suggest one strength and one limitation of each approach.

Postmodernism

Both positivists and interpretivists believe that it is possible to collect objective data and, by so doing, to make reliable and valid statements about behaviour. **Postmodernism** is slightly different in that it is not a scientific methodology. As Usher and Edwards (1994) argue, it is 'a different way of seeing and working, rather than a fixed body of ideas, a clearly worked out position or a set of critical methods and techniques'. Postmodernism is a critical worldview based on the idea that people construct stories (*narratives*) through which to make sense of the world. These personal narratives are neither true nor false; they simply *are* and can, of course, be revealed by sociological research. However, of greater interest here is the associated concept of metanarratives – the 'big stories' a society constructs to explain something about the nature of the world. Examples of metanarratives include religions (such as Buddhism or Islam), political philosophies (such as socialism or conservatism), nationalities (Pakistani, Mauritian or Nigerian for example) and science.

KEY TERM

Postmodernism: microsociological perspective that rejects the modernist claim that the social world can be understood rationally and empirically. Focus is on understanding how people construct personal narratives (stories), through which they make sense of the world.

At different times and in different societies, different metanarratives explaining 'how the world works' come to the fore. In pre-industrial (or pre-modern) societies,

religion is the dominant metanarrative. In industrial (or modern) societies, science is increasingly prominent as it challenges, and in some respects replaces, religious explanations of the world. Postmodern societies (those that develop 'after modern societies'), however, are characterised by what Lyotard (1979) calls an 'incredulity towards metanarratives'. For a variety of reasons, people stop regarding these 'big stories' as believable or sustainable.

It is important to note that postmodernism is not 'anti-science'; rather, it argues that the significance of metanarratives in not whether they are true or false, but how people view them. From this position, postmodernism examines 'science as metanarrative' – as a worldview struggling to establish its leadership (*hegemony*) over other metanarratives. Accordingly, postmodernism suggests a range of practical and theoretical criticisms.

Theoretical criticisms focus on ideas such as **objectivity**. For example, Polyani (1958) argues that 'all observation is theory-dependent'. What he means is that to understand what we are seeing, we must already know what it is. To observe a table we must already have a theory that describes what it looks like. This casts doubt on positivist versions of science, in which theoretical explanations are *produced* by observations tested during the research process. Postmodernism also questions positivist conceptions of social reality as something waiting to be discovered (just as something like electricity or gravity existed before science discovered it). Postmodernism, like interpretivism, argues that knowledge about the social world is actively created by people going about their daily lives; the world cannot exist independently of their activities.

KEY TERM

Objectivity: freedom from personal or institutional bias.

Postmodernists do, however, include interpretivism in this criticism. Interpretivists claim to actively *create* knowledge rather than merely revealing its existence. This follows because according to postmodernists, it is impossible to study people in small groups without changing their behaviour in some way. The act of 'doing research' – whether it involves asking people questions (positivism) or participating in the behaviour being researched (interpretivism) – changes that behaviour.

9

Does participating in the behaviour you are studying change that behaviour?

ACTIVITY

Postmodernists suggest that people no longer view science and scientists as beneficial bringers of progress. Working in a pair or small group, identify as many positive or negative aspects of science as you can. Use these ideas as a basis for arguing for and against the extent to which you think people see science as a broadly beneficial or broadly harmful enterprise.

Sociological research is not, therefore, getting at 'the truth'; it merely presents different *versions* of truth. The only way to decide between them is by making subjective judgements. To decide if one version is superior to another – i.e. that it has a greater claim to 'truth' or 'validity' – we must measure each version against certain criteria. For example, based on the criteria of 'objective testing and proof', science is superior to religion. However, if we change the criteria to 'faith', then religion is a superior truth to science. For postmodernists, therefore, concepts such as truth are inherently subjective because they are based on power relationships. Those with the power to define the criteria against which the status of knowledge is measured effectively decide what is true.

Postmodernists have also criticised the association between scientific knowledge and 'progress' – the idea that science improves people's lives. These critics claim that science is not necessarily a dispassionate, objective 'search for truth'. As Campbell (1996) has suggested, science can also be seen 'as the vanguard of European exploitation, a discipline run amok, instigators of nuclear and other weapons systems, the handmaiden of big business and the defilers of nature'. These ideas force us to consider the notion of a scientific ethos, with Prelli (1989) questioning the extent to which scientists actually conform to a 'community of values'. As Martinson et al. (2005) discovered, scientific fraud appears widespread; 33 per cent of 3,200 US scientists 'confessed to various kinds of misconduct – such as claiming credit for someone else's work, or changing results because of pressure from a study's sponsor'.

The uses of sociological knowledge: the role of values in sociology

The role of values

Earlier in this chapter, we suggested that sociological knowledge differed from other forms of knowledge – from journalism, through personal experience to everyday conversation and thinking – because it deals in facts. To establish sociological knowledge, data is collected and then analysed or tested objectively. In other words, the data collected and presented is 'value-free' – it has not been influenced by the values, beliefs or prejudices of the researcher. More correctly, it is value-neutral, since it is not possible to truly 'act without values'. The best we can do is recognise the various points at which values potentially intrude into the research process and adjust our research strategy to limit or neutralise their effect. It is possible to outline a range of points at which values potentially intrude into the research process.

Research considerations

To carry out research, sociologists have to make certain practical choices. Researchers must choose a topic, and decisions about who or what to study are influenced by their personal values. For example, while Goffman (1961) chose to study inmates in an asylum, Caplan (2006) chose to study changes in food consumption in Tanzania and Chennai in southern India. These values will also determine whether a researcher studies the activities of the powerful – as in Pearce's (1998) study of corporate criminality in the chemical industry – or the relatively powerless. Davis (1985), for example, studied the social processes involved in becoming a prostitute. In addition, these choices are influenced by personal views about danger and difficulty. For example, powerful people tend to value their privacy, so gaining access to their world may not be easy.

Topic choice is also influenced by funding considerations. Those paying for the research may not only influence *what* is studied but also *how* it is studied. This situation raises ethical questions (see below) about whether a researcher should be held responsible for the purposes to which their research is put. For example, 'Project Camelot' was research funded by the US government and military in the 1960s, designed to influence internal politics and development in Chile. Solovey (2001) argues that the proposed involvement of sociological researchers in the project was ethically questionable.

Decisions about the method of research used are also influenced by values because they inform a researcher's beliefs about how best to achieve reliability and validity in sociological research. As we have seen, different sociologists have different ideas about the respective value of quantitative and qualitative data. Where questions are asked of a **respondent**, judgements are made about who to question, what to ask and how that person is permitted to respond. Positivists may prefer to limit respondent choice by giving them a list of answers from which to choose – perhaps closed questions, where the answers are easy to quantify. Interpretivists may encourage a respondent to answer in their own words by asking open-ended questions. Values also influence data analysis: the researcher must make decisions about what data to include and what to exclude from the completed research.

KEY TERM

Respondent: a person who is the subject of a research process or who responds to the research.

Coser (1977) argues that while choice is always value-relevant (influenced by values), once choices about what to study and how to study it have been made, value-neutrality involves the researcher *acknowledging* their values. Sociologists should clearly state the value-relevant assumptions in their work and make explicit the values they hold so these assumptions may be questioned, challenged or changed by other researchers.

TEST YOURSELF

What is the difference between value-freedom and value-neutrality?

The uses of sociological knowledge

The uses of sociological knowledge are many and varied. The section below looks at some of the contrasting ways in which this knowledge has been applied.

In classical sociology, knowledge involved the development of grand theories that sought to explain ideas such as social order and change:

- Marx (1867) developed theories about capitalism, economic and social exploitation and inequality.
- Weber (1905) developed theories of modernisation.
- Durkheim (1893) explored the social forces that produced and inhibited change.

More recently, the focus has moved onto a range of *social issues*:

- **Feminism** highlighted the effects of patriarchy on **gender** relationships – work that indirectly contributed to the development of social policies in Europe and North America relating to issues such as sexual (and, for black feminists in particular, racial) discrimination and equal pay.
- Townsend and Abel-Smith's (1965) UK poverty research also changed the way governments defined poverty. There was a move away from definitions of an absolute poverty line based on minimum nutritional needs, towards a relative definition that took account of 'minimum expected living standards' in a particular society.
- In a global context, research has started to focus on areas such as the social and environmental costs of development. In 1984, for example, a gas explosion at the US-owned Union Carbide plant in Bhopal, India, caused nearly 4,000 deaths. More widely, there is an increasing sociological interest in the issues raised by economic, political and cultural forms of globalisation. Examples of this include the convergence of global (capitalist) economic systems, the development of large-scale political communities, such as the European Community, and the various forms of changes that arise from the meeting and mixing of different cultural ideas and behaviours.

KEY TERMS

Feminism: a broad range of approaches dealing with male–female relationships from the perspective of the latter.

Gender: the social characteristics different societies assign to individuals based on an understanding of their biological or social differences. Where biological sex refers to ideas like male and female, gender refers to ideas about masculinity and femininity.

In this respect, the uses of sociological knowledge have evolved to encompass things such as contributing to and informing public debates – making people aware of social issues and highlighting different perspectives. For example, Cohen's (1972) concept of moral panic and Wilkins' (1964) description of a deviancy amplification process – whereby relatively minor deviant acts can turn into criminal social problems – have arguably become part of mainstream discussions about crime and deviance over the past 50 years.

> ### TEST YOURSELF
>
> Summarise the change in focus of ideas about the uses of sociological knowledge over the past 150 years.

One contemporary use of social knowledge is in relation to **social policy** (see below). While sociology does occasionally make direct inputs into policy through research commissioned by government departments and agencies, its contribution is more frequently felt indirectly. Sociological research can, for example, highlight particular social issues. Townsend and Abel-Smith (1965) challenged the accepted belief that poverty had been largely eradicated in the UK; indirectly, their research led to a range of policy initiatives designed to limit the extent of poverty. A further indirect area of influence is the way in which sociological knowledge can inform how governments define and measure particular issues and ideas. In recent years, for example, criticism of the validity of official crime statistics has led to the development of measures with greater validity, such as the UK British Crime Surveys.

> **KEY TERM**
>
> **Social policy:** a set of ideas and actions pursued by governments to meet a particular social objective. A housing policy, for example, sets out the various criteria required to solve a perceived social problem.

By collecting comparative evidence about different societies, sociologists may also help to influence social policy. For example, Stephens (2009) compared the UK and Nordic (Scandinavian) welfare models to explore ideas about social inclusion and exclusion reflected in a range of UK government policies over the previous 10 years, from childcare to welfare benefits

and care of the elderly. Another indirect role involves the testing of social policies through sociological research. The intention here is to monitor and evaluate the success of the policies in tackling particular issues. A further contribution sociology makes to the evaluation process is an understanding of the intended and unintended consequences of social policy. Stephens, for example, states that an intended consequence of recent developments in the UK welfare model has been to use means-testing to allocate help where it is most needed, which largely excludes the middle classes. However, an unintended consequence has been to increase feelings of social exclusion among both the very poor and the middle classes by reducing contact between them.

> ### ACTIVITY
>
> *In small groups, identify possible examples of sociological research that you think are always, sometimes or never unethical. Each group should share its examples with the other groups and briefly justify its categorisation of each research example. What conclusions can be drawn from this about the role of values in sociological research?*

Sociology and social policy: the differences between sociological problems and social problems

Sociological and social problems

The difference between a 'social' and 'sociological' problem is significant. It affects how we understand the sociological enterprise, the nature and purpose of social policy and the contribution of sociologists to such policies.

A variety of behaviours, including crime, poverty and unemployment, have the potential to be considered **social problems**. However, Carter (2001) suggests that behaviour

> **KEY TERM**
>
> **Social problem:** behaviour seen to 'cause public friction and/or private misery', usually involving some form of 'public outcry or call for action' (Stanley, 2004). A social problem is always defined from the perspective of the powerful.

is only 'a problem' when it is defined as such 'according to the beliefs and values of some influential or dominant group in society'. A social problem, therefore, is behaviour of which powerful social groups disapprove. This suggests that it is a relative concept – what may be considered a social problem by one group may not be seen as such by another.

Sociological problems fall into two broad categories. The first is the idea that societies have to solve certain fundamental problems – for example, food, shelter, socialisation – if they are to survive. Issues such as the nature of social order, social control and social change are, therefore, *sociological* problems but not necessarily *social* problems. Some sociologists apply a different definition to sociological problems. Willis (2011), for example, suggests that a sociological problem is simply a question 'that demands explanation'. By this definition, social problems and sociological problems can sometimes be the same (synonymous). In general terms, though, sociological problems are considered in light of how and why behaviour comes to be defined as a social problem in the first place.

An example of this distinction is provided by the concept of 'disability'. Adomaitiene (1999) notes how 'the disabled' face a number of *social problems*, from discrimination and lack of facilities to unsuitable building environments. In addition, 'the disabled' are frequently labelled, especially in the media, as a social problem in themselves. A sociological problem here might be why discrimination occurs or how disability is constructed as a social problem. If sociologists simply accepted that their role was to provide solutions to social problems and a social problem was whatever powerful people said it was, then the role of sociology would be fundamentally different.

It may not be the sociologist's job to solve social problems, but sociological research can have practical, real-world applications that help us understand and deal with social problems. Painter and Farrington's (1997) study of the relationship between street lighting and crime pointed out that the better lit an area the less crime it experienced. This not only addressed the sociological problem of how changes to the physical environment alter individual behaviour, it also suggested solutions to a social problem.

How is the social problem of crime different from the sociological problem of crime?

Sociology and social policy

Calvert and Calvert (1992) define social policy as 'the main principles under which the government directs economic resources to meet specific social needs', such as housing, education, crime prevention and help for the elderly.

Social policy is an area where social and sociological problems frequently meet. However, the distinction between social and sociological problems is not simply academic. If sociologists think only in terms of social problems they risk over-identifying with a particular social group – those to whom certain types of behaviour are problems. This potentially affects value-neutrality. If sociologists simply accept the 'definitions of the powerful' they risk failing to investigate the possible role of these groups in *creating* social problems.

In over-identifying with the interests of the powerful, sociologists can be accused of being agents of **social control**, researching ways to uphold the *status quo*. This reduces the study of human behaviour to a narrow, 'problem-based' perspective and raises questions about the

13

TEST YOURSELF

Briefly explain the difference between a social and a sociological problem.

KEY TERM

Social control: the various mechanisms, such as rewards and punishments, that individuals and societies use to maintain order.

scope of sociological research. For example, Mills (1959) argued that an 'unimaginative view' of sociology as 'solving social problems' reduces sociology to 'the accumulation of facts for the purpose of facilitating administrative decisions'. Sociologists, therefore, need to be constantly aware of their relationship to both powerful and powerless groups.

TEST YOURSELF

Suggest two arguments against using sociological research to solve social problems.

Feminist theory

In recent times, feminist research has focused on a range of policy issues and practices designed to highlight the inequality faced by women all over the world. Pascall (1997), for example, has charted how social policies that reduce the state's welfare role result in a rise in 'women's unpaid work' as carers. In addition, Misra (2000) highlights how social policies relating to employment, poverty reduction and child birth in the USA have been influenced by women's activism. Misra also points out that these social policies are connected. For example, the development of 'family friendly' employment policies can be linked to areas such as poverty, where single parents are often unable to take advantage of the new employment policies. Although feminist theory mainly tries to identify and address the social disadvantages experienced specifically by women, other sociologists have pointed out that 'disadvantaged groups' are often the target of social policies (the 'social problem' approach) or politically marginalised. In this respect, Becker (1967) argues that it is impossible to achieve value-neutrality when it comes to social issues. Sociologists should make a choice about how and why their research is used – to promote the interests of the disadvantaged or to support the activities of the state.

From a left-wing perspective, Tombs and Whyte (2003) argue that rather than conducting research to inform social policy, the sociologist's role is to empower the powerless by providing the information required to challenge policies that do not benefit them. Sociologists should 'take the standpoint of the *underdog* [and] apply it to the study of the *overdogs*'.

From a new-right perspective, Marsland (1995) argues that sociology should address 'social problems' as they are defined and identified by the political consensus in democratic societies. He states that 'sociological research has a necessary, important, and constructive role to play in relation to policy formulation, implementation, and evaluation'. In this respect, Marsland believes that a 'fully engaged' sociology is one that takes a commitment to social policy seriously. A sociology that refuses to become involved in social policy allows other social sciences, such as psychology and economics, or powerful vested interest groups, to go unsupported and unchecked by objective research.

ACTIVITY

The Joseph Rowntree Foundation (www.jrf.org.uk/) publishes research on welfare and poverty that can be used to illustrate how sociological studies can contribute to social policy. Choose one piece of research from the site and write up to:

- *150 words identifying the key arguments in the research*
- *150 words explaining how the research could contribute to the development of social policy.*

The diversity of human behaviour and cultural variation

Murdock (1945) argued that one feature of human societies is that they share a large number of 'cultural universals'. By this he was referring to behaviours that are common to all societies, past and present, such as groups defined by:

- age
- family
- language
- status
- symbols
- beliefs
- practices.

While these features may be universal, it is evident that different societies interpret them in different ways.

- When European people meet, it is often acceptable to shake hands. In Japan, it is more acceptable to bow.

- In the Arab world, shaking hands with someone of the opposite sex may be unacceptable.
- To beckon someone with the palm facing upwards and crooking your index finger is an acceptable way of calling someone towards you in the USA. In India this action is an insult.

In this respect, while we may be able to talk on one level about cultural uniformities, we also need to think about cultural diversity in two main ways: cross-cultural and intra-cultural.

Cross-cultural diversity refers to differences *between* societies. For example, broad cultural differences between the UK and Mauritius include things such as language, political organisation (while both are democracies, the UK has an unelected monarch as head of state, while Mauritius is a republic with a president elected by parliament), and different social, political and economic histories. We could, of course, note many other differences, ranging from cuisine, through cultural products such as music, dance and literature, to religious festivals.

Another example of cross-cultural diversity involves personal space:

- Germans like to maintain a circle of space of that extends roughly 60 cm around the body. People feel uncomfortable if others enter this space uninvited.
- In Hungary, personal space extends around 40 cm.
- In Argentina personal space can be so small as to be almost non-existent.

Attitudes to relationships between people of a different sex and those of the same sex also vary. For example, in Saudi Arabia, a man holding another man's hand in public is a sign of mutual respect. In Europe, if two men were holding hands, people would assume that they were (sexual) partners. In countries where homosexuality is a criminal offence, they might be arrested and imprisoned.

While most societies recognise only two sexes – male and female – some recognise a 'third sex' (transgendered individuals). In some Native American tribes certain males (*berdache*) take on the gender identity and social status of females.

TEST YOURSELF

Identify two cultural differences between your own and any other society.

Mauritius is a republic with a president elected by parliament

Intra-cultural diversity involves differences *within* the *same* culture. We can consider this using examples from a range of social categories.

Class

We can identify distinct class groupings in **modern industrial society** (working, middle and upper class, for example). Each of these classes has its own cultural characteristics. In relation to work, manual occupations (plumber, road sweeper) are working class, while professional (non-manual) occupations (dentist, accountant) are middle class. Different classes also typically have different levels of educational achievement. Middle-class children, for example, are much more likely to attend university than their working-class peers, while middle-class cultural lifestyles are more likely to include leisure activities such as opera, theatre and fine dining.

KEY TERM

Modern industrial society: type of society characterised by particular forms of political, economic (mass production, manufacturing) and cultural (science, reason) beliefs and practices.

Lifestyles are related to income differences that come from higher levels of education and work – for example, the middle classes occupy more middle and senior managerial positions. Lifestyles are also based on cultural tastes. High culture, for example, refers to the idea that some cultural products and practices are

15

superior to others: classical music, opera and the works of Shakespeare are *high cultural* forms, whereas pop music, cinema and the works of J. K. Rowling (e.g. Harry Potter) are not. As Gans (1974) puts it, high culture relates to 'The art, music and literature ... that were (and are) preferred by the well-educated elite'. Katz-Gerro et al. (2007) suggest that this view of high culture sees societies as 'culturally stratified'. It indicates a basic division between a small, cultured elite at the top and a large mass of people at the bottom who embrace popular culture. Giddens (2006) defines popular culture as 'entertainment created for large audiences, such as popular films, shows, music, videos and TV programmes' (the very opposite of high culture). This is the 'culture of the masses' – a term used to suggest a shallow, worthless and disposable form of culture.

While an elite could, even in the past, separate itself from the masses physically and culturally, in many countries today it is increasingly difficult to distinguish someone's status on the basis of how they speak, behave or dress. However, it might still be possible to identify differences based on a person's cultural products and ideas. The cultural elite claims that 'taste' cannot be bought or learnt – it is bred over several generations.

Country	Male–Female	Male–Male	Female–Female
Canada	14	18	14
Chile	14	18	18
France	15	15	15
Guyana	13	Illegal	Illegal
Iran	Must be married	Illegal	Illegal
South Korea	13	13	13
Saudi Arabia	Must be married	Illegal	Illegal
Spain	13	13	13
Tunisia	20	Illegal	Illegal
UK	16	16	16

Table 1.1   Age of consent in selected societies

permissions – children are allowed to exhibit behaviours, such as play, that are discouraged in adults – and denials: children are not allowed to do things, such as have a sexual relationship, that are open to adults. Table 1.1 highlights the cultural differences between societies in relation to ideas about sexual maturity and sexual orientation.

Youth includes a range of cultural categories, such as pre-teens ('teenies'), teens and young adults, that reflect differences in things like consumption. Not only do different categories of youth have different cultural tastes, but young people also tend to have different tastes from both children and adults in areas such as music, fashion, food and language. Youth lifestyles are also more likely to be played out in public, in the street or pubs and clubs, whereas elderly lifestyles are generally played out in private – inside the home.

Adulthood involves cultural differences constructed around *rights* – such as marriage and full-time work – and *responsibilities*, such as childcare. These characteristics set adulthood apart from other age groups. Although there are cultural variations in how old age is perceived in Western societies such as the UK, Europe and the USA, it is frequently seen as a diminished identity. This means that it has 'lost something' – such as the ability to earn an independent living because of compulsory retirement – in the transition from adulthood. In this respect, old age is frequently regarded as undesirable and problematic. Gianoulis (2006) argues that the 'medicalisation' of old age contributes to this process: 'Instead of viewing the disorientations of older people as being the result of personal and social change, they are viewed as symptoms

TEST YOURSELF

Identify three types of television programme that are likely to be watched by the working class and three that are likely to be watched by the middle class.

Age

Cultural diversity, both within and between societies, is expressed through age in a number of significant ways: firstly, in the notion of different biological age groups (child, youth, adult, elderly) and, secondly, in the cultural characteristics associated with biological age. This includes different assumptions about how people of a particular age should behave.

Childhood, for example, involves a range of cultural differences. These differences relate to issues such as of "senility".' Many people, therefore, see old age as an inevitable process of decline, senility, helplessness, withdrawal from society and loneliness. In some non-Western societies, such as Tamil Nadu in India, the (illegal) practice of *thalaikoothal* is perhaps an extreme example of such 'undesirability'. In this practice, elderly family members may be murdered (*senicide*) by their relatives when they are considered to be an economic burden.

This process of decline in old age is not, of course, inevitable. Cultural variations within societies mean that, for some, old age brings changing patterns of consumption and leisure, especially among the wealthier members of society. Others might have a different interpretation of 'being old' and the elderly might refuse to conform to conventional stereotypes of old age. Barrett et al. (2003) also argue that different societies produce different subjective experiences of ageing. Americans and Germans, for example, 'tend to feel younger than their actual age … but the bias toward youthful identities is stronger at older ages, particularly among Americans'.

However, in some non-Western societies old age is viewed differently. Kagan (1980) notes how in Columbia (South America) the elderly are valued for the knowledge and experience they are able to pass on to younger members of society. For the Sherbro of Sierra Leone, increasing age brings the individual 'closer to God' and is something to be welcomed.

Gender

People of different classes, ages and ethnic backgrounds may display widely different cultural behaviours even though they share the same gender.

One way of considering gender is in terms of 'life chances'. Dahrendorf (1979) defines this as an individual's *relative chances* of gaining the kinds of things a society considers *desirable*, such as a high standard of living, and avoiding those that society considers *undesirable*, such as low social status. A working-class woman's life chances are lower than an upper-class man's. Equally, an upper-class woman has greater life chances than a working-class man. Conversely, Stanworth (1984) argues that the life chances can vary even between men and women of the same class, age and ethnicity. Within families, for example, men in many different cultures take the greater personal share of 'family' resources.

While some obvious gender differences exist in most societies – men and women dress differently, have different attitudes to cosmetics, body decoration and so on – there is also a range of less obvious differences. Some of these are related to patriarchal ideologies

(ideas that support the domination of women by men), which result in differences in how men and women are treated, both by each other and by society as a whole. For example, in many societies a range of gender inequalities exist within families. These range from women doing more domestic labour, through having greater responsibility for care of the children, the sick and the elderly, to suffering higher levels of domestic violence. There are also differences in attitudes to children. In the UK, for example, Self and Zealey (2007) report that around 20 per cent of women remain 'childless by choice'.

Some technologies have specifically gendered associations in many societies. An iron and ironing board, for example, are typically associated with female domestic labour

In terms of education, girls in the UK generally outperform boys at every level, although class and ethnic factors also play a part. Asian boys, for example, outperform both white British and Afro-Caribbean girls. For women, however, better educational performance does not automatically mean better employment options. In the USA, there are no restrictions on women taking on paid employment, but in Saudi Arabia a woman must have permission from a male guardian to work outside the home. Eitzen and Baca-Zinn (2003) argue that while 'women perform 60% of work world wide', they earn '10% of income'. Scott (2004) suggests that one explanation for this is that female life chances are affected by asynchronies. This means that family responsibilities restrict the opportunities women have to 'synchronise' their life with other social requirements, especially work. Childcare, for example, does not fit easily with full-time work; responsibilities in the home also limit a woman's chances to develop the social networks that help many men to promotions throughout their careers.

Ethnicity

Ethnicity refers to cultural differences between social groups that, as Winston (2005) suggests, involves people 'seeing themselves as being distinctive in some way from others' on the basis of a shared cultural background and history. Song (2003) states that ethnic groups have a 'common ancestry' and 'memories of a shared past' constructed around a variety of 'symbolic elements … such as family and kinship, religion, language, territory, nationality or physical appearance'. Examples of ethnic groups are many and varied. In India it is possible to identify around 2,000 distinctive ethnicities based on religion (such as Hindu, Buddhist, Jain, Christian and Sikh) and language.

Another example is noted by Self and Zealey (2007): 'Historically the population of Britain has predominantly consisted of people from a White British ethnic background'. However, this does not mean that the majority ethnic group is all the same (*homogeneous*). This main group is actually made up of a range of ethnicities – English, Scottish, Welsh and Irish – some of which could be seen as minority ethnicities within the white majority. In terms of wider ethnic diversity, immigration over the past 50 years has produced a range of distinct ethnic minorities (Table 1.2).

Minority group	Percentage
Other white	2.5
Indians	1.8
Pakistanis	1.3
Mixed ethnicity	1.2
Black Caribbean	1.0
Black Africans	0.8
Bangladeshis	0.5

Table 1.2   UK ethnic minorities

This pattern of ethnic diversity is further complicated by 'other ethnicities', such as Chinese, and people who live and work in the UK but are officially resident elsewhere. Favell (2006), for example, estimates that around 200,000 French people live and work in and around London. As he notes, 'London is now the fourth largest French city after Paris, Lyon and Marseilles.' As another example, Mauritius consists of four major ethnic groups: Indo-Mauritian, Creole, Sino-Mauritian and Franco-Mauritian.

Religion

There are wide variations in religious beliefs, practices and organisation both within particular societies and between different countries. For example:

- Christianity, Judaism and Islam involve the worship of a single god (monotheism).
- Other forms of religion (such as paganism) involve the worship of many different gods (polytheism).
- Some belief systems do not involve a 'god' at all; the North American Sioux understand the world in terms of *Waken* – Beings or Powers – the expression of anything incomprehensible.

In terms of practices, some religions allow direct communication with their god(s) through prayer, but others do not. McGuire (2002) suggests that cultural variations exist because all religions have a 'dual character'. On an individual level they involve a diversity of beliefs, practices and ways to 'be religious', some of which include communal practices, such as attending religious ceremonies, while others do not. It is possible, for example, to be Christian without ever setting foot inside a church. Different religions also require different levels of personal commitment, such as attendance at services or praying a certain number of times each day.

On a wider social level, religions perform particular **functions** – such as socialisation (into a range of moral beliefs and values, for example), social solidarity and social control. This last may involve both direct control – what people may wear or eat, for example – and indirect control, such as providing a moral template for how people should lead their life 'in accordance with God'.

KEY TERM

Functions, manifest and latent: manifest functions are the intended consequences of an action; latent functions are the hidden or sometimes unintended consequences of that same action.

In a global context, religious diversity exists at three main levels:

1 There are differences *between* religions, such as Christianity, Islam, Hinduism, Buddhism or Shinto.
2 There are differences *within* religions: for example, Islam has three major belief systems (Sunni, Shia and Sufi).
3 There are differences of belief, practice and organisation within this second level. Protestant Christianity, for example, *includes* groups such as Presbyterians, Baptists and Methodists, while within Islam there are groups such as Wahhabi and Alawite.

A further dimension involves religion and ethnic identity. Winston (2005) notes that many ethnic groups are 'defined mainly in terms of religion (e.g. Jewish or Muslim people)'. This combining of religious and ethnic identity may be strengthened or weakened by an ethnic group's geographical location. O'Beirne (2004) suggests that religion is a relevant factor 'in a person's self-description, particularly for people from the Indian subcontinent' living in the UK. She suggests that immigrant groups use religion as a way of maintaining a sense of cultural and ethnic identity when moving to a different country.

Analysis of the UK Census (2001) shows that:

■ Christians ranked religion the 7th most important aspect of their identity, while Muslims, Sikhs and Hindus ranked it 2nd.
■ White Britons ranked religion as the 10th most important aspect of their identity, but South Asians ranked it 2nd.

It is important to note that even when comparing two apparently similar ethnic groups (such as Indian and Pakistani, often grouped as 'South Asians'), differences of affiliation exist. The various forms of affiliation (Hindu, Muslim and Sikh, for example) found among Indian ethnicities suggests a higher level of religious *fragmentation* among this group than among their Pakistani counterparts.

TEST YOURSELF

Identify two cultural differences between groups in your society. To what extent do these cultural differences reflect differences in status and power?

Global culture

A wider dimension to diversity involves the idea that all societies are increasingly characterised by a globalised culture. This refers to the rapid global movement of cultural ideas, styles and products that can be picked up, discarded and adapted to fit the needs of different cultural groups.

There is a great variety of cultural products to choose from and people are no longer limited to local or national cultural choices. In this respect, cultural products are malleable (open to manipulation and change), and where people are exposed to a range of cultural influences and choices, a 'pick-and-mix' approach to culture may develop. This can result in the creation of something new, different and unique – a process known as cultural hybridisation.

Global cultural forms have been expressed in two main ways:

1 **Globalised** culture reflects how local or national cultural developments can spread, to be picked up, shaped and changed to suit the needs of different groups. The driving force here is information technology – the development of cheap personal computers and mobile phones as well as with the evolution of the internet.
2 An alternative interpretation suggests a process of convergence and similarity *within* cultural groups; cultures are becoming more alike:

   ■ sharing the same language (English)
   ■ doing the same kinds of things (watching American films, wearing American clothes, visiting similar websites)
   ■ consuming similar products (from film and television, through social networking websites, to food and drink – Big Macs, Pepsi, Coke …).

KEY TERM

Globalisation: various processes – economic, political and cultural – that occur on a worldwide basis.

Alongside this cultural globalisation, we find diversity *between* cultural groups: like-minded individuals share cultural similarities across national boundaries, but these groups are many and varied. In this way, cultures resemble 'strands of influence'. For example, some young people in the USA, Japan and India may develop *common cultural bonds* based on a shared interest in sport, music or computer games. Others may develop cultural bonds based on Pokemon cards or Manga comics.

How are social networking sites such as Facebook evidence of global cultural convergence?

Sklair (1999) argues that to understand global cultural development we need to think about three processes:

1 Localised globalism means that some forms of globalised culture are adapted and changed by particular (local) cultural behaviours. Regev (2003), for example, suggests that 'rock music' – a global product of US origin – is now consumed and filtered through many different cultural influences, which has resulted in new 'local varieties of rock'.

2 Globalised localism involves some features of *local* cultures, parts of their uniqueness and individuality, becoming part of globalised cultures. Rather than seeing the globalisation of culture as making everything *the same*, globalisation creates new and diverse cultural forms.

3 Global cultural convergence is, for Bryman (2004), demonstrated by what he calls the 'disneyisation' of culture: 'The process by which the principles of Disney theme parks dominate more and more sectors of American society as well as the rest of the world'. While disneyisation celebrates diversity in consumption, lifestyle and notions of freedom and choice, it presents standardised, homogeneous versions of these ideas – just like Disney World itself presents a sanitised version of things like 'the Wild West'. In this respect, the global trend is for cultural differences to gradually disappear as all societies start to adopt ideas and attitudes broadly similar in style and content.

Plumb (1995) argues that the process of globalisation is accelerated because culture has become a commodity – something to be bought and sold. Similarly, Lechner (2001) suggests that the economic power of global companies such as Coca-Cola, Nike and McDonald's creates a consumer culture where standardised commodities are promoted by global marketing campaigns to 'create similar lifestyles'.

Ritzer (1996) calls this the 'McDonaldisation of self and society'; cultural products are *standardised* and *homogenised*. Wherever you are in the world, if you buy a Big Mac you will get the same basic product. Global economics means that consumer products must be created to appeal to the widest possible range of tastes across the widest possible range of cultures – from Britain to Bosnia and Bangalore. Berger (1997) characterises this as 'McWorld culture'; the idea that global culture is increasingly Americanised: 'Young people throughout the world dance to American music, wearing T-shirts with messages about American universities and other consumer items. Older people watch American sitcoms on television and go to American movies. Everyone, young and old, grows taller and fatter on American fast foods.'

ACTIVITY

Find examples from your society to illustrate each of the three processes noted by Sklair. Do you think that these examples represent problems for society, or its healthy development?

The nature of social order, social control and social change

At the start of this chapter we suggested that concepts of social order were at the heart of sociology's development. Now we are going to look at how two contrasting approaches – **functionalist theory** and **Marxist theory** – provide different interpretations of how order and control are created and maintained. Both perspectives are **structuralist** (or **macrosociological**), and argue

KEY TERMS

Functionalist theory: major, if dated, sociological theory that argues that consensus is the overriding principle on which societies are based. Focus is on institutional relationships and the functions they perform for the individual and society.

Marxist theory: philosophy or social theory based on the ideas of Karl Marx.

Structuralist: form of sociology, such as functionalism and Marxism, that focuses on analysing society in terms of its institutional relationships and their effect on individual beliefs and behaviours.

Macrosociology: large-scale sociological approach where the focus is on social structures and institutions.

that how societies are organised at the level of families, governments and economies (the institutional or system level), determines how individuals view their world and behave within it (structural **determinism**). This perspective presents society as a powerful force that controls and shapes how people think and behave.

KEY TERM

Determinism: the claim that human behaviour is shaped by forces beyond the immediate control of individuals, such as social structures or 'society'.

Consensus structuralism

Functionalism

For functionalists, any explanation of how order and stability are created and maintained involves looking at how societies are organised at the level of the social system. This involves the idea that the various parts of a society (family, education, work, etc.) function in harmony. Each part is dependent on the others. Just as the different parts of the body – such as the heart, lungs and brain – work together to form something more complex than the sum of their individual parts (a living body), the different

parts of a society work together to form a social system. Parsons (1937) argues that every social system consists of four 'functional sub-systems' – political, economic, cultural and family. Each of these sub-systems performs a different but related function that addresses certain 'problems' faced by every society.

The connections between the various parts of the social system – family, culture, work and government – are created by institutional purposes and needs. For a *family institution* to exist (and perform its *functions*) its members *need* to survive. The *work institution* performs this survival function by allowing family members to earn money to buy the food (among other things) that they consume; conversely, to fulfil this *purpose*, work *needs* families to produce socialised human beings.

While order is created at the institutional level through these relationships, Parsons (1959a) explains how *individuals* fit into the overall structure of society on the basis of functional prerequisites – things that *must* happen if society is to function properly. For individuals to survive and prosper, they need to be part of larger co-operative groups – they must *combine* to solve fundamental problems. Every social institution, from families to schools to workplaces, must develop ways to ensure that individuals conform to the needs of

21

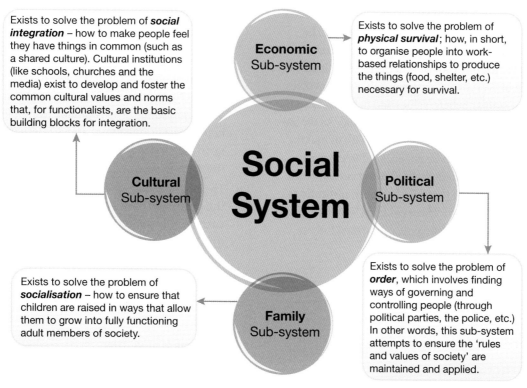

Functional sub-systems

Source: Parsons, 1937

both the institution and society as a whole. For Parsons, institutions do this by developing ways to solve 'four problems of their existence'. We can illustrate this using the example of education.

1 Goal maintenance: institutions must provide people with goals to achieve, such as academic qualifications.

2 Adaptation: to achieve institutional goals, people need a co-operative environment, such as a classroom and teachers, within which people can work.

3 Integration: people must be motivated to achieve (educational) goals, and one way to do this is to encourage a 'sense of belonging', to both wider society, where educational qualifications are used to sift and sort (differentiate) adults in the workplace, and to the education system itself. A school, for example, makes people feel they 'belong' to the institution and that they have things in common with other pupils and teachers.

4 Latency: conflicts within an institution must be managed and rules created to encourage desirable behaviour and punish rule-breaking (deviance). In schools these rules cover things like attendance, behaviour and dress. They are designed to maintain a particular way of life in the institution.

Societies and their institutions can only function if people feel they are part of a much larger community. If millions of individuals simply acted in their own selfish interests, things would quickly fall apart. We must, therefore, be compelled to behave in ways that are reasonable, consistent and broadly predictable if social order is to be maintained for the benefit of everyone. Control of behaviour involves people sharing similar beliefs, values and behaviours so they are effectively working towards a common goal. As we have already noted, institutions must also find ways of making people conform. People can be encouraged to conform willingly by convincing them that following certain rules is in their best interests. If that fails, however, institutions might use agents of control. These could be 'soft' (for example, teachers) or hard (the police or armed forces).

TEST YOURSELF

Briefly explain the meaning of the term 'functional prerequisite'.

Conflict structuralism

From this perspective, societies are generally considered stable because powerful groups impose order on relatively powerless groups. Although conflict is at the heart of all

social relationships, Marxism theorises this in *economic* terms (such as **economic determinism**), with different social classes battling against each other. Feminism expresses this conflict in *gender* terms: men and women battling against each other.

KEY TERM

Economic determinism: idea that the form taken by economic relationships (such as master and serf in feudal society or employer and employee in capitalist society) is the most significant relationship in any society. This determines the form taken by all other political and cultural relationships.

Marxism

For Marxists, work is the most important activity in any society because no other social activity (politics, family or culture) can exist without people first having found a way to survive. Thus, how work is socially organised (who does it, what they do and who benefits from it) is the key to understanding how all other social relationships are organised. Marxists refer to a relationship between 'base and superstructure'. By this they mean the relationship between economic, political and ideological institutions, which they claim is the basis for social order and control:

- The economic base is the foundation on which society is built. It is the world of work and involves particular types of *relationships* (the **relations of production**), such as owner, manager, wage labourer and *organisation*. The capitalist workplace is organised hierarchically, one group above another. Those further up in the hierarchy had more power and control than those lower down.

- The political and ideological superstructure 'rests' on the economic base and involves political institutions, such as *government* and agencies of social control (the police, judiciary and courts) and *ideological institutions* including religion, education and the mass media.

KEY TERM

Relations of production: in Marxist theory, the social relationships into which people *must* enter in order to survive, to produce and reproduce their means of life. In capitalist society, the main relations of production involve owners and non-owners.

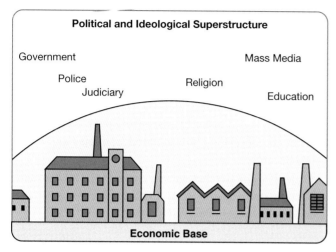

Political and Ideological Superstructure

Government

Mass Media

Police

Religion

Judiciary

Education

Economic Base

The relationship between base and superstructure in capitalist society

The workplace is a key area of conflict because of its organisational structure. In capitalist society, the 'means of economic production' – the tools, factories and machines that are used to create wealth – are owned by one class (the bourgeoisie, or ruling class). The majority own little or nothing and so are forced to sell their ability to work. This ability is known as their labour power. It is part of what Marxists call the **forces of production**: how labour power is organised to produce wealth by harnessing it to various forms of technology – from simple tools to advanced machinery.

> **KEY TERM**
>
> **Forces of production:** in Marxist theory, this refers to how everything – from raw materials, through labour power to machinery – is organised in the productive process.

In capitalist societies, members of a small bourgeois class become very rich because they keep the profits made from goods and services and most people own nothing but their ability to work for wages. The emphasis on conflict suggests that capitalist societies are inherently unstable. However, this is not the case – Marxists argue that the ruling class is not only economically powerful but also politically powerful. It controls what Althusser (1972) calls 'repressive state apparatuses' (RSAs) or ways of compelling people to conform by force. This can range from hard policing (the police and armed forces as agents of social control) to soft policing (social workers and welfare agencies 'policing' the behaviour of the lower classes).

Ownership and control of institutions such as the media also allow the ruling class to influence how others see the world. Althusser calls these institutions that deal in ideas 'ideological state apparatuses' (ISAs). The education

system, for example, does not just teach knowledge and skills, it also teaches values of competition, individualism ('educational success' is measured by how successfully pupils compete against each other) and respect for authority. All these ideas fit neatly into a capitalist economic system that most benefits the bourgeoisie.

Order and stability are maintained at a system level through the institutions that make up the political and ideological superstructure. These, in turn, are controlled by a ruling class whose power comes from ownership of the economic base. Most people are locked in to capitalist society by the need to earn a living for themselves and their family. They are also locked in by a range of ideas that support the status quo, which are spread by the media, education, religion and other institutions.

Socialisation, therefore, is an effective form of control – a type of ideological manipulation that seeks either to convince people that the interests of the ruling class are really the interests of everyone or to present society as impossible for the individual to influence or change. Socialisation may be more effective in the long term because people incorporate the basic **ideology** of capitalism into their personal value system. However, also involves making economic and political concessions to the lower classes to ensure their co-operation.

> **KEY TERM**
>
> **Ideology:** a system of related beliefs.

Feminist theory

Although there are many forms of feminist theory, they all share the belief that contemporary societies are patriarchal to some degree; the interests of men are always considered more important than those of women. In basic terms, therefore, order and control are based on male power, expressed in two ways. *Interpersonal power* refers to things like physical violence or the various ways female labour is exploited within the family group. *Cultural power* focuses on how male-dominated societies are structured to oppress and exploit women. Men dominate the highest levels of economic, political and cultural institutions.

Different types of feminism emphasise different forms of control as the way to understand a male-dominated social order. For **liberal feminism**, the key form of control

> **KEY TERM**
>
> **Liberal feminism:** type of feminism that promotes gender equality.

23

is sexual discrimination, while for **Marxist feminism**, class inequality provides the context in which female oppression, exploitation and discrimination occur. In a competitive, capitalist society men are encouraged to exploit any 'weaknesses' in women's market position (the fact that women may be out of the workforce during and after pregnancy, for example) to their own advantage.

> ### KEY TERM
>
> **Marxist feminists:** type of feminism that focuses on challenging capitalism as a route to freeing women from oppression and inequality.

For **radical feminism**, patriarchy is the source of female oppression. Patriarchy is a feature of all known human societies and results in men dominating the social order in two spheres: the *public* – such as the workplace, where women are paid less and have lower status, and the *private* – the home, where women carry out the majority of unpaid domestic work.

> ### KEY TERM
>
> **Radical feminism:** form of feminism that sees female oppression in terms of patriarchal relationships.

> ### TEST YOURSELF
>
> Suggest two differences between consensus and conflict approaches to explaining social change. Also identify one strength and one limitation of each approach.

Action approach

This general approach, also called interactionism, claims that order and control are created 'from the bottom up'. It is based on the idea that people create and re-create 'society' on a daily basis through their daily routines. People constantly, if not always consciously, produce and reproduce social order through their individual and collective behaviour. From this viewpoint, 'society' is merely a term people use to explain the limits they place on behaviour. Although society does not exist *physically*, it does exist *mentally*. People act as though society is a real force having an effect on them, limiting and controlling their behaviour. This creates order and stability.

To understand how order is maintained, therefore, we must examine the *socio-psychological* processes through which social groups and a sense of society are constructed. From this perspective, social life involves a series of *encounters* – separate but linked episodes that give the appearance of order and stability; they exist for as long as we *act* in ways that maintain them. Garfinkel (1967) demonstrated the fragile nature of our beliefs about social order by disrupting people's daily routines and observing how agitated, confused and angry people became.

Order is more psychologically desirable than disorder, and people strive to impose order through the meanings given to behaviour in two ways:

1 To interact, people must develop shared definitions of a situation. In a school classroom, if a teacher defines the situation as a period of time for teaching, but her students define it as a time for messing around and having fun; this will almost certainly result in disorder.

2 Where meanings are negotiated they can easily change. The identities associated with masculinity and femininity have changed dramatically over the past 30 years.

If society is not a 'thing' acting on behaviour – if it has no *objective reality* beyond social interaction – it becomes a convenient label applied to the pressures, rules and responsibilities that arise from social relationships. The idea of labelling (or naming) is important because it shows how order is created through interaction. For example, labelling theory argues that when something is named, such as categorising people as 'young' or 'old', the label is associated with a set of characteristics. Knowledge of these characteristics is used to influence or control behaviour. The characteristics assigned to the label 'student', for example, lead people to expect certain things from that person. In the same way, they would expect different behaviour from someone labelled as a 'criminal'.

Social change

As with explanations of order and control, there are different perspectives when it comes to explaining social change. Functionalism, for example, explains major forms of social change using what Parsons (1937) called structural differentiation. This is the idea that where social systems consist of connected sub-systems, changes within one causes changes in the others.

In the UK in the 18th century, cultural changes began with the rapid development of scientific ideas that revolutionised the workplace through the introduction of machines and industrial forms of production. These changes meant employers needed literate and numerate workers – which the family institution could not supply. This led to what Merton (1938) calls social strains – tensions and pressures build up in society when the needs of one institution, in this instance the workplace, cannot be met by another institution, the family. This tension was released by the intervention of government (the political sub-system) and the development of a new cultural institution – education – in the late 19th century, to provide the skills required by more advanced work processes. As we can see, major social changes such as moving from a pre-industrial to industrial society are the gradual result of changes within and between institutions. Structural differentiation also means that some institutions, such as the family, lose functions while others, such as education, gain new ones.

How is the development of education systems evidence of structural differentiation?

Marxism and social change

For Marxism, social change comes about through conflict and the clash between the contradictory interests inherent in capitalist forms of economic production. While conflicts exist everywhere in a society – between different ethnic groups, age groups and genders – Marxists believe that the existence of different classes is the main source of conflict. Capitalism is a competitive economic system. Businesses compete against other businesses for customers, workers compete against other workers for jobs – and competition leads to conflict. Owners want to keep as much of their profit as possible – the less they pay in wages, the more houses, cars and mobile phones they can buy. At the same time, non-owners also want the desirable things society has to offer; it is in their interests, therefore, to demand more from employers. Therefore, conflict is expressed at all

levels of society, from the small-scale, everyday (micro) level, where workers may strike for more money, to the large-scale (macro) level, where conflicts lead to wider political and economic changes.

Feminism and social change

Different forms of feminism have slightly different explanations of social change. For liberal feminism, change can be created through the legal system. Liberal feminists in the UK and the USA have promoted a range of *anti-discriminatory* laws which, they argue, redress the historical gender imbalance. In the UK, legislation such as the Sex Discrimination Act (1975, updated in 2003), which made discrimination in the workplace illegal, and the Equal Pay Act (1970), are examples of this approach. In addition, female inequality can be addressed by changing male attitudes to family life and through the continued development of anti-discriminatory laws and practices.

Marxist feminists link gender inequality to economic or class-based inequalities. They argue that the development of patriarchal ideas, attitudes and practices (such as sexual discrimination) are the product of cultural differences in the way males and females are raised. Men are not naturally exploitative of women. Rather, it is the economic system (capitalism) that encourages and rewards sexist attitudes and behaviour. Improving the position of women, therefore, requires a radical change at the economic level – capitalism needs to be transformed.

For radical feminism, capitalism is not the whole problem. If all known societies are patriarchal, a change in female lives can only come about by overthrowing the ideas and practices on which male domination is based. One form of change, therefore, involves overthrowing the ruling sex class (men). Men are defined as the 'gender enemy' because they have always exploited women. Women must establish a *matriarchal society,* in which the current (patriarchal) roles are replaced by equality and mutual respect between males and females.

Action theory and social change

From this perspective, social reality is not something fixed and unchanging but rather fluid and malleable. This follows from the various ways in which people negotiate reality through meanings that are open to change.

On a micro level, evidence of relatively small-scale social change includes things such as changing attitudes to gender. For example, Western societies have seen recent movements towards greater gender equality in areas such

25

as employment and education. Globalisation has also produced a wide range of cultural changes, as increasing contact between different societies has led to the exchange of ideas and practices and their incorporation into different cultures. Enjoying Indian, Chinese and American food, for example, has become a major feature of European culture over the past 50 years.

While change at the macro level is harder to explain, the focus on meanings has led to an examination of the role of cultural institutions – and religion in particular – in the process of change. Weber (1905), for example, argued that Calvinism, a 16th-century offshoot of Protestant Christianity, helped promote a strong and lasting social transformation in the shape of capitalism. More recently, Robinson (1987) has argued that there are 'six conditions that shape the likelihood of religion becoming a force for social change':

1 a religious worldview shared by the revolutionary classes
2 a theology (religious teachings and beliefs) that conflicts with the beliefs and practices of the existing social order
3 a clergy closely associated with revolutionary classes
4 a single religion shared by the revolutionary classes
5 differences between the religion of the revolutionary classes and the religion of the ruling classes (such as one being Catholic and the other Protestant)
6 channels of legitimate political dissent blocked or unavailable.

Examples of change resulting from these conditions being met include the Iranian Revolution in 1979, where the (secular) regime of the Shah of Persia was overthrown and the Civil Rights Movement in the USA where, from the 1960s onwards, social change was promoted and supported by black religious activists and leaders such as Martin Luther King.

ACTIVITY

One way to gain an understanding of how different sociological perspectives view society is by analogy – likening them to something familiar. For each of the following perspectives and analogies, list five characteristics (such as five characteristics of a human body for functionalism).

For each characteristic, briefly explain how it can be applied to society (for example, just as a human body has connected organs that work together, the different parts of society, such as families and schools, are connected and work together):

1 *Functionalism – human body*
2 *Marxism – league table (e.g. school exam results)*
3 *Action theory – a play*
4 *Feminism – war*
5 *Postmodernism – theme park.*

Summary points

○ **Sociology evolved to answer two key questions:**
  - How is social order created and maintained?
  - How and why do societies change?

○ **Three key sociological perspectives are based around:**
  - consensus: functionalism (Comte and Durkheim)
  - conflict: Marxism (Marx)
  - social action (Weber).

○ **Science is a way of producing a particular type of knowledge, one that is:**
  - reliable
  - valid.

○ **The production of scientific knowledge is governed by:**
  - procedural rules, such as the hypothetico-deductive method
  - ethical rules, such as Merton's scientific ethos.

○ **Two major types of sociological methodology are:**
  - positivism
  - interpretivism.

○ **Postmodern approaches are critical of positivist and interpretivist conceptions of science as metanarrative.**

○ **The role of values in sociological research relates to areas such as:**
  - choice of topic
  - choice of method.

○ **The uses of sociological knowledge relate to:**
  - large-scale theories that seek to explain social order and social change
  - smaller-scale theories used to explain a range of social issues.

○ **Sociological and social problems may not be the same:**
  - A sociological problem is a question 'that demands explanation'.
  - A social problem involves behaviour that creates a 'public outcry or call for action' to resolve the problem.
  - Social problems are not necessarily sociological problems.

○ **In terms of its diversity, human behaviour always varies in terms of:**
  - class
  - age
  - gender
  - ethnicity.

○ **Three key sociological concepts include understanding:**
  - social order
  - social control
  - social change.

○ **These can be understood in terms of three major sociological perspectives:**
  - consensus: functionalism
  - conflict: Marxism and feminism
  - social action: Weberian and interactionist (neo-Weberian).

Exam-style questions

a What is meant by the term 'sociological problem'? [2]

b Describe how any two uses of sociological knowledge may be linked to social policy. [4]

c Explain the concept of cultural diversity in relation to class, gender or ethnicity. [8]

d Assess functionalist explanations of social order. [11]

Total available marks 25

Chapter 2:
Socialisation and the creation of social identity

Learning objectives

The objectives of this chapter involve understanding:

- the difference between structuralist and interactionist views of the relationship between the individual and society
- how individuals become competent social actors – the nature–nurture debate and concepts of Self, Other, 'I'/'Me' and the presentation of self
- sociological, biological and psychological explanations of how individuals become competent social actors
- the process of socialisation and the contribution of socialising agencies: the family, education, peer group, media and religion

- the contributions made by culture, roles, norms, values, beliefs, ideology and power to the social construction of reality
- the social construction of identities based around social class, gender and ethnicity
- modernist and postmodernist theories of identity formation.

Introduction

The focus of this chapter is the relationship between the individual and society, initially in terms of structuralist and interpretivist perspectives. This leads into an analysis of how the individual becomes a competent social actor in the general context of the **nature versus nurture debate** – the extent to which human behaviour can be satisfactorily explained by cultural influences. This involves looking at what people need to learn, such as **roles, values and norms**, as well as the socialisation process through which they learn it. This process is further examined through the contributions made by socialising agencies such as the family and the media. The chapter concludes by examining the concept of identity based on social class, gender and ethnicity, and how modernist and postmodernist perspectives interpret the process of identity formation.

KEY TERMS

Nature versus nurture debate: a debate in the social sciences about whether human behaviour can be explained in biological/genetic (*nature*) or cultural (*nurture*) terms.

Roles: expected patterns of behaviour associated with each status that we hold, such as friend, pupil or teacher.

Values: beliefs or ideas that are important to the people who hold them. A value always expresses a belief about how something *should* be.

Norms: socially acceptable ways of behaving when playing a particular role.

Structuralist and interactionist views of the relationship between the individual and society

In the previous chapter we looked at different ideas about the relationship between the individual and society based on concepts of structure and action. These concepts are part of the **domain assumptions** (or key ideas) of the structuralist and **interactionist** perspectives. In this section, we examine the concepts of structure and action in more detail before looking at how the structuralist and interactionist perspectives can be combined.

KEY TERMS

Domain assumptions: fundamental assumptions on which a particular perspective or ideology is based. The domain assumptions of Marxism, for example, include economic exploitation and class conflict.

Interactionist: an approach focused on the behaviour of individuals that refers to three related perspectives (phenomenology, ethnomethodology and symbolic interactionism), based on the concept of social action.

Structuralist theories originated in the work of Durkheim and Marx. From a structuralist perspective, social action is the product of deep, underlying forces in society that reach beyond the level of individual consciousness and control. These structural forces shape our behaviour and have a major influence on our thought processes. Marx claimed that the capitalist relations of production were the main structural force in modern industrial societies. The way in which capitalist production of goods and services is organised, with the workers separated from ownership of land and factories, can be seen as an invisible mechanism that controls the way in which all other aspects of a society operate. By contrast, the functionalist perspective sees the structure of society more in terms of the institutional arrangements required to ensure the smooth running of society. So, for example, institutions such as the family, education and government are associated with established patterns of behaviour that together create an order and structure in society.

For structuralists, the established social order represents a powerful force that the individual has little or no freedom to oppose. For various reasons, people accept the established institutional patterns of behaviour as if they were a hidden force controlling their actions. By conforming to social rules in this way, each person's actions reflect the dominant influence of the social structure. For structuralists, therefore, sociology should be the study of the effects of the structure of society on social life. In other words, sociologists should adopt a macro, or large-scale view. The actions of the individual should be explained in terms of the influences of the overall structure or organisational arrangements of a society. For example, a structural explanation might identify poverty (which can be seen as part of the structure of society) as the cause of an increase in the crime rate. Likewise, differences in suicide rates might be explained in terms of differences in beliefs and practices between religious groups (religious institutions being part of the structure of society).

29

Is society, like gravity, an invisible force acting on us all?

The idea of social structure becomes a little clearer if we think about the different ways in which behaviour is governed by informal rules or norms that define expected behaviours in any given situation:

- Every relationship we form, such as making a new friend, becoming a parent or getting a new boss, involves playing a role – an idea that refers to people 'playing a part' in society. Just as an actor performs a role in a play, people take on and perform various roles (such as student, sister, brother, friend and employee) in their day-to-day life.
- Each role has certain associated values or beliefs about how something *should* be. For example, we may believe that friends *should* keep the secrets we tell them. There are also norms associated with each role, such as friends helping us if we are in trouble.

Every time we play a role, therefore, we experience the *effect* of social structures – rules that shape our behavioural choices. This suggests that social structures exert a significant influence on how we behave.

TEST YOURSELF

Identify two values associated with any two roles that you play.

Interactionism

Interactionism is a general term for a **microsociological** approach that focuses on the behaviour of individuals. Interactionism refers to three related perspectives (**phenomenology**, **ethnomethodology** and **symbolic interactionism**) based on the concept of social action – an idea we can illustrate using a distinction drawn by Weber (1922).

KEY TERMS

Microsociology: type of sociology focused on the study of individuals and small groups.

Phenomenology: interactionist approach that argues that the social world consists of *phenomena* whose meaning is both negotiated and interpreted through interaction.

Ethnomethodology: sociological approach that argues that all social interaction is underpinned by a search for meaning; if we can understand the meanings people give to a situation we can understand their behaviour in such situations. In this respect, it is possible to discover the nature of social order by disrupting it.

Symbolic interactionism: interactionist perspective that analyses society and situations in terms of the subjective meanings people impose on objects, events and behaviours.

Behaviour becomes action when it is directed towards other people in ways that take account of how those people act and react. In other words, social action involves a knowledge of how our behaviour might affect the people at whom it is directed. Whenever we have a conversation, for example, we are engaging in social action; how we behave is influenced by how the other person behaves, and vice versa.

If the concept of structure focuses on how behaviour is governed by constraints that control or, at times, determine how we behave, social action focuses on our ability to make choices about how to act. Interactionists therefore reject the determinist tendencies of structural approaches.

Interactionists argue that to explain human behaviour we need to study people's interactions at the micro level – that is, as they go about their daily lives – because, as Schutz (1962) argues, 'subjective meanings give rise to an apparently objective social world'. Societies are constructed through social interaction and this, in turn, is based on meanings. We live in a complex, symbolic world in which the meaning of our actions, our choice of clothes or the

30

language we use is always open to interpretation. The meaning of something, whether a physical object such as a mobile phone or a symbolic system such as language, is never self-evident and its meaning can be changed by the social context in which it appears. Wilson (2002) argues this point from a phenomenological perspective, claiming that 'we experience the world with and through others'. In other words, the social world – with its 'social artefacts and cultural objects' – consists of *phenomena* whose meaning is both negotiated and interpreted through interaction.

Briefly explain how objects like mobile phones may be seen as status symbols.

To understand how social context can determine or change the meaning of something, consider two people fighting:

■ If the fight occurs in the street we might interpret this as unacceptable and call the police.

■ If the two people were fighting in a boxing ring rather than disapproving, we might cheer and encourage our favoured fighter.

While this example demonstrates that meanings must always be interpreted, it also suggests that interaction is based on shared definitions of a situation, which themselves may be the product of negotiation. Social interaction, therefore, does not simply involve obeying rules without question, because the meaning of behaviour can change depending on its social context. Wrong (1961) criticises what he calls an '**over-socialised conception of man**'. He rejects the idea that human behaviour is governed entirely by the effects of socialisations. For Wrong, people are able to exercise a degree of freedom from the influences of their social environment.

KEY TERM

Over-socialised conception of man: criticism of the claim that human beings are simply the product of their socialisation and that behaviour can be understood as merely a response to external stimulation.

Garfinkel's (1967) ethnomethodological 'breaching experiments' demonstrate this idea. He deliberately set out to upset people's definition of a situation to show how they 'construct reality'. In one experiment he sent researchers into restaurants and told them to deliberately mistake

customers for waiters. While they were doing so, Garfinkel secretly observed the reactions of the waiters (amusement, confusion and anger). This line of argument concludes that society is not a 'thing' or 'force' acting on our behaviour, since it has no objective reality beyond social interaction. Rather, as Schutz argues, society has a subjective reality – we experience it through social interaction. Society is simply a label we give to the rules and responsibilities arising from our relationships.

Could 'society' be just a label we give to social interaction?

The idea of labelling demonstrates how interactionists view society as the product of social interaction. Labelling theory argues that when we name something, such as categorising people as 'male' or 'female', we associate the name with a set of characteristics that are then used to guide our behaviour. These characteristics influence our behaviour and attitude to the named person, object or situation. If the meaning of something is only developed through interaction, then meanings can change. For example, male and female social identities have changed over the past 50 years. In Western societies female identity has changed dramatically. Previously, a woman was defined almost exclusively in terms of marriage, motherhood and caring for others. Today, there is a wider range of definitions, such as the single career woman, which reflects changing ideas about equality and perceptions of women.

Structuration

Concepts of structure and action are both important in helping us understand the relationship between society and the individual. Although we are all individuals, our behavioural choices are influenced, limited and enhanced by the framework of rules and responsibilities (social structures) that surround us. Just as we cannot conceive of society without individuals, it is impossible to think about people without referring to the ways in which their behaviour is structured. Giddens (1984) developed a perspective called **structuration**, which outlined the importance of both structure and action in considering the relationship between society and the individual.

> **KEY TERM**
>
> **Structuration:** theory, developed by Giddens, which argues that structure and action are equally significant in terms of our ability to understand the relationship between the individual and society.

The key to structuration is the idea that as people develop relationships, the rules they use to govern their behaviours are *formalised* into routine ways of behaving towards each other (*practices*). Through the huge range of practices in our lives, a sense of structure develops in our social world – and this involves rules. This idea is important because it indicates the way our actions create behavioural rules and demonstrates how such rules become *externalised* (they seem to take on a life of their own, separate from our individual behaviours). Thus, although we may exhibit rule-making behaviour, these rules 'reflect back' (*reflexivity*) on our behaviour in ways that suggest or demand **conformity**.

> **KEY TERM**
>
> **Conformity:** behaving in a socially acceptable way.

In explaining why some rules are created and accepted while others are discarded, Giddens uses the idea of social resources and power relationships. Some rules are *negotiated*; friendship, for example, is based on a series of unwritten and unspoken rules that develop over time. Other rules, such as laws governing punishments for murder, are *non-negotiable*; they are simply imposed on individuals by powerful groups.

> **ACTIVITY**
>
> *Think about the groups to which you belong (such as family, school or college, work, friends and peers) and answer the following:*
>
> 1 *How do these groups shape my behaviour?*
> 2 *How does my behaviour shape the behaviour of other people in these groups?*
> 3 *Which groups have most influence on my behaviour?*

The processes of learning and socialisation: how the individual becomes a competent social actor

Socialisation is a process that describes how we are taught the behavioural rules we need to become both a member of a particular society/culture and a competent social actor. Genetics suggests that behaviour may be guided by instincts based on biological imperatives (commands that cannot be ignored). From this viewpoint, people are born with certain abilities that are part of 'human nature'.

> **KEY TERM**
>
> **Socialisation:** process through which people learn the various forms of behaviour consistent with membership of a particular culture. Young children, for example, must learn the roles, norms and values they will need to become a fully functioning member of their society; these are things children do not acquire 'naturally'.

At one extreme, instincts are fixed human traits. These are things we are born knowing, such as a 'mothering instinct', and our cultural environment plays little or no role in the development of these instincts. A weaker expression of this idea is that people are born with certain capabilities that are then realised through environmental experiences. 'Nature' gives us strong hints about behavioural rules, but people are free to ignore those hints. If women have greater child-nurturing capabilities than men, then it makes genetic sense for them to take on a caring role within a family. However, this is not something their genes force them to do. One way to test whether nature, in the form of instincts, or nurture, in the form of socialisation, is the more important factor is to take advantage of a naturally occurring form of experimentation – the study of unsocialised or feral children.

Feral children

Evidence of human infants raised by animals is rare and not always reliable, although there is one notable example – that of Saturday Mthiyane, who was discovered in 1987, aged five, living with a pack of monkeys in South Africa. However, evidence of children raised with little or no human contact is more common. A well-documented example is 'Genie', a 13-year-old Californian girl discovered in 1970. Pines (1997) notes that Genie had

32

been 'isolated in a small room and had not been spoken to by her parents since infancy. She was malnourished, abused, unloved, bereft of any toys or companionship.' When Genie was found, 'she could not stand erect … she was unable to speak: she could only whimper'.

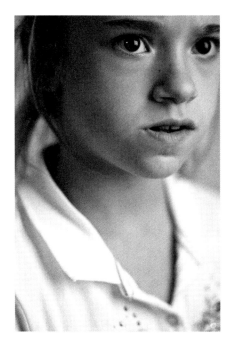

How do feral children like Genie, or Dani who was discovered in Florida in 2005 (pictured here), demonstrate the importance of socialisation?

Feral children are sociologically significant for two main reasons. First, when children are raised without human contact they fail to show the social and physical development we would expect from a conventionally raised child – for example, walking upright, talking, using eating implements. Second, if human behaviour is instinctive it is not clear why children such as Genie should develop so differently from children raised with human contact. We would also expect that, once returned to human society, feral children would quickly pick up normal human behaviours. This, however, is not the case.

Further evidence for the significance of socialisation is the fact that different cultures develop different ways of doing things. If human behaviours were governed by instinct, we would expect there to be few, if any, differences between societies.

Sometimes cultural differences are relatively trivial. Billikopf (1999) discovered through his own experience that 'in Russia, when a man peels a banana for a lady it means he has a romantic interest in her'. At other times cultural differences are more fundamental. Wojtczak (2009) argues that in Victorian Britain most women 'lived in a state little better than slavery'. As she notes: 'women's sole purpose was to marry and reproduce.' This is not a situation we would recognise in British society today.

If human behaviour was instinctive, it would be much the same, regardless of place or time. The fact that this is not the case suggests as Podder and Bergvall (2004) argue, that 'culture isn't something we're born with, it is taught to us'.

TEST YOURSELF

Briefly explain how feral children can be used to test the influence of nature or nurture on human behaviour.

The 'I' and the 'Me'

Basic human skills have to be taught and learnt. the symbolic interactionist George Herbert Mead (1934) argued that the same was true of more advanced social skills. He claimed that how people behave is conditioned by the social context in which behaviour occurs. While self-awareness – the ability to see ourselves as others see us and react accordingly – is often seen as an instinctive human attribute, Mead argued that it is in fact learnt. It involves developing a concept of Self, and this is what sets humans apart from animals. For Mead, 'the Self' (an awareness of who we are) has two related aspects:

- An 'I' aspect based around our opinion of ourselves as a whole. We each respond to the behaviour of others as an 'I'. Mead called this the 'unsocialised self'.
- A 'Me' aspect that consists of an awareness of how others expect us to behave in a given situation. Mead called this the '**social self**' because it develops through socialisation.

KEY TERM

Social self: an awareness of how others expect us to behave in given situations means that our sense of Self – who we believe ourselves to be – is created through social interaction and exchange.

We can illustrate these ideas in the following way. If you accidentally put your hand in a fire, the 'I' is expressed by how you react to the pain. The 'Me', however, specifically conditions how you choose to express that pain; your reaction will be conditioned by factors such as:

- who you are – whether you are male or female, adult or child, etc.
- where you are – alone at home or in a public place
- who you are with – such as family, friends or strangers.

33

If you are a young child, for example, your reaction to being burnt may be to cry. If you are a young man, you may feel that crying is not a socially acceptable reaction – so you may swear loudly instead. Swearing loudly may be acceptable if you are at home by yourself, but may not be acceptable if you are fixing a stranger's fire as part of your job. Similarly, if you had been messing around with friends when you burnt your hand, their reaction may be to laugh and make fun of your pain. Laughter would not be an appropriate reaction if it was your child who had burnt their hand.

The presentation of self

If the social context of an act changes both its meaning and how people react, it follows that an awareness of self is constructed and developed socially. Goffman (1959) argues that who we believe ourselves to be – our sense of identity – is also constructed socially through how we present ourselves to others.

Goffman proposed a model of self and identity in which he described social life as a series of dramatic episodes. People are *actors*. Sometimes they write and speak their own lines – this is their personal identity. Sometimes they follow lines that are written for them – the external influences that inform how people behave in particular situations and roles. For example, because we understand how our society defines masculinity and femininity, we know how we are expected to behave if we are male or female. As Barnhart (1994) puts it: 'Interaction is a performance, shaped by environment and audience, constructed to provide others with impressions' about how the actor wants to be seen.

The idea of creating an impression is also significant in relation to how we present ourselves in different situations. Goffman suggests that when we adopt a particular identity, we 'perform' to others in order to 'manage' the impression they have of us. Identity performance, therefore, is about achieving a desired result: when you want to create a favourable impression on someone you 'act' in ways you believe they will like.

Fifty years before Goffman, Cooley (1909) suggested that in the majority of social encounters other people are used as a **looking-glass self**. They are like mirrors

KEY TERM

Looking-glass self: theory that argues that our sense of self develops from how we are seen by others; we understand who we are by looking in the 'mirror' of how others behave towards us.

reflecting 'our self as others see us'; when we 'look into the mirror' of how others behave towards us we see reflected an image of the person *they* think we are.

The presentation of self always involves two characteristics of social **action theory**:

1. The importance of interpretation: identities are broad social categories whose meaning differs both historically and cross-culturally.
2. The significance of negotiation. Identities are always open to discussion; what it means to be male, female, young, old and so forth is constantly changing as people 'push the negotiated boundaries' of these identities.

KEY TERM

Action theory: sociological perspective focusing on individuals and how their interactions create and re-create a sense of society.

TEST YOURSELF

Suggest one way you try to manage the impression people have of you.

Alternatives

Not all scientific disciplines place the same emphasis on socialisation when explaining how individuals become competent social actors. For example, biological ideas about evolution have sometimes been used to explain social development. These ideas range from relatively crude forms of 'social Darwinism', based on the idea that social life simply involves 'the survival of the fittest', to the more sophisticated arguments of sociobiology. In these, biological principles of natural selection and evolution are applied to the 'human animal' to produce what Wilson (1979) argues is a 'biological basis' for all human behaviour. He claims that although human behaviour is not genetically determined, it is strongly influenced by 'biological programming'.

These 'biogrammers' suggest that we are predisposed to behave in a particular way. For example, men and women are biologically programmed with different traits that lead them to perform different cultural roles:

- Women are passive, nurturing and caring, which makes them best suited to child-rearing.
- Male traits of aggression best suit them to a 'providing role' that translates into paid work in contemporary societies.

A similar argument is found in the work of functionalist sociologists such as Parsons (1959a). He argues that in most societies, family roles are organised to reflect the belief that women play an expressive role – that of caring for others. Men, however, play an instrumental role – one geared towards providing for the family. Both of these roles are based, in part, on evolutionary biological principles.

While males and females can choose not to fulfil these roles, behaviour that opposes this biological instinct is generally a less efficient way of organising human cultural relationships. As a result, sociobiologists claim that attempts to limit the effects of biological programming – such as social engineering – will cause social problems.

KEY TERM

Social engineering: cultural manipulation of individuals to produce particular social outcomes, such as gender equality.

Evolutionary psychology explains contemporary psychological and social traits in terms of the general principles of natural selection: those behaviours that are evolutionarily successful are selected and reproduced. In this way, various forms of social behaviour, such as family development and gender roles, can be explained as evolutionary adaptations occurring over many centuries. They represent successful adaptations to problems common to all human societies, such as how to raise children while also providing the things family members need for survival.

Psychology is, however, a diverse field and there are many different explanations for human development. These range from those focused on genetics (such as evolutionary psychology), through disciplines such as neuropsychology, to social psychological approaches broadly similar to the interactionist theories found in the works of Mead and Goffman.

The relatively recent development of neuropsychology, for example, focuses on the functions of the brain and how they influence behaviour. Traditionally, this has involved comparing 'normal' and 'abnormal' (damaged) brain functioning to explain behavioural differences. Bruce and Young (1986), for example, investigated the relationship between brain damage in soldiers and prosopagnosia (face recognition problems). More recently, neuropsychology has been used to investigate things such as criminal behaviour. Cauffman et al. (2005)

argue that differences in juvenile brain functioning play a part in antisocial behaviour. Wortley (2011) suggests that neuropsychological factors can explain crimes committed by different types of offender. These factors include how our brains react to punishment or being denied something desirable, as well as whether some brain functions are not working as they should. Wortley argue that while 'genes may be responsible for certain behavioural predispositions, they do not themselves produce behaviour'. Fallon's (2006) neurological research had already revealed that the brain structure of psychopathic killers was not always significantly different from the brain structure of people who did not engage in violent, risky, behaviours. The crucial difference was the social environment in which such people were raised. For example, people who were abused as children were much more likely to develop murderous impulses in adulthood.

Social psychology places greater stress on how environmental factors, such as family and work relationships, affect the development of genetic or psychological predispositions. Meins et al. (2002) noted that although there exists a genetic impulse for babies to become attached to their primary care-giver, this impulse can be affected by environmental factors. The most important of these is the ability of the care-giver to empathise with and understand the needs of the child (*mind-mindedness*). Maternal mind-mindedness, for example, predicts whether the attachment will be secure or insecure – something with significant consequences for a child's emotional, psychological and social development. Van IJzendoorn (1997) argues that there is strong evidence to suggest that insecurely attached infants have more problems forming secure attachments with other adults later in life. They find it more difficult, for example, to regulate 'negative emotions', such as anger, or manage the delicate emotional balance between 'self-confidence and a concern for others'.

ACTIVITY

Make a list of anything you think might be instinctive human behaviour (such as eating, sleeping, crime, childcare etc.). Remove an item from the list if people have a choice about whether or not to do it (such as crime) or how and when we do it (such as eating). What do the remaining items on your list tell you about the influence of instincts and culture on human behaviour?

35

Agencies of socialisation: family, education, peer group, media, religion

We previously noted Podder and Bergvall's observation that culture 'isn't something we're born with, it is taught to us'. This means that learn the rules for interaction with one another through socialisation – a process that takes two main forms:

1 According to Cooley, primary socialisation occurs within primary groups involving 'intimate face-to-face association and cooperation'. This type of socialisation is critical to the development of behaviours we recognise as fundamentally human, such as learning language. The first primary relationship we form is usually with our parents. This is followed by primary attachments to people of our own age (friends) and, subsequently, with other adults, such as work colleagues. Primary socialisation is necessary because human infants need other people in order to develop both as human beings and as members of a particular culture. We do not just need to learn general human behaviours, we must also learn about social relationships, how to play roles, etc.

2 Secondary socialisation involves secondary groups and is characterised, according to Berger and Luckmann (1967), by 'a sense of detachment from the ones teaching socialisation'. Secondary socialisations are situations in which we do not necessarily have close, personal contacts with those doing the socialising. Parsons (1959a) argues that one of the main purposes of secondary socialisation is to 'liberate the individual from a dependence on the primary attachments and relationships formed within the family group'. In contemporary societies, where the majority of people we meet are strangers, it would be impossible and undesirable to treat them in the same way we treat people we love or know well. This is why we develop instrumental relationships – those based on what people can do for us, or what we can do for them, in particular situations. Berger and Luckmann suggest that while primary socialisation involves 'emotionally charged identification' with people such as our parents, secondary socialisation is characterised by 'formality and anonymity'. You do not, for example, treat a stranger who asks you for directions as your closest friend.

How does forcing people to dress identically contribute to their socialisation?

Social control

The process of socialisation brings *order, stability* and *predictability* to people's behaviour. If a child is socialised into a 'right' way of doing something, such as eating with a knife and fork, there must also be a 'wrong' or deviant way (such as eating with their fingers), which should be discouraged. Socialisation, therefore, is a form of social control that Pfohl (1998) characterises thus: 'Imagine *deviance* as noise – a cacophony of subversions disrupting the harmony of a given social order. *Social control* is the opposite. It labours to transform the noisy challenge of difference into the music of conformity.'

Social control is linked to the idea that human behaviour involves a life-long process of rule-learning, underpinned by sanctions – the things we do to make people conform:

- Positive sanctions (*rewards*) are the pleasant things we do to make people behave in routine, predictable, ways. These range from smiling, through praise and encouragement, to gifts.
- Negative sanctions (*punishments*) are the reverse. They include not talking to people if they annoy us, putting people in prison and the ultimate negative sanction – killing someone.

Social controls take two basic forms:

1 *Formal controls* involve written rules, such as laws, that apply equally to everyone in a society. They also include non-legal rules that apply to everyone playing a particular role in an organisation (such as a school or factory). Sanctions are enforced by agencies of social control – for example, the police and the legal system. Formal controls tell everyone within a group *exactly* what is and is not acceptable behaviour. Infringement of these

TEST YOURSELF

Identify one difference between primary and secondary socialisation.

rules (deviance) may result in formal sanctions – such as a fine or imprisonment for breaking the law, or being sacked for breaking a company's organisational rules.

2   *Informal controls* reward or punish acceptable/ unacceptable behaviour in everyday, informal, settings (such as the family). These controls do not normally involve written rules and procedures. Rather, they operate through informal enforcement mechanisms that might include ridicule, sarcasm, disapproving looks or personal violence. Such controls mainly apply to the regulation of primary relationships and groups. However, there are exceptions because primary relationships can occur within secondary groups – a teacher, for example, may also be a friend or even a relative. Informal controls also relate to the 'unofficial rules' we create in casual groups. A few of these rules might be applied generally – for example, unless you are in a boxing ring, punching someone in the face is generally regarded as unacceptable. However, the majority of unofficial rules are specific to a particular group. Swearing among friends, for example, may not invite sanction, but swearing at your mother or father might.

Agencies of socialisation

We can look at selected agencies of socialisation in terms of the roles, values and norms they try to teach and the sanctions they impose.

Primary

Family: Although there are only a small number of family roles, these tend to be played out over long periods and involve complex forms of role development, especially in societies that allow divorce and remarriage. Adults may have to learn roles ranging from husband/wife to parent/ step-parent. Child development also involves a range of

Within a family, how do children play their roles differently from adults?

roles: baby, infant, child, teenager and, eventually perhaps, an adult with children of their own.

The ability to develop roles within the context of a group mainly governed by relationships based on love, responsibility and duty, means that we can make mistakes and learn lessons as we go without causing too much harm. Mead refers to parents as **significant others**. They shape both our basic values, such as how to address adults, and our *moral values* – for example, our understanding of the difference between right and wrong. Basic norms, such as how to address family members (e.g. *Mum*, *Dad*), when, where and how to eat and sleep, and definitions of acceptable behaviour are normally taught within the family. Sanctions are mainly *informal*, with positive sanctions involving things like:

- facial expressions (smiling, for example)
- verbal approval/reinforcement ('good boy/girl')
- physical rewards (such as gifts).

> **KEY TERM**
>
> **Significant others:** people who are important to us and whose opinions we value.

Negative sanctions are similarly wide-ranging – from showing disapproval through language (such as shouting) to physical punishment.

Functionalists often see primary socialisation as a one-way process that passes from adults to children. However, socialisation involves more than an unquestioning acceptance of the behaviours we learn within the family group. Although children are socialised by *copying* behaviour (Hartley (1959) argues that imitation of adult family behaviours, such as girls 'helping mum' with domestic chores is an important part of socialisation) they are also actively involved in negotiating their socialisation. For example, children do not always obey their parents. Children may also receive contradictory socialisation messages: a relative may reward behaviour that a parent would punish.

Peers: Peer groups are made up of people of a similar age, such as teenagers. They can be considered primary agencies of socialisation because we usually choose friends of a similar age, and personal interaction with them influences our behaviour – from how we dress and talk to the things we love or hate. Peer groups can also be secondary agencies because they may be used as a reference group – what Hughes et al. (2002) call 'the models we use for appraising and shaping our attitudes, feelings and actions'. In the recent past this has included youth **sub-cultures** such as hippies, skinheads and punks. Although we may never personally interact with these groups, our own behaviour may be influenced by things like the fashions and the general behaviour of people our own age. This is an example of peer pressure as a form of social control.

KEY TERM

Sub-cultures: a culture within a larger culture. Sub-cultures take many forms, such as religious groups, fans of a particular singer or actor, school gangs, etc. Sub-cultures usually develop their own norms and values, although these do not necessarily conflict with those of the wider culture within which they exist.

How do your friends influence your behaviour?

We play a range of peer-related roles, depending on our age group and situation. 'Friend', for example, expresses very personal role play, whereas at school or work we may have a variety of acquaintances. In the workplace, too, we are likely to play the role of colleague to at least some of our peers. Similarly, the values we are taught within a friendship or peer group vary with age and circumstances. However, we will probably carry the value of friendship with us throughout our lives.

Peer-group norms often relate to ideas about age-appropriate behaviour. Young children, for example, are not allowed to smoke or buy alcohol. Conversely, it is generally not considered age-appropriate for the elderly to take part in extreme sports or wear clothes designed for younger people. Peer-group sanctions, or **social sanctions**, are generally informal and include things like disapproving

looks and disparaging comments. This is mainly because peer-group norms vary considerably, and the same behaviour may result in different responses depending on the situation. Swearing at a grandparent will probably be met with disapproval; swearing among friends may be perfectly acceptable. Approving gestures and language, laughing at your jokes and seeking out your company may represent positive sanctions. Refusing to speak to you, rejecting your friendship or engaging in physical violence are negative sanctions associated with peer groups.

KEY TERM

Social sanctions: rewards and punishments designed to exert social control and enforce conformity to roles, norms and values.

Secondary

Agencies of secondary socialisation include schools, religious organisations and the media. In some cases, such as education, we are in daily contact with other members of the group without ever developing a primary attachment to them. In other examples, such as admiring a particular actor or musician, we may never meet them, yet we might be influenced by their behaviour in several ways.

Education: Education involves two kinds of curricula:

- a formal curriculum that specifies the subjects, knowledge and skills children are explicitly taught in school
- a hidden curriculum that Jackson (1968) describes as the things we learn from the experience of attending school, such as how to deal with strangers, obedience to adult authority and respect for the system.

School is also a place where we 'learn to limit our individual desires' – to think about the needs of others rather than our own. School may be one of the first times that children are separated from their parent(s) for any length of time. It provides both *opportunities* (to demonstrate talents to a wider, non-family, audience) and *traumas* – the need to learn, for example, how to deal with people who are not family and *authority figures* such as teachers.

Parsons (1959a) argued that school plays a particularly significant role in secondary socialisation for two reasons:

1 It 'emancipates the child from primary attachment' to their family. It eases children away from the affective relationships found in the family and introduces them to the instrumental relationships they will meet in adult life.

2 It allows children to 'internalise a level of society's values and norms that is a step higher than those learnt within families'. Through interaction with 'strangers' in the educational system, a child begins to adopt wider social values into their personal value system. This process loosens the hold of primary groups and allows children to gradually integrate into adult society, something that also promotes social solidarity and value consensus.

Like any institution, schools involve a range of roles, such as teacher and pupil, which are themselves linked to a range of related roles called a role-set. This further extends the idea of cultural relationships because we become locked into a range of *expected behaviours*. A pupil, for example, plays this role in relation to the roles others are playing in the school environment:

- other pupils in their class
- pupils of different ages
- their subject teachers
- teachers of other subjects
- caretaking staff
- administration staff
- parent(s)/guardian(s).

Schools project a range of values. These range from the idea that pupils should work hard to achieve qualifications to ideas about individual competition for academic rewards, teamwork, conformity to authority (not questioning what is being learnt and why it is necessary to learn it) and achievement on the basis of merit. In many education systems, one 'covert value' is that academic ability, such as a talent for writing essays, is more highly valued than vocational ability, such as bricklaying. Many of these values relate not just to education but also to the wider social world, especially that of the workplace.

From a Marxist perspective, Bowles and Gintis (2002) argue that there is a *correspondence* between school norms and workplace norms: 'Schools prepare pupils for adult work rules by socialising them to function well, and without complaint, in the hierarchical structure of the modern corporation.' This correspondence theory is evidenced through school norms like:

- the daily need for attendance
- always being in the place you are supposed to be at certain times
- the right of those in authority to give orders that must be obeyed.

These ideas are backed up by positive sanctions that include the gaining of grades, qualifications and prizes, as well as more personal things such as praise and encouragement. On the negative side, schools use detentions, suspensions and exclusions. Failure to achieve qualifications or gaining a reputation as being unintelligent also function as negative sanctions.

TEST YOURSELF

Suggest two further examples of the connection between school and work. Also suggest arguments against the idea that there is a correspondence between school norms and workplace norms.

Mass media: The media is a slightly unusual secondary agency because our relationship with it is *impersonal*; we are unlikely to meet those doing the socialising. While there is little evidence that the media has a direct, long-term effect on behaviour, there is stronger evidence of short-term effects. Advertising, for example, aims to make short-term changes in behaviour by encouraging people to try different consumer products. Potter (2003) suggests that short-term effects include:

- imitation, such as copying behaviour seen on television
- desensitisation – the idea that constant and repeated exposure to something, such as violence or poverty, progressively lowers our emotional reaction
- learning, in which we are introduced to new ideas and places.

Does repeated exposure to images of violence, poverty or racism desensitise us to such issues?

39

There is also some evidence for *indirect* long-term effects. Chandler (1995) argues that 'television has long-term effects, which are small, gradual, indirect but cumulative and significant'. Potter claims that these include things such as:

- **consumerism** – the active and ever-increasing pursuit of goods and services that define lifestyles and identities in contemporary capitalist societies
- fear – where 'heavy exposure to negative and violent' media leads some people to overestimate things such as the extent of crime or their likelihood of being a victim
- agenda setting – Philo et al. (1982) argue that the media determines how something will be debated; in the UK, for example, immigration is framed in terms of 'numbers of immigrants' and Islam is frequently discussed in the context of 'terrorism'. The media sub-text here is that 'Muslim = terrorist'.

KEY TERM

Consumerism: repeated exposure to affluent lifestyles and desirable consumer goods that suggests that 'happiness' is something that can bought.

The extent to which the media can impose values on behaviour is uncertain. However, the media is undoubtedly influential in supporting or marginalising certain values. It has a loud voice in debates over nationality (what it means to be 'British' or 'Chinese', for example). It also promotes certain values while devaluing others – for example, many English newspapers take an 'anti-European Community' stance. Potter suggests that media influence comes about through a process of habituation: the more people are exposed to certain images and ideas, the more likely it is that they will incorporate them into their personal value systems. In relation to norms, the media has what Durkheim (1912) called a 'boundary-marking function'. It publicises acceptable and unacceptable forms of behaviour to reinforce perceptions of expected behaviours. The media may try to preserve particular ways of behaving, through campaigns to 'save the family', for example, but it may also promote changes in behaviour, such as campaigns against racism. To reinforce its message, the media employs a range of sanctions. Positive sanctions involve the use of praise, flattering pictures and uncritical features. Negative sanctions might include being pictured in an unflattering pose, critical articles or behaviour being held up to public ridicule.

Religion: Whether or not we see ourselves as 'religious', religion plays a significant role in the general socialisation process in many societies, particularly in relation to ceremonial functions, such as marriages and funerals. It can also be argued that important moral values – very strong beliefs about how people should behave – are influenced by religious values. For example, several of the Ten Commandments in Christian religions are reflected in legal systems around the world.

In terms of moral beliefs, few people would argue that murder or theft are acceptable. However, many of the world's major religions, from Christianity to Islam, are accused of promoting patriarchy through both their general organisation (many religions have an exclusively male clergy) and the gender values they encourage. Despite this, Swatos (1998) argues that contemporary religions are undergoing fundamental changes that make them more 'female friendly'. For example, God is increasingly portrayed as loving and consoling rather than as authoritarian and judgemental, and clergy are seen as 'helping professionals' rather than as 'representatives of God's justice'.

Religious values are powerful forces for those who believe. Religion can be regarded as a 'design for living' – a force that provides help and guidance to live a life in accord with God, but religious beliefs and values can also be a source of conflict:

- between religions, such as the history of conflict between Christians and Muslims dating back to the 11th century
- within the same religion: Northern Ireland, for example, has experienced major conflicts between Protestant and Catholic Christians over the past 50 years.

Religious values are frequently displayed through styles of dress, such as the Muslim hijab or Sikh turban, something that indicates both religiosity (a measure of people's commitment to religion) and ethnic identity. Religious values are also expressed through notions of patriarchy and social control. Although, as Steggerda (1993) notes, Christianity promotes concepts of love and care that are attractive to women, and Daly (1973) argues that in a 'male-dominated world' religions provide women with a sense of shelter, safety in a threatening world and belonging; the price they pay for these benefits is submission to patriarchal control.

Religions apply positive sanctions on their followers in different ways:

- Hinduism involves a belief in *reincarnation* (when you die you are reborn into a new life) based on how well you observed religious laws in your previous life; the reward for good behaviour in one lifetime is rebirth into a higher social position.

- Notions of *sin* in Christian religions can also be significant features of religious control, because the believer is encouraged to live a life free of sin in the hope of heavenly reward.

Negative sanctions are also many and varied. Catholicism, for example, has the sanction of excommunication (exclusion from the church), whereas some forms of Islam specify a range of punishments for those who break Shari'ah law. Such punishments may also be applied to 'non-believers' in theocratic societies, such as Iran, where government is dominated by religious authorities.

ACTIVITY

Draw a spider diagram centred on any role you play to illustrate its role-set. What does this diagram tell you about how you present yourself to society or a particular social group? What types of influence are making you take on the role, and why? See example below.

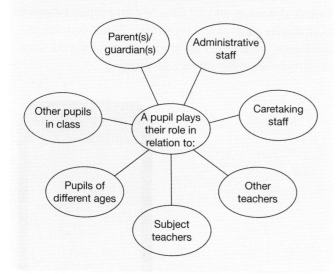

Culture, roles, norms, values, beliefs, ideology and power as elements in the social construction of reality

In previous sections we have referred generally to ideas such as 'society' and 'culture'. In this section we are going to explore these ideas in more depth.

Defining society

While 'a society' is a concept that is easy to reference – we all probably understand what is meant by Indian, Mauritian, Nigerian or British society – it is more difficult to define. One key feature, however, is that people see themselves as having something in common with others in their society and, by extension, they consider themselves to be different from people in other societies. In this respect, different societies involve two types of *space*:

1 Physical space, in the sense of a distinctive geographical area marked by either a physical border, such as a river, or a symbolic border – perhaps an imaginary line that marks where one society ends and another begins.

2 Mental space, which separates people based on the beliefs they have about the similarities they share with those in 'their' society and the differences from those in other societies.

It seems straightforward to define a society in terms of physical space – Mauritius occupies a certain geographic area, Nigeria another and India yet another. Yet in itself this space is a *mental* construction; we are simply giving a particular meaning and significance to what is effectively a line on a map.

Anderson (1983) captures the significance of this idea when he categorises societies as 'imagined communities' – things that exist only in the mind. He points out that 'the members of even the smallest nation will never know most of their fellow members, meet them, or even hear of them, yet in the minds of each lives the image of their communion'. Societies are mentally constructed by:

- geographic borders that set physical boundaries – we might, for example, consider that everyone born within these borders belongs to a particular society

- a system of government, which may involve a monarchy, parliament and civil service, for example

- common language, **customs** and traditions that people share

- a sense of belonging and identification that involves developing an awareness of 'our' society as different from other societies; Indians, for example, may see themselves as different from Pakistanis or Bangladeshis.

41

KEY TERM

Customs: established and accepted cultural practices and behaviours.

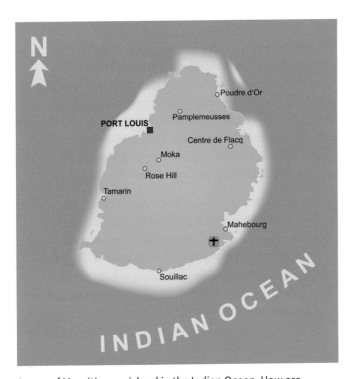

A map of Mauritius, an island in the Indian Ocean. How are societies 'imagined communities'?

The social construction of reality

If societies are mental constructions, it follows that their reality is socially constructed. To understand how this occurs we need to explore the concept of culture. We have previous referred to culture as a distinctive 'way of life' that has to be taught and learnt through primary and secondary socialisation. We can develop this concept to understand how culture contributes to the **social construction of reality**. Dahl (2000) defines culture as 'a collectively held set of attributes, which is dynamic and changing over time' that structures the social world. In this respect, all cultures have two basic components:

■ Material culture involves the physical objects ('artefacts'), such as cars, phones and books, that a society produces and that reflect cultural knowledge, skills, interests and preoccupations.
■ Non-material culture consists of the knowledge and beliefs valued by a particular culture. This includes religious and scientific beliefs as well as meanings people

give to material objects. Merton (1957) suggests that objects such as cars, houses and clothes can function in two ways. Their *manifest function* refers to the purpose for which they exist; clothes, for example, function to keep you warm. Their *latent function* however, may be hidden or obscured. Material objects might function as status symbols – owning something a culture feels is desirable says something about you to others.

TEST YOURSELF

Identify an example of material and non-material culture in your society.

The idea that cultural objects can have different meanings suggests that cultural interaction, especially in contemporary societies, is both sophisticated and complex. The more sophisticated the interaction in any society, the more open it is to misinterpretation.

In order to make sense of cultural interaction, therefore, we need to create common meanings and establish a structure within which behaviour can be played out in predictable ways. For a society to function it must have order and stability, and for these to exist people's behaviour must display patterns and regularities. While cultures may develop differently, they are all constructed from the same basic materials: roles, values and norms.

An essential tool of communication or a beautiful object of desire?

Roles

Roles are a building block of culture for two reasons:

1 They are always played in relation to other roles. For someone to play the role of teacher, for example, others must play the role of students. Roles contribute to the

creation of culture, therefore, because they demand both social interactions – people have to co-operate to successfully perform certain tasks – and an awareness of others. In this respect, roles help individuals develop *sociality*, the ability to form groups and communities, particularly when they are grouped into role-sets. This adds a further dimension to the cultural framework because it locks people into a range of relationships, each with its own routines and responsibilities.

2   Every role has a name (or label). This name identifies a particular role and carries with it a sense of how people are *expected* to behave in any situation.

Values

These common expectations provide a sense of order and predictability because role play is governed by behavioural rules in two ways:

1   All roles have a prescribed aspect based on beliefs about how people *should* behave. Role play, therefore, is governed by values that provide general behavioural guidelines – a teacher *should* teach their students, a parent *should* care for their child, etc.

2   Values are a *general* structuring agency; they provide only broad guidance for role behaviour. For example, it is understood that someone playing the role of teacher should teach, but values do not tell them *how* to play this role. The specific behavioural guides that tell people how to successfully play a role are known as norms.

Norms

Thio (1991) argues that 'while norms are specific rules dictating how people should act in a particular situation, values are general ideas that support the norm'. Norms, therefore, are behavioural rules used to perform roles predictably and acceptably. This is important, according to Merton (1938), because without order and predictability, behaviour becomes risky and confusing. He used the term *anomie* to describe a condition where people who fail to understand the norms operating in a particular situation react in a range of ways – from confusion, through anger to fear.

Goffman (1959) argues that norms are more open to interpretation and negotiation than either roles or values. This means they can quickly adapt to changes in the social environment. There are many ways to perform a teaching role, depending on a range of personal and cultural factors – including the behaviour of those in the teacher's role-set. Some teachers interpret their role as strict disciplinarians; others adopt a more friendly approach. However, these interpretations are not set in

stone; even the strictest teacher may relax their approach at certain times.

How do different teachers interpret their roles differently?

Beliefs

Roles, values and norms provide an important framework within which relationships can be ordered and made broadly predictable. A further layer of cultural structuring involves beliefs. These are the fundamental, deep-rooted ideas that shape our values and are, in some respects, shaped by them. While all values express a belief, beliefs do not necessarily express a value. They are more general behavioural guidelines that include ideas, opinions, convictions and attitudes. These may or may not be true; what matters is that they are *believed* to be true. Beliefs in contemporary societies are many and varied, but they perform a significant structuring role when combined with systems or ideologies.

Ideologies

Joseph (1990) argues that all ideologies are constructed around a set of fundamental beliefs whose ultimate purpose is to explain something. This might be:

■   the meaning of life (scientific and religious ideologies)
■   the nature of family organisation (familial ideologies)
■   the superiority/inferiority of selected social groups (sexist or racist ideologies).

Blake (2004) notes that ideology has come to mean something 'not to be believed' – referring to beliefs as 'ideological' suggests that they involve a partial, or biased account. However, the *function* of ideology is more important here than its form or content. All ideologies include elements of propaganda, as those who believe in a particular ideological viewpoint seek to convince others.

Henderson (1981) takes the concept of ideology a little further when she argues that 'an ideology is a pattern of ideas,

43

both factual and based on values, which claims to explain and legitimise the social structure and culture of a particular group in society'. In other words, ideologies provide the justification for particular attitudes and behaviours.

Critical theory argues that ideologies have a manipulative element: a capitalist-controlled media directly attempts to influence its audience by constructing and presenting a version of reality favourable to the ruling class. Adorno and Horkheimer (1944), part of the Marxist Frankfurt School, argued that ruling-class ideology is transmitted through a culture industry that creates forms of popular culture – film, magazines, comics, newspapers, etc. – which are consumed uncritically and passively by the masses. By controlling the culture industry, a ruling class controls the means of mental production – how people see and think about the social world.

KEY TERM

Critical theory: theory developed by and associated with Marxism that seeks to understand, criticise and change the nature of capitalist societies or some feature of such societies.

Ideologies are important in the social construction of reality because they play an overarching structural role in any society. They represent complete systems of belief – something Chibnall (1977) suggests is important because 'ideological structures permit events to be "mapped", i.e. located within wider contexts and related to similar events'. In this sense, ideologies are mental maps that tell us not only where we have been – our cultural history – but also where a society wants to go in terms of economic, political and cultural development. Ideologies are powerful structuring agencies because they pull together and make sense of the various strands of our individual and cultural existence and give the social world meaning, stability and order. Jones and Myhill (2004) argue that this occurs because ideologies not only involve related beliefs and justifications for those beliefs, they also specify objectives for social action and instructions for how to realise these objectives.

TEST YOURSELF

Suggest an example of an ideology in your society and identify some of its related beliefs. Assess the extent to which this ideology influences behaviour in your society.

Power

Power is an important, but often elusive, concept. Dugan (2003) defines power *actively*, suggesting that

it involves 'the capacity to bring about change'. Lukes (1990), however, defines power *passively*, arguing that one definition involves the power to 'do nothing' by making others believe nothing has to change. Power also has many sources. Weber (1922) distinguishes between two types:

1 coercive power, where people are forced to obey under threat of punishment
2 consensual power (authority), where people obey because they believe it right to do so.

KEY TERM

Power: the ability to make others do what you want, even against their will.

Authority can be further sub-divided:

- Charismatic power involves people obeying because they *trust* the person issuing a command.
- Traditional power is based on custom and practice – the way things have always been done.
- Rational/legal power expresses the idea that people expect commands to be obeyed because their position in an authority structure gives them the right to demand compliance.

Power also has a number of dimensions. We can define power in terms of decision-making. It involves:

- the ability to make decisions – teachers, for example, can decide what their students do in the classroom
- preventing others making decisions – a teacher can stop their students doing things they might like to do (such as gazing out of the window)
- removing decision-making from the agenda – the ability to 'do nothing' because others are convinced that no decision has to be made.

Giddens (2001) suggests that power relates to the social construction of reality through 'the ability of individuals or groups to make their own concerns or interests count, even where others resist'. This means that those with power can impose their definition of reality on others. In doing so, they can bring about order and stability.

However, Foucault (1983) argues that power in modern societies is different from power in past societies because it is opaque, or 'difficult to see'. People are unaware of the power that other individuals or groups such as governments have over them. This has occurred because the way people think about and experience power in everyday life has changed. In the past, social control was mainly based on raw (coercive) power – from a monarch exercising supreme power to prison systems that maintained total control over the body. In modern societies, Foucault claims, power is exercised in increasingly subtle modes ways, such as technological surveillance – both 'from above', such as CCTV, and 'from below' – smartphones, for example, that can be used to record people's behaviour.

Foucault further argues that knowledge about the social world and the language we use to express such knowledge are both aspects of belief systems that control behaviour by influencing how people *think* about the world. If, for example, we believe in ideas like 'male' and 'female' this conditions how we behave both *as* males and females and *towards* other males and females.

Although reality is socially constructed, the construction process itself involves a complex relationship between beliefs, ideologies and power on one side (the broad structural elements of culture) and everyday ideas about roles, values and norms on the other.

ACTIVITY

To illustrate how the social construction of reality takes place on an everyday basis, take a walk around your school or college and record the different ways you classify the people you meet. For example, you will probably meet some or all of the following classes of people: strangers, acquaintances (people you recognise but don't really know very well), friends, close friends, best friends. There will, of course, be other categories to discover. How does this classification affect your behaviour towards the people you encounter?

Social class, gender and ethnicity as elements in the construction of social identities

This section examines the ways that people use concepts such as class, gender and ethnicity to create identities that fix them within particular cultures and societies.

KEY TERM

Social identity: collective or group identities applied to important roles. Cultures classify, group and give meaning to broad identities, such as male or female, that define how 'men' and 'women' are generally expected to behave.

TEST YOURSELF

Briefly describe two social identities.

Class identities

Social class can be difficult to define, but Crompton (2003) suggests that occupation is a good general indicator that can allow us to define simple class groupings, such as working, middle and upper class. Occupation can also suggest ways in which class identities develop out of different work-related experiences.

Lower class

Traditional working-class identities are fixed (or centred) around manual work and the manufacturing industry. Such jobs were widely available in Britain, even in the later part of the 20th century. A further dimension to class identity came from the largely urban and close-knit *communities* within which the traditional working class lived. Here, people of a similar class, occupation and general social outlook had their cultural beliefs continually reinforced through personal experience and socialisation: the 'working-class Self' could be contrasted with the 'middle-/upper-class Other'. In such circumstances, class identity was built not just around what people were or believed themselves to be, but also around what they were *not*. More recently, however, Crompton has suggested changes to the nature of work:

- a decline in traditional manufacturing industries
- a rise of service industries such as banking, computing and a range of lesser-status service jobs.

This has led to the emergence of a new working class. Goldthorpe et al. (1968) argued that this section of the working class developed new forms of identity:

- privatised or home-centred
- instrumental: work was a means to an end – the creation of a comfortable home and family life – rather than an end in itself.

In terms of general class identity, however, Devine (1992) suggests that there were still important differences between the new working class and the middle classes. The former, for example, retained a strong sense of 'being working class'.

Middle class

Middle-class identities are constructed around a range of occupational identities. These include:

- professionals such as doctors, whose identity combines high levels of educational achievement

45

with personal *autonomy* (freedom of action) and decision-making

- managers involved in the day-to-day running of private and public companies – an identity, Brooks (2006) suggests, that combines career progression, decision-making, power and control over others and the organisation of work routines
- intellectuals, such as university lecturers, who reflect an academic identity dealing with knowledge and information services
- consultants focused on selling knowledge, information and skills across both national and global markets
- routine service workers (such as shop assistants), who represent an expanding identity group situated at the bottom of the middle-class hierarchy; they may have lower earnings and levels of skill than some higher working-class occupations, but they qualify as middle class on the basis of their *non-manual* work and, in the case of occupations such as nursing, higher levels of *social status* (a significant factor in all types of middle-class identity).

Upper class

Upper-class identities are based on two major groupings:

- The landed aristocracy is a relatively small group whose traditional source of power is its historic ownership of land and its political connections to the monarchy. In the past, this made it the most significant section of society. Over the course of the 20th century, the economic power and influence of the aristocracy may have declined, but there remains a significant upper-class section of society.
- The business elite now represents a major section of the upper class – one characterised by immense income and wealth based on ownership of significant national, international and global companies.

Self and Zealey (2007) note that:

- 21% of the UK's total wealth is owned by the wealthiest 1% of its population
- 7% of the nation's wealth is owned by the least wealthy 50%.

In India, a similar pattern of income equality emerges:

- The top 10% of wage-earners earn 12 times more than the bottom 10%
- 42% of India's 1.2 billion population live on around $1.25 a day.

On a global scale, Davies et al. (2008) note that the world's richest 1% own 40% of the total global wealth. Of this 1%, 60% live in just two countries: the USA and Japan.

The blurring of class identities

Peele (2004) argues that recent global economic changes have resulted in 'a blurring of traditional class identities'. We can see this in cultural changes in taste and consumption. In particular, a convergence of working-class and middle-class tastes makes it increasingly difficult to define class identity clearly. Distinctive boundary lines between working-, middle- and upper-class identities have changed dramatically, although they have not disappeared completely.

What are the elements of working- and middle-class taste cultures in the 21st century?

Prandy and Lambert (2005) suggest that there has been a gradual shift from people 'seeing themselves as working class to middle class', and Savage (2007) argues that although people still use class categories as a source of identity, the meaning of these categories has changed. Greater emphasis is placed on individual, rather than collective, experiences. As a result, working-class identities in particular have become more varied. This reflects the idea that class identity is becoming increasingly fluid – based on someone's ability to choose who they are or who they want to be. Brooks argues that we can push the idea of a 'coherent, stable and unified' middle-class identity a little too far. Higher-level professional workers may have little or nothing in common with lower-level shop workers. However, it is possible to identify three general cultural themes that contribute to middle-class identity:

1 Not working class: this reflects the idea that 'the middle classes' occupy an ambivalent and precarious class position:

   - 'Above the working class' and wanting to remain separated from them. As Brooks puts it: 'The construction of middle-class identities has primarily been related to the claim that one is 'not working class.'

- ■ 'Below the upper class' but aspiring to be like them.

2 Disgusted subjects: Lawler (2005) argues that 'expressions of disgust at perceived violations of taste' are a consistent and unifying feature of middle-class identities. The 'ownership of taste' allows the middle classes to distinguish themselves from those below and above; the upper class can be categorised in terms of 'vulgar and tasteless shows of wealth'. As Bourdieu (1984) put it: 'Social identity lies in difference, and difference is asserted against what is closest, that which represents the greatest threat.'

3 Social capital: this refers to how people are connected to networks (who you know) and the value these have for what Putnam (2000) calls 'norms of reciprocity' – what people are willing to do for each other. Catts and Ozga (2005) call this the 'social glue that holds people together in communities and gives them a sense of belonging'. They argue that the middle classes are in the best position to integrate into significant social networks, such as those found in schools or the workplace, that reinforce their sense of identity and difference. One important aspect of this is what Bourdieu (1986) calls cultural capital. This refers to non-economic resources, such as family and class background, educational qualifications, social skills and status, that give people advantages and disadvantages over others.

TEST YOURSELF

Describe three cultural practices in your society that are commonly used to identify class distinctions.

Gender identities

Connell et al. (1987) argue that we are not born a 'man' or a 'woman'; we become 'men' and 'women' through the social construction of gender identities. In other words, while biological sex refers to the physical characteristics that cause people to be labelled male or female, gender refers to the social characteristics given to each sex. Lips (1993) argues that differences in male and female identities do not occur naturally from biological differences. Gender identities differ historically and cross-culturally, which means that they are both learnt and relative. Connell (1995) suggests that there are two forms of dominant gender identities:

1 Hegemonic masculinity, where 'traditional' forms of masculinity are based on a variety of physical

and mental characteristics. For example, men are encouraged to adopt a particular body shape that, *ideally*, emphasises physical strength and physique. Mental characteristics include ideas about about men as 'leaders', 'providers', being unemotional, rational, calm, cool, calculating, etc. Connell and Messerschmidt (2005) argue that even in societies where different masculinities exist, one is always dominant.

2 Emphasised femininity relates to the idea that female identities were traditionally defined by how they could accommodate the interests and needs of men. The *dominant* identity was one that 'matched and complemented' hegemonic masculinity. Women were regarded as essentially passive, emotional beings whose identity was expressed in the service of others. Kitchen (2006) characterises this as a 'complicit femininity', because it is defined by male needs and desires.

Male identities

If one form of masculinity is always dominant, it follows that alternative masculinities exist. Schauer (2004) suggests these take different forms:

- ■ Subordinate masculinities are generally seen as 'lesser forms' of masculinity, particularly for men who are unable or unwilling to perform hegemonic masculinity, such as those with physical disabilities.
- ■ Subversive masculinities involve an alternative masculinity that challenges and undermines hegemonic masculinity. An example here might be the 'serious student' who works hard at school rather than being part of a gang that is disruptive in class.
- ■ Complicit masculinities refer to newly feminised masculinities such as the 'new man'; men who combine paid work with their share of unpaid housework. This type of masculinity sees women as equals and occurs, Connell (1995) argues, because 'as women have become more powerful, male identities have begun to change'.
- ■ Marginalised masculinities refer to men who feel they have been 'pushed to the margins' of family life due to long-term unemployment, for example; they no longer feel able to perform what they see as the traditional masculine roles of breadwinner and family provider. Willott and Griffin (1996) noted this type of masculinity developing among the long-term unemployed working class as traditional beliefs about 'the good family man' providing for wife and kids collided with an inability to provide for their partner and children.

47

How does this behaviour challenge notions of hegemonic masculinity?

Crisis

Benyon (2002) argues that contemporary global societies are experiencing a crisis of masculine identity caused by a combination of:

- long-term unemployment
- the loss of traditional male employment in manufacturing industries
- lower educational achievement relative to girls
- the rise of female-friendly service industries.

Male identities once focused on traditional ideas such as providing for a family, but this is no longer the case. Marginalised masculinities cannot demonstrate traditional male qualities because they no longer control the economic resources on which such masculinity was based. This male identity crisis has resulted in the rise of two particular forms of exaggerated masculinity that try to reassert traditional forms of male identity:

1 Retributive masculinities aim to reclaim traditional masculinity from their 'emasculated' peers. Typical behaviours include binge drinking, fighting and womanising. These behaviours are based on an idealised version of a traditional masculinity – when 'men were men and women were glad of it'. This identity is:

- rigidly patriarchal
- aggressive, both physically and verbally
- oppositional, in the sense of rejecting complicit masculinities
- reclamational – it seeks to 'reclaim masculinity' as an identity.

2 Hypermasculinity is a form that Wolf-Light (1994) characterises as 'authoritarian and autocratic,

impersonal, contemptuous and violent ... the very image of patriarchy'. Robinson (2006) argues that this identity particularly appeals to 'white, middle-class and middle-aged men primarily because of its ability to provide a degree of certainty about what it means to be a man ... a belief in an essential and unchanging "deep masculinity"'.

Female identities

There three main forms of feminine identity in contemporary societies:

1 Contingent femininities are framed and shaped by male beliefs, behaviours and demands:

- Normalised identities, for example, involve women learning to play a secondary role to men – as mothers, girlfriends, partners and the like. Chambers et al. (2003) argue that such identities continually struggle with the problem of 'producing a femininity that will secure male approval'.
- Sexualised identities are fashioned through male eyes and fantasies. In these types of identity, women are sexual objects that exist for male gratification.

2 Assertive identities reflect the changing position of women in many societies. They involve women breaking free from traditional ideas about femininity, but not completely setting themselves apart from their male counterparts. Froyum (2005) suggests that assertive femininities are adopted to 'resist male power without actually threatening to overthrow such power'. Different types of assertive identity include:

- 'Girl power' identities. Hollows (2000) suggests that these emphasise 'sex as fun' and the importance of female friendship. These identities represent a way of 'coping with masculinity', but older women are excluded from this identity.
- Modernised femininities that relate to a slightly older age group. These locate new-found female economic and cultural power within the context of family relationships. The *assertive* aspect here is a desire for personal freedom and expression – what McRobbie (1996) terms 'individualism, liberty and the entitlement to sexual self-expression' – within the context of traditional gender relationships.
- Ageing femininities, which assert the right of elderly women to be fashionable, active and *sexual* beings.

3 Autonomous femininities, which involve *competition* with men, on female terms. Evans (2006), for example,

points to a female individualism as part of a 'new gender regime that frees women from traditional constraints', such as pregnancy and childcare. Autonomous women are likely to be:

- highly educated
- successful
- professional middle class
- career-focused.

They also tend to form non-committal heterosexual attachments. These may involve marriage but are unlikely to involve children.

TEST YOURSELF

Identify and explain two types of female identity in your country. Assess the extent to which female behaviour can be explained in terms of these identities.

Ethnic identities

When thinking about ethnic identities it is helpful to keep two things in mind:

1 Ethnicity is not the same thing as race. As Ossorio (2003) argues, 'the simple biological notion of race is wrong' – there is no credible scientific evidence of genetically different 'racial groups'.

2 Avoid thinking about ethnicity in terms of 'minorities'. The Center for Social Welfare Research (1999) states: 'For all of us, identity is in some sense "ethnic" in that we have diverse origins ... related to how we are perceived and treated by others'.

Ethnicity, therefore, refers to a combination of cultural differences, in areas such as:

- religion
- family structures
- beliefs
- values
- norms.

Winston (2005) suggests that ethnic identities develop when people 'see themselves as being distinctive in some way from others' because of a shared cultural background and history. Song (2003) claims that this is often expressed in terms of distinctive markers such as a common ancestry and 'memories of a shared past'. A sense of ethnic identity is based on 'symbolic elements ... such as family and kinship, religion, language, territory, nationality or physical

appearance'. Ethnic identity does not necessarily relate to 'any actual evidence of cultural distinctiveness as a group'. The key factor is whether people are 'conscious of belonging to the group'.

Ethnicity as a source of personal and social identity is built on a range of ideas that include referencing:

- country of birth and the sense of a common geographic location
- traditions and customs that contribute to unique cultural practices that distinguish one ethnic group from another
- shared histories and experiences as a defining sense of identity, as with victims of slavery in the case of Black Caribbean and African identities or the Nazi holocaust in the case of Jewish identities
- religious beliefs, celebrations and traditions that connect people on the basis of shared cultural practices, such as common forms of worship.

Unlike racial identities, ethnic identities are negotiable. Their nature and meaning can change to external and internal factors. External factors might include contact with other cultures; internal factors might be a clash of ideas and experiences between different age, class or gender groups within a particular ethnic group. For this reason, ethnic identities require constant maintenance through collective activities, such as festivals, celebrations or religious gatherings, and a variety of material and symbolic cultural artefacts, such as traditional forms of dress, food and crafts.

Wimmer (2008) argues that an important aspect of ethnic identities is how they are defined in relation to other ethnic groups by constructing a sense of *difference*, which establishes boundaries for a particular identity. Ethnic boundaries may be positive, conferring a sense of belonging to a definable cultural group, or defensive – a way of fighting racism and discrimination, for example. Boundaries may also be imposed through cultural stereotypes about ethnic groups and identities. This may in fact reinforce a stereotyped group's sense of identity.

Another way in which ethnic identities can be imposed relates to how *minority* identities can be defined by *majority* ethnicities in terms of their 'Otherness': how 'They' are different from 'Us'. While this relationship strengthens both majority and minority ethnic identities, it can also result in minority ethnicities being portrayed as a threat in two main ways:

- cultural, where minority beliefs and practices are framed as challenges to a particular way of life

49

- physical, where in countries like Britain and the USA, following the 11 September 2001 World Trade Center attacks, the media framed and referenced this threat in terms of 'Muslims' and 'terrorism'.

While this *oppositional* dimension is significant – the idea that some ethnic groups partly or wholly construct their sense of Self through opposition to the Other – a further dimension involves two types of hybrid ethnic identities:

1 Conventional hybridisation suggests that the mixing of distinctive ethnic styles produces new and unique identities. This mixing tends to take place on the margins of identity, involving the combination of specific *features* of ethnic identities rather than a complete change. Examples include things such as:

  - food, Indian, Chinese and Italian cuisine, for example, have become a key part of British culture, often with subtle changes that give them a unique 'British' identity twist
  - clothing, where the American style of jeans and T-shirts has been incorporated into a variety of global ethnic identities
  - music, such as *Bhangra,* which displays cross-over styles to produce unique musical fusions and genres.

2 Contemporary hybridisation suggests that ethnic identities undergo constant maintenance, change and development under the influence of two main processes:

  - immigration, where different ethnic groups physically meet
  - cultural globalisation, where, through agencies uch as the internet, ethnic cultures and identities are increasingly exposed to different cultural influences.

Rather than creating new and different hybrid identities, cultural changes result in gradual alterations to an *established* identity. In this way, ethnic identities are constantly drawing on new influences and re-establishing old identities in the face of new challenges. White English youth identities have, for example, *incorporated* aspects of other cultures relating to:

- music, such as rock, pop, rap and hip-hop
- food, such as hamburgers, Asian cuisine and German beer
- language, especially slang terms associated with youth cultures and sub-cultures
- clothing that includes jeans and T-shirts.

While these cultural imports have undoubtedly changed these identities, this involved incorporation and modification to an existing sense of cultural identity

and style, rather than the creation of a new and unique identity as is seen to happen in the case of conventional hybridisation.

ACTIVITY

Use the internet and other forms of media to find representations of different class, gender and ethnic identities. In small groups, take it in turns to present your representations to one another. Explain clearly what the various elements of the image say about the social identity of the individual or individuals represented. Also assess how far the image matches what you see as the social reality.

Theories of culture and identity with reference to modernism and postmodernism

At the start of this unit, we noted how sociology developed as the product of **modernity**. This was a new type of society characterised by industrialisation, urbanisation and the development of science and reason, which began with the Enlightenment in Europe and gradually replaced pre-modern, pre-industrial, societies. Modernity introduced different ways of understanding social order, stability and change. In this section, we are going to look at how modernist sociological perspectives have theorised culture and identity. We are then going to investigate the postmodernist perspectives that explain the decline of modern societies and their gradual replacement by a new type of post-industrial, post-rational society.

 KEY TERM

Modernity: a stage in historical development characterised by things like industrialisation, urbanisation and the development of science and reason.

Modernist theories

One way to look at culture and identity from a general modernist perspective is to consider what culture and identity *do*, how they are *used* and what they *mean*.

Function

Consensus approaches, such as functionalism, have identified a range of functions for both culture and identity. In other words, they exist because of what they do for – and in some senses to – people. Fisher (1997), for example, argues that culture is shared behaviour that 'systematises the way people do things, thus avoiding confusion and allowing cooperation so that groups can accomplish what no single individual could do alone'. Mazrui (1996) suggests that culture performs seven important functions:

1 Communication: culture provides the context for the development of communication systems such as language.

2 Perception: culture shapes how people see the world. Offe (2001), for example, argues that Western cultures generally believe that 'the future' is not predetermined, whereas 'some African societies believe in a predetermined future not controllable by individuals'.

3 Identity: culture influences how people see themselves and others, in terms of different social and personal identities. For Durkheim (1912), these are an important part of social solidarity and integration.

4 Value systems: cultural institutions, such as education, the media and religion, are a source of values that influence behaviour through socialisation.

5 Motivation: cultural values and norms involve sanctions that promote and discourage particular behaviours. They also set behavioural boundaries to maintain certain standards of behaviour – for example, laws specify acceptable and unacceptable behaviour.

6 Stratification: cultures develop ways of differentiating and ranking individuals through categories such as class, gender and age. Lenski (1994) argues that stratification is 'inevitable, necessary and functional' because it generates the 'incentive systems' required to motivate and reward the people who are best qualified to hold the most important positions within a cultural system.

7 Production and consumption: culture defines these practices in terms of what people 'need, use and value'.

1	Communication	4	Value Systems
2	Perception	5	Motivation
3	Identity	6	Stratification
		7	Production and Consumption

Mazrui's seven functions of culture

Alongside culture, Adams and Marshall (1996) argue that identities perform five complementary functions:

1 Identities provide individuals with a structured context for social actions – a 'framework of rules' that guides behaviour when playing certain roles. This helps people understand their relationship to others.

2 Identities generate a sense of individual purpose by setting behavioural goals. For example, student identity involves the desire to achieve goals such as educational qualifications.

3 Identities create a measure of self-control in terms of deciding what we want and how to achieve it. When faced with a variety of choices, a clear sense of identity allows people to select and process information relevant to particular roles and identities. For example, a student might note down what a teacher says in the classroom, but may not record a conversation they had if they met in the street.

4 When we take on an identity we must ensure the commitments we make are consistent with our personal values and beliefs. A student who believes education is a waste of time is unlikely to perform their role successfully.

5 As part of a general goal-setting function, identities allow us to see likely or hoped-for outcomes. A student identity, for example, has a 'future orientation' – wanting to perform the role successfully in order to achieve a certain type of job.

TEST YOURSELF

Briefly describe, using examples, any two functions of culture.

Use

Conflict theories, such as Marxism, are based on the idea that contemporary societies contain competing cultural groups, with their own affiliations, products and consumption patterns. One focus here, therefore, is on how culture and identity are *used*, both to enhance the 'sense of Self' and the social cohesion of a dominant social class, and to lower the social status of other, competing, classes. We can see these ideas in practice in relation to concepts of high and low (popular or mass) culture.

High culture: High culture refers to the idea that some cultural products and practices are superior to others and that those who prefer high cultural products see themselves as 'socially superior'. To understand why culture and identity is important here, we need to examine how they are used.

In the past, it was easy to maintain a status distinction between the ruling and the lower classes. Status was fixed by birth, marriage, inheritance and law. However, mass education and the growth of higher-paid jobs mean that in many modern societies 'the masses' (or lower classes) can work their way up the social scale. This relatively new situation, in which someone of lowly social origins can become hugely wealthy or politically powerful, has led to an identity crisis among elite groups. They are increasingly unable to maintain their sense of superiority on the basis of wealth and income alone.

Cultural attributes such as taste and 'breeding', however, cannot be bought or learnt; they are either acquired by elites over many generations or, as Hobsbawm and Ranger (1992) argue, simply invented. In globalised societies where it is increasingly difficult to maintain status distinctions on the basis of how people speak, live or dress, differences can be maintained through the consumption of cultural products and ideas.

Elite cultural identity is not only reflected in consumption, it is also bound up in questions of leadership. As Cooney (1994) argues, elites see themselves as 'determining what happens in society'. An elite group identifies those aspects of culture that are 'the best in thought and deed' – a judgement that happily coincides with the cultural products they consume and separates them from, as they define it, the worthless: the mass-produced and the artificial (low culture). By taking ownership of these forms and elevating them to a position of cultural superiority, an elite group:

- asserts its own cultural identity: 'this is who *we are* and who *you are not*'
- establishes its cultural hegemony over questions of taste: the elite decides what counts as 'high culture'
- creates a strong 'taste barrier' between itself and the masses, especially those who aspire to join the ranks of the elite.

Low culture: Low, **popular** or **mass culture** is the opposite of high culture. It is defined by a ruling class as shallow, worthless and disposable. It is manufactured by

'culture professionals', such as music and film producers and television executives, on an industrial scale. In other words, it is mass-produced – the opposite of the 'individual crafting' of high culture. Elite groups often contrast modern low culture with the historical folk culture of the peasant class. While this was crude, bawdy and in many respects brutalised, it was at least *authentic* – a culture consumed by those who created it. Modern popular culture is often considered *inauthentic*; its creators have no great interest or emotional investment in their products. Such products are artificial, requiring no great effort to understand, and *formulaic* – once a cultural product becomes a popular success the 'winning formula' is simply reproduced in order to churn out increasingly inauthentic copies.

Low culture is further criticised for its commercialism – the only objective of its producers is to make money – and mass appeal. Low cultural products are aimed at the widest possible audience, not to enrich their lives but simply because the larger the audience, the greater the chances of a commercial success. To be as inclusive and profitable as possible, these products must appeal to the lowest common denominator. This means they have to be:

- intellectually undemanding
- predictable
- inoffensive
- simple to understand.

Davis (2000) notes that while high culture is 'the preserve of very few in society' and involves 'art, literature, music and intellectual thought which few can create or even appreciate, popular culture is regarded as mediocre, dull, mundane entertainment to be enjoyed by uneducated and uncritical "low-brow" hordes'.

How do some forms of popular culture appeal to the lowest common denominator?

While high culture must be unchanging and challenging, because it represents the height of cultural achievement in a society, popular culture does have its uses. It is a way of distracting the working classes from the real causes of their problems in capitalist society – low wages, exploitation and a lack of power. A popular culture that encourages passive consumption of the pre-packaged products of big business destroys vital communal aspects of folk culture. It also provides the lower classes with a false sense of happiness, togetherness and well-being. This stops them thinking too closely about how they are economically exploited by a ruling class.

TEST YOURSELF

Suggest one example of high culture and one example of popular culture in your society.

Meaning

We can also consider culture and identity in terms of what they *mean* in relation to things such as 'conspicuous consumption': what Jensen et al. (2000) describe as 'consumption that serves the principal purpose of impressing on others who and what you are'. One way of expressing cultural identity, therefore, is through a display of wealth that emphasises an individual's social status and position. More generally, consumption is linked to identity because it represents a 'background presentation' of the self. The consumption of goods and services comes with a 'substance of stories and experiences attached to them'. What we buy, how we dress and where we spend our leisure time all reveal something about who and what we are.

Brusdal and Lavik (2005) suggest that consumption in modern societies no longer simply involves people satisfying basic needs. Rather, it involves 'creating meaning and purpose in their life'. As Wearing and Wearing (2000) put it, commodities are increasingly used for what they mean 'in terms of identity and status'.

Neo-Marxist theory has also examined the meaning of culture and identity in terms of consumption in modern societies. Aldridge (2003), for example, notes that consumption in capitalist societies has two dimensions:

1 It involves the satisfaction of needs: 'the instrumental purchase of goods and services for practical purposes – the car as a means of transport'.

2 It has symbolic meaning: 'people exchange messages about class, status and identity – the car as status symbol'.

KEY TERM

Neo-Marxist theory: more recent form of Marxism, sometimes called hegemonic Marxism, that gives greater importance to cultural factors in explaining human behaviour than traditional Marxism (where the emphasis is on economic relationships).

This approach suggests that people in modern societies are socialised into a set of pre-existing identity categories, such as gender, age and class. As a result, consumption choices are used to enhance people's general perception of both their own and other people's identities.

Postmodernist theories

For postmodernism, the 'old certainties' of modernity give way to the 'new uncertainties' of postmodernity – an idea illustrated by changing ideas about identity.

Centred identities are clear, relatively fixed and certain in terms of what is expected by others. In modern societies, for example, people have a clear (*centred*) idea about what it *means* to be 'a man' or 'a woman' because there are relatively few *choices* available to them in how these categories are defined. The social rules governing how to be young or old, male or female, upper class or working class are clear, consistent and rigidly enforced. Postmodernists argue that a key social change is the development of *global* economic and cultural influences, which have opened up societies, communities and individuals to new and different experiences, behaviours and ideas. In the UK, for example, just as people eat food from the USA, India and Thailand, wear clothes from China and listen to mp3 players from Japan, they have imported a range of cultural ideas, styles and fashions from around the globe. This cultural trend has resulted in fragmented identities.

Primary sources of identity such as class, age and gender have become less important as ways of defining 'the Self'; other sources, such as consumption, green and cyber identities, have become increasingly significant. Through exposure to different ways of living, behaving and being, traditional identity sources can no longer be sustained as *monolithic* entities (the idea that there is a correct way to 'be female' or 'elderly'). In postmodernity, there are so many ways to be these things that it is no longer possible to support, sustain and control simple, centred social identities. As a result the rules governing the correct way to play out these identities ('real men don't cry', 'a woman's place is in the home') are relaxed as people develop the freedom to both invent and adapt identities to their personal tastes and styles.

One outcome of fragmentation is that identities become decentred; people are less certain about how to behave. If there are many ways to be 'middle class', which is the 'right' way? Identity categories are also more easily combined to create a whole new range of hybrid identities. Some young British Asians, for example, define themselves as *Brasian* – a mix of both British and Asian cultures and identities. The downside to almost unlimited choice from which we pick and mix identities is uncertainty and confusion about who we are and how we are supposed to behave.

How does the idea of choice produce uncertainty?

People are still socialised into a variety of roles, values and norms, but social identities no longer set certain standards of belief and behaviour. Rather, individuals shape their lives through the development of personal identities that are always unique in some way, shape or form. While individual development (or *personal narrative*) is influenced by others, it is in no sense *determined* by these relationships. Whereas for structuralist sociology socialisation regulates the behaviour of the individual, postmodernists believe that socialisation encompasses a range of possibilities. Every

time new choices are added, the pattern of socialisation changes. Eventually, even tiny changes to an individual's life can have a significant outcome. This explains how and why those socialised in the same family in apparently very similar ways develop different adult personalities.

The decentring of culture and identity means that people are increasingly open to and accepting of different experiences, both 'the new', in the literal sense of something not previously seen or done, and 'the newly different', in the sense of changing how we relate to existing experiences. Rampton (2002) suggests that identity construction in postmodern societies is 'something that involves assembling, or piecing together a sense of identity from many changing options'. Each individual creates their identity through their consumption choices and practices – something illustrated by the difference between shopping at a market stall in a small village (modernity) and a vast mall situated on the edge of town (postmodernity). The market stall presents a narrow range of goods from which to choose, as was the case with identities in the past. Shopping malls present people with the freedom to browse huge spaces filled with a wide range of consumer goods – where they 'shop for identities'. As 'identity consumers', people have an expanding range of choices about who to be and how to express their sense of self. As Phillips (2003) puts it: 'Consumption is changing … It is now just as important to buy things for what they *mean* as what they *do*. Consciously or unconsciously, consumers make decisions about their purchases based on their identity or the identity they wish to project or communicate to others.'

ACTIVITY

Assess the extent to which your social identity is shaped by the things that you own. What other factors influence your social identity?

Summary points

- **The relationship between the individual and society can be understood in terms of three different approaches:**
  - structuralism, or macrosociology: society as a social force constraining behaviour
  - interactionism, or microsociology
  - structuration.

- **The 'nature–nurture' debate involves considering:**
  - biological and genetic (nature) influences.

- **Explanations for social development include:**
  - sociobiology and biogrammers
  - evolutionary psychology and social selection
  - neuropsychology and brain development and function
  - social psychology and the relationship between genetic and social factors
  - cultural learning (nurture).

- **Different types of socialisation include:**
  - primary
  - secondary.

- **Agencies of socialisation include:**
  - family
  - education
  - mass media
  - peer group
  - religion.

- **Societies are socially constructed as:**
  - physical spaces
  - mental spaces
  - imagined communities.

- **Cultures have two components:**
  - material
  - non-material.

- **Cultural order and stability are socially constructed around:**
  - roles
  - values
  - norms
  - beliefs
  - ideology
  - power.

- **Individuals locate themselves within cultures and societies through three types of social identity:**
  - class
  - gender
  - ethnic.

- **Modernist theories of culture and identity involve:**
  - certainty
  - centred identity
  - high and low/popular culture
  - taste cultures
  - conspicuous consumption
  - presentation of self
  - symbolic meaning.

- **Postmodern theories of culture and identity involve:**
  - uncertainty
  - decentred identity
  - fragmented identities
  - pick-and-mix identities
  - consumption cultures and choices
  - identity shopping.

Exam-style questions

a What is meant by the term primary socialisation? [2]

b Describe how any two values may be linked to social roles in a society. [4]

c Explain why individuals have to be socialised into acceptable standards of behaviour. [8]

d 'Neither structure nor action fully explains the relationship between the individual and society.' Assess this claim. [11]

Total available marks 25

Chapter 3:
Methods of research

Learning objectives

The objectives of this chapter involve understanding:

- the difference between primary and secondary data and between quantitative and qualitative data

- the range of different research methods and sources of data used by sociologists and an assessment of their strengths and limitations

- the stages of research design: deciding on research strategy; formulating research problems and hypotheses; sampling and pilot studies; conducting the research; interpreting the results and reporting the findings.

Introduction

This chapter looks at the research process in terms of how sociologists design their research, from initial thoughts about what to study to ideas about how to study it. As part of this process we need to understand different types of data and their respective strengths and limitations, as well as the range of methods available to sociologists in their research.

The distinctions between primary and secondary data and between quantitative and qualitative data

Primary data

Primary data involves information collected *personally* by a researcher. They may use a range of methods, such as questionnaires, interviews and observational studies.

KEY TERM

Primary data: information collected *personally* by a researcher.

Strengths

The researcher has complete control over how data is collected, by whom and for what purpose. In addition, where a researcher designs and carries out their own research they have greater control over the reliability and validity of the data, as well as how representative it is.

Limitations

Primary research can be time-consuming to design, construct and carry out, especially if it involves personally interviewing large numbers of people. Primary research can also be expensive. In addition, the researcher may have difficulty gaining access to the target group. Some people may refuse to participate or, in the case of historical research, potential respondents are no longer alive.

Secondary data

Secondary data is data that already exists in some form, such as documents (government reports and statistics, personal letters and diaries) or previous research completed by other sociologists.

KEY TERM

Secondary data: data that already exists; data not personally generated by the researcher.

Strengths

The researcher is able to save time, money and effort by using existing data such as official government statistics about crime, marriage or divorce. There may also be situations, where secondary data is the *only* available resource, such as when researching suicide. Secondary data is also useful for historical and comparative purposes. Aries (1962), for example, used historical paintings and documents to support his argument that childhood was a relatively recent invention.

Some forms of secondary data, such as **official statistics**, may be highly reliable because the data is collected consistently, in the same way from the same sources. This type of data is also more likely to represent what it claims to represent. Many countries, including Britain, India and Mauritius, conduct a census of every household every 10 years, which collects representative data that can be used as a reliable secondary source.

KEY TERM

Official statistics: government-generated secondary source of data on areas such as crime, marriage and employment.

Limitations

Secondary data is not always produced with the needs of sociologists in mind. For example, official definitions of poverty, class or ethnicity may be different from

Why might personal websites involve unreliable secondary data?

57

sociological definitions. Sources, such as personal documents, can be unreliable. Official crime statistics may not measure all crimes but only those reported to the authorities. Some forms of secondary data, such as historical documents, may only reflect the views of a single individual rather than representing wider opinions.

Quantitative data

Quantitative data expresses information numerically, in one of three ways:

- a raw number, such as the total number of people who live in a society
- a percentage, or the number of people *per 100*, in a population; for example, around 80% of Indians follow the Hindu religion
- a rate, or the number of people *per 1,000* in a population; a birth rate of 1, for example, means that for every 1,000 people in a population, one baby is born each year.

KEY TERM

Quantitative data: information expressed numerically that captures the 'who, what, when and where' of behaviour.

Strengths

The ability to express relationships statistically can be useful if the researcher does not need to explore the *reasons* for people's behaviour – if they simply need to compare the *number* of murders committed each year in different societies. Kruger (2003) argues that quantitative data 'allows us to summarize vast sources of information and make comparisons across categories and over time'. Statistical comparisons and **correlations** can test whether a hypothesis is true or false. They can also track changes in the behaviour of the same group over time (a longitudinal study).

KEY TERM

Correlation: a statistical relationship between two or more variables that expresses a level of probability. A high (positive) correlation suggests the strong probability of a relationship; a low (negative) correlation suggests the probability of little or no relationship.

Matveev (2002) argues that quantitative research is more reliable because it is easier to repeat (*replicate*) the study. Standardised questions that do not change, for example, can be asked of different groups or the same group at different times. The results can then be quantified and compared. If the answers are the same, or very similar, then the research is more likely to be reliable. Quantitative data also makes it easier for the researcher to remain objective. They not need to have a close personal involvement with the subjects of the study, so their *personal biases* are less likely to intrude into the data-collection process.

Quantitative data, such as that collected from questionnaires, is intended to limit subjective judgements by posing uniform questions and even the choice of responses. Does quantitative data minimise subjective judgements?

Limitations

Quantification is often achieved by placing the respondent in an 'artificial social setting' in order to control the responses and the data collected. People rarely, if ever, encounter situations where they are asked to respond to a list of questions from a stranger, or have their behaviour observed in a laboratory. Some argue that it is impossible to capture people's 'normal' behaviour or collect 'real' responses when the subjects are placed in such an artificial environment.

A further problem is that quantitative data only captures a relatively narrow range of information. Day (1998) calls this the 'who, what, when and where' of people's behaviour. Quantitative data does not usually reveal the *reasons* for behaviour because it lacks depth; the more detailed the behavioural data, the more difficult it is to quantify. As a result, quantitative data is often seen as superficial. As Kruger argues, it's 'difficult to get the real meaning of an issue by looking at numbers'.

McCullough (1988) suggests that a significant limitation of quantitative data is that 'issues are only measured if they are known prior to the beginning of the research'. To quantify behaviour, the researcher must decide in advance what is and is not significant in terms of the behaviour being studied. There is no opportunity to develop the research beyond its original boundaries. A final limitation is what Sorokin (1956) calls 'quantophrenia' – quantification for its own sake, regardless of whether it tells us anything useful about the behaviour being quantified.

TEST YOURSELF

Briefly explain the idea that quantitative data captures only the 'who, what, when and where' of behaviour.

Qualitative data

Qualitative data aims to capture the *quality* of people's behaviour by exploring the 'why' rather than the 'what, when and where'. It involves questions about how people feel about their *experiences* and can be used to understand the meanings applied to behaviour. For example, in the USA Venkatesh (2009) studied a juvenile gang from the viewpoint of its members, while Goffman (1961) examined the experiences of patients in a mental institution. Both were trying to capture the *quality* of people's behaviour: what the subjects understand, how they feel and, most importantly, why they behave in particular ways in different situations.

KEY TERM

Qualitative data: non-numeric data that expresses the quality of a relationship.

Strengths

The objective of qualitative behaviour is to understand people's behaviour, so they must be allowed to talk and act freely. This allows the researcher to capture the complex reasons for behaviour. Qualitative methods, such as **participant observation** involve the researcher

KEY TERM

Participant observation: research method that involves the researcher participating, openly or secretly, in the behaviour they are studying.

establishing a strong personal relationship or rapport with respondents in order to experience their lives. By collecting qualitative data in this way, researchers have greater freedom to study people in their 'normal' settings. The results are more likely to show how people really behave and what they really believe. The ability to capture the *richness* of people's lives through qualitative data is also an important strength. Matveev suggests that qualitative methods and data allow the researcher to gain a 'more realistic feel of the world that cannot be experienced through numerical data and statistical analysis'.

Limitations

Qualitative research focuses on the intensive study of relatively small groups, which may limit the opportunity for applying the data more widely – such groups may not be representative of anything but themselves. For similar reasons, it is difficult to compare qualitative data across time and location because no two groups will ever be qualitatively the same (the research does not compare 'like with like'). The depth and detail of the data also makes such research difficult to replicate, which means its reliability is generally lower than that of quantitative research.

TEST YOURSELF

Why is qualitative data useful for capturing the meaning of people's behaviour?

ACTIVITY

Which of the following types of data do you think is most suitable to collect in sociological research? Give reasons for your answer.

1 *quantitative*

2 *qualitative*

3 *quantitative and qualitative.*

Make a list of the strengths and limitations of each type of data.

Quantitative and qualitative methods and sources of data

Primary quantitative methods

Questionnaires

Questionnaires consist of written questions that take one of two forms:

- Postal questionnaires are normally completed in private; respondents write their answers without the presence of, or guidance from, the researcher.
- Researcher-administered questionnaires are completed in the presence of the researcher, with respondents answering questions verbally.

> **KEY TERM**
>
> **Questionnaire:** research method consisting of a list of written questions. Closed-ended questions provide possible answers from which the respondent can choose, while open-ended questions mean the respondent may answer in their own words.

Questionnaires involve two basic types of question. *Closed-ended* or pre-coded questions involve the researcher providing a set of answers from which the respondent can choose. The researcher limits the responses that can be given, as in the following example:

Do you own a sociology textbook?	Yes	No	Don't Know
Code	[1]	[2]	[3]

There are variations on this type of question, such as those that measure respondent attitudes, but their defining characteristic is that they do not allow the respondent to develop an answer beyond the listed categories.

In *open-ended* questions, the researcher does not provide possible answers. Rather, the respondent answers in their own words. For example:

'What do you like about studying sociology?'

This type of question finds out more about the respondent's opinions and produces a limited form of qualitative data – although the main objective of a questionnaire is usually to *quantify* responses. Some questionnaires contain a mix of open and closed questions.

TEST YOURSELF

Identify two differences between open and closed questions.

Strengths: Pre-coded questions make it easier to quantify data, because the options are already known, they are limited in number and easy to count. Such questions are also quick and easy to code and interpret; in some cases this is just a simple count of the number of responses. Pre-coded questions are useful when the researcher needs to contact large numbers of people quickly and efficiently. The respondents do the time-consuming work of completing the questionnaire.

Questionnaires can result in highly reliable data; because everyone answers the same questions, it it easy to replicate the research. The fact that respondents often remain anonymous means that the validity of the research is improved, especially when it involves questions about potentially embarrassing or criminal behaviour. In addition, without face-to-face interaction, there is less risk that the respondent will give biased answers or try to anticipate what the researcher wants to hear.

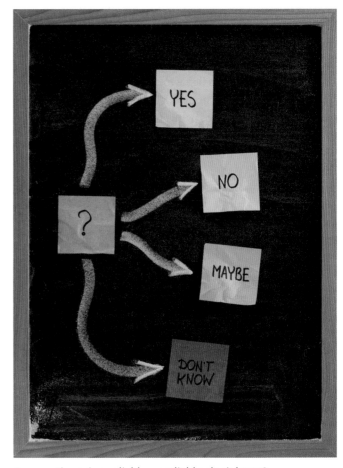

Are questionnaires reliable, unreliable, don't know?

60

Limitations: One significant practical problem with questionnaires is a low response rate, where only a small proportion of those receiving a questionnaire return it. This can result in a carefully designed sample becoming unrepresentative, because it effectively selects itself. There is also nothing the researcher can do if respondents ignore questions or respond incorrectly, such as choosing two answers when only one was requested.

The questionnaire format makes it difficult to examine complex issues and opinions. In addition, the lack of detailed information means that potentially significant data is not collected. These factors can limit the validity of the research. Another weakness is the fact that the researcher has to decide at the start of the study what is and is not significant. There is no opportunity to amend this later on.

The researcher has no way of knowing whether a respondent has understood a question properly. The researcher also has to trust that the questions mean the same thing to all respondents. While anonymity may encourage honesty, if someone other than the intended respondent completes the questionnaire, it will affect the validity and representativeness of the research. Some of these problems can be avoided by pilot studies (see below), but they cannot be totally eliminated.

A further problem involves (unintentionally) biased questions. These can take a number of forms:

- If a question has more than one meaning (*ambiguity*), people will be answering *different questions*. 'Do you agree most people believe the Prime Minister is doing a good job?', for example, is actually two questions; you could agree or disagree that the Prime Minister is doing a good job, but you could also agree or disagree with 'most people's belief'.
- Leading questions suggest a required answer; by saying 'most people believe', for example, the question challenges the respondent to go against the majority.
- When giving respondents a range of answers, they must be weighted equally to avoid leading answers. The following possible answers to the question 'How do you rate Sociology as a subject?', for example, are too heavily weighted in favour of a *positive* answer:

Brilliant!	Incredible!	Fantastic!	Marvellous!	Not bad

- If an option is not precisely defined, it will mean different things to different people. For example, people may define the word 'occasionally' in different ways.
- Hypothetical questions ask respondents to imagine themselves in a position they do not actually hold ('If you were the Prime Minister how would you run the country?') – and imaginary questions run the risk of producing imaginary answers.

Suggest one reason why biased questions lower the validity of data collected using a questionnaire.

Structured interviews

A **structured interview** is where the researcher asks questions to respondents in person. To achieve consistent and comparable results, the same questions are asked in the same order each time.

 KEY TERM

> **Structured interview:** set of standard questions asked by the researcher of the respondent. It is similar to a questionnaire, but is delivered by the researcher rather than completed by a respondent.

Strengths: One strength of the structured interview format is that potential reliability problems, such as respondents misunderstanding or not answering questions, can be resolved by the researcher. In addition, it avoids the problem of unrepresentative samples – the response rates will be 100%.

Limitations: Structured interviews involve prejudgements about people's behaviour and, like questionnaires, can also contain unintentionally biased questions. The lack of anonymity in an interview also contributes to two related limitations:

1. The interview effect occurs when a respondent tries to 'help' the researcher by providing answers designed to please. This reduces validity because respondents simply provide answers they *think* the researcher wants. This can be caused by a 'halo effect', a situation Draper (2006) describes as occurring when the *novelty* of being interviewed and a desire to reward the interviewer for giving the respondent the chance to experience it, results in *unintentionally* dishonest answers. Conversely, prestige bias occurs when a respondent gives an answer designed to *not make themselves look bad*. Opinion polls, for example, sometimes show respondents saying they would willingly pay more taxes if it helped to improve hospitals or care of the elderly, but in reality they vote for political parties that promise to reduce taxes.

61

2 The **researcher effect** refers to how the relationship between researcher and respondent may bias responses:

- *Aggressive* interviewers, for example, may introduce bias by intimidating a respondent into giving answers they do not really believe.
- *Status* considerations, based on factors such as gender, age, class and ethnicity, may also bias the data. A female respondent may feel embarrassed about answering questions about her sexuality posed by a male researcher.

KEY TERM

Researcher effect: also called the interviewer effect, this refers to how the relationship between researcher and respondent may bias responses and lead to invalid data.

TEST YOURSELF

Suggest one similarity and one difference between a structured interview and a questionnaire.

Content analysis

Content analysis has both quantitative and qualitative forms. What both types have in common is the study of *texts* (data sources such as television, written documents, etc.). Quantitative analysis of media texts, for example, uses statistical techniques to categorise and count the frequency of people's behaviour using a content analysis grid (Table 3.1).

KEY TERM

Content analysis: research method used for the systematic analysis of media texts and communications.

Although the grid below is a simple example, content analysis can be complex and wide-ranging. Meehan's (1983) study of US daytime television, for example,

identified and analysed the stereotypical roles played by female characters in soap operas. Harwood (1997) used content analysis to demonstrate that television viewers generally prefer to watch characters of their own age.

Strengths: Content analysis can identify underlying themes and patterns of behaviour that may not be immediately apparent. *Recurrent themes*, such as female associations with housework, in complex forms of social interaction can also be identified. Hogenraad (2003) used computer-based analysis to search historical accounts of war in order to identify recurring themes and words in the lead-up to conflicts. This suggests that quantitative analysis can have predictive qualities. By identifying a pattern of past behaviour that always leads to war, it would be possible to predict future conflict. Similarly, Kosinski et al. (2013) used content analysis of Facebook to show how a user's personal characteristics, such as their intelligence quotient (IQ), sexuality and political views, could be inferred from the things they 'liked'.

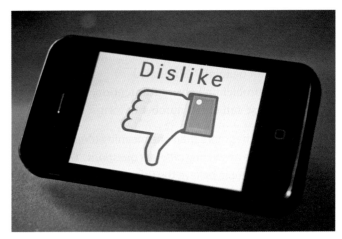

Content analysis can be used to reveal hidden social processes, such as how websites collect private information

Content analysis can also be used for 'concept mapping'. Page (2005) tracked how media professionals portrayed global warming in order to show how far global warming was reported in terms of 'natural' or 'social' causes. The quantification of such behaviour allows researchers to draw complex conclusions from quite simple data-collection techniques. The use of a *standardised framework* (the *grid*) also means that data can be checked and *replicated*.

Limitations: In some types of content analysis reliability may be limited because researchers must make subjective judgements about behaviour. Not only do they have to decide which categories will and will not be used, they may also have to judge which

Character	Gender	Age	Place and purpose	On screen
Azir Khan	Male	25	Office (employee)	30 seconds
Safiq Dhonna	Male	56	Office (customer)	43 seconds
Angelique Basson	Female	37	Shop (customer)	84 seconds

Table 3.1   Simple content analysis grid to record the behaviour of characters in a television programme

forms of behaviour fit which categories. This raises questions about whether all observed behaviour can be neatly categorised, In this instance, data can be difficult to replicate because different researchers studying the same behaviour may not categorise it in the same way.

Content analysis does not tell us very much about *how* or *why* audiences receive, understand, accept or ignore themes and patterns discovered by the research. This is why content analysis is often used in combination with a qualitative method such as semiology (see below).

Experiments

Experiments involve testing the relationship between different **variables** – things that can change under controlled conditions. The researcher changes (manipulates) independent variables to see if they produce a change in dependent variables that are not changed by the researcher; any changes must be caused by a change in the independent variable.

KEY TERM

Variables: factors that can be changed (manipulated) by the researcher to understand their effect on behaviour.

Experiments, therefore, are based on changing an independent variable and measuring any subsequent change in a dependent variable. This relationship that can be one of two types:

1. Correlations occur when two or more things happen at roughly the same time. These only *suggest* a relationship, however, because it is possible for them to occur by chance. For example, waking up in bed fully clothed may correlate with feeling unwell – but that does not mean the former *causes* the latter. A third factor, such as drinking a lot of alcohol the previous evening, might be a cause of both.

2. **Causation** involves the idea that when one action occurs, another *always* follows. Causal relationships are powerful because they allow a researcher to predict the future behaviour of something.

KEY TERM

Causation: the idea that when one action occurs, another *always* follows because the latter is caused by the former.

It is not always easy to distinguish between correlation and causation in the real world of sociological research, because things often happen at the same time by chance

or coincidence. However, there are two ways to separate correlation from causality:

1. Test and retest a relationship. The more times a test is replicated with the same result, the greater the chances that the relationship is causal.

2. Use different groups with exactly the same characteristics:

   - an **experimental group** whose behaviour is manipulated
   - a **control group** whose behaviour is not.

KEY TERMS

Experimental group: the subjects of an experiment. The researcher changes different variables to test their effect on behaviour.

Control group: in an experiment, the characteristics of the control group exactly match those of the experimental group. While the behaviour of the experimental group is manipulated in some way, no attempt is made to similarly manipulate the control group. This allows comparisons to be made between the control and experimental groups.

Laboratory experiments

Bandura et al.'s (1963) 'Bobo doll' experiment, designed to measure the relationship between media violence and violent behaviour in young people, used four groups:

- Three experimental groups were shown a film depicting different types of violence
- A control group was not shown violent behaviour.

Each group was observed to see whether those *shown* violent behaviour then *played* violently with a specially designed inflatable doll. The experimental groups demonstrated violent behaviour, but the control group did not. This suggested at worst a correlation and, at best, a causal relationship between seeing violence and acting violently. A control group can be used to check that changes in the experimental groups' behaviour were not the result of chance. Without a control group, Bandura et al. could not have been sure that the violent behaviour of the groups shown violent films was not simply their normal behaviour.

This research is an example of a **laboratory experiment**, one that takes place in a closed environment where conditions

KEY TERM

Laboratory experiment: experiment that takes place in a closed environment where conditions can be precisely monitored and controlled.

can be precisely monitored and controlled. This ensures that no 'outside' or uncontrolled variables affect the relationship between the dependent and independent variables.

Field/natural experiments

Laboratory experiments are rare in sociology, because they raise ethical issues and questions about validity. Therefore, a more common type is the **field experiment**, which is conducted outside of a closed, controlled environment.

> **KEY TERM**
>
> **Field experiments:** experiments that take place in the 'real world', beyond the closed, controlled environment of the laboratory.

> **TEST YOURSELF**
>
> Briefly explain the difference between a laboratory and a field experiment. Suggest one strength and one limitation of each type of experiment.

A specially designed inflatable doll can be used in laboratory experiments to test triggers for violent behaviour in young people

It is very difficult to control all possible independent variables in a natural setting, which means that natural experiments tend to establish correlations rather than causation. However, the basic principles of the experiments are the same. Researchers use dependent and independent variables to test a hypothesis or answer a research question:

- To test the hypothesis that teachers' expectations influence how well their pupils do in school, Rosenthal and Jacobson (1968) conducted a study of low educational achievement in Mexican children. The dependent variable was their level of achievement and the independent variable was the expectations teachers had about the ability of their pupils. Rosenthal and Jacobson manipulated the independent variable by pretending to be psychologists who could, on the basis of a sophisticated IQ test, identify children who would display 'dramatic intellectual growth'. In fact, they tested the pupils and then *randomly* classed some students as 'later developers'. The researchers informed the teachers of their 'findings'. They retested the pupils at a later date and discovered that the IQ scores of those pupils whose teachers believed were 'late-developing high flyers' had significantly improved.
- Garfinkel's (1967) breaching experiments showed how people 'construct reality' through everyday routines and assumptions. In one experiment, student researchers (the independent variable) were sent home with

instructions to behave as if their parents (the dependent variable) were strangers and to observe and record how the parents' behaviour changed towards their 'oddly behaving' offspring.

Strengths: Laboratory experiments are easier to replicate than field experiments because the researcher has more control over both the research conditions and the variables being tested. Standardised research conditions give experiments a high level of reliability. Experiments can also create powerful, highly valid statements about behaviour based on cause-and-effect relationships that can be extended from the lab to understand people's behaviour in the real world. Similarly, field experiments can be used to manipulate situations in the real world to understand the underlying reasons for everyday behaviour.

Limitations: It can be difficult to control all possible influences on behaviour, even in a laboratory setting. A simple awareness of being studied, for example, may introduce an uncontrolled independent variable into an experiment. The **Hawthorne (or observer) effect**, named after a study by Mayo (1933) at the Hawthorne factory in Chicago, refers to changes in people's behaviour directly resulting from their knowledge of being studied. The working conditions at the factory were manipulated in different ways, such as changing the brightness of the lighting and the temperature in the factory. However, the results were always the same: the productivity of the workers increased. As Draper argues, 'the important effect here was the feeling of being studied'.

KEY TERM

Hawthorne (or observer) effect: changes in people's behaviour that result from their knowledge of being observed.

The ecological validity of experiments can also be questioned because they take place in an artificial environment. A controlled experiment is an *unusual* situation and respondents may behave differently in a laboratory or field setting. One solution to this problem is to conduct the experiment secretly, as in the case of Milgram (1974) or Rosenhan (1973), but this raises ethical questions about the right to experiment on people who may be unwitting (and unwilling) participants.

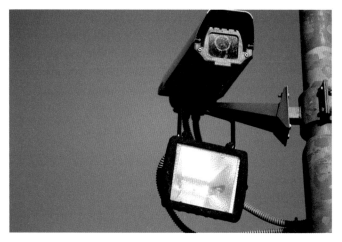

How might the knowledge of being watched change people's behaviour?

Longitudinal surveys

These are a form of comparative analysis that involves tracking changes among a representative sample over time, from a few months to many years. The same group is analysed at different stages in their lives, using methods ranging from questionnaires to non-participant observation.

Like participant observation studies (see below), longitudinal surveys are carried out over a significant period of time; they can last many years. However, in longitudinal surveys the researcher remains detached from the study group, having contact with the research subjects only on a limited basis at set intervals. By contrast, with participant observation studies the researcher usually maintains more or less complete

contact with the study group throughout the period of the research.

KEY TERM

Longitudinal survey: a form of comparative analysis that involves tracking changes among a representative sample over time.

Strengths: Kruger argues that one strength of longitudinal surveys is that they can be used 'to summarize vast sources of information and facilitate comparisons across categories and over time'. This is because they exploit the ability of quantitative methods to identify and track personal and social changes. Hills et al. (2010), for example, used data from the English Longitudinal Survey of Ageing to analyse the relationship between mortality rates and levels of wealth. The study found a strong correlation between low wealth and premature death. This demonstrates a significant strength of longitudinal studies: the ability to reveal trends that would otherwise remain hidden.

A further advantage of longitudinal surveys is that they can generate reliable representative samples to suggest causal relationships. Power et al.'s (2011) 10-year study of 200 families raising children in highly disadvantaged neighbourhoods, for example, found a 'clear cause and effect between physical or environmental improvements to an area and the well-being of its families'.

Limitations: Sample attrition, or the number of people who withdraw from the original sample over time, is a major limitation of these surveys. High levels of attrition can reduce the representativeness of the sample over time – a problem that grows the longer the study lasts.

While longitudinal studies can identify trends or allow researchers to make correlations and causal connections between phenomena, such as income and life expectancy, they are only ever a glimpse of behaviour at any given moment. They can, therefore, be criticised for lacking depth and validity.

TEST YOURSELF

Suggest one reason why a researcher might want to study the same group at different times.

Cross-sectional surveys

This type of survey is explicitly designed to produce a 'snapshot' of behaviour at any given time:

- Qualitative forms are generally descriptive, with the objective being to illustrate a particular type of behaviour. It may involve, for example, looking at a certain

65

population characteristic, such as suicide, income or poverty, applied to a single country, a large area within a country or a specific feature of different countries.

■ Quantitative forms, the most common type, are analytic: the objective is to analyse both correlations and causations between different phenomena. Durkheim's study of suicide, for example, used cross-sectional surveys taken from different societies to build up a comparative analysis of variable suicide rates. He used these as the basis for a theoretical explanation of different types of suicide.

> **KEY TERM**
>
> **Cross-sectional survey:** research method focused on identifying groups that share broad similarities, such as level of education, and measuring differences in a single variable; whether, for example, people with a high level of education have higher rates of suicide than those with a lower level of education.

Both types of **cross-sectional survey** normally require representative samples because one of the main objectives is to make generalisations about behaviour. In this respect, cross-sectional surveys tend to focus on identifying groups that share broad similarities, such as income, education and gender. They measure differences using a single variable, such as death or suicide rates. By comparing standardised groups, it is possible to explain differences in death or suicide rates using variations in standardised variables – whether, for example, people with a high level of education have higher rates of suicide than those with a lower level of education.

Secondary quantitative methods

Official statistics

Official statistics created and published by governments are a major source of secondary quantitative data used by sociologists to examine trends and patterns within and between societies:

■ Patterns of behaviour may be picked up by statistical analysis because they provide a broad overview of behaviour across potentially wide areas: local, national and international. Durkheim (1897), for example, identified distinct patterns to suicidal behaviour based on a **comparative analysis** of official suicide statistics across a range of different societies.

■ In terms of trends, statistical data drawn from different years can be used to understand how something has

changed. For example, education statistics can track changes in levels of achievement. Statistics can also be used to track changes in behaviour, such as before and after the introduction of a new law.

> **KEY TERM**
>
> **Comparative analysis:** a comparison of different cultures, cases and situations to understand their similarities and differences.

Statistics can be used for comparisons within groups, such as differences in middle- and working-class family size, and between societies. Bakewell (1999) suggests that official refugee statistics are useful because they quickly and easily demonstrate the size and scale of an international social problem.

Strengths: In practical terms, official statistics may be the only available source covering a particular area of study, such as suicide. In addition, data that would be costly, time-consuming and difficult to collect, such as statistics on marriage, divorce or crime, is readily available – especially since the development of the internet. Another strength of official statistics is their representativeness. As Marshall (1998) notes, statistical 'data are almost invariably nationally representative, because they are obtained from complete censuses or very large-scale national sample surveys'.

More theoretically, many official statistical sources, in areas including crime, unemployment, marriages, births and divorces, are recorded by law. Data is usually collected in the same way from the same sources (*iteration*). This adds to its reliability because research can be replicated and compared. Although definitions, of areas such as 'unemployment' may change over time, most – such as 'birth' or 'murder' – remain the same. Some statistical data has low validity, but this is not true of all official statistics. For example, data about marriage, divorce, birth and death can record these events with a high degree of accuracy.

Sociologists use the term 'hard statistics' to refer to quantitative data that demonstrates such accuracy. For example, statistics about the number of divorces in a society can be viewed as 'hard' evidence. This is because a divorce has to be legally registered and so clear and accurate records are available. Statistics that are considered to be less accurate are referred to as 'soft statistics'. Official statistics about the unemployment rate may be 'soft' in, because there are different ways of defining 'unemployment'; depending on which definition is used, the figures may vary greatly.

Limitations: Apart from not providing any great depth or detail, official statistics involve of problems of validity due to what governments include in or exclude from published data. Such data may only give a *partial picture of reality* for two reasons:

1   While official crime statistics provide valuable data about crimes reported to the police, they tell us little or nothing about the 'dark figure of crime' – crimes that are not reported or recorded. Research has shown that in many societies as much as 75% of all crime 'is in the dark figure'.

2   Statistical data does not reveal much about the *reasons* for people's behaviour. For example, although we have a reasonably precise figure for the number of year-on-year murders in countries around the world, this data tells us little about *why* people kill each other.

Although quantitative data is normally considered more *objective* than qualitative data, its significance must always be *interpreted* by researchers; they have to decide what the data *means*. A statistical rise in crime, for example, may be the result of:

■   a real rise

■   a different way of defining and counting crime

■   police targeting certain types of crime and arresting more people.

Governments occasionally change the definition of key concepts. Different governments may also define a concept differently, as Bakewell discovered in relation to official definitions of 'a refugee' around the world. Such changes and differences bring into question the reliability of the data, because when making statistical comparisons the researcher must ensure they are comparing like with like. Two further problems arise over how behaviour is officially categorised:

■   To estimate the extent of 'knife crime', data is increasingly taken from *hospital records* because victims do not always report the incidents. While this official data gives us an idea of the general extent of knife wounding, it does not distinguish between deliberate and accidental wounding, for example.

■   The categories used by governments to define things such as social class or poverty are not necessarily the same as those used by sociologists.

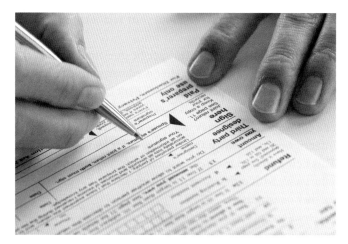

Does having to legally record statistical information make it more reliable?

Primary qualitative methods

Semi-structured ('focused') interviews

Nichols (1991) defines this method as 'an informal interview, not structured by a standard list of questions. Researchers are free to deal with the topics of interest in any order and to phrase their questions as they think best.' **Semi-structured interviews**, therefore, allow a respondent to talk at length and in depth about a particular subject. The focus or topic of the interview is decided by the researcher. The interview has a structure or 'interview schedule' – the areas the interviewer wants to focus on – but there is no list of specific questions. Different respondents may be asked different questions on the same topic, depending on how the interview develops. The objective is to *understand* things from the respondent's viewpoint, rather than make generalisations about behaviour.

KEY TERM

Semi-structured interview: research method in which a respondent is encouraged to talk at length about a particular subject. Also called focused interviews because the topic is decided by the researcher and is the focus of their questions.

Open-ended questions are frequently used in semi-structured interviews. Some of these are created before the interview, while others arise naturally from whatever the respondent wants to talk about. For example, if the interview focused on understanding family life, the interviewer might begin with a question like: 'Tell me about your family.' If the respondent then mentions their children the interviewer might decide to continue with

67

a question such as: 'Tell me about your relationship with your children.'

Strengths: As there are no specific questions prepared, there is less risk of the researcher predetermining what will be discussed. Where the respondent can talk about things that interest them it is possible to pick up ideas and information that may not have occurred to the interviewer or of which they had *no prior knowledge*. This new knowledge can be used to inform subsequent interviews with different respondents and to suggest further questions.

By allowing respondents to develop their ideas, the researcher tries to discover what someone really means, thinks or believes. The focus on issues that the *respondent* considers important results in a much greater depth of information. This may increase the validity of the data as it is more likely that the research will achieve its real aims. Oatey (1999) suggests that 'freedom for the respondent to answer how they wish is important in giving them a feeling of control in the interview situation'. Within limits, face-to-face interaction allows the researcher to help and guide respondents. To explain, rephrase or clarify a question or answer, for example, may improve overall validity.

TEST YOURSELF

Suggest two differences between structured and semi-structured interviews.

Limitations: This method demands certain skills in the *researcher*, such as asking the right questions, establishing a good rapport and thinking quickly about relevant question opportunities. It also requires skill from the *respondent*; an inarticulate respondent will probably be unable to talk openly and in detail about the research topic. Oatey also argues that open-ended questions 'can cause confusion either because of the lack of understanding of the question or by the lack of understanding of the respondent's answer'.

Semi-structured interviews are not only more time-consuming than questionnaires but the large amounts of information they produce must also be analysed and interpreted. This data is rarely tightly focused on a particular topic, so a researcher may spend a lot of time analysing data that has little or no use to the study.

A theoretical problem is the idea that all interviews are *reconstructions*. Respondents must *remember* and *recount* past events, and this creates problems for both researcher and respondent. While a researcher has no way of

knowing if someone is telling the truth, a further problem is *imperfect recall*; it can not only be difficult to remember things that may have happened months or years ago, but memories can also be *selective* – respondents only recall those things that seem important to them.

Finally, semi-structured interviews lack *standardisation*; the same questions are not necessarily put to all respondents and similar questions may be phrased differently. Can reduce the reliability of the data and make it difficult to generalise the research.

Unstructured interviews

Unstructured interviews are built on a general idea or topic that the researcher wants to understand. Respondents are encouraged to talk freely about the things they feel are important. Kvale (1996) states that 'behaviour is understood from the perspective of those being studied; their perceptions, attitudes and experiences are the focus'.

KEY TERM

Unstructured interviews: free-form interview method where the objective is to get the respondent to talk, without prompting or interruption, about whatever they feel is important about a topic.

Strengths: The researcher's limited input means that data reflects the interests of the respondent. It is therefore more likely to be an accurate and detailed expression of their beliefs. Hamid et al. (2010) used this method in their study of young Pakistani females because 'unstructured interviews helped elaborate on the topics of participants' choice [marriage and sexuality] and probed further their concerns'. This technique avoids the problem of the researcher prejudging what constitutes important or irrelevant data.

The researcher must establish a strong *rapport* with respondents. If this rapport is achieved, people who may be naturally wary of being studied can open up to the researcher, allowing sensitive issues to be explored in depth. Hamid et al. established a relationship with their respondents by meeting them a number of times before their research started. This 'helped the participants to open up … and discuss sensitive issues regarding sexuality and growing up with reference to their marriage and other related topics of their choice'. If the research is relatively informal it can take place somewhere the respondent will feel at ease, such as in their own home. For Hamid et al. this helped 'overcome the barrier of talking about sensitive issues'.

How are unstructured interviews like a conversation?

Limitations: Unstructured interviews demand skills of both the researcher and the respondent. The researcher must resist the temptation to influence, encourage or interrupt. Respondents must be able to express themselves clearly and understandably. The researcher, by design, has little control over the direction of the interview and the conversation may stray into areas that later prove irrelevant to the research. The interviews are time-consuming in themselves, but so is analysing and interpreting all the data they generate. Reliability also tends to be low because the *non-standardised* format makes the interview impossible to replicate.

A more severe limitation is the argument that all forms of interviewing are inherently biased by interview effects. Cohen and Taylor (1977) argue that the most significant of these effects is that through the act of questioning people, a series of *status manipulations* come into play. The outcome of this is that respondents try to please the researcher by telling them what they believe they want to hear.

TEST YOURSELF

Suggest two advantages to understanding behaviour from the respondent's point of view.

Group interviews

Group interviews (also called focus groups) involve respondents gathering to discuss a topic decided in advance by the researcher. These groups may be selected as representative samples – a cross-section of society,

KEY TERM

Group interviews: also called focus groups, these involve respondents discussing a topic as a group rather than individually.

for example – or they may simply represent a group the researcher wants to explore in detail. Nichols suggests that focus groups may also be same-sex and from similar backgrounds to prevent gender and class variables affecting the reliability and validity of the data. For Morgan (1997), the effectiveness of group interviewing is based on:

■ an interview structure with clear guidelines for the participants, to avoid arguments within the group
■ predetermined questions through which the experiences of participants can be explored
■ interaction within the group, which Gibbs (1997) argues gives 'unique insights into people's shared understandings of everyday life'.

Strengths: In group interviews, the researcher can help the discussion. They can:

■ control the pace and scope of the discussion
■ plan a schedule that allows them to focus and refocus the discussion
■ intervene to ask questions, stop or redirect aimless discussions
■ create a situation that reflects how people naturally share and discuss ideas.

Gibbs argues that one strength of this method is the ability to 'draw on respondents' attitudes, feelings, beliefs, experiences and reactions'. In a group, respondents are encouraged to elaborate and reflect on their beliefs. Pain et al.'s (2000) study of the fear of crime used this format to:

■ generate large amounts of detailed information quickly and efficiently
■ uncover attitudes, beliefs and ideas that would not have been revealed by less flexible methods.

Kitzinger (1995) suggests that group interaction 'enables participants to ask questions of each other, as well as to re-evaluate and reconsider their own understanding of their specific experiences'. Respondents can also 'explore solutions to a particular problem as a group rather than as individuals'. Morley (1980) felt that individual interviews were 'abnormal situations' for most people, but that group interviews created an environment that encouraged people to talk at length.

Limitations: The researcher must control the behaviour of the group to allow people to speak freely and openly about an issue while maintaining the focus of the research. This, Gibbs notes, means 'good levels of group leadership and interpersonal skill are required'. The more people there are to co-ordinate, the more likely it is that there will be

69

problems with resources, such as time, money and effort. There may also be problems with representativeness: if in a carefully selected group of ten, one person does not show up, the sample becomes unrepresentative.

Morgan argues that any failure to stop individuals and alliances taking control and 'setting their own agenda for discussion' raises questions about reliability. Researchers have less control over the data because they have less control over the group and the direction of the discussion. This may also affect validity because the focus of the interview may end up moving away from the researcher's intended focus. Group interviews are also at risk from another type of 'interview effect' – one that Janis (1982) calls 'Groupthink'. This refers to the pressure people feel to arrive at 'desired outcomes', such as saying what they believe the researcher wants to hear. Group interviews also run the risk of simply reflecting a 'group consensus' rather than revealing what individuals really believe.

What practical advantages do group interviews have over individual interviews?

Observation

Observational methods are based on the idea that data is more valid if it is gathered by *seeing* how people behave, rather than taking on trust that people do what they *say* they do. There are two main observational techniques: non-participant and participant.

Non-participant observation

Non-participant observation involves observing behaviour *from a distance*. This sometimes takes place

 KEY TERM

Non-participant observation: when the researcher observes behaviour without participating in that behaviour.

literally – when the research subject does not know they are being observed. However, non-participant observation usually means that the researcher does not become personally involved in the behaviour they are studying. In this way, the researcher's presence cannot influence the behaviour of those being watched. As Parke and Griffiths (2002) noted in their study of gambling: 'Non-participant observation usually relies on the researcher being unknown to the group under study … [they] can study a situation in its natural setting without altering that setting.'

Strengths: Access is one practical advantage of non-participant observation. It allows research on people who may not want to be studied because their behaviour is illegal, secret or personally embarrassing, for example. People may also be suspicious of a researcher or, as in the case of the gamblers Parke and Griffiths studied, 'dishonest about the extent of their gambling activities'. Since the researchers could not simply ask gamblers about their behaviour, one solution was to observe them 'at work'.

When the researcher does not participate in the behaviour being observe, respondents can be objectively studied in a natural setting. The researcher gets to see 'everyday behaviour' just as it would normally occur – a technique Yule (1986) used to discover how mothers *really* treated their children in public places.

How does this picture illustrate the idea that we can't always trust the evidence of our own eyes?

Limitations: Observational studies cannot be easily or exactly replicated because the characteristics and composition of a group may change over time. Observing people 'from a distance' may also produce data that fails to capture the depth, richness and intimate details of their behaviour. This type of study also raises ethical questions, because people are being observed without their permission. Parke and Griffiths argue that this method requires certain practical skills, such as 'the art of being inconspicuous'. They found that 'if the researcher fails to blend in, then slot machine gamblers soon realise they are being watched and are highly likely to change their behaviour'.

What advantages are there to watching rather than questioning people?

Participant observation

Participant observation is when the researcher takes part in the behaviour being studied. It is based, in part, on what Weber (1922) termed **verstehen** – 'to understand by experiencing' or, as Mead (1934) described it, the researcher's ability to *take the part of the other* and see things from their viewpoint (*empathy*). Participant observation reflects what Downes and Rock (2003) call 'the claim social behaviour cannot be understood unless it is personally experienced' or, as Parker (1974) puts it, 'by cornering people in classrooms to answer questionnaires the sociologist misses meeting them as people in their normal society'. Participant observation can take two forms: overt and covert.

KEY TERM

Verstehen: research strategy central to participant observation, which takes advantage of the researcher's ability to see things from the subject's viewpoint (*empathy*).

Overt observation involves participating in the behaviour of people who *know* they are being studied. The researcher joins the group *openly*, and usually conducts the research with the *permission* and *co-operation* of the group (or significant members of the group).

KEY TERM

Overt observation: participant observation in which those being studied are aware they are being researched.

Strengths: On a practical level, recording data is relatively easy because the group knows and understands the role of the researcher. The researcher can ask questions, take notes and observe behaviour openly. With groups that have *hierarchical structures*, such as large businesses, the researcher can gain access to all levels – the boardroom as well as the shop floor.

It can be difficult to gain access to some groups, so researchers may use *sponsorship* to find a way in. This involves gaining the trust and co-operation of an important group member. Venkatesh's (2009) study of a black American gang, for example, was only possible because a middle-ranking gang member called 'JT' 'sponsored' and protected Venkatesh while he observed

the gang and eventually gained access to some of its more powerful members. This situation echoed Whyte's (1943) entrance into an Italian street gang through the sponsorship of its leader, 'Doc'.

Sponsorship makes it easier to *separate* the roles of participant and observer. It reduces the chance of the researcher becoming so involved in a group that they stop observing and simply become a participant (*going native*). Even so, Venkatesh found there were times when his involvement was so complete that he acted 'like one of them' and effectively ceased to be an objective and impartial observer.

The ability to ask questions, observe individual behaviours and experience the day-to-day life of respondents helps the researcher to build up a highly detailed picture of the lives they are describing. This '360-degree' view means the researcher not only gets to understand what people 'say they do', but also witnesses and experiences what people *actually* do. This can increase the validity of the data.

Where the observer's role is clearly defined there is also less risk of involvement in unethical, criminal, dangerous or destructive behaviours. The researcher can, for example, withdraw from risky situations without necessarily losing the trust or arousing the suspicions of those being studied.

What advantages are there to experiencing behaviour rather than simply observing it?

Limitations: If a group refuses the researcher permission to observe it, then the research cannot be carried out. In addition, overt observation requires substantial amounts of time, effort and money. Venkatesh, for example, spent around eight years on his study of a single gang in a small area of one US city.

Theoretical criticisms initially focus on the observer/Hawthorne effect and the extent to which knowledge of being watched changes how people behave. While people may be studied in their natural environment, an awareness of the presence of the researcher may make them behave unnaturally. Venkatesh witnessed a staged punishment beating designed to demonstrate the limits of his observational role; higher-level gang members were 'putting on a show' for his benefit.

A further limitation is the researcher's level of involvement:

- Without full participation, researcher involvement may be too superficial to allow a true understanding of behaviour.
- Ethical concerns, such as not participating in illegal behaviour, may affect the extent to which the researcher is truly experiencing how people normally behave.
- There is a risk that the researcher will become *too* involved and effectively 'become the story' they are reporting. Their presence becomes the *focal point* around which people orientate their behaviour. Venkatesh was given 'special treatment'; he was invited to meetings and was introduced to people he would not have met if he had not been known as a researcher sponsored by a powerful gang member.

Overt participant observation is impossible to replicate; others must trust that the researcher saw and experienced the behaviour they document. In addition, it can be difficult for a researcher to accurately record behaviour while they are in the middle of it. No researcher can record and document everything that happens, which means this method will always involve the selection, interpretation and reconstruction of ideas and events.

In **covert observation**, the researcher secretly (covertly) joins the group, so the subjects are unaware that they are being studied. The main objective is to experience behaviour in its 'natural setting'; to watch people behave as they normally behave. Unlike overt participation, the researcher must balance the roles of researcher and participant without revealing their true role to other group members.

Strengths: Covert observation may be the only way to study people who would not normally allow themselves to be researched. Such people may include:

- Criminal or deviant groups: Ward (2008) 'was a member of the rave dance drugs culture' when she began her five-year study 'in London nightclubs, dance parties, bars, pubs and people's houses'. Her knowledge of the 'dance scene', coupled with her friendship with those involved meant she was able to gain easy access to this world.
- Closed groups: Lofland and Stark (1965) secretly studied the behaviour of a religious sect because this was the only way to gain access.

- Defensive groups: Ray (1987) covertly studied Australian environmental groups who would have been suspicious of his motives if he had tried to study them openly.

 KEY TERM

Covert observation: those being studied are unaware they are part of a research project.

Full participation in a group, where the researcher lives, works and socialises with the people they are studying, means this method produces highly detailed, insightful, personally observed and experienced, data. Covert participation also avoids the observer effect – the subjects' behaviour is largely unaffected by the researcher's presence.

Through personal experience, the researcher gains valuable insights into the meanings, motivations and relationships within a group. These can explain *why* people behave in certain ways. The ability to experience things from the point of view of those involved, coupled with the sociological insights a researcher brings to the role of observer, means they can make sense of behaviour even in situations where group members may not fully understand the reasons for that behaviour. As Parke and Griffiths note, it is possible to overestimate 'the subjects' knowledge and understanding of their own behaviour' and their ability to explain why they do something in an interview or questionnaire.

Limitations: Goffman's study of a US mental institution identified three major problems for the covert participant observer:

1 Getting in: while gaining covert entry to any group can be a problem, some groups are more difficult to enter than others:

- Entry to some groups is by invitation only. Unless the researcher is invited, they cannot join.
- Some groups have entry requirements. To covertly study accountants or doctors, the researcher would need to hold the qualifications these professions require.
- The characteristics of the observer must match those of the observed. A man, for example, could not covertly participate in a group of nuns. (There are, however, ways around this problem. Goffman, while neither a doctor nor mentally ill, was able to covertly observe by taking a manual job within the institution.)

A police officer in uniform is intended to stand out from the crowd. Why are the characteristics of the researcher and the group significant in covert participant observation?

2 Staying in: once inside, the researcher may not have access to all areas. For example, an observer posing as a school student could not freely enter places, such as staffrooms, reserved for teachers. Someone being where they are not supposed to be would raise suspicions, and the researcher runs the risk of being discovered by 'gatekeepers' – those whose job it is to restrict access.

The researcher has to quickly learn the culture and dynamics of a group if they are to participate fully. This can require a range of skills, including the ability to mix easily with strangers, create and maintain a plausible and convincing 'back story' (past) and to think quickly on their feet when questioned or challenged. For example, Parker had to make instant decisions about whether or not to participate in the criminal activities of the gang of youths he was secretly studying.

If a researcher lacks the 'insider knowledge' they *should* have, they risk exposure. Parke and Griffiths, for example, noted how 'street knowledge about slot machine gamblers and their environments', such as the terminology players use, machine features and gambling etiquette, is an essential requirement for covert participation in the gambling world.

The ability to successfully blend into a group carries its own problems. It can be difficult to separate the roles of participant and observer, especially if the researcher is well integrated into a group:

■ At one extreme, the researcher may have to choose between participation and observation, such as if a group participates in criminal activities.

■ At the other, the researcher may become so much a part of the group they *go native* and stop being an observer, which can raise doubts about the validity of the research. Whyte, for example, became so involved with the lives of gang members he came to see himself as 'one of the gang' and not as a researcher.

3 Getting out: it can be difficult to stop participating. A member of a criminal gang, for example, cannot simply leave. In other groups leaving may raise ethical questions, such as the effect of deserting people who have grown to trust and depend on the researcher. This type of research raises further ethical questions, such as whether a researcher has the right to pretend to be one of the group or use its members for their own purposes.

In addition to problems of entrance, acceptance and departure, further limitations include:

■ research cannot be replicated
■ we have to trust that the researcher saw what they claim to have seen
■ recording data is frequently difficult; the researcher cannot take notes, ask too many questions or openly record conversations
■ the impossibility, as Parke and Griffiths note, of studying 'everyone at all times and locations', where it becomes 'a matter of personal choice as to what data are recorded, collected and observed', all things that affect reliability and validity.

TEST YOURSELF

Identify two differences between overt and covert participant observation.

Case studies

This type of research studies the characteristics of a particular group or 'case', such as Westwood's (1984) 12-month participant observation study of female workers in a 'Stitchco' factory. A **case study** is not really a research method, but rather a research *technique,* in which different methods can be used to generate data. Such studies are usually based on qualitative methods.

KEY TERM

Case study: in-depth, qualitative, study of a particular group or 'case'.

73

Type	Overt or covert	Participation	Characteristics
Non-participant	Overt/covert	None/minimal	Complete observer
Covert participant	Covert	Full	Complete participant
Overt participant	Overt	Full	Participant-as-observer

Table 3.2   Types of observation

Source: Brewer (2000)

Strengths: The focus on a single group studied over time provides great depth and detail of information that has greater validity than simple quantitative studies. In cases where the sample is relatively small and self-contained, such as a factory (Westwood), a school (Lacey, 1970) or even a restaurant (Marshall, 1986), large amounts of data can be collected in a relatively cost-effective way.

Such studies help to uncover the meanings people give to everyday behaviour. They often make use of participant observation, but other methods are also used in case studies. The research objective is normally to develop narrative data that 'tells a story' about the people being studied, so qualitative methods are usually most useful.

A significant strength of case studies is that they allow an in-depth understanding of how people see and understand their particular world, using their own eyes, words and experiences. People can 'speak for themselves' through the channel of sociological research. Small-scale case studies can also be used as pilot studies to allow a researcher to develop hypotheses, test data-collection methods and identify potential problems in preparation for a larger study.

Limitations: Case studies have a range of practical limitations that depend to some extent on their size and scope. Large-scale, in-depth studies can take a lot of time, effort and money. Regardless of their size, the intensive and detailed nature of case studies means that they make higher demands on the skills of researchers, who may spend months or years living and working with their subjects, and respondents, who may be subject to extensive and detailed questioning and observation throughout the study.

It is difficult to generalise from case studies because they tend to focus on small groups that may only be representative of themselves. It might, however, be possible to draw comparisons between similar groups. The validity of such criticism depends on the researcher's aims. If the sample (or case) *is* the target population, and the aim is to simply provide a detailed insight into the behaviour of a particular group, there is no need for the research to be generalised.

Semiology

Semiology is the study of the cultural meanings embedded in media forms. Stokes (2003) suggests that semiology is frequently combined with content analysis to produce a more rounded picture of behaviour through its ability to explore and interpret the 'hidden messages' within texts. The theoretical justification for this is the idea that texts always involve two levels of understanding:

- The *denotative* refers to what something *is*; a literal representation, such as picture of a bunch of roses.
- The *connotative* refers to what something *means* and this can vary between individuals, groups and cultures. In some cultures, for example, a man giving a woman 12 red roses might symbolise his love. Doing the same in Russia symbolises death – *even* numbers of flowers are only given to people at funerals.

KEY TERM

Semiology: the study of cultural meanings embedded in media forms, often used to explore and interpret 'hidden meanings' embedded within texts.

These features of language and culture are significant because it is possible to examine both behaviour and texts, such as television programmes and websites, on two levels:

- what it claims to be (denotative level)
- what it means to others (connotative level).

For example, the Glasgow Media Group (1976) showed how semiological analysis can identify the assumptions that lie behind the presentation of television news. Its analysis of how industrial disputes were portrayed illustrated subtle (and not so subtle) forms of bias:

- Employers were generally filmed in a relatively calm environment, such as in an office, behind a desk, and the reporter would ask respectful questions that the employer was allowed to answer without interruption.
- Employees, often simply identified as 'striking workers', were often pictured outside and the questioning was more aggressive, with an emphasis on the employee having to justify their actions.

Strengths: Rose (2007) argues that semiology has a number of practical advantages: it requires very few resources, is relatively cheap to carry out and can be applied quickly and efficiently to very large samples.

Semiology also provides useful tools for analysing the meaning of media texts, to demonstrate how the media constructs realities and identities, from selling products to selling ideas. Marxism, in particular, has used semiology to reveal how the media in capitalist societies has presented various social conventions, such as social and economic inequality, as 'natural', inevitable and unchangeable. Various studies have used semiology to show how 'hidden meanings' are embedded in texts:

What is the connotation (meaning) of these pictures to you? Think about the cultural meanings embedded in the images

- Cumberbatch (1990) found that TV adverts used male and female identities in different ways. Older men and younger women were more likely to be used than other age groups. Older men featured heavily when an advertiser wanted to convey authority, especially when an advert featured technical expertise, while young women were used to convey sexiness.
- Best (1992) demonstrated how pre-school texts designed to develop reading skills are populated by sexist assumptions and stereotypes about males and females.

Although it is an interpretive method, semiology can be grounded in empirical research and can be easily combined with different types of content analysis:

- Conceptual analysis focuses on the concepts or themes embedded in texts – an extension of quantitative content analysis. Philo and Berry (2004), for example, identified recurring themes in news reports of the Israeli–Palestinian conflict, such as language differences when referring to similar forms of behaviour: Palestinians were often described as 'terrorists', while Israeli settlers were called 'extremists' or 'vigilantes'.
- Relational analysis examines how texts encourage the reader to see something in a particular way by relating one idea to something different. Hall (1980) calls this a 'preferred reading' the way text is constructed through language, pictures and illustrations 'tells' the audience how to interpret the information presented.

Limitations: Rose suggests that a researcher needs a thorough grounding in their subject matter if they are to identify and understand the underlying meaning of texts or behaviours. A semiological analysis of multiplayer video games, for example, would be difficult for a researcher with little or no experience of online gaming.

More fundamental limitations relate to the idea that we cannot simply assume that because a researcher uncovers 'hidden meanings' in a text, a casual audience would do the same. Similarly, semiology is based on the belief that media messages are layered in terms of denotations and connotations – 'core ideas' are embedded in layers of seemingly inconsequential ideas. The 'real message' of advertising, for example, is not about choosing one product over another but about creating a consumption culture in which people define themselves in terms of what they buy.

However, this argument assumes that 'real' messages can be found by peeling back the layers and that the researcher has a privileged position in this process as someone who 'knows the real meaning' of media messages. Hebdidge, for example, states that some youth sub-cultures wore Nazi swastikas in an 'ironic way', while Young argues that this is unsupported by evidence and that semiological analysis runs the risk of the researcher projecting their own interpretations and prejudices on the study.

75

	Official	Organisational	Individual
Sources	Governments	Private companies and organisations	**Personal documents**
Historical and current types	Official reports; court reports; academic studies; websites	Newspapers (local/national); film; magazines; books; church records; academic studies	Letters; diaries (paper and video); oral histories; personal websites; biographies; autobiographies; social networking sites; photographs

Table 3.3   Types and sources of documentary evidence

Secondary qualitative methods

Documentary sources

There are many documentary sources available to sociologists and it is difficult to classify them in any meaningful way. We can, however, think about documentary evidence (Table 3.3) in terms of different *sources* and types.

Strengths: In terms of practical strengths, documentary sources give the researcher access to data that would cost a lot of money, time and effort to collect personally. Such sources can provide secondary data in situations where it is not possible to collect primary data (about things that happened in the distant past, for example). Historical documents can also be used for comparative purposes; contrasting how people once lived with how we live now is useful for tracking and understanding social change. Historical analysis also reveals the diversity of people's behaviour – things we now take for granted may have been seen differently in the past, and vice versa.

More theoretically, documents can provide qualitative data of great depth and detail. For example, diaries such as those of Samuel Pepys, who recorded life in England during the 1660s, or Anne Frank, who recorded her life in hiding from the Nazis in Amsterdam during the Second World War, provide extensive and valuable details about people and their daily lives. In addition, it is sometimes possible to compare accounts across time to test the validity of current accounts of social behaviour. Comparisons of past and present accounts of family and working lives can help us understand the continuities and changes in individual and institutional behaviour. Pearson (1983), for example, used media accounts going back over 100 years to demonstrate that 'hooligan' or 'yobbish' behaviour is not a recent phenomenon in the UK.

Documents can also be used for semiological analysis that compares their literal (what they actually say) and metaphorical meanings – what they tell us about the hopes, fears and beliefs of whoever produced them.

Personal documents: secondary source of data covering areas such as personal letters, diaries, oral (verbal) histories, websites, social networking sites and photographs.

Newspaper articles, for example, may tell us more about their writers and how they see social problems than they do about the topic of the article.

TEST YOURSELF

Suggest one reason why official government websites may not be a valid source of data.

Limitations: Practical limitations tend to focus on the availability of documentary sources – they are not always easy to find – and where they come from. Paper documents can be forged and a researcher needs to know whether they are originals or copies that may have been changed by other authors. Similar considerations apply to digital text, photographic and video sources. We do not always know why or by whom a document was created, which means we cannot always be sure if it is a credible source. Did the author have first-hand experience of the things they describe, or are they simply repeating something they heard?

More theoretically, documents pose reliability problems in that they may be:

- incomplete
- inaccurate
- unrepresentative – diaries, for example, may simply be one individual's view.

These problems make documents difficult to generalise. This may not be an issue if there are a large and diverse number of sources from which to reconstruct social behaviour, but it is a problem if the researcher is dealing with a single documentary source.

A simple way to do some sociological research is to take a short walk around the area where you live or go to school. As you walk, make a note of the people and things you see. What sort of sociological picture of your area have you discovered? Order your observations into meaningful categories, such as:

- *housing*
- *car ownership*
- *evidence of crime*
- *population density*
- *cultural life (theatre, museums, type of shops etc.).*

Once you have collected your data, write up a short report outlining the sociological profile of your area, explaining what common patterns of social organisation you have seen.

Research design

This section looks more generally at the design of sociological research. Oberg (1999) suggests there are four interconnected stages of research design:

1 Planning is where the researcher decides on the strategy – such as what to research and how to research it – and formulates research hypotheses or questions.
2 Information gathering involves identifying a sample to study, conducting an initial pilot study and applying research methods to collect data.
3 Information processing relates to the idea that once data has been gathered, its meaning must be analysed and interpreted.
4 Evaluation involves both an internal analysis that asks questions about how the research was conducted (whether the research method was appropriate, for example) and an external analysis, whereby conclusions are reported to a wider public audience for their analysis and criticism.

This outline can be developed to show a more detailed representation of research design across a range of categories.

The research problem

This is the initial stage, when the sociologist decides things such as the general topic to study and then develops more specific ideas about what aspect to study. This may be accompanied by a review of previous research in the area

under consideration. A review like this may generate ideas about what to study, whether to replicate previous research and how to avoid errors made in previous research.

Research hypothesis *or* question

This is the research focus that sets the basic theme for a study:

- If a hypothesis is used – Ginn and Arber's (2002) analysis of how motherhood affects the lives of graduate women was based on the hypothesis 'The effect of motherhood on full-time employment is minimal for graduate women' – it must be *tested* and this means using research methods suitable for this purpose.
- If a research question is used – Conway's (1997) examination of parental choice in secondary education was based on the question 'Does parental choice help to strengthen the advantage of the middle classes over the working class?'– the research method used must be capable of generating high levels of descriptive data.

Suggest two reasons why a researcher might want to review previous research in the area they plan to study.

77

Collecting data

Before data can be collected, the researcher needs to identify the people – or respondents – who will be the subject of the research. Although it would be ideal to select and study everyone in a particular group (the target population), this is not always possible. For example, if the target population was 'doctors in India', the size and geographic distribution of such a population would make it impossible to observe or question everyone personally. This is where **sampling** enters the research process.

A sample is a relatively small proportion of people who belong to the target population. In the example above, the researcher might choose 1,000 doctors and, by studying their behaviour draw certain conclusions about *all* doctors. However, this only works if the sample is *representative* of the target population. Representativeness may be more significant than sample size because it relates to whether the characteristics of the sample accurately reflect those of the target population. If:

- 60% of the *target population* are male
- 60% of the *sample* should be male.

If the sample is representative anything discovered can be generalised to the target population. A researcher can make statements about a group they have not studied (the target population) based on the behaviour of a group they *have* studied (the sample).

Sampling frame

Constructing a representative sample often requires a sampling frame. This is a list of everyone in a target population, such as an electoral or school register, and it is used for two main reasons:

1   Unless everyone in the target population can be identified, the sample drawn may not accurately reflect the characteristics of the population.

2   For a researcher to contact people in their sample, to interview them for example, they must know who they are.

However, simply because a sampling frame exists does not mean a researcher will automatically have access to it. This may be denied for reasons of:

■   legality: names cannot be revealed by law
■   confidentiality: a business may deny access to its payroll records, for example
■   privacy: some groups do not want to be studied.

There are a number of representative forms of **sampling technique**.

KEY TERM

Sampling and sampling techniques: a sample involves a small number of subjects drawn from a much larger (target) population. Sociologists use a variety of random and non-random sampling techniques.

Simple random sampling

This is based on the *probability* that the random selection of names from a sampling frame will produce a representative sample. For the sample to be truly random, *everyone* in the target population must have an *equal chance* of being chosen. A simple random sample, therefore, is similar to a *lottery*:

■   Everyone in the target population is identified on a sampling frame.
■   The sample is selected by randomly choosing people from the frame until the sample is complete.

A 30% sample of a target population of 100 people, for example, would involve the random selection of 30 people.

Random samples are based on chance distributions

Systematic sampling

This is a variation on simple random sampling that is often used when the target population is very large. It involves taking a sample directly from a sampling frame. For a 25% sample of a target population containing 100 names, every *fourth* name would be chosen. This technique is not truly random – for example, the fifth name on the list could *never* be included in the sample so not everyone has an equal chance of inclusion. However, it is random enough for most samples.

Stratified random sampling

Although simple and stratified random samples can be used in many research situations, problems can occur when a target population is made up of small groups, such as a population with numerous age groups. A biased sample can easily occur by chance, with some groups *over-represented* and others *under-represented*.

Stratified random sampling avoids these problems by dividing (*stratifying*) the target population into groups whose characteristics are *known* to the researcher, such as different age groups. Each group is then treated as a separate random sample in its own right. We can illustrate this by considering:

■   a target population of 100 people (80 females and 20 males)
■   a 10% sample.

To exactly represent the gender balance of the target population, the researcher needs a sample of eight females and two males. To ensure its randomness this involves:

■   splitting the target population into two groups: 80 females and 20 males
■   selecting 10% of *each*:
    ❑   eight females from the 'female only' group
    ❑   two males from the 'male only' group.

When combined, the sample is representative of the target population.

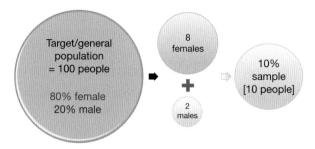

A simple worked example of stratified random sampling

Stratified quota sampling

This variation uses the same basic technique, with two main differences:

1   Although a sampling frame is always useful, it is not strictly necessary. It is enough just to know the characteristics of the respondents in order to construct a sample. Using the previous example, the selection of females and males from their respective groups is done on an *opportunity basis*. The researcher goes through the group of 20 males, asking each in turn to be part of the sample. Once two males have agreed, the quota for the males-only sample is complete and no further males can be selected.

2   This technique is not truly random because not everyone in the target population has an equal chance of being selected. If the first two males agree to be part of the sample, the remaining 18 have no chance of being selected.

Non-representative sampling

Researchers generally find representative samples useful, but there are times when a non-representative sample serves the purpose. For some types of research the sociologist might not want to make generalisations about a very large group based only on a small sample. They might simply be interested in the behaviour of the group itself, rather than what it represents. Case studies, for example, involve studying the behaviour of a particular group (or *case*) in great detail and can be used to illustrate how a non-representative sample works: the 'sample' *is* the target population. In Ward's research on rave participants and Venkatesh's gang study, the fact that each group was only representative of itself was unimportant, since neither researcher wanted to generalise their findings; they simply wanted to understand a particular group in depth.

Opportunity sampling

In some circumstances it may not be possible to create a representative sample. Here, the researcher may be forced to settle for opportunity sampling, a general type of sampling – with two main sub-divisions:

1   Best opportunity sampling involves *deliberately* choosing a sample that gives the best possible opportunity to test a hypothesis. If the hypothesis is false *for this group*, it will probably be false for other similar groups. Goldthorpe et al. (1968), for example, wanted to test the claim that the working class in the UK was becoming indistinguishable from the middle class. Their best opportunity sample consisted of highly paid car-assembly workers in Luton. This group was chosen because if *any* working-class group was likely to show lifestyles similar to their middle-class peers, it would be these 'affluent workers'.

2   Snowball samples work on the principle of 'rolling up' more and more people to include in the sample over time. The researcher would identify someone in the target population who was willing to participate in their research. This person then suggests more people who are also willing to participate. These then suggest further possible participants, until the researcher has a usable sample. Although this technique is unrepresentative, it may be the only option in certain situations:

    ■   Wallis (1977) used snowball sampling to contact (ex-)members of the Church of Scientology when his request to interview current members was rejected.

    ■   In Sappleton et al.'s (2006) research into gender segregation, 'respondents were enlisted through personal referrals, prior contacts and cold calls'.

Opportunity sampling can be a useful technique when no sampling frame is available and the researcher knows little or nothing about the characteristics of their target population.

Pilot study

Before embarking on a full-scale study, many researchers choose to run a **pilot study** to test the various elements of their research design. Pilot studies are a research *tool* normally used for one of two reasons:

1   As a 'mini version' of a full-scale study designed to test the feasibility of carrying out such a study. In other words, before embarking on a study that may take up

> **KEY TERM**
>
> **Pilot study:** 'mini version' of a full-scale study designed to test its feasibility.

large amounts of time, money and effort, a researcher may conduct a smaller study to identify any problems, such as access to respondents, that may occur in a larger study. A pilot study is also helpful in determining the resources, such as staffing and finance, needed for a study. The results of a pilot study can be used to demonstrate to funding bodies that a full study would be feasible and worthwhile.

2   To pre-test a research method, such as a questionnaire. This might involve testing different types of question, examining and analysing the data it produces to ensure the questions will elicit the data required, and identifying and eliminating possible sources of bias or unreliability, such as leading or ambiguous questions.

TEST YOURSELF

Identify and explain one difference between a stratified random and a stratified quota sample.

Data analysis

Foucault (1970) argues that data 'can never speak for itself'; it has to be analysed, by bringing together and categorising related ideas, and interpreted: what, in short, does the data mean? In this respect, analysis and interpretation takes place on three levels:

1   Private/internal analysis involves using concepts like such as reliability and validity to ensure data is logical and consistent.

2   Practical analysis relates to the *purpose* of data collection – the idea of *doing something* with the data. Wilkinson and Pickett (2009), for example, used comparative data drawn from secondary sources to make extensive correlations between social inequality and crime. These suggested a possible causation: the more unequal a society, the higher its relative level of crime.

3   Public/external analysis relates to the idea that all research represents the outcome of a process of social

construction. Not everything the researcher saw, heard or recorded is presented for public consumption. This is partly because it would result in lengthy reports and partly because some data may be considered irrelevant to the research objectives.

Presenting completed research

Glaser and Strauss (1967) suggest that the final stage of the design process involves four related elements:

1   analysing related research to discover common themes and trends in the data

2   reflecting on the research itself; does it, for example, support or disprove the hypothesis?

3   is it possible to discover patterns in the data?

4   does the research suggest ways the data can be linked to create an overall theory?

Once the data has been analysed and interpreted it can be presented in terms of its:

- findings
- conclusions about, for example, the hypothesis (has it been disproven?)
- limitations, which might include discussion of various research problems that may have affected the study
- suggestions for further research
- improvements to the research design.

ACTIVITY

Design a poster that identifies and explains the different stages of research design. Once you have done so, choose a sociological topic that interests you, and think about how you would approach the research of this topic, based on your poster. Make a clear connection between the outcomes you want from the research and the methods employed to get to those outcomes.

Summary points

- **There are two different types of data:**
  - primary
  - secondary.

- **Each can take one of two different forms:**
  - qualitative
  - quantitative.

- **Primary quantitative methods include:**
  - questionnaires (postal)
  - structured interviews
  - content analysis
  - experiments
  - longitudinal surveys.

- **Secondary quantitative methods include official statistics.**

- **Primary qualitative methods include:**
  - semi-structured ('focused') interviews
  - unstructured interviews
  - group (focused) interviews

- non-participant observation
- overt participant observation
- covert participant observation
- cross-sectional surveys
- semiology.

- **Secondary qualitative methods include documents:**
  - personal
  - official
  - historical.

- **The four stages of research design are:**
  - Planning:
    - the research problem
    - hypothesis **or** question
    - pilot study
    - sampling:
      - simple random
      - systematic
      - stratified
      - non-representative.
  - Information gathering.
  - Information processing and analysis.
  - Evaluation.

Exam-style questions

a What is meant by the term primary data? [2]

b Describe any two differences between quantitative and qualitative data. [4]

c Explain how primary quantitative methods can be used to generate sociological data. [8]

d 'The strengths of qualitative methods lie in their ability to generate highly valid data.' Assess this claim. [11]

Total available marks 25

81

Chapter 4:
The relationship between theory and methods

Learning objectives

The objectives of this chapter involve understanding:

- positivist, interpretivist and realist approaches to the relationship between sociological theory and methods
- practical, ethical and theoretical research considerations
- concepts of validity, reliability, objectivity and representativeness
- triangulation and methodological pluralism.

Introduction

This chapter expands on the relationship between theory and methods by focusing on the concept of methodology. This initially involves outlining how different theoretical approaches, such as positivism, interpretivism and realism, construct this relationship. We then broaden the perspective to include methodological concepts, such as reliability, validity, objectivity and representativeness, as ways of assessing the value of different research methods. This chapter further examines how practical, ethical and theoretical considerations may influence the construction and conduct of sociological research. We conclude with an explanation of how methodological pluralism and triangulation can be used to improve data reliability and validity.

Positivist and anti-positivist approaches

We can examine the relationship between theory and methods in more detail by showing how three different theoretical approaches – positivism, interpretivism and realism – construct this relationship.

Positivism

According to this approach, it is both possible and desirable to study social behaviour using similar methods to those used when studying natural world. We can examine this belief by identifying some of its key ideas, beginning with the basic principle that social systems are made up of structures that exist independently of individuals.

Institutions represent behaviour at the macro (very large group) level of society. As individuals we experience social structures as forces bearing down on us, pushing us to behave in certain ways and shaping our behavioural choices. Although we have a measure of choice in our daily lives, this is limited by social structures.

For positivists, where social action is determined by structural forces it makes sense to study the causes of behaviour. This means looking at the structural forces that make people choose one action over another, rather than studying their effects – the choices themselves. Social structures are seen as real, objective forces; people cannot stop these forces from acting on them. Durkheim (1895) described structural forces in terms of the **collective conscience**.

Just as natural scientists have observed the effects of 'unseen forces' such as gravity or electro-magnetism, social structures are unseen forces whose effect can be observed using similar techniques to those of the natural sciences:

- systematic observation
- rigorous testing
- quantitative measurements that create reliable knowledge.

More specifically, knowledge is created by:

- observing social behaviour
- developing and testing hypotheses
- analysing and evaluating evidence.

This systematic process culminates in the development of theories that explain the initial observations and predict future behaviours.

How do we explain why some children achieve more than others?

KEY TERM

Collective conscience: the expression of a society's 'collective will', which bears down on individuals, shaping their beliefs and behavioural choices.

83

TEST YOURSELF

Identify two methods used in sociological research that positivists would favour.

Since this version of science is concerned only with what *is*, rather than how we might *want* something to be, scientists must be personally objective. They do not participate in the behaviour being studied, so they do not bias or influence the data-collection process. Quantitative methods are *favoured* because they allow for the collection of objective and reliable data. Questionnaires, structured interviews, experiments or comparative and observational studies offer higher levels of reliability than qualitative methods. They also allow the researcher to maintain a high level of personal objectivity by 'standing apart' from the behaviour being researched. Research methods, therefore, should not depend on the subjective interpretations of a researcher, and research should be *capable* of exact replication.

In summary, positivist methodology involves these key ideas:

- The primary research goal is to explain, not describe, social phenomena.
- Scientific research involves the ability to discover the 'general rules' (or structures) that determine individual behaviour.
- The social scientist must personally be objective – their research must not be influenced by their values, beliefs, opinions and prejudices – and systemically objective; that is, they should use objective methods.
- Scientific research involves the ability to quantify and measure behaviour.

Interpretivism

For interpretivists, the crucial difference between society and physical nature is that social reality is formed through the interaction of people who have consciousness. This awareness of ourselves and our relationship to others gives us the ability to *act*. People are able to exercise **free will** over the choices they make about how to behave in different situations, rather than simply *react* to outside (structural) stimulation. In this

KEY TERM

Free will: the argument that because humans have consciousness they can make free and informed choices about their actions.

sense, people are unpredictable – they do not always react in the same way. This means that behaviour cannot be studied and explained in the way natural scientists study and explain the non-human world.

For interpretivists, unpredictability is constructed through meanings. 'Society' does not exist in an *objective* form; it is *experienced* subjectively because we give it meaning through behaviour. In other words, people create and re-create a 'sense of the social system' on a daily basis. Society is not something 'out there' to be objectively observed but something 'in here' to be experienced and understood.

Society is created through everyday behaviour and the interactions between individuals in social settings

The construction and reconstruction of social reality is based on both the choices people make and the choices others make for them. If you are caught stealing something from a shop, then others in the criminal justice system will make choices about your future behaviour. They may restrict your freedom of action by sending you to prison. Choices are not, therefore, made in a cultural vacuum; they are influenced by cultural contexts that shape behaviour. How we interpret a situation restricts our range of behavioural choices. In addition, we assess how other people might react to our choices and modify our behaviour accordingly. If you do not want to be arrested then you may decide not to steal something.

An awareness of our choices, and the fact that we understand the consequences of our actions, helps to explain why societies are generally ordered and stable. We consciously limit our behavioural choices to make them broadly predictable and understandable to others. For this reason, facts about behaviour can be established, but they always depend on context – they will not apply to all people, at all times, in all situations.

Suggest another example to illustrate how the interpretation of people's behaviour depends on context.

The fact that people actively create the social world makes it impossible to establish causal relationships either in theory or in practice. If behaviour is conditioned by how people personally interpret their world (and no two interpretations can ever be exactly the same), it follows that 'simple' causal relationships cannot be empirically established. There are too many possible variables involved. Where social contexts define the meaning of behaviour, the best a researcher can do is describe reality from the viewpoint of those who define it, whether they are in a classroom, a family or a mental institution.

If researching social behaviour involves understanding how people individually and collectively experience and interpret their situation, research methods must reflect this social construction of reality. The aim of interpretivist research, therefore, is what Laing (2007) calls 'the recovery of subjective meaning'. The role of the researcher is to help respondents 'tell their story' and, by so doing, understand and explain their behavioural choices.

How do semi- and unstructured interviews facilitate the recovery of subjective meaning?

We can summarise interpretivist methodology as follows:

- The primary aim is to describe social behaviour in terms of the meanings and interpretations of those involved.
- Behavioural rules are context bound; they shift and change in subtle ways depending on the situation.
- Uncovering and describing behavioural rules involves the close study of people's behaviour; the researcher must

gain a good understanding of the context within which such rules are created. This is why researchers in this methodology often use participant observation.

- If, as Humphries (1970) argues, participation is *desirable* because the researcher gets a deeper insight into behaviour, the kind of 'objective detachment' valued by positivists is explicitly rejected.
- While reliability is important, interpretivists place greater emphasis on achieving *validity*.

Realism

A realist approach reflects two ideas:

1. The existence of objective social structures (like *positivism*): this involves understanding what something *is*, such as empirical evidence of crime.
2. Subjective experience and the social construction of reality (like *interpretivism*): this involves understanding what something *means* – for example, how people think about and explain crime.

While positivism and interpretivism emphasise the importance of one or other of these dimensions, realism argues that both are important. To adequately study crime, we must combine an understanding of its empirical reality with its meaning to different individuals.

Realism is sometimes described as 'post-positivism'. Both positivism and realism believe that societies have objective features that can be studied scientifically. Social structures exist independently of the people who create them and are 'real forces' that influence behaviour. By understanding how these structures work, therefore, it is possible to establish causal relationships.

The influence of social structures on behaviour is, however, modified and changed by individual experiences, meanings and interpretations. While social structures influence everyone in a society, they do not affect all individuals in exactly the same way. This fact must be reflected in methods of studying the social world. Realist methodology is based on a belief that the social world consists of both structures with an empirical reality and actions with meaning.

To fully understand and explain human behaviour, sociologists must be able to study the influence of both structure and action. This involves:

- using different methods, quantitative and qualitative
- combining different forms of data. While qualitative and quantitative data can be defined separately, they are inseparable within the research process; quantitative

data is only useful if it has meaning, while qualitative data is only useful if it has an objective

- the idea that *what* is discovered is more important than *how* it is discovered; in other words, the sociologist should be flexible when it comes to choosing research methods, and be prepared to use whatever methods are most likely to produce a reliable research study with valid results
- valid knowledge is created by studying the social world in its *totality*, in terms of social structures, social actions *and* their relationship.

You can think about research methods in terms of a toolbox. Are research methods more than just tools with a single purpose?

ACTIVITY

Think about the subjects you are studying at A level. Make a list of your reasons for choosing these subjects (think about how other people influenced your choice as well as the things you might plan to do with your qualifications). How does this list illustrate either positivist or anti-positivist arguments about the nature of the social world?

The theoretical, practical and ethical considerations of research

Theoretical research considerations

When faced with a problem such as hanging a picture, we reach for a hammer – the most appropriate tool for the job. When carrying out sociological research, therefore, it makes sense to adopt a similar approach: choose a research topic and then select the most appropriate method of collecting data. Unfortunately, although some methods are better suited than others to certain types of research, Ackroyd and Hughes (1992) argue that we should not see these methods as 'tools' that are somehow appropriate or inappropriate for particular tasks. Research methods do not have a clear, single and straightforward purpose. In addition to this – as we have seen – sociological research is surrounded by theoretical beliefs about both the nature of the social world and how it can be studied. When collecting data, therefore, a researcher has to make initial decisions about factors such as what counts as data. Should the data be statistical or descriptive? Should the research test a hypothesis or simply report what respondents say? When deciding how to carry out research, sociologists need to confront and resolve a range of theoretical questions relating to choice of topic and research method.

Topic choice

At a theoretical level, topic choice involves a number of considerations. The intended *audience* of the research may influence (and in some cases actually dictate) topic choice. While Jessop's (2003) 'Governance and Meta-governance: On Reflexivity, Requisite Variety, and Requisite Irony' is perfectly acceptable for an academic audience, it would be impenetrable to a non-academic audience. The *purpose* of research is also important. If the objective is to test a hypothesis, the topic is likely to be narrower in scope than if the objective is a descriptive account.

In both the social and natural worlds there are many potential topics to study, but the general process is the same. What is considered 'worthy of being studied' is influenced by a researcher's values. These are:

- personal – if poverty holds no attraction, for example, then a researcher is unlikely to study it
- institutional – universities and governments are important sources of **research funding**. In the UK, for example, university-based research is overseen and funded by the Economic and Social Research Council, which, in turn, is mainly funded by the UK government. If a government sponsor values quantitative statistical data, therefore, qualitative research is unlikely to be acceptable.

 KEY TERM

Research funding: the source of funding for academic research.

Choice of method

This is similarly surrounded by theoretical considerations, in particular the researcher's perspective:

- Interactionists tend to avoid using statistical methods, mainly because they are not trying to establish causality.
- Positivists are more likely to take the reverse view, mainly because they not interested in descriptive accounts.

We can, therefore, suggest an *association* between interpretivism and qualitative research methods, such as focused interviews or participant observation. Similarly, we can suggest an association between positivism and quantitative methods, such as questionnaires and laboratory experiments. However, this is a simplified distinction that cannot be applied in all circumstances.

A mix of methods (data triangulation) can be used to satisfy different types of research question within the same topic. Although an interpretivist interested in understanding why people fear crime will choose a primary method that gives in-depth, qualitative data, this does not mean they will never employ quantitative methods. Before doing their main research, the researcher might carry out a small study using a simple (quantitative) questionnaire to discover if people actually *do* fear crime; if they do not then further research is probably unnecessary.

A researcher's beliefs about the reliability and validity of particular methods will also play a part in which approach they choose for their research. Such decisions may reflect a researcher's **value judgements** about how something should be studied. If, like Polsky (1971), the researcher believes that covert participation is both unethical and methodologically invalid, they are unlikely to choose this method.

> **KEY TERM**
>
> **Value judgements:** judgements based solely on the values of those making a decision; value judgements are, by definition, subjective.

TEST YOURSELF

Suggest two ways a researcher's theoretical perspective might influence their choice of method.

Practical research considerations

Topic choice

Practical considerations can influence a researcher's choice of topic in a number of ways. Large-scale research carried out over a long period of time may be expensive.

Those who commission and pay for it may have an important say in the choice of topic, method and overall conduct of the research. In addition, in the UK and the USA, where government agencies or departments fund social research, it is usual to commission and fund research designed to help policy-makers make decisions. Research that does not aid this process might not win funding.

Time can be a practical consideration in terms of the depth and scope of the research. Large-scale longitudinal research, such as the Peterborough Adolescent Development Study (2002–10) designed to understand how families, schools and communities shape young people's social development, can be time-consuming to carry out and manage. The principal investigator in this example, Per-Olof Wikstrom, had to manage a team of more than 30 student investigators and academic collaborators over a 10-year period.

A researcher may know what topic they *want* to study, but it may not be possible to do so. Two of the most important practical considerations when choosing a research topic are:

- access to research subjects (individuals)
- their co-operation in the research.

Researchers bring their own personalities to the research process. What problems might there be with managing a large team of researchers?

Both of these factors may be denied. A researcher might choose to continue anyway by carrying out *covert* research – Goffman (1961), for example, studied the patients and medical staff in a US mental institution while posing as a member of the cleaning staff. However, some argue that such research is ethically questionable. The problem of co-operation may be solved by sponsorship: a member of the group being studied vouches for and

87

'protects' the researcher. More cynically, perhaps, problems of access and co-operation may explain why a lot of sociological research focuses on the activities of the *powerless*, people who cannot say no, rather than the powerful, who can and often do resist being studied.

Choice of method

Researchers must deal with a range of practical issues in assessing how and why various methods are 'fit for the purpose' of testing a hypothesis or answering a research question. As Dunican (2005) suggests, fitness for purpose 'reflects how well the chosen research method is suited to the context of study. This is measured in terms of how well it is suited to answering the issues posed in the research question.' We can use Venkatesh's study to illustrate this idea. He originally began 'armed only with a questionnaire and a desire to learn more about the lives of poor black people'. However, he asked only one question – 'How does it feel to be black and poor?' – before his research subjects made him realise that in order to understand what it was like, he needed to experience it for himself.

Choice of method is also affected by practical considerations such as the topic being studied. Some topics lend themselves more easily to one method than another. Quantitative methods are useful when the researcher wants reliable data to establish statistical relationships. An example of this is Kessler's (2000) study of the relationship between sponsorship and small business performance, where the main objective was to test whether 'those who are sponsored are more successful than non-sponsored individuals'. Alternatively, in studies

such as Diken and Laustsen's (2004) analysis of tourist behaviour in Ibiza and Faliraki, a qualitative approach was more appropriate, because the nature of the research was more descriptive.

Time is another consideration, because some methods are more time-consuming than others. Participant observation may involve years of research: Whyte (1943) spent around four years gathering extensive information about the behaviour of one youth gang in Boston, USA, and Venkatesh took around eight years documenting the lives of the black residents – gang members and non-members alike – in a small area of Chicago.

The amount of funding available may directly influence a researcher's choice of method. Questionnaires are generally cheaper than in-depth interviews, which, in turn, may be cheaper than participant observation. This depends, of course, on the size and scope of the study. Funding levels also influence the size of any research team. Similarly, the size and composition of the group being studied is a factor: questionnaires are suitable for researching large, widely dispersed groups, while participant observation may be more appropriate for the study of small, geographically localised groups. Dunican observed that 'it seems logical that the selection of any research method should be based on the nature of the research question'. However, Boaz and Ashby (2003) note that the *source* of research funding can also be a practical consideration. While 'sensitivity to the sponsor's requirements can contribute to the fitness for purpose of research, it can equally introduce biases that conflict with the aim of producing objective, good quality evidence.'

Practical considerations are clearly important in the conduct of sociological research. If a researcher cannot gain access to research subjects to administer questionnaires, organise interviews and experiments or participate in the behaviour of a group, then other considerations are irrelevant. Similarly, if a researcher has neither the time nor the funding to support themselves through a year-long observational study then, once again, this research avenue is closed. Once these initial issues have been overcome, a researcher faces another set of considerations – **ethical issues** relating to how the research should be carried out.

In Diken and Lausten's study, using a qualitative approach yielded in-depth descriptions of why people acted the way they did when on holiday. What might be the advantages of a qualitative approach in this situation?

KEY TERM

Ethical issues: 'ethics' refers to the morality of doing something. Ethical questions relating to sociological research involve beliefs about what a researcher should or should not do before, during and after their research.

Suggest two ways in which practical research considerations might influence a researcher's choice of topic.

Ethical research considerations

Ethics refers to the morality of doing something. Ethical considerations apply to choices about the *type* of research being undertaken such as whether it is ethical to study people without their knowledge, and to researcher *behaviour* – whether it is, for example, ethical to deceive people about the purpose of a research study. Ethical issues, therefore, guide choices about how people are persuaded to participate in research, and how they are physically and psychologically protected during and after the study. In this respect, both legal and safety considerations influence the choice of topic and method, and the conduct of the research.

Legal considerations

Legal considerations can be a particularly significant factor when research involves observing or participating in illegal behaviour, such as Ditton's (1977) study of workplace theft. In terms of topic, the researcher must decide whether it is ethical to research something like criminal behaviour in the first place. Choice of method may also be influenced by the level of the researcher's involvement. To avoid an ethical dilemma, for example, a researcher may choose to avoid immersive methods such as participant observation when studying criminal behaviours.

In addition, the researcher must consider their ethical responsibilities to both perpetrators and possible victims of crime. Participants should also be made aware of the possible consequences of their co-operation, such as adverse media publicity. A researcher should gain the informed consent of those being researched in order to avoid ethical questions about the conduct of the research. Finally, relationships need to be based on *trust* and *personal integrity*. If the researcher promises *anonymity*, disclosing identities to the authorities or the media would be unethical.

Safety

The *physical* and *psychological* safety of everyone involved in a project is an important aspect of the research process. Some types of research involve methods, such as covert participant observation, that require deep involvement with respondents. A researcher must take care not to cause distress to potentially vulnerable people at the end of the study. For example, if the research involves regularly meeting and interacting with elderly people, it would be unethical to simply break contact with them once it is complete. A researcher not prepared for this type of involvement will, therefore, choose an alternative method.

Ethical practice

While both legal and safety considerations are important, Pimple (2002) argues that sociological research is generally bound by a code of ethical practice that involves the researcher using their values to guide them in answering three research questions:

1 Is it true? At its most extreme, unethical behaviour here involves things like the researcher deliberately making up (fabricating) data or falsifying their results.

2 Is it fair? Unethical behaviour here covers how others in the research process are treated and refers to things such as:

- ownership: for example, who can ethically claim to be the author?
- plagiarism: passing off the work of others as your own.

3 Is it wise? This refers to wider questions about whether research can be *morally justified* and whether a different research topic or method would have greater moral justification. This, Pimple argues, involves three tests:

- Does the research improve the human condition or damage it?
- Does it lead to a better or a worse world?
- Would it be better to pursue other lines of research?

The relationship between those doing the research and those being researched is equally important. Even when there are no legal or safety issues involved, there are morally ambiguous areas. These involve researchers making decisions about the conduct of their research on issues such as:

- Studying people who do not want to be studied: Wallis (1977) wanted to research Scientology but the church leaders refused him access to current members. He contacted former members and based his research on their opinions and experiences.

89

- Tricking people into co-operating: Rosenhan (1973) suspected that doctors could not accurately diagnose schizophrenia and sent students displaying *fake* symptoms into hospitals to test his hypothesis.
- Experimenting on people who do not know they are being studied, or causing them distress: in Milgram's (1974) study of authority, respondents were convinced they were giving electric shocks to 'learners' whenever the learners gave an incorrect answer to a question. While no shocks were given and the 'victims' were pretending to react, some respondents broke down in the face of the pain they believed they were inflicting.

ACTIVITY

Identify and assess the possible practical, ethical and theoretical considerations involved in the study of the following:

a *suicide*
b *lifestyles of the rich and famous*
c *the culture of the police*
d *the family life of teachers.*

Validity, reliability, objectivity and representativeness in research

An important aspect of the relationship between theory and methods is that there is no general agreement about how to collect data about the social world. Different methodological approaches develop their own ideas about scientific sociology.

Sociological research is also complicated by people's awareness of both themselves as the object of research and their relationship to others, such as those carrying out the research. It is further complicated by the fact that different sociologists see the social world differently. Human relationships have a moral dimension, and this moral dimension extends to the way we believe should study human relationships.

For some sociologists, conducting secret experiments on people can be morally justified by because the results of the research may prove valuable. For others, this behaviour is both morally wrong and

scientifically misconceived because to truly understand behaviour we must understand how it is subjectively experienced. Such different views lead to different research approaches based on different beliefs – the most fundamental of which is *what we believe exists*. Those who believe the social world consists of instinctive responses to social stimulation will study it in a different way from those who believe it is socially constructed through everyday behaviour and meanings.

TEST YOURSELF

Briefly explain the meaning of a 'cause-and-effect' relationship. Use an example to illustrate your answer.

Reliability

Reliability refers to how effective a research approach is at collecting consistent data. This is related to whether a researcher can *check* the accuracy of their data by repeating or replicating the research. If they get two different answers, the research approach is *unreliable* and any conclusions drawn from it will be limited. Reliability can be improved by *standardising* the research approach, as this allows less scope for differences to occur in the way that different researchers ask questions and collect data. If a standardised approach is used to collect information from people who have the same or similar characteristics, the same study results should be achieved each time.

 KEY TERM

Reliability: this generally refers to the effectiveness of the research approach in generating consistent data. A researcher can *check* the reliability of their research by repeating (*replicating*) the research to see if they get the same, or very similar, results.

It is easier to achieve a standardised approach using quantitative research methods, such as questionnaires and structured interviews. For this reason, quantitative methods are often regarded as 'reliable'. However, research based on a quantitative approach is not automatically high in reliability. There may be weaknesses in the way that the research was designed and/or carried out that make replication difficult. Moreover, when replicating a study, it may be difficult to ensure that the subjects have the same characteristics as the original group.

Reliability is an important methodological consideration – obviously, it is preferable for research to be reliable rather than unreliable. However, questions of reliability are not always straightforward. Knight (2001), for example, suggests that the quest for high reliability in sociological research comes at a cost: 'reliability pushes us towards simplicity and certainty' – two conditions that may be incompatible in social research.

Validity

Validity is a further concept that is used to assess different research methods and data, albeit one that has numerous forms designed for different applications. For our current purpose, however, we can outline two basic types:

1 *Construct validity* refers to the idea that methods and data are only useful if they actually *measure* or *describe* what they claim to be measuring or describing. Unemployment statistics, for example, may or may not have a high level of construct validity, depending on what they claim to measure.

2 *Ecological validity* refers to the extent to which research methods reflect the world being studied – the idea that the closer we get to studying people in their natural environment, the more likely we are to get valid data. Questionnaires have low ecological validity because this type of research may be unusual and strange for most respondents. Covert participant observation, on the other hand, has much higher validity.

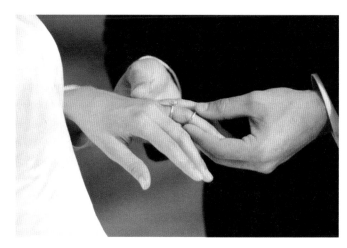

Do marriage statistics have a high or low construct validity?

KEY TERM

Validity: the extent to which a research method measures what it claims to measure.

TEST YOURSELF

Suggest two reasons why interviews might lack ecological validity.

Validity is a useful concept because it reminds us to consider the *accuracy* of different data types (primary, secondary, qualitative and quantitative). However, it is difficult to generalise about the validity of different data types and research methods for two reasons:

1 There is a wide range of validity tests that can be applied in different ways. Official statistics may have construct validity – there is little reason to doubt the validity of UK marriage and divorce statistics – but it may lack ecological validity; official crime statistics do not really measure crime, but rather a subset of criminal activity, those crimes that are reported to official agencies.

2 Taylor (2011) argues that qualitative research is not automatically valid: 'Qualitative sociologists are quite convinced methods such as participant observation and in-depth interviews provide the "true story" of people's experiences. But the psychology of perception and the work of Elizabeth Loftus on memory suggests "telling it like it is" may not be quite that simple.' In other words, 'seeing for yourself' is not always as valid as interpretivists believe. Researchers may simply see the things they want or expect to see.

Bryman (2004) suggests that this problem can be limited by 'respondent validation'. The subjects of the research are used to check the validity of the researcher's observations and interpretations. This can improve the credibility of a study, but it is not without its problems. Emerson and Pollner (1988), for example, suggest these issues include respondents:

■ failing to fully read or understand the research
■ being unwilling to criticise the research because of their friendship with the researcher
■ fearing possible wider consequences of agreeing or disagreeing with the research.

91

Can we always trust the evidence of our own eyes? This question is always relevant in designing and conducting sociological research

Objectivity

One of the things that distinguishes sociological knowledge from journalism or common sense (what everyone knows) is the ability to make objective statements about behaviour; facts are methodologically superior to opinions. Personal objectivity is a particularly significant factor. The researcher not only has no personal stake in the truth or falsity of the behaviour they are testing or describing, they also try to avoid unduly influencing that behaviour. A researcher must try to maintain an objective detachment.

Personal objectivity has a number of dimensions, from trying to objectively observe and record at one extreme to not deliberately falsifying data at the other. Personal objectivity is something all sociologists – positivist, interpretivist and realist – must actively try to achieve. Without it, sociological research has no greater reliability or validity than any other form of knowledge. Although we must, therefore, assume that all sociologists are objective, there are still theoretical arguments about the nature of objective social research. Positivism and interpretivism, for example, have different interprestations of 'research objectivity'.

Positivists argue that we can study objective features of the social world (institutions such as families or educational systems) because they are solid and permanent. Objectivity involves the idea that social

structures are real, exist independently of the observer and can be experienced directly or indirectly using particular indicators of their existence. Sociological research, therefore, involves *discovery* – the ability to progressively uncover the principles on which the social world is based. Discovery is achieved by the researcher distancing themselves from the behaviour being studied. Objectivity requires the researcher to place themselves 'outside' the behaviour they are studying – theoretically, if not always practically. Their personal values and beliefs should not influence what they see; they must study the social world as a detached observer.

Interpretivists take a different view of objectivity. Where positivism sees a single reality that can be discovered through systematic research, interpretivism argues that there are many realities, expressed through the various ways in which people see and understand the social world. This world is not something 'out there' waiting to be discovered. It exists only as interpretations people make (how they understand behaviour). It follows,

Slum dwellings present grim daily challenges for those living within them. What social forces are at work here?

therefore, that the aim of social research is subjective understanding. The researcher's role is that of an objective channel through which individuals 'tell their story' to uncover how and why people see the social world in particular ways. This interpretation suggests that sociologists should use their ability to empathise in the research process. As Murphy (1988) argues, *how* we *see* something is always based on our values; it cannot be separated from how we *interpret* what we see. From this position, positivist notions of objectivity prevent the researcher questioning how and why their values are part of the research process. Objectivity, in this respect, involves sociologists 'striving to understand the value base of data, rather than searching for ways to purge values from research'.

Although interpretivists believe that values can never be entirely removed, a researcher should still strive for personal objectivity. Williams (2005) argues that we should see objectivity and subjectivity as part of a continuum – a line with 'pure objectivity' at one extreme and 'pure subjectivity' at the other. Sociological research is *more* value-laden than natural scientific research, but this does not automatically make it unreliable and invalid, for two reasons:

- 'Pure objectivity' is an *ideal* that can never be attained because *all* research, social and natural scientific, involves some degree of value commitment.
- If sociologists recognise how values impact their work, by identifying the assumptions under which they are working, this research is less value-laden, more reliable and valid than the opinions of the non-sociologist.

While these ideas make an important contribution to our understanding of objectivity and its role within the research process, Spencer et al. (2003) make the point that 'there is considerable agreement that objectivity is particularly problematic in qualitative research'. This is mainly because of the active 'involvement of the researcher in the research setting and inevitable selectivity of data collection, analysis and interpretation'. In other words, it is more difficult for interpretivist research to maintain the necessary levels of personal objective detachment required to accurately report people's feeling, beliefs and behaviours.

TEST YOURSELF

Briefly explain why quantitative research may have greater objectivity than qualitative research.

Representativeness

In broad terms, **representativeness** refers to two related ideas:

1 The characteristics of the people used in a sample should accurately reflect those of the target population they represent. Positivists, for example, see representativeness as the ability to *generalise* observations made about one relatively small sample group to the much larger target population it represents. The importance of representativeness can be illustrated by the example of postal questionnaires. Response rates for this research method are almost invariably low, which can create problems in two areas:

- There is an increased chance of **sampling error** created by an unrepresentative self-selected sample (a sample that 'selects itself' – those who bother to reply).
- Survey-based research based on an unrepresentative sample will lack validity; the findings of the research cannot be validly generalised to the target population.

KEY TERMS

Representativeness: extent to which the characteristics of a sample population accurately reflect those of the target population.

Sampling error: anything in the research design that causes a sample intended to be representative of a target population to become unrepresentative; a self-selected sample, for example, is a form of sampling error.

TEST YOURSELF

Suggest two reasons why a self-selected sample may lack representativeness. Consider whether representativeness should be an important consideration in all sociological research studies.

2 Data collected during a research process should accurately represent whatever the research claims to represent. While this is true for both positivism and interpretivism, interpretivists believe that representativeness can be an end in itself. The research data represents a reliable, valid and objective account of some form of behaviour.

While interpretivists may not be so concerned with representativeness as a means towards generalisation, it is

93

sometimes the case that similar groups will develop at least some similar behaviours. 'Generalisation within a case', for example, involves the idea that it might be possible to apply the findings in a case study of one particular group to other, similar, groups. Dale's (2002) interviews with Pakistani and Bangladeshi women in Oldham, for example, revealed a significant pattern of gendered ethnic discrimination. Many of the respondents suggested that employers used covert forms of discrimination, expressed through the questions they asked prospective employees. While Dale noted that her respondents were 'not representative of the Pakistani and Bangladeshi population of Oldham', nor of the town itself, her study had wider representational value because the balance of probability suggests that the experiences of ethnic-minority groups are likely to be similar, whatever their specific location within the same country.

ACTIVITY

A simple way to visualise the reliability and validity of different methods is to create a methodological square such as the one below. Place all of the research methods you have studied in the appropriate segment.

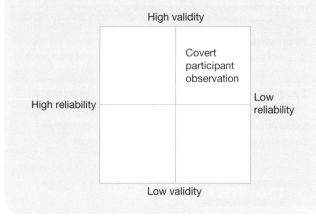

Triangulation and methodological pluralism

Throughout the first four chapters we have suggested an association between positivism and quantitative research methods, and interpretivism and qualitative methods that goes some way beyond the personal preferences of particular sociologists. Wood and Welch (2010) sum up this idea: 'Some researchers stick to what they call "quantitative" research, and others stick to "qualitative" research'. The general implication here is that quantitative methods *are* positivist while qualitative methods *are* interpretivist and the two should not be mixed. However, this argument is open to question.

Methodological pluralism

While it may be necessary to differentiate between different sociological methodologies, positivism and interpretivism do not each occupy their own unique social space, with no shared features. The notion that 'positivists' do not use qualitative methods because they lack reliability, while interpretivists do not use quantitative methods because they lack validity is overly simplified.

The basic principles of methodologies are not set in stone. It is more useful to see them as mental constructs created for theoretical convenience. Wood and Welch argue that 'there is now increasing awareness that both quantitative and qualitative styles of research may have a contribution to make to a project, which leads to the idea of *mixing* methods.' This can be expressed as **methodological pluralism**, something Payne et al. (2004) define as 'tolerance of a variety of methods'.

 KEY TERM

Methodological pluralism: combining research methodologies, such as positivism and interpretivism, in ways that allow each to complement the other to improve research reliability and validity.

The logic of this argument is that different research methods have different methodological strengths and weaknesses. Questionnaires may produce reliable data, but this data has low validity, while the reverse may be true for covert participant observation. Rather than approaching research methodology from the perspective of a 'design problem' – how to test a hypothesis (positivism) or answer a research question (interpretivism) – we can approach it from a methodological perspective. This involves considering *how* to collect data with the highest possible levels of reliability and validity, regardless of the methods or data types used.

Triangulation

If methodological pluralism represents the theoretical justification for using mixed methods, **triangulation** is the means through which this theory is put into practice. It refers to the various ways in which a researcher can attempt to improve research reliability and validity.

 KEY TERM

Triangulation: the use of two or more research methods where the weaknesses of one method, such as a quantitative interview, can be offset by the strengths of another, such as qualitative participant observation, to improve overall research reliability and validity.

Methodological triangulation involves the use of two or more research methods. Denzin (1970) suggests that this allows the researcher to offset the weaknesses of one method with the strengths of another. For example:

■ A general weakness of questionnaires is that the researcher must assume a respondent is telling the truth.
■ A researcher could offset this by using an observational method, such as participant observation, to check that respondents actually do what they say they do.

Alternatively, the researcher could compare the results from *two different methods* used on the same people (such as a semi-structured interview and a focus group). If the conclusions drawn are broadly the same, this helps confirm the reliability and validity of the data. Hughes et al.'s (1997) examination of 'the appeal of designer drinks to young people', for example, used focus groups and structured interviews. The data from one was used to cross-check and confirm data from the other (such as each showing a strong pattern of age-related differences in attitudes to designer drinks). This approach can be further sub-divided:

■ Within-method triangulation is a technique that Bryman characterises as 'the use of varieties of the same method to investigate a research issue'. On a simple level, this might involve asking open and closed questions in the same questionnaire.
■ Between-method triangulation is characterised by what Bryman calls the use of '*contrasting* research methods, such as a questionnaire and observation'.

Harvey and MacDonald (1993) summarise the use of researcher-focused methodological triangulation as involving any combination of:

■ two or more researchers using same research technique
■ one researcher using two or more research techniques
■ two or more researchers using two or more research techniques.

Methodological triangulation can take different forms:

■ *Researcher triangulation* can be used in studies that rely heavily on a researcher's interpretations to generate data. If different researchers using the *same* research method arrive at the same results, this

can confirm the reliability of the data. Alternatively, using researchers from different ethnic, age, gender and class groups can help check for factors such as observer and interviewer bias that may lower reliability and validity.

■ *Data triangulation* involves gathering information through different sampling strategies – such as collecting data at different times, in different contexts and from different people. This can be extended to include gathering data from both the individuals involved in a particular situation and the researcher's own experiences in that situation. Venkatesh, for example, was able to make sense of certain forms of behaviour, such as drug dealing, and experiences, such as being black and poor, in ways that would not have been possible if he had not been intimately involved in the world he was studying. He gathered data from both those involved and from his own experience of living in their world.

■ *Theoretical triangulation* is based on the idea that just as research methods are inherently open to errors, so too are theoretical positions. There are strengths and weaknesses to different theoretical perspectives, and these can be used to the researcher's advantage. By looking at the social world in realist terms, considering *both* structure and action, we can arrive at the best possible representation and explanation of social behaviour.

TEST YOURSELF

Suggest some advantages of triangulation.

To illustrate these ideas we can point to a variety of sociological research that has used methodological triangulation to good effect.

■ Barker (1984) used overt participant observation, questionnaires and semi-structured interviews in her research on the Unification Church ('Moonies').
■ Hey (1997) studied girls' friendships in two London schools using a combination of participant observation and personal documentation. Some of the girls allowed her to read their diaries and she was also given access to the notes the girls passed between each other in the classroom.
■ MacKeogh (2001) studied the 'micro-politics of family viewing' in relation to how young people used television and their parents' attempts to control

how and what they watched. Her primary method was overt participant observation, because she wanted to understand the critical awareness young people had about the media they consumed. Her observation notes were complemented by those made by her respondents, as well as semi-structured interviews to explore some of the issues raised in the observations.

■ Garforth and Kerr (2010) examined 'women's under-representation in science', using a mix of interviews, focus groups and participant observation.

Methodological pluralism and triangulation are, therefore, frequently employed by sociologists because they improve research reliability and validity. As Parke and Griffiths (2002) argue: 'One obvious advantage of non-participant observation is that it relies only on observing behaviour. Since the researcher cannot interact in the behavioural processes, most data collected will be qualitative, interpretative, and to some extent, limited. However, by using other methodological research tools (e.g. structured interviews), suspicions, interpretations and even hypotheses can be confirmed.' In addition, by gathering different types of data and sources (such as respondents and participant observers) the researcher is more likely to get a complete, fully rounded (*holistic*) picture of the behaviour they are studying.

Using different methods and sampling strategies, a researcher can generally improve overall the reliability of a research approach and the validity of the data collected. More specifically, data collected using higher reliability methods, such as questionnaires, can offset the weaknesses in observational methods; the reverse applies to validity. Finlay (1999), for example, compared accounts of the same events given by different respondents in semi-structured interviews and added a further check by comparing 'the oral record of those events with the contemporary documentary record in local newspapers'. Finally, a researcher's confidence in the accuracy of their data can be increased using triangulation. As Bechhoffer and Paterson (2000) argue: 'If we are able to base part of an explanation on unstructured interview material, on documentary evidence and on the results of a survey, our confidence in our findings is likely to be greatly increased'.

Identify one way methodological pluralism and triangulation might improve research reliability or validity.

Arguments in favour of methodological pluralism and triangulation are convincing, but these techniques still have practical problems. Triangulation adds another layer of time, effort and expense to research, in terms of things such as:

■ the time needed to analyse different data types created from a number of different methods
■ the need to employ more researchers
■ the general co-ordination of a much larger research project.

In terms of theoretical problems, Bryman notes that triangulation is sometimes seen as a way of getting at 'the truth' by throwing a vast array of resources, methods and data at a problem, based on the (naive) idea that 'there can be a single definitive account of the social world'.

In addition, collecting and comparing different types of data can be complicated. Such data may not always be easily and neatly compared. As Bryman argues: 'Triangulation assumes data from different research methods can be unambiguously compared and regarded as equivalent in terms of their capacity to address a research question.' This assumption may, of course, be incorrect: differences arising between the data from a structured interview and a focus group may have less to do with the reliability and validity of each method and 'more to do with the possibility that the former taps private views as opposed to the more general ones that might be voiced in the more public arena'. More specific problems of reliability and validity link from the above in the sense that where a researcher gets contradictory data from two different sources it can be difficult to distinguish 'truth' from 'falsity'. If the researcher receives two opposing accounts of the same thing, which account is true? And more importantly, how can the researcher tell?

Summary points

For positivist approaches to sociological research, the key ideas are:

- structure determines action
- explanation
- science:
  - systematic observation
  - rigorous testing
  - quantitative methods
  - reliability
  - objectivity
  - causality.

For interpretivist approaches the key ideas are:

- subjective meaning
- interpretation
- understanding
- qualitative methods
- validity.

For realist approaches the key ideas are:

- objectivity *and* subjectivity
- structure and interpretation
- holistic approach
- methodological pluralism.

Theoretical research considerations:

- Choice of topic:
  - audience
  - values:
    - personal
    - institutional.
- Choice of method:
  - perspective
  - quantitative, qualitative, both?
  - data triangulation
  - reliability
  - validity
  - representativeness.

Practical research considerations:

- Choice of topic is influenced by:
  - funding
  - time
  - access
  - co-operation.
- Choice of method is influenced by:
  - fitness for purpose
  - topic
  - reliability and validity
  - time
  - funding.

Ethical research considerations:

- legality
- safety:
  - physical
  - psychological.

The value of different methods of research can be assessed in terms of:

- reliability
- validity
- objectivity
- representativeness.

Methodological pluralism involves combining aspects of different research methodologies, such as quantitative and qualitative methods.

Triangulation

- methodological: two or more research methods.
  - within-method.
  - between-method.
- data: different sampling strategies
- theoretical: structure and action.

Exam-style questions

1. **a** What is meant by the term feral children? [2]

   b Describe how any two norms may be linked to social values in a society. [4]

   c Explain why individuals generally conform to accepted standards of behaviour. [8]

   d 'The role played by socialisation in shaping human behaviour has been overstated.' Assess this claim. [11]

2. 'Sociological theories that focus on the structure of society reveal far more than those that emphasise the role played by individual actors'. Explain and assess this claim. [25]

3. Explain and assess the view that the strengths of quantitative research methods outweigh their limitations. [25]

Total available marks 75

97

Chapter 5:
The family

Learning objectives

The objectives of this chapter involve understanding:

- how the family can be defined, different types of family and the difference between families and households
- different family and household structures
- the family and social change, focusing on industrialisation, urbanisation and globalisation
- the 'fit thesis' and post-industrial society
- the diversity of contemporary family forms and relationships
- whether the nuclear family is a universal feature of societies

- alternatives to the conventional nuclear family
- the relationship between the family and other social institutions such as the economy
- changing family functions
- the roles of parents, children and grandparents
- debates about gender equality within the family
- changing patterns of marriage, cohabitation, separation, divorce and childbearing
- how family life impacts on individual family members
- the social construction of childhood and old age
- the experience of childhood.

Introduction

This chapter examines the concept of the family, from how it is defined, through the functions it performs to its relationship with other social institutions such as the economy. The focus is on two related areas: firstly, the family as an institution that serves certain purposes and satisfies particular needs for both the individual and society; and secondly, families conceived as social groups that differ in both their structure and the ways in which individuals perform their roles and relationships. (Please note that much of the research in this area has been conducted in the UK.)

The family and social change

The distinction between households and families, and between types of family

To understand the significance of families as a major social institution (a pattern of shared, stable, behaviour that persists over time) it is necessary to define the concept of the family both in terms of what it is and how it differs from other types of communal living, such as **households**.

KEY TERM

Household: residential unit consisting of unrelated individuals.

Families

Murdock's (1949) conventional definition of a family suggests that it is characterised by:

- common residence
- economic co-operation and reproduction
- adults of both sexes, at least two of whom maintain a socially approved sexual relationship
- one or more children, own or adopted.

This functionalist definition is *exclusive* because it is based on the idea that families have characteristics that make them different from other social groups, such as schools. This definition is flexible enough to accommodate different types of family relationship and organisation. For example, families do not have to be **monogamous** (one man married to one woman); they can also be **polygamous**. One man can be married to a number of women (**polygyny**) or one woman married to a number of men (**polyandry**).

KEY TERMS

Monogamy: having a single sexual or marriage partner at any given time.

Polygamy: having more than one sexual or marriage partner at the same time.

Polygyny: one man married to a number of women.

KEY TERM

Polyandry: one woman married to a number of men.

Exclusive definitions can be useful for distinguishing between family and non-family groups. However, they may exclude household forms, such as single-parent and homosexual (gay and lesbian) households, that are considered to be families in many modern societies. Popenoe (1988) suggests that a contemporary exclusive definition can encompass both single parents and homosexual relationships, while Giddens (2006) suggests an alternative, *inclusive*, definition that focuses on kinship and the general relationships that make families different from other social groups. Kin relationships, for example, can be based on:

- biology, such as mother and child
- affinity, such as two adults living together
- law, such as **marriage**.

KEY TERM

Marriage: union between two people, recognised by law.

According to Giddens, families are defined through people directly linked by kin connections, where adult members take responsibility for childcare. One advantage of an inclusive definition like this is that it covers a variety of possible family forms and relationships. There is a drawback, however – if the definition is too broad, it may include groups that most people would not normally consider to be families.

Ambert (2003) suggests that an alternative definition should focus on both *kinship* (inclusive) and *function* (exclusive). Families involve two or more people, bound by ties of mutual consent, who assume responsibility for:

- the physical maintenance and care of group members
- procreation or adoption
- socialisation and social control of children

99

- the production, consumption and distribution of goods and services
- affective nurturance (childcare).

Households

A household can be defined as one or more people living in a particular dwelling. This definition includes families, of course, but while all families are households, not all households are families. This idea can be illustrated by looking at three different types of household structure:

1 Single-person households are where an adult lives alone, either because of the death of a partner, the breakdown of a relationship or through personal choice.

2 Couple households consist of two people without children. Such households may include:

   - couples who have not yet started a family
   - those whose children have left home
   - those who have chosen to remain childless.

Roseneil (2006) suggests that an additional category in this type of household is 'couples who live apart'. These are people who are in a stable relationship and who spend a significant amount of time together, but who do not share a home. Some couples do this because work demands and different routines would make it difficult to live together. Other couples choose this lifestyle because they want to maintain some independence.

3 Shared households involve a group of unrelated people living together. This may be temporary, such as when students live together, or permanent, such as people who live in **communes**.

Commune: shared household involving a group of largely unrelated people living together.

TEST YOURSELF

Identify and explain one difference between a family and a household.

Types of family

Just as there are different types of household structure, there are also different types of family structure.

Nuclear families consist of parents and their children (two generations). Contact with wider kin, such as

grandparents, tends to be infrequent and impersonal (by telephone, for example) rather than meeting regularly in person. This type of family is a self-contained economic unit whose members are expected to support each other socially and psychologically. It is sometimes called the *isolated* nuclear family to reflect its physical separation from wider kin and its economic isolation from the rest of society.

KEY TERM

Nuclear family: family unit based on two generations – parents and their dependent children.

There are some variations on this two-generation structure. These include **reconstituted** or *step*-families resulting from the break-up of one family, due to death or **divorce**, and its reassembly as a new family through marriage or cohabitation outside of marriage (sometimes called a **common-law family**). Step-families may include children from both old and new families. A more recent variation on the traditional nuclear family involves same-sex (gay or lesbian) couples. In these cases, the children of the family may be adopted, come from a previous (heterosexual) relationship or from fertility treatments. In the UK, same-sex couples have been able to form a **civil partnership** that gives each partner similar legal rights to married heterosexual couples since 2005. In 2014 a new law was introduced that allowed same-sex couple to legally marry in civil ceremonies.

KEY TERMS

Reconstituted family: sometimes called a step-family, this involves the break-up of one family and its reassembly as a new family through marriage or cohabitation.

Divorce: legal dissolution of a marriage.

Common-law family: adult couple and children living together as a family without the adults being legally married.

Civil partnership: same-sex relationship giving the participants similar legal rights to married couples.

Partnership: being part of a couple, often living as married people but without any legal ties.

TEST YOURSELF

Suggest two reasons for the increase in the number of reconstituted families in modern industrial societies.

Why might nuclear families be seen as isolated in modern societies?

A **lone-parent family**, involving a single adult plus dependent children, is sometimes called a *broken nuclear* family, especially when it arises from the break-up of a two-parent family (through death, separation or divorce). **Single-parent families**, while headed by a lone parent, are an important variation because they do not result from a family break-up.

KEY TERM

Lone-/single-parent family: both consist of a single adult and dependent children. Lone parenthood is usually distinguished from single parenthood on the basis of factors such as divorce or the death of a partner, rather than choice.

Extended families are a different type of family structure that takes two basic forms:

- Vertically extended families involve three or more generations (grandparents, parents and children) living in, or close to, the same household. **Matrifocal families** are a female-focused variation on this – for example a female grandparent, parent and children. **Patrifocal families** are focused on men.
- Horizontally extended families are those with branches *within* generations, such as aunts and uncles, living with or close to each other.

KEY TERMS

Extended family: family structure containing more than the parents and children of nuclear structures. A vertically extended family, for example, involves three or more generations, such as grandparents, parents and children.
Matrifocal family: family that focused on women, such as a female grandparent, parent and children.
Patrifocal family: family structure focused on men.

Both types of extended family exist in contemporary industrialised societies, but Gordon (1972) suggests that the norm for this type is now the **modified extended family**. In this form, wider family members keep in touch both *physically*, through visits or exchanges of help and services, and *emotionally*, via telephone and email perhaps, without necessarily having frequent personal contact. Willmott (1988) further suggests three variations on the modified extended family.

- Locally extended types involve 'two or three nuclear families in separate households' living close together and providing mutual help and assistance.
- Dispersed-extended types involve less frequent personal contact between family members.
- Attenuated-extended types include 'young couples before they have children', gradually separating from their original families.

KEY TERM

Modified extended family: contemporary form of extended family: family members maintain contact but rarely live in close proximity to one another.

TEST YOURSELF

What is the difference between a dispersed-extended family and a locally extended family?

ACTIVITY

Draw a kinship diagram to show members of your immediate and extended family.

Changes in family and household structure and their relationship to industrialisation, urbanisation and globalisation

The diversity of family and household structures in contemporary societies indicates that both are sensitive to social change. We can explore how major forms of change, including industrialisation, **urbanisation** and globalisation, have influenced the nature of family and household structures.

KEY TERM

Urbanisation: the development and growth of towns and cities.

To begin with, we need to be clear about these three ideas:

1   Industrialisation refers to a process in which machines are widely used in the production of goods (*mechanisation*). One result of mechanisation is the development of factories and the ability to mass produce consumer goods such as clothes, cars and mobile phones.

2   Urbanisation involves the movement of a population away from relatively small-scale rural (village) living to larger communities based in towns and cities. This is sometimes called social migration from the countryside to towns – urban areas that developed alongside industrialisation and factory production.

3   Globalisation takes a number of forms – economic as well as political – but here the focus is more on cultural globalisation. This involves rapid global movement of different ideas, styles and products that can be picked up, discarded and, most importantly, *adapted* to fit the needs of different cultural groups.

Industrialisation and urbanisation are closely associated with the idea of modern industrial societies. Globalisation is more closely linked to the idea of a postmodern, post-industrial society. In such a society, the ability to create and distribute *services*, from security to software, is more important than the ability to build and manufacture physical goods. Taking Britain (the first country to industrialise) as an example, there are two ways of applying these concepts to explain the changes in family and household structures. These are the 'fit' thesis and post-industrial society.

The 'fit' thesis

This argument suggests that industrialisation and urbanisation contribute to changes in the family and household. As these processes developed between the late-17th and late-19th centuries, they radically changed the nature of work and economic production. Economic change, from the land-based, rural, family-centred organisation of pre-industrial society to the capital-intensive, urban, factory-centred organisation of industrial society, produced a gradual structural change. This was characterised by a shift from a mainly extended family organisation to one dominated by nuclear families.

In terms of the fit thesis, industrialisation involves the development of factories and the growth of large urban centres (urbanisation) to support and supply labour for industrial production. The extended families of pre-industrial society were ideally suited to the demands of family-based subsistence farming. However, as industrialisation spread, these extended families were replaced by nuclear families that fitted two crucial

economic requirements: geographic mobility and labour flexibility – they could move to wherever jobs were located in urban areas. People were gradually forced to change the way they lived to accommodate new forms of economic production.

In the late 20th century, a similar pattern began to emerge with the emphasis on family fragmentation and diversity. The nuclear family structures created by industrialisation and urbanisation are being disrupted by the needs of global economic systems and work processes. Nuclear family structures are also changing because of de-industrialisation (a decline in the importance of manufacturing) and de-urbanisation (movement away from towns and cities to the countryside). Such process have been caused by the development of computer technologies that allow people to work when and wherever they like.

Evidence for the 'fit' thesis has been put forward by traditional functionalist writers, such as Parsons (1959b) and Goode (1963). These sociologists claim that extended family structures were the norm in pre-industrial society because families and households were:

- multi-functional – a wide family network performed a range of functions related to the economic and social well-being of family members
- kinship-based – the extended family had a common economic position that involved working together, mainly as subsistence farmers but also in various craft trades, brewing and baking, in and around the home
- economically productive – the extended family provided the only viable means of physical survival.

The idea of the family group as economically productive is related to three further factors:

- Labour-intensive subsistence agriculture required as many people as possible – men, women and children – to work the land.
- The ability to move away from the family group was limited by poor communications (no railways or cars and rudimentary road systems). This meant that family members were physically unable to move far from the family home, even if they wanted to.
- Elderly, infirm and sick family members relied on their kin for care in the absence of any well-developed, universal welfare system.

As industrialisation and urbanisation took hold, nuclear families gradually became the dominant family structure. There were several reasons for this. One of the most significant was that people had to be mobile in order to find and keep work in the new industrial processes. There was a huge population movement away from rural areas to the developing towns and, in such a situation, the extended family gradually broke down and small, highly mobile, nuclear family units became the norm. Alongside these changes, new opportunities arose for social mobility and economic advancement, as different types of work developed.

A further contributing factor to the breakdown of extended families was the decline of nepotism (favouring friends and relatives over others). The new industries demanded specific skills and knowledge, so people could no longer be promoted simply because of their family connections.

Agricultural workers in the 18th century. Why was the extended family well suited to this type of existence?

Arguments against the 'fit' thesis

Finch (1989) examined the idea that before the Industrial Revolution family obligations were much stronger and family members provided greater support for each other than in the industrial and post-industrial eras. She found little evidence to support this view of the pre-industrial family. For example, she found no evidence that people automatically assumed responsibility for elderly relatives in pre-industrial times. Also, in their wills parents often made little or no financial provision for children other than the eldest son. Historical studies have also shown that there was a wide range of household types in the pre-industrial period – there is no evidence that extended families were the norm. Such studies have led some sociologists to question the idea of a 'fit' between the nuclear family and the process of industrialisation. One alternative suggestion is that industrialisation and urbanisation first occurred in Western Europe *because* pre-industrial family structures were mainly nuclear. As a result, they could respond to the new economic opportunies requiring family mobility and flexibility. In other words, pre-industrial family structures, without unbreakable ties to extended kin, were a contributory *cause* of industrial development. The relatively large number of extended households, which included servants who had few, if any, emotional ties to their employers, were relatively flexible structures that could easily adapt to changed economic conditions.

Carlin (2002) argues that 'most households in early modern Western Europe were nuclear family households; all the blood relations they contained were one couple and their children'. Although extended families existed, they were not as common, nor as dominant, as 'fit theorists' have suggested, because:

- average life expectancy was low (around 35–40 years) and the majority of parents rarely lived long enough to become grandparents
- evidence about those who did survive into 'old age' suggests they were expected to retire into households separate from their children.

Carlin also notes that some parts of Western Europe with similar birth and death rates to the UK contained more **verticalised** (sometimes called *stem*) extended families. This suggests, at least in part, that people in the UK were *choosing* not to live in extended family structures.

KEY TERM

Verticalised: form of extended family that reaches up and down the generations. A classical vertically extended family involves grandparents, parents and children living together or in close proximity.

Laslett (1965; Laslett and Wall, 1972) argues that upper-class dwellings often included both wider kin and servants, mainly because there was enough room for them within the house. Lower-class households, although frequently nuclear because of high mortality rates among the elderly, probably included 'lodgers' (who are likely to have been kin) staying in the home temporarily. Laslett estimates only 10% of pre-industrial households contained more than two generations of kin. Similarly, Gordon (1972) suggests that arguments about the pre-industrial dominance of the extended family confuse *temporary* family extensions, such as a relative living within a nuclear family for a short period, with *permanent* extended family structures. This, he argues, 'is seldom actually encountered in any society, pre-industrial or industrial'.

Harris (1983) argues that nuclear family structures were necessary for industrialisation because the process required an inheritance system that concentrated wealth, making capital (investment money) available to relatively small numbers of people. This was made possible in a close-knit nuclear structure linked with a system of *primogeniture* (inheritance by the first-born son). In addition, those who did not inherit were forced to move out of the family home. Wegge's (1999) research on peasant population movements in Germany supports this idea. She notes, 'it is the primogeniture institution which better promotes emigration'.

For fit theorists, industrial and urban development occurred because of the geographic movement of people. However, statistics show that the population of England and Wales trebled between 1700 (6 million) and 1851 (18 million), with a population explosion in urban areas that suggests there was a large, landless, workforce. In other words, urbanisation was not a consequence of the break-up and migration of extended rural families; it was caused by rapid population growth in the early industrial period.

Anderson (1995) also argues that no single family or household structure was dominant during the industrialisation process. Both reconstituted and lone-parent families existed in pre-industrial societies, mainly because of high death rates among the poor. However, the evidence does suggest that changes gradually occurred in relation to social class and the increasing diversity of family and household structures.

The working class

Anderson suggests that during the process of industrialisation, the working class developed a broadly extended family structure, mainly as a consequence of urbanisation.

As towns developed around factories, pressure on living space resulted in extended families that satisfied a number of purposes:

- The lack of government help for the sick or unemployed meant working-class families relied on a strong **kinship network** for their care and survival.
- Most people could barely read or write, so kinship networks helped secure jobs for family members by recommending them to employers.
- If both parents worked, relatives played a vital part in childcare.
- Death rates were high, but orphans could be absorbed into the extended family structure.
- Children worked from quite a young age, so young relatives were used to supplement family income.

KEY TERM

Kinship networks: family relationships, based on biology, affinity or law, that form distinctive patterns (grandparents, parents, grandchildren) and networks; members of kinship groups may feel a special bond with and responsibility for other kin.

The middle and upper classes

Middle-class family structures tended to be nuclear. In part this was because the importance of education – and the cost of good schooling – meant that middle-class families were smaller than those of the working classes. In addition, the managers employed in the new industries were usually from the middle class and geographic mobility weakened extended family ties.

Gomm (1989) argues that upper-class family structures have historically been a mixture of nuclear and extended types. There was enough room for extended kin such as elderly relatives within the family home, and evidence suggests that it was quite common for the vertically extended family to exist in this class.

TEST YOURSELF

Suggest one argument for and one argument against the 'fit' thesis.

Post-industrial society

Globalisation has affected family structures all over the world in a number of ways, particularly in relation to geographic mobility. Across Europe, economic and political globalisation has resulted in greater opportunities for the free flow of labour across national borders. Improved communications, from email to mobile phones and voice-over-internet (VOI) technologies, have also made it easier for migrants to maintain close and extensive contacts with their (modified) extended families. Today, family and household structures are arguably more complex, fragmented and diverse than ever before.

Although nuclear family structures are the dominant form, they involve a range of different relationships. A single-parent family contains a different set of relationships from those in a reconstituted family, for example. The question, therefore, is the extent to which either or both these structures can be characterised as nuclear families. Definitions of nuclear and extended family structures also determine, to some degree, how we view the relationship between them. Willmott's (1988) concept of a dispersed-extended family, for example, seems to accurately characterise many types of family relationship today. The basic nuclear structure surrounded and supported by extended family networks has come about for three main reasons:

- Social changes, such as relatively easy access to divorce, have led to greater numbers of reconstituted/lone-parent families and single-person households.
- Lifestyle factors, such as greater social acceptance of single-parent and same-sex family structures, have also resulted in structural diversity.
- Increased life expectancy, more active lifestyles and changes to the welfare system have created changes within family structures. These include a new style of grandparenting, in which grandparents play a greater role in the care of grandchildren.

These trends have led to what Brannen (2003) calls the **beanpole family**. Beanpole structures arise in developed societies that have low or declining birth rates and increasing life expectancies. With fewer children being born, horizontal (intra-generational) family extensions are weak. At the same time, higher life expectancies lead to stronger vertical extensions between grandparents, parents, children and grandchildren.

KEY TERM

Beanpole family: an inter-generational, vertically extended family structure with very weak intra-generational links. This structure develops in societies with low or declining birth rates and increasing life expectancies.

Luscher (2000) suggests that such changes are making people increasingly uncertain about family structures and relationships. As divorce has increased, there are more lone-parent and reconstituted families. This can cause family relationships to weaken, has people distance themselves from previous family relationships. Luscher argues that families are seeking 'to put geographical distance between different family generations'.

The structure of a beanpole family

Another striking feature of contemporary societies is the growth of lone-person households. Beaumont (2011), for example, notes that nearly one third (29%) of British households contain one person – the second most common household structure after two-person households (35%). Over the past 50 years, one-person households have increased around 2.5 times, up from 12% in 1961.

TEST YOURSELF

Suggest one way in which modern technology has made it easier for families to maintain contact.

105

ACTIVITY

In a small group, design a poster to demonstrate either the 'fit' thesis or post-industrial society. Present it to the class and explain the rationale behind it.

Diversity in family forms according to class, ethnicity, religion, family size, marital status, age and family life cycle

We have talked in general terms about 'the family', but DeVault (1994) argues that 'the family is a falsely monolithic concept'. Rather than seeing it as a simple, homogeneous ('all the same') social group, we need to understand **family diversity** across a range of categories.

> **KEY TERM**
>
> **Family diversity:** expression of the range of family types in a society, from nuclear through extended and reconstituted to single-parent.

Class

O'Neill (2002) makes several observations about single (never married) parents when compared to two-parent families. Single parents are more likely to have working-class origins. They are also more likely to have lower average incomes and to live in poverty than two-parent families of the same class.

While beanpole family structures are less common in middle-class families, the average age of working-class mothers when they have their first child is much lower. As a result, four- or occasionally five-generation families are more likely to develop.

Family relationships also show high levels of class diversity. Adult relationships in middle-class families are more likely to be **symmetrical** – an idea developed by Willmott and Young (1973) to describe relationships characterised by **joint conjugal roles**. These involve lower levels of **gender inequality** in terms of both paid and unpaid (domestic) work. In contrast, working-class families are more often characterised by **segregated conjugal roles**, with the female role focused on home and children and the male role on paid work. In this situation, men have more power and control over women, and family roles and relationships reflect the needs of male family members. Such patriarchal relationships are expressed in a range of ways – from the threat or reality of violence, to dominance through decision-making. However, the extent to which gender equality exists in middle-class families has been questioned. For example, a study by Pahl and Vogler (1994) found that men make the most important financial decisions in middle-class families, whereas women make decisions about everyday domestic spending, such as food and clothing.

Lareau (2003) suggests that parents of different classes interact with their children in different ways. Middle-class parents generally adopt a 'deliberate' parenting style that 'actively fosters children's individual talents, opinions and skills'. Working-class parents are more likely to adopt a parenting style based around natural growth: 'Parents care for their children, love them, and set limits for them, but within these boundaries, they allow the children to grow spontaneously … children generally negotiate institutional life, including their day-to-day school experiences, on their own'. Lareau claims that this results in middle-class children gaining 'an emerging sense of entitlement' that makes them better equipped to meet the demands of higher education and the workplace. This cultural advantage translates into economic advantage. While both approaches are child-centred, the middle and upper classes can invest a wider range of family resources in their child's development. For example, Reay et al. (2004) argue that middle-class women are much more actively involved in their children's education through monitoring school progress and questioning teachers about their children's school performance.

> **KEY TERMS**
>
> **Symmetrical family:** relationship in which family roles are shared equally within the home.
>
> **Conjugal roles:** male and female roles played within the home.
>
> **Joint/segregated conjugal roles:** joint conjugal roles involve adults within the family sharing domestic duties. Segregated conjugal roles involve a clear separation between family roles; this traditionally involves women having responsibility for domestic labour and men for paid work outside the home.
>
> **Gender inequality:** unequal relationship between males and females, usually expressed in favour of men.

Age

Age diversity involves differences within and between generations (roughly defined in 25-year intervals).

Grandparents raised during the 1940s have the experience of war, rationing and restrictions on personal and sexual freedom. Their grandchildren, raised during the 1990s, may have developed very different attitudes and lifestyles. The family experience of a young couple with infant children is also different from that of an elderly couple without children.

Age and family structure come together when we think about dependent children. Beaumont (2011), for example, notes that in the UK:

- 76% of dependent children live in a dual-parent nuclear family, with only Belgium, Latvia and Estonia having a lower European percentage.
- 20% live with a lone mother. Among European states only Latvia (30%) has a higher percentage of lone-parent mothers (OECD, 2010).
- 3% live with a lone father.
- 1% have alternative living arrangements – mainly children's homes but also communes.

Wider social changes related to age also influence family forms. Such factors include:

- family formation – when to start a family
- size – the number of children born and raised
- structure – children have different experiences based on the type of family structure in which they live.

In addition, families with school-age children are more likely to be what Rapoport and Rapoport (1969) term 'dual-income families'. In this family form, 'both heads of household pursue careers and at the same time maintain a family life together'. This experience is different from that of a lone-parent family or a single-income dual-parent family.

Throughout the industrialised world, people both live longer and enjoy a more physically active old age than they do in other parts of the world. This affects family forms and relationships in a range of ways, such as:

- a greater likelihood of divorce – where the length of marriage increases, so too does the likelihood of it ending
- changes in childbearing – family formation is starting later and women are producing children at a later stage in the family life-cycle
- changing patterns of grandparenting – as people are more active into old age, they are better able to contribute to family life through things like child-minding.

What contribution can grandparents make to contemporary families?

Ethnicity

Ethnic diversity relates to differences within and between cultural (or ethnic) groups, expressed in terms of attitudes and lifestyles – especially those related to religious norms and values. The decline in the influence of organised religion (secularisation) among *some* ethnic groups partly accounts for things such as:

- an increase in cohabitation outside of marriage
- a decline in the significance of marriage
- an increase in divorce rates
- the availability of remarriage after divorce.

For other ethnic groups, religion may place great emphasis on marriage and disallow divorce.

More specifically, ethnic differences are found in areas such as family size, where different ethnicities have greater or lesser numbers of children and extended family members. Differences can also be seen in marriage – whether this is arranged by the parents or freely chosen by the participants; and the division of labour – whether family roles are patriarchal, **matriarchal** or symmetrical.

KEY TERM

Matriarchy: female-dominated family unit.

In the UK, Dale et al. (2004) found clear differences between ethnic groups in relation to female paid employment, family roles and responsibilities. Black women are more likely to 'remain in full-time employment throughout family formation' than either their white or

Asian peers. Within minority ethnicities, Indian women generally opt for part-time paid employment once they have a partner, but both Pakistani and Bangladeshi women are more likely to stop paid work once they marry and produce children.

Mann (2009) notes that the UK's *Asian* and *Black Caribbean* populations make up around 70% of the minority ethnic population. However, there are some key differences within and between these groups. For example, Black Caribbean families are characterised by:

- lower marriage rates – Modood et al. (1997) note that around 40% of Black Caribbean adults under 60 were in formal marriages (compared to 60% of White adults)
- cohabitation outside of marriage – Mann (2009) notes that Black Caribbean families with dependent children 'had the largest proportion of cohabiting couples'
- higher rates of separation, divorce and single parenthood – Mann notes that 45% of Black Caribbean families were headed by a lone parent, usually the mother, compared with 25% of White families; Hughes (2009) also reports that around 56% of dependent children lived with a lone parent – a situation that explains the smaller average Black Caribbean family size (2.3 people).

A further feature of Black Caribbean families is the much larger numbers of 'absent fathers' – those not living within the family home but maintaining family contacts. Family structure in this group, therefore, is more likely to be matriarchal. Chahal (2000) suggests that this reflects an emphasis on 'individualism, independence and physical and emotional space' as essential components of family life.

In contrast, South Asian (Indian, Pakistani and Bangladeshi) families are characterised by the following:

- Higher marriage rates, with a greater likelihood of *arranged marriage* (especially among Muslims and Sikhs). Berthoud notes that around 75% of Pakistani and 65% of Indian women are married by their mid-twenties.
- Lower rates of cohabitation outside of marriage – according to Mann, cohabitation 'is less usual amongst Asian populations' and they have lower rates of divorce and single-parent families.
- Self and Zealey (2007) note that around 10% of Pakistani/ Bangladeshi and 5% of Indian families are headed by a lone parent. Hughes notes that around 15% of all dependent children live with lone parents, the lowest for all ethnic groups. This helps to explain larger family sizes, with Bangladeshi and Pakistani ethnicities having the largest families.

In South Asian families, men are more likely to have power and authority (**patriarchy**). This is reflected in 'traditional' family roles. A majority of Pakistani and Bangladeshi women, for example, look after home and family full time. Chahal (2000) notes that among Pakistani and Bangladeshi ethnicities, older family members supported cultural traditions involving multi-generational households, traditional divisions of labour and arranged marriages.

KEY TERM

Patriarchy: male-dominated unit or society.

TEST YOURSELF

Suggest two differences between Black Caribbean and South Asian families.

Life cycle

When looking at how social categories such as class, age and ethnicity influence family life, it is easy to overlook the fact that families are dynamic groups that have life cycles. As Foster (2005) points out, people have different family experiences at different stages in their lives.

Pre-family: Pre-family formation involves young adults leaving their family of origin to begin a new family. Rosenfeld (2007) suggests that this new 'independent life stage' is something that 'really distinguishes modern family life from previous eras'. Young adults are separated from their family of origin:

- geographically – a young couple may move away from the area in which their parents live
- residentially, in terms of living apart from a family of origin
- socially, in terms of forming new friendships and relationships.

Family: Family formation itself is a developmental stage involving:

- different roles, such as parenting and grandparenting
- an evolving set of statuses, such as baby, child, adolescent and so forth.

Individual family members not only have different personal experiences of the same family life, but these experiences and relationships constantly shift and change.

Adults at different stages in family formation also have very different experiences. The family form of a young couple with dependent children is different from that of an elderly couple with independent children. Family structures are also significant: lone-parent families are different from dual-parent families, and a reconstituted family consisting of step-parents and step-children is different from a nuclear family consisting of a single child and its natural parents.

Post-family: Post-family formation is a further life-cycle dimension and includes the phenomenon of 'boomerang kids'. This is where adult children *leave* the parental home, then return for one of several reasons:

- a lack of employment opportunities
- high levels of personal debt
- a lack of affordable housing
- relationship breakdown or divorce.

This phenomenon shows that family formation and duration is not a linear, progressive and inevitable process. Families break up and reconfigure – family members adapt to a changed set of circumstances and take on new roles. This is not simply the outcome of family breakdown. There may also be a shift in family roles if dependent children leave home and start families of their own. Westland (2008) highlights the phenomenon of 'both-end carers'. This is a pivot or 'sandwich' generation of women aged 50–70 ('the grandmother generation'), who are expected to take on a central role in providing informal family services – looking up the family tree to the care of the elderly and down to the childcare needs of adult children.

TEST YOURSELF

Briefly explain what is meant by a 'family life cycle'.

Family size: The size of a 'completed family', one into which no more children will be born or adopted, has an impact on both family form and relationships. Historically, class was a significant factor in family size: the lower the class, the larger the family. However, in recent times this difference has become less pronounced. We can identify examples of long- and short-term changes in family size based on the average number of children in each family.

In modern industrial societies, the long-term trend has been a decrease in average family size. Hughes

notes that women in the UK born in 1937 averaged 2.4 children, while their children's generation averaged 1.9 children. Average family size in the UK continued to decline in the 20th century to a low point of around 1.7 children in 1999. Since that time, there has been a slight increase in average family size in the UK. By way of comparison, the average Mauritian family size according to the 2000 Census was 3.9 people, while Zambia has one of the largest family sizes in the world, with an average of 6 children.

A range of factors may explain the *long-term decline* in family size. To begin with, social attitudes to very large families have changed. Such attitudes are influenced by factors such as the extension of dependent **childhood** due to a higher school leaving age. Whereas in the past children contributed to family income – they were an *economic asset*, especially to working-class families – they are now more likely to be a *drain* on family resources. As children become more expensive to raise, their numbers fall. Womack (2006) also reports that rising living costs 'have led many people to choose to enjoy the lifestyle they have instead of adding more pressure with the cost of bringing up a child'.

KEY TERM

Childhood: socially variable period of pre-adulthood.

Childlessness is increasingly common among both single females and couples. Many single women choose to pursue a career rather than having children. McAllister and Clarke (1998) found that the reason couples gave for childlessness included:

- choice: not wanting children
- equivocation: being unsure about whether to have children
- delay: uncertainty about wanting children now, but not discounting *ever* having them.

Women now stay in education longer than they did in the past. They also have many more career opportunities. As a result, women are now having their first child later in life than they used to (an average of 29 years old), which means there is less time for larger families to develop. Having children later in life also gives women a chance to establish a career that they can return to after childbirth. This means they are less likely to settle for a traditional 'mother and child-rearing' role. Finch (2003) notes that while *younger* women have moved towards later childbirth this has *not* been offset by *older* women having more children, something that 'results in a decrease in the average family size'. The increasing availability of cheap and reliable contraception has also contributed to reduced family size, giving people greater choice over whether or not to have children.

Why is childlessness significant for career women?

ACTIVITY

Compare and contrast the diversity in family life in the UK with the diversity in family life in your own culture. Is there more or less diversity in your own culture? Suggest reasons for your answer.

TEST YOURSELF

What evidence is there of long-term decline in family size?

The debate about the postulated universality of the nuclear family

Contemporary debates about the universality of the nuclear family begin with the work of Murdock (1949) and his 'survey of 250 representative human societies'. From this, he concluded: 'The nuclear family is a universal human social grouping, either as the sole prevailing form of the family or as the basic unit from which more complex familial forms are compounded.' This characterisation has two main threads:

1 Structural *convergence,* or the idea that family structures are historically moving toward the 'nuclear norm', which will eventually become the 'sole prevailing' family form.
2 A *dominance* thesis, in which the nuclear family is simply the main family structure in all societies.

Convergence

Convergence arguments are built on modernisation theory. This is the idea that human development has followed a broadly linear route, from economically, politically and culturally undeveloped pre-industrial societies, through developed industrial societies, to fully developed post-industrial societies. For classical functionalists, development was theorised in terms of different *stages*, from primitive to advanced, through which all societies pass. The driving force behind this change is institutional differentiation. As institutions such as work and education developed to meet changing social needs, they forced changes in institutions such as the family. Parsons (1951) argued that these changes focused on institutional specialisation. Families lost many of the functions they had traditionally performed, such as the education of children and the long-term care of the sick and the elderly. Instead, they focused on the two functions that they were uniquely equipped to manage – socialisation and stabilisation.

If modernisation is an inevitable, linear process, all societies are converging in terms of their economic, political and cultural structures. This extends to the family because economic and cultural changes have historically produced changes in family structures (the 'fit' thesis). Skolnick (1995) suggests that family convergence across all societies is based on two claims:

- The family group is best placed to perform certain functions, such as childcare.
- There is a **functional fit** between the nuclear family and industrial society. Independent of the kin network, the 'isolated' nuclear family is free to move as the economy demands.

KEY TERM

Functional fit: the idea that social institutions, such as the family, education and work are closely related. The functional fit between the family and work is such that while the family produces socialised individuals for the workplace, work provides the physical means for family survival.

In addition, the intimate nuclear family is well suited to serving the emotional needs of adults and children 'in a competitive and impersonal world'. For convergence to be valid, functionalists would need to show that the extended family structures of pre-industrial societies had been replaced by a nuclear family structure adapted to the needs of industrial society. However, the evidence presented by historians such as Laslett and Anderson does not support this argument.

This does not necessarily invalidate Murdock's claim to nuclear universality. He argues that the nuclear family structure is not only 'the first and most basic' but also the building block for all other types of family structure: 'Among the majority of the peoples of the earth, nuclear families are combined, like atoms in a molecule, into larger aggregates.' In other words, all family structures – whether extended or polygamous – are based on a nuclear core of 'husband and wife'. Extended families are nuclear families with temporary extensions, while polygamous families 'consist of two or more nuclear families affiliated by plural marriages. That is, by having one married parent in common.' Similarly, a lone-parent family structure represents:

- a 'broken nuclear' form, in the case of the death or divorce of a partner
- a reformation of the nuclear family in the case of the formation of a reconstituted family
- a structure that cannot be sustained without outside support – either from kin or the state.

If we accept the argument that conventional alternatives are merely variations on the nuclear norm, it opens up another line of criticism involving unconventional alternatives.

TEST YOURSELF

Briefly explain what is meant by the nuclear family being 'the building block for all other types of family structure'.

Alternatives

Examples drawn from tribal societies suggest that it is possible for family structures to exist that are very different from the nuclear norm:

- Gough's (1959) analysis of the Nayar of Malabar (*Kerala*) in southern India revealed a complex system of family and marriage-type relationships based on two practices. First, a joint **matrilineal** family structure (*tharavad*) involving common family ancestors living 'together'; women lived in the main part of the house with men occupying separate rooms or houses. Second, Schwimmer (2003) notes how 'on reaching puberty, a woman could entertain an indefinite number of lovers, usually between three and eight, without any public concern over sexual

fidelity or paternal responsibility.' A form of arranged marriage (*sambandham*) resulted in the woman taking 'responsibility for raising children within matrilineally constructed households, focusing on mothers, daughters, and sisters. The domestic group also included the women's brothers'.

KEY TERM

Matrilineal: tracing ancestral descent through the female line.

- The Lakker of Burma (*Myanmar*) provide a further variation in that, as Keesing (1976) notes, they 'do not see children as having any blood relationship to the mother. The mother is only a container in which the child grows. Children of the same mother and different fathers are not considered to be related to each other and sexual relationships between them are not considered incest.'
- Herndon (2004) argues that the Ashanti of West Africa developed a matrifocal family system where 'Children belong legally to the mother and her clan.' Upon marriage, the man takes on some family responsibilities, but family assets and property are owned and controlled along the female line. The father's role, in this respect, is to provide 'material support', although 'two thirds of couples do not share common residence because they cannot afford to'.

While these examples seem to challenge the idea of the universal nuclear family, they can actually be used to *support* the argument because they refer to pre-industrial societies; as societies modernise, the nuclear norm is established. A more critical alternative would be one that exists in modern industrial societies, such as a commune.

The Shaker/Oneida community developed in 19th-century Boston (USA). According to Hillebrand (2003), it adopted a communistic culture based on *complex marriage* – 'every man married to every woman' – with two principles:

1 Male–female cohabitation required the consent of a third commune member.
2 No two people could have exclusive attachment with each other.

At its height, the Oneida community was made up of a few hundred members in different locations. It was effectively dissolved in 1881.

A longer-lasting example is the Israeli **kibbutz**, which is based around principles of communal living, property ownership and child-rearing:

- Couples could engage in monogamous sexual relationships.
- They did not share the common residence and economic co-operation characteristic of nuclear families.
- The product of their work was shared among the community.

The few remaining members of a Shaker community, USA, 1965. Is this type of community an argument against the universal nuclear family?

While the kibbutz carries out many, if not all, of the functions of a nuclear family, it may not be accurate to describe it as a nuclear or composite nuclear family. Although each kibbutz *functions* as a family, it is not a family as defined by Murdock. This type of communal living is not the norm in Israeli society – only around 5% of the population live in this way.

A more extreme form of communal living was the attempt by the Soviet Union in the 1920s, to 'abolish the family' in favour of communes, with married women being allowed to live separately from their husbands. Some attempts were made to collectivise the care of children, but the extent to which this was fully realised is open to doubt. This experiment in abolition was ended in the 1930s.

New World Black family: This family type is relatively common in the Caribbean and parts of the United States. It involves a matrifocal extended family consisting of a single woman and her children, supported by an extended family network centred on the grandmother. This structure is frequently seen as a legacy of two processes: slavery, where males were separated from females, and extreme levels of poverty, which meant that Afro-Caribbean males were more likely to live away from the family home because they were unable to provide for their family.

The development of an extended kin network, however, allowed family members to help and support each other. This arrangement meant that 'single' mothers could work while their children were cared for by other female kin. It was, and still is, not uncommon for fathers to maintain both an emotional and economic relationship with their family. While this family type is often cited as a viable alternative some experts argue that it is a *composite nuclear family*, despite the fact that there is no common residence or economic co-operation between adult partners.

The extent to which the nuclear family can be seen as a universal family structure depends on how we view the evidence for alternative family forms. While kibbutzim and the New World Black family seem to offer viable alternatives, in recent times the rules governing communal living in kibbutzim have gradually eased. Children are now allowed to spend more time with their natural parents. The New World family structure might also be considered specific to a particular time, place and set of economic circumstances. In the UK, for example, while relatively large numbers of Afro-Caribbean children live with their mothers, they generally lack the extended family support found in the New World.

Universal dominance

A further dimension to the argument is that nuclear families are dominant because the structure fits most easily with the demands of modern industrial society: small, self-contained, flexible and mobile. Goode argues that nuclear families serve 'the needs of the modern industrial system'. However, this argument is questionable for two reasons:

1 The inflexibility of the extended family has been overstated, partly because the terms 'nuclear' and 'extended' are frequently used too rigidly. Gordon

claims that the 'classical extended family' 'is seldom actually encountered in any society, pre-industrial or industrial'. Hareven further suggests that the flexibility of extended families 'that enabled households to expand when necessary and to take people in' has been underestimated. Litwak (1960) goes even further, arguing that we can no longer talk about 'truly extended' or 'truly nuclear' families in industrial societies; all family structures are based around a form of 'modified nuclear family'.

2 The dominance of the nuclear family in industrial societies was not caused by industrialisation but by capitalism. The argument here is that the nuclear family gradually became an 'ideal' and to some extent *idealised*, form that brought it to cultural dominance in industrial societies for political and ideological reasons. Nuclear families solved important questions of **patrilineal** descent and inheritance, particularly among the upper and middle classes. It came to dominance not because of a functional fit with economic production but rather because it was a family structure that fitted more closely with the interests of powerful social groups. In particular, it suited the needs of a capitalist class of (male) owners who wanted to ensure their wealth was passed down the generations through legitimate heirs. Stacey (1998) also suggests that the 'traditional' nuclear family is a 'political, not biological, construction'. It acts in the interests of men by enhancing and perpetuating social inequalities, maintaining class hierarchies and transferring social, cultural and economic capital from one generation to next.

KEY TERM

Patrilineal: tracing ancestral descent through the male line.

ACTIVITY

Design an alternative form of communal living that is not based on the nuclear family, but which satisfies all the necessary functions of the family. What are the advantages and disadvantages of the commune you have designed?

Different theories about the relationship between the family and the economy

This section examines consensus and conflict approaches to the relationship between the family and the economy.

Consensus

Approaches such as functionalism are based on the idea that any social system (or society) consists of four sub-systems:

- the economic (work)
- the political (government)
- the cultural (education, religion and media)
- the family.

Each sub-system has a specific role, but the system as a whole functions because the connections between the sub-systems depend on purpose and need. For the economy to function, it *needs* the family to produce socialised individuals orientated towards work. The role of the family, therefore, is theorised in terms of two types of co-operation: *between* institutions, such as family and work, and *within* institutions, such as the relationship between adult partners. In this respect, Murdock (1949) identified four **functional prerequisites** of the family – the things it must perform to fulfil its role in society:

1 Sexual control involves the idea that adult married or cohabiting couples do not have sexual relations with anyone other than their current partner, something that provides 'stability through exclusivity'. By showing commitment to each other and their family, adults work towards ensuring the survival of *their* group. By 'looking inward' to the needs of *their* family, adults also 'look outward' to the needs of the social system.
2 Reproduction involves families 'reproducing society' by creating new members to replace those who die.
3 Socialisation involves children being taught values and norms.
4 Economic provision involves the idea that families have to organise themselves to ensure the group's survival. They must develop a division of labour involving paid employment and unpaid domestic work.

KEY TERM

Functional prerequisites: the things that any institution, such as a family, must perform if it is to continue to function successfully.

TEST YOURSELF

Briefly explain and evaluate the concept of a 'functional prerequisite'.

113

Alongside these ideas, Parsons and Bales (1956) argued that whereas in the past the family was *multi-functional* (performing different functions), it became increasingly specialised in modern societies. The development of 'new' social institutions, such as education, meant that families gradually suffered a **loss of functions**. Parsons (1959b) believed that these changes were consistent with family evolution because they left families free to concentrate on two essential (or irreducible) functions:

- **Primary socialisation** – families are socialisation 'factories whose product is the development of human personalities'. This function links to social order and system stability as the mechanism through which new family members come to understand and learn the values and norms needed to successfully play their adult roles.
- The stabilisation of adult personalities involves adult family members providing physical and emotional support. Family relationships provided both the motivation for paid work and the emotional and sexual comforts that came from the development of affective relationships.

114

KEY TERMS

Loss of functions: situation in which functions that were once performed by an institution are now performed by another institution. The educational function of the early-industrial family has been taken over by schools in late-modern societies.

Primary socialisation: teaching and learning process normally first carried out within the family.

Fletcher (1973) drew these functional strands together by arguing that contemporary families performed two types of function:

1. Core functions cannot be performed by either individuals working alone or by any other institution. Family groups provide a necessary context for both childbearing and child-rearing. This involves ensuring a child's physical and psychological survival and its social development into adulthood (primary socialisation). A child's natural parents are best suited to this process because they have a personal investment in their child's survival and development. The family also provides both a 'physical home' (nurture and shelter for the child) and an 'emotional home' in terms of the child's psychological well-being; children feel wanted and loved. The regulation of sexual behaviour involves norms relating to permissible sexual relationships that contribute to family stability and, by extension, wider social order and stability.

2. Peripheral functions are things that, while still performed by some families at some times, have been largely taken over by other institutions. These include education, health care and recreation.

Neo-functionalism

Traditional functionalists saw the links between families and other institutions in broad terms: the economy needs socialised individuals and it is the purpose of the family to provide them. Neo-functionalist approaches focus more specifically on the processes involved in linking the individual to society. Horwitz (2005), for example, argues that the family functions as a bridge connecting the 'micro world' of the individual with the 'macro world' of wider economic society, whereby 'families help us to learn the social rules necessary for functioning in the wider world'. The family is, therefore, 'a school for learning social norms'. By learning behavioural rules within the family, children create a template 'for other intimate relationships and the more anonymous relationships' found in the workplace. The family is crucial in this process because it represents a 'secure base' from which 'children can learn both explicitly, through instruction, and implicitly, through experimentation, the rules that do and should govern behaviour in the broader social world'. For Horwitz, the family 'is a superior site for learning these rules of behaviour' for three reasons:

- Rules transmitted and enforced by people who share a deep, emotional commitment are more likely to be effectively taught and learnt.
- Emotional closeness provides incentives to develop co-operative behaviour – for example, children want to please their parents.
- Rule-learning can be taught subconsciously by children observing and imitating adult behaviour, thereby 'adopting the implicit rules that are at work'.

TEST YOURSELF

Suggest one way in which the family is a bridge between the individual and society.

Conflict

Approaches such as Marxism also adopt a systems approach to understanding the family's relationship to the economy. In this approach, the family's general role is to support a capitalist economic system across three dimensions:

1 Ideologically – families propagate ideas favourable to both capitalism and a ruling class. Althusser (1970), for example, argues that the family is an ideological state apparatus (ISA) through which children learn norms and values broadly supportive of the economic and political status quo. Zaretsky (1976) argues that socialisation involves the transmission of a ruling-class ideology. This encourages a largely unquestioning acceptance of 'the capitalist system' and the rights of a ruling class through beliefs about competition, the importance of the work ethic and the requirement to obey legitimate authority.

2 Economically – families perform a *productive* role beneficial to capitalism by not only producing 'future workers' but, more importantly, by taking on the substantial costs of replacing '*dead labour*' (those who literally die and those who become too old or sick to work). Althusser also argues that the family has a *consumption* role in modern societies. In the past it was a unit of production, creating the things people needed to survive; now it buys most of what it needs, from food and shelter to leisure, and this means family members have to find paid employment. Zaretsky also argues that families are important targets for advertisers; by encouraging consumption, the family has progressively become a major source of profit.

3 Politically – the family role is closely related to the needs of capitalist economies. It acts as a stabilising force that helps maintain the order needed for companies to function profitably. Family responsibilities also lock people into capitalist economic relationships, because family members have to work in order to support each other and their children financially; taking responsibility for family members also acts as a political stabilising force. Zaretsky argues that the growth of the **privatised family** encourages family members to focus on private problems rather than wider social concerns such as social inequality. 'Seeing the world through a private family lens' discourages political engagement and action against an exploitative

economic system. The family becomes a safety valve for adult frustrations. Where most people are relatively powerless in the workplace, this condition is disguised by the power they exert – economic, psychological and occasionally physical – over their family. Political frustrations, therefore, are directed away from their causes – social and economic inequality – and onto family members.

Neo-Marxism

This perspective adds a cultural dimension to the relationship between the family and the economic system. It highlights how different types of family capital confer advantages and disadvantages on children of different classes. Bourdieu (1986) uses the concept of cultural capital – non-economic *resources* that can be 'spent' to give some families advantages over others – to argue that parents are differently positioned to invest in their children. Silva and Edwards (2005) argue that middle- and upper-class parents equip their children with the knowledge and skills necessary for an easy transition to the workplace. Bourdieu argues that cultural capital operates through the family to give some children a 'head start' in education, because parents can motivate their children by transmitting the attitudes and knowledge needed to succeed educationally. Willis (1977) also demonstrates how a *lack* of cultural capital consigns working-class children to educational failure and explains 'why working-class kids get working-class jobs'.

Institutional investment refers to the time, money and effort (emotional labour) parents put into their child's education. The greater the investment, the more likely children are to achieve the qualifications they need for the highest-status universities. This makes it easier for them to get higher-paid jobs and contributes to a process of class reproduction – how middle- and upper-class parents, for example, ensure their offspring maintain or advance their family's class position. Parents also invest in a range of cultural goods and services – from books and computers, through extra tuition, to getting their child into the 'right' school – that give them educational advantages. Sullivan (2001a) tested this effect on GCSE performance and concluded that cultural capital transmitted within the home had a 'significant effect on performance'.

Social and symbolic capital

Social capital is another form of family capital that refers to people's connections within a social network and the value these connections have for what Putnam (2000) calls

115

KEY TERM

Privatised family: structure that is home-orientated, child-centred and built on emotional relationships between adults and children.

'norms of reciprocity' – what people do for each other. As Cohen and Prusak (2001) argue, high levels of social capital involves 'the trust, mutual understanding, shared values and behaviours' that bind wealthy families into networks reinforced by mutual self-interest and co-operation. In this respect, middle- and upper-class families have greater access to *significant* social networks, in schools or the workplace, that give their children economic advantages.

Symbolic capital, on the other hand, relates to the characteristics that upper-class children develop, in particular:

- authority – directing the efforts of others in the expectation of being obeyed
- personal charisma used to manipulate others' behaviour.

> ### KEY TERMS
>
> **Social capital:** how people are connected to social networks (who you know) and what people do for each other.
>
> **Symbolic capital:** how upper-class children in particular learn self-confidence, a strong sense of entitlement and self-worth within the family that they then apply in the workplace.

How does cultural capital give some children an advantage over others?

Feminism

The feminist approach has traditionally focused on conflict within the family and, in particular, on how women are exploited through 'traditional gender roles' enforced and reinforced for the benefit of men. From this perspective, the family is an oppressive structure, imprisoning women in a narrow range of *service* roles and responsibilities, such as domestic labour and childcare.

The links between the family and the economy are generally *indirect*. Female family roles and responsibilities allow men to exercise economic power through 'free' family services paid for by women's **domestic labour**.

Marxist feminists emphasise the relationship between female exploitation through the notion of a **dual burden**. Women are doubly exploited in the public sphere (workplace), as paid employees whose labour contributes to ruling-class profits, and in the private sphere (the home) as unpaid workers whose labour mainly benefits men. Duncombe and Marsden (1993) argue that women now perform a **triple shift**, the third element being the time and effort women invest in the *psychological* well-being of family members. Female investment in their children's and partner's emotional well-being not only benefits men within the home but also contributes to wider economic stability.

> ### KEY TERMS
>
> **Domestic labour:** work done within the home, often performed by women.
>
> **Dual burden (double shift):** the idea that women perform 'two shifts', one inside the home as domestic labourers and one outside the home as paid employees.
>
> **Triple shift:** where a female double-shift refers to women's roles as domestic and paid labourers, a third element of female responsibility is the emotional work they do; investing time and effort in the *psychological* well-being of family members.

Feminists argue that women increasingly suffer from two main types of exploitation: patriarchal as domestic labourers and capitalist as paid employees. Bruegal (1979) argues that women are a 'reserve army of labour' – women are called into the workforce when there is a shortage of (male) labour and forced back into the family when there is a surplus. One aspect of this 'reserve status' is that women are generally a *marginalised workforce*, forced into low-pay, low-status employment on the basis of sexual discrimination. Finally, feminists also claim that women's family lives are oppressive. Even though many women happily perform the role of housewife feminists argue that the connection between domestic labour and femininity is imposed by a patriarchal society.

> ### TEST YOURSELF
>
> Identify two ways in which the family supports a capitalist economic system.

<!-- -->
ACTIVITY

Check your understanding of the four types of capital:

- *economic*
- *cultural*
- *social*
- *symbolic.*

What do you think is the most important for determining:

- *the school you attend*
- *the person you will marry*
- *the occupation you will achieve?*

Family roles, marriage and changing relationships

Changes and continuities in family functions

Families have always been a social space in which children are born and raised. Although reproduction occurs in alternative areas, the family performs this core function in most modern societies. However, the *way* in which the family performs this function has arguably changed due to changes in both **family functions** and wider society. In pre-industrial times, family members took sole responsibility for physical survival. Today, a range of complementary agencies, such as hospitals, schools and welfare agencies, play a part in this process. There is also now a greater emphasis on the psychological development and well-being of children, and several outside agencies, from the media to psychologists, play a part in child development.

KEY TERM

Family functions: the various purposes the family group exists to perform in society, such as primary socialisation.

Although primary socialisation remains important, its nature and purpose have changed as societies have altered, economically, politically and culturally. In pre-industrial societies, the family was a more self-contained unit, with fewer connections to wider society. Most people worked within and around the home, and children were taught the roles and responsibilities they needed to take their place in this economic arrangement.

In contemporary industrial societies, however, the family as a unit of economic production has been largely taken over by paid work outside the home. This has resulted in changes to how and why children are socialised. The contemporary focus is more on individual psychological development; a child is encouraged to learn certain norms and values relating to how they deal with others rather than learning specific skills.

Essentially, the family has shifted from being a unit of production to being one of consumption – buying rather than making the things it needs for survival, comfort and leisure. This change is significant because of how it has affected both family roles and the relationship between the family and wider society – the functional linkages between families and other institutions. The skills required for adulthood have changed. There is more emphasis on establishing emotional attachments because the contemporary family no longer functions as a workplace or school. The nature and extent of childhood has also changed and this, in turn, has altered the focus of primary socialisation. Agencies such as the media and the peer group have taken on significant socialisation functions, which both complement and compete with the family. However, as Horwitz argues, a child's natural parents still play an important role in primary socialisation because of their 'personal investment' in their child's survival and development.

Parsons (1959b) argues that in industrial societies the stabilisation of adult personalities is a major family function. Family members provide physical, emotional, psychological and economic comfort, security, support and companionship. They do this through the development of affective relationships based on love and a sense of belonging to a social group with strong kinship bonds. The family is also the only institution in industrial society that is based on **particularistic values**, where people treat others differently based on their particular relationship. Family members, for example, are usually more inclined to trust each other than a complete stranger. This contrasts with the **universalistic values** that apply to wider society – for example, the idea that everyone is treated equally by the law.

KEY TERMS

Particularistic values: how people such as family members or work colleagues treat others differently based on the value of their particular relationship.

Universalistic values: values that apply to everyone, regardless of their particular situation. The idea that everyone is equal under the law is an example of a universalistic value.

The theory that affective bonding is the basis of modern family relationships contrasts with the suggestion that the pre-industrial family was built on economic relationships. People married because they had a strong economic interest in forming such relationships, not necessarily because they 'fell in love':

- For the upper classes, marriage was particularly focused on ensuring that family wealth was consolidated and, if possible, enhanced, through arranged marriages between wealthy families.
- For the lower classes an economic marriage made sense in a society based on subsistence farming; the more adult members of a family there were, the easier it was to manage the necessary distribution of labour.

Stabilisation, therefore, has two specific meanings. In the past, economic stability was significant, whereas in contemporary societies, emotional stability is more important. Despite this, there are still some **empty-shell marriages**, where a married couple stays together even though they are no longer in love. There are several reason why people do this – from providing their children with a stable home to maintaining the appearance of being married. The 'emotional home' is now more child-centred, and children are children valued for psychological and emotional reasons rather than economic ones. This change has not only affected the nature of the child–parent relationship, it is also reflected in family roles and the domestic division of labour – who does what in the home. Willmott and Young (1973) describe the following three types of family:

- The pre-industrial family (before about 1750) was a relatively stable structure in which men and women worked together inside and outside the home. Although family members were not equal – men generally headed the household – women were not simply domestic labourers.
- The asymmetrical family that developed after this time was disrupted by industrialisation; the home and the workplace were separated as men moved into paid work outside the home and women became domestic labourers and child-carers.
- The symmetrical family, which developed around the middle of the 20th century, was characterised by joint conjugal relationships.

KEY TERM

Empty-shell marriage: when a couple continues to live together, even though the marriage may be effectively over, for reasons other than love.

TEST YOURSELF

Identify two core family functions.

Peripheral functions

One of the most striking changes in contemporary families is the extent to which functions they once performed have been taken over by other institutions:

- Education is now handled by a school system.
- Health care has been largely handed over to a range of professional practitioners, from doctors and nurses to social workers.
- Recreation and leisure, once focused on the family, has become either more individualised or something that is pursued outside the home.

Changes have undoubtedly occurred. However, some experts argue that these former functions have not been completely lost. They have simply been modified:

- Many parents, especially among the middle classes, are actively involved in their children's education.
- Families play an important care role – non-critical illnesses are largely treated within the family, and families may carry out long-term care of the elderly. However, this responsibility still mainly falls to women.
- Many families, especially those with young children, share leisure and recreation, although this may be largely consumed outside the home as part of the leisure industry. Some argue that where leisure occurs inside the home, through things such as television, computers, gaming consoles and mobile phones, it is actually becoming more individualised; contemporary families may no longer share leisure activities.

Debates about the relationship between the family and the state

Families are seen as important, if not crucial, to social order and stability. However, the relationship between the family and the state is generally theorised as one in which governments support both the family generally and, in some instances, particular family structures, roles and relationships. Family life is surrounded by:

- legal norms, governing things such as marriage and divorce
- moral values that shape ideas about what a family *is* and *should be*, what it *does* and *should do*.

In other words, families are influenced and shaped by a family ideology. This ideology defines the family as both a public institution supported by government and a private institution where family members should be left alone to work out their relationships.

The managerial state

This tension between the two is captured, for Dean (2006), by the concept of a managerial state. The role of the state in modern industrial societies involves *managing* the development of family groups and relationships. Family policy is built on a general assumption of 'privacy'. It is the job of the state to set behavioural *boundaries* by encouraging certain forms of behaviour, such as marriage, and discouraging others, such as single parenthood. It must carry out this job without becoming directly and coercively involved in how people live out their family lives. An example of a coercive or state-directed approach is China's 'one-child' system introduced in 1979, which limits couples to one child (although there are exceptions to this law). The idea of a managerial relationship between the family and the state is reflected in a range of sociological approaches.

China operates a one child per family policy in order to limit population growth. How is this an example of a state-directed approach to family life?

Consensus

Traditional functionalist approaches stress the role that families play in maintaining order. The family group performs certain essential functions for both individuals and wider society, which makes it crucial to any social system. The relationship between the family and political institutions is, however, an ambivalent one. Throughout much of the industrialised world, the state has progressively removed a range of functions from the family, especially peripheral functions in areas such as education and welfare. At the same time, a variety of state policies, such as the introduction of free nursery provision for all three-year-olds in the UK in 2004, have an impact on family life.

Similarly, a range of economic policies, from housing to taxation, affect family life. In the UK, for example, Child Tax Credit is paid to parents in full-time education or training who are also caring for children.

New right

In the USA, Eichner (2010) argues for a 'supportive state' model, where political institutions act to 'support families in performing their caretaking and human development functions'. These ideas relate to neo-functionalist/new-right arguments about the fundamental importance of the family group in any society. The managerial role of the state here relates to encouraging 'socially beneficial' family structures and relationships and discouraging those seen as 'socially detrimental'. Government policies should be directed at supporting 'traditional family relationships'. Neale (2000) notes that this involves stable family relationships created within married, heterosexual, dual-parent nuclear families.

These structures provide emotional and psychological benefits to family members. At the same time, personal and social responsibilities are created, which benefits society in general. Children are given clear moral and behavioural guidance, which makes them less likely to engage in deviant behaviour, and each adult partner plays a role that involves both personal sacrifice and commitment to others.

From the new right perspective, family structures and relationships such as single parenthood can only be sustained with government support – something that encourages a dependency culture:

- economic – without state support this 'family choice' could not exist
- moral – its existence depends on the tolerance of those who eventually pick up the bill for women who choose to have children outside marriage.

Single parenthood, therefore, is considered both immoral and unproductive. It produces poorly socialised, **dysfunctional** children who go on to live adult lives dependent on state benefits, crime or both.

119

TEST YOURSELF

Suggest reasons why the state should not support some forms of family structure.

Conflict

Conflict perspectives such as Marxism and feminism take a more critical approach to the relationship between the family and the state. Marxism focuses on relating what the family group does, such as socialisation, to how it benefits powerful groups. For example, it might point to how a ruling class benefits from 'free family services', such as bearing the costs of raising children, because they are future employees. For Marxists, the relationship between the family and the *capitalist* state is based on how the family helps to maintain and reproduce social inequalities by presenting them as 'normal' and 'natural' within the socialisation process.

The state, as part of the political and ideological superstructure, supports and promotes the family group as a stabilising force. The financial and moral responsibilities people take on when they create family groups lock them into capitalist economic relationships. For example, people have to work to provide for family members. Having this responsibility also acts as an emotionally stabilising force. In this respect, Althusser portrays families as an ideological state apparatus. Through primary socialisation children learn values, such as the importance of the work ethic, and norms, such as work itself – both paid and unpaid, that integrate them into capitalist society.

How does capitalism lock individuals into family relationships?

More generally, the relationship between the family and the state is regulated by, for example, rules governing who can marry (*bigamy*, being married to more than one person at the same time, and *incest*, marrying a close relative, are illegal in most countries) and a minimum legal age for marriage. Similarly, there are rules about divorce, which is legal in western Europe, but not in all countries.

Conflict approaches, therefore, argue that the state/family relationship in contemporary societies is geared towards the protection of ruling-class interests. Critics of the conflict approach, however, have pointed out that the development of a welfare state, through free universal education and health care, has produced widespread and long-lasting benefits to working-class families.

TEST YOURSELF

Identify two ways in which a ruling class benefits from the family.

Feminism and the state

Feminist sociology has traditionally focused on the family group as patriarchal and oppressive, imprisoning women in a narrow range of *service* roles and responsibilities, such as domestic labour and childcare. Different forms of feminism have different perspectives on the relationship between the state and the family. Liberal feminism has traditionally looked to the state and legal agencies as a way of redressing gender imbalances in family life through social policies that will break down barriers to female emancipation. These might include equality in political representation, equal pay and anti-discrimination polices, and protection against domestic violence. Similarly, the legal system has been seen as both a source of protection for women and as a way of enforcing equal gender rights.

More specifically, liberal feminists have looked to the state in terms of polices that recognise female dual roles – as both family carers and paid employees. These include the development of nursery schooling and childcare facilities that allow women to work and have family responsibilities. They also cover a range of polices aimed specifically at the family group, from family planning to pregnancy and childbirth.

Finch outlines a general problem with managerial approaches: 'Governments are always in danger of presuming a standard model of family life for which they can legislate, by making the assumption that most families do in fact operate in particular ways.' Social policies affecting the family are always created and enacted within the context of certain ideological beliefs. However, many social policies focus less on trying to impose a particular family form 'from above' and more on trying to create the conditions in which there is a 'flexibility in family life' that ensures 'people have maximum opportunity to work out their own relationships to suit the circumstances of their own lives'. This view may be valid, but it ignores the idea that not all sections of a population are treated equally. Some, particularly the poor and the powerless, are subject to greater levels of government regulation and intervention in family life than others.

The relationship between the family and the state in contemporary democratic societies is, therefore, a complex one. It must work alongside ideological beliefs about the desirability of particular family forms as well as a general desire not to intervene directly in the private life of the family except in exceptional circumstances, such as **domestic violence** and child abuse. However, while governments have great control over the relationship between the state and the family, this is not simply a one-way process; we must also recognise that the family is a fluid and dynamic institution.

KEY TERM

Domestic violence: any form of physical or verbal abuse towards family members within the home.

TEST YOURSELF

Identify two ways in which women may benefit from state involvement in family life.

ACTIVITY

Design a poster that shows the different perspectives on the relationship between the family and the state. Based on what you have depicted, how do you think the state should benefit the family and vice versa?

Roles and responsibilities within the family, including the roles of parents, children and grandparents

This section outlines the various experiences shared by family members in terms of their general roles and responsibilities.

Parents

One way to understand parental roles is to think about them in terms of social and personal identities. How individuals interpret and play parental roles is conditioned by what this role means in two ways: what a society expects parents to do and how individuals interpret their role in the *personal* context of family relationships. Considering parental roles in this way helps us understand two key ideas:

1 Parental roles are not fixed and unchanging. In the past, social identities were dominant. They provided clear behavioural guidelines for family roles: the mother worked in the home, raising children; the father's role was mainly outside the home as economic provider. There were not many opportunities to develop personal identities that differed from the social norm. Indeed, the penalties for breaking away from the norm were severe, ranging from male violence against women who tried to reject or renegotiate their role within the family, to general social disapproval.

2 Contemporary gender roles still have some connection to those of the past. The role of 'mother' is usually marked out differently from that of 'father'. They are, however, not as constrained by social identities as they once were. Rather, as Mann argues, they are open to negotiation. People have more personal freedom to decide how they want to interpret parental roles. James (1998) suggests that the home is now 'a spatial context where identities are worked on' and roles, as Fortier (2003) puts it, are 'continuously re-imagined and redefined'.

With this distinction in mind, we can illustrate continuities and changes in parental family roles in relation to domestic labour. This refers to the maintenance of a home and family, and involves a range of day-to-day tasks, such as cooking, cleaning and childcare. Several observations about contemporary patterns of domestic labour within the UK emerge from recent studies.

■ Gershuny et al. (2006) observe that women of all ages, ethnicities and classes do more domestic labour than men. Women spend more time on routine domestic tasks, while men spend more time on jobs such as repairs and gardening. This division of labour reflects both traditional assumptions about parental roles and the fact that men, on average, spend more time in the paid workforce.

■ Kan (2001) found that while levels of female housework were marginally reduced by paid employment, retirement or unemployment increased female housework and reduced that of her partner.

■ Ramos (2003) notes that domestic labour is more likely to be equally distributed when the male is unemployed and his partner works full time.

■ Pleck (1985) argues that where parents hold 'traditional gender beliefs' women do more housework than in families where beliefs reflect sexual equality.

■ In households where partners hold conflicting beliefs, men do less domestic work and where there are no clear gender associations with particular tasks, such as pet care, these are performed equally.

Why do women do more domestic labour than men?

Although more women are now in paid employment, women still do the majority of work within the home. This is particularly evident in families with dependent children. Women in this situation generally perform many of the mundane aspects of childcare, such as feeding and clothing, while men focus on the less mundane, such as playing with their children. Willmott (2000), however, argues there is less reliance on 'traditional roles when dividing up tasks in the home'. Changing family (and wider social) relationships mean that domestic labour is 'negotiated by every couple depending on their individual circumstances'. The significant factors in determining 'who does what' in the family are time and inclination 'not whether they are a man or a women'.

Cultural beliefs about male and female abilities and roles may also help explain domestic labour differences. Pilcher (1988) found that older people, unlike their younger counterparts, did not talk about 'equality' but instead thought about gender roles, responsibilities and relationships in treaditional ways about gender roles. This reflected their socialisation and life experiences, where 'men undertook limited household work, married women

had limited involvement in paid work and a marked gendered division of labour was the norm.'

Children and parents

Children's family roles are intimately connected to their relationship with their parents. We can gain a clearer understanding of the contemporary role of children by noting what Archard (2004) calls 'a *dissimilarity* in ideas about childhood between past and present'. How parents relate to children has changed, not just in terms of their different roles in pre-industrial and industrial societies, but also in relation to postmodernity. Fionda (2002), for example, suggests that adults in contemporary societies view children in several different ways:

■ As objects of concern requiring care and protection *from* their parents. In the UK, much recent family policy casts children in this role, with the state 'stepping in' to reduce the damage done to a child's physical, emotional and psychological development by 'dysfunctional' family relationships (child abuse is an extreme example of this kind of relationship).

■ As autonomous possessors of rights who should enjoy similar levels of freedom to adults and who should not be denied the rights adults take for granted, such as protection from assault. This interpretation makes children accountable for their actions – if they demand or are given adult rights in terms of what they do, how they do it and with whom it is done, they must take responsibility for their behaviour.

■ As lacking moral consciousness. Their status as children means they cannot be expected to show full moral responsibilities. They should therefore not be subject to the same reprisals (such as criminal law) as adults.

These ideas reflect a basic uncertainty about the status and role of children in contemporary families. Are they individuals in their own right or dependent on adults? Aries (1962) argues that in pre-industrial societies the relationship was more clear-cut: children were 'little adults', considered an economic asset to the family. They dressed, lived and worked like adults. Robertson (2001), however, argues that we have reached a stage in post-industrial society where children have become 'economically worthless and emotionally priceless'. This marks a significant status change that has altered parent–child roles and relationships. While children may have less paid employment now than in the past, they make some economic general contribution to family life through domestic labour. Although Bonke (1999) argues that in most cases this is a relatively small contribution, Howard (2010) reports that substantial numbers of children in the UK – between 100,000 and 700,000 – take on 'caring responsibilities such as dressing, washing or bathing family members'.

What does the idea that children are 'economically worthless and emotionally priceless' mean?

Postman (1994) argues that modern communication systems, such as television, the internet and mobile phones, have changed the child–adult relationship that developed throughout the modern industrial period. In terms of their criminality, sexuality and dress, children have become more like adults – similar to their status in pre-industrial society. Adults, however, have become more like children by equating 'youthfulness' with health, vitality and excitement.

Robertson argues that as the distinction between child and adults becomes less clear, family roles and relationships are more focused on allowing children to find their own general way in life. According to Mann, this involves the 'rise of more democratic forms of parent–child relationships … children are having an input in decision making'. However, his relationship can be both uneasy and uncertain. In modern societies, technology means that children have access to a wealth of knowledge about the adult world. Robertson suggests that roles and responsibilities in postmodernity are rapidly changing, with children increasingly seeing the world through the eyes of *consumers*, encouraged to buy

goods and services, such as mobile phones, formerly the preserve of adults.

Advertisers target 'children's markets', which leads to a consumption culture that encourages children to locate their identity and sense of self in what they consume. In the postmodern society, children develop a status as autonomous individuals rather than dependent beings; they acquire 'rights' formerly only extended to adults. As a result, children become more rebellious, sexually precocious and active. They become involved adult world that requires them to be increasingly sophisticated and less 'child-like'. These changes, in turn, affect how children are raised. They may have greater control over their own social development, but they must also take responsibility for their mistakes.

These changes are linked to contemporary ideas about the role of fathers. In some ways, parent–child relationships in postmodernity resemble those of the past, particularly the idea of children as 'little adults' with rights and responsibilities. However, the situation has not entirely reverted to that of pre-industrial societies – children are banned from numerous 'adult' experiences, such as drinking, smoking and sexual activity. This 'postmodern ambivalence' is reflected in changes to perceptions of parental roles. In particular, the role of the father has become more uncertain. Is his role one of economic provision, emotional and psychological provision, a combination of both – or neither?

Grandparents

Grandparents were once considered an economic and emotional drain on family resources. Today, however, Bengston (2001) argues that grandparents represent 'a valuable new resource for families', particularly in relation to childcare. Grandparenting is not a new phenomenon, as Anderson's study of 19th-century Lancashire revealed: 'Most working mothers had a co-resident grandmother who looked after the children in return for her own keep.' It is the extent of grandparenting in modern societies that is new. Wellard, for example, notes that around 30% of UK families 'depend on grandparents for childcare'. This figure increases to nearly 50% in lone-parent families.

Smallwood and Wilson (2007) argue that has led to modifications in family structures. While 'the once classic extended family is now almost extinct', extended family networks that include grandparents have become more important. Rake (2009) argues that we should not see families in terms of *either* nuclear *or* extended structures, but rather in terms of 'whole family' extended networks. She notes that grandparents now provide childcare for 'more than two million British families' with around '200,000 grandparents as sole carers'. As work pressures leave mothers with less time for childcare, communal parenting 'will become commonplace in many families', for reasons that include:

- more women working
- parents working long and unsociable hours
- the high cost of childcare
- longer active life expectancy.

The contribution of grandparents is not restricted to childcare. Rake estimates that '90% of grandparents now provide some form of financial support for their grandchildren', and Broad et al. (2001) suggest that inter-generational ties are important for sociability and emotional support. This relationship is not, however, one-way. Brannen notes that longer life expectancy in industrial societies results in more children returning to the family home to provide financial and domestic care for their parent/s.

Grandparents have become an increasingly valuable family resource, especially in an age in which more mothers have to work for a living

Mann argues that family roles and responsibilities are increasingly open to negotiation. The breakdown of rigid social identities in postmodernity means there is no longer a 'right' and a 'wrong' way to perform such roles. This applies to grandparents as well as parents and children. Negotiation, however, is a two-way process and, as Mann

argues: 'Most grandparents want to help out, but they do not necessarily want to provide child care on a full time basis. Grandparents can no longer be taken as "door mats".'

While negotiation and choice are clearly important, the influence of wider social factors should not be ignored. The American Academy of Child and Adolescent Psychiatry (2011) reports that while 'an increasing number of children in the United States live in households headed by a grandparent', this is mainly due to:

- high rates of divorce, lone parenthood and teenage pregnancy
- parental illness, disability, imprisonment or death
- parental abuse or neglect.

TEST YOURSELF

Briefly explain why 'we shouldn't see families in terms of *either* nuclear *or* extended structures'.

ACTIVITY

Farson (1974) argues for 'a children's liberation' where every child has the right to:

- *exercise choice in their own living arrangements*
- *information that is accessible to adults*
- *choose belief systems, including to educate oneself*
- *sexual freedom*
- *work*
- *vote*
- *freedom from physical punishment*
- *justice*
- *own property*
- *travel independently*
- *whatever drugs their elders use.*

Which of these 'rights' do you agree or disagree with?

Conjugal roles and debates about gender equality within the family

Functionalism

Traditional functionalist approaches see family development in evolutionary terms. From this perspective, asymmetrical gender relationships, where males and females have separate roles characteristic of the early industrial family, gradually give way to symmetrical relationships based on joint conjugal roles in late/post-industrial society. This is based on the idea that as societies pass through different stages of industrialisation, gender roles gradually converge through a process of what Willmott and Young (1973) call 'stratified diffusion'. As conjugal roles in the upper class moved towards greater equality, these changes 'trickled down' the class structure. They were adopted next by middle-class families and, by the middle of the 20th century, the working class.

On this basis, Sullivan et al. (2008) suggest that industrial societies have experienced a 'quiet revolution' in conjugal roles based on a general acceptance of gender equality. Evidence for this can be seen in:

- increased male housework
- decreased female housework
- men devoting more time to childcare
- the family group becoming more home-centred.

Two further developments include the **new man** – an identity that developed in the 1980s when men began to take on a greater share of domestic work – and the New Father, someone who combines a traditional masculinity with being 'a good, caring and responsible' father. McMahon (1999), however, calls the new man a 'fantasy – most men have little interest in changing the patterns of child care and housework'.

KEY TERM

New man: someone who combines paid work with their share of domestic labour.

Neo-functionalism

Traditional functionalism theorises men and women playing different family roles. Men generally take an **instrumental role**, dealing with people in an objective, unemotional way, based on a mutually beneficial relationship. For men to be successful in their provider role outside the family, they need instrumental orientations. Because they traditionally spend more time within the family, women tend to take an **expressive** role; dealing with family members on the basis of love and affection.

KEY TERM

Instrumental/expressive role: instrumental roles involve dealing with people in an objective, unemotional way, based on what they can do for us and what we can do for them. Expressive roles are the opposite – they involve dealing with people on the basis of love and affection.

Swenson (2004) offers a different interpretation of conjugal roles. He focuses on adults, including lone parents, as providers of a safe, stable family environment for primary socialisation. From this perspective, parents give their children a knowledge of both expressive and instrumental relationships and it does not matter which partner provides which; For Swenson, conjugal roles in contemporary families can be fluid. Women can provide instrumental values and men expressive values (or vice versa depending on specific family conditions and relationships). Same-sex families can perform these roles. Lone-parent families are not automatically excluded since the parent may successfully combine both roles or they may have help from others, such as extended family members, who provide the alternative role. For example, grandparents may play an expressive role while the parent's role is instrumental. Swenson does believe that the source of 'antisocial behaviour' in children is the *instability* of family roles and relationships. 'Optimal socialisation' takes place in stable (married) families where both parents play complementary roles.

What's new about neo-functionalism?

Marxism

Marxist analyses focus on families as social spaces involving complex conflicts and power struggles. Morgan (2001) illustrates this through three 'family economies':

1 The political economy centres on the economic aspect of family life. According to Pahl (2007), this involves understanding how money is 'received, controlled and managed before being allocated to spending'. This involves a resource theory where power struggles are an inevitable part of conjugal relationships; those

who control the most valued resources, such as family income, have the greatest power. In this respect, financial decision-making indicates where power lies, and Pahl and Vogler (1994) found men made the most important financial decisions. Other areas of major decision-making in dual-earner families relate to whose work has the greatest priority when, for example, the family relocates due to a change in employment. Hardill (2003) found that women were more likely to be the 'trailing spouse', revealing that male occupations had greatest priority.

2   The moral economy refers to the values and norms relating to the conjugal roles and responsibilities of different family members. The female partner can exercise high levels of power through her ability to organise family resources and behaviours even where her partner may be the only breadwinner.

3   The emotional economy relates to interpersonal relationships and what Dallos et al. (1997) call 'affective power'. If someone 'loves you' this gives you power. Pahl suggests that this 'family power' can be subtle. It can shift depending on such factors as who 'loves' the other the most: the partner who 'loves least' can use this to exert power over the one who 'loves more'.

Like any institution in capitalist society, families involve power struggles. These might take place openly, in the form of domestic violence, or covertly in the form of decision-making. Domestic violence involves a range of behaviours, both physical and emotional, aimed at aggressively controlling another family member. The extent of domestic violence is difficult to estimate, as many victims do not report the attacks. Kirkwood (1993) notes that there are several possible reasons for this:

■   the victim's low self-esteem (a belief that they 'deserve it')
■   economic or psychological dependence on the perpetrator
■   fear of further consequences (*repeat victimisation*).

Nicholas et al. (2007) note that around 75% of victims are female and Coleman et al. (2007) suggest that around 40% of victims experience domestic abuse more than once.

TEST YOURSELF

Suggest one reason why domestic violence is a 'crime prone to repeat victimisation'.

Feminism and conjugal roles

Different types of feminism have slightly different perspectives on conjugal roles.

Liberal: Liberal feminism is based on the idea of equality of opportunity. In a conjugal relationship, men and women should be free to choose both their roles and how these are performed in a family context. This 'softer' form of feminism promotes 'practical and realistic' ways of creating a gender balance within the family. This recognises that some women choose to focus on domestic and child-rearing responsibilities, others focus on a career and some want (or need) to combine family and work responsibilities. Equality of opportunity is based on the idea that men and women can compete equally in both the private and public domains. Other forms of feminism argue that male cultural capital, resulting from ingrained patriarchal ideas about 'male and female capabilities', gives them an advantage in both the home and the workplace.

Marxist: This applies Marxist ideas about economic equalities to an explanation of gender inequalities in conjugal roles in capitalist societies. Women perform a service role in the family, which gives them the status of 'unpaid servants'. This role is sometimes performed willingly, but more often they take on this responsibility because their partner is unable or unwilling to do so. With more women now entering paid employment they may be doubly exploited, in the public sphere as paid employees and in the private sphere as unpaid workers whose labour primarily benefits men. As noted earlier, Duncombe and Marsden (1993) argue that women may perform a triple shift – through the emotional work they invest time and effort in the psychological well-being of family members.

Marxist feminists, therefore, argue that women increasingly suffer from two forms of economic exploitation: *patriarchal*, as unpaid domestic labourers whose work benefits men and *capitalist* as paid employees whose labour creates profits for a ruling class. In this respect, capitalism is the 'real cause of female oppression' because it involves relations of domination, subordination and oppression. Female exploitation inside and outside the family will continue for as long as capitalism exists. Gender is a 'secondary' form of exploitation – one that will disappear once primary (economic) forms of exploitation are resolved.

Radical: Radical feminism sees patriarchy as the primary source of male domination within the family. It believes that this problem can be resolved in a range of ways. Firestone (1970) argues that biology is the essential gender difference from which all cultural differences flow. The fact that women experience pregnancy and are forced to depend on men creates a 'culture of sex discrimination'. If technology can free women from this biological dependency, by enabling children to be born outside the womb, an essential gender difference will be eliminated and male powers of discrimination will disappear.

A second argument believes that should exploit the 'values of femininity' such as a sense of community, family, empathy and sharing. These are the characteristics that make them different from men, whose interests are built on patriarchal values of aggressiveness, selfishness and greed. Women should embrace the power reproduction gives because, for Stanworth (1987), it is 'the foundation of women's identity'. Stanworth argues that women must reject the technologies embraced by writers such as Firestone as a further source of male power and domination – by taking away one of the most important differences between men and women – the ability to reproduce.

Frieden (1963) and Millett (1969) see the patriarchal structures and practices of the family itself as the source of female oppression. Friedan argues that 'a housewife is a parasite' because she is forced to depend on men for her social existence. The solution to gender inequality is either the abandonment of the patriarchal family or the development of matriarchal family structures and conjugal roles that exclude men through, for example, lesbian relationships.

Post-feminism rejects the claim that any single theory can explain the position of women in society. The social position of different groups of women varies considerably so it is futile to try to construct a theory that explains the position of *all* women. Sociological explanations of gender inequality, for example, need to be more tailored to particular groups of women, such as those from the middle class or from a specific ethnic background. Post-feminists argue that female histories and experiences are too diverse and fragmented for *all* women to have common interests as a sex class.

KEY TERM

Post-feminism: post-feminist theory is an approach to understanding gender inequality that seeks to avoid single, over-arching explanations of the position of women.

For post-feminism, alternative feminist perspectives ignore or downplay the idea of women making choices – to be

Is gender just a matter of performance?

mothers or childless career women, for example. Butler rejects the idea that 'biology is destiny' – men and women do not have 'essential natures' (the former as aggressive and competitive, the latter as compassionate and nurturing). Rather, the key to changing conjugal roles is understanding how gender is performed. The rigid separation of work and home that developed in modern industrial societies cannot be sustained in postmodern, post-industrial societies. Both men and women move freely into and out of the public domain today.

Contemporary families, therefore, develop around a gender understanding in which conjugal roles are based on rational choices about 'who does what and when'. Men and women perform different, complementary and interchangeable conjugal roles. Specific family roles, such as childcare, are no longer the responsibility of one gender.

Post-feminists believe that Marxist and radical feminists have ignored important changes in male and female family lives, roles and relationships over the past 50 years. With increasing numbers of women rejecting motherhood, for example, it is natural that many women no longer see themselves in these terms. Women can construct their personal identities in a range of ways, one of which involves 'reclaiming femininity from men'. Women can be both 'feminine', in terms of seeking and gaining pleasure from the care of others, and 'careerist' in the sense of wanting economic independence and security. Post-feminists, therefore, argue that conjugal roles are about how different men and women construct and negotiate their lifestyles and identities. Unlike other feminisms, this approach suggests we should not underestimate a woman's urge to be closely involved in the nurture and care of her

127

children, nor should we disrespect women for making such choices.

Changing patterns of marriage, cohabitation, separation, divorce and childbearing; the causes and consequences of these changes

Our evidence for changing forms of family association across a range of social categories is based, for illustrative purposes, on statistical data drawn from the UK.

However, explanations for these patterns can be applied to a range of modern industrial societies.

Marriage

Marriage patterns are often complicated by **serial monogamy** (people can marry, divorce and remarry). This makes simple comparisons between past and present less reliable because we may be counting the same people more than once. Marriage statistics such as those in Table 5.1 do, however, tell us something about general marriage patterns.

While raw numbers are useful, they are also sensitive to population changes; the larger the population, the higher the number of potential marriages. For this reason, it is better to look at marriage rates (the number of marriages per 1000 in a population); something we can compare with selected European countries (Table 5.2).

Year	All marriages ('000s)	1st marriage ('000s)	Remarriage ('000s)	Remarriage as % of all marriages
1901	360	–	–	–
1950	408	330	78	19
1960	394	336	58	15
1970	471	389	82	17
1990	375	241	134	36
1999	301	180	121	40
2000	306	180	126	41
2004	311	190	121	39
2006	250	149	101	40
2007	242	143	99	41
2009	235	151	84	36

Table 5.1   Marriage patterns (England and Wales)

Source: Adapted from Self and Zealey (2007); Hughes and Church (2010); Beaumont (2011)

Country	Marriage rate per 1000 people
Cyprus	7.8
Denmark	6.7
Malta	5.9
United Kingdom	5.2
EU average (27 countries)	4.9
Sweden	4.9
France	4.5
Belgium	4.1
Slovenia	2.9

Table 5.2   Marriage rates in the European Community, 2005

Source: Self (2008)

Although there has been a consistent overall decline in marriage and a steady decline in first marriages, this has been offset to some extent by remarriages. Remarriages peaked in the 1980s and have since slowly declined, but as a percentage of all marriages, remarriage has *doubled* in the past 50 years, peaking around the turn of the 21st century and slowly declining over the past 10 years.

Causes of marital changes: Explanations for marital changes fall into two broad groups. The first suggests that the general decline can be explained by demographic changes rather than a change in people's behaviour. Marriage in the UK was most popular just after the Second World War and during the 1970s. During these periods, there was a 'baby boom' when a greater than average number of babies were born over a relatively short time. The Second World War prevented many couples starting a family, and by the 1950s the average span for family completion (from first to last child) was a historically short 10 years. *Family compression* produced a population bulge – a rapid, if temporary, increase in the number of children. This goes some way to explaining both an increase in marriage and childbirth during the 1950s and the numbers marrying in the 1970s and 80s as the 'baby boom generation' reached adulthood.

A related explanation is that, in any society, some age groups (cohorts) are more likely than others to marry. This means there are 'peak periods' for marriage (the age range at which marriage is *more likely*). Hughes (2009), for example, reports that in 1977 the average

age at first marriage for women was 23. By 2007, this had increased to 29. The more people there are in this age range, the more marriages there are likely to be. The relationship between this marriageable cohort and other age cohorts is also significant, because the number of children or elderly in a population affects marriage statistics. Children are not legally allowed to marry in most countries and the elderly are less likely to marry. The UK, in common with many industrial societies, has an ageing population, in which the elderly outnumber the young. The size of these two cohorts affects marriage statistics. If we focus on those *most likely* to marry – the marriageable population – we find only a relatively small decline in marriage rates over the past 30 years.

A second set of explanations focuses on wider influences on people's behaviour. There is now less stigma attached to having children outside marriage and there is also less social pressure to get married. Women now have more career opportunities, which allows them greater financial independence. As a result, there is less economic pressure for them to marry. Oswald (2002) argues that increased female financial, career and personal independence means that marriage is now a 'lifestyle choice', and women are less likely to enter a relationship that restricts their ability to work and develop a career.

Cohabitation (see below) as an alternative to marriage has increased in recent years and although many cohabiting couples eventually marry, many do not. Self and Zealey suggest that *falling* marriage and *rising* cohabitation are the result of more people choosing to delay marriage until later in life. Similarly, Hughes and Church note that in 2010 around 10% of families with dependent children were single (never-married) mothers, compared to 1% in 1971. There has also been an increase in those choosing to remain single and childless.

Secularisation processes, whereby the influence of religious beliefs has generally declined, leads to changes in the meaning and significance of marriage. As secularisation has spread, there is less pressure to marry and the importance of the institution of marriage has declined. Finally, Beck (1992) argues that people in postmodern societies increasingly assess the *likely* risks and consequences of their actions. The statistical likelihood of divorce, with its attendant emotional and economic consequences, can lead to the *avoidance of risk* by not marrying.

129

TEST YOURSELF

Identify two long-term trends in UK marriage.

Cohabitation

Although Gillis (1985) argues that common-law marriage, where a couple live together 'as if married', was extensively practised in the past, **cohabitation** is not legally recorded in the UK and this limits the reliability of the data. Over the past 25 years, however, survey methods have produced more reliable estimates, with Hughes and Church (2010) identifying a broad increase in cohabitation, from 10% of couples in 1986 to 25% in 2006. Around 25% of young people (25–29) now cohabit, compared with around 18% in the mid 1990s. There has also been a generational increase in female cohabitation. Of those aged 55–59, 1% had cohabited before the age of 25; of those aged 25–29, 25% currently cohabit. The proportion of cohabiting couple *families* has also increased significantly in the past 10 years – from 9% to 15% of all families.

KEY TERM

Cohabitation: a relationship where two people live together as if they were married.

In a general sense, increases in cohabitation are explained by factors such as:

- reduced social pressures to marry
- lower levels of stigma attached to living with someone without being married
- the wider availability of contraception/abortion.

Causes: Smart and Stevens (2000) suggest four main reasons for recent upward trends in cohabitation:

1   Changing attitudes to marriage: these range from indifference to the institution of marriage itself to uncertainty about whether a partner is 'suitable' for marriage.
2   For some, cohabitation represents a trial for their partner to prove they can settle down, gain and keep paid work and interact successfully with the mother's children. Self and Zealey suggest that later marriage is a factor here; before marriage, males and females move into and out of serial cohabitation – one cohabiting relationship followed by another.
3   Many cohabiting parents are either unwilling to enter into a legal relationship or they believe it is easier to leave a cohabiting relationship if it does not work out.
4   There may be a philosophical opposition to marriage, and some people believe that cohabitation leads to more equal relationships. Smart and Stevens note two basic forms of 'commitment to cohabitation': contingent, where couples cohabited 'until they were sure it was safe or sensible to become permanently committed or married', and mutual, where couples felt as committed to each other and their children as married couples.

TEST YOURSELF

Identify one long-term trend in cohabitation.

Divorce

Keeping in mind that divorce has been both a legal and financial possibility for most people in the UK for only around 60 years, we can begin by looking at a statistical breakdown of divorce (Table 5.3).

Year	No. of divorces ('000s)	Average age at divorce	
		Males	Females
1921	3	–	–
1941	7	–	–
1947	47	–	–
1951	29	–	–
1961	20	–	–
1971	80	39	37
1981	160	38	35
1991	180	39	36
2001	157	42	39
2007	129	43	40
2008	136	44	41
2009	127	44	42

Table 5.3   Divorce in the UK

Source: Office for National Statistics (2000–2010)

In the early to mid 20th century, there was a relatively small number of divorces. An anomaly occurred in the late 1940s, as people who married in haste during wartime realised their mistake when the war ended. However, over the past 40 years, divorce has become more common, peaking in the 1990s. In recent years there has been a general decline in divorce, although since 1981 there has been a doubling of 're-divorces' – people experiencing multiple marriages and divorces. One clear pattern is that divorcees have been getting older – a fact that reflects the later average age of marriage.

As with marriage, raw numbers are also sensitive to population changes. Ignoring any other factors, the higher the number of marriages, the greater the likelihood of a *proportion* ending in divorce. For this reason, it is more reliable to look at divorce rates, which peaked at the turn of the 21st century and have since gradually declined.

Causes: Patterns of divorce are affected by a range of social factors. One of the most significant of these factors is legal change: each time divorce is made easier or more affordable, the number of divorces increases. However, it is important to note that changes to the rules about of divorce can create reliability problems. For example, the 1969 Divorce Reform Act in the UK, introduced 'irretrievable breakdown of marriage' as the only requirement for divorce. Before that, one partner had to 'find fault' (such as adultery) with the other. We do not know how many people in 1968 *would* have divorced if the new rules had applied then.

TEST YOURSELF

Suggest two long-term trends in divorce.

In this respect, economic changes probably play a more crucial role than legal ones. In 1949, legal aid was made available to divorcing couples, which meant that divorce was no longer something that only the rich could do. As more women became financially independent, divorce also became a viable option for them. The development of the welfare state meant that the partner who took on sole care of any children after divorce was also provided for financially. Hughes notes that around 35% of divorces today are childless, which makes dissolving a marriage less complicated, both emotionally and financially.

More generally, the process of secularisation means that many couples no longer regard marriage as a 'sacred institution' that must be preserved. There is also less stigma attached to divorce. In addition, increasing life expectancy in modern societies means that a marriage has longer to last, which may place greater strain on a relationship, increasing the chances of divorce. Clarke and Berrington (1999) identify a number of other risk factors in relationships that can lead to **marital breakdown**:

- Young (especially teenage) couples are statistically more likely to divorce.
- Populations with a large proportion of married couples involve higher divorce risks.
- Short courtships: Becker et al. (1977) argue that *stable* marriage relationships occur when each partner is well matched; short courtships do not give couples enough time to ensure they are well suited.

KEY TERM

Marital breakdown: the ending of a legal marital relationship for reasons other than the death of a partner.

Finally, contemporary ideas about marriage are arguably governed by romantic individualism. Couples enter a relationship seeking to fulfil their *personal interests* in the partnership in one of two ways:

- Romantic love, where the love given to a partner is unconditional, but if one partner 'falls out of love' there is nothing to hold the marriage together.
- **Confluent love** where love is *contingent* – one partner gives it in return for something else. For example, one partner may marry because they believe this will enhance their social status (what Coverman calls 'status enhancement'). If this fails to happen or changes over time, there is nothing to keep the couple together.

KEY TERM

Confluent love: refers to the idea of love being contingent; it is given in return for something else.

Marriage, therefore, is increasingly a search for personal happiness rather than a moral commitment, and this may explain the increase in *remarriages*. Divorcees are not unhappy with *marriage*, they are unhappy with the person they married. Becker et al. argue that a mismatch between what someone *expects* to happen in a marriage and what *actually* happens is likely to result in divorce. People may have romanticised ideas about love and family life. When they realise that such ideas are unrealistic, they choose divorce as a way out of an unhappy experience.

Divorce Decree

Is divorce just a result of falling out of love?

Childbearing

Chamberlain and Gill (2005) note that the total number of live births in the UK fell from a peak of just over 1 million at the start of the 20th century to around 700,000 at its end. Statistically, there has been a general overall decline in live births, even taking into account the significant increases that followed the two World Wars ('baby booms') and a further spike in the mid 1960s as the children of the post-war baby boom had children of their own.

Over the past 50 years, changing patterns of childbearing can be summarised in terms of:

- a decline in birth rates, from around 30 live births per 1,000 people in 1900 to around 10 in 2010
- a decline in family size from an average of 3 to 1.6 children, although this has *risen* slightly over the past decade
- an increase in the average age at which women have their first child
- births outside marriage now account for nearly half of all births.

However, by looking at the average number of children born to women of childbearing age (roughly between the ages of 15 and 44), it is possible to get a more reliable picture of changes in family size in terms of **fertility rates** (Table 5.4).

KEY TERM

Fertility rate: a measure of the number of children born to women of childbearing age (usually taken as 15–44) in a society each year.

Number of children born per 1,000 women of childbearing age (usually taken to be 15–44)	
1959	2.60
1969	2.40
1979	1.80
1989	1.70
1999	1.60
2000	1.65
2001	1.63
2005	1.70
2008	1.97
2009	1.96

Table 5.4   Fertility rate, England and Wales

Source: Office for National Statistics (2010)

By way of comparison, India has a long-term rising birth rate (Table 5.5), although it is significant that over the past 25 years this has started to stabilise.

Year	Millions
1964	19.0
1971	22.0
1991	27.0
2001	27.1
2009	27.2

Table 5.5   Live birth statistics: India

Source: United Nations (2010a)

Fertility rates in India have fallen significantly in both the long and the short term, just as they have in the UK. (Table 5.6).

Number of children born per 1000 women of childbearing age (usually taken to be 15–44)	
1959	5.90
1969	5.70
1979	4.90
1989	4.10
1999	3.30
2000	1.65
2005	2.90
2009	2.70

Table 5.6   Fertility rate, India

Source: United Nations (2010a)

Causes: In the later part of the 20th century, there was an increase in female workforce participation. This applied to what Rapoport and Rapoport (1969) term 'dual-career families', where both partners work, as well as single career women. One consequence of this is that women are marrying and having children later in their lives. This trend towards 'later family formation' partly explains a general decline in childbearing. Women have a limited fertility span and are unlikely to have large families during their 30s and early 40s. Economic and cultural factors also play a part in smaller family sizes. For example, it is becoming increasingly expensive to raise children, and many women choose to remain childless – the Organisation for Economic Co-operation and Development (OECD) reports that the UK has one of highest levels of childlessness in Europe.

The reasons for this are linked to factors such as female career development and the fact that many people now feel that parenthood would disrupt their lives. Tiffen and Gittins (2004) argue that women are now less likely to accept personal and social identities built around the home and motherhood, while McAllister and Clarke note that highly qualified women are more likely to remain childless. They suggest that many women deliberately choose independence over the constraints of childcare and material security over financial risk.

Concepts of risk and security help to explain both current birth rates and, by extension, the trend towards smaller family sizes. Smithers (2012) reports that the cost of raising a child in the UK is more than £200,000. While the reliability and validity of such calculations

is can be questioned (estimates tend to be worked out by insurance companies who have a vested interest in inflating costs), it is reasonable to assume that cost is a consideration for many prospective parents. In a society where, as Graham notes, there is 'less need for children as a protection against old age and illness', risk can be managed through birth control – either contraception or abortion. Beaumont reports that that 21% of all conceptions in England and Wales are legally terminated.

Why do contemporary families have less need for children as 'insurance against old age'?

Consequences: While the evidence we have presented points strongly to significant changes in family formation over the past century, the consequences of these changes are much more difficult to define. Neale (2000) asks: 'How are we to view the diversity and fluidity of contemporary patterns of partnering, parenting and kinship? With optimism or as a cause for concern?'

New right: cause for concern

A fundamental principle of the new-right approach is the idea that the 'traditional nuclear family' consisting of two, heterosexual, married adults, with clearly defined gender roles and relationships is the institution best equipped to provide the foundation on which all other social relationships are built. Diversity represents a family breakdown that has significant consequences for both individual members and wider social relationships. Essentially, the new approach states that stable nuclear family relationships provide emotional and psychological benefits to family members. In turn, these benefit society as a whole because each adult partner

133

plays a role that involves both personal sacrifice and commitment to others.

From this perspective, the idea that all types of family structure are equal (*moral relativism*) is wrong, because it challenges the moral commitment to others that lies at the heart of social responsibility. The new right endorses social policies that encourage 'beneficial' family structures and discourage forms such as single parenthood that are regarded as damaging to both individuals and communities. Morgan's (2000) argument against cohabitation, for example, illustrates this interpretation of family diversity as a source of social problems by suggesting that cohabitation suffers from three important deficiencies when compared to marriage:

1   It is lightweight and 'always more likely to fracture than marriages entered into at the same time, regardless of age and income'. Another reason for instability is that cohabiting couples are more sexually promiscuous than married couples; they 'behave more like single people than married people'.

2   Cohabitation outside of marriage is fragmentary, because cohabitants with children who marry are more likely to divorce. Of those who never marry, '50% of the women will be lone unmarried mothers by the time the child is ten'. One reason for this is that cohabitation for women is 'not so much an ideal lifestyle choice as the best arrangement they can make at the time'.

3   The relationship is more likely to be abusive: both women and children are at greater risk of physical and sexual abuse 'than they would be in married relationships'.

More generally, new-right approaches argue that family and relationship diversity is undesirable, dysfunctional and indicative of family breakdown because it is confusing to individuals. This can lead to a 'moral anarchy', in which some behaviours, such as abortion practices that take no account of the 'rights of the unborn', produce morally undesirable results.

A counter to family breakdown, therefore, is 'family uniformity'. The traditional heterosexual nuclear family is more desirable than other family structures because it provides social, economic and psychological stability, family continuity and successful primary socialisation. In such an environment, 'traditional' family values can be emphasised and reinforced, creating a sense of individual and social responsibility that forms a barrier against 'rampant, selfish, individualism'. As Horwitz

(2005) argues, within the traditional family, children and adults learn *moral values* that they take into wider social relationships. Traditional nuclear families, therefore, are a vital source of both individual happiness and social stability because they have a moral core that involves:

- caring for family members
- taking responsibility for both their own behaviour and that of their children
- unconditional economic co-operation
- the development of stable, successful, interpersonal relationships.

Even in the midst of great social changes, families still have a role in providing social care for one another

Critics of the new-right approach argue that it is based on an idealised view of white, middle-class families as the desirable norm. It advocates a 'one size fits all' family in a society no longer characterised by moral and normative consensus and conformity. It also ignores the darker side of traditional family life. Making divorce more difficult for example, may indeed persuade some to try to make their marriage work, but it also traps others in a loveless relationship characterised by violence and abuse.

TEST YOURSELF

Why is 'family breakdown' seen as a problem by the new right?

Postmodern optimism

Finch (2003) argues that while new-right approaches presume 'a standard model of family life' for which governments must, if necessary, legislate – people must be made to follow an approved set of choices – postmodern approaches involve a radically different interpretation of family diversity; 'a family' is whatever people want it to be. This rejects the idea of '*the* family' and argues that people construct relationships in ways *they* believe are acceptable and appropriate. Family groups, therefore, are arenas in which individuals play out their personal narratives (*life stories*). The emphasis here is on choice; people increasingly make behavioural decisions that suit their particular needs, desires and circumstances, regardless of what others may believe or think. In this respect, postmodern societies are characterised by several different family forms, each of which is *exclusive*. In every family, people work out their personal choices and lifestyles as best they can. As Stacey (2002) puts it: 'Every family is an alternative family.'

For Elkins (1992), postmodernity is characterised by a permeable family that 'encompasses many different family forms':

- traditional or nuclear
- two parents working
- single parent
- blended (reconstituted)
- adopted child
- test-tube
- surrogate mother
- co-parent.

She argues that the modern family, involving the 'traditional family structure' that the new right encourages is 'one that spoke to our need to *belong* at the expense, particularly for women, of the need to *become*'. The **postmodern (*permeable*) family**, however, 'celebrates the need to *become* at the expense of the need to *belong*'. Suematsu (2004) goes further by questioning the usefulness of family groups in postmodernity: 'A family is essentially a unit of support. There were days when human beings could not survive without it. Those days are over.' As Zeitlin et al. (1995) argue, postmodernity frees people from the constraints of the past and offers new ways of *thinking*, *acting* and *being* that are played out in families.

How do postmodern families speak to our need to *become*?

From this perspective, there is no single, correct, way to 'be a family'. Families are simply 'individual organisations', tailored to their members' specific needs and desires. As such, it makes no sense to talk about their 'functions' or 'oppressive and exploitative structures'. Rather, we should 'celebrate difference'. Family diversity should be embraced, either because it points towards an *optimistic* change in family roles and relationships, or because we are powerless to prevent it. Postmodern societies are increasingly global sites of conflict, where what happens in one has significant consequences for others.

The constant exposure to new ideas, through global cultural agencies such as the internet, makes people question traditional ways of thinking and behaving. Custom and tradition – the way things have always been done – have less influence than they once did. Diversity follows from the awareness and freedom to make different choices, including ones that were once denied – from divorce to same-sex families. Traditional types of family relationship, such as marriage and children, co-exist with newer forms, such as childlessness or living apart while maintaining family relationships. As exposure to different cultural ideas increases, what was once new and exotic becomes routine; individuals and societies gradually become more accepting of single-parent, surrogate-mother and **gay and lesbian families**. In the globalised world, Jagger and Wright (1999) argue, attempts to 'recapture an idealised "nuclear" version of family life where time stands still and traditional values are re-vitalised' is no longer an option.

KEY TERM

Postmodern family: idea that in postmodernity the focus of family members is on individual self-development.

KEY TERM

Gay and lesbian families: family group involving same-sex parents (gay males or lesbian females) and children, such as those from a previous heterosexual relationship.

Members of a Pakistani family in Chitral District. How does this ethnic group embody 'old-fashioned family values'?

For Neale, postmodernism involves a relational approach to understanding diversity, one where family relationships are increasingly played out in micro-networks. People negotiate their relationships to take account of their own personal needs and responsibilities, rather than worrying about what others in the community might think. Where a diversity of family roles, relationships and structures exists, it becomes more difficult to justify morality-based judgements about one way of living being better than another. Society in general becomes less judgemental about how others choose to form family relationships. These ideas reflect two recent processes that are a consequence of globalisation:

1   People are liberated from the constraints of traditional norms and values.

2   They exercise greater levels of choice and control over their personal relationships and sense of self; there are now more ways to 'be male or female' or 'a good partner'.

This individualisation of self and society ('what's right for me') means that social norms surrounding marriage, divorce or sexual freedom have changed. Mann (2009)

suggests that one result of this is greater freedom and flexibility in relationship choices: 'People are far more able to choose the intimate relationships that are important to them, and are more likely to end them if they no longer accord with their personal preferences and objectives.'

This interpretation is not, however, uncontested. Berthoud, for example, suggests that different ethnic groups embrace or reject these changes to different degrees:

■   At one extreme are those who cling to 'old-fashioned values', such as marriage, as a way of reinforcing a particular ethnic identity in a rapidly changing and confusing world. In the UK, Pakistani and Bangladeshi ethnicities are closest to this point.

■   At the other extreme are those who embrace 'modern individualism', where single parenthood or divorce are openly embraced. In the UK, both Black Caribbean and White ethnicities are closest to this point.

Other critics suggest that postmodernists overstate the extent to which people are disconnected from family and social networks. Although there is greater freedom of choice in contemporary societies, most people live and behave in broadly conventional ways, while recognising and tolerating 'unconventional' behaviours. Postmodernists confuse this toleration of 'life at the margins' with the idea that everyone embraces it unquestioningly. Similarly, choice is not unlimited; different classes, genders, ethnicities and age groups rarely have the same freedom of choice, and the consequences of making these choices are different for different groups. Divorce, for example, will have a different meaning to the non-religious than to someone whose religion looks unfavourably on it.

TEST YOURSELF

Briefly explain what is meant by the 'permeable family'.

ACTIVITY

Organise a class debate with the motion of 'This house believes the family has outlived its usefulness.' Select a new-right, feminist or postmodernist perspective and prepare your speech for the debate.

The impact of family life on individual members

How family life affects individuals is a matter of some sociological debate. Consensus theorists generally believe that the benefits of family life outweigh the drawbacks, while conflict theorists take the opposite view.

Consensus

Functionalists and neo-functionalists usually stress the positive aspects of family life, where the *benefits* outweigh the possible *costs*. They recognise that the family is not a perfect institution – it may be dysfunctional to some family members and some families have a 'darker side' of domestic violence and child abuse (Bell and Vogel, 1968). However, they believe it is the best we have in terms of fulfilling a range of needs and functions:

- companionship
- security (emotional, physical, sexual, psychological and economic)
- raising children.

Fletcher (1973) characterises the 20th-century family as a 'rewarding institution catering for individual self-realisation and autonomy'. We can develop this idea by illustrating the family's positive impact on individuals.

Postmodernist

While functionalists such as Parsons (1959b) argue that contemporary families play an important stabilising role for both the individual and society, postmodernists focus on *individual* psychological stability. This involves questions about identity – 'who we are' and how we understand our position in society.

Cultural globalisation has given people more choice about their everyday behaviour. However, the disadvantage of this almost unlimited choice is that it can cause uncertainty about who we are and how we are supposed to behave. The old certainties of class, gender, age and ethnic social identities no longer guide us on how to behave 'appropriately' in any given role, so our sense of identity has become increasingly decentred. Family life can also suffer from this decentring process, but people now have more choices about how to be a 'father' or 'daughter', for example, and their unique construction around kinship ties allows family members to centre identity on this group. In other words, families are a strong focal point that provides a much clearer sense of who we are and how we relate to others.

Stable family relationships provide significant emotional and psychological benefits to family members when we orientate our identity towards other family members. For example, adults frequently put the interests of their children or their partner above their own interests. In turn, the sense of personal and social responsibility created within families has wider benefits for the community because children are given clear moral and behavioural guidance. This general process also involves a sense of moral commitment to others that forms the basis of social responsibility. Within the family, adult partners play roles based on domestic labour and care for others, shared economic provision and so forth, indicative of both personal sacrifice and commitment to other family members. In return, Becker (1991) suggests, families generate 'psychic income' for their members – the psychological pleasures people gain from a relationship with those who share a sense of personal commitment, love and affection. In a wider sense, Anderson (1989) argues that families provide support networks that confer psychological and social benefits no longer provided by other social institutions. This includes ideas such as love, comfort and security to more practical concerns ranging from childcare to financial help.

What benefits do families bring to individual members?

TEST YOURSELF

Suggest two ways family benefits outweigh family costs.

Conflict

The conflict interpretation argues that the *costs* of family life outweigh its *benefits*. Within this approach, there are three general views – those who see the family as:

- psychologically destructive
- socially oppressive and exploitative of women
- violent and abusive institutions.

137

Critical theory

The first of the three views listed above is advanced by critical theorists:

- Leach (1967) argues that the close-knit family group is a source of social and psychological conflicts that damage people's lives.
- Laing and Esterson (1970) see the family as an 'emotionally exploitative' institution, and problems created within it are reproduced in society as a whole.
- Cooper (1972) suggests that the family group is an institution that stunts the individual's social/psychological development, restricts freedom of expression and results in the 'murder of their selves'.

This approach highlights the 'darker social and psychological side' to family life – Laing and Esterson (1970), for example, focus on the psychological damage family life does to children – and suggests the 'abolition of the family' as a solution.

However, the critical theory does not locate the family group within the structure of society as a whole to consider whether families serve a useful social purpose, regardless of how the lives of its individual members may be affected. More significantly, it does not suggest any viable alternative that would eliminate the psychological traumas that supposedly characterise contemporary family life. As we have seen, the attempt to abolish the family in the Soviet Union in the early 20th century was not a success.

Marxist feminism

The second viewpoint is advanced by Marxist feminists when they draw attention to the oppression and exploitation of women within the family. Most women take on an exploited role as 'unpaid servants' to their partner and children. This service role, especially when part of a double shift involving work inside and outside the home, contributes to the patriarchal exploitation of women as domestic labourers through the provision of 'free' physical, psychological, sexual and emotional services. In addition, women's lives within the family are oppressed in terms of:

- the 'housewife role': even though many women happily perform this role, willingness to identify domestic labour with femininity is a result of patriarchal ideology and socialisation
- violence within the family, where women are the main victims.

These interpretations propose *abolition* of either the family itself or the patriarchal family as a solution to the problem.

A different interpretation argues that while the benefits outweigh the costs for the *majority* of family members, *some* families are dysfunctional in terms of domestic violence and child abuse.

Why might many women willingly perform this role?

Domestic violence

Jansson et al. (2007) note that 3% of all women and 2% of all men in the UK experience either minor or severe violence at the hands of their partner. Dodd et al. (2005) report that 16% of *all* violent incidents involve domestic violence, with the majority of victims being female. Around 100 women each year – 40% of all female murder victims – are killed by a current or former partner; the comparable figure for men is around 6%. World Health Organization (2002) figures reveal that this pattern has a global dimension (Table 5.7), with around 70% of female murder victims killed by their male partner.

Country	%
Canada	29
Egypt	34
Nicaragua	28
Paraguay	10
Philippines	10
South Africa	13
Switzerland	21
United States	22

Table 5.7 Proportion of physical assaults by intimate partner

Source: World Health Organization (2012)

In the UK, women are more likely to be sexually assaulted than men. Around 50,000 women are raped each year, nearly half by their current partner. The World Health Organization estimates that around 25% of all women worldwide 'experience sexual violence by an intimate partner in their lifetime', although there are wide variations across different countries (Table 5.8).

Country	Prevalence (%)
Finland	25
Hungary	10
Japan	6
Lithuania	18
Netherlands	28
Sweden	19
Switzerland	12
Peru	47
Thailand	30
Zimbabwe	25
USA	8

Table 5.8   Proportion of women experiencing rape or sexual assault within domestic settings in their lifetime

Source: Kelly and Regan (2003)

Child abuse

Child abuse is a further aspect of the 'darker side' of family life. Humphreys and Thiara (2002) argue that child abuse has strong links to domestic violence. Men who are violent towards their partner are also violent and abusive towards children in their care.

- Around 80 children are killed each year by parents or carers.
- The most likely abuser, according to the National Commission of Inquiry into the Prevention of Child Abuse (1996), is someone known to the child, particularly a male parent or step-parent.
- In 2012 around 46,000 children were considered to be 'at risk' of parental abuse, both physical and psychological.
- Of the most serious offences, the Home Office (1996) found that 25% of all recorded rape victims are children.
- Rooney and Devis (2009) report that 'the highest homicide rates are in infants', the vast majority of which occur within the family.

Suggest two ways in which families might be dangerous for their members.

Your curiosity is aroused by various incidents in a neighbour's house. You suspect domestic violence. Identify and discuss the reasons you would/would not intervene by contacting the relevant authorities.

The social construction of age

The social significance of divisions based on age groups

Age illustrates the sociological relationship between an objective characteristic (biological ageing) and the meanings that different cultures attach to it. Age groups reflect different cultural assumptions about appropriate behaviour and these assumptions affect individual perceptions of age. This occurs in two main ways:

139

1 Through identification with people of a similar biological age. In pre-modern societies this involves relatively simple group identities such as 'young' and 'old', while in contemporary societies we can suggest four main groups – child, youth, adult and elderly. However people of a similar age are grouped and labelled, the function is the same: to create what Durkheim (1893) calls social solidarity – a sense of belonging to a specific grouping with its own particular values, norms and behaviour.

2 Through pressure to conform to an age grouping. For example, children are denied some of the opportunities open to adults, while the elderly are similarly denied opportunities to behave in 'age inappropriate' ways, such as participating in sporting activities.

We can investigate the significance of age divisions by outlining four different *phases* in our biological development associated with different cultural meanings and identities.

Children

Childhood is the first social identity consciously experienced by 'immature humans'. During this period, whose length differs across cultures, children are first exposed to primary socialising influences from adults (mainly parents) and, increasingly, secondary sources such as the media. In our society, 'childhood' can have several different meanings, from the idea of 'innocence' to children being in need of adult care, supervision and protection – something that supports Jenks' (1996) argument that 'childhood is not a natural but a social construct'. Childhood also involves socially constructed ideas about:

- *Permissions* – children can exhibit behaviours, such as play, that are discouraged in adults.
- *Denials* – children are not allowed to do things such as marry.

What are some of the permissions and denials of childhood?

Youth

The next stage reflects a range of identities, including pre-teens ('teenies'), teens and young adults. These identities have come into existence in recent years to reflect social changes in areas such as education, work and consumption. Hine (2000), for example, argues that 'teenagers' did not make much of an appearance in the UK until the mid-to-late 1950s and their development is the result of social changes such as the extension of education and the increase in consumer goods (music and fashion in particular) aimed at a specific post-child, pre-adult market. Functionalists such as Parsons (1964) and Eisenstadt (1968) argue that 'youth' provides a 'period of transition' between childhood and adulthood. Industrial societies create concepts of 'youth' in which young people move gradually away from childhood identities and into adult identities – particularly through the phenomenon of **youth cultures** and sub-cultures (versions of which include hippies, punks and goths).

> **KEY TERM**
>
> **Youth culture:** cultural norms, values and identities particular to specific groups of young people.

Adult

Adult identities are generally built on rights and responsibilities that set them apart from other identities. Adults are allowed to do certain things (marry, work full time, drink, smoke, etc.) while also taking on roles (such as family and work) that involve care and responsibility for others. In this respect, adult identities avoid many of the forms of discrimination experienced by children and the elderly (the concept of **ageism**). Adulthood, therefore, represents a general identity defined by how individuals construct fully formed personal identities separate from those that controlled their youth and childhood. It marks a shift in individual identity focus – away from the forces that shape children and young adults and towards what Magolda (2004) calls a sense of 'what to make of themselves within the context of the society around them'.

> **KEY TERM**
>
> **Ageism:** discrimination on the basis of age.

Elderly

Old age in contemporary societies is generally seen as a special category of adulthood. It is one that while retaining some of the social statuses associated with adults, is sufficiently different to be considered an age category in its own right. This identity increasing significance because of the twin trends of an ageing population and longer life expectancy gained through improved medical treatment, care, diet and exercise. One consequence of these processes is, however, an increased **dependency ratio**. There are more retired, economically inactive elderly relying on the economically active young.

> **KEY TERM**
>
> **Dependency ratio:** relationship between the economically inactive section of a population and those who are economically active. A high dependency ratio means, for example, that there are more elderly people who depend on fewer younger people to maintain things like state pensions or health services funded through taxation.

In some tribal societies, the elderly gain increased family status as patriarchs or matriarchs, valued for their knowledge and experience. However, in Western industrial societies, old age came to be seen as a diminished identity, characterised by a loss of status. Mutran and Burke (1979) note that 'old persons have identities which, while different from middle-aged persons, are similar to young adults: they see themselves as less useful and less powerful than middle-age individuals'. Part of the reason for this is the stigma attached to old age. People see it as an inevitable process of decline, senility, helplessness, withdrawal and loneliness. The elderly come to be perceived as a deviant minority group – a process hastened by the medicalisation of old age. Here, medicine is used to define and manage the elderly and any disorientations they show are not the result of personal and social change but rather evidence of 'senility'.

Conversely, higher life expectancy and more affluent lifestyles have contributed to the reinvention and fragmentation of elderly identities. These involve distinctions between the old and the very old, changing patterns of consumption and leisure, and different interpretations of the meaning of 'being old', where the elderly reject conventional stereotypes and social identities.

The oldest (93) runner in the 2008 London Marathon. Have cultural changes closed the gap between young and old identities?

Barrett et al. (2003) argue that different societies produce different subjective experiences of ageing. Americans and Germans, for example, 'tend to feel younger than their actual age … but the bias toward youthful identities is stronger at older ages, particularly among Americans'.

There is no clear *historical* or *cross-cultural* agreement about the age at which the individual loses one identity and takes on another. Settersten (2006) suggests the significance of age divisions in contemporary societies involves two ideas.

- Age identities have a formal, organisational, importance (*salience*) as a way of structuring 'rights, responsibilities, and entitlements' between, for example, adults and children. Informally, individual age divisions 'shape everyday social interactions', such as those between a parent and child, and provide a basic structure to these social exchanges.

- The passage of *biological time* anchors the passage of *social time* (defined by Halbwachs, 1980 as the 'temporal rhythms of everyday life') when societies give certain age-related events, such as an 18th birthday or retirement from work, a social significance as markers signifying the transition from one phase in the life course to another. This process is sometimes termed a **rite of passage** that takes different forms in different cultures.

> **KEY TERM**
>
> **Rite of passage:** rituals that denote transitions from one phase in the life course to another.

For Aborigines, one transition is marked by 'walkabout'. At age 13, the child spends six months in the Australian Bush and on their return they are accepted into adulthood. In Jewish culture, this transition is marked by the *Bar mitzvah* for boys (aged 13) and the *Bat mitzvah* for girls (aged 12). Other rites of passage include marriage ceremonies and funerals. For Settersten (2006), biological age itself is relatively unimportant here: 'What matters is what the age indexes – the important experiences that happen at those times.'

Social significance extends to two further ideas:

1 Age divisions come bundled with normative expectations (the types of behaviour expected from different age groups) that are used as a 'life map'. Polkinghorne (1991), for example, suggests that 'individuals construct private and personal stories linking diverse events into

141

unified and understandable wholes. They are the basis of personal identity and they provide answers to the question "Who am I?".' In other words, people come to understand their personal identity by linking age-related experiences to create a life narrative.

2 Riach (2007) suggests that people use knowledge of how age divisions are organised to both upset normative expectations of 'age-appropriate' behaviour and 'pre-empt possible forms of marginalization'. She suggests that in situations where ageism is (literally) at work, people may take conscious steps to avoid 'embodying the older worker'.

What is meant by the term 'rite of passage'?

Age stratification

Age groups always exist in some sort of status hierarchy (ranked above or below each other on the basis of their social standing – adults, for example, have a higher status position than children). Theoretical explanations for why societies are age stratified fall into three broad categories, which are described below.

Modernisation

Modernisation theory suggests that the significance of **age stratification** varies in relation to *social change* and, in particular, the transition from pre-industrial (pre-modern) to industrial (modern) society. In the former, where class-based forms of stratification are absent, age-grading systems develop with peer groups forming **age sets** – each generation has certain rights and responsibilities. Johnson and Tumanka (2004) note that age-setting is still common in some traditional societies, such as the Maasai in Kenya. Modernisation theory argues that economic changes produce cultural changes. The need for trained labour, for example, produces an education system that creates age-stratified groups, such as 'youth'. Similarly, the idea of 'retirement' produces concepts of old age.

How is age-setting functional for the Maasai?

Cohorts

Cohort theory focuses on societies having what Marshall (1996) terms an 'age structure associated with different roles and statuses'. In this respect, age is considered as a *group* rather than an individual construct; the relative status of whole groups (*cohorts*) changes with age. Stratification by cohort, therefore, is a flexible interpretation of structural differences in age groups. As each cohort ages (biologically/chronologically) it attracts socially produced roles, self-concepts and identity changes in the form of normative expectations. Zhou (1997) suggests that 'age is a basis for acquiring roles, status, and deference from others in society. When people become old, they exit roles as workers and take on roles as retirees'. In addition, Riley (1994) argues that people born into the same cohort have similar 'experiences in time and may share meanings, ideologies, orientations, attitudes and values'. This theory reflects how social changes affect different cohorts in different ways, at different times. The life experiences of a young adult today are very different from those of a young adult a century ago.

Life course

Life-course analysis suggests that the concept of chronological age is increasingly blurred in modern societies. It argues that a more useful concept is that of social age – the idea that, over an individual's lifetime, certain structured life events mark the divisions between different phases and experiences. Mitchell (2003) suggests

Age stratification: system of social ranking by age. Children, for example, may be ranked lower than adults because they have fewer rights.

Age set: people of a similar age who share certain rights and responsibilities because of their age.

Life-course analysis: the examination of differences and changes over the course of an individual's lifetime. An individual's family experiences as a child and an adult are, for example, very different.

that social age involves thinking about transitions – how major life events, such as starting work or retirement, affect individual age identities. Norms are constructed, in terms of both general social perceptions of 'age-related appropriate or inappropriate' behaviour and specific ideas about how individuals interpret, incorporate or reject these norms and perceptions. Societies not only develop normative rules associated *with* age categories, they also develop ideas *about* age categories – for example, the point at which childhood changes to adulthood.

TEST YOURSELF

Give three examples of ageism.

ACTIVITY

For each of the following groups, make a list of their permissions and denials in your society:

- *children*
- *adults*
- *the elderly.*

Choosing an example from each group, what happens when people defy the expected permissions and denials?

Childhood as a concept that is socially constructed

Archard (2004) argues that every human society has developed a concept of childhood, but societies differ in their definitions of childhood and, by extension, adulthood. If childhood was a simple biological category, we would expect every society to see it in a similar way. The fact that they do not suggests that childhood is socially constructed rather than biologically determined.

The work of Aries has stimulated extensive debate about the changing nature of childhood and the status of children. Although some of Aries' claims have been questioned, his work helps to focus on a number of areas relating to the historical analysis of childhood. Aries argues that 'childhood' as a distinctive phase in social development is a consequence of modern societies. Childhood as both a social and biological category only came into existence around three centuries ago. Childhood as a special status, therefore, is linked to social change and, more specifically, the change from pre-industrial to industrial society. While there were

'non-adults' in pre-industrial society, they were neither called 'children', nor treated in ways we would currently recognise as appropriate to this stage in an individual's life. Aries suggests that changing beliefs about children developed as the Christian church popularised the idea of them as 'fragile creatures of God'. Childhood became defined as a phase of 'uncorrupted innocence', to be nurtured and encouraged. Children were not to be seen as 'little adults', but as beings who needed the protection of adults.

While in pre-industrial society, 'children' lived and worked alongside their parents, the development of industrial society saw a gradual physical and cultural separation between children and adults. In the UK, the development of an education system in the late 19th century resulted in being 'progressively removed from adult society'.

Pollack (1983) attacks the suggestion that there was no conception of childhood in pre-industrial society, and Archard argues that 'Aries claims to disclose an absence of the idea of childhood, whereas he should only claim to find a dissimilarity in ideas about childhood

'Portrait of a Young Girl', Adriaen van der Linde (c. 1570–1609). Why were children treated as 'little adults'?

between past and present'. However, it is evident that the status of children changed in the transition to modern societies, just as it has changed, according to Jenks (1996), throughout the modern period. He notes the existence of two basic historical childhood statuses:

- The Dionysian child is constructed as 'a wilful material force … impish and harbouring a potential evil'. This view suggests that adults must control children to prevent them falling victim to their essential 'badness'.
- The Apollonian child, on the other hand, is constructed as 'angelic, innocent, untainted by the world it has recently entered. It has a natural goodness and a clarity of vision'. This view suggests that the role of adults is to create the conditions under which children can develop their essential 'goodness'.

Adult attitudes towards childhood and children (which are not necessarily the same thing) tend to shift between these two extremes of characterisation. Fionda suggests that in modern industrial societies children are variously seen as:

- objects of concern requiring adult protection
- autonomous possessors of rights
- lacking moral consciousness
- aware of and accountable for their actions.

These ideas reflect a basic uncertainty about the status of children. They need to be simultaneously controlled and given the freedom to develop 'naturally', away from the corrupting influence of adult society. Uncertainty about how children should be seen and treated is nothing new. Hendrick (1990) has identified a range of transformations in the status of children and childhood since 1800:

- The Delinquent child appeared in the mid 19th century, reflecting concerns about how to deal with law-breaking children and provide protection and care.
- The Schooled child involved ideas about the need for education – moral and spiritual as well as technical – the literacy and numeracy required for the newly emerging industrial culture.
- The Psycho-medical child was constructed towards the end of the 19th century with the development of psychological theories. This stressed the unique

nature of childhood and constructed it as a time of biological and emotional 'stress and turmoil'. The concept of **adolescence** as a distinctive phase of childhood also developed through the work of writers such as Hall (1904).

- The Welfare child emerged in the 20th century, stressing children's vulnerability and ideas about delinquent behaviour being shaped by neglect, abuse and poverty.
- The Psychological child emerged in the late 20th century, focused on children having their own needs, which, in turn, should be protected and encouraged.

Fionda summarises this general progression: 'Concepts of who and what children are and what childhood consists of have changed over time'. Heywood (2001) reinforces this when he notes: 'Childhood, according to the seventeenth-century cleric Pierre de Bérulle, "is the most vile and abject state of human nature, after that of death". It is tempting to agree – not least as an antidote to all the sentimental nonsense surrounding the supposedly pure and innocent child of the Victorian era … Such extremes serve to remind us that childhood is a social construct, which changes over time and varies between social and ethnic groups'.

The cross-cultural dimension

The cross-cultural dimension is also significant because if childhood was a simple, biologically determined category, we would expect different societies to have similar perceptions. However, evidence suggests that this is not the case. Malinowski's (1922) study of the Trobriand Islanders of Papua New Guinea argues that pre-industrial tribal societies differed from their industrial counterparts in three main ways:

- Children were given more responsibility and accorded more rights.
- Adult – child relationships were closer, less authoritarian and more supportive than is typically the case in modern societies.
- Children were encouraged to explore their sexuality. There was less guilt attached to 'sex play' and adults were more tolerant of sexual discovery through play.

Mead's (1928) study of the Pacific Island of Samoa looked specifically at female experiences of adolescence, which she characterised as far less stressful than that of children in the USA. She attributed this situation to differences in Samoan attitudes towards sex and child-rearing.

Comparative studies of this kind are important because they allow us to test competing explanations of childhood

KEY TERM

Adolescence: distinctive phase of childhood, first theorised by Hall (1904), which starts with the onset of puberty and ends at the beginning of adulthood.

development. In this instance, adolescence in industrial societies is frequently characterised as involving 'stresses, strains, tensions and tantrums' that are attributed to biochemical changes during puberty. However, Mead suggests that these are *cultural* in origin – social time, in this respect, is more important than biological time. In modern societies, family life is child-centred, and biological parents have certain rights over their child, but Mead's (1935) study of the Mundugumor of New Guinea provides evidence of alternative child-rearing patterns. Children were looked after by family relatives or other young girls within a household. As a result, the 'parent–child' relationship was much looser.

More recent studies in South America, Asia, Eastern Europe and Africa have revealed a diverse range of child–parent relationships. Hecht's (1998) ethnographic study of the 'unconventional childhood' of Brazilian street children shows that, while many children find themselves living and working on the streets from an early age, they still maintain links with parents and wider family. This relationship frequently takes the form of helping to provide for the family by begging or selling bottles, cans and cardboard.

Both historical and cross-cultural evidence points to the **social construction** of childhood, an idea underlined by a range of views concerning the nature of childhood in contemporary industrial societies. One significant argument is that childhood, as we have generally understood it over the past 50 years, has disappeared. Postman argues that a major reason for this is the development of 'open admission technologies' that expose children to images of adulthood (sex, violence, news) that make it more difficult to define where childhood ends and adulthood begins. The internet, for example, gives children access to information and images that, in former times, were denied until adulthood. The 'virtual world' also has two unique features:

1 Age distinctions are difficult to maintain; it is easier for adults and children to interact on equal terms in ways that would not be possible in the physical world.

2 It is not compartmentalised. Children and adults can mix freely, blurring distinctions made in the physical world, such as status differences and the interaction norms that usually govern adult–child relationships.

Robertson suggests that a further factor in the disappearance of childhood is that children are encouraged to see the world through the eyes of *consumers*, using goods and services that were formerly available only to adults (for example, mobile phones). Advertisers target 'children's markets' in increasingly sophisticated ways, and this has led to the development of a 'consumption culture' among children that mirrors that of the adult world.

Postman links the disappearance of traditional childhood with its reappearance in another form, in which the child–adult distinction is increasingly blurred and where 'adults have a different conception of what sort of person a child is, one not unlike that which prevailed in the 14th century: that they are miniature adults'. This changing status of children, Robertson argues, changes how they are defined and treated by adult institutions, such as the legal system, schools and the workplace. O'Donnell and White (1998) discovered that around 25% of working children in North Tyneside in England were under the age of 13 (such employment is illegal in the UK except for actors or models).

A third perspective on how childhood is socially constructed argues that, although there are changes in the way children are perceived and treated, this is neither *one-way* (children effectively becoming 'little adults') nor necessarily evidence of the disappearance of childhood. Rather, childhood is being reinvented in postmodern societies, as it adapts to wider social changes. While children are increasingly consumers of products, they also *shape* those products. Instead of being passive receivers of 'adult culture', they develop relatively sophisticated 'childhood cultures'. The postmodern child inhabits a world quite different from their modern predecessor (of even a generation ago). They are exposed to a far wider and richer range of experiences, albeit ones still markedly different from the adult world.

TEST YOURSELF

Suggest two ways in which childhood is socially constructed.

KEY TERM

Social construction: behaviour that is culturally, rather than naturally, produced. Sociologists believe behaviour is socially constructed because it varies both historically and across different societies.

ACTIVITY

Design a poster or verbal presentation to illustrate Hendrick's 'transformations in the status of children and childhood'.

Class, ethnicity and gender as factors affecting the experience of childhood

Although historical and cross-cultural perspectives are necessary and useful, a further dimension is that of divisions *within* contemporary societies. This is the idea that children of different classes, genders and ethnicities have different experiences of childhood. Jenks argues that 'childhood is not a natural but a social construct' – it is always associated with a variety of meanings and experiences. We also need to note that childhood is transgressive; when talking about childhood and class, for example, we also need to consider gender and ethnic differences *within* this category.

Class

The economic class into which a child is born has a major impact on their experience of childhood. Hecht's study of Brazilian street children highlights this by making a distinction between the 'nurtured' and the 'nurturing' child. The former are the offspring of the wealthy, for whom childhood is a time when they are looked after (*nurtured*) – by parents, teachers and servants. The 'nurturing child' is the offspring of the poor, for whom childhood is largely spent looking after others (*nurturing*) – parents, siblings and wider kin. The nurtured child is one who *draws* upon family capital while the nurturing child is one who *contributes* substantially to that capital.

In societies without such extremes of wealth and poverty this distinction is played out more subtly, although class-based experiences are always related to inequality – economic as well as cultural. In many countries some upper-class children attend private boarding schools, which gives them a very different experience of childhood from their working- or middle-class peers. According to Bourdieu, the economic inequality on which this is based (boarding school fees can sometimes cost almost as much as average full-time yearly earnings) confers a range of cultural advantages based on social capital. That is, how people are connected to social networks and the value that these connections have in adult life.

Historically, middle- and upper-class families were more child-centred, with family resources, attention and effort invested in a child's physical and social development. This cultural capital consists of non-economic resources, such as the knowledge, skills and personal motivations, that see their children successfully through the education system. In this respect, working-class childhood is frequently focused on the 'here and now' and immediate gratification. That is, taking something whenever it is offered, such as leaving school at the earliest

Children at an independent school in India. How is education an important source of social and cultural capital?

opportunity to take paid employment. Middle-class childhood is characterised by a future orientation and deferred gratification – such as staying in education to get qualifications that will lead to professional careers. By accepting a lower standard of living during this period of education, the middle-class child aims to achieve a higher living standard over the course of their lifetime.

Gender

The argument that boys and girls have different experiences of childhood is based on the concept of differential gender socialisation. Parents *assume* boys are psychologically and emotionally different from girls and treat them in different ways. Will et al. (1976) demonstrated this by observing young mothers interacting with a baby called Beth. They offered her a doll to play with and used words like 'sweet' to describe her. When introduced to a similar baby called Adam they offered him a train and he received fewer smiles. Despite being treated quite differently, Beth and Adam were the *same* child dressed in different-coloured clothes.

Parents consciously and subconsciously treat their children in different ways by associating different objects, behaviours and expectations with different genders. Smith and Lloyd (1978) found that toys were used to reinforce gender ideas: girls are associated with dolls and domestic toys because they reflect a future caring role. Boys are associated with active, mechanical and scientific activities, girls with reflective, non-mechanical pastimes. This research concluded that parental behaviour was based on perceptions of gender.

Parents often expect girls to do more domestic chores, and girls' behaviour outside the home is more tightly controlled. McRobbie and Garber (1976) argue that young female lifestyles are more likely to conform to the 'culture of the bedroom – experiments with make-up, listening to records [music], sizing up boyfriends', whereas young male lifestyles are traditionally played out in public places.

Martin and Ruble (2004) suggest that children are 'gender detectives'. They search for clues about gender-appropriate behaviour from primary sources – parents, peers – and secondary sources such as the media. They also seek to discover 'why girls and boys differ'. Peers shape and reinforce gender identities and different experiences of childhood through things such as games that are traditionally played by one gender or another. Sports such as football and rugby have masculine associations and participation reinforces notions of masculinity, while exclusion reinforces notions of femininity.

Similarly, shared activities and pastimes have gender connotations and expectations. For example, a common interest in cars or heavy metal music (boys) or fashion, cosmetics and shopping (girls) creates gender bonds and reinforces identity barriers. Individuals who cross those invisible boundaries (the girl who likes heavy metal, the boy who likes fashion) risk being *negatively sanctioned* for breaking identity norms. In this respect, peer pressure can be an important influence an individual's experience of childhood. Negative sanction may range from being bullied to exclusion from valued peer and friendship groups.

TEST YOURSELF

Suggest one way in which children might imitate their parents.

Ethnicity

Ethnicity refers to cultural differences between social groups. Where different ethnic groups have their own sense of history, tradition and custom, these differences translate into how childhood is constructed and interpreted. As we have seen, different ethnic groups define the duration and extent of childhood differently, particularly the point at which childhood ends and adulthood begins. Different ethnicities also develop their own ideas about childhood divisions. In North America and Western Europe, for example, the notion of childhood has gradually been extended through factors such as participation in compulsory education. This has resulted in the development of different childhood categories, especially those used to describe later childhood behaviours, such as 'teenager'.

In this respect, childhood in contemporary societies has become increasingly fragmented. There is now a range of categories baby, toddler, child, tween, teen as different ethnic groups not only develop different concepts of childhood itself but also different interpretations about aspects of childhood. The concept of adolescence, for example, arguably went unrecognised until psychology developed as an academic discipline. Similarly, Hine (2000) suggests that the 'teenager' was an American media invention in the late 1940s to describe an apparently 'new breed of American youth'.

One feature of the distinction between childhood and adulthood across all ethnic groups is the power that adults have to control children's sense of time, space and body. Pilcher (1995) argues that the 'daily temporal rhythm of children's lives is tightly controlled by adults', something that relates to a diverse set of ideas – from the times children sleep and eat to the time spent on schoolwork or leisure. Adult control of space refers to where children should be at certain times, such as in school or at home. The sense of 'legitimate space' – where children are allowed to go – differs between ethnic groups. Katz (2004) showed how Sudanese children were allowed to roam freely around their home village and associated areas. This contrasts with the tight restrictions placed on children's freedom of movement in many European and American towns and cities. Time and space also relate to control of children's bodies – from what they can wear, how they style their hair, whether, when and where they can use make-up, pierce or decorate their skin, to who may touch their bodies.

Control of children's time, space and body is also closely related to class and gender. Different ethnic groups may experience different levels of poverty and affluence that place restrictions on, or provide opportunities for, childhood experiences. Ethnic groups develop different ideas about how their children should dress, speak to adults and with whom they can associate. Brannen and Oakley (1994), for example, found that Asian parents placed greater restrictions on their children's freedom of movement

147

and association, particularly with their daughters, than their English counterparts. They do, however, treat sons differently from daughters in this respect.

Song (1999) also notes the significance of 'the family as workplace' for some ethnic minority children in the UK, particularly Chinese ethnicities, but also extending into Italian and Asian identities. This relates to how children are co-opted into the family work space. In the case of Chinese families running takeaway restaurants in the UK, Song notes how 'children contribute their labour [and] come to understand and believe in "helping out" as part of a "family work contract"'.

Debates about the social position of the elderly in different societies

Like childhood and adulthood, old age is also socially constructed. Different societies interpret the start, meaning, significance and status of old age in different ways. The differences can be found in all areas, from social markers, such as compulsory retirement in industrial societies, to interpretations of the social position of the elderly.

Cross-cultural comparisons of the status of elderly people show some disparity between societies. The most obvious example of this can be seen in a comparison between modern and pre-modern societies. There are, however, also comparative differences *within* these categories. Modern societies such as the UK and the USA demonstrate differences in the relationship between the elderly and other social categories.

Victor (1987) suggests that the status of the elderly depends upon a number of factors. These include the nature of social organisation – an idea most clearly illustrated by nomadic societies, where the elderly are considered a burden when they are no longer able to easily follow the nomadic lifestyle. In these societies, the elderly

are often neglected and may even be killed once they start to become a hindrance. In more settled societies, the elderly's knowledge and skills may be considered vauable to the family group or society as a whole. In Kagan's (1980) study of a Columbian (South America) village, the elderly remained socially and economically active, as far as physically possible. She argued that they did not constitute a gerontocracy (where the elderly are social leaders because of their age) but they were nevertheless seen as valued and respected members of their communities.

Other forms of value that enhance the status of the elderly relate to the control of social resources. The status of the elderly is higher in societies that value the knowledge and skills they possess. In many American Indian tribes, for example, elderly males are valued for their skills of leadership and their intimate knowledge of tribal folklore and ceremony. In Europe and America, those elderly who have control over economic resources also have higher status. The key to social status, therefore, is control over valued social and economic resources.

Cultural attitudes to the afterlife also play a part here. In some societies, old age is valued because the elderly are closer to death and the spiritual afterlife. The older a person gets, the greater the respect accorded to them. Among the Sherbro of Sierra Leone, a person's status increases as they become more incoherent because they are believed to be communicating directly with their ancestors. In other societies, the signs of old age are welcomed because they symbolise the fact that the elderly will soon begin their 'real life' after death. In such cultures, where life is seen as a preparation for the next world, the status of the elderly increases as they grow older.

What knowledge and skills can the elderly contribute to societies?

Suggest two differences in the social position of the elderly in different societies.

In modern industrial societies, the status and social position of the elderly is arguably different, although social position in modern societies is not simply a function of age but is complicated by concepts of class and gender. To be 'old and wealthy' represents a different social position to being 'old and poor'. In the same way, elderly men may have greater social status than elderly women. However, in general, the elderly are represented as social problems – a burden on the young. They also tend to attract negative labels based on ideas about senility and forgetfulness, illness (both mental and physical) and unattractiveness (physical and sexual).

These ideas reflect a symbolic annihilation of the elderly, through which their social position is degraded by 'making them different'. This is further enhanced by the elderly being excluded from the workplace through forced retirement. Here, 'old age' is both separated from general notions of adulthood and an identity in its own right, which becomes increasingly significant through the twin trends of an ageing society and longer life expectancy. Retirement from work can, therefore, be a significant rite of passage marking a diminished identity.

Theories

There are different theories about the position of the elderly. Modernisation theories, for example, suggest that the lower social position of the elderly in industrial societies is explained by the fact they are a distinctive **status group**. Avramov and Maskova (2003) argue that modernisation theory has successfully identified 'changes in society that are likely to reduce the status of older people', such as those suggested by Cowgill (1974) – the elderly as 'underemployed, untrained in the latest technologies and separated from family/community networks'. These features lower the social position of the elderly because modern societies are structured to reflect ageism. Abrams (2005) argues that 'age prejudice between the generations' is more common than sex or race discrimination, something that holds true across both gender and ethnic boundaries.

KEY TERM

Status group: social group sharing similar levels of status and often similar lifestyles or occupations.

However, it can be argued that age boundaries have less distinct in recent times. Kiemo (2004) suggests that social and economic changes do not have a uniform impact, which makes it difficult to see 'the elderly' as a distinctive stratum in modern societies in any but the broadest sense. Meadows (2003) further argues that job performance does not significantly deteriorate with age and 'there is no evidence to support the view older workers are inherently less productive than younger workers'. She notes, however, that older workers do not always receive the same levels of workplace investment and training as younger colleagues. Where they do receive training they 'reach the same skill standards'.

A related explanation is based on control over social resources. Here, the social position of the elderly is not so much a function of age itself – the elderly do not have a lower social position because they are old – but rather of the different levels of resources controlled by different age groups. Political economy theory relates age to work – the lower status of the elderly comes, Townsend (1986) argues, from their 'progressive removal from the workplace'. Hockey and James (1993) note how this denies them social resources such as an earned income. Turner (1989) argues a variation here – exchange theory – that suggests the marginalisation of different age groups is related to a general failure to control a variety of social resources, not just those relating to work.

Postmodern explanations focus on two arguments about life choices. The first is that the declining social position of the elderly is not inevitable and irreversible. The second is that although certain *age markers* still exist, the meaning of age in postmodern societies is increasingly fluid. People are no longer restricted to rigid, age-categorised role behaviours since, as Grusky (1996) suggests, concepts of age no longer have a 'privileged position'. We must seek to understand how and why the elderly exercise a range of choices over how their identities are constructed and represented.

Modernisation theories represent old age as a master status, which defines how others see 'the elderly' and interpret their behaviour as appropriate or inappropriate. In contrast, postmodernists argue that ideas about age-related characteristics and statuses differ widely in contemporary societies, where traditional ideas and associations are gradually broken down by cultural globalisation. People are increasingly exposed to alternative ideas and lifestyles relating to age. As traditional notions of age-related roles and statuses break down, changing lifestyle choices open up new social spaces – 'non-traditional behaviours', for example, that different age groups claim as their own.

While ageist ideas may persist, they are balanced by ideas that reinvent elderly statuses, in ways that relate to things like the fragmentation of elderly identities (distinguishing between the old and the very old, for example), changing patterns of consumption and leisure, and different interpretations of the meaning of 'being old', whereby the elderly refuse to conform to conventional stereotypes and social identities. From this perspective, chronological age is far less significant than social age.

We can illustrate these ideas through three further theories. These suggest that changing social positions are the result of a combination of pressures 'from above' – how societies construct elderly identities and status – and 'from below' – how the elderly themselves construct their identities and statuses.

- *Disengagement theory* suggests that as people biologically age they progressively disengage from social relationships, both consciously, in the sense of a gradual withdrawal from extended social networks (work being the most obvious example), and subconsciously. The older one becomes, the greater the likelihood of family and friends disengaging through death. Disengagement in this respect is a two-way process: individuals progressively disengage from their general involvement with society and society disengages from the individual; people interact with the elderly on increasingly fewer occasions.
- *Activity theory* focuses on how people learn and choose to play age-related roles, and from this position, **disengagement** occurs continuously as people make different choices about their behaviour and the groups to which they belong. This process also involves 'active re-engagements' in social interactions as people leave some groups and join or develop others.

- Finally, *social generational theory* examines the impact of biological ageing processes on individual self-perceptions and identities. In particular, it suggests that behavioural choices are conditioned by values that fail to adapt to social and technological changes. The elderly become, in Dowd's (1986) phrase, 'immigrants in time'. They lose social status because their life experiences are rooted in the values, norms and customs of the *past*. As society moves on, they remain trapped in the identity conferred by their past experiences, both in their own eyes and those of others. Cultural separation between age groups is reflected in a social distance between those 'from the past' and 'those in the present', with the social position of the latter rising as that of the former declines.

Summary points

- **'A family' can be defined:**
  - exclusively
  - inclusively.
- **Different types of households:**
  - single person
  - couples
  - shared.
- **Different types of family structure:**
  - nuclear
  - lone-parent
  - reconstituted
  - extended
  - modified extended families.
- **Changes to family and household structures are closely linked to:**
  - industrialisation
  - urbanisation
  - globalisation.
- **Family diversity is evidenced across a number of social categories:**
  - class
  - ethnicity
  - religion
  - family size
  - marital status
  - age
  - family life cycle.
- **Alternatives to the nuclear family:**
  - tribal societies
  - communes
  - New World Black family.
- **Consensus perspectives such as functionalism and neo-functionalism emphasise the positive effects of the family.**
- **Consensus approach stresses the role of the family in maintaining social order through carrying out essential functions and by acting as a support for the state. Conflict perspectives emphasise the negative effects of family life and the support that the family provides for ruling class interests.**

- **The relationship between family members focuses on:**
  - parents
  - children
  - grandparents.
- **Debates about conjugal roles and gender equality are organised around a number of consensus and conflict perspectives:**
  - functionalist
  - neo-functionalist
  - Marxist
  - feminist.
- **The darker side to family life can be examined in relation to:**
  - domestic violence
  - child abuse.
- **Age divisions within families involve various socially constructed categories:**
  - children
  - youth
  - adult
  - elderly.
- **Childhood as a social construction can be considered in two ways:**
  - historically
  - cross-culturally.
- **Class, ethnicity and gender affect the experience of childhood. Primary gender socialisation, for example, involves four processes:**
  - imitation
  - identification
  - role learning
  - conditioning.
- **The social construction of old age involves:**
  - cross-cultural comparisons
  - historical comparisons
  - control of social resources
  - class and gender differences
  - rites of passage.

Exam-style questions

Section A

a What is meant by the term 'basic and irreducible functions'? [2]

b Describe two ways in which the existence of family structures may benefit capitalism. [4]

c Explain how the family may contribute to value consensus. [8]

d Assess the view that the family exists more to benefit society rather than individual family members. [11]

Section B

a 'Marriage has less importance in modern industrial societies than it has in traditional societies'. Explain and assess this view. [25]

b Explain and assess the view that in modern industrial societies family structures are becoming increasingly similar. [25]

Section A

a What is meant by the term 'domestic violence'? [2]

b Describe two reasons for the increase in divorce in modern industrial societies. [4]

c Explain how the family may contribute to gender inequality. [8]

d Assess the view that class is the most significant influence in shaping family relationships. [11]

Section B

a 'The modern family is in decline'. Explain and assess this view. [25]

b Explain and assess the diversity of family structures in contemporary societies. [25]

Total available marks 150

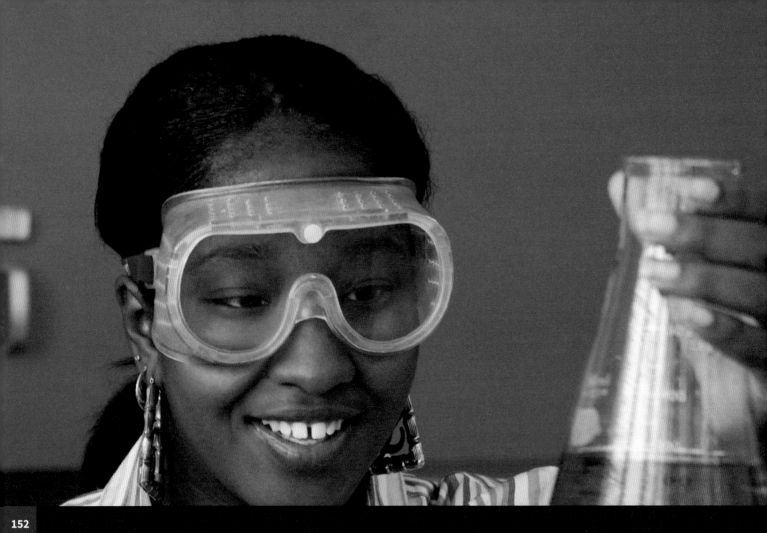

Chapter 6:
Education

Learning objectives

The objectives of this chapter involve understanding:

- different perspectives on the relationship between education and the economy
- how intelligence is defined and measured
- different perspectives on the relationship between intelligence and educational achievement
- consensus and conflict approaches to the relationship between education and social mobility
- the relationship between different forms of social inequality (class, gender and ethnicity) and educational achievement

- how concepts of knowledge and learning are socially constructed
- deschooling and cultural capital
- power and control in modernity and postmodernity
- language codes and the language of education
- labelling, the hidden curriculum and the gendered curriculum as explanations for differential achievement
- examples of pro- and anti-pupil sub-cultures.

Introduction

This chapter focuses on the relationship between education, wider social institutions, such as the family and workplace, and the individual. These are examined in terms of 'outside school' processes, such as how education relates to economic change and social mobility, and 'inside school' processes, including ideas about the nature of the formal and hidden curriculum, the effects of school segregation through streaming, setting and banding, and the development of pro- and anti-pupil sub-cultures. These two themes are brought together through a discussion of differential academic achievement that examines ideas about intelligence, language and the significance of economic, social and cultural capital.

Education in social context

Theories about the links between education and the economy

The relationship between **formal education** systems and the economy is both complex and multidimensional. This is partly because the structure and organisation of education always reflects ideological beliefs about its meaning, purpose and relationship to other social institutions. This complexity is also due to the way in which economic systems of production, distribution and exchange have developed historically.

Why was there a new need for a literate and numerate workforce with the onset of industrialisation?

> **KEY TERM**
>
> **Formal education:** education that takes place within the formal setting of the school. It involves learning a specific range of subjects (the formal curriculum), mastery of which is tested through formal examinations.

Mass education, where the majority of a population experience formal schooling, is a feature of most modern industrial societies. The relationship between mass education and economic development is not accidental. In pre-industrial societies, when most people lived and worked in and around the home, there was no economic need for education. It was only when industrialisation and factory production increased the demand for a literate and numerate workforce that the pressure for mass education arose. Education systems are thus closely linked to economic systems, but the precise nature of their relationship is open to debate. We can explore this debate by looking at three sociological approaches to the relationship between education and work in contemporary industrial societies.

Functionalism

Functionalism sees society as a social system consisting of different institutions (family, work, education, etc.). These institutions are functionally connected in two ways:

1 Each institution performs certain essential (*core*) functions, such as providing the means of survival (work) or secondary socialisation (education).

2 To perform these functions, each institution needs certain things from other institutions. In contemporary societies, where the workplace usually requires a certain level of knowledge and skill, the education system needs to provide individuals with the necessary social and intellectual foundations. Schools perform this function by accrediting certain levels of knowledge and skill through qualifications.

The relationship between education and work is one of dependency. The workplace needs the education system to perform its allotted roles in order for society to function successfully.

The development of mass education is, therefore, explained in terms of functional differentiation: institutions develop to perform particular functions, such as 'work' and 'education'. If the needs of one institution are not being adequately met, tensions develop within the system that threaten its stability and ability to function. For example, industrial forms of work require a literate and numerate workforce; without these skills, the economy cannot function. Institutions such as the family cannot meet this new requirement, so the stability of the system is threatened. It can be restored in one of two ways:

- An existing institution, such as the family or religion, evolves to perform the required function. This involves differentiation that occurs *within* individual institutions; different roles need to be developed if the institution is to perform its new function.
- A new institution, such as formal education, arises to fulfil the need.

Although it is possible for an existing institution to evolve, the scale of economic change that occurs as societies industrialise is often too great. Existing institutions cannot adapt quickly enough or in all the necessary ways to deal with the new demands. At some point in their development, therefore all societies will develop a specialised institution (education) that can restore stability in such situations.

TEST YOURSELF

Explain the term 'functional differentiation'.

In the UK, the 1944 Education Act that established free, universal education explicitly addressed the relationship between education and the workplace through a distinction between:

- academic pupils, destined to move on to university and professional employment
- vocational pupils, who were destined to follow a practical or technical route into the workforce.

Secondary (ages 11–15) education was organised into a tripartite system. Pupils were allocated to one of three types of school after taking an intelligence test at age 11. The types of school not only mirrored contemporary beliefs about the nature of **intelligence**,

they also reflected current economic needs in terms of types of labour:

- Grammar schools provided a wholly academic education and were geared towards the needs of professional occupations, such as doctors and accountants, based on particular qualifications.
- Secondary modern schools provided a mix of vocational (work-related) and academic education geared towards the needs of the service sector.
- Secondary technical schools provided a work-related technical/vocational education and were geared towards the development of skilled manual occupations. In fact, this section was never fully established and its function was largely taken over by secondary modern schools.

KEY TERM

Intelligence: capacities and abilities related to the acquisition and demonstration of knowledge and skills, such as problem-solving and decision-making.

The argument that this type of division is functional and necessary is reflected in secondary education systems worldwide:

- India has both academic and vocational (school and profession-based) routes through secondary education.
- Pakistan has similarly developed academic and technical routes.
- Mauritius organises secondary education in a slightly different way, but has also developed a distinction between academic routes into the workplace and a form of basic education intended to be a route into vocational training, for around 5% of the school population.

The separation of academic and vocational educational routes reflects a belief in two basic forms of work:

1 professional careers, requiring higher levels of abstract knowledge and lower levels of practical expertise
2 non-professional work, requiring higher levels of practical expertise and lower levels of abstract knowledge.

These ideas are reflected in Davis and Moore's (1945) argument that those who are most able and talented intellectually are allocated work roles that offer the highest rewards in terms of income, power and status. In other words, the most functionally important economic roles must be filled by the most capable and competent members of society. There is a clear relationship between education and the economy: 'Education is the proving ground for ability and hence the selective agency for placing people in different statuses according to their abilities.'

Neo-functionalism/new right

Neo-functionalist or new-right perspectives acknowledge the basic relationship outlined by writers such as Davis and Moore. However, they also argue that this kind of society and economy no longer exists. The rapid social and economic changes that have occurred over the past 40 years as a result of globalisation have changed our understanding of the relationship between education and the economy.

For example, Bell (1973) argues that post-industrial societies developed first in heavily industrialised parts of the USA and Western Europe and subsequently spread across the world.

There has been a steady rise in general service industries and, more recently, a rapid rise in computer-based service technologies. In post-industrial society, therefore, services and knowledge are the dominant productive industries, and these are characterised by their flexibility and speed of change. This brings into question the academic/vocational distinction in modern education systems. Neo-functionalists argue that this type of division is too inflexible to meet the needs of a globalised economy.

Luhmann (1997) adopts a similar systems approach, but criticises traditional functionalism as being too 'mechanical' in its theorising of the relationship between education and the economy. He questions, for example, the idea that an economy simply *exists* – that it has unity and coherence as a system – and that people are simply allotted places within it depending on such criteria as educational qualifications. While Luhmann sees *social* systems as interconnected networks, questions of inclusion or exclusion from an ever-changing system of social and economic relationships are the key to understanding *education* systems. They must be as flexible as the workplace if they are to function coherently. In many education systems, these ideas are reflected in recent changes to different types of academic and vocational qualifications, with various attempts to:

- break down rigid distinctions between 'academic' and 'vocational' subjects through the development of new qualifications and routes to competence
- move away from a curriculum wholly focused on subject knowledge towards one based on *functional* knowledge and skills, such as the ability to work with others and

solve problems rather than simply 'remember names and dates'
- narrow the distinction between different types of knowledge and skills.

Neo-functionalist and new-right perspectives argue that economic behaviour in the 21st century is very different from 50 – let alone 150 – years ago. Various globalising processes have caused a long-term decline in manufacturing and a rise in the financial and service sectors. This has changed both the nature of economic production and, as a consequence, the nature of education systems.

TEST YOURSELF

Which type of economic activity is most significant in modern societies?

Evaluation: 'Functional importance' is the idea that different adult roles are measured according to their social contribution. For example, accountants have higher social status and pay than road sweepers because their role is functionally more important for society. Tumin (1953) questions the idea that we can objectively measure functional importance. He argues that this is something we can only establish subjectively and that it represents an ideological justification for the functionalist analysis of education and its relationship to the economy. Such arguments are based on a tautological argument (one that contains its own proof). Accountancy has greater functional significance because it requires high-level academic qualifications; the demand for advanced academic qualifications are proof that this occupation is functionally important to the economy.

A second line of criticism focuses on the assumption that modern education systems 'sift and sort' students into different types of education and qualifications in a meritocratic way – that is, based on each student's merits. These merits might be higher levels of intelligence, or a willingness to work hard and make personal sacrifices to pursue an education. However, there is little evidence that a genuinely meritocratic system exists in modern industrial societies. These societies are marked by inequality, which affects who is able to succeed in the education system. For example, wealthy people can send their children to fee-paying schools, which effectively buys them social status rather than children earning it through their own talents.

Parkin (1971) suggests that the functionalist view is merely an ideological attempt to justify inequality in society. The idea of **meritocracy** has been criticised by both interactionists, who focus on school processes to show that education is not meritocratic, and Marxists, who argue that the 'meritocracy myth' obscures underlying processes of class reproduction. Willis (1977) claims that working-class children get working-class jobs not because these are the jobs to which they are best suited but because middle-class children get the middle-class jobs.

KEY TERM

Meritocracy: system based on equality of opportunity; those with ability and talent achieve their just rewards regardless of their social characteristics.

Luhmann argues that traditional functionalism does not consider how modern social systems operate. Ideas that were relevant to education 100 or 50 years ago no longer apply.

Social democratic theory

Social democratic theory looks at the relationship between education and the economy in terms of two related processes in modern societies:

1 Technological changes in the workplace, involving both a decline in traditional manufacturing and the rise of service industries in areas such as finance, computing and information technology. In the UK, for example, the tripartite system produced a small percentage of highly qualified university entrants (around 15% of 18-year-olds) and a large number of poorly qualified school-leavers. This situation failed to meet the economic need for a better-qualified service-industry workforce.

2 Social changes focused on ideas about equality in gender, sexuality, ethnicity and class. The tripartite system failed to meet the requirements of social fairness because it was based on ideas about intelligence that were increasingly divided along class lines.

KEY TERM

Social democratic theory: political theory that advocates technocratic and meritocratic solutions to the problem of differential educational achievement.

The solution to these problems in the UK was **comprehensive education**, which was designed to address social inequality and technological change. Social democrats believe that comprehensive schools fulfil the ideal of a meritocracy. These schools contain a broad class mix, in which all children – regardless of prior academic achievement – receive the same secondary education. In the UK, the introduction of comprehensive schools was intended to establish a system of 'contest mobility'. Turner (1960) states that its objective was 'to give elite status to those who earn it'. Equality of opportunity was not only seen as socially fair, but in addition, competition would produce larger numbers of better-qualified workers to serve the new technological requirements of a changing economy. From this perspective, therefore, education is the means through which problems of technological change and social inequality can be addressed and managed. A truly meritocratic system would result in a fairer distribution of economic and social rewards, increased social mobility and a decline in social inequality.

KEY TERM

Comprehensive education: system where schools are open to all children, regardless of their ability to pay, where they live or prior educational achievement.

More recently, social democratic theory has argued for the need to retrain and refocus the workforce in contemporary societies to address both economic and social changes. As Chitty (2009) notes, this involves

Which of these people does the most functionally important work?

156

seeing 'education and training' as the means through which industrial societies are 'transformed from low-skill, low-wage economies into a high-skill, high-wage and technologically advanced economies'.

Evaluation: While social democrats see comprehensive schooling as a way of reducing class inequality by creating more opportunities for working-class children, Marxists argue that this misunderstands institutional relationships in capitalist societies. Fundamental economic inequalities are not affected by educational changes. Bowles and Gintis (2002) argue that the reverse is true – economic inequality drives educational inequality.

We can see evidence of this idea when considering the claim that comprehensive schools promote social mixing by abolishing selection by intelligence test. Critics argue that this system has been replaced by an even more unequal selection process, in which middle-class children attend middle-class schools and working-class children attend working-class schools.

In this respect, social democratic theory confuses change with equality: the idea that making schools more meritocratic or compensating working-class children for their social disadvantages overcomes wider social inequalities and economic disadvantages. However, Wilkinson and Pickett (2009) argue that social inequality in the UK is greater now than at any time in the past 50 years.

Marxism

Bowles and Gintis (2002) argue that the structure and organisation of the workplace is mirrored in the organisation of schools. Workplace inequalities are reflected and reproduced through the education system in a range of ways:

1 The school disciplines students to the demands of work and the 'crucial ingredient of job adequacy'. This involves behaviour such as regular attendance and the regulation of personal time and space – where pupils should be and when they should be there.

2 Social relationships within the school copy the relationships found at work. There is, for example, a hierarchy within the school similar to that in the workplace, with teachers exercising authority over pupils.

3 Just as workers have no control over or ownership of the things they produce, so too are pupils alienated in the education system. They have no control over:

- the educational process as a whole: they must simply do as they are told
- the content of education: this is decided by others

- the teaching and learning process: pupils are encouraged to compete against each other for grades and qualifications rather than see knowledge and understanding as worthwhile goals in their own right.

For Bowles and Gintis, the **correspondence principle** is maintained at all levels of the education system, usually through streaming, setting or banding (see below):

- For those destined for lower levels of work, 'rule following' is emphasised; pupils are given little responsibility and made to do simple, repetitive tasks.
- For those destined for middle levels of work, reliability and some ability to work independently is emphasised.
- For those destined for higher levels of work, there is an emphasis on working independently and taking some control over their academic work.

 KEY TERM

Correspondence principle: neo-Marxist theory that argues that the organisation of schools closely corresponds to the organisation and demands of the workplace.

The relationship between education and the economy, therefore, is based around **cultural reproduction** – the means through which higher social classes reproduce their economic domination from generation to generation.

KEY TERM

Cultural reproduction: Marxist idea that higher social classes try to reproduce their leadership and privileges by investing time, money and resources in the education of their offspring.

For Bourdieu (1986), meritocracy is a myth. The education system works in favour of a ruling elite in various ways. Some involve the ability to pay for exclusive forms of education such as private schooling and tutoring, while others relate to educational practices such as **streaming**, where children of different abilities are taught separately. Meritocracy is, however, a *legitimating myth* for Bourdieu; the education system has the appearance of fairness, equality and merit, when in fact it is the opposite.

KEY TERM

Streaming: situation in which groups of children of different measured ability are taught separately in all subjects on the formal curriculum.

Cultural reproduction

The formal curriculum plays an important part in cultural reproduction because it allows children of different classes to be separated into different employment streams at an early age. In this way, cultural reproduction is disguised as a consequence of the choices children make and their differing levels of ability or aptitude. For Althusser (1971), schools are an **ideological state apparatus** (ISA) that involves social learning. Teachers 'transform pupil consciousness' by encouraging them to accept not just 'the realities of life', that the workplace is unequal, but also their likely future social positions. In this respect, vocational education within schools has two main advantages for ruling elites:

- It eliminates working-class children as competitors for higher-level occupations.
- It gives the appearance of being chosen by the working class, either through deliberate choice or because they have failed to reach a required level of academic achievement.

>
> **KEY TERM**
>
> **Ideological state apparatus (ISA):** Marxist concept that argues that institutions such as schools encourage values favourable to the interests of a ruling class in capitalist societies.

How do teachers 'transform pupil consciousness'?

Bates and Riseborough (1993), for example, argue that a significant feature of contemporary forms of vocational education in the UK (sometimes called the new **vocationalism**) is that most (white) middle-class students follow the academic route into professional employment,

whereas (white and black) working-class students are encouraged along the vocational route to lower-paid/lower-status work.

> **KEY TERM**
>
> **Vocationalism:** the knowledge and skills required for specific types of employment.

Marxists have generally been critical of both vocational education and work-based training schemes. For example, Finn (1988) argues that youth training schemes involved cheap labour that employers could use for a short time and then discard without penalty. Bonded trainees who left a job risked losing state benefits and were effectively tied to a particular employer, whatever the conditions of the job.

Many trainees were either placed on 'work-creation schemes' devised and funded by the government or in work offering no prospect of further employment once the training period was over and the government subsidy ended. Finn argues that training was minimal to non-existent in many types of work placement and, where training was given, it did not cover the skills required for work in a high-technology, service-based economy. For Bates and Riseborough the new vocationalism is more about social control. It takes potentially troublesome unemployed youth 'off the streets' and subjects them to workplace discipline, lowers wages for all young people by subsidising some employers, and lowers unemployment figures. Similar criticisms have been made about recent forms of government-sponsored work-based training schemes:

- Work-experience programmes are designed as 'voluntary' schemes for those who take unpaid work for up to six months. While they receive an allowance during their placement, if they leave the job their benefits are stopped.
- Mandatory schemes are compulsory. The longer-term unemployed must take unpaid work and a failure to complete the programme results in a loss of state benefits.

As Davies (2012) reports, such schemes have been accused of being 'modern slave labour' that involves little or no training.

Evaluation: Criticism of Marxist approaches has focused on the connection they make between education and the economy. Young (1981), for example, has called this approach 'left functionalism': the idea that education functions to 'meet the needs of a ruling class'. Marxists have also been criticised for seeing working-class pupils as passive and for making the assumption that everything that is taught in schools is necessarily learnt. Willis's (1977) study of working-class students in the UK showed that they were not passive – they strongly resisted attempts by teachers to make them conform to school rules and values. The claim that schools prepare people for working life is also problematic. In the USA, Gloria Joseph (1988) showed that there is a large body of Black and Latino people who are not in employment at all. Poor school records and low levels of educational achievement partly explain why the unemployment rate is so high among these ethnic groups. Neo-Marxists such as Poulantzas (1978) argue that schools are relatively autonomous institutions, which can interpret the curriculum in ways that make it difficult to see how a precise correspondence between education and work can develop.

A different level of criticism focuses on the ability of individuals to make choices about their education. This involves the idea that the choices made by working- and middle-class pupils reflect their different interests and experiences. Schools should be responsive to these choices by making different types of academic and vocational education available.

Heath (1997) argues that Marxist approaches tend to reject all forms of vocational education because they encourage class-based cultural reproduction. She notes that, by demanding equal opportunities, some forms of vocational education have helped women in areas of schooling and eventually work that were traditionally male preserves.

TEST YOURSELF

Give two examples of a correspondence between school and work.

Feminism

From a general feminist perspective, the relationship between education and the economy is one in which males and females are channelled into different types and levels of work. Women are at a disadvantage because of horizontal and vertical workplace segregation that filters down through the education system.

Horizontal segregation refers to the idea that many occupations are *sex segregated*, or mainly performed by either males or females. Female-dominated occupations include teaching, nursing, shop and secretarial work, while their male-dominated occupations include engineering,

computing and construction. This concept is reinforced by dual labour markets:

- Male-dominated primary labour markets involve companies with high levels of job security, career prospects and wages.
- Female-dominated secondary labour markets involve worse working conditions, job security and considerably lower wage levels.

Female over-representation in secondary labour markets is, for Sommerlad and Sanderson (1997), partly explained by the idea that 'primary markets are conceptualised as male and characterised by male ways of working and career norms'. Even where women are present in a primary market, they occupy a *secondary position*, based on the idea of vertical workplace segregation – men dominate higher managerial positions, for example.

Subject choices: These ideas are important for feminists because the way economies are structured sends messages to pupils about how different occupations are gendered. This translates into gendered curriculum choices. In terms of the most popular choices:

- Girls choose subjects such as English, Psychology, Art and Design, Sociology and Media Studies.
- Boys choose subjects such as Physics, Business Studies, Geography and Physical Education.

KEY TERM

Gendered curriculum: situation in which males and females choose, or are given, different subjects to study.

This difference in subject choice at school level translates into differences at undergraduate level. Self and Zealey (2007) note that:

- more women than men studied subjects allied to medicine, such as nursing
- more men than women studied business and administrative services, engineering and technology subjects and computer sciences.

The Equal Opportunities Commission (2007) argued that educational achievements – girls consistently

KEY TERM

Educational achievement: a narrow interpretation of this idea refers to the gaining of different levels of educational qualification.

159

outperform boys at all levels of the UK education system – 'are not necessarily helping women into well-paid jobs'. They suggest that one cause of the discrepancy between achievement and occupation is **gender stereotyping**, the idea that boys and girls have different educational and occupational aptitudes. As Warrington and Younger (2000) note, male and female career aspirations reflect traditional gender stereotypes, such as childcare, nursing, hairdressing and secretarial for girls, and computing, accountancy and plumbing for boys.

> **KEY TERM**
>
> **Gender stereotyping:** the practice of assigning particular characteristics to whole gender groups, such as males and females, regardless of their individual differences.

Is science a male subject?

One area in which gender stereotyping appears most fully embedded into the school curriculum is in vocational education and work-based training. In the school curriculum, there is evidence that work experience places boys and girls into traditionally stereotyped jobs. Mackenzie's (1997) study found that:

- 45% of girls were allocated to caring placements, but these did not always reflect their choices.
- Boys who did not get their preferred placement tended to be allocated to occupations that they considered as either neutral or traditionally male.
- Girls who were unsuccessful in their preferred placements were allocated to traditionally female occupations.

In this respect, vocational training is more likely to result in both males and females being channelled into 'traditional' forms of gendered employment.

Kampmeier (2004), however, argues that while there are greater opportunities for stereotyping and segregation in vocational training, because of a relatively narrow range of occupational types covered, 'academic education' does not necessarily guarantee a lack of stereotyping and segregation.

Across Europe 'gender segregation in the labour market has not been considerably reduced during the last decades, as far as 'typical' male and female occupations – such as electricians and nursery nurses – are concerned'. The argument here, therefore, is that one role of vocational education is to reinforce gender (and class) stereotypes and divisions in ways that are not quite so apparent with academic forms of education, mainly because they do not necessarily channel males and females into particular forms of work at a relatively early age.

Evaluation: The relationship between work and education is a complex one, and female over-representation in secondary labour markets may reflect wider social processes, such as family roles, responsibilities and choices, that have little or nothing to do with education.

> **ACTIVITY**
>
> *Design a poster to show how the organisation of schools might correspond to the demands of the workplace. For example: school uniforms and work uniforms. Also discuss examples of where there is no correspondence between schools and work.*

Explanations of educational achievement and intelligence

What is intelligence?

It might seem that 'intelligence' is relatively easy to describe and demonstrate. However, Sternberg (1987) suggests that, not only is it very difficult to define, but its meaning is also vigorously contested: 'There seem to be almost as many definitions of intelligence as there are experts asked to define it.' For convenience, however, we can group these definitions into two broad categories:

1 Capacities: This general categorisation of intelligence is based on the idea that humans have certain faculties, aptitudes and competences that allow them to behave 'more intelligently' than other animals. Sternberg's (1986) triarchic theory, for example, argues that intelligence has three related components:

- Meta-components involve the capacity to solve problems and make informed, correct, decisions.

- Performance components involve the ability to actually carry out meta-component actions, such as seeing a relationship between two or more ideas.
- Knowledge-acquisition components refer to the capacity to acquire new information and make logical choices between different options.

From this perspective, intelligence is defined in terms of the ability to use each capacity to process information and choose appropriate responses, depending on the particular situation.

2 Abilities: This is a narrower definition that focuses on the ability to perform particular tasks or solve specific problems. Binet (1916), for example, the creator of one of the first tests to measure intelligence, defined it as 'the capacity to judge, reason and comprehend well'. Jensen (1973) argues that while human intelligence is complex and difficult to define precisely, it is possible to test and quantify some important aspects of what he calls 'general intelligence' or the 'g' factor, a subset that relates to 'abstract reasoning ability'. By focusing on abilities, therefore, it is possible to develop tests that measure the extent to which individuals are able to do things like identify rules, patterns, reasons and logical principles in three particular areas:

- mathematical
- verbal or comprehension
- spatial.

While categories based on capacities or abilities recognise different dimensions to 'intelligence', it is still something conceptualised in the singular. Someone is either intelligent or they are not. Gardner (2003), however, has introduced a further layer of complication through his theory of multiple intelligences. This questions the assumption that 'intelligence is a single entity' passed between generations, with children inheriting their parents' general intelligence.

Gardner (1999) argues there are at least seven distinct types of intelligence, ranging from the conventional linguistic, mathematical and spatial abilities, through musical intelligence to interpersonal intelligence – the extent to which an individual can empathise with others. Interpersonal intelligence is sometimes called emotional intelligence and, as Ogundokun and Adeyemo's (2010) study of Nigerian secondary school students found, it is possible to measure and quantify it. They found a strong correlation between levels of emotional intelligence and academic achievement.

Why is it difficult to define intelligence?

Measuring intelligence

While there is a general agreement that something called 'intelligence' exists and can be defined, there are serious disagreements about what it is and how it *should* be defined. As we have seen, although it is possible to measure some *aspects* of intelligence, such as mathematical or verbal abilities, there are different views about what is being measured and how it can be reliably and validly measured. In an educational context, however, the most common tests use something called an **intelligence quotient (IQ)**; this is a measure, not a definition, of individual intelligence, where an IQ of 100 is taken as the average for any population.

KEY TERM

Intelligence quotient (IQ): a specific measure of individual intelligence, where a score of 100 is the average, conventionally based on tests of mathematical, verbal and spatial skills.

161

Mathematics has been a traditional arbiter of intelligence. Why might this be a limiting perspective on intelligence?

Purpose of IQ tests: The purpose of IQ testing in education varies around the world. In the UK it was extensively used between 1950 and the mid 1970s to separate children into different schools at the age of 11. Those who passed the 11-plus exam were eligible to attend grammar schools and follow a broadly academic curriculum. Those who failed attended secondary modern schools that followed a broadly vocational curriculum. Although most children currently attend comprehensive education, for which there is no entry test, grammar schools still exist in some parts of the country and 11-plus IQ tests are used to control entry to these schools. In the USA, entrance to higher education is partly controlled through Scholastic Aptitude Tests (SATs) that cover the skills of critical reading, essay-writing and mathematics.

Although IQ tests are just one of a range of tests used in education systems, they are important because they claim to be objective tests of innate intelligence: they not only reliably and validly measure 'intelligence', they do so independently of cultural influences such as class, gender, age or ethnicity. Those who support IQ tests believe that are an important tool for revealing the natural variations in intelligence within and between different individuals and populations. This is based on the theory that people are born with a certain level of intelligence, inherited from their parents, which does not vary greatly throughout their lifetime.

> **KEY TERM**
>
> **Ethnicity:** expression of the cultural background of different groups, which includes factors such as religious affiliations, country of birth and residence, cultural beliefs, traditions and customs.

These ideas have significant implications for the relationship between intelligence and educational achievement. If an education system is meritocratic, any differences in achievement can be explained by natural variation in intelligence.

Internal evaluation: Internal criticisms of intelligence testing focus on the construction and application of the tests themselves, mainly about their claim to be 'culture-free' or 'culture-neutral'. The argument here is that rather than being a measure of 'natural intelligence', IQ tests actually measure cultural learning.

Where IQ tests are timed, for example, students who are familiar with the question formats are likely to perform better than those who are not. In other words, students who practise answering IQ tests have an advantage, because to answer a question, the student first needs to understand what it is asking. Those who have to spend time thinking about *how* to answer a question have less time in which to actually answer it. Murray (2013) argues that the ability to pay for private test tuition gives children 'from more affluent families

an unfair advantage over those from less well-off backgrounds'.

A further criticism is that tests of verbal reasoning and comprehension, especially in societies with a diverse range of ethnicities, make cultural assumptions that disadvantage children from ethnic minorities. For example, certain questions might assume that something is common knowledge, whereas it may not be known to those from minority cultures.

Another criticism of IQ tests relates to differences in cultural learning between those born and raised within the same society, but who are separated by differences in class and ethnicity. Dove (1971), for example, demonstrated that IQ tests assume particular kinds of cultural knowledge that bias them towards particular (in this instance, white American) ethnic groups. One consequence of this bias is that those familiar with the cultural assumptions contained in the tests have higher measured IQ scores. Dove also showed how, by reversing these assumptions in favour of minority, culturally different and disadvantaged groups, levels of measured intelligence could be reversed.

Kaplan (1998) claims that 'how well a person does on an IQ test depends on a variety of factors besides intelligence'. These include:

- education
- reading habits
- experience with and attitudes towards taking tests
- cultural upbringing
- mental and physical health.

He concludes: 'Count me among those who regard the study of intelligence as more pseudo-science than science.'

External evaluation: External criticisms of IQ testing relate to wider ideas about the validity of such tests. These criticisms take a number of forms relating to both the nature of 'intelligence' and what, if anything, IQ tests actually measure. Burden (2004), for example, argues that the concept of 'intelligence' is both problematic – it is too complex to be reduced to simple forms of 'intelligence testing' – and context dependent: 'It's a hypothetical construct psychologists have used to describe how people behave. How I would behave in the Amazon jungle is a lot less intelligently than I would in my job as a psychology professor. And if something goes wrong with my car I open the bonnet and hope someone will come and help me.'

Other types of criticism focus on the construct validity of IQ tests. Flynn (1987), argues that 'psychologists should stop saying IQ tests measure intelligence. They should say that IQ tests measure abstract problem-solving ability (APSA), a term that accurately conveys our ignorance'. In other words, while IQ tests used in education systems claim to measure something called 'intelligence', what they actually measure are two possible *types* of intelligence – those that involve linguistic and logical-mathematical abilities.

This is significant in the context of understanding the relationship between intelligence and educational achievement because it suggests that out of all the possible measures that *could* be used, decisions have been made about which are considered valid. This implies that what counts as 'intelligence' and how it relates to educational achievement are culturally loaded constructs. Any relationship between the two is biased in favour of those social groups who have the power to both define how intelligence is measured and how it is realised or expressed in terms of educational achievement.

What IQ tests measure, therefore, is at best a subset of 'intelligence'. This raises important questions about why they are designed to measure some abilities but not others. One explanation is that they measure those abilities most valued by powerful social groups (what Marxists call the 'ruling class'). IQ testing is part of a process of cultural reproduction in which the power to define and objectively measure intelligence is a valuable social resource, for two reasons:

1   Intelligence is defined in ways that reflect the particular class, gender or ethnic interests of powerful groups.
2   If subordinate social groups accept, or are unable to challenge, this definition it both cements their lower position (they are 'less intelligent') and justifies any differential treatment they receive. Children of the upper and middle classes, for example, achieve more not because of their privileged position but because they are simply 'more intelligent' and so more deserving. It similarly serves as a justification for both social and academic segregation because it is based on 'objective' criteria.

From this perspective, IQ tests and the concepts of intelligence they embody are part of the ideological state apparatus. Convincing people that natural intelligence differences exist and can be objectively measured, is a powerful form of social control. Gardner, for example, calls this 'the IQ way of thinking: that people are either smart or not, that there's nothing much you can do about it, and that tests can tell you if you are one of the smart ones'.

Additional criticisms of the cultural biases of IQ tests focus on their ecological validity. One problem with IQ testing is that it takes place under artificial conditions – not just those of the test itself but also, as Flynn argues, the premises on which such intelligence testing is based: 'We know that people solve problems on IQ tests; we suspect that those problems are so detached, or so abstracted from reality, that the ability to solve them can diverge over time from the real-world problem solving ability called intelligence; thus far we know little else'. To put this another way, what IQ tests measure is the ability to complete IQ tests.

TEST YOURSELF

List the pros and cons of using IQ tests to measure intelligence in education.

Intelligence and educational achievement

Keeping in mind that definitions of both intelligence and achievement may be socially constructed, explanations for their relationship generally take three forms: agnostic, positive and negative.

Agnostic: This explanation argues that we do not know if there is a real relationship between intelligence and achievement for two reasons:

1   There is no generally agreed definition of intelligence so we do not know what is being measured.
2   Even if we select a quantifiable subset of intelligence, there is no general consensus about how it can be reliably and validly measured.

Further problems arise if intelligence is conceptualised as a *relationship*. This means it is seen as something fluid and dynamic, created by individuals as they go about their lives and expressed in different ways and contexts, rather than as a permanent quality. This position suggests that intelligence develops through cultural practices and ways of learning, rather than being something we are born with. As Kaplan argues: 'Intelligence is difficult to define precisely, but we can all agree that it refers to intellectual *ability* as opposed to intellectual achievement.' People can be intelligent without necessarily being able to demonstrate their intelligence by passing exams.

Positive: This explanation argues that we can assume IQ tests measure significant aspects of intelligence in the form cognitive skills. These include the ability to solve mathematical problems or understand logical arguments. Since these skills are very similar to those valued in both education and the workplace, it makes sense to test the relationship between intelligence and achievement in this

163

way. From this perspective, IQ clearly correlates positively with educational achievement:

- Deary et al. (2007) found a 0.8 correlation (1 = a very strong, possibly causal relationship and 0 = no relationship) between 'cognitive ability tests taken at 11 and national school examinations taken at 16'. Their main finding was 'the large contribution of general mental ability to educational achievement'.
- Mackintosh (2002) notes that 'schoolchildren's IQ scores correlate in the range 0.5 to 0.7 with their current and subsequent educational attainment: the correlation between 11-year-olds' IQ scores and their GCSE grades at age 16 is over 0.5'.

Although this evidence of a positive relationship is significant, it should be noted that the difference between 0.5 and 0.8 is actually very large.

In general, this approach makes a positive connection between social selection on the basis of educational qualifications and intelligence. In the USA, for example, Murray and Herrnstein (1994) argue that race is linked to intelligence (roughly running from black at the bottom, white in the middle to Asian at the top) and this explains why black Americans achieve less than their white or Asian peers.

In the UK, Saunders (2002) argues that intelligence, while not determined at birth, differs between social classes. Social and developmental factors mean middle-class children are, on average, significantly more intelligent than their working-class peers. Social selection based on class differences in intelligence, therefore, operates in two ways:

1 Middle-class parents in professional employment have demonstrated their higher levels of intelligence. They have achieved high employment status by competing with their working-class peers.
2 The knowledge and experience parents gain through this social process gives their children an advantage. This is partly because they have more to lose by educational failure (downward social mobility) and partly because middle-class parents instil in their children the importance of educational qualifications, because this is how they achieved their current social status.

According to Saunders, social selection ensures that those who are the most academically able rise to the top of the class structure. Intelligent working-class children are educationally successful and rise into the middle class. Middle-class children who fail to capitalise on their social advantages fall back into the working class. This process

means that middle-class children will, on average, always be more intelligent than working-class children.

Negative: Explanations here generally follow two lines of reasoning:

1 It would be surprising if there was no positive correlation between IQ test scores and educational achievement, mainly because the skills valued and taught in schools and tested in public examinations are those measured in IQ tests.
2 Educational achievement is not related to intelligence; rather, it is related to a range of cultural factors inside and outside the education system that allow some pupils to do well, while severely limiting the ability of others to do the same. This achievement is simply validated by higher measured levels of IQ. In other words, cultural factors relating to class, gender and ethnicity explain higher IQ and achievement levels. As Goleman (1995) argues: 'The vast majority of one's ultimate niche in society is determined by non-IQ factors, ranging from **social class** to luck'.

KEY TERM

Social class: the individual's position in a class-based system of social stratification, conventionally defined by occupation.

Petty (2011) argues that a defining feature of IQ tests is that they 'reflect the social order' because 'the people who make up the IQ tests are from the educated middle class. What they are saying to others who score high on IQ tests is, 'You must be intelligent, you think just like me'. The values that are reflected in IQ tests are those of the middle class.'

ACTIVITY

Discussion: If intelligence, attainment and employment are closely related (the brightest achieve the most and get the best jobs), why are there so few women in higher-income professional work?

The relationship between education and social mobility

The relationship between education and **social mobility** is a complex one. To begin with, it is important to understand what 'social mobility' means and how it is measured. Aldridge (2001) suggests that the concept 'describes the movement or opportunities for movement between different social groups'. In late-modern industrial societies this involves two ideas:

1 social classes and how they are ranked in a system of stratification that allows people to move up or down the class structure
2 how social class can be tested or measured using various indicators, usually a person's occupation.

KEY TERM

Social mobility: the ability to move up or down the class structure.

Social mobility can be defined in different ways, but for our purposes it is most helpful to think in terms of relative mobility which, for Aldridge, 'is concerned with the chances people from different backgrounds have of attaining different social positions'. This means that is a measure of how movement varies according to someone's starting position in the class structure. It is an appropriate definition to use in the context of education because we can relate individuals to educational qualifications and different occupations – and therefore to upward or downward social mobility. There are two main ways to measure relative social mobility:

1 Inter-generational mobility refers to movement between generations, such as the difference between a parent and their adult child's occupational position.
2 Intra-generational measures refer to an individual's mobility over the course of their life, comparing the position of someone's starting occupation with their occupation on retirement, for example.

Underlying all this is the idea that contemporary industrial societies are broadly based on achieved social status and mobility. The individual's position in society is not fixed (or ascribed) by characteristics such as age, gender or ethnicity; rather, it is earned or achieved on the basis of factors such as educational qualifications.

Consensus approaches

Functionalism: Functionalist arguments about the relationship between education and social mobility focus on how education systems represent a bridge between the family and the economy:

1 Social mobility is functionally necessary: people must be allowed to move up – or fall down – the occupational and social structure. This ensures that important social positions are filled by those who are most qualified.

2 Upward mobility is earned through demonstrations of individual merit. In modern societies, which contain a wide variety of occupations, from unskilled workers such as road sweepers at the bottom, to highly skilled professionals such as doctors and accountants at the top, people must fill these positions on the basis of their knowledge and skills.

Meritocracy: It is inevitable that mass education systems develop in modern industrial societies, because their primary function is differentiation – allowing individuals to 'demonstrate their differences' in objective ways. For education systems to perform this role effectively, they must be meritocratic. Rewards such as well-paid, high-status occupations are earned and allocated through individual abilities and efforts in the education system. Such systems are, by definition, competitive. However, competition must be based on equal opportunities. If some people are disadvantaged – because of their sex, race or social class, for example – then society cannot be sure that 'the best people' will end up in the most important or prestigious adult roles. Meritocratic systems involve, therefore, inequalities of outcome. Parsons (1959a) summarises this idea as follows: 'It is fair to give differential rewards for different levels of achievement, so long as there has been fair access to opportunity, and fair that these rewards lead on to higher-order opportunities for the successful.'

Schools develop inequalities of outcome through testing and examinations. In a meritocratic system, these must be objective tests that everyone has an equal opportunity to take and pass. This is because role allocation is a mechanism through which those who are intellectually most able and talented achieve work roles that offer the highest rewards in terms of income, power and status. As Davis and Moore argue: 'Education is the proving ground for ability and hence the selective agency for placing people in different statuses according to their abilities.'

Harris (2005b) suggests that for traditional functionalism, social mobility develops out of the way people are encouraged to perform different roles, some of which are more important, skilled and difficult to learn than others. The promise of higher levels of status, income and job satisfaction by working for educational qualifications, therefore, represents *necessary* motivations and rewards. These rewards lead to the development of social hierarchies – some jobs are more important than others and this creates functionally necessary social inequalities. For Davis and Moore, the inequalities that flow through social mobility represent 'an unconsciously evolved device by which societies ensure the most important positions are conscientiously filled by the most qualified people'. Lenski's (1994) analysis of 'Marxist social systems' such as China and North Korea supports this position. It argues that **social inequality** is inevitable, necessary and functional because 'incentive systems' are required to motivate and reward the best-qualified people for occupying the most important positions within a social system.

> **KEY TERM**
>
> **Social inequality:** unequal and unfair distribution of resources in any system such as education. Inequality of educational opportunity, for example, refers to the way some children are treated unfairly in the education system on the basis of subjective criteria such as class, gender and ethnicity.

Poor children share textbooks at a monastery school in Burma (Myanmar). Is education entirely meritocratic?

Evaluation: As we have seen, inequalities of educational outcome that affect social mobility are justified by meritocratic competition. However, it can be argued that education systems in modern industrial societies are not meritocratic. Some groups, such as the working class and some ethnic minorities, experience systematic disadvantage. Paterson and Iannelli (2005), for example, argue that in Scotland: 'Many studies have shown education and the acquisition of educational qualifications are important means through which middle-class families pass on their social and economic advantage to their children. In these circumstances, education, rather than promoting greater social mobility, may in fact reduce it'.

While meritocratic systems should involve contest mobility, neo-Marxists such as Bowles and Gintis argue that modern education systems are characterised by 'sponsored mobility'. By this they mean that upper-and middle-class children enjoy a range of cultural advantages

over their working-class peers, such as the ability to buy high-quality, high-status private education. Their progress from school to high-paid, high-status employment is effectively sponsored by their parents' class background. Breen and Goldthorpe (1999) have demonstrated that social mobility is not as great in modern societies as it *should* be if it were based on merit alone. In this respect, social class is a variable that promotes or hinders social mobility.

In addition, although a meritocracy involves open competition for social resources such as educational qualifications or adult employment, Breen (1997) argues that this only occurs at the lower levels of society. The higher social levels are marked by social closure – they are closed to the vast majority and no real competition takes place within these levels. Social closure is related to high levels of **social capital** – the networks and connections built through membership of elite private schools, such as Winchester and Eton in the UK or the Lawrence School, Sanawar, in India and universities such as Oxford and Cambridge in the UK or Harvard and Yale in the USA.

> **KEY TERM**
>
> **Social capital:** extent to which people are connected to social networks (who you know) and how this can be used to the individual's advantage.

> **TEST YOURSELF**
>
> Why do functionalists believe that education systems must be meritocratic?

Neo-functionalism/new right: This approach to education and mobility combines the concept of meritocracy with individual life choices. If societies provide the same opportunities to their members through a meritocratic schooling system, then educational success or failure results from the different choices people make.

Saunders (1996), for example, argues that social mobility is related to education in the sense that it reflects the life choices made by different individuals and groups. In any competitive system there must be 'winners and losers'. Some people will have more of the 'good things in life' than others. Who these winners and losers turn out to be in modern, meritocratic societies is determined by the choices they make, not by factors such as class, gender or ethnicity. Saunders argues that middle-class parents invest heavily in their children's education and this 'investment choice' combined with hard work by the children themselves, is rewarded by higher educational qualifications. This does not guarantee that such children will be upwardly mobile, but it usually guards against downward mobility.

Murphy (1990) argues that in an education system that provides **equality of opportunity**, differences in achievement are the result of unsuccessful students choosing not to participate. Where individuals end up in the class structure is also the outcome of their life choices – for example, the difference between choosing to work consistently in school to gain qualifications or leaving school at 16, getting pregnant and becoming a single parent.

KEY TERM

Equality of opportunity: the absence of discrimination within institutions such as schools.

More generally, neo-functionalist/new-right approaches argue that where individual choices are the key to mobility through education, schools should be privately owned rather than state controlled. This would ensure that consumers (parents and their children) have the widest possible choice. This idea is related to **marketisation** and follows from the idea that private companies are consumer-capture organisations; they must respond to consumer demand by continually innovating and improving their service to attract and retain customers.

KEY TERM

Marketisation: process whereby the supply and consumption of educational goods and services are opened up to private and public competition.

This approach sees consumer choice as being limited by 'producer capture'. This limits a child's chances of mobility, especially children from the lower levels of society who cannot afford to pay for an alternative education to that offered by the state. Pateman (1991) notes: 'Teachers have set their own agendas for schools when it should be parents who set agendas for teachers.' From neo-functionalist/new-right perspectives, one way to increase social mobility is through selection by ability:

- It identifies those most suited to different types of education – academic for those who want to pursue a professional route into work, vocational for those whose talents lie elsewhere. This requires rigorous selection processes to ensure that individual pupils are placed in

the right type of school and on the right type of course for their particular needs.
- It selects children objectively on the basis of their natural talents and benefits those lower down the social scale because it promotes social mobility through competition.

Meritocratic forms of selection are preferable to the covert methods that take place in 'non-selective' education systems. The very rich, for example, self-select their children by paying for private education. Those from the middle class self-select by making sure their children attend the schools with the best academic reputation. Intelligent working-class pupils who lack the economic, family, social and **cultural capital** available to other classes are left to attend schools that fail to recognise their talents. As a result they are consigned to academic failure and a lack of mobility.

KEY TERM

Cultural capital: anything in the individual's cultural background that gives them advantages over others; higher educational qualifications, for example, are a form of cultural capital the individual tries to exchange for advantages in the workplace, such as high-pay, high-skill jobs.

167

Evaluation: The focus on schools as selective agencies has been questioned, in particular the assumption that school diversity means more choice and greater opportunities for social mobility. The argument here is that neo-functionalist/new-right approaches confuse social selection, where schools choose parents, with consumer choice, where only those with substantial economic resources can choose private education.

In the UK, Shepherd and Rogers (2012) carried out an analysis of Christian faith schools, which are allowed to select students on the basis of parental faith. The results showed that these schools take a lower proportion of working-class children than their catchment area suggests they should: 'England's faith state schools are on average failing to mirror their local communities by shunning the poorest pupils in their area.' In this respect, consumer choice is only really available to those who have the money and resources to make such choices. Where schools select their pupils through interviews and tests, it is largely middle-class parents, those with the cultural capital to play the selection game successfully, who benefit at the expense of the working class.

The evidence for 'bright working-class children' benefiting from objective forms of selection is hotly debated. While critics argue that IQ testing brings little or no benefits to working-class children, supporters such as Saunders (1996) claim that to see 'middle-class children outperforming working-class children' in objective tests and to 'deduce from this that the system itself was unfair and needed changing' misses the point. Middle-class children are, he argues, simply more intelligent.

Conflict approaches

Marxism: While consensus approaches generally see open, competitive and meritocratic education systems as the most important source of social mobility in modern industrial societies, conflict approaches take the opposite view. Education is not a source of social mobility but rather the means through which a bourgeois class is able to cement its privileged social position. It does so by ensuring that social inequality is reproduced through a system that appears to be fair but which is really biased in their favour.

For Marxists, the main role and purpose of education is cultural reproduction. Althusser, for example, argues that the reproduction of capitalism involves each new generation being taught the skills, knowledge and ideas required in the workplace. Schools do not just select, allocate and differentiate children in the interests of society as a whole. They role is to help the children of the ruling class to achieve the levels of education required to follow in their parents' footsteps. For Marxists, therefore, the role of education is to educate most people 'just enough' to be useful employees and a small number 'more than enough' to take up high-powered elite working roles.

Aldridge (2004) argues that a key feature of modern industrial societies is a lack of occupational mobility for those lower down the class structure. To understand how and why this is the case, Marxists argue that what happens in the education system cannot be separated from the demands of the economy. Education is a way of reproducing the social inequalities found in the capitalist workplace.

Powell (2002) sees social closure in terms of 'restrictions placed on people's ability to engage in certain occupational endeavours' that are reflected by 'criteria restricting entry into the practice of all but the most menial and unrewarding of occupations'. This results in 'collective entry requirements for practising various occupations and professions that effectively work to limit social mobility'. In other words, social mobility is restricted because certain occupational groups can close off entry to 'outsiders' – those lower down the social scale. The well-connected and influential social classes can ensure that their offspring

are recruited into high-level professional occupations such as dentistry or accountancy.

Aldridge argues that social closure does not merely limit upward intra-generational social mobility, 'from manual occupations to higher status professional and technical occupations', it actually causes it to decline. A tightening of entry requirements across 'higher-status occupations' means they are 'closed from below'. This means that it is impossible to enter these occupations without having been through a particular educational process, from A levels, through undergraduate and postgraduate qualifications to professional entrance exams. Where outside entry is not possible, long-range intra-generational mobility across the class structure is curtailed, as are certain forms of short-range mobility from within the middle classes, since transfers from lower-status to higher-status professions are similarly difficult.

TEST YOURSELF

1 What does the term 'cultural reproduction' mean?
2 What evidence might be used to show that cultural reproduction exists?

The argument here is that education is not a particularly strong source of social mobility because as a population becomes 'more educated', powerful groups simply raise the entry requirements for elite occupations. Thus, while children may gain more and better educational qualifications than their grandparents, the economic value of these qualifications declines. Occupations such as nursing that once required a relatively low level of educational qualification (such as GCSEs) now require much higher levels (such as an undergraduate degree).

For Althusser, the formal curriculum taught in schools is the main way in which education restricts social mobility and enhances elite class reproduction. This involves the following.

- Access to different types of knowledge, academic and vocational, being restricted through elite control of the formal curriculum. The higher a child goes in the education system, the greater their access to the forms of knowledge required for professional occupations.
- Restricting the ambitions and expectations of different social classes by structuring knowledge. Academic (theoretical) knowledge is valued more than practical (vocational) knowledge because the former is most useful for professional workers.

- Children learning to accept authority because this is a valued workplace skill. The higher children go in the education system, the *looser* the social controls on their behaviour. After the age of 16, for example, they can be trusted to 'do the right things'. Those who 'cannot be trusted' have already been excluded, either through failing to reach the required educational level or through self-selection – leaving school at the earliest opportunity.

How are some occupations closed to lower-class pupils?

Neo-Marxism: Traditional Marxists such as Althusser see education as a tool used by a ruling class to maintain its domination and control. Neo-Marxists claim that the relationship between education and cultural reproduction is based on legitimate leadership with the 'consent' of the led. As Strinati (1995) puts it: 'Dominant groups in society maintain their dominance by securing the 'spontaneous consent' of subordinate groups'. This is achieved, for example, through their control of the media. If people can be made to believe that education is meritocratic, with achievement based on individual intelligence and hard work, then the system cannot be blamed. The individual is responsible for their own failure.

For Bowles and Gintis (1976, 2002), cultural reproduction is secured through the correspondence between workplace and educational **inequality**. Education systems play a gate-keeping role in society, allowing those with the 'right' orientations and attitudes through and excluding those with the 'wrong' orientation to work. Education is not so much a test of ability as a test of conformity. Those who 'play the game' progress through its various levels, while those who do not are systematically eliminated. Macdonald and Jónsdóttir (2008) further suggest that playing the game successfully involves 'the necessary understanding of the rules of the game, to understand what is expected of you' and this is something middle-class children, equipped with higher levels of cultural capital, understand more easily.

KEY TERM

Inequality: any situation that lacks equality; this may be due to natural differences, such as inequalities of height, or social differences (see *social inequality*).

Hegemonic (ruling-class) control also explains why *some* working-class pupils are successful. By overcoming the barriers systematically placed in their way, they prove that they are willing to accept the values on which elite hegemony is based. These pupils who succeed 'against the odds' also help to maintain the 'myth of meritocracy'.

Evaluation: The correspondence between education and work in contemporary societies is methodologically weak. It is based on superficial similarities; almost anything that happens in the workplace can be made to correspond to school processes.

The role of education as an institution charged with creating well-socialised, docile, future workers is also questioned by Willis's study of working-class 'lads'. This research suggests that some pupils are well aware of the limitations of education and work. They 'see through' the system, for example, and consciously rebel against it. The main question when evaluating this view is how far the experience of education socialises pupils into an acceptance of capitalist ideology. Where traditional Marxism casts teachers in the role of 'agents of ideological transmission and control' – directly responsible for shaping the perceptions of pupils – an alternative interpretation is that many pupils realise they are destined for low-status work and see little point in learning the lessons offered by the education system. Chien and Wallace (2004) also suggest that teachers are not entirely to blame because their 'entire upbringing and experiences have subtly shaped their opinions about how students should be taught and what type of knowledge is valuable and should be taught in schools'.

ACTIVITY

Use the internet to research the educational background of the top politicians, business people and celebrities in your society. What does your research tell you about the relationship between education and social mobility?

169

Debates about the links between social inequality (class, gender, ethnicity) and educational opportunity and achievement

In this section, we will consider in more detail the sociological explanations for differential educational achievement – how and why children of different classes, genders and ethnicities achieve different levels of qualifications. We will also look at possible interrelationships between these factors.

Functionalism

Traditional functionalist approaches generally assume that modern educational systems are meritocratic. As such, explanations for differential achievement focus on family and economic processes. Since meritocracies are, by definition, competitive, education systems are not designed to eliminate social disadvantages. Their function is to efficiently sort people into different economic positions based on their individual merits.

Class: Explanations for working-class underachievement focus on **cultural deprivation** and the idea that working-class family life lacks the attributes that contribute to middle-class success. Douglas (1964), for example, notes the impact on educational attainment of variables such as:

- parental attitudes, expressed in terms of levels of encouragement and interest in a child's education
- family size – larger working-class families mean fewer parental resources for each child
- position within the family – older children achieve more than younger members of large families
- deficient care of babies in large families with fewer social and economic resources to devote to their care and upbringing. Desforges (2003) also argues that the weight of evidence supports the claim that 'at-home good parenting' has a positive effect on achievement.

> **KEY TERM**
>
> **Cultural deprivation:** as a cause of educational underachievement, cultural deprivation suggests a lack of important cultural resources, such as parental encouragement.

Cultural deprivation has two main applications in terms of achievement:

1. Working-class children encounter difficulties adjusting to the middle-class norms and values found in schools.

Bernstein (1971) argued that working-class **restricted speech codes** clashed with the **elaborated speech codes** of middle-class teachers. This, in turn, influenced teachers' assessments: middle-class students, able to express themselves in 'the **language** of education', were consequently over-represented in top streams, sets and bands (see below).

2. Wider economic pressures on family life result in working-class children leaving school at the earliest opportunity. Parental attitudes and economic pressures combine to create a tendency towards **immediate gratification**. This has traditionally involved males moving into full-time manual work and females into part-time work and having a family of their own. In contrast, middle-class families are future orientated and their children tended towards **deferred gratification**. They see education as a 'means to an end' of higher-status employment. Goodman and Gregg (2010) found that around 80% of the most affluent mothers assumed their child would go to university, while around 40% of the least affluent mothers 'hoped' their child would go to university. They also found that children from poorer families believed they were 'less academic' and were consequently less concerned about doing well academically than their middle-class peers.

> **KEY TERMS**
>
> **Restricted and elaborated speech codes:** Bernstein argues that elaborated codes involve complex vocabulary and ideas and subtle meanings that can be used and understood in a wide range of different situations. Restricted codes use simple language to convey direct meanings. They are predictable, express relatively simple, straightforward ideas and are directed towards an audience that already understands most of what is being expressed.
>
> **Language:** communication system that, in humans, involves both verbal and non-verbal cues.
>
> **Immediate/deferred gratification:** deferred gratification involves not taking something immediately in the hope that by waiting you will receive something better. Immediate gratification involves taking something as soon as it is offered. In education, for example, leaving school at the earliest opportunity may bring immediate gratification in the sense of being able to earn money sooner; however, by staying in school to earn higher qualifications the individual's long-term earning power is likely to be much greater.

Contemporary ideas about cultural deprivation have focused on ways of compensating working-class children for their dysfunctional family life to give them an equal

170

opportunity to compete with their culturally advantaged middle-class peers. In the UK, examples of **compensatory education** have included:

- Education Action Zones, involving clusters of primary and secondary schools joining forces with parents, councils and local businesses to improve educational services.

- Sure Start programmes, introduced in 2000, designed to improve services to the poorest pre-school children and families to prevent truancy and increase achievement. Additional schemes were aimed at pregnant teenagers to help them back to education or training.

- Extended schools that offer services, such as crèches, support for parents and leisure opportunities for pupils outside the traditional school timetable, designed to engage parents in their child's education. Wilkin et al. (2002), for example, found a positive impact on lower-class 'attainment, attendance and behaviour' when schools offered activities that increased 'engagement and motivation'.

KEY TERM

Compensatory education: supplementary educational programmes designed to compensate children for their deprived home background.

Neo-functionalist/new-right underclass theories argue that a combination of material and cultural factors are the cause of educational failure among those increasingly disconnected from mainstream society. For Murray and Phillips (2001), the underclass involves 'people at the margins of society, unsocialised and often violent … parents who cannot provide for themselves, whose children are the despair of the teachers'. In this respect, 'the socially excluded are no longer just poor but the victims of anti-education, anti-marriage policies which have undermined personal responsibility'.

The argument here is that the underclass is responsible for its own underachievement. Parents fail to take moral responsibility for childcare and socialisation, and their children socially select themselves out of education through truancy, misbehaviour and 'anti-education' beliefs.

Ethnicity: Notions of cultural advantage and disadvantage focused on the family are also used to explain differences in achievement within minority ethnic groups. The relative failure of Black Caribbean working-class boys in the UK, for example, has been variously related to:

- the high number of female-headed single-parent families that fail to provide role models for male children

- the development of 'anti-education' sub-cultures and the effects of large-scale unemployment, Ball et al. (2012) report that with black unemployment currently running at 50% in the UK, there is little chance of boys getting paid work as adults so they see little point to educational qualifications.

Sewell (2010) summarises this general argument when he suggests that black children's educational performance is undermined by:

- poor parenting
- 'anti-school' peer-group pressure
- an inability to take responsibility for their own 'anti-school' behaviour.

Asian and Indian pupils in the UK achieve more highly. This is explained in terms of cultural and family values of educational success and extended family structures that support children throughout their schooling. Chua (2011) also suggests that the higher achievements of Chinese pupils can be partly explained by 'tiger mothers', who push their children relentlessly towards educational success.

Neo-functionalist/new-right arguments suggest that the 'disproportionate representation' of ethnic minorities in the underclass is related to failures in their cultural organisation. Some black ethnic minorities 'disadvantage themselves' through dysfunctional family structures that correlate with differential educational achievement. Black Caribbean families, for example, have the highest rates of single parenthood and the lowest rates of educational achievement.

High levels of Indian and Asian achievement are explained by close, stable and supportive extended families. In this respect, Saunders (1990) argues that underclass life, both black and white, is characterised by dependency cultures involving a passive acceptance of low status. This creates a cycle of deprivation that carries from parents to children in the form of low educational and work expectations.

Gender: This perspective suggests that cultural deprivation explains differences in female educational achievement *between* classes. Middle-class boys achieve more than working-class girls, for example. Differences *within* classes, where working-class girls generally outperform boys, can be explained by linking social and economic change to gender socialisation. Wilkinson (1994), for example, argues that the gradual change from

171

manufacturing to service industries has given rise to a 'knowledge-based' economy that 'values brains more than it does brawn'. The skills women have traditionally demonstrated in the home, such as conflict resolution and interpersonal communication, are increasingly valued in the workplace.

Economic change, with a large increase in the proportion of women working both full and part time, has resulted in a slow but steady change in parental attitudes towards female education. Whereas in the past, most girls would expect to spend most of their life outside paid employment, the reverse is increasingly true. Higher levels of female educational achievement reflect the greater need for qualifications to take into the workplace.

One of the main neo-functionalist/new-right educational concerns is male underachievement resulting from social and economic changes that have tipped the educational balance unfairly in girls' favour. Francis and Skelton (2005) note that male underachievement is often explained by natural differences between boys and girls. For example, curriculum changes have been characterised by a move away from testing 'more difficult' male subjects and forms of knowledge towards 'softer' feminine subjects. These developments have progressively disadvantaged boys. The feminisation of schooling also favours girls. This refers to factors such as the lack of male role models in primary schools, 'female-friendly' teaching practices, curricula and assessment criteria, such as coursework rather than final exams. Feminisation also expresses itself in the classroom by, for example, punishing natural exuberant male behaviour. This may result in the development of 'anti-pupil' sub-cultures and behaviours, such as truancy, that damage boys' educational chances. These arguments about gendered differential achievement come together around three main points:

- Male underachievement results from the 'feminisation of school and work'.
- Teaching and testing regimes favour female ways of thinking and working.
- Male underachievement results from the school's failure to develop ways to engage boys effectively and actively.

Evaluation: Nell Keddie (1971) criticises the concept of cultural deprivation because it implies that the culture of working-class pupils is in some way deficient. Keddie argues that it is actually the education system that often discriminates against working-class pupils. Schools are run by the middle class, which rejects any cultural views that differ from its own. Keddie argues that schools

Many educational theorists believe we need to differentiate between male and female learning styles to get the best out of every individual

should recognise 'cultural difference', not deprivation. If working-class culture was recognised and valued by teachers, working-class pupils would have a better chance of achieving educational success.

Hanafin and Lynch (2002) suggest that the idea of deficiency, in the form of ethnic-minority or working-class parents not valuing education, is both misplaced and misdirected. They argue that many working-class parents, both black *and* white, take a keen interest in their children's education, but 'felt excluded from participation in decision-making' within schools. In contrast, the middle-class women in Reay's (2000) study were better positioned to involve themselves in school decision-making. Mirza (2001) also cites the development of 'Saturday Schools' among Black Caribbean communities as evidence for a commitment to education going unrecognised within the state school system.

Underclass explanations have also been criticised for their ideological bias. MacDonald and Marsh (2005) found 'no evidence of a distinct, deviant, underclass culture' in their research in Middlesbrough, England. What they found was a complicated picture of 'marginalised youth' struggling to come to terms with their low status and **social exclusion**. Mac an Ghaill (1996)

 KEY TERM

Social exclusion: being excluded from participation in social institutions such as education or employment.

also argues that working-class underachievement is not explained by the culture of working-class boys but by changes in the labour market. For example, the decline in manufacturing jobs have effectively excluded such boys from their traditional forms of industrial employment and left them as a relatively marginalised group within the education system.

> **TEST YOURSELF**
>
> Give two examples of cultural deprivation.

Marxism

Marxist explanations for differential achievement have generally focused on two main areas: **material deprivation** and cultural capital.

> 🔑 **KEY TERM**
>
> **Material deprivation:** as a cause of educational underachievement, material deprivation refers to factors such as poverty, a lack of physical resources and so forth.

Class: Traditional Marxist approaches favour materialist explanations, with poverty and deprivation as the main source of differential achievement. Material deprivation, for example, involves a combination of factors that give working-class pupils a disadvantage in education:

- poor diet/nutrition
- the lack of private study facilities and resources
- the need to work to supplement family income.

While these forms of deprivation are significant in regions such as Europe and North America, Ramachandran argues that, in India, material deprivation is more acute:

- 50% of schools have a leaking roof or no water supply
- 35% have no blackboard or furniture
- 90% have no functioning toilets.

She further argues: 'Malnutrition, hunger and poor health remain core problems, which comprehensively affect attendance and performance in classes. The added burden of home chores and child labour influence a large number of children, especially girls, to drop out of school'.

The development of different class cultures built around different norms, values, beliefs and attitudes, flows from material advantages and disadvantages.

- For the middle class, educational qualifications are an important way of reproducing individual class positions.
- For the working class, the work-based route to money and status has always been more important.

Class sub-culture theory takes this a step further by arguing that education systems are dominated by middle-class norms, values, beliefs and ideologies. While some working-class sub-cultural groups succeed by adapting successfully to this environment, others do not. Underachievement, therefore, is a by-product of rejecting school values through things like truancy and exclusion.

> **TEST YOURSELF**
>
> Suggest two ways in which material deprivation may disadvantage working class pupils.

An alternative explanation involves situational constraints. Working-class children find it more difficult to translate values into social behaviour and, by extension, educational qualifications. As Westergaard and Resler (1976) argue, while working-class parents 'have a high and increasing interest in their children's education they lack the means to translate that interest into effective influence on their children's behalf'. This idea can be linked to neo-Marxist concepts of class reproduction, which argue that the underlying purpose of education is to ensure the continued hegemony of a ruling class.

While Willis talks about how 'working-class kids get working-class jobs', the opposite is also true: upper-class kids are destined to get upper-class jobs. Mac an Ghaill, for example, argues that a person's class origins are the best predictor of educational success or failure, while Demack et al. (1998) suggest that 'Social class differences are still the largest differences of all and the children of professional parents have the largest advantage of all.' One reason for this is the heavy investment made by middle- and upper-class parents in their children's education:

- Economic investment involves things like buying private education or tuition.
- Emotional investment involves middle-class parents being able to influence the focus and direction of a child's education decisively. Mothers, in particular, invest time and effort in their children's education. This emotional labour includes not just help with homework but also making sure that the school is providing appropriate levels of support, teaching and testing.

173

How does material deprivation affect an individual's education?

Gender: Marxists generally frame gender differences in achievement in terms of social class. Murphy and Elwood, for example, note how historical improvements in female achievement are 'not shared by girls from low socio-economic backgrounds'. Gorard et al. (2001) also note that:

- there is little measurable difference in male/female attainment in maths and science
- there is no significant gender difference at the lowest attainment levels for all other curriculum subjects
- girls do better than boys among 'mid-to-high-achievers', and that there is a closer correlation between achievement and class than there is between achievement and gender.

Neo-Marxists argue that questions of underachievement should be reframed in terms of working-class boys and changing male identities:

- Jones and Myhill (2004) argue that male identities that emphasise physical strength, sexual virility and aggressiveness are not conducive to educational achievement. Such masculinities create problems for teachers in the classroom and downplay the value of educational qualifications.
- Changes in both female identities and the workplace mean that some working-class boys consider education to be irrelevant to their future as, Epstein et al. (1998) argue, they lose control of both their unique identities and lives.
- Platten (1999) takes issues of identity further by arguing that boys are increasingly victims of negative gender stereotyping, which translates into lower teacher expectations and educational underachievement.

Ethnicity: Demack et al. argue that class is a good general predictor of educational attainment across all ethnic groups. In the UK, for example, Black and South Asian

(Pakistani and Bangladeshi) minorities are relatively *over-represented* in the lower social classes, and there is widespread evidence of their lower educational attainment. However, one exception to this is the educational performance of Indian children who make up one of the most educationally successful groups.

Explanations for Black and South Asian underachievement focus on material deprivation. Blair et al. (2003), for example, note how within the same ethnic groups, higher levels of poverty and deprivation are consistently associated with lower educational achievement.

Gillborn and Gipps (1996) also argue that those from the higher social classes achieve more, regardless of their gender or ethnic background.

Various forms of racism, from overt to cultural and institutional have also been cited as factors in black underachievement. Mac an Ghaill argues that the popularity of 'Saturday Schools' amongst Black Caribbean communities suggests there is a general dissatisfaction with 'white institutions' that regularly fail black children.

Evaluation: Douglas argues that material deprivation is too broad an explanation for all forms of underachievement, because some materially deprived children manage to succeed. Working-class attainment also tends to fall throughout a child's education. This implies that school processes, such as **labelling**, stereotyping and low teacher/pupil expectations are potentially significant explanations. Gazeley and Dunne (2005) suggest that schools can make a difference; levels of working-class achievement can be raised, but the behaviour and expectations of teachers can also compound the levels of material and cultural disadvantage many working-class children bring to the school.

KEY TERM

Labelling: a process that involves naming something and, by so doing, associating it with a specific set of social characteristics.

While Lupton (2003) concludes that 'neighbourhood poverty' and 'poor schooling' are inextricably linked, the question is which comes first: are schools 'poor' because the ability of their students is low or do schools fail to inspire and educate working-class pupils?

Feminism

Over the past 50 years, there has been a shift in emphasis in feminist education research. It has moved away from female underachievement in modern industrial societies and now focuses more explaining how girls learn to cope with and overcome a range of school and workplace disadvantages. Eichler (1980), for example, highlights how gendered socialisation helps to construct different gender identities expectations about the role girls will play as adults.

In the past, schools contributed to how women saw their primary adult role, as mothers and housewives, by placing more importance on male education. Female horizons have widened, but traditional assumptions about masculinity and femininity continue to influence both family and work relationships, especially for working-class girls. One aspect of this idea is how the choice of subjects studied after the age of 16 is broadly gendered. (Table 6.1).

Subject	% Males	% Females
Physics	76	24
Computer Studies	73	27
Economics	70	30
Design and Technology	65	35
Mathematics	60	40
Biology	38	62
English Literature	30	70
Social Studies	30	70
Modern Languages	30	70
Drama	30	70
Art and Design	30	70
Home Economics	06	94

Table 6.1 UK A Level or equivalent entries for young people
Source: Babb et al. (2006)

There is also evidence of changes in female primary socialisation. Carter and Wojtkiewicz (2000), for example, found that parents are getting much more involved in their daughters' education than they have in the past. In terms of how socialisation influences concepts of femininity, Crespi (2003) argues that there is now a range of gender identities available to adolescent girls, whereas previously these roles had been largely restricted to part-time or domestic work. Girls have more opportunities to express a range of different 'femininities', including ones that involve a career. In addition, workplace changes reflect back onto family socialisation processes. For example, parents, change their perception of their children's future adult roles and, consequently, the relative importance they place on male and female educational achievement. Educational choices are further reflected in

career choices. In most industrial societies, engineering is male-dominated while nursing or secretarial work is female-dominated. These patterns point towards the idea of underlying social and educational processes that push males and females into different career paths.

Explanations for increasing levels of female educational achievement in contemporary societies relate closely to 'concerns' about male underachievement. Francis and Skelton, for example, note how explanations for female achievement are frequently discussed in terms of male underachievement focused around three main ideas:

- Natural differences, such as differences in brain functions between boys and girls, explain differences in achievement.
- The feminisation of schooling gives girls distinct advantages over boys. Ideas here range from the lack of male role models to 'female-friendly' teaching practices, curricula and assessment criteria that reflect a form of **positive discrimination** in favour of girls.
- Gender constructions and interpretations 'produce different behaviours that impact on achievement'. This includes both teacher expectations (assuming girls will be better behaved) and interpretations – girls are increasing seen as likely to achieve more than boys.

175

KEY TERM

Positive discrimination: preferential treatment based on the individual's class, gender, ethnicity and so forth.

A further problem for feminists is the idea that where female educational achievement is generally rising this applies to all girls, regardless of class and ethnicity. Jones and Myhill, for example, argue 'educational underachievement' is defined by teachers in ways that are increasingly likely to identify boys – particularly white and black working-class boys – as 'potential underachievers'. Ideas about what counts as 'underachievement' also vary in terms of gender. For example, female underachievement among working-class and minority ethnic-group girls is often overlooked in the rush to identify and explain male underachievement. In addition, teachers rationalise achievement differences in terms of their perceptions of the nature of male and female abilities:

- Female achievements are characterised in terms of 'performance': understanding what an examiner wants and delivering it.
- Male achievements are characterised in terms of 'ability'.

These differences embody cultural beliefs about boys being 'naturally more intelligent' than girls, who compensate for this deficiency through their ability to learn the mechanics of passing exams. We can also note that, in many societies, patriarchal beliefs about the abilities, aptitudes and roles of males and females favour male education over female education.

Evaluation: A major criticism is that arguments about female achievement are based on the misconception that because girls as a group achieve more than boys, all girls do better than all boys. Warrington and Younger found little difference between the percentage of boys and girls who leave school with no qualifications, and there are clear class and ethnic differences in achievement. At the very least, upper- and middle-class girls do better than both working-class boys and working-class girls.

Gillborn and Mirza (2000) also argue that gender differences in achievement are negligible compared to class differences in achievement. Underachievement by working-class and minority ethnic girls is frequently ignored by feminists and non-feminists alike.

TEST YOURSELF

Which curriculum subjects are most and least popular with boys?

The interrelationship between class, gender and ethnicity

Although, for the sake of illustration, we have looked at explanations for differential achievement in terms of class, gender and ethnicity as separate categories, in reality all these factors are combined in every individual. There is necessarily an interplay between them and each category is affected by the others. There are, however, important arguments about their relative significance – that is, whether we should see them in combination or as separate categories.

Combination: Combination approaches are particularly associated with Marxist perspective. They argue that class is the primary source of educational disadvantage, with gender and ethnicity as secondary sources that appear *within* classes:

- Claire (2004) notes 'a strong direct association between class background and success in education: the higher a child's class, the greater their attainments'.
- Mac an Ghaill argues that social class origins remain the single best predictor of educational success or failure, using parental occupation as an indicator of class (Table 6.2).

Percentages	2008	2002	1989
Higher professional	81	77	52
Lower professional	75	–	–
Intermediate/skilled manual	61	52	21
Lower supervisory	47	–	–
Routine manual	43	–	–
Other/not classified	37	32	12

Table 6.2   Five or more GCSE grades A*–C or equivalent at age 16
Source: Hughes and Church (2010)

Evidence for this interpretation is based on comparing differences in gender and ethnic attainment within the *same* classes. Taking the UK as an example, among those at the lower end of the class scale, there is no decisive evidence that girls outperform boys *within* this group. The picture is broadly similar across all class groupings; although in the 7–14 age range there are substantial differences between girls and boys in English (averaging around 10%) the same is not true for maths and science (an average 2% difference).

In terms of ethnicity, Asians and Indians achieve higher-than-average educational qualifications when compared to most other ethnic groups. However, this group also has higher-than-average levels of educational *underachievement*, which again suggests that social class is a more significant determinant of achievement.

Overall, Gillborn and Mirza argue that of 'these three best known dimensions of inequality', in terms of disparity in achievement:

- gender is the *narrowest*
- ethnicity is in the middle
- class is the *highest*.

They caution, however, against 'the trap of simply arguing *between* various inequalities': how and why inequalities combine and are compounded is more significant than simple class *or* gender *or* ethnic differences.

Separation: The main argument here is not that gender and ethnicity are *necessarily* more significant than class in determining educational achievement; rather, gender and ethnicity are important dimensions of inequality that must be considered as factors *in their own right*. Evidence to support this argument comes from holding social class constant and measuring achievement differences in terms of gender and ethnicity. From this perspective, there are small but consistent gender differences in attainment across all social classes.

Select two students, one tall, one short. Their educational future rests on a single target – whoever reaches highest wins.

1   *Is this test fair? If not, why not?*
2   *Should the smaller pupil be compensated for their 'lack of height'?*
3   *Should the taller pupil be penalised for being 'too tall'?*

Structures and processes within schools

The social construction of knowledge and learning; power and social control as factors influencing the structure, content and development of the curriculum

Weber (1922) argues that all societies develop beliefs about what 'is worthy of being known'. This suggests that knowledge is not something that is simply 'out there', waiting to be discovered, taught and learnt. One context for understanding this idea is to look at how knowledge is socially constructed in education systems: what kinds of knowledge should be taught, to whom and for what purpose. This involves examining ideas relating to power and control through the structure, content and development of the school curriculum. One way to do this is by locating the development of education systems in the contexts of modernity and postmodernity.

Modernity

One aspect of debates surrounding how both education and knowledge are socially constructed is the idea of schools as modern institutions that originally developed to meet the needs and requirements of modern industrial societies.

From traditional Marxists perspectives, schools are places where particular relations of power and control flow from the nature of economic relationships in capitalist societies. As we have noted, for Althusser, cultural reproduction involves the ability of a ruling class to pass on its political and economic domination from one generation to the next. Education, characterised as an ideological state apparatus (ISA), is an important institutional mechanism for social learning. Teachers are agents of ideological control, who 'transform pupil consciousness' by trying to get them to accept 'the realities of life' and their likely future social positions.

Cultural institutions such as education, the media and religion are seen as *instruments* of class oppression and domination through the power they have over what people learn and how they learn it. Our view of the world is conditioned by what we learn in school in a range of ways:

- Through formal learning: children must learn the skills and knowledge needed in the workplace.
- Access to knowledge is restricted through control of the curriculum. The higher an individual goes in the education system, the greater their access to knowledge.
- Preparing children for the differing levels of knowledge in the workplace means creating different levels of knowledge in the school. This is reinforced through rigorous and periodic testing.
- Academic (theoretical) knowledge has more value than practical (vocational) knowledge because it is more useful to the professional middle classes – those who control both what is taught and how it is taught.
- Some forms of knowledge are more valid than others. In the UK curriculum, for example, English, maths and science have a special status.
- Children must learn to accept 'authority' because this is important in the workplace.
- Commodification is the idea that knowledge must have an economic value so it can be bought and sold. This is achieved through educational qualifications.

Young (1971) further argues that what counts as educational knowledge always has an ideological dimension. Knowledge is socially constructed from a particular viewpoint and for a particular purpose. How schools are organised reflects the idea that knowledge can be:

- Categorised in terms of 'subjects' that have their own unique body of knowledge. This implies that one subject is not relevant to another. The ability to categorise knowledge in terms of both subjects and subject content is a powerful ideological tool. It allows control over what is being learnt, how it is learnt and how pupils can validate their learning.
- Presented in particular ways through a formal curriculum. Knowledge is conceptualised as something to be given, not discovered. It is protected by gatekeepers, such as teachers, exam boards and politicians, and learning is a process of gradual revelation. Teachers not only choose when to reveal certain types of knowledge, they also choose which pupils will receive that knowledge.
- Validated through examinations. Knowledge must be continually assessed and evaluated to ensure that pupils

177

reach approved levels. This leads to 'credentialism' – knowledge is only valid if it can be quantified in the form of qualifications. It also leads to the idea that certain types of knowledge have greater validity than others.

Why do schools validate knowledge through written tests?

For Young, therefore, the ideological construction of knowledge is part of a wider hegemonic process. The ability of powerful groups to manufacture or impose a consensus about what knowledge is and how it can be validated means that pupils can be assessed against their knowledge and understanding in ways that appear:

- objective: since there is agreement about what constitutes knowledge, testing can be measured against known standards of competence
- fair: pupils can be evaluated in terms of whether they reach certain standards, for example, general literacy and numeracy or exams such as A levels
- meritocratic: success or failure in reaching 'agreed standards' can be expressed in terms of individual characteristics; if standards exist and children have an equal opportunity to achieve them, success or failure is down to their individual merits.

Young goes on to argue that the formal school curriculum reflects the interests of a ruling class in capitalist societies in the way knowledge is:

- selected: involving decisions about which subjects appear on the curriculum and the content of each subject
- stratified within the classroom, school and society: this involves questioning things like why theoretical knowledge is considered superior to practical knowledge, the division between vocational and academic subjects and why subjects are separated rather than integrated within the curriculum.

Bernstein adds a further dimension to this argument, by stating that how knowledge is organised ('classified and framed') (Table 6.3) affects the messages pupils receive about the nature and purpose of education.

TEST YOURSELF

Suggest one way in which knowledge is categorised in schools.

Characteristics of strongly classified and strongly framed knowledge	Characteristics of weakly classified and weakly framed knowledge
There are right answers that are already known.	There are no right answers. Education is a process of explanation and argument.
Personal experience is largely irrelevant, unless specifically requested as an example and then it will be right or wrong.	The personal experiences of pupils are always important.
Knowledge is divided into subjects. When one is being studied, other subjects are irrelevant.	Subject boundaries are artificial. Pupils should link various forms of knowledge.
Education is what happens in school.	Education happens everywhere.
Teachers determine the time and pace of lessons.	The pace of learning is determined by the pupil and their interests.
Education involves matching the individual performance of pupils against fixed standards.	Education is a process of personal development, unique to each individual learner.

Table 6.3   The classification and framing of educational knowledge
Source: Bernstein (1971)

Bernstein suggests that most types of education are characterised by the strong classification and framing of knowledge, because it reflects wider social themes of power and control. Steiner schools, based on the educational philosophy of Rudolf Steiner (1861–1925), are an example of weak classification and framing that produces a 'different kind of message' about education. In Steiner schools:

- the curriculum reflects the needs of the child at each stage of their development
- children enter classes according to their age rather than academic ability

- subject material is presented in an individual way that aims to interest the learner
- children are encouraged to discover and learn for themselves
- learning involves the development of 'practical, emotional and thinking capacities'.

Reactions to modernity: deschooling

Illich (1973) is similarly concerned with how and why education systems developed in modern societies. However, he approached these questions from a different perspective. His view is a reaction to modernity that is both radical – the need for the '**deschooling**' of societies – and conservative (many of his ideas refer to idealised notions of childhood, education and the destructive processes of modernisation). Illich's basic ideas about power and control can organised into there broad categories:

 KEY TERM

Deschooling: alternative form of education proposed by Illich based on the abolition of formal schools.

1 Institutionalisation: modern education systems destroy individual creativity and, though qualifications, allow education to become a commodity. Education systems were modern institutions that developed to control access to knowledge and the behaviours of children in industrial societies. They also validated the power and control of the professional middle classes (as teachers) and their effective sponsors, the upper classes, who had a significant interest in controlling people's views of the world.

   Illich linked the institutional development of schools with the development of new, different and destructive concepts of childhood: 'If there were no age-specific and obligatory learning institution, 'childhood' would go out of production.' It was, in his view 'only by segregating human beings in the category of childhood could we ever get them to submit to the authority of a schoolteacher.'

2 Professionalism: the criticism of modern education systems relates in part to his general criticism of the professional middle classes and their ability to shape the structure, content and development of the curriculum in their own image and for their own needs. Criticism of the role of teaching professionals in the organisation of teaching and learning is similar to his criticism of professional doctors. For example, Illich argues that the general assumption that medicine involves an inevitable progression from ignorance about disease to enlightenment about the nature and causes of illness

ignores the fact that people are routinely 'made ill' by the medical profession through the use of ineffective, toxic and unsafe treatments.

   In a similar way schools exist for the benefit and advancement of teaching professionals rather than those they teach. Teachers protect their interests by using qualifications to allow only certain groups access to particular professions. This is also significant in terms of control over knowledge; profesional teachers decide what counts as legitimate knowledge and how it can be validly expressed. Institutionalism and professionalism also give particular groups the power to control how legitimate knowledge can be acquired – by attending school.

3 Commodification: both institutionalism and professionalism have as their objective the commodification of learning. This means turning something abstract such as 'knowledge' into something concrete such as qualifications, which have a wider cultural currency in terms of buying entry into professional occupations.

   For Illich, this process of commodification was the real meaning and purpose of education. It echoed Dewey's (1916) distinction between education and training:

- Education should be *transformative*, focusing on individuals and their social, psychological and moral development as people in ways that enable them to achieve their 'full potential'.
- Training is the mechanical and repetitive 'learning' of a narrow range of 'undisputed facts'.

Illich believes that modern schools are simply places where students 'learn how to pass exams' rather than being taught how to create things, think problems through or develop their human potential.

TEST YOURSELF

Briefly explain what is meant by 'the commodification of learning'. Also suggest two weaknesses with the idea that learning has been commodified.

Cultural capital

Where traditional Marxists saw ownership of economic capital as the key to understanding both social and economic inequality, neo-Marxists such as Bourdieu (1973) argue that in late/postmodern societies, the mechanisms of cultural reproduction are more varied and more subtle. Bourdieu's concept of cultural capital, for example, provides a significant mechanism for cultural reproduction that is carried out by the education system.

179

'Cultural capital' refers to the different advantages and disadvantages conferred by people's cultural histories. It was initially developed to explain differences in educational achievement in terms of a range of non-economic factors that help or hinder individual life chances. These include family history and status, and the extent to which family members invest time and effort in their children's social and educational development. From this perspective, cultural reproduction works 'in the background' of the education system. It is not its main or its only purpose, but it is a significant purpose for those who understand and exploit the system.

Otsuka (2005) illustrates this idea in terms of 'cultural differences between values, beliefs and practices' that affect educational achievement among Indo- and ethnic Fijians. Indo-Fijian culture places a high value on education as 'the only way to success'. In this respect, their cultural orientation is individualistic, meaning that parents interpret their role as one of helping and encouraging their children to achieve qualifications.

In contrast, ethnic Fijian culture has a greater communal orientation. Parents think it is more important to encourage children to 'become good members of their community … somewhat at the expense of their children's education'. Otsuka concludes that one consequence of this different parental orientation is that 'Indo-Fijian students generally become better educational performers than their ethnic Fijian counterparts.'

Bourdieu is critical of the idea that schools operate along meritocratic lines, because differences in cultural capital influence both the relative starting points of students as they enter the education system and their relative progress through that system. The cultural capital that middle- and upper-class children bring to their education gives them a distinct advantage. Just as Crozier et al. (2004) noted how middle-class parents were able and willing to invest more time, money and effort in their children's education than their working-class peers, Mariaye (2008) found a similar process operating in countries such as Mauritius. There, middle-class parents exploited their knowledge and understanding of how the higher levels of the education system worked to ensure their offspring were better prepared, both financially and culturally, for its demands.

Postmodernity

The explanations previously outlined all emphasise the idea of education systems acting upon individuals in various ways to produce different outcomes. They give little or no consideration to how those within the system, both teachers and pupils, recognise the various processes involved and act in ways that challenge or negate their influence and operation. Postmodernists see education in a different way – in terms of the relationship and tension between two competing, increasingly opposed, processes.

First, institutions such as schools grew out of the development of modern society. As such, they exist to serve purposes which, for Foucault (1977), are based on power. The power principle here relates to how the modern state tries to exert social control over a population through institutions such as education.

Second, we should note the increasing resistance of students and teachers to the centralising tendencies of modernist education systems. Teachers and pupils are questioning their roles and demanding greater control.

The tension between these two processes has important implications for both the social construction of knowledge and learning, and how power and control are exercised and experienced. For example, postmodernists argue that control operates on two levels:

Mental control involves how people think and act in several ways:

- The school curriculum specifies which subjects and knowledge are worthy of being known, and its content is controlled down to the finest detail.
- Knowledge is also controlled in terms of what pupils are taught within specific subjects. English literature, for example, involves learning 'high culture' texts, such as Shakespeare, and largely excludes *popular culture* – the books and magazines most people actually read, the computer games they play and the films they watch.
- A general form of cultural control also operates. Schools are not simply organised for 'education', but also for institutionalising the culture of powerful groups. They distribute and legitimise particular forms of what Provenzo (2002) identifies as language, practices, values, ways of talking and acting, moving, dressing and socialising.

Physical control involves control over things such as the following:

- Bodies, which relates to what pupils and teachers can and cannot do. This involves ideas such as compulsory attendance and where pupils should be at certain times. Once in those lessons, students are restricted in when they can speak, who they can speak to and how they speak to them. There are also movement restrictions on where pupils can sit and when they can legitimately leave the classroom.
- Space: many schools use closed-circuit television (both inside and outside the classroom) to patrol and control space; who is allowed to be in certain spaces, such as classrooms, corridors and staffrooms, when they are allowed to be there and what they are allowed to do once there.

How do schools control bodies and space?

More generally, Sizer (1984) argues that the structure, content and development of the school curriculum is based on principles of:

- uniformity: the emphasis is on a narrow definition of achievement – how many tests are successfully passed – rather than the quality of learning and understanding
- quantification: the value of a school, its teachers and its students is assessed only in ways that can be quantified; targets are set for both individual and whole-school exam passes
- fragmentation: the school day is rigidly divided into unconnected lesson segments, and what is taught is not open to negotiation
- control: individual responsibility is limited, learning is controlled by the demands of the curriculum and testing regimes; there is little scope for individual development or expression, and pupils are expected to learn similar things, at similar times, in similar ways.

The other side of this centralising process is changes in people's behaviour prompted by globalising processes such as cross-cultural contacts and exchanges. Taylor (2004), for example, argues that students all over the world are increasingly active consumers rather than passive recipients of education. Their general outlook on education is increasingly consumer-oriented, wanting instant gratification, adaptable to new situations, sceptical and cynical.

These characteristics embody the tension between:

- Producers: education is increasingly a tightly controlled, patrolled and policed system that specifies what, how, when and by whom something should be learned. Modern education systems are homogenised – one size fits all. Hanafin and Lynch argue that this type of system is disabling; the main objective is to progressively measure, fail and exclude.

- Consumers who are becoming more independent and individualistic. Postmodern pupils are increasingly heterogeneous; they have a wide mix of differences. Elkins (1998) suggests that students increasingly want to be recognised and treated as individuals rather than as groups defined in terms of class, gender, age or ethnicity: 'Whereas modern childhood was defined in terms of differences *between* age groups, postmodern childhood is identified with differences *within* age groups.'

The significant economic, political and cultural changes presented by globalisation mean that, for Young (1999), the form and content of the school curriculum must change (Table 6.4). It must move away from that 'of the past', and towards one 'of the future' that keeps pace with changes occurring both nationally and globally.

Curriculum of the past	Curriculum of the future
Knowledge and learning 'for its own sake'	Knowledge and learning 'for a purpose'
Concerned with transmitting existing knowledge	Focus on creation of new knowledge
Little value placed on relationships between subjects	The interdependence of knowledge areas
Boundary between school and everyday knowledge	Link between school and everyday knowledge

Table 6.4   Curriculum characteristics
Source: Young (1999)

ACTIVITY

Imagine three people (one French, one Indian and one English) go into a shop in France (the 'dominant culture', in this respect, would be French). The French person speaks the language, the Indian person knows a little French, the English person knows no French.

The objective is to buy 7 oranges, 1 kilo of flour and 1 litre of cooking oil.

1 *Write a brief explanation (100–200 words) explaining how cultural capital advantages or disadvantages each person in this situation.*

2 *Imagine the French person is like an upper-class child, the Indian a middle-class child and the English a working-class child. Write a further brief explanation (200+ words) explaining how their cultural capital advantages or disadvantages them within the school environment.*

Language, deprivation and knowledge

We can extend and refine ideas about power and control within education by thinking about different aspects of the 'language of education'. We can consider this both literally, in the sense of different types of language use conferring educational advantages and disadvantages, and metaphorically, in the idea that middle- and working-class pupils not only 'speak different cultural languages' but also that educational achievement is based on the ability to 'speak the language of education' itself.

TEST YOURSELF

Briefly explain the difference between cultural deprivation and material deprivation.

Language codes

Bernstein was one of the first to investigate how the use of language gave students certain cultural advantages and disadvantages. He argued that education systems were based on a particular language code that needed to be either used or learnt if pupils were to succeed in the terms set by modern educational systems. In this respect, Bernstein argued there are two basic language codes – restricted and elaborated – that, while not class-specific, are used in different situations and for different purposes.

Elaborated codes are:

- complex in their use of vocabulary and the expression of ideas
- subtle in terms of the range of meanings they express and convey
- abstract in terms of their ability to grasp and express meanings
- individual in the sense of clearly 'spelling out' meaning. They are context independent and can be used and understood in a wide range of different situations
- inclusive by elaborating meaning in situations where something has to be clearly explained.

Restricted codes are:

- simple in their use of language to convey direct meanings
- predictable because an audience already understands the meaning
- concrete in their expression of relatively simple, straightforward, ideas
- collective in the sense that ideas do not need to be explained openly; an audience already understands the general meaning, they are context dependent because meaning is restricted to the specific situation in which they are used

- exclusive: meanings do not need to be elaborated because language is directed towards an audience that already understands most of what is being expressed.

Bernstein argues that restricted codes are used by all social classes. When conversing within families, for example, no one would say 'Greetings to you, that individual of the female sex to whom I am directly related by ties of kinship and personal affection' when they could just say 'Hello, Mum'. However, elaborated codes are more likely to be used by the middle classes, and this is significant because education systems are based on the use of both restricted *and* elaborated codes. As such, middle-class children have a significant educational advantage because education involves:

- the development of new knowledge
- new, higher, levels of understanding
- abstract thinking and reasoning
- moving away from simple shared meanings
- a requirement to use elaborated codes.

This is significant for two reasons:

1 Working-class pupils must first learn the elaborated code of the school *before* they can learn the knowledge being taught.

2 The restricted codes of working-class speech clash with the elaborated codes of middle-class teachers. A good, if literal, example here is Mauritius, where teaching may involve a mix of languages – English, French and Creole. Middle-class pupils who are more fluent in English and French (the elaborated codes of the school) have an advantage because of their familiarity with these languages. Middle-class pupils, able to express themselves in 'the language of education', are less likely to find themselves placed in the lowest streams, sets and bands through teacher assessments.

Evaluation: Although Bernstein's analysis moves the debate away working-class 'deficiencies' and deprivations, it does raise a number of questions.

While the kind of 'class-based speech differences' Bernstein isolated were, at the time, a relatively important feature of life in the UK, the same is not necessarily true in the 21st century. Working- and middle-class speech patterns have arguably flattened, and middle-class youth in particular now use restricted forms of speech that were once used mainly by the working class.

More significantly, Edwards questions whether 'classrooms are normally predicated upon elaborated codes'. He argues that the normal mode of classroom interaction involves a system of restricted codes. The aim of these codes is simply to convey as clearly as possible sets of received knowledge to children. There is little or no opportunity for students to question or evaluate this knowledge.

The language of education

Bernstein acknowledged that his research only showed *differences* between working- and middle-class language codes. It leaves open the question of how to explain class-based achievement differences. They could be interpreted as cultural *deprivation*: a failure by working-class children to integrate fully into the education system. Or they could be explained by schools failing to develop a truly meritocratic system. This is not an easy question to answer, but investigating what happens in schools and classrooms can help explain differential achievement.

Labov's 'long-term participant-observation with a number of black adolescent peer groups' in the USA suggested that, contrary to the idea that 'black children from the ghetto area receive little verbal stimulation, hear very little well-formed language, and as a result are impoverished in their means of verbal expression', the reverse was true. While Labov noted that working-class black children 'spoke a different dialect' (Black English Vernacular), he concluded 'they have the same basic vocabulary, possess the same capacity for conceptual learning, and use the same logic as anyone else who learns to speak and understand English'. Their language codes were *different* but *equal* to the codes used by their middle-class peers.

In addition, longitudinal studies that hold the measured IQ of a particular child cohort constant at the start of their educational career and examine their achievement levels at the end of their schooling suggest a significant 'school effect':

- The Robbins' Report (1963) argued that social class was a significant factor in achievement: of UK students with a similar IQ – more than twice as many middle-class pupils went on to study at degree level than their working-class peers.
- Duckworth and Seligman's (2005) study of 13–14-year-old pupils with similar IQ levels but different levels of measured *self-discipline* – how they applied themselves to their studies – achieved at different levels.
- Murayama et al.'s (2012) German study of mathematical achievement found that IQ was only important in the initial development of mathematical competence. In the long term, measured intelligence showed no relationship to mathematical achievement. One conclusion was that 'students' competencies to learn in math involve factors, such as motivation and study skills, that can be nurtured by education'.

This evidence links into a wider debate about 'the language of education', the extent to which schools are 'middle-class institutions' and whether this confers hidden advantages to middle-class children. Bourdieu (1986), for example, argues that education reproduces the power and domination of ruling social classes through a combination of habitus and cultural capital.

> **TEST YOURSELF**
>
> Suggest two things that studies of pupils with the same measured IQ tell us about the relationship between intelligence and educational achievement.

Habitus

Habitus is similar to the idea of a *habitat*, the environment in which a group lives and flourishes. Bourdieu (1973) believes that schools are the 'natural habitat' of the middle and upper classes. The working-class child entering a middle-class institution is immediately disadvantaged because their interests, beliefs, values and norms are not only different but actively conflict with those of both teachers and the education system. This not only leads to their eventual relative failure in academic terms, but the failure appears to be their own fault, not the fault of an education system that neither represents nor favours this class. Middle-class children, however, are immediately advantaged because their cultural beliefs, norms and values are similar to those of the teachers and the general ethos of the school. Beron and Farkas (2001) found that linguistic differences disadvantaged working-class and black children because they did not 'speak the middle-class language' of schools and teachers.

Just as different classes have different access to financial resources they also have differential access to cultural resources in the shape of cultural capital. Light (2013) defines this as 'fluency in a society's elite culture' or 'high cultural knowledge that ultimately redounds to the owner's financial and social advantage'. Knowledge is instrumental in cultural reproduction, but this refers more to knowledge acquired *about* schooling than knowledge acquired *in* schools. In other words, it is about knowing how to 'play' the education system successfully.

Cultural capital takes numerous forms but is acquired, Light argues, 'in the family and in formal schooling'. In this respect, 'When the school curriculum reinforces the home curriculum, as it routinely does for children of the affluent, students obtain additional access to their own culture in school. Conversely, when the school curriculum contradicts or subverts the home culture, as it does for poor, immigrant,

183

How does extreme wealth shape a child's cultural capital, and how does this differ from that of a poor family?

ACTIVITY

Elaborated language codes are like a 'secret language' that must be decoded if they are to be understood. Try decoding the following phrases taken from some well-known films:

The Terminator: *I'llway ebay ackbay!*

Star Wars: *Aymay ethay orcefay ebay ithway ouyay!*

Forrest Gump: *Ifelay isway ikelay away oxbay ofway ocolateschay. Ouyay evernay owknay atwhay ou'reyay onnagay etgay.*

Star Wars: *Aay onglay imetay goay, niay aay alaxygay arfay arfay wayay...*

Want to know the secret?

If the word begins with a vowel, add 'way' to the word, otherwise move the first consonant(s) to the end of the word and add 'ay'.

How might a pupil's understanding of the 'language of schools' give them an educational advantage?

or ethnic-minority children, students have to master a foreign culture at school while mastering their own at home'.

Different forms of capital, both economic and cultural, are contingent. For neo-Marxists such as Poulantzas (1978), possession of economic capital is always the most significant factor. The greater the individual's ability to draw on economic capital, the higher their levels of cultural capital. Cultural reproduction involves the conversion of cultural capital into economic capital through the education system in the shape of educational qualifications. Shapiro (2004) how economic and cultural capital are linked: 'racial inequality is passed down from generation to generation through the use of private family wealth' in the USA, with the white upper and middle classes in the best position to provide their children with the social, economic and educational support that gives them a range of advantages over other ethnic groups.

Teacher–pupil relationships: streaming, labelling, hidden curriculum, the gendered curriculum

Previous sections have focused on how schools relate to other institutions and the impact this has on aspects of teaching and learning. This section takes a different perspective, examining what happens inside schools and using school processes to explain differential achievement.

Teacher–pupil relationships

There are several aspects to the relationship between teachers and pupils, from labelling to the hidden and gendered curriculum. However, we can begin by noting pupil orientations to different types of teaching.

Cano-Garcia and Hughes (2000) argue that the teacher–pupil relationship is significant in terms of the extent to

which pupils 'switch on' or conform to particular teaching styles. How information is delivered is an important part of the teacher–pupil relationship. It also has consequences for pupil orientations to both education and their personal experience of schooling. We can note four basic teaching styles, each of which relates to Bernstein's notion of power and control in the classroom – from strong controls and knowledge framing at one extreme, to weaker controls and knowledge framing at the other:

- teacher-centred, where the teacher directs and informs the class
- demonstrator, where although the class is teacher-centred and controlled, there is an emphasis on demonstrating ideas and encouraging students to experiment
- student-centred, where the role of the teacher is defined as helping (or facilitating) the student to learn by giving them responsibility for their own learning
- delegation styles, in which students work independently on teacher-designed tasks, at their own pace.

Teaching styles are not particularly related to academic achievement – no single style is necessarily superior to any other. However, Cano-Garcia and Hughes argue that the most academically successful students are those who can work independently of the teacher within a fairly rigid set of teacher-controlled guidlines and procedures. Successful pupils understand what the teacher wants and develop 'teacher-pleasing behaviours' to provide it.

The reverse of this idea is what Barrett (1999) calls 'switching off'; where pupils fail to see what they are learning as 'useful now, as well as in the future', it turns a large number off the idea of learning. Switching off also occurs when pupils feel they lack the power to influence the scope, extent and purpose of their studies. This is something that may be influenced by different teaching styles and their related teacher–pupil relationships. Seaton (2004) suggests that pupil orientations to both teaching styles and academic learning are reflected in two types of response:

1 Learned dependence, where the educationally successful pupils are those who quickly learn to work in accordance with whatever the teacher demands.
2 Experienced alienation relates to pupils who see the school, teachers and even the concept of 'education' itself as something alien and strange, simultaneously both irrelevant and threatening.

Although for Seaton these responses have their origins *outside* the school, in the norms and values of different home lives, they are expressed *inside* the school through teacher–pupil relationhips. He argues that 'studies show that, through their experiences of schooling, many students 'learn' to see their role not as thinking, but 'doing what is expected and working hard''. This involves 'learning':

■ that good grades go to students who follow rules
■ to allow others to make decisions for them
■ obedience to authority.

These ideas suggest that the main message pupils are sent is an instrumental one. Educational success is not simply a question of 'intelligence' but also depends on how successfully the pupil can adapt to the educational process. It could be argued that middle-class children gain no more or less satisfaction from their schooling than working-class children. Barrett, however, suggests that middle-class children are more likely to tacitly agree with teachers that the purpose of education is to gain qualifications. Such students are also more inclined to display teacher-pleasing behaviour. Working-class pupils are more likely to break this tacit agreement. At its most extreme, this can be seen in the higher numbers of working-class pupils, particularly boys, who are expelled or suspended from school for assaults on teachers and fellow pupils.

TEST YOURSELF

Identify two things that pupils informally learn 'from the experience of attending school'.

The hidden curriculum

These aspects of the teacher–pupil relationship are one part of the informal or **hidden curriculum**. This is a concept that Jackson (1968) defines as the things children learn from the experience of attending school. Skelton (1997) suggests that **informal education** involves a 'set of implicit messages relating to knowledge, values, norms of behaviour and attitudes that learners experience in and through educational processes'. The hidden curriculum, therefore, refers to the idea that schools transmit certain value-laden messages to pupils. Paechter (1999) suggests that these messages have two dimensions:

■ Intended consequences are the things that teachers 'actively and consciously pursue as learning goals'. These include encouraging particular values, such as politeness, the importance of order and obedience to authority, while discouraging others, from bullying and sexism, through questioning the role and authority of the teacher to a lack of effort or attendance.
■ Unintended consequences include the messages pupils receive through the teaching and learning process. This includes status messages, such as whether boys appear to be more valued than girls, and messages relating to beliefs about ability: whether teachers believe it is 'natural' or the product of 'hard work', for example.

KEY TERMS

Hidden curriculum: the things pupils learn through the process of attending school. These may be both positive, such as how to make and keep friends, and negative, such as learning the consequences of disobeying adult authority.

Informal education: the things children learn through the experience of attending school that are not part of the formal curriculum. These include ideas about the value of learning, norms of behaviour within the school, attitudes to authority and so forth.

In general, the messages transmitted within schools as part of a hidden curriculum fall into two broad categories.

Socialisation messages relate to what is required from pupils if they are to succeed in education. Some ideas refer explicitly to how pupils should behave. These include various classroom processes that involve order and control, such as attendance and punctuality. Others relate to the things pupils must demonstrate in order to 'learn how to learn'. In part this involves learning conformity to formal school rules. However, it also means understanding the informal rules, beliefs and attitudes perpetuated through the socialisation process, such as recognising the teacher's authority and not questioning what is being taught. Children also learn ideas about:

- individualism – learning is a process that should not, ultimately, be shared
- competition – the objective is to demonstrate you are better than your peers through various types of testing; assessment is also an integral part of the hidden curriculum because it suggests knowledge is only useful if it can be quantified
- knowledge – to pass exams the pupil must conform to what the teacher presents as valid knowledge, realised and tested through formal written examinations.

Status messages relate to the ideas that pupils develop about their 'worth'.

- The type of school a child attends influences the individual's self-image and sense of self-worth. In some societies, for example, a small band of private, fee-paying schools have the highest social status. More generally, schools are given a status as 'good' or 'bad' based on their exam results.
- Practices such as segregating children in different streams, bands and sets (see below) affect pupil self-perceptions in terms of membership of high-achieving or low-achieving academic groups.
- The idea that academic (higher) and vocational (lower) subjects have different statuses in the curriculum and school. Hill and Cole (2001) argue that the hidden curriculum excludes particular groups, especially working-class children, but also such groups as the mentally and physically disabled. Gillborn (1992) also argues that the hidden curriculum affects ethnic, as well as gender and class identities through citizenship teaching. Here, the subject content – ideas about democracy or racial equality for example – frequently clashes with the 'learned experiences' of black pupils.

Labelling

A further dimension to the hidden curriculum is positive and negative labelling. This refers to the way in which teachers classify and stereotype students, which affects pupil self-perceptions. Padfield (1997), for example, explores how 'informal reputations', such as being labelled a 'swot' (a very hard-working student) or 'naughty child', gained within the school influenced official definitions of pupils. Labelling theory examines how school processes shape meanings, in terms of ideas such as:

- the purpose of education
- roles and relationships within schools

- pupils' self-perceptions developed through processes such as streaming, banding and setting.

Labelling processes have two distinctive features. First, Brimi (2005) suggests that they involve cultural capital. A student's home and family background has a significant impact on their experience of education and how successfully or otherwise they negotiate the various barriers to success, such as exams or negative labelling.

Second, Nash (1972) suggests that 'success' or 'failure', in exams, is not simply a matter of a person's background or how wealthy there parents are. There are more subtle processes at work in the classroom, relating to how teachers and students manage their impressions of each other. If a student can employ sufficient cultural capital to conform to the teacher's perception of a 'good pupil', they may be able to overcome particular disadvantages in their home background. This explains why some pupils from disadvantaged social backgrounds succeed in the education system. We can illustrate these ideas by looking at how labelling processes operate within schools.

Streaming

This practice, once very common in the UK but increasingly discarded in favour of setting and banding (see below), involves allocating children to different year groups or streams within the school on the basis of 'academic ability'. The streams are ranked hierarchically and pupils are normally tested at the end of each academic year and re-assigned to the same or different streams. The evidence suggests that streaming not only has significant consequences for the individual pupil, but it can also reinforce educational inequalities and differential achievements.

Hargreaves' (1967) study of Lumley School noted that boys were streamed on the basis of 'academic ability'. After the first year at secondary school, it was almost impossible for a boy allocated to the bottom stream to later move into the top stream. While Hargreaves found a close correlation between social class and streaming, with middle-class children in the top and working-class children in the bottom streams, he also found the experience of streaming made each child feel they were a 'success' or a 'failure'. The lack of movement between streams also encouraged the development of pupil sub-cultures. This led not only to conflicts between teachers and pupils but also to 'inter-stream', pupil-to-pupil, conflicts. Hallam et al. (2001) also highlight how high- and low-stream pupils attracted different stigmatising labels, such as 'thick'/'dumb' (stupid) and 'boffin'/'clever clogs' (intelligent).

Keddie (1971) found that the academic label attached to a pupil followed them through their schooling and was a crucial influence on how they were perceived by new teachers. Their behaviour and ability was interpreted in the light of the label pupils brought to the classroom rather than simply assessed anew.

Banding and setting

Two common variations on streaming involve banding, and **setting**. In banding, pupils are allocated different 'bands' when they enter secondary school on the basis of reports from teachers in their primary schools. In setting, pupils are streamed on a subject-by-subject basis. For example, a pupil may be in the top set for physics, a middle set for biology and the bottom set for French.

> **KEY TERM**
>
> **Setting:** process by which pupils are streamed on a subject-by-subject basis.

Setting, in particular, avoids some of the more common social consequences of streaming. For example, it tends to avoid the development of strong sub-cultural relationships and groups. Hallam et al. note that it has both benefits, and drawbacks. Benefits include minimising disruptive behaviour. Drawbacks include stigmatising lower-set pupils as 'academic failures' and the long-term association between lower sets and unemployment, higher sets and good exam grades. Keddie also notes how teachers give 'more creative work and privileges to higher set students while restricting lower sets to tedious, routine tasks'. Power et al. (2003) argue that setting created the belief, even among relatively successful grammar school pupils, that those in the lowest sets were failures. Lupton's (2004) study confirmed this idea when she noted how one head teacher abandoned banding 'principally to counter problems of low self-esteem among pupils in the lower band'.

While streaming, setting and banding are part of a social process that heightens or diminishes a child's expectation of educational success or failure, this is not the whole story. Associated with such practices are attitudes, perceptions and beliefs that teachers have about children that are transmitted, consciously and unconsciously, through classroom interaction. As Keddie argues, this creates a situation where those in the top streams, set or bands come to understand 'the nature and boundaries of what is to count as knowledge. It would seem to be the failure of high-ability pupils to question what they are taught in schools that contributes in large measure to their educational achievement.'

> **TEST YOURSELF**
>
> Briefly explain the difference between streaming and setting.

Self-fulfilling prophecies

School processes such as streaming, setting and banding are a significant source of positive and negative labelling. This is, in itself, an important part of the process of a pupil's self-perception based on reference groups – the people we compare ourselves to in whatever role we are playing.

Teachers are an important part of a pupil's reference group. Their opinions are always significant because they have the power to create and impose labels that relate directly to individual self-perceptions. Teachers are not alone in this role. Fellow pupils are also part of the school reference group and may have a significant impact on how the role of education is defined through pro- and anti-pupil sub-cultures. The educational significance of teacher labelling is partly expressed in terms of **self-fulfilling prophecies**: a prediction about something, such as 'ability' that, by being made, causes it to occur.

- Nash studied how teacher's beliefs about 'good' and 'bad' pupils were transmitted to students through teacher attitudes and behaviour. He concluded that teacher expectations are a determining factor in a student's educational success or failure. 'Certainly children of low social origin do poorly at school because they lack encouragement at home, because they use language in a different way from their teachers, because they have their own attitudes to learning and so on. But also because of the expectations their teachers have of them'. Teachers made conscious and subconscious 'predictions' about the ability of their pupils that affected the behaviour of those students. Where they associated working-class pupils with low levels of attainment, they reinforced this cultural stereotype through their lowered expectations.
- Rosenthal and Jacobson (1968) tested the effects of teacher labelling and expectations on pupil's academic performance by telling teachers they could predict which children in a class would develop academically; the pupils they identified showed greater academic achievement than their classmates. However, they had simply identified

> **KEY TERM**
>
> **Self-fulfilling prophecy:** prediction that, by being made, causes it to come true.

'potential high achievers' randomly and the changes they observed were the result of a self-fulfilling prophecy; the teachers consciously and subconsciously communicated positive and negative beliefs about individual pupils, who picked up on these ideas and eventually saw themselves in terms of the labels they were given.

What assumptions do teachers make about their pupils?

The idea of a self-fulfilling prophecy also applies to whole classes of students, who may find themselves negatively labelled through practices such as streaming, setting, banding or through processes such as class, gender and ethnic stereotyping. Willis (1977) and Ball (1981), for example, documented the effects of negative labelling on the educational achievement of working-class pupils, while both Wright (1992) and Troyna and Hatcher (1992) studied similar effects on ethnic-minority children.

Explanations for gender differences in achievement that focus on labelling and stereotyping suggest that girls increasingly experience positive labelling as high achievers who work hard and have least behavioural problems. Boys are increasingly negatively labelled in terms of underachievement, laziness and behavioural problems. Jones and Myhill suggest that teachers identify boys as 'potential underachievers' and redefine and re-evaluate their role in terms of how to stimulate boys' 'natural' interests and abilities. One frequent consequence of this is that working-class and minority ethnic girls start to underachieve.

Francis (2000) argues that changes within the school and wider society have altered the way in which girls construct femininity (they no longer see it mainly in terms of 'husband and home'), whereas concepts of masculinity have remained largely unchanged. This shift is significant in the context of economic changes such as a rapid decline in male-dominated manufacturing industries and a rise in female-friendly service industries.

While labelling is generally directed at individuals and groups, whole schools may also find themselves positively or negatively labelled. In many countries the most expensive private schools generally attract positive labels while comprehensive schools, especially those in poor inner-city areas, often attract negative labelling. Gewirtz (1998) argues that the type of school attended can create a self-fulfilling prophecy of success or failure even before a pupil enters the classroom. Top-performing schools, whether private or state-maintained, create a climate of expectation that pushes pupils into higher levels of achievement.

TEST YOURSELF

Using an example to illustrate your answer, explain what is meant by a 'self-fulfilling prophecy'.

Evaluation: A major methodological problem with labelling explanations is that they are both a *cause* and a *consequence* of differential achievement. This follows because:

- for teachers to label working-class boys as 'underachievers', they must already be aware of differences in educational achievement
- if differential achievement *causes* teacher labelling, such labelling cannot be an initial *cause* of differential achievement, although it may subsequently contribute to it.

Concepts such as labelling and self-fulfilling prophecies are also criticised for being too deterministic as explanations for underachievement. They suggest general processes that, once set in motion, are almost impossible to reverse. These concepts are also infinitely adaptable as explanations:

- In the past, female underachievement in the UK was the result of negative labelling.
- In the present, female overachievement results from positive labelling.

While interactionist approaches reintroduce the notion of human agency to the role of education by looking at relationships within the school, they both over-determine the importance of labelling and underplay the influence of wider social processes on educational achievement. Micro school processes, such as teacher labelling, tell us a great deal about how and why individual pupils 'succeed' or 'fail'. However, social processes, relating to areas such as the economic relationships that create the situation in which concepts like success and failure are constructed in the first place, are marginalised.

While interactionists consider power to be a significant variable, it is seen in the context of individuals – for example, teachers who have the power to impose labels on pupils; pupils who have the power to reject. There is little sense of power being located in wider economic, political and ideological relationships which Marxists, for example, argue determine the role of education systems.

The gendered curriculum

The hidden curriculum and labelling processes are both expressed through the subjects that individuals choose to study. Males and females make different subject choices. Self and Zealey, for example, note that among undergraduates 'a higher proportion of women than men studied subjects allied to medicine [such as nursing], while a greater proportion of men studied business and administrative services. Higher proportions of men also studied engineering and technology subjects and computer sciences.'

Explanations: We can outline a selection of different explanations for the gendered curriculum.

Eichler emphasises how different socialisation experiences and social expectations about males and females help to construct different gender identities and expectations about adult roles. In the past, for example, the education system contributed to the way women saw their primary adult role in the *private sphere* of the family, as mother and housewife. Although female horizons have widened over the past 25 years, feminists argue that traditional assumptions about masculinity and femininity continue to influence both family and work relationships in areas such as the following:

- Textbooks and gender stereotyping: males appear more frequently and are more likely to be shown in *active* ('doing and demonstrating'), rather than *passive*, roles. Best (1992), for example, demonstrated how pre-school texts designed to develop reading skills remain populated by sexist assumptions and stereotypes.

- Subject hierarchies: both teachers and pupils quickly appreciate that some subjects are more important than others, both *within* the formal curriculum, such as English, maths and science, and *outside* the curriculum; subjects *not* considered worthy of inclusion and hence *knowing*. The argument here is that gender hierarchies reflect these subject hierarchies, with males opting for higher-status subjects in far greater numbers.

Norman et al. (1988) argue that teacher expectations, especially in early-years schooling, emphasise female roles related to the mother/carer. While this may no longer

automatically see their primary role as one of caring for their family, work roles continue to be framed around the idea of different male and female capabilities, both mental and physical. This can result in gendered subject choices. Bamford (1989), for example, notes how certain subjects attract gendered labels – sciences such as physics and chemistry were seen as masculine, while social sciences were seen as feminine. These gendered perceptions may explain lower levels of female participation and general achievement in science subjects.

Abbot and Wallace (1996) also suggest that concepts of masculinity and femininity are influenced by factors such as academic hierarchies – how schools are vertically stratified, with men normally occupying the higher-status positions. Mahony (1985) argues that staffing structures reflected male importance in the workplace; the highest-status teaching jobs were and remain occupied by men. As Mirza et al. (2005) note: 'Women make up 53% of the secondary teaching population, but are still under-represented in secondary school senior management positions, particularly headships'; around 30% of secondary heads are women. In the nursery/primary sector, although only 16% of teachers are male, 34% of *head* teachers are male.

ACTIVITY

Draw a picture of an iceberg; the top quarter should be above sea level, the rest is submerged. To the top part, add the things you think pupils are supposed to learn in school (the formal curriculum); to the submerged part, add the things you think pupils learn from 'the experience of attending school' (the hidden curriculum). Share and discuss your ideas with the class.

Which part of the iceberg is most influential on children, in your opinion, and why?

Pupil sub-cultures and attitudes to education

As we have seen, the experience of many young people in education is shaped by a range of school processes. This section explores how these experiences lead to a range of pro- and anti-pupil sub-cultural responses.

Pro- and anti-pupil sub-cultures

Woods (1976) argues that there is a range of sub-cultural responses or adaptations to school culture, with *ingratiators* at one extreme – the most positive adaptation that involves pupils who try to earn the favour of teachers – and *rebels*

189

at the other – those who explicitly reject the culture of the school and may even develop a **counter-school culture**.

The sub-cultural responses in Mac an Ghaill's study were a more subtle outcome of a complex interplay of class, race and sexuality:

- Although macho lads eagerly looked forward to leaving school at the earliest opportunity and entering paid work, in reality this type of work had all but disappeared, creating what Mac an Ghaill called 'a crisis of masculinity'.
- White working-class males clung to an outdated mode of masculinity focused on traditional forms of manual waged labour that no longer existed. They frequently employed racist explanations ('the blacks have taken our jobs') to explain and rationalise this situation.

In contrast, pro-school youth took the form of:

- Academic achievers, similar to Willis's conforming 'earoles'. These pupils had a strong school and work ethic and looked to academic qualifications as a route to social mobility.
- New enterprisers, who rejected the academic route to mobility. They focused instead on developing practical skills, particularly in business and IT, that they hoped would be rewarded in the changing labour market.

Blackman (1995) also captured how tensions within the school contribute to sub-cultural development:

- Boffin boys were generally conformist and pro-school, with a group identity based on working hard and aspiring to social mobility.
- Boffin girls worked hard and were pro-school, although their conformity was occasionally instrumental; if what they saw as poor teaching, for example, clashed with their academic aspirations, the latter took priority.
- New Wave girls shared this instrumental approach, but had a more ambivalent attitude to the school. While Boffin girls 'specialised in academic superiority', New Wave girls had wider interests and tastes. They generally conformed academically but unlike Boffin girls, they were sexually active and more confident in their ability

to challenge ideas and practices, particularly those they saw as patriarchal and sexist.

- Mod boys were similarly ambivalent, walking a fine line between deviance and conformity. These boys were generally anti-school but pro-education; they wanted academic qualifications but did not particularly value their schooling.

Sewell (2000) examined how black youth adapted to the experience of schooling in terms of four main responses:

- Passive accepters were those African-Caribbean boys who unconsciously accepted the white cultural values of the school. They were generally pro-school and accepted the conventional wisdom that it was 'black kids' who gave the school a bad name.
- Active accepters 'acted white' in the school. Sewell found this to be the most common pro-school strategic response.
- Passive resistors developed innovative ways of maintaining a delicate balancing act between satisfying the demands of their **peer group**, through minor acts of deviance, while simultaneously avoiding direct and open confrontation with teachers. This type was particularly characteristic of black girls and was *neither* pro- *nor* anti-school.
- Active resistors used what they saw as the racist assumptions of the school to rebel against their teachers.

Shain (2003) examined the sub-cultural responses of Asian girls:

- The Gang were generally anti-school. They adopted an 'Us and Them' approach that involved a positive assertion of Asian identity. They generally opposed the dominant culture of the school, which they saw as white and racist.
- The Survivors were pro-education and pro-school. They were generally seen as 'ideal pupils', who worked hard to achieve success, avoided confrontation and were positively labelled by teachers as 'nice girls' and 'good workers'. This group played up to the stereotype of Asian girls as shy and timid, while being actively engaged in a strategy of self-advancement through education.
- The Rebels were generally pro-school and their rebellion was against their own cultural background. They adopted

Western modes of dress and distanced themselves from other Asian girl groups. Their survival strategy was one of academic success, and they equated school with positive experiences that they did not find in their home life.

- Faith girls developed their identities around religion rather than ethnicity. They were pro-education in the sense of fostering positive relations with staff and students and pursuing academic success. They were, however, aware of racism in the school as a major source of oppression and this made some of them anti-school.

TEST YOURSELF

Suggest two ways in which pupil sub-cultures influence attitudes to education.

How are attitudes to education shaped by pupil sub-cultures?

Pro- and anti-education sub-cultures

While pupil sub-cultures focus on orientations to schools as institutions, some sub-cultures develop around orientations to the idea of education itself. Lees (1993), for example, described:

- Pro-school girls, who valued school as an enjoyable place for socialising with friends, but who were generally anti-education; qualifications were not particularly important.
- Pro-education girls, who fell into two main groups: those who valued education as enjoyable and worthwhile and those who took a more instrumental approach to their studies; qualifications were a necessary means towards a desired end. They did not value school 'for its own sake'.
- Anti-education girls, who were anti-school and anti-education; school was a waste of time, a disagreeable and uncomfortable period in their life that they had to get through before escaping into the adult world of work and family.

A number of studies have also found young people who are pro-education but anti-school:

- Mac an Ghaill identified what he called 'Real Englishmen', a group of middle-class pupils who aspired to university and the professional careers enjoyed by their parents. This group played an elaborate game of ridiculing school values while simultaneously working hard, mainly in private outside school. They believed that this was achieving success on their own terms.
- Power et al. examined how some groups of middle-class children who found themselves in lower sets and streams were pro-education but still did not value their school experience.
- Fuller (1984) found that the black girls she studied were strongly pro-education, but were still anti-school. They valued qualifications but resented the negative labelling by some teachers. This made them work harder to 'disprove the label'.

> **KEY TERM**
>
> **Pupil sub-cultures:** groups that develop within schools around similar interests, beliefs and behaviours.

TEST YOURSELF

Briefly explain the difference between pro-school and pro-education sub-cultures.

Influences on educational performance

While these studies provide general evidence of a relationship between pupil sub-cultures and educational performance, it is useful to look more specifically at the impact of both school and pupil–teacher relationships across categories of class, gender and ethnicity.

Class: Permanent exclusion from school is a major influence on educational performance. Hughes and Church, for example, note that there are currently around 8,000 permanent exclusions from UK schools each year. The majority of excluded pupils are working-class. Around 50,000 pupils each day take unauthorised absence from school; again, the majority are working-class and these pupils are, according to Babb et al., highly likely to leave school with no qualifications at all.

A more subtle form of exclusion involves 'ability grouping'. This involves practices such as streaming, setting and banding. As seen above, Hallam et al. noted how some pupils were stigmatised as 'thick' – by both teachers and peers – through the association between lower sets and unemployment and higher sets and good exam grades. Teachers also gave 'more creative work and privileges to higher set students while restricting lower sets to tedious, routine tasks'.

Teacher labelling also affects educational performance. Gazeley and Dunne (2005) argue that 'teachers and trainee teachers often hold stereotypical ideas about pupils and parents according to their social class'. The 'class expectations' some teachers hold – working-class pupils as low-achievers, middle-class pupils as high achievers – translate into classroom practices that 'located the source of a pupil's underachievement within the pupil or the home'.

This research also found that some teachers held fatalistic views about the ability of working-class children. These children were thought to be 'destined to fail' because of their class and family backgrounds, regardless of the teacher's efforts. Not all teachers held these views, however. As Gazeley and Dunne put it: 'I believe there is a danger in setting low expectations of a child. If a child already does not expect to do well the last thing a teacher should be doing is reinforcing that view.'

Gazely and Dunne also discovered that 'middle-class pupils and parents were viewed more positively' and 'teachers had higher expectations and aspirations for the future for middle-class pupils than for working-class pupils'. These ideas are particularly interesting in the context of the observation that 'pupils identified positive relationships with teachers as crucial to their learning'.

Ethnicity: The hidden curriculum affects the experience of education for ethnic-minority groups in a range of ways. Low post-16 participation rates in the UK suggest that racism plays some part in the black experience of schooling in two ways:

1 Overt racism: Aymer and Okitikpi (2001) argue that Black Caribbean boys are more likely to report negative abuse and harassment from their peers. Kerr et al. (2002) found that British students had less positive attitudes towards immigrants than many other countries. This, they argued, shaped peer-group interaction and black pupils' experiences of education. Mirza sees the development of Supplementary (Saturday) Schools as evidence of a general dissatisfaction, among black parents and children, with 'white institutions' and teachers that seem regularly to fail them.

2 Cultural racism (ethnocentrism) is a more subtle form expressed in areas such as the following:

- An **ethnocentric curriculum** that involves teaching practices and expectations based on cultural norms, histories and general cultural references unfamiliar to many ethnic-minority pupils.
- Role models: Blair et al. point to a lack of role models within schools for ethnic-minority pupils. Ross (2001) estimates that 5% of teachers are drawn from ethnic minorities, while around 15% of UK school pupils have an ethnic-minority background.

> **KEY TERM**
>
> **Ethnocentric curriculum:** school curriculum based on the cultural norms, values, beliefs and history of a single ethnic group. In a multicultural society, an ethnocentric curriculum is likely to favour the majority ethnicity.

In terms of teacher–pupil relationships, the Runnymede Trust (1998) claims that a range of hidden processes occur within schools that 'deny equal opportunities' and negatively affect the educational performance of ethnic-minority pupils. These processes include high levels of control and criticism from teachers, as well as stereotypes of cultural differences, communities and speech that betray negative and patronising attitudes.

A significant feature of the educational experience of Black Caribbean boys in the UK is that as they move through school, achievement seems to fall until, at GCSE, they have the worst academic performance of all children. Reasons here include:

- Masculinity defined in terms of rebellion against 'white' schooling and teachers. Foster et al. (1996) suggest that the over-representation of Black Caribbean boys in low-status sets and bands is the result of 'unacceptable behaviour' rather than any particular lack of academic ability.
- Discipline: Hinsliff (2002) has argued that 'a failure by teachers to challenge disruptive behaviour leads to an escalating situation which results in black boys being excluded from school. Black Caribbean boys are more frequently excluded than any other ethnic group'.
- Family structure: children from single-parent families generally have the worst educational experiences across all ethnic groups; Black Caribbean families have the highest rates of single parenthood and the lowest rates of educational achievement.

The various forms of subtle labelling and stereotyping do seem to influence ethnic experiences of education. Generally positive teacher attitudes to Indian pupils, based on knowledge of their high levels of attainment, may be offset by negative beliefs about Black Caribbean pupils. Figueroa (1991) suggests that teachers frequently limit ethnic-minority opportunities through the use of culturally biased forms of assessment, such as how students are expected to speak and write, and by consigning pupils to lower bands and sets on the basis of teacher assessment. Teachers also have lower opinions of the abilities of some ethnic-minority groups, which results in a self-fulfilling prophecy or vicious circle of underachievement. The low expectations of teachers transmits to pupils, who come to see themselves as having little talent or ability. These students stop trying to achieve because they believe there is no point if their teachers have already given up on them. The subsequent failure to achieve simply confirms the initial teacher assessment.

However, Gillborn (2002) argues that schools are institutionally racist, especially terms of curriculum developments 'based on approaches known to disadvantage black pupils':

- Selection by setting – black pupils are routinely assigned to the lowest sets.
- Schemes for 'gifted and talented' pupils where white pupils are over-represented.
- Vocational schemes for 'non-academic' pupils where black pupils are over-represented.

Gillborn claims that teachers 'generally underrate the abilities of black youngsters' based on outmoded racial stereotypes about ability, intelligence and effort (young black males characterised as 'lazy', for example). This results in them being assigned to low-ability groups, a restricted curriculum and entry for lower-level exams.

Gender: The influence of gender identities on educational performance has been documented in a range of ways. Epstein et al. argue that the 'feminisation of school and work' involves the idea that wider changes in the workplace and female behaviour have caused young males to control of their unique identities and their lives. As a result, some boys now see education as irrelevant to their future for two main reasons:

- Females have more opportunities to express a range of different 'femininities', including those that involve a career, rather than just part-time work and family responsibilities.
- Workplace changes reflect back onto family socialisation processes. Parents, for example, change their perception of their children's future adult roles and, consequently, the relative importance they place on male and female educational experiences.

Francis argues that changes within the school and wider society have altered the way girls construct femininity; they no longer see it mainly in terms of the home. Concepts of masculinity have, however, remained largely unchanged. Walker (1996) similarly identifies changing conceptions of masculinity, in terms of 'finding a role in a fast-changing world' as a challenge many young men are unable to resolve in the education system. In this respect, hypermasculinity is an exaggerated form of masculinity ('laddishness') that emphasises and values things such as physical strength and sexual virility. Such ideas are at odds with educational achievement. Hughes and Church note that boys make up 75% of permanent exclusions.

Finally, in terms of labelling and stereotyping, it has been suggested that educational experiences have changed, with a reversal of traditional forms of gender labelling:

- girls are increasingly positively labelled as high achievers who work hard and have least behavioural problems
- boys are increasingly negatively labelled in terms of underachievement, laziness and behavioural problems.

193

ACTIVITY

Use your experience of education to identify pupil sub-cultures you have encountered or know about. Make a list of the general social characteristics of each group (such as their gender, class and ethnicity), whether they are associated with different streams, sets or bands and the types of behaviour they display. In your opinion, are these groups pro- or anti-school, pro- or anti-education?

Summary points

- **The relationship between education and the economy has been theorised from a number of different perspectives:**
  - functionalist
  - neo-functionalist/new right
  - social democratic
  - Marxist
  - feminist.

- **There is no consensus about how the concept of 'intelligence' is:**
  - defined
  - measured.

- **The relationship between intelligence and achievement can be summarised in three ways:**
  - positive
  - negative
  - agnostic.

- **The relationship between education and the economy can be examined through two approaches:**
  - consensus
  - conflict.

- **Debates about the links between inequality, educational opportunity and achievement can be considered from three main perspectives:**
  - functionalism and cultural deprivation
  - Marxism and material deprivation/cultural reproduction
  - feminism and differential socialisation.

- **The interrelationship between class, gender and ethnicity can be considered in two main ways:**
  - combination approaches
  - separation approaches.

- **The social construction of knowledge involves two main approaches:**
  - Modernist: how knowledge is:
    - categorised
    - presented
    - validated
    - weakly and strongly framed and classified.
  - Postmodernist and forms of control:
    - mental
    - physical.

- **Deprivation can be related to ideas about language and knowledge:**
  - language codes
    - elaborate
    - restricted.
  - habitus
  - cultural capital.

- **The teaching and learning process involves considering:**
  - individual relationships:
    - teacher–pupil interaction
    - labelling
    - self-fulfilling prophecies.
  - school processes:
    - hidden curriculum
    - streaming, setting and banding
    - gendered curriculum.

- **Pupil sub-cultures and attitudes to education can be expressed in two main ways:**
  - attitudes to the school attended:
    - pro-school sub-cultures
    - anti-school sub-cultures.
  - attitudes to education:
    - pro-education sub-cultures
    - anti-education sub-cultures.

- **Pupils can be 'pro-school' but 'anti-education', and vice versa.**

Exam-style questions

1 **a** Explain why the educational performance of girls has improved compared with that of boys in many modern industrial societies in recent years. [9]

   b Assess the view that the main factor influencing educational achievement is the social class background of the pupil. [16]

2 **a** Explain the processes within education through which pupils are encouraged to accept the core values of society. [9]

   b Assess the view that the main role of education is to promote social equality. [16]

3 **a** Explain how teachers may discriminate against some pupils. [9]

   b Assess the usefulness of new-right theories in understanding educational inequality. [16]

4 **a** Explain how the labels teachers attach to students are an important factor in determining educational success. [9]

   b 'Those who shape the curriculum also determine which pupils will succeed and which fail.' Assess this claim. [16]

Total available marks 100

Chapter 7:
Global development

Learning objectives

The objectives of this chapter involve understanding:

- how development can be defined through a range of social and economic indicators, including the two-world, three-worlds and many-worlds systems

- modernisation, neo-modernisation, underdevelopment/ dependency and world-system theories of development

- public and private forms of aid, including 'trade as aid'

- development debates focused around neo-liberal and interventionist approaches

- global and regional trends in population growth

- debates about the consequences of global population growth, both pessimistic (Malthusian and neo-Malthusian) and optimistic (demographic transition and Marxist approaches)

- demographic change in the context of migration, employment, health and education

- the strengths and limitations of absolute and relative definitions of poverty

- a range of cultural/individualistic and structural explanations of the causes and consequences of poverty

- the economic, political and cultural dimensions of globalisation

- examples of transnational agencies and corporations

- the role of transnational agencies and corporations in national economic and cultural systems.

Introduction

This chapter is based on the related themes of development and social inequality, beginning with ideas about how development can be defined and used as a starting-point for different theoretical approaches. The concept of globalisation – central to understanding contemporary forms of development – is explored along with the role of transnational agencies and corporations. This theme is complemented by an examination of population development and demographic change, with particular reference to migration, employment, health and education in a global context. Finally, the theme of inequality is investigated in two ways: first, through the concept of poverty and different explanations for its existence and persistence, and second, through ideas about the role of aid and trade in global development.

Development and inequality

Concepts of development

The concept of **development** is relatively easy to describe as something that involves the change from small-scale, pre-industrial societies to large-scale industrial societies. However, defining the concept in a theoretically meaningful way is more difficult because there are two key areas of disagreement:

1 How the concept can be operationalised (*measured*) and explained. This relates to the indicators and measures used to express different levels and rates of development.

2 The meaning of 'development' itself, which Leinbach (2005) describes as a process and a condition:

 ■ Condition means it is possible to identify societies at different stages in their development. Conventional conditions, for example, involve differences between undeveloped, developing and developed societies.

 ■ Process means describing and explaining how and why societies change from one development stage to the next.

KEY TERM

Development: process by which societies change from underdeveloped, through developing to developed societies.

To understand development, therefore, we need to think about two things:

1 the different characteristics of each developmental stage (condition)

2 the various processes involved in the change from one condition to the next.

TEST YOURSELF

Briefly explain how development is both a process and a condition.

Characteristics

Thomas (2000) suggests that development can be defined in terms of three key characteristics:

1 Scale: the focus here is on identifying and understanding large-scale change, such as society-wide improvements in areas such as:

 ■ economic production
 ■ economic consumption
 ■ income
 ■ wealth.

2 Evolution: change is both continual (it occurs over an extended period) and cumulative (it involves improvements in economic, political and cultural life). This relates to change at both the individual level, such as increased life expectancy, and the societal level, such as increased economic production.

 Evolutionary changes can also take two forms:

 ■ Planned – as the intentional outcome of social policies, such as governments taking deliberate steps to develop economic, political and cultural environments.

 ■ Unplanned – arising from general behaviour within a society. The Industrial Revolution in Britain during the 18th century is an example here. A huge range of scientific and technological developments combined to produce rapid and widespread economic, political and cultural changes that were not consciously planned.

3 Direction: although development is usually characterised in terms of positive social changes, this is not necessarily the case. Negative changes may also occur. Human societies can develop and, in terms of their power and influence on a world stage, decline. Change does not, therefore, always progress from underdevelopment to development.

There are two main problems with defining development in terms of social changes linked with social improvements:

1 'Improvement' and 'development' are subjective concepts and sociologists cannot agree on how they are defined. A social change regarded by one group as an improvement may not be seen as such by another group.

2 Even when there is broad agreement about what 'development' means, there are still questions about how it should be measured:

- There are both economic and social aspects to development. As such, there are debates about what indicators should be used in measuring it and where it should be measured in purely economic terms. Debates surround not only things like the choice of economic indicators, but also whether development should be measured in purely economic terms.

- Quantifiable measures, such as historical changes in income levels, poverty or living standards, are relatively easy to objectively identify, access and construct. However, qualitative measures, such as 'quality of life' or 'happiness' are more difficult to define and standardise within and across societies.

Keeping these qualifications in mind, the sections below look at some of the different ways in which development

has been operationalised across two broad categories: economic and social.

Economic indicators

Barbanti (2004) notes that the conventional way to understand development since the 1950s is in terms of economic growth. In other words, development has traditionally been measured in terms of economic indicators such as:

- Gross domestic product (GDP), or the total value of economic goods and services created by a society over a particular period.
- Gross national income (GNI), which includes net income from abroad, such as the value of foreign investments.

This type of broad economic indicator is a useful measure of development for three reasons:

1 It provides a way of classifying different societies in terms of their general income/living standards and can be used to estimate the level of other social indicators, such as education, healthcare and literacy.

2 It uses objective, quantifiable data that allows broadly reliable historical and cross-cultural comparisons of economic standing and growth.

3 Different societies can be ranked in terms of their different levels of development (Table 7.1).

TEST YOURSELF

Suggest two economic indicators of development.

The use of economic indicators also allows countries to be broadly grouped into developmental categories on a global scale.

Region	Highest	Lowest
Africa	South Africa ($10,710)	Democratic Republic of Congo ($340)
Europe/Scandinavia	Luxembourg ($64,110)	Kyrgyz Republic ($2200)
North and Central America	USA ($48,820)	Nicaragua ($3730)
Latin America	Brazil ($11,420)	Bolivia ($4890)
Asia	China ($8390)	Nepal ($1260)

Table 7.1 Gross national income 2008–12 by region: US$ millions, adjusted for purchasing power parity (PPP)

Source: World Bank (2013)

Note: PPP is a measure of the relative purchasing power of different currencies. An international dollar has the same purchasing power as a US dollar has in the USA.

Three-worlds system

This classification involves dividing the globe into three distinct worlds, based on levels of economic wealth and political ideology:

1 First world: The wealthy, industrialised, technologically developed, capitalist economies of Western Europe, North America and Japan.
2 Second world: The relatively poorer industrial and semi-industrial communist societies, such as China and countries of the former USSR.
3 Third world: The relatively impoverished pre- and semi-industrial nations with low levels of technological development in Africa, South America and South East Asia.

Although this classification is still occasionally used, it has largely outgrown any significance it might once have had. There are two main reasons for this. Firstly, the break-up of the former USSR has made the concept of a 'second world' based around communism largely redundant. Secondly, this system of classification is too broad to reflect accurately the developmental differences within and between these worlds.

Two-worlds system: the North–South divide

An alternative classification proposed by the Independent Commission on International Development Issues (1980), more commonly known as the Brandt Report, focused on the idea of a North–South global divide. The most developed and wealthiest economies are largely found in the northern hemisphere and the poorest, least developed, in the southern hemisphere.

Do cities such as London reinforce the argument of a global North–South divide?

This broad division arguably reflects the global distribution of economic development and consumption. In 2005, for example, the most economically developed 'northern' countries consumed around 80% of the world's economic resources. However, there are two main problems with this classification:

1 The divide is not geographically accurate. For example, Australia – a highly developed economy – lies in the southern hemisphere. This suggests that geographic location may not necessarily be economically significant.
2 The growth of economies in China and South East Asia, such as India, has invalidated a simple North–South divide. The World Bank now ranks China as the second-largest economy in the world after the USA in terms of GDP (Table 7.2).

Ranking	Country	North or South?
1	USA	North
2	China	South
3	Japan	South
4	Germany	North
5	France	North
6	Brazil	South
7	United Kingdom	North
8	Italy	North
9	India	South
10	Canada	North
11	Russian Federation	North
12	Spain	North
13	Australia	North
14	Mexico	South
15	Korean Republic	South

Table 7.2 Largest economies by GDP (US$)

Source: World Bank (2013)

Many-worlds system

Characterises development in a more sophisticated way. It uses more categories and recognises that the majority of societies have experienced some form of economic development since the Second World War. The many-worlds

198

system is based on a 'sliding scale' of development that includes categories such as:

- MEDCs: more economically developed countries
- LEDCs: less economically developed countries
- LLEDCs: least economically developed countries
- NICs: **newly industrialising countries**.

KEY TERM

Newly industrialising country: a less developed country currently undergoing industrialisation.

Although not tied to notions of geographic space, this system is still problematic. The use of a 'sliding scale' reflects the dynamic nature of economic development, but there is still a strong correlation between MEDCs and the first world/North, and LLEDCs and the third world/South.

In addition, although this system allows a large number of different levels of development to be defined, the system still does not allow for a definitive economic definition of development. This fragmented approach could, for example, include relative levels of:

- manufacturing and service industries
- consumption patterns
- the price of a standardised product in different societies.

The Hamburger Standard

As an example of the third idea, we can look at the Hamburger Standard. This takes a global commodity, such as a 'Big Mac' hamburger, manufactured to exactly the same standard worldwide (in India the Maharaja Mac, a chickenburger, is substituted), and compares its relative cost in different societies to arrive at a general estimate of economic development. The more developed a society, the greater the purchasing power of its currency. In an economically strong country, a Big Mac would cost relatively less (Table 7.3).

Highest purchasing power	Lowest purchasing power
Norway	Egypt
Switzerland	Hong Kong
Brazil	South Africa
Canada	India

Table 7.3   The Hamburger Standard

Source: The Economist (2013)

How useful is the 'Hamburger Standard' for assessing a country's state of development?

These different classifications demonstrate the strengths and weaknesses of economic indicators as measures of development. Although they provide an objective range of quantifiable criteria against which to rank different societies, Thirlwall (2002) has questioned their usefulness as measures of development. The main reason for this is because they fail to take into account non-economic factors that impact on a society's overall development. These include levels of:

- health care
- income distribution
- literacy.

Relatively simple economic indicators such as GNI also tell us little or nothing about how incomes are distributed throughout a society. These systems also encourage the misconception that the characteristics of a group must be the characteristics of individuals within that group. For example, the USA has an average GNI of around US$50,000, but this hides major differences in levels of income. Wolff (2012) estimates average US household income as:

- top 1% = $1.3 million
- bottom 40% = $17,000.

Indicators such as GNI/GDP also present problems of reliability, because they are not necessarily defined or calculated in the same way in all societies.

It is also important to note that economic development often comes at a price, in terms of factors such as pollution, environmental degradation, long-term unemployment and poverty. We should not, therefore, assume that economic indicators measure social development.

Social indicators

Although economic development is important, it does not tell the whole story. For example, we can note a range of non-economic indicators.

Political indicators: Badri (1994) suggests that development can be measured by political indicators relating to the level of control people have over their lives. There are three key measures:

1 Freedoms, such as:

- democratic elections
- peaceful protest
- speech
- religion.

2 Rights, such as:

- legal representation
- a fair trial
- free assembly
- free association.

3 Relationships, such as:

- respect for borders
- sovereignty of other nations
- conformity to international laws
- acceptance of international treaties.

On a wider scale, Leinbach highlights the concept of 'distributive justice'. This refers to development measured in terms of the satisfaction of basic human needs that include public goods and services, such as health care and education. This concept also includes general measures of need relating to demographic variables such as:

- infant and child mortality rates: whether children survive into their first and fifth years, respectively
- death rates, including the chances of dying from both natural and non-natural causes, such as murder or suicide
- life expectancy: the average age to which people live can indicate a range of developmental factors.

While Palacios (2002) notes that global average life expectancy rose during the 20th century, from 50 to 66 years, there are differences between regions, societies (Table 7.4) and groups within societies. For example, women have greater life expectancies in nearly every society.

Region	Highest	Lowest
Africa	Tunisia: 74	Central African Republic: 46
Europe	Sweden: 80	Ukraine: 65
North and Central America	Canada: 79	Guatemala: 67
South America	Costa Rica: 77	Brazil: 70
Asia	Japan: 79	India: 63

Table 7.4 Average life expectancy at birth (years)

Source: United Nations (2010b)

Cultural indicators: Badri identifies a range of cultural indicators that can help us understand different levels of development. These include:

- levels of adult literacy
- educational opportunities
- access to basic services such as shelter, clean water and electricity.

Using this type of measure, countries such as the UK and India, which have broadly similar levels of economic development, would be classed very differently in terms of social development. For example, literacy and educational opportunities are more evenly distributed across the UK than the Indian population.

Social indicators can be a valid measure of development and provide a range of goals against which to measure progress in meeting certain universal life standards. However, cultural indicators can also be problematic:

- Questions of reliability and validity arise over how particular countries produce statistical data in areas such life expectancy and child mortality. This creates problems of comparability.
- Social indicators are subject to distortion within and between societies:
  - Young, black, urban, working-class males in the USA, for example, have lower average life expectancies because of high murder and suicide rates.
  - In developing countries, average life expectancy can be lowered by high rates of infant and female mortality during childbirth.

TEST YOURSELF

Suggest two social indicators of development.

Social and economic indicators

In 1990, the United Nations (UN) developed the **Human Development Index (HDI)**. This was an attempt to combine social and economic indicators to assess and rank countries across three economic and cultural areas:

- life expectancy
- knowledge, as measured by adult literacy and educational provision
- living standards measured by GDP per capita.

KEY TERM

Human Development Index (HDI): measurement tool developed by the United Nations that combines social and economic indicators to assess and rank countries across three economic and cultural areas: life expectancy, knowledge and living standards.

The advantage of the HDI is that it does not rank countries according to a predetermined 'development scale', such as globalised standards of development/ underdevelopment. Instead, it compares societies using a set of objective, quantitative criteria that reflects qualitative criteria. For example, 'levels of knowledge' are measured by literacy rates.

The index also takes into account one of the main criticisms of development scales – their ideological bias towards Western societies with high levels of economic development. Using the HDI, countries with high levels of economic capital but low levels of investment in human capital through, for example, education, can be ranked as 'less developed' than economically poorer societies that invest more in social and educational welfare. In this respect, the HDI measures the *ends* of social development – what it means in terms of raised living standards, for example, rather than the *means* to achieve such ends (economic growth). The index can also measure indicators of overdevelopment: the illnesses and diseases, such as heart disease and obesity, that affect affluent societies and reduce average life expectancy.

There are drawbacks to the HDI, including questions about its reliability and validity. Other problems arise from the fact that it needs to be used in combination with other indexes, including:

- human poverty indexes (HPI) that measure of social inequality

- gender development indexes (GDI) that reflect the fact that gender differences exist in most societies in terms of how economic and cultural development is experienced.

ACTIVITY

In small groups, choose one of the following and devise a scale to express different levels of social development in your society:

- *shelter*
- *health*
- *politics*
- *economics*

Compare your continuum with that of other groups.

Different theories of development: modernisation theory, underdevelopment theory, world-system theory

In the opening section we looked the different ways in which development has been defined and measured. This section develops these ideas by examining three main theoretical explanations of development.

Modernisation theory

Modernisation theories are based on the idea that development follows a broadly linear path. Societies pass through different stages, from undeveloped to fully developed, through a cumulative effect; the achievements of one stage become the platform from which to launch the next. Sociologically, the work of Comte, Marx and Weber generally reflects this type of **modernisation theory**.

KEY TERM

Modernisation theory: theory that explains how societies pass through different stages of development, from undeveloped to fully developed.

Comte (1853) saw development in terms of ideological changes in how the world was explained. He claimed that all societies passed through three developmental stages, from superstition to science:

1 Theological: religion was the main form of explanation.
2 Metaphysical: a transition stage between religion and science.

201

3 Scientific ('positive'): scientific knowledge is the dominant form of explanation.

Marx (1867) saw development in economic terms. Societies moved from one epoch to another as the means of economic production changed. Unique **modes of production** characterised three major developmental phases:

1 feudalism
2 **capitalism**
3 communism.

🔑 **KEY TERMS**

Modes of production: Marxist concept that argues that societies pass through different and successive stages of development, each of which is characterised by a different and unique form of economic organisation.

Capitalism: economic system based on private ownership and profit.

Weber (1905) saw development in terms of a change from traditional, or pre-modern, society to modern industrial society which, once started, followed an inevitable process whose features included:

■ industrialisation
■ urbanisation
■ rationalisation: behaviour and social organisation based on scientific principles.

Although these theorists viewed modernisation in different ways, they shared a number of ideas about development. For example, they all believed that is was:

■ phased – or characterised by different, separate (*discrete*) stages
■ cumulative – each stage built on the preceding one
■ linear – societies move from underdeveloped through developing to developed
■ progressive – each stage was superior to the previous one
■ inevitable – modernisation, once started, could not be stopped or reversed.

Stages of growth: Contemporary modernisation theories similarly theorise development as a linear process. For Rostow (1960), this involves the idea that all societies pass through five discrete stages:

1 *Traditional society* is characterised by:

■ religion and magic as the dominant ideological forms
■ agricultural production, with no industrial development

■ rigid political hierarchies with little or no social mobility; social relationships are largely fixed at birth (ascribed) and based on family and kinship.

2 *Preconditions for take-off*: this stage is triggered by the development of relationships with other societies in areas such as:

■ trade, where goods and services are exchanged in the marketplace
■ aid: developed societies provide underdeveloped societies with grants and loans.

The precondition stage has three basic characteristics:

■ In terms of ideology, scientific ideas and practices develop. These lead to technological developments, such as inventions or the application of technologies introduced by more developed societies.
■ Industrial production develops, initially as a form of **proto-industrialisation**. A common example of this is the 'putting-out' or 'domestic' system. In this system, a merchant makes an agreement with family groups that they will assemble garments or shoes, for example in return for payment (sometimes called 'piece work' – people are paid only for the 'pieces' they produce). Other forms of industrial production focus on labour-intensive industries such as mining, although this may depend on relationships with other, developed, societies. For example, developed societies may introduce different forms of manufacturing, such as shipbuilding or car production. Agriculture is still significant, but it begins to decline in importance.
■ Politically, societies develop as recognisable nation states, often ruled by elites such as a monarch or military/civilian dictatorship. A key development is the emergence of a bourgeois (capitalist) class, with the knowledge, skills and motivation to exploit economic opportunities. They must be able and willing to invest capital and reinvest profits. This lays the foundations for stage 3.

🔑 **KEY TERM**

Proto-industrialisation: stage leading up to industrialisation in any society. This may involve the development of economic practices, such as the 'putting-out' system in 17th-century Britain, which laid the foundations for industrialisation.

3 *Take-off*: at this stage, economic growth becomes self-sustaining. Levels of capital investment and

productivity reach a stage where economic expansion can be sustained. The general characteristics of this stage are as follows:

- The rapid expansion of manufacturing and a sharp decline in the social and economic significance of agricultural production. Agriculture is also modernised through various technologies that produce *agribusinesses* – large-scale agricultural production run on industrial lines.
- Political and cultural institutions develop more mature forms: a **democratic transition** to representative government in the former, and education systems providing skilled, literate and numerate workers and managers in the latter.

Democratic transition: part of the 'take-off' stage in Rostow's theory of development, in which political institutions develop more mature forms, such as representative democracy.

4 *The drive to maturity*: this is a consolidation phase, in which science and technology are increasingly applied across different economic sectors:

- Economic behaviour becomes more diversified, producing a wider range of goods and services for both internal consumption and export. Service industries develop as a significant economic sector.
- Political reforms are consolidated with the extension of democratic processes. A range of social reforms, such as government-sponsored welfare systems, are introduced.

5 *Maturity*: the final phase involves what Rostow called the 'age of high mass consumption'. This situation is characterised by:

- advanced levels of economic activity and development, relating not just to manufacturing and service industries but also to the development of knowledge industries, such as computing and communications.
- an increasing range of choices about development, such as the type of society in which people want to live, and the society they envisage for their children; these choices are exercised two levels:
  - ❏ the individual level, in terms of consumption patterns

- ❏ the institutional level, in terms of the social infrastructure: how things like education and welfare systems are developed, structured and financed.

Can modernisation theory be likened to the development of air travel?

Criticisms: Modernisation theory, as both a description of and explanation for the development process has been criticised in a number of ways.

To begin with, modernists see development as a linear process that, once started, proceeds along a set path towards a specific end. It is an 'inevitable historical process' that forms the basis for a **convergence theory** of development: all societies are moving towards the same developmental stage. Although this may reflect the experiences of the first societies in Europe to modernise, they did so under different conditions to those faced by contemporary societies in Asia and Africa. Most significantly, developed societies now exist and have an interest in the economic and social **exploitation** of less developed societies.

Convergence theory: theory that all societies are moving towards the same developmental stage.
Exploitation: using others for your own needs or gain.

When Britain modernised in the 17th and 18th centuries, it was one of the first nations to undergo this process. In countries such as China and India today, modernisation is occurring in the context of already-developed societies. The behaviours and demands of these developed nations mean that modernisation is taking place under qualitatively different terms and conditions. We cannot assume, therefore, that a theory explaining modernisation in Western societies will reliably and validly explain modernisation in non-Western societies.

203

A second line of criticism involves the idea that, according to modernisation theories, all societies are gradually *converging* in terms of their social, economic and political structures. The problem here is that 'modernisation' is not so much a theory to be tested as a statement to be accepted, with the 'Western model' as the blueprint. The theory describes the stages of development in Western societies and the development of Western societies 'proves' the theory.

A further problem arising from this characterisation is that it argues there is only one way – the Western way – to achieve development. This can be used to justify a range of economic, political and cultural interventions by developed countries in the internal affairs of underdeveloped countries on the basis these are necessary for 'modernisation'. The theory also enhances the hegemony of developed societies by prescribing what underdeveloped societies *must* do to modernise. As Coury (1997) argues, development 'is defined in terms of very specific Western societies' with a number of non-negotiable features:

- individualism
- democracy
- capitalism
- science
- secularism
- stability.

Capitán and Lambie (1994) argue that contemporary modernisation theories equate development to economic change and growth, regardless of the social and political consequences for a population: 'Social and political factors are held to be less important and are simply assumed under broad concepts such as modernity and freedom'.

TEST YOURSELF

Identify and explain two criticisms of modernisation theories of development.

Neo-modernisation: Structural change, or neo-modernisation theories recognise that the process of development is affected by the fact that developing countries are locked into a set of global economic, political and cultural relationships that affect their development. We should not, therefore, look for a uniform model of development that will suit all societies.

For neo-modernists, the main difference between underdeveloped and developed societies is a structural one. Whereas the former are predominantly agricultural societies, the latter are industrial or post-industrial societies. This key economic difference explains why some societies develop while others remain relatively underdeveloped. Initially, therefore, industrialisation is the most important feature of development, because industrial societies create:

- high-value economies developing and trading a range of products
- investment and reinvestment opportunities that promote economic growth
- high-productivity economies with profits for reinvestment and higher wage levels that encourage domestic consumption.

The problem of how underdeveloped societies initially develop in the context of already-developed nations is resolved by what Redding (1990) calls a 'cultural trigger'. These are ideas that set off the development process. Borrego (1995), for example, notes how neo-modernisation theorists argue that religions, such as Confucianism in China and Shinto in Japan, provide the cultural ideas that trigger development through the spread of beliefs conducive to capitalist development:

- a high value placed on education
- a commitment to meritocratic personal advancement
- the need for hard work.

These beliefs encompass the qualities needed to take advantage of Western developments. In Japan, for example, development increased once companies started to make cheap copies of US electrical goods. Todero and Smith (2005) argue that the ability to produce a diverse range of goods and services, combined with profits for reinvestment in areas such as new machinery, research and products, represents the key to understanding development. The focus is on how structural relationships constrain development.

Internal constraints include:

- geographic factors, such as the availability of natural resources to develop extraction/manufacturing industries, or physical location (whether a country is landlocked, for example)
- human capital factors, such as the size and demographic composition (for example age and gender) of the population; this also includes things like levels of general education and skills
- government ideologies in terms of attitudes to foreign investment, aid and trade, as well as economic and

cultural development – inward foreign investment, for example, is likely to be attracted to low-wage economies at the expense of widening social inequalities.

External constraints relate to political, economic and cultural relationships with other countries. For example, economic development in Cuba has been hindered because, as Hillyard and Miller (1998) note, 'the United States government has maintained an economic embargo against Cuba for some 38 years; in 1996 the Helms-Burton Act extended the territorial application of the existing embargo to apply to foreign companies trading with Cuba.'

International constraints generally relate to factors such as the ability to attract foreign investment and technology, as well as the nature of political relationships with neighbouring countries. Crucially, developing countries also need access to foreign economic markets for trade. Structural change theory recognises how international relationships and the existence of countries with different levels of development affect undeveloped countries.

As with traditional modernisation theory, the key is industrial production. Development is seen as both *self-generating* (as profits are created they are reinvested to create further profit) and *self-perpetuating* (once industrialisation has begun, it takes on a life of its own, with successive developments building cumulatively in a relatively linear, evolutionary, fashion).

However, this situation depends on the reinvestment of capital, either from indigenous or foreign investors – and this may not happen because of 'capital flight'. This means that foreign investors may have little or no interest in the development of the country in which they invest. Instead, profits are exported to an investor's home country.

Dependency/underdevelopment theory

Dependency/underdevelopment theory broadens the focus to examine the relationship between developed and underdeveloped societies, advancing the view that underdevelopment arises as a consequence of the relationships that form between underdeveloped and developed societies. Chaliand (1977), for example, argues that underdeveloped societies are those with 'distorted

> **KEY TERM**
>
> **Dependency/underdevelopment theory:** Marxist theory of development that argues that underdeveloped and developing societies are kept in a state of economic dependency by the behaviour of developed societies.

and highly dependent economies' dependent on developed nations in terms of:

- producing primary products for consumption in the developed world
- providing markets for their finished goods
- gearing economic development to the needs of industrialised societies
- product prices being determined by large businesses from economically dominant Western countries.

Dual development: This form of development theory sees global development as uneven in two ways:

1 *Core or centre economies*, characteristic of developed nations, dominate world trade. Their relationship with underdeveloped nations is exploitative. For example, **transnational corporations (TNCs)** from developed nations may operate within an underdeveloped nation to extract natural resources, such as oil, or exploit cheap labour. Western clothing companies such as Calvin Klein and Primark manufacture many of their products in countries such as Bangladesh.

2 *Periphery economies* are dependent on developed nations in three main ways:

   - Ideologically: ideas about economic and social development are imposed by developing countries.
   - Culturally: Capitán and Lambie argue that developing countries adopt 'behavioural and consumption' features from developed nations, from how to dress, through films and magazines to fizzy drinks.
   - Technologically: underdeveloped nations import technology rather than developing 'indigenous technologies'.

> **KEY TERM**
>
> **Transnational corporations (TNCs):** corporations based in a specific territory that operate in a range of countries and markets across national borders.

Ferraro (1996) suggests that 'two key arguments' of the dual development approach are:

- coexistence: 'powerful and wealthy industrialized nations compete with weak, impoverished peasant societies in the international economy'
- persistence: unequal and exploitative relationships do not gradually disappear; dependency is a condition of the relationship itself.

Dominant societies have a long-term interest in 'creating and maintaining underdevelopment. They do so by establishing TNCs within the dependent society, and giving aid to develop economic and political infrastructures that help the TNCs to function.

In addition to this, the lending practices of world banking organisations limit the ability of underdeveloped countries to develop modern, industrialised economies. Instead the weaker countries are simply locked into dependent political and economic relationships with developed societies.

Colonial dependence: This form of dependency is theorised in two main ways. Traditional Marxist perspectives focus on the earliest periods of aggressive capitalist development, in terms of military conquest, colonialism and exploitation. Neo-Marxist approaches focus on contemporary forms of hegemonic colonisation.

> **KEY TERM**
>
> **Colonialism:** situation of dependency in which one country governs and controls another country/territory, through things like conquest. India, for example, was once a British colony.

Hegemonic colonisation refers to situations in which underdeveloped societies become 'client states' for a dominant power through economic, political and cultural penetration. For example, the relationship between the USA and its relatively underdeveloped neighbour Mexico is, Thompson (2004) argues, based on relations of dominance and dependence. Mexico is economically dependent on the USA because '85% of the goods and services exported are sold in the USA' and the USA is 'the dominant global economic and military power'.

Colonial dependency theory focuses on how developed capitalist economies use their dominant economic position to exploit the natural and human resources of underdeveloped countries to keep them in a state of underdevelopment. This is achieved in several different ways:

- direct political rule by dominant powers
- indirect political rule through the support of (corrupt) local elites who make political and economic decisions that favour the interests of dominant nations
- trade agreements that give exclusive access to raw materials, such as oil, to TNCs
- only providing aid on the condition that the underdeveloped society allows access to its internal markets.

Evaluation: Dependency theories not only locate development within a global context, they also focus on the idea that international investment and trade are not necessarily mutually beneficial. In some situations, they can be exploitative. As Capitán and Lambie put it, this represents 'a situation in which the economy of certain countries is conditioned by the development and expansion of another country to which it is subservient'. From a Marxist perspective, inequalities between developed and underdeveloped societies are inherent in global capitalism. Put simply, the developed dominate at the expense of the underdeveloped.

Until 1947, India was a British colony (here we have a scene from modern Mumbai). What were the benefits and costs of this relationship for each society?

It can be difficult for underdeveloped societies to break free from this dependence. However, some have managed to achieve decolonisation, including India and many African states. This suggests that the relationship between developed and underdeveloped nations may not always be one of simple dependency. While colonial dependency emphasises the exploitative relationship between colonisers and colonised, it is not only or always the colonisers that benefit. Colonies may benefit from the development of their political and economic infrastructure. Moreover, in the post-colonial era, developing countries may benefit from their relationship with former colonisers, with the latter providing privileged access to technology, markets, expertise and capital investment.

> **KEY TERM**
>
> **Decolonisation:** the process a country undergoes to free itself politically, economically and culturally from a colonial past.

Dependency theory claims that local elites are co-opted into the exploitation process as agents of international capitalism. However, critics of dependency theory have pointed out that while elite corruption may contribute to underdevelopment, this is not always or necessarily the case; indigenous political movements have succeeded in developing the political and economic structures of formerly dependent countries while simultaneously developing a more equitable relationship with developed countries.

Finally, some actions by developed nations to aid underdeveloped nations are not always prompted by economic self-interest. The promotion of political stability, the alleviation of human suffering and the advance of environmentalist policies are all aspects of a less exploitative relationship.

TEST YOURSELF

Identify and explain two differences between modernisation and dependency theories.

World-system approach

The **world-system theory** states that development must be seen in the context of global systems and networks, and should focus on how nations are politically and economically interdependent. Frank (1995) suggests two historical and contemporary aspects of 'world systems' development:

- Politically, in terms of the spread of various empires, from ancient Rome to modern Britain and the effect of these empires on international relationships. This aspect includes the use of African slaves, exploited by Britain in particular throughout the 17th and 18th centuries. Frank suggests that industrial development in this period was largely based on **slavery**.
- Economically, where **globalisation** has encouraged the development of a global capitalist economic system in which every country has a stake. Capra (1983) claims

KEY TERMS

World system theory: theory that argues development must be understood in the context of global systems and networks, with the focus on understanding how nations are locked into political and economic relationships that make them interdependent.

Slavery: economic system in which some people are considered to be the legal property of others. They can be bought and sold, made to work unpaid and have few, if any, legal rights or freedoms.

Globalisation: various processes – economic, political and cultural – that occur on a worldwide basis.

that this is because world systems are 'integrated wholes whose properties cannot be reduced to those of smaller units [such as nation states]'.

According to world systems theory, therefore, development is based on the complex interplay between political, ideological and economic relationships that characterises the globalised modern world. For Wallerstein (1974), these relationships their roots in Western Europe as far back as the 16th century. At this time, individual states began to experience greater political and economic cohesion. This consolidation laid the groundwork for modernity, where the development of industrial capitalism led to rapid and extensive economic expansion among many European states, as they searched for new sources of raw materials, labour and markets.

Wallerstein believes that this was the beginning of what came to be a complex and interdependent world economic system. We can only make sense of ideas such as development and underdevelopment in the overall context of two types of relationship between nations:

- direct, such as one country trading with another
- indirect, such as the effect of one country trading with another to the exclusion of other nations.

Regions: Wallerstein's original formulation suggested a three-pronged regional world economic system:

1 Core regions include the most highly developed economies. They were the first to develop full capitalist economies and are characterised by:

   - strong central governments
   - highly developed industrial bases
   - well-developed bureaucratic administrations.

2 Periphery regions include underdeveloped countries defined in relative terms by their unequal relationship with core regions. Peripheral states are characterised by weak governments controlled by indigenous elites or, where such states are colonies, representatives of the core regions. In relation to core regions, peripheral states serve as sources of raw materials, surplus labour and captive markets.

   Chase-Dunn and Grimes (1995) suggest that underdeveloped status is maintained because these regions are locked into a world political and economic structure reproduces the subordinate status of peripheral states. To be part of a world system, peripheral regions must accept economic ideas and behaviours that, in the long term, maintain their dependence on developed nations.

3 Semi-peripheral regions occupy a space somewhere between the core and the periphery. Such regions may aspire to core membership or they may be former members of the core whose economic development has stalled or declined. Either way, they are significant elements in the world system. Although frequently exploited by core regions, they often attempt to exploit those on the periphery of the world economy. In some situations, such as the former Soviet Union, societies could stand 'outside' the general world system – but only for as long as their political and economic hegemony could be maintained over client states (those that were occupied by another country or had pledged loyalty to one).

World systems theory, therefore, puts development and underdevelopment within a global context, where political and economic relationships are governed by a nation or region's position in the global marketplace. To understand how or why societies develop or fail to develop we must consider the constraints and pressures acting on them in a global context.

More specifically, this approach sees capitalism as a 'world economic system' because it dominates all forms of global production, distribution and exchange. The development of any society – core, semi-periphery or periphery – is, therefore, constrained by the need to participate in this economic system. As such, only capitalist societies can belong to the world economic system – a requirement that ensures a continued situation of domination and dependency.

Complexity: Complexity theories are a development of the general world system approach. They see contemporary dependency as a mix of political, cultural and economic hegemony. Urry (2002), for example, argues that the development of global capitalism involves not only economic interdependencies, but also a range of additional political and ideological dependencies. For example, the European Community began as an economic trading bloc in the 1950s and has gradually developed into a political bloc of 27 nations with varying degrees of political participation and ideological co-operation. Some member states are part of a single currency system (the Euro), whereas others are not (including the UK).

According to complexity theories, dependency is not simply 'one-way', from the periphery to the core. It also has dimensions and consequences that relate to how the behaviour of semi-peripheral and peripheral nations affect those core nations and vice versa. This can be expressed

in relation to **environmentalism**, for example. Rapid industrialisation in semi-peripheral regions such as China has both favourable and unfavourable consequences:

- Economically, core regions such as the USA benefit because their major industries can take advantage of very low labour market costs to produce cheap consumer goods.
- Politically, core regions have to deal with the environmental costs of China's rapid industrialisation. There may also be unfavourable consequences for core regions in terms of things like unemployment.

KEY TERM

Environmentalism: political/ideological philosophy and movement concerned with safeguarding, conserving and improving all aspects of the human and natural environment for future generations.

TEST YOURSELF

Identify and explain two differences between modernisation and world-systems theories.

ACTIVITY

Choose one of the following models of development:

- *modernisation*
- *neo-modernisation*
- *underdevelopment*
- *world systems.*

On a postcard, summarise the main claims of the model and identify one strength and one limitation. Exchange your postcards with other students to build up a revision list of key ideas, strengths and limitations.

Debates about aid and development

We can give some initial context to debates over the role of **aid** in the development process by defining its meaning.

KEY TERM

Aid: various forms of public and private assistance given to promote economic development and social welfare across the globe.

The OECD (1995) defines aid as assistance given to promote 'economic development *and* social welfare' across the globe. This can take a number of forms:

- non-repayable grants
- repayable loans that must have:
  - a lower interest rate than current market rates
  - a grant element: the norm is around 25% of the loan
- non-monetary assistance such as technological and military help, advice and training
- development finance: this involves aid in the form of credit, guaranteed by a developed nation, through which developing nations can establish trading links.

Aid can be divided into two broad categories: public and private.

Public aid

Public or official development assistance takes two main forms:

1 Bilateral or direct aid given by one government to another. Its main purpose, according to the American Congressional Budget Office (1997), is 'to encourage equitable and sustainable economic growth in developing countries'. The concept of sustainable growth reflects the idea that economic aid should be directed towards the specific development needs of the receiving country. The long-term goal of this is to establish self-sustaining economic growth. Other forms of bilateral aid may, however, have different objectives.

Military assistance can be:

- economic, such as the provision of loans, grants and credit agreements to enable a developing country to purchase military hardware from the country providing the assistance
- political, ranging from things like providing military advisors and trainers to a military presence in the developing country.

Humanitarian assistance includes the following:

- Donations made by a government to ease suffering in situations of war or natural disaster, usually, but not necessarily, in a developing country. In 2011, for example, the USA provided $500 million of 'emergency assistance' to the eastern Horn of Africa, including $50 million assistance for famine relief in Somalia.

- Co-operation between countries. Anshan (2010), for example, notes that China has provided both emergency medical assistance and long-term co-operation to 44 African countries since 1963.
- Physical aid such as food and clothing provided either directly or indirectly through non-governmental organisations (NGOs), such as charities.

TEST YOURSELF

Identify and briefly explain two types of bilateral aid.

2 Multilateral or indirect aid is assistance channelled through international agencies, such as the International Monetary Fund (IMF) and the World Bank, both established in 1944. These are economic agencies whose primary development role is to lend money at concessional rates to low-income countries. They also lend money at non-concessional rates to middle-income countries that find it difficult to raise loans in private markets. In 'exceptional circumstances' the IMF will lend money to developed nations; the UK, for example, required an emergency £2.3 billion loan in 1976.

Receiving countries have to meet certain political and economic conditions before assistance is given. These conditions vary, but Greenhill (2004) points out that 'the World Bank is still lending money to developing country governments on condition they adopt specific economic policies such as privatisation'. This means that in order to qualify for a loan, receiving countries must allow private companies to develop/run industries such as water, gas and electricity generation and supply that were formerly provided by governments.

Ideology

The argument here is that financial organisations such as the IMF and World Bank provide assistance to developing nations as part of an ideological agenda. This promotes not just capitalism as the solution to developmental problems, but a particular form of neo-liberal capitalism. This is based on the desire to ensure the widest possible role for the private sector in determining the political and economic objectives of governments. It includes ideas such as:

- private ownership of all areas of the economy
- the liberalisation of trade between countries
- access to internal markets for TNCs.

209

How do organisations such as the IMF promote global development?

The United Nations is another multilateral aid agency that promotes a global development agenda through programmes such as the Millennium Development Goals (MDGs). Clemens et al. (2004) note that these represent 'a set of quantitative, time-bound targets' for every country to attain by 2015 (Table 7.5).

Target		Key indicators	
1	Eradicate extreme poverty and hunger	1	Halve the number of people living on less than 60p a day. Act to reduce slum dwelling
2	Universal primary education	2	Both boys and girls to complete primary school
3	Promote gender equality	3	End discrimination in primary and secondary schooling
4	Reduce child mortality	4	Reduce by two-thirds
5	Improve maternal health	5	Reduce by 75% the number dying in childbirth
6	Combat HIV, malaria and other diseases	6	Halt and begin to reverse the spread of HIV
7	Ensure environmental sustainability	7	Halve the number of people without access to safe drinking water
8	Development as a global partnership	8	Develop a fair and open trading system, providing debt relief or working for democracy

Table 7.5　The Millennium Development Goals

Source: United Nations (2000)

It is unlikely that every country will achieve all these goals by 2015, but the most recent United Nations (2012) report suggests targets have been met in terms of:

- poverty reduction
- access to safe drinking water
- improving the lives of slum-dwellers in urban areas.

A final aspect of public aid is the commitment made in 1970 by 23 of the major developed nations to a target of contributing 0.7% of GNI to official development assistance. However, UN data (2012) shows that only four nations – Sweden, Norway, Netherlands and Luxembourg – have consistently hit this target. In 2011, the world's largest economy, the USA, contributed 0.2% of GNI to assistance.

Private aid

Private or unofficial development assistance ranges from specific targeted project work to acting as channels for both government and privately donated humanitarian aid. This type of assistance is mainly related to NGOs that perform a range of services (Table 7.6).

Type of assistance	Example NGO
Poverty reduction	Oxfam
Medical	Médecins sans Frontières
Humanitarian	Danish Refugee Council
Educational	Barefoot College
Business creation	One Acre Fund
Microfinance	Bangladesh Rural Advancement Committee

Table 7.6　Role of NGOs

Advantages

Modernisation theory suggests that aid may help developing societies achieve 'take-off'. Neo-modernisation theory suggests that carefully targeted economic aid may represent an important way for societies to stimulate the industrialisation process. This would allow them to make the crucial transition from agricultural to industrial society. Similarly, from world-system perspectives, aid is one of the ways in which peripheral and semi-peripheral societies develop their industrial base in order to contribute to global economic markets.

More generally, if the overall objective is to encourage developing countries to industrialise and reduce their dependence on developed countries, aid can help deal with rapid industrialisation and bring developing countries into the world political infrastructure. Aid gives donor countries political leverage which might, for example, be used to ensure that environmental targets are met. Further arguments in favour of aid include the following:

- Reconstruction projects can promote development following conflicts. US aid, for example, has played a role in the reconstruction of Iraq following the Second Gulf War.
- Aid has helped reduce diseases such as polio and to eradicate smallpox.
- Humanitarian aid in areas such as Africa and South East Asia has lessened the effects of natural disasters. NGOs have also worked towards reducing the impact of drought and famine by helping developing populations improve their farming methods and sanitation, as well as to increase their levels of education.
- Aid helps to develop economic infrastructures, such as sanitation and waste disposal, when private companies are unwilling to intervene because there is no profit to be made.

Disadvantages

Despite the benefits, not everyone sees aid as either wholly beneficial to the recipient or altruistic on the part of the donor. There are three main criticisms of aid programmes:

1 *Exploitation* relates to the dependency theory argument that development assistance contributes to the client status of receiving states. Developing nations are locked into a cycle of economic development that mainly benefits companies from the donor country. According to the US Agency for International Development (USAID) (2005): 'The principal beneficiary of America's foreign assistance programs has always been the United States; 80% of Agency contracts and grants go directly to American firms'. USAID also claims that 'US foreign assistance has always had a twofold purpose': furthering America's foreign policy interests in expanding democracy and free markets, and improving the lives of the citizens of the developing world.

2 *Inefficiency*, for new-right/market liberal approaches, involves the argument that 'trade rather than aid' represents the most efficient and cost-effective solution

to the problems of development, dependency and industrialisation. Although some forms of humanitarian aid may be useful, the only long-term development solution is to incorporate these countries into the global market economy. This involves allowing TNCs to operate freely in developing countries in order to:

- develop natural resources, such as coal, oil and gas
- generate employment
- develop indigenous economic infrastructures.

3 *Effectiveness* relates to whether aid is the best way to promote political and economic development. Will it achieve the desired goals? Will it create more problems than it solves in the receiving society? Collier and Dollar (2002), for example, argue that whether or not aid stimulates economic growth depends on the political situation. Developing nations with stable political and government structures benefit from aid; those where the political situation is unstable do not. This raised questions about whether aid could and should be used to assist the development of stable political and economic structures in the first place. Easterly et al. (2003) found no significant empirical relationship 'between the amount of aid and economic growth of the recipient countries'.

There is also an argument that aid is sometimes used in ways that bring no long-term economic or cultural benefits to the receiving country. For example, building roads to develop communication systems has no benefit if a country does not have the financial or material resources to maintain the roads.

Trade as aid

From a new-right perspective, Bauer (1971) argues that, historically, when aid has been given directly to governments, ruling elites use it to consolidate their power base through things like patronage and corruption. As a result, many people now believe that money and assistance is not the more efficient or cost-effective way to encourage development, except in the case of humanitarian disasters. The meaning of 'aid' has changed from the idea of 'donation' to the idea of promoting trade as the route to (self-) development.

Industrialisation is seen as the key to development, so helping countries to industrialise by helping them trade in global markets is an important step towards solving the problem of underdevelopment. Development must be sustainable, so 'aid through trade' promotes long-term, self-sustaining, economic stability and progression. Governments and NGOs generally agree that sustainable development is the route to take, they disagree about what role trade should take in this process. This can be illustrated by two opposing interpretations: neo-liberal (free market) and state interventionist.

Neo-liberal approaches

This approach argues that long-term sustainable development can only be assured through free-market trading policies between nations. These policies need to be based on some fundamental principles:

- Trade liberalisation involves opening national markets to international competition. This gives developing countries access to lucrative markets in the developed world, while TNCs gain access to markets and resources in the developing world. Developing countries gain access to both capital investment and newer forms of technology.
- Competition is the most effective way to encourage development through new and cost-effective ways of producing goods and providing services. The developed world must abandon protectionist policies such as:
  - high taxes on goods from developing nations
  - state subsidies to inefficient industries
  - preventing access to developed markets. In Europe, for example, a Common Agricultural Policy that provides subsidies, guaranteed prices and markets for agricultural products, is seen as a barrier to trade liberalisation.
- State ownership and control distorts the workings of free markets by giving some companies an unfair advantage (through cheap loans, for example). Private companies, working in a competitive market, are the key to economic development.
- Although the state plays a role in banning and policing unfair competitive practices, it should not over-regulate business behaviour. Business discipline comes from the need to be competitive in free markets.
- People should be allowed to keep as much as possible of their earned income because this provides both individual and structural incentives for businesses to invest and innovate. Low taxation is essential for development.

Morrison (2000) notes that China, with the highest recent levels of economic growth in the world, has adopted a range of free-market initiatives, from the gradual privatisation of state-owned enterprises (SOEs) to the development of 'private enterprise zones' with lower rates of business taxation and less strict labour laws. Similarly,

the rapid growth of the 'tiger economies' of Hong Kong, South Korea, Singapore and Taiwan has been attributed to the adoption of free-market policies in the 1960s that led to rapid industrialisation. However, Borrego argues that cultural factors, such as the religious values of Confucianism in China and Shinto in Japan, have played a key part in sustainable development.

KEY TERM

Tiger economies: fast-growing economies of Southeast Asia, including Hong Kong, South Korea, Singapore and Taiwan.

Critics also note that 'free-market policies' are encouraged and imposed on developing countries, while developed economies such as the USA use a range of policies to protect their industries and services against foreign competition. In addition, free-trade policies give developed nations and TNCs significant economic advantages that can negatively affect industrial development in developing countries. TNCs may exploit the markets, resources and cheap labour that they have access to.

Governments also have a role to play in regulating businesses to limit their environmental impact. The state also has a role to play in banning uncompetitive practices, getting rid of corruption and preventing the development of monopolies and *cartels*, where a group of companies agrees not to compete against each other to maintain high prices.

Interventionist approaches

These approaches argue that the state should be able to intervene to control both economic activity and the behaviour of private corporations. If states can play what Justino (2001) calls a conflict-management role, the economic power of developed nations can be channelled and restricted to provide a strong development strategy that takes into account the needs of all nations. More specifically, interventionist approaches focus on trade as a significant dimension of aid. From this perspective, it is essential for developing nations to participate equally in a global trading system. There are two main reasons for this:

1 International trade encourages the development of indigenous industry and sustained self-development. This is how the world's poorest nations can move away from aid dependence.

2 Trade represents a standard development model followed by the world's richest nations – it is a *proven* strategy.

For interventionists, governments play a significant political and economic role in areas such as:

- trade agreements, giving developing countries access to developed markets
- regulation of economic activity to encourage competitive business practices
- encouraging economic diversity by helping developing countries move away from monocultural production – an overdependence on a single product that makes them vulnerable to price collapses on world markets
- the financial development of indigenous industries.

Interventionists criticise free-market approaches which argue that economic development and, by implication, political and cultural development, should be left to market forces. As evidence of the problems this creates, they point to various experiments in free-market liberalisations in South America in the 1990s. Countries including Chile, Brazil and Argentina were encouraged to follow neo-liberal economic policies proposed by writers such as Friedman (1962) and von Hayek (1973). The result was a level of economic development, but it came at a cost of political repression.

TEST YOURSELF

Suggest one similarity and one difference between neo-liberal and interventionist approaches to trade.

Three-dimensional approach

Short (2001) argues that both free-market and interventionist polices may act more in the interests of developed countries and TNCs than those of developing nations. In developed countries, privatisation policies often price services so high that the poor cannot afford them. In developing nations, 'Trade liberalisation can harm the low-skilled and hit the poor disproportionately hard'. A more recent approach to the 'trade–aid' debate, therefore, has been a three-dimensional approach.

In this approach, trade and aid are located within a developmental context that the Brundtland Commission (1987) says 'meets the needs of the present without compromising the ability of future generations to meet their own needs'. This means reconciling four imperatives:

- economic development
- social cohesion
- North/South equity
- environmental protection.

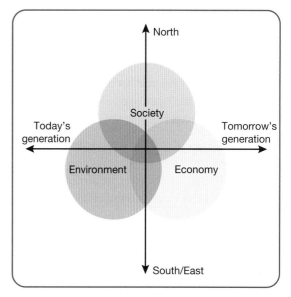

The 3D approach to sustainable development: von Stokar and Steinemann (2004)

Von Stokar and Steinemann (2004) argue that different regions and generations face contrasting but interlinked problems that require a three-dimensional solution. We must consider three related dimensions of development through trade: economic, social and environmental.

For developing countries in the South, the primary need is to develop trade while protecting the environment. In the developed North, strong economies and some measure of environmental protection already exist; the main problem for these nations is twofold:

- adjusting to cultural lifestyles that encourage environmental protection, such as producing less waste and developing fuel-efficient transport, for the benefit of future generations
- offering greater opportunities for economic development in the South.

ACTIVITY

In groups, research the economic, political and cultural advantages and disadvantages of both aid and trade. As a class, discuss whether or not you believe aid, trade or a combination of both provides the best strategy for development.

Population growth and development

This section examines a range of historic and contemporary population trends, and considers the consequences of continued global population growth.

213

Trends

Population growth is broadly measured in terms of the relationship between two variables:

1 Crude birth rates, or the number of live births per 1000 in a population per year. Such rates are affected by a range of demographic factors:

- Economic value of children – this tends to be higher in developing countries, where children in agricultural and early industrial societies are an economic resource. In developed nations, children tend to be an economic drain on families, as economically inactive childhood is gradually extended through education.
- Economic cost of children – this is much higher in developed countries, where children tend not to enter the labour force until their late teens.
- Female employment – in developed nations, where more women are employed outside the home, fertility rates tend to be lower. Developed nations have higher levels of female professional workers with relatively lower fertility rates because they marry or start families at a later age. The average age of first marriage for women in the UK is 29; in India and China it is 22.
- Child and infant mortality – where these rates are high, families tend to have more children as 'insurance' against both the likelihood of loss and poverty in old age.
- Availability and cost of reliable birth control – this includes both contraception and abortion.

2 Death rates: these, too, are affected by various demographic factors, including:

- health care and avoidance of infectious diseases
- general living standards, including nutrition and hygiene standards
- access to clean water
- levels of global conflict, such as war
- levels of local conflict, such as violent neighbourhoods.

Population growth, therefore, is broadly measured in terms of 'natural increase' – the numbers of births minus the number of deaths.

TEST YOURSELF

Briefly explain why global population growth is not simply a matter of calculating birth rates.

Global

For most of human history, global populations have been relatively small (Table 7.7):

- In 1500, the total was less than half a billion.
- Around 1800, the population passed 1 billion.
- In 2011, the global population stood at 7 billion.

Year	Billions
1500	0.5
1750	0.7
1804	1.0
1927	2.0
1960	3.0
1975	4.0
1987	5.0
1999	6.0
2011	7.0

Table 7.7   World population growth

In the time it takes to read this sentence, the world population has increased by 25: 42 births minus 17 deaths.

On current trends, the United Nations (2004) estimates that the global population in 2050 will be:

- High: 10.6 billion
- Medium: 8.7 billion
- Low: 7.4 billion

To put this into context, these projections suggest that each year the 'world population will expand by about as many people as now live in Italy' or, over a 50-year period, 'more than twice the current population of China'. While this suggests substantial population growth over the next half-century, we must take into account population spread. There is a difference of around 3 billion people between the highest and lowest projections and this raises questions of reliability. The figures and assumptions on which growth projections are based can and do change. The 2008 revision of these projections, for example, suggests a high of 10.5 and a low of 7.8 billion.

When explaining trends in global population growth, experts refer to primary and secondary drivers:

- Primary drivers include broad historical processes such as industrialisation and urbanisation. The application of industrial processes to agriculture, for example, vastly increases the population that can be supported. Urbanisation allows greater numbers of people to live in smaller areas. In 1800, around 3% of the world's population lived in cities. By 2010, it was more than 50%.

- Secondary drivers include the kinds of factors we have noted in relation to birth and death rates. Industrialisation, for example, leads to higher sustainable populations by:
  - raising the economic value and cost of children
  - increasing female employment
  - lowering child and infant mortality
  - allowing greater access to health care
  - controlling infectious diseases
  - establishing higher nutrition and hygiene standards.

Regional trends

Global population trends are an important factor when considering development. However, we need to remember that these trends are *global*. Societies have not all developed at the same time and the same rate. This means we need to look at the consequences of differential development. While societies such as the UK, Germany and the USA developed in the context of developing nations, the reverse is also true. British and Indian development, for example, has been closely linked for the past 250 years, but it has not been the development of equals. Britain, as a colonial ruler, benefited far more than India. The consequences of being a developed nation in a developing world are very different from those of being a developing nation in a developed world.

To explain the consequences of global population trends, we need to understand how primary drivers of modernisation and development not only have an overall global impact but, more importantly, how they affect various regions differently. Rosling (2013) that rather than making a strong distinction between population growth in developed and developing nations, contemporary population projections show a clear distinction between four groups:

1 Developed nations (such as the UK) with zero or negative population growth.
2 Higher developing nations (such as China) with zero population growth.
3 Lesser developing nations, such as India, with falling population growth.
4 Underdeveloped nations with sharply rising population growth (Table 7.9).

For a population to exactly replace itself (zero population growth), an annual total fertility rate of 2.1 is needed

(Table 7.8). Comparing developed nations with developing nations shows rapid progress towards a growing convergence.

Country	1970	2000	2010
UK	2.43	1.64	1.98
USA	2.48	2.06	1.93
EC average	2.42	1.48	1.58
OECD average	2.76	1.68	1.74
Brazil	4.06	2.39	1.94
China	5.51	1.74	1.60
India	5.49	3.12	2.65

Table 7.8   Total fertility rates

Source: OECD (2013)

Development type	Region	Projected % population change: 2000–50
Most developed	North America	−0.4
	Europe	−4.7
Developing	Asia	−0.8
	Latin and Central America	−0.1
Least developed	Africa	+8.3

Table 7.9   World population distribution by region

Source: United Nations (2008)

Global population growth is uneven. The least developed nations are mainly African and they account for nearly all of the projected global population increase over the next 40 years.

Addressing the problems of the underdeveloped world is, therefore, the key to controlling population growth. While this may involve various forms of aid and sex education, a more effective form of population control is to follow the development lessons of the rest of the world. It is possible to manage population growth by changing the social conditions, such as extreme poverty, lack of political representation and economic exploitation, that drive the need for large families. In the long term, therefore, political and economic change drives population control.

215

Population growth affects social policy at every level, and remains one of the biggest global challenges of the future

TEST YOURSELF

What is the trend for total fertility rates in Brazil, China and India?

216

Explanations

It is also important to understand the *consequences* of population growth. This is usually considered on a global basis, in terms of the number of people who can be physically supported by the planet's resources.

Classical Malthusian model

Malthus (1798) developed a mathematical model of the relationship between human populations and physical resources. His model is based on the claim that human behaviour is governed by two 'natural laws': to eat (subsistence) and to reproduce. Malthus argued that, in their 'unchecked state', these natural conditions inevitably collide:

- Populations increase geometrically (1, 2, 4, 8, 16…).
- Subsistence, or the ability to produce food, increases arithmetically (1, 2, 3, 4, 5…).

By this calculation, the rate of population increase over even a few generations inevitably outstrips the ability of a population to feed itself. This creates increasingly severe consequences, beginning with increasing levels of poverty. Ultimately, this natural collision of

opposing forces would have catastrophic consequences. At this point population growth would be checked in two ways:

1   Negative or preventative checks to lower the fertility rate:
- sexual abstinence
- later marriage.

2   Positive checks on population growth that lower both life expectancy and populations:
- disease
- famine
- war.

However, Malthus's formulation has been criticised for several reasons.

1   Technological developments, starting with the Industrial Revolution, soon made it clear that claims about the 'arithmetic progression' of food production were unreliable.

2   While Malthus considered preventative checks on population growth, such as contraception and abortion, as 'immoral vices', these are increasingly accepted as effective population restraints. In developed nations in particular they have made his model of geometric population progression untenable.

3   There is a clear sense that Malthus' theory is based on a moral critique of the poor. For example, he was critical of the poor for what he saw as their 'unchecked sexuality', which outstripped their economic ability to provide for their offspring.

4   Reproduction is not simply a human reflex. Choices about whether to have children and how many to have can be seen as rational choices taken in the context of changing economic, political and cultural circumstances. In particular, the model ignores the effects of demographic transition – the argument that economic growth reduces population growth.

Neo-Malthusian models

While Malthus's mathematical model proved unreliable, neo-Malthusian approaches argue that the fundamental problems he addressed have not disappeared.

The population bomb: Erlich (1968) updated Malthus's claim that population growth inevitably outstrips food production, stating that:

1   Catastrophic outcomes were imminent: 'The battle to feed all of humanity is over. In the 1970s hundreds of millions of people will starve to death.'

2 Although it was already too late – 'nothing can prevent a substantial increase in the world death rate' – radical solutions could be applied to address the long-term problems of population growth. These measures included:

- a tax on 'additional children'
- luxury taxes on childcare products
- mass sterilisation
- prenatal sex choice – where male children are more highly valued in many societies, allowing parents to choose a male child would limit family size
- expansion of contraception, abortion and sex education.

Erlich's predictions about the effects of population growth have generally been disproven both by events and circumstances. Although many in Africa have died of starvation over the past 40 years, the causes were war and natural/man-made disasters rather than overpopulation. Similarly, the prediction that India would not be able to feed around 200 million people 'by 1980' was disproven.

The limits to growth: A more sophisticated neo-Malthusian approach to the consequences of population growth is provided by Meadows et al. (1972). They accept the underlying principles of the classical Malthusian model, but they expand and change the variables:

- Any one of five variables – world population, industrialisation, pollution, food production or resource depletion – increase geometrically.
- Technology and the ability to increase resource production increases arithmetically.

It should be stressed that 'limits to growth' is a *model* not a theory. It shows the probable outcome of a specific course of action rather than predicting that it will necessarily occur. Any model is only as good as the data it uses and, as we have seen with assumptions about population growth, these can be unreliable.

When testing the population-growth variable, Meadows et al. found that, at some point, technological advances in food production would no longer sustain a given global population. The world would then experience an uncontrolled, potentially disastrous economic and political decline.

Carrying capacity

A different interpretation of the relationship between populations and environments argues that any environment with a finite level of resources has a certain population 'carrying capacity': the number of people it can support without being gradually degraded. In this respect, there is always an upper limit to population growth, both regional and global. Unlike related neo-Malthusian approaches, however, carrying capacity suggests that there is no particular tipping point. The important factor is how people use physical and cultural resources to support population growth.

An environment's carrying capacity, therefore, is not fixed. It can be expanded by technological developments and resource management. It will, however, always be degraded for future populations by actions in the present, such as extracting and using oil. The more people there are, the closer an environment gets to its carrying capacity and the more likely conflict becomes, as increasing numbers of people compete for fewer resources.

A simple way to illustrate this idea is to imagine five islands, each of which can comfortably support 100 people. This nominal capacity is increased or decreased by a range of demographic factors, such as the age structure of the population (adults consume more resources than children) and consumption patterns (people consuming less increases capacity, while higher consumption reduces capacity). Improvements in food technology may, over time, increase each island's carrying capacity, One island may also decide to invade, conquer and enslave the inhabitants of a neighbouring island, thereby increasing their carrying capacity at the expense of their neighbour. As we can see from this simple example, carrying capacity is a complex, flexible calculation:

1 At some point in the future, the carrying capacity of the globe will inevitably be exceeded by unchecked population growth.
2 The carrying capacity of future generations is affected by environmental decisions taken by previous generations; at some point, for example, there will be no more oil left in the planet to extract.

While some argue that resources can be cultivated, husbanded and preserved to support current global carrying capacity, others take a more pessimistic view. Catton (1982), for example, argues that a population's current attitudes to the environment and the exploitation of finite natural resources are shaped by a 'cultural heritage' rooted in the past, when the planet's carrying capacity far exceeded its human load. However, this, is no longer the case. Global population growth has effectively exceeded the planet's carrying capacity and the human load can only be carried by using up natural resources – something that cannot be sustained in the long term.

This theory suggests, therefore, that while it is important to limit population growth through things like family planning, it is also necessary to understand how irreversible changes to the environment are a factor in the population equation. Urbanisation, for example, may drive population growth, but it also:

- limits biodiversity
- involves the loss of agricultural land
- affects hydrological systems
- influences local climate systems.

In a way, population growth is seen as an effect rather than a cause of global problems. The real cause is a cultural inability to recognise, understand and act on the facts of environmental carrying capacities.

The tragedy of the commons

The problem of overpopulation in relation to shared and sustainable resources was addressed by Hardin (1968) in terms of how 'common resources' on which everyone in a group or population depends can be depleted by individual self-interest. In this case, individual self-interest means countries with large and growing populations that can only be sustained by taking resources away from other countries. From this perspective, the 'tragedy of the commons' can be seen as a criticism of the behaviour of developed nations and their relationship to underdeveloped and developing nations. 'Tragedy' is applied in the classical sense to refer to how an individual is eventually destroyed by a fatal weakness or personality flaw.

One interpretation of this idea is that the planet is a shared, finite resource that can sustain a very large global population for as long as the resource is cultivated, managed and shared equitably. The problem is that some nations, driven by economic and political self-interest, act independently. To 'take more of the common' to enhance their interests while simultaneously being aware such behaviour is destructive and ultimately against the long-term interests of all. Once one nation behaves in this way, other nations will inevitably follow. Hardin believes that there is 'no technical solution to the problem'; rather, the solution involves 'mutual coercion mutually agreed upon'. People's 'economic self-interest' must be artificially limited 'in their own best interests', through mechanisms such as international agreements. The European Community, for example, has negotiated quotas on the number of fish that can be caught each year. While this places artificial limits on what individual fishing companies can catch, it prevents over-fishing and preserves fish stocks for future generations.

There are several general criticisms aimed at neo-Malthusian models and theories, particularly in relation to unreliable and invalid predictions. More specific criticisms focus on two areas that can be addressed by examining alternative explanations of the consequences of population growth.

> **TEST YOURSELF**
>
> What is the key variable for Malthusian and neo-Malthusian explanations?

Demographic transition

One criticism of neo-Malthusian approaches is that population-growth projections generally predict the future based on the past, along the lines of average population growth over the past 25 or 50 years projected into the next 25 or 50 years. However, it is important to note that such predictions can be seen as ahistorical, because they ignore how societies actually evolve. Newson et al. (2005) suggest that this idea is addressed by demographic transition models, where historical development is characterised as a progression from high mortality and high fertility to low mortality and low fertility.

These trends are part of a general **demographic change** that occurs in the transition between four basic stages and transformations in a society's historical development:

1 pre-industrial or pre-modern
2 early industrial or early modern
3 late industrial or late-modern
4 post-industrial or postmodern.

> **KEY TERM**
>
> **Demographic change:** changes in population statistics over time.

The argument here is that birth, death and population rates correlate with these stages across all developed nations (Table 7.10).

The reasons for these demographic changes are many, varied and complex. However, one of the most important is modernisation, with industrialisation driving the process. As McFalls argues: 'Most societies eagerly accept

Stage	Birth rate	Death rate	Population
1	High	High	Low
2	High	Falling rapidly	Growing
3	Falling	Low	Increasing
4	Low	Low	High

Table 7.10   Demographic transitions: all industrialised countries

Source: McFalls (2003)

technological and medical innovations, as well as other aspects of modernization, because of their obvious utility against the universal enemy: death. Social attitudes, such as the high value attached to having many children, are slower to change. It can take generations for people accustomed to high childhood mortality to recognize that low mortality means that they no longer need to have eight children to ensure that four will survive to adulthood.'

In other words, the transition between different stages of development produces technological changes, such as the ability to create more resources. It also makes cultural changes from, for example, absolute levels of poverty or literacy, to relative levels that, while still indicative of social inequality, change the demographic nature of societies. This means that while different societies in different stages of development have different demographic characteristics, the general trend is towards a global situation of low birth and death rates combined with historically high global population.

KEY TERM

Social inequality: the unequal and unfair distribution of resources in any society.

This suggests that population growth is sensitive to development. It also suggests that population growth can be managed in the short and long term. While global populations may be historically high, an increasing number of highly developed nations, such as Sweden and the UK, have already achieved or are rapidly approaching an *additional stage* to demographic transition, one that involves:

- low birth rates
- low death rates
- zero/negative population growth.

Demographic regulation

Bogue (1969) adds to the transition model by arguing that societies are capable of recognising and regulating population growth in line with particular norms that adapt to changes in economic conditions. This means that societies develop ways to regulate populations that do not rely on 'Malthusian catastrophes'. The existence of developed countries provides a broad population development template in terms of:

- understanding the need for population regulation
- contemporary communication systems that spread ideas about population control quickly around the globe
- advances in population control techniques, such as contraception.

TEST YOURSELF

Summarise the demographic difference between Stage 1 and Stage 4 societies.

Marxist models

Marxists move the debate away from population growth as the primary reason for underdevelopment. Instead, they blame the global distribution of resources between rich and poor societies. Malthusian approaches implicitly identify the behaviour of lesser developed and developing countries as problematic – producing too many people they are unable to feed. Marxist approaches argue that developed countries are the real problem. This is not, therefore, a problem of overpopulation but one of under-resourcing. Developed countries not only consume too many resources, they do so in ways that negatively affect developing nations.

This relates to the concept of hyper-consumption. An important feature of this is overeating; not just in terms of personal consumption, but also due to the inefficient production and processing of food. Meadows (1999), for example, notes that Americans consume '700 kilos of grain per person per year'. Most of this is fed to pigs and chickens to produce meat; nearly 40% of the world grain crop is fed to animals. This is an inefficient use of resources because the food value of grain is much higher than that of meat.

Consumption and its relationship to population growth is, in this respect, a problem of contemporary capitalism with its hyper-intensive modes of consumption, rather than of population. The global community is able to maintain or exceed its current level as long as there is a more even distribution of resources and a more rational approach to their consumption. The solution is to embrace **sustainable development** models in which social, rather than technological, development will lead to a decline in population growth, ecological damage and development costs.

Overall, therefore, Marxist approaches reject the claim that global population growth inevitably means more people consuming more resources and eventual biological and ecological catastrophes. A large global population can be supported and sustained through changes in capitalism and consumption, with developed countries taking less and developing countries receiving more of the total level of global **wealth**.

KEY TERMS

Sustainable development: economic theory related to the relationship between trade and aid, which argues that the objective of development should be the promotion of long-term, self-sustaining, economic stability and progression.

Wealth: economic concept that describes the total extent of possessions owned by individuals and societies. While income is one aspect of wealth, the concept also includes those things, from ownership of factories through stocks and shares to fine art, that can produce an income for their owner.

TEST YOURSELF

Identify and briefly explain one key difference between neo-Malthusian and Marxist explanations of the consequences of population growth.

ACTIVITY

Divide into groups. Each group should illustrate the consequences of global population growth from one of the perspectives illustrated in the text. Each group should present its findings to the class.

Global issues

Migration, international employment patterns and demographic change

This section examines **migration** and employment patterns in the contexts of demography, the study of human population characteristics, and demographic

KEY TERM

Migration: relatively large-scale movement of people from one place to another. This usually occurs across societies, but may also occur within societies, usually on a temporary basis.

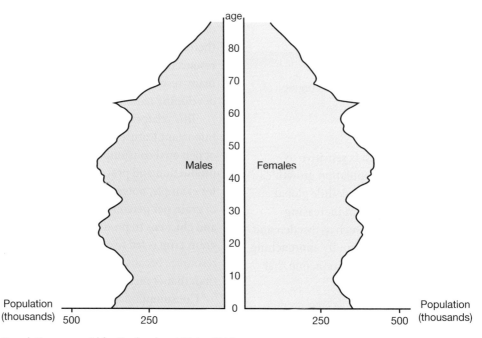

Population pyramid for England and Wales 2013

Source: ONS (2013)

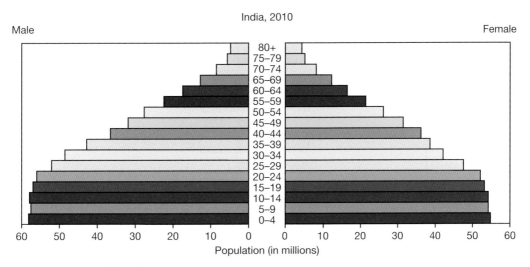

India, 2010

Male   Female

Population (in millions)

Population pyramid for India

Source: US Census Bureau (2013)

changes, statistical analyses of population structures in terms of variables such as:

- geographic distribution
- employment
- health and disease
- birth and death rates
- age and sex distributions.

Demographic differences

Demography involves understanding populations through their objective, quantifiable characteristics. These can be used comparatively to create a picture of both difference and change. We can demonstrate this by looking at the differences between developed and developing societies.

Developed societies: The population structure of developed nations has a range of important features. These features can be seen in an age–sex pyramid, a type of population pyramid that reflects, for example, a steady population growth. The US Population Reference Bureau (2006) links this to development; 'Pyramids where the proportions of the population are fairly evenly distributed among all age groups are representative of many highly industrialized societies'. This general shape is indicative of:

- falling long-term birth rates
- smaller average family size
- falling fertility rates
- low child and infant mortality rates
- falling death rates
- increasing average life expectancy (as shown by the number of people aged over 80).

Developing societies: The demographic features of developing nations show important comparative differences. Population structure, as reflected in India's age–sex pyramid, is significantly different in both its overall shape (a classic pyramid) and its characteristics. This population shape is indicative of:

- a younger population, with generally higher birth rates than in developed nations
- lower average life expectancy, due to a combination of disease, lower living standards, and poorer working conditions
- higher numbers of women dying during childbirth
- higher fertility rates
- higher average family size
- higher child and infant mortality rates – a classic 'adaptation to poverty strategy', where higher birth rates compensate for anticipated higher child and infant mortality rates.

TEST YOURSELF

Summarise the demographic difference between developed and developing nations.

Demographic changes

The evidence of demographic difference suggests that other processes are at work. In order to understand how and why these changes occur, we need to understand demographic changes at the structural level. This can be illustrated by looking at a historic age–sex pyramid for a developed nation such as the UK. This shows a similar

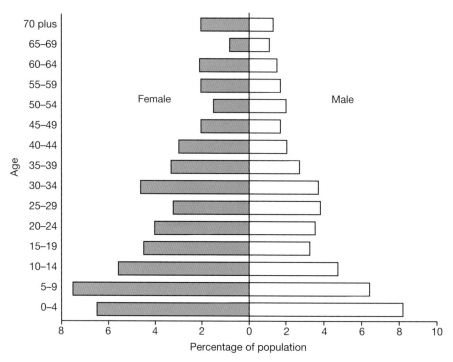

Age–sex pyramid from Stoke-upon-Trent, England 1701

Source: Gatley (2001)

profile in terms of fertility, life expectancy, family size and infant mortality to present-day population demographics in developing nations.

The consequences of demographic differences (life expectancy, poverty, etc.) are important, and we can understand some of their causes by looking at demographic changes in areas such as migration, employment, health and education.

Migration: Migration refers to the movement of people from one area to another. This occurs two main ways:

- Internal migration involves movement within a specified border, usually a nation but in some cases, such as the European Community, a region or continent.
- External migration (*immigration/emigration*) involves movement across political borders, from one country or region to another.

Migration is a key dimension of demographic change, both in its own right and in terms of its wider consequences for things such as employment, education and health. However, there are other aspects to migration that make it difficult to break down into 'types'. Despite this, a broad typology (Table 7.11) can be constructed around a range of economic, political and cultural types and sub-types:

- Permanent: migrants settle in their new location.
- Semi-permanent: migrants settle for short periods in their new location and then return to their country of origin.

- Temporary: migrants move to a new location for very short periods, usually days or weeks, before returning to their country of origin.

This typology, although limited, helps us to understand and explain some of the key drivers of migration: industrialisation, urbanisation and globalisation.

Industrialisation: This is a significant driver of migration in the sense that greater populations can be supported by the same amount of land. Britain, for example, had a population of around 4 million in 1601. By 1901, the population had risen to around 30 million and has since doubled to around 60 million. Also, new forms of factory-based production processes require large amounts of productive labour that migrates from the countryside to towns and cities. Initially, therefore, industrialisation creates large internal population migrations from rural to urban areas.

Urbanisation: The general process of social migration from rural to urban areas established by the industrialisation process is the result of two types of structural pressure. These can be applied to both the transition between pre-industrial and industrial society and more general migrations in the late industrial and early post-industrial periods:

1 Push factors are pressures that force people away from rural living and into towns, or force them to make cross-border migrations. Examples of push pressure include:

   - industrialisation
   - war

Type	Sub-type	Example
Economic	Permanent	Workers relocating to new country
	Semi-permanent	Migrant workers moving to a different country for a relatively short period in search of work (*seasonal migration*)
	Temporary	A series of short, but regular, migrations between an individual's point of origin and their ultimate destination (*step migration*)
Political	Permanent	Refugees – people forced out of their home country by war, persecution or natural disasters
	Semi-permanent	Internally displaced people (IDPs) may be forced away from their home through war but then return at the earliest opportunity
	Temporary	Natural disasters, such as Hurricane Katrina in New Orleans, USA in 2005, force people to move temporarily until it is safe to return
Cultural	Permanent	Retirement to another country; many elderly British people, for example, retire to countries such as Spain or France, where the climate is warmer and the cost of living lower
	Semi-permanent	In 2010, around 400,000 students arrived in the UK to study at university (around 15% of them from India) for between three and five years
	Temporary	Tourism – both internal and external

Table 7.11   Typology of migration

- natural disasters
- population pressures
- lack of physical resources
- unemployment.

2   Pull factors are the things that attract people to towns, cities and countries. These include the following:

- Economic factors such as the availability of work and the promise of higher incomes and an improved standard of living. The World Bank (2005), for example, suggests that people move 'from rural areas in search of jobs and opportunities to improve their lives and create a better future for their children'.
- Cultural factors such as freedom from ethnic/religious persecution.

Urbanisation is an important driver of migration:

- in 1800, 2% of the population lived in towns and cities
- in 1950, 30% lived in urban areas
- by 2050, 70% of the world's population are projected to be urban-dwellers.

Fragmentation

While around 80% of the populations of the UK and Argentina live in urban areas, around 40% of Argentina's population live in a single city (Buenos Aires). Fragmentary urbanisation is also expressed in terms of megacities with over 5 million inhabitants in developing

nations. According to the US Population Reference Bureau (2005): 'By 2015, 59 megacities will exist, 48 in less developed countries' and, of these, '23 cities are projected to hold over 10 million people; all but four will be in less developed countries'. Migration and development are, in this respect, part of a continuous cycle.

Fragmented industrialisation, where development is concentrated in a few areas, attracts migrants from rural areas, which leads to further industrial concentration. One consequence of this migration to the (mega)city is unemployment and low-wage work. Huge urban populations chase a limited number and range of jobs in the manufacturing and service industries. As Khosla et al. (2002) note, in developing nations 'there is little evidence of growing investments in industrial infrastructure that could absorb the influx of urban population. Unlike at the time of the Industrial Revolution when the enormous rise in factory production and investment offered jobs to the urban migrants, today's developing world migrants often have few employment opportunities'. One consequence, according to the US Population Reference Bureau (2005), is that migrants 'often end up not finding the opportunities they are looking for, but become part of the urban poor'.

TEST YOURSELF

Identify and explain two migration 'push factors'.

Globalisation

Contemporary migration trends are increasingly driven by globalising processes. The free movement of capital around the globe, for example, the relocation of many manufacturing industries to developing countries, increasingly requires fewer restrictions on the movement of labour. The UN Department of Economic and Social Affairs (2012), for example, notes a range of these contemporary migration trends. The majority are driven by economic rather than political factors – refugees, for example, make up around 7% of global migration:

- South–South migration is almost as common as South–North migration; each has around 75 million migrants per year.
- North–South migration, although increasing, is much less common: around 13 million people move from developed to developing nations.
- South–North migration has been the main driver of global migration, with this type of movement now outnumbering South–South migration.
- Contemporary patterns are marked by the interchange of global migrations; while 20 million migrated from Asia to Europe in 2010, 8 million made the reverse journey.

Further evidence for the economic basis of global migration comes in the form of 'bilateral migration', or movement between nearby countries. For example, Germany currently hosts the 'largest bilateral migrant stock from the South residing in Europe'.

Tourism

Mass tourism is a different, but increasingly significant, form of temporary cultural migration. Where overseas travel and the concept of 'a holiday' were once only available to the wealthy, the advent of cheap air travel, growing affluence and a greater knowledge of the world has opened up tourism all over the world.

In terms of development, tourism is significant because it is a consumption process in both *non-material* terms (the consumption of leisure) and *material* terms (the things people buy). In addition, tourism reinforces and changes the identity of the places people visit. For example, the development of the 'seaside holiday' dramatically changed the nature of UK coastal resorts. In Spain, cheap package holidays to places such as Majorca led to their reinvention as 'British spaces' – places where the tourist could speak English, consume familiar food and drink, and mix with people of their own nationality and class. More recently, as

Diken and Laustsen (2004) note, places such as Ibiza have been 'transformed from a "paradise island" of alternative holidays in the 1960s, first into a bastion of package tourism and then into a clubbers' Mecca of unchallenged hedonism'.

Sheller and Urry (2004) analyse the relationship between tourism, consumption and change in terms of the re-creation and reinvention of places as:

- paradises that rapidly lose this characteristic through mass tourism
- global heritage sites, where places are redesignated as 'respectful playgrounds'
- remade playful places, whereby global cities such as London, Hong Kong and Barcelona have 'refashioned their built environments to perform as 'attractions' on a highly competitive global stage of 'world-class' destinations'
- new playful places involving the exploration of 'unexpected sites', such as the slums and tenements of inner-city urban landscapes across the world; these are 'places of danger and enthralment, monotony, and awesomeness; the new places of play for a kind of 'postmodern middle class' both fascinated and repelled by their indescribable, indistinct, yet atmospheric post-apocalyptic urbanism'.

One of the ironies of tourism in late/postmodernity is suggested by Urry (2001). He argues that Western tourism increasingly involves the search for authentic experiences involving the discovery of 'new' and 'unspoilt' places. Through their 'discovery' and exploitation they become inauthentic destinations – changed by mass tourism and then discarded as tourists move on to the next 'authentic location'.

In what ways does tourism have a transformative effect on popular destinations?

Employment patterns

In terms of general employment patterns and trends, we can briefly examine some major areas of difference between developing and developed nations. The most clear example of this is between different types of employment.

While global employment patterns in the 21st century are becoming increasingly complex under the influence of economic globalisation, for most of the 20th century, one of the major areas of difference was between:

- industrialised, developed nations, characterised by a rapid decline in levels of agricultural employment, a gradual levelling-off/slow decline in manufacturing and a steep rise in service-sector employment, and
- non-industrialised, developing nations, where the main source of employment was agriculture and, in the case of the least developed nations, subsistence farming where production is for family consumption.

In the later part of the 20th century, changing economic conditions in the developed world caused a significant demographic change – a move away from manufacturing and towards service employment. The development and spread of information technologies, from personal computers through the internet to mobile technologies, has led to a further demographic development, the rise of large-scale knowledge-based industries and employment. These changes have resulted in two significant developments:

1 Changing employment patterns in developed nations have seen an increasing number of women entering the full-time workforce.

2 Manufacturing, once the staple form of employment for developed nations, has increasingly moved to middle-income developing nations. Polaski (2004) believes that the impact of globalised economic processes on employment patterns and trends has occurred in two major areas:

- Global labour-market supply – there is 'currently a global surplus of workers', with China, for example, having around 200 million unemployed or underemployed workers. To put this into perspective, the UK currently has a total employed workforce of around 30 million.
- Integrated labour markets – markets are seen in global (*integrated*) rather than national (*segmented*) terms. Where there was once only competition *within* nations for work, now there is competition *between* nations for labour.

The globalisation of labour markets has had three main consequences for international employment patterns:

1 The expansion of employment emigration, which involves workers in *different nations* competing for a limited number of jobs. This process, sometimes called 'off-shoring', is when work that was once done in a developed nation, such as call-centre monitoring or financial services, is moved to a developing nation, such as India, where:

- employment regulations are weaker
- employment benefits and wages are lower
- governments offer a range of financial and political incentives for the relocation of jobs.

Off-shoring tends to take place between highly developed and lesser developed nations – countries such as India, with the economic, political and cultural infrastructure to compete for and win service and knowledge-based work.

2 Labour mobility occurs in two ways:

- Labour movements between developed nations. This is taking place increasingly within the European Community, where there is a relatively free movement of labour between the 27 member nations. Polish workers, for example, are free to find employment in countries such as England or Germany, and vice versa.
- The recruitment of labour from developing countries to fill gaps in some economic sectors of developed nations. This has traditionally involved work at the lower end of the economic spectrum, such as migrants doing work that the indigenous people do not want to do. Increasingly, however, it involves work in the middle and upper employment ranges, such as doctors from developing countries working in the National Health Service in the UK.

3 Unemployment in lesser developed countries, resulting from the economic practices of developed nations. Polaski notes that farmers in developing countries find it impossible to compete in world markets because of 'agricultural subsidies to high-income farmers in the United States and Europe'. In addition, although the International Labour Office (2003) argues that 'employment is the way out of absolute poverty' in developing nations, this is not necessarily the case. A more important factor may be where or not work provides a living wage that enables individuals and families to exist above the poverty line. The International Labour Organization (2005) states that 'in 1997 around

25% of the employed labour force in developing countries were working poor'. By 2005, half the world's workers 'did not earn enough to lift themselves and their families above the $2 a day poverty line – just as many as ten years ago. Among these working poor, 520 million lived with their families on less than $1 a day'.

Globalisation is a significant cause of higher labour mobility between nations, but Ghose (2000) argues that mobility is actually restricted by a range of political, economic and cultural factors. In the USA, proximity to relatively impoverished Mexico has proven to be a powerful 'push factor', as economic migrants from Mexico seek (illegal) employment in the USA. However, beyond this example, 'the share of migrant workers in the international labour force showed generally insignificant growth and actually declined in several countries. More importantly, annual immigration flows were declining'.

While labour mobility may have economic advantages for migrants who gain employment and wages that were unavailable in developing nations, it can have serious consequences for indigenous labour forces. Competition for employment lowers the of them finding and keeping work, as well as causing a drop in wage levels.

Human capital

Ghose suggests that the fact that developed nations can 'pick and choose' the labour they require from developing nations has a more significant impact on those nations. It results in a 'brain drain', whereby 'the average skill level of the migrants from developing to industrialised countries tends to be much higher than that of the population of their home countries'. This alters the balance of human capital in favour of developed nations. Barro and Lee (1994), for example, consider human capital an 'integral aspect of economic growth'. Losing this capital seriously hinders the economic prospects of developing nations.

TEST YOURSELF

Identify and explain one difference in employment patterns between developed and developing nations.

Health

Robbins (2005) observation that 'each historical period has its characteristic illnesses' that 'reveals how we live largely defines the kinds and frequencies of diseases to which human beings are susceptible' suggests that health is an important dimension of both development and demographic change. Some forms of illness, such as lung diseases, can be related to industrial processes. Others such as obesity leading to heart disease, can be related to post-industrial consumption patterns.

Developing countries are particularly susceptible to the demographic impact of poverty. Braveman and Gruskin (2003), for example, note that globally there are 'strong and pervasive links between poverty and health. For centuries, powerful associations have been noted between health and an absolute lack of economic resources'. The US Population Reference Bureau (2005) argues that in both the developing world and, to a lesser degree, the developed world, 'poverty is both a cause and an outcome of disease'. There is, therefore, a reflexive relationship between the two. Poverty creates disease and disease, in turn, creates poverty through factors such as an inability to work or the death of a family provider. From this perspective, ill health is not randomly distributed across and within populations. The chances of contracting typhoid, for example, increase under conditions of poverty and poor sanitation.

Part of the demographic problem in this relationship is the fact that individual levels of personal spending on health care are much lower in developing countries. The British Medical Association (2005) notes: 'Roughly 1.2 billion people survive on less than 60p a day and have access to little or no healthcare. Poverty also causes an increased susceptibility to disease through malnutrition and lack of access to lifesaving treatment'.

Levels of government health spending (Table 7.12) are also a significant factor. Developed nations spend significantly more, whether viewed as total health expenditure or as a percentage of GDP.

Rank	Country	Total per capita health expenditure (PPP)	Total health expenditure as % of GDP
1	USA	7,960	17.6
10	Germany	4,219	11.7
17	UK	3,438	9.8
69	Brazil	921	8.8
79	Mauritius	714	5.6
111	China	347	5.1
148	India	124	4.2

Table 7.12   Global health expenditure

Source: World Health Organization (2012)

While higher levels of public and private expenditure in developed countries do not guarantee good health, they do promote:

- greater access to care and medical provision
- highly trained medical staff
- greater knowledge of disease transmission
- higher levels of sanitation and clean water
- higher levels of nutrition and balanced diets.

Education

Education – and literacy in particular – is an important demographic factor in terms of overall social development and individual development within societies. Education makes significant demographic contributions to gender relationships, health and employment, for example. Patrinos and Psacharapoulos (2002) argue that education represents an 'important economic asset' for both individuals and nations. Archer (2006) identifies two practical contributions that education makes to both development and demographic change:

1 Participation in decision-making processes, in both the private and public spheres, increases. This is particularly important for gendered involvement – female participation in community life, for example, increases by level of education.

2 Educational participation is strongly connected to a decline in infant mortality and improved child health. Cameron and Cameron (2006) argue that child and adult literacy produces significant micro (individual) and macro (structural) economic benefits: those 'who had completed literacy courses were more willing to take initiatives in developing their livelihoods'. Smith and Haddad (2001) argue that education is linked to the 'empowerment of families to break the cycle of poverty' because female earnings are '10–20% higher for every year of schooling completed'.

In addition, child and adult educational programmes help reduce the spread of HIV/AIDS. The Global Campaign for Education (2004), for example, claims that HIV/AIDS 'is spreading fastest among young women (aged 15–24) because they have little access to knowledge, economic resources and decision-making power'. Furthermore, Smith and Haddad note that 'young women with a primary education are twice as likely to stay safe from AIDS'.

ACTIVITY

1 *Use the typology of migration table to research examples of different types of migration in your society.*

2 *Divide into three groups and use the migration examples you've researched to show how they are related to:*
   - *industrialisation*
   - *urbanisation*
   - *globalisation.*

The causes and consequences of poverty

Before we examine cultural and structural causes and consequences of **poverty**, it is necessary to define the concept. We can do this by divding it into two main categories: absolute and relative.

 KEY TERM

Poverty: state of being poor, as measured in absolute or relative terms.

Absolute poverty

This definition is based on identifying the minimum conditions needed to maintain human life. Seebohm and Joseph Rowntree (1901) were among the first to identify a minimum subsistence level below which people were to be considered 'poor'. They also distinguished between:

- Primary poverty – individuals or families lacking the means to provide the basic necessities of life, such as food, clothing and shelter.
- Secondary poverty – although people have sufficient means to sustain life, they fail to do so because they spend at least part of their income on things that are not essential.

Gordon et al. (2003) update this idea, defining poverty in terms of **basic needs**:

- clean water
- sanitation
- shelter
- education
- information
- food
- health.

KEY TERMS

Basic needs: minimum requirements to sustain human life, such as clean water, food and shelter.

On this measure, they argue: 'If the household or individual does not have access to a particular basic need, they are defined as "deprived". Those who are deprived of two or more of the seven basic need indicators are defined as being in **absolute poverty**'. They conclude that around 35% of children in the Middle East and North Africa lived in absolute poverty.

KEY TERMS

Absolute poverty: a measure based on the idea of the minimum necessities needed to sustain life, such as food.

Strengths: Measuring poverty in absolute terms has certain advantages:

- Definitions of poverty can be standardised because people have similar biological needs wherever they live.
- Falkingham (2000) argues that once minimum human needs are objectively standardised, their definition and measurement does not change. The same definition of poverty is used wherever and whenever it is measured.
- Absolute definitions can be applied consistently across all societies to compare levels of poverty on a global scale, regardless of different levels of social and technological development.

The UN Human Poverty Index (HPI) measures absolute poverty across three dimensions:

- healthy life expectancy
- access to education
- living standards.

Using a range of indicators for these criteria, countries can be ranked in terms of their comparative rates of poverty. In 2013, for example, Sweden had the lowest rate of any country:

- 1st   Sweden
- 26th   UK
- 101st   China
- 136th   India.

Absolute measures allow historical changes to poverty levels to be tracked. Sweden has consistently maintained the lowest level of global poverty over the past 25 years.

Limitations: Absolute definitions are less useful for measuring levels of poverty within particular societies. For example, historical and cross-cultural differences in living standards make it difficult to apply a standard 'minimum needs' test in any meaningful way. An individual's experience of poverty in India is very different from the experience of poverty in the UK. Compared to India, therefore, 'minimum subsistence level' tests in the modern UK find very little poverty. This suggests that concepts of poverty – what it means to 'be poor' in different societies – reflect a society's beliefs about what is an acceptable standard of living. As living standards rise, people's expectations change and concepts of poverty also change.

In this respect, Falkingham questions the concept of 'needs'. Can they be defined biologically, having just enough to eat for example, or do we need to consider needs in relation to the quality of life in different societies?

Relative poverty

Because of these limitations, some people argue that poverty must be defined and measured by the standards of specific societies. Townsend and Abel-Smith (1965), for example, argue that poverty in relatively wealthy, developed societies is not simply a matter of minimum needs. There is a cultural dimension to poverty in such societies, and a person should be considered poor if they lack the resources to participate fully in the social and cultural life of their society. Therefore, poverty is not a cultural absolute but a cultural variable. Mack and Lansley (1984) claim that it must be measured in the context of 'an enforced lack of socially perceived necessities'. That is, what one society regards as unnecessary may, in another society or at another time, be seen as a necessity.

From this perspective, societies all have different living standards and therefore different perceptions of poverty at different stages of historic and cross cultural development. It also suggests that demographic differences within the *same* society result in differences between social groups. A normal and acceptable living standard for a teenager may not be viewed in the same way by an elderly person.

Strengths: Relative definitions reflect historical and cross-cultural perceptions and experiences. Poverty in the UK, for example, does not mean the same as poverty in India. Because these definitions attempt to measure a variety of dimensions of life and lifestyle, they are more likely to accurately represent people's behaviour, attitudes and expectations. In this respect, poverty is not simply about being economically poor; any measure must accurately reflect the quality of an individual's life. For example, a high life expectancy is relatively meaningless if that life is lived in abject poverty.

Relative definitions can evolve and change in line with wider social-developmental changes. As we have seen, in the developed world, absolute measures of poverty are likely to be historically unreliable because living standards and lifestyles have changed significantly over the past century.

Limitations: The flexibility of relative definitions can be a methodological limitation. Maxwell (1999), for example, notes how the meaning of 'poverty' has evolved to include a range of ideas:

- deprivation – a general measure of poverty
- relative deprivation – a measure that takes account of the relationship between social groups; a millionaire in a society of billionaires would be 'relatively deprived'
- participation in social activities
- social inclusion and exclusion from areas of society, such as work and education.

While all these concepts measure something, it is not clear whether they actually measure 'poverty'. This diversity of meaning also makes it difficult to standardise poverty measures across societies. In addition, absolute measures can be objectively defined and quantitatively measured. However, some relative measures, such as whether people 'feel poor', are subjective, qualitative and difficult to measure reliably.

A major criticism of relative definitions, therefore, is that they measure social inequality rather than poverty. In an affluent developed society, people can enjoy a relatively comfortable standard of living compared to those in underdeveloped nations, but they may still be classed as 'relatively poor'. Poverty, in this respect, becomes a function of definition rather than fact. Using a relative measure poverty can never be eliminated.

> **TEST YOURSELF**
>
> Briefly explain the difference between absolute and relative definitions of poverty.

Causes of poverty

We can outline causal explanations for poverty in terms of two broad categories: cultural and structural.

Cultural explanations

Cultural or individualistic explanations focus on the qualities possessed by individuals and the groups to which they belong. In this respect, poverty is caused by an individual's cultural background as well as the life choices they make.

Underclass theory: This general theory is probably the most individualistic of all explanations of poverty. It suggests that the very poor constitute a 'class apart' – they exist 'outside' mainstream society. However, while many in poverty are socially excluded in terms of income and opportunities, this theory suggests that the poverty of this underclass is explained by their life choices. O'Brien and Briar (1997) argue that this approach makes an important ideological distinction between two groups:

- The deserving poor who, through little fault of their own, find themselves in poverty and who try to lift themselves out of this situation.
- The undeserving poor who are happy to exist on the margins of society, living off state or charitable handouts, begging and indulging in petty crime – these people choose this lifestyle and make no effort to involve themselves in mainstream society.

Jencks (1989) notes that underclass theories see poverty in terms of three types of 'individual failure':

- moral – through routine engagement in deviant/criminal behaviour
- economic – because they are unwilling to work
- educational – they lack cultural and educational skills and qualifications.

The failure to pursue educational qualifications leads to economic marginalisation and the development of a morality based around criminality or a dependence on welfare systems to support deviant lifestyles.

Culture of dependency: This related theory argues that state welfare systems both support and trap the poor in a culture of **welfare dependency**. This occurs for three main reasons:

1 Welfare payments are so high that they provide the underclass with a comfortable existence for little or no effort.

2 Where welfare payments do not provide a comfortable lifestyle, they offer a baseline income that gives people the freedom to work in the hidden economy, where they pay no tax on earnings, or to engage in various forms of economic crime.

3 Where the underclass lack the educational skills and qualifications to find highly paid work, their

229

options are limited to low-skill, poorly paid work. Generous welfare payments means it is not in their economic interests to work; welfare is, in this respect, a major disincentive.

KEY TERM

Welfare dependency: new-right theory that argues that generous welfare payments create a disincentive among those who receive them to find work or live their lives independently of government support.

Dependency cultures can also be created or enforced by government behaviour. In any means-tested welfare system where people receive different levels of benefits based on their income and savings, the problem of a **poverty trap** frequently arises. This creates a massive disincentive to work, because the income difference between working and not working is relatively small. In some cases, the individual may have a lower income by working and losing state support.

KEY TERM

Poverty trap: situation in which the costs of working outweigh any economic benefits to the individual. If someone's income rises as they find work and their welfare benefits are consequently reduced, this can result in the individual having a lower overall income.

Culture of poverty: Lewis's (1959, 1961) studies in Mexico and Puerto Rico examined how the poor adapted to and coped with poverty. He argued that poverty was not caused by random events, such as illness or disease, or natural forces striking different people at different times. Instead, the persistence of poverty across generations proved that it should be seen as a socialisation process. Adults who experience poverty as a set of objective conditions or consequences, such as long-term unemployment, low rates of pay or illness/disability, learn to cope with living in poverty and pass this knowledge on to their children. The persistence of poverty, therefore, is explained by one generation socialising the next into the knowledge and skills required to live in poverty. A **culture of poverty** develops because it is functional in terms of:

- informal economies involving moneylenders as a way of budgeting limited resources, or informal borrowing and lending arrangements with friends and neighbours

- informal living arrangements involving a lack of commitment to institutions such as marriage, which means trying to provide for others as well as oneself.

KEY TERM

Culture of poverty: situation that explains poverty in terms of the idea that the poor adapt to their poverty and teach the skills required to survive to succeeding generations.

Lewis argues that a culture of poverty is ultimately self-defeating. By 'adapting and coping', the poor do not address the problems that create poverty, such as unemployment and low wages. However, the poor often have no choice but to adopt this strategy if they are to survive.

Cycle of deprivation: A related explanation claims that the persistence of poverty through successive generations is due to a range of social and economic factors that combine to limit the life choices exercised by the poor. Some versions of this theory suggest that 'poor life choices', such as unmarried teenage pregnancy, are significant factors in the cycle. Deprivation is usually considered in terms of material factors, such as a low family income, having cumulative effects:

- parents living on a low income (material deprivation) means…
- children have a poor diet, which causes…
- health problems and missed schooling that leads to…
- educational failure (cultural or **social deprivation**) and…
- low-paid, low-skill work that leads to…
- parents living on a low income.

KEY TERM

Social deprivation: situation in which some members of a society are prevented, through things such as poverty, illness or disability, from full participation in the society in which they live.

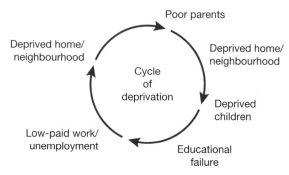

The cycle of deprivation

One of the main problems with all these theories is that they see 'the poor' in terms of a stable group. People not only live in poverty over the course of their lifetime, but their behaviour and life choices perpetuate poverty in generational terms: poor parents produce poor children. While poverty may be difficult to escape in developing nations, this is not supported by the evidence of developed nations. The reality of poverty is one of 'churn': people move into and out of poverty at different stages in their life cycle. As Jarvis and Jenkins (1997) note: 'Although only a minority of the population have a low income in any given year, many more people experience low income at least once over a four-year period'.

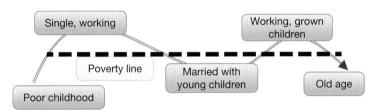

The poverty line

The 'victim-blaming' approach to poverty that these cultural theories take has also been criticised. This approach can be summed up as follows:

- The causes of poverty are located in individual failings that involve the poor actively contributing to the fact of their poverty through moral and cultural failings.
- Governments and the affluent are absolved from either blame or responsibility.
- The problem of poverty cannot be solved by government action or changes to the behaviour of the rich and powerful; it is the poor themselves who must change.
- Problems of national poverty and underdevelopment are not caused by the behaviour of developed nations and TNCs. Browne (2006), for example, argues: 'Poor Africans are condemned to live in poverty so long as they and their governments are encouraged to blame the West for all their problems, rather than confronting the real causes of poor governance, corruption and poor education'.

TEST YOURSELF

Identify and explain two features of cultural explanations of poverty.

Structural explanations

Structural explanations suggest that the causes of poverty can be found in the economic and political structures of contemporary societies. In order to solve the problem of poverty, therefore, we must change the social structures that *create* poverty. This approach examines how individual behavioural choices are limited or extended by structural factors, such as the demands of the capitalist economic system and the interests of the ruling elite.

Labour-market theory: This focuses on how structural changes in the labour market, largely related to globalisation, have affected levels of employment and wages in developed countries and, as a direct consequence, developing and underdeveloped countries. For example, developed countries have experienced two major labour-market changes: a sharp decline in manufacturing industries and a rise in service industries. This has resulted in two long-term processes that create poverty:

1 The loss of secure, well-paid, manufacturing work that has impacted disproportionately on working-class wages and employment. Resulting factors such as long-term unemployment push people into poverty.
2 The creation of insecure, poorly paid service work, such as in call centres, or marginal forms of irregular self-employment, such as window-cleaning, performed by those who would once have had secure well-paid work.

Underdeveloped societies may benefit from the relocation of manufacturing industries from developed nations, but any advantages are usually accompanied by low wages and poor working conditions. TNCs only gain from relocation to developing nations if labour costs are lower. Gribben (2003) notes that the decision of the British-based manufacturer Dyson to switch production to Malaysia, with the loss of 900 UK jobs, only made economic sense because production costs 'are 30% lower'.

The argument here is that labour-market changes affect developed and underdeveloped nations in different ways. However, the end result is increasing profits for TNCs and declining wage or employment levels that lead to poverty across all countries.

Capitalism: This explanation, related to labour-market changes and the impact of economic globalisation, argues that poverty is an inevitable outcome of capitalism. Where competition for economic resources is the norm, differences will always exist, because capitalist societies

231

are characterised by unequal distribution of wealth and income. Marxists, therefore, see poverty as an inevitable condition of capitalism.

Income differences are not only an integral part of capitalist economics, but the poor and unemployed also function as a reserve army of labour. They are called into and excluded from the labour force as necessary, and they function to drive down wage levels and enhance profitability. This partly explains why poverty may vary over the course of a person's life, as they are drawn into and then discarded from the paid workforce.

The causes of poverty, therefore, relate to economic organisation and the relationships that create and sustain both wealth and inequality. People fall into or fail to escape from poverty *not* because of their individual and social deficiencies but because society is structured to keep them in poverty. Capitalism needs poor people, but they do not have to be the same poor people over extended periods of time.

Risk mapping: This approach relates structural and cultural factors to each other and then to poverty. Structural factors such as unemployment and low wages force individuals to culturally adapt to their social situation:

- some choose crime and the hidden economy
- some retreat into drug or alcohol addiction
- some struggle to survive by adapting to the demands of the labour market, such as working at more than one job.

By identifying the structural factors that lead to poverty, we can identify different social groups at greater or lesser risk of poverty. Risk mapping, therefore, moves away from explaining poverty in terms of the characteristics of 'the poor' and onto the idea that poverty itself is a structural relationship. Although the identity of those living in poverty may change, but the condition of poverty itself remains.

Memberships theory: This approach refines the general concept of risk by relating it specifically to structural factors. Durlauf (2002), for example, explains how poverty is related to membership of two types of group and how this limits and enhances behavioural choices:

1 *Exogenous* groups include gender and ethnic memberships with certain ascribed characteristics. In societies that practise various forms of sexual, religious or racial discrimination, for example, the chances of entering or escaping poverty may be related to factors

beyond an individual's control. Examples include practices such as the British class system, the Hindu caste system and apartheid in South Africa (1945–94) under white rule.

2 *Endogenous* groups relate to the individual's specific social and economic circumstances and their impact on life chances. Durlauf suggests that these may include things such as:

- family
- where people live
- the type of school, if any, they attend.

Memberships theory, therefore, explains poverty in terms of the interplay between these structural factors in terms of hierarchies of influence and risk.

Economic factors, such as wage levels, broadly determine the extent of poverty in any given society. In the UK, general living standards are much higher than in some parts of Africa and South America. While the UK may experience **relative poverty**, countries in Africa and South America are more likely to experience absolute poverty. Economic factors influence the behavioural choices of people who are not classed as poor and this in turn, limits the behavioural choices of the poor. This effectively traps them in poverty through their own group memberships and apparent behavioural choices.

 KEY TERM

Relative poverty: measure of poverty that argues that poverty has to be defined and measured relative to the accepted living standards of particular societies. It includes the idea that someone should be considered poor if they lack the resources to participate fully in the social and cultural life of their society.

Schools in poor neighbourhoods, for example, may have lower status and funding, which perpetuates lower educational achievement and lessens the individual's chances of finding secure, well-paid, work. Thus, structural factors determine the development of membership groups that, in turn, perpetuate the risk of poverty.

TEST YOURSELF

Suggest two differences between cultural and structural causes of poverty.

Bridging the gap: inter-generational transmission (IGT)

Moore (2001) notes that individualistic approaches 'suggest people become and remain poor due to their beliefs and behaviours'. Although poverty clearly has a cultural dimension, this must be located within the overall structure of society. To explain poverty, it is necessary to understand both:

- 'cultures of coping among the poor'
- 'cultures of wealth among the rich and middle class'.

The first helps us understand how people adapt to poverty; the second helps us understand how the behaviour of the wealthy contributes to the creation of poverty.

Inter-generational transmission (IGT) represents a bridge between cultural and structural explanations. It suggests that the persistence of poverty is the result of a complex interplay between a range of cultural *and* structural factors that can only be explained in terms of inter-generational transmissions. Moore defines this as the transfer or absence of transfer of different forms of capital between generations (Table 7.13).

Type of capital	Examples
Human	Investment of time and capital in education/training
	Knowledge/skills useful as part of coping and survival strategies
Economic	Money, assets and debt
	Inheritance, bequests
Environmental	Pollution and ill health
	Lack of affordable transport
Cultural	Parental experience and investment in child's education
	Traditions and value systems
Political	Ethnicity/gender/class
	Family background

Table 7.13   Inter-generational transmission of capital
Source: Moore (2001)

Consequences

The consequences of poverty are many and varied across different developed and developing nations. However, some general themes emerge, involving the idea that the poor and non-poor have different life chances. These refer to an individual's 'long-term prospects' – their chances of gaining the things a society considers desirable, such as a high standard of living, and avoiding those things considered undesirable, such as poverty. Mills (1959) suggests that life chances include things like the chance to:

- stay alive during the first year after birth
- view fine art
- remain healthy
- get well again quickly after sickness
- avoid becoming a juvenile delinquent
- complete an intermediate or higher educational grade.

In this respect, some general consequences of poverty relate to areas like the poor having lower life chances in terms of:

- employment: getting and keeping secure, well-paid, long-term, work
- consumption, involving a range of essential and non-essential goods, from food and shelter to ownership of transport
- health: living a long, healthy and active life
- crime: being the perpetrator or victim
- education: gaining the knowledge and skills that help people to break away from poverty.

Segregation: Further consequences of poverty relate to sequences of segregation:

- economic segregation based on poverty leads to …
- social segregation, where poor and non-poor do not meet culturally, and …
- physical segregation: the poor and non-poor not only experience different lifestyles, they also live and work in different worlds that rarely, if ever, meet.

In the USA for example, private gated communities create a physical barrier to interaction between rich and poor on anything but a service basis. They only meet as master and servant.

Gender

A further aspect of poverty relates to gender and the idea that poverty is increasingly linked to both female lives, as heads of households, and experiences of low-paid, part-time work. As Ruspini (2000) argues, men and women, even of the same social class or ethnic grouping, experience poverty in different ways. The consequences of being female and poor are:

- greater poverty than men
- worse poverty than men
- an increasing trend to greater poverty.

233

Children

Poverty also has consequences for children:

- Howard and Garnham (2001) argue that poverty is likely to last longer for children. Those born into poverty find it difficult to escape; they carry poverty with them into adult life.
- Lewis (1959) also suggests that children are 'robbed of their childhood' by poverty. He notes how, at an early age, children are expected to 'earn their keep' and contribute, if they could, to a family income.
- Hecht's (1998) study of Brazilian street children also suggests that one consequence of poverty for children is that they cease to be nurtured by their family and instead become responsible at a very early age for nurturing that family by 'begging and selling bottles, cans and cardboard'.

ACTIVITY

Discussion

'Some people are rich and some are poor, just as some people are hard-working and others are lazy. This has always been and always will be the case; it's just the way people are and we shouldn't feel bad about or responsible for poverty'.

Split into two groups, one to suggest evidence that supports this view, one to suggest evidence that rejects this view.

Discuss the statement as a class.

Sociological theories of globalisation and its effects

This section explores the concept of globalisation and its effects across three interrelated dimensions: economic, political and cultural.

Globalisation

Globalisation refers to the speed with which connections can be made between:

- people: such as the ability to travel quickly anywhere in the world
- goods and their rapid movement around the globe
- services, made possible by the speed of computer technology
- information transferred instantaneously
- ideas that travel rapidly from society to society.

Globalisation describes a process that, through the speed of its occurrence, transforms the nature of other processes. In so doing, it becomes synonymous with changes that have global consequences. Scholte (2000) claims that these consequences include:

- the internationalisation of 'cross-border relations between countries'
- the liberalisation of political and economic relationships, such as 'removing government-imposed restrictions on movements between countries'
- the universalisation of cultural forms, such as television, that spread 'various objects and experiences to people of all corners of the earth'
- modernisation, involving the spread of the social structures of modernity, such as capitalism, scientific rationalism and industrialism, across the world.

Concpetualising globalisation as speed involves a number of social processes. Giddens (1990), for example, argues that a major feature is the separation of time and space (*distanciation*). Various forms of global communication, from telephones through television to the internet, take place instantaneously across *the globe*. It is as if people occupied the same physical space. For Virilio (2000) states that globalisation makes concepts of distance and physical space irrelevant in the contemporary world and Harvey (1990) argues that time and space are compressed. The speed at which things can be done shortens the time required to do them and effectively renders concepts of distance meaningless.

Disembedding

Distanciation and compression represent vital preconditions for disembedding – the idea that things are separated from their original surroundings and contexts. These include:

- objects, such as credit cards, disembedded from their original physical context of coinage
- processes, such as the electronic transfer of money into and out of a bank account
- people, in three ways:
  - global communication between strangers is both possible and takes place in indeterminate areas such as 'cyberspace', something that has no physical existence
  - physical disembedding, such as how people define themselves in terms of national/global identities
  - cultural disembedding in relation to the development of hybrid cultures that involve mixing elements of different cultures to produce something new and different.

Baudrillard's (1998) concept of simulacra – 'representations that refer to other representations' – captures the concept of disembedding. A credit card is a *simulation* of coinage which, in turn, is a simulation of something like a piece of gold. Where disembedding takes place, the 'origins of the original' are lost or concealed in time and space. The simulation has the same general status as whatever it is simulating – both are 'as real' as each other; a telephone call or an email are 'as real' as talking to someone in the flesh.

Can you think of any other kinds of simulacra?

Disembedding is a significant globalising process that has consequences for a range of economic, political and cultural relationships. This is especially true for what Scholte calls 'deterritorialisation' or 'supraterritoriality'. In this respect, 'globalization entails a reconfiguration of geography, so that social space is no longer wholly mapped in terms of territorial places, territorial distances and territorial borders'. Therefore, social interactions are no longer limited by notions of territory – places fixed in time and space. Political and cultural identities are no longer necessarily and intimately tied to physical spaces such as countries and capitalist forms of production. In addition, distribution and exchange operate on a global scale, crossing national and international borders.

Giddens suggests that disembedding and deterritorialisation cause individuals and nations to become increasingly connected in new and important ways. Events on one side of the world can have significant and unforeseen consequences on the other. We can develop these ideas by looking at a range of globalised economic, political and cultural interrelationships.

TEST YOURSELF

Identify three key features of globalisation.

Economic

One feature of globalisation is the impact it has had on economic interrelationships in terms of mobility – the increasingly global nature of stock markets and trading blocs based on:

- capital mobility, where companies and investments move into and out of different countries as profitability and economic policy dictate
- labour mobility, as people physically move around from place to place
- information mobility that helps the development of a range of global financial services.

The globalisation of economic relationships in the physical world is reflected in transnational corporations. These are corporations that, while based in a specific territory, such as the UK or the USA, operate in a range of countries. Although TNCs are a feature of modern society, first established in countries such as the USA in the 19th century, Smith and Doyle (2002) suggest that globalisation has increased their power, influence and status in world economic terms. Economic trading blocs, such as the European Union and the North and South American Trading Alliance, represent a further example of the economic links between societies. In these examples, nation states develop political agreements and alliances around preferential trading privileges for member nations, for example.

The development of the internet has complicated the nature of economic interrelationships, because economic activity increasingly takes place in virtual trading communities. These networks involve the production, distribution and exchange of:

- physical products
- financial products
- services
- knowledge.

One consequence of virtual networks is the breakdown of distinctions between the local, national, international and global. Disembedding, for example, is both encouraged and accelerated in areas such as economic exchange, initially through the development of credit cards and increasingly through electronic money transfers. It also occurs in production and distribution – goods and services created in one country (or, in some instances, many countries) are distributed and sold around the globe.

Sporer (2000) suggests that 'globalisation is the latest stage in the permanent process of social change

235

that started as industrialisation and modernisation in Europe but now is spreading globally'. The eventual outcome of this process will be an 'integrated world economy'. McMichael (2004) claims that involves the development of global commodity chains: networks of production, distribution and exchange that are linked across national boundaries. It means that individual producers and consumers are locked into a global chain of economic events.

This network is significant because it creates economic hierarchies. Highly developed countries are positioned at the top of the global commodity chain, exploiting the fact that clothes or electrical goods can be manufactured using relatively cheap labour in developing countries. Unequal economic relationships also create dependency networks that are difficult to break. Developing countries become a source of relatively cheap production, whereas developed countries come to depend on the flow of (cheap) goods to maintain living standards. The nature of global networks, complexities and dependencies is illustrated by the fact that 'the Japanese eat poultry fattened in Thailand with American corn, using chopsticks made with wood from Indonesian or Chilean forests. Canadians eat strawberries grown in Mexico with American fertiliser. The British and French eat green beans from Kenya and cocoa from Ghana finds its way into Swiss chocolate'.

Globalised capitalism

Castells (1997) argues that economic behaviour has entered a new phase with the development of a new form of globalised capitalism. Where older forms

of capitalism focused on the production of *things*, newer forms focus on knowledge, information and systems. Castells believes this has caused a reordering of economic production, with information now the *primary* product. This has come about because of computer networks that traverse the globe. As Smith and Doyle (2002) argue: 'Today's most technologically advanced economies are knowledge based'. This claim suggests globalisation is the driver for a new phase of capitalist economic production, distribution and exchange.

However, while there is a general agreement that *something* is changing in global economic interrelationships, there is disagreement about exactly what that is. For some, globalisation is partial or regional. Thompson (2000), for example, argues that the world is divided into three major regional economic blocs: North and Central America, Europe and Asia. While economic globalisation may be taking place *within* each regional bloc, there is no competition between them. Apart from a very small number of truly global trading companies, such as Nike, most TNCs and nations trade predominantly and substantially within each bloc.

A more radical argument suggests that economic globalisation is defined by 'the production and distribution of products and services of the same type and quality on a worldwide basis'. Rugman and Hodgetts (2000) suggest that this leads to globalisation being portrayed as encouraging the 'dominance of international business by giant, multinational enterprises (MNEs) selling uniform products from Cairo, Illinois to Cairo, Egypt and from

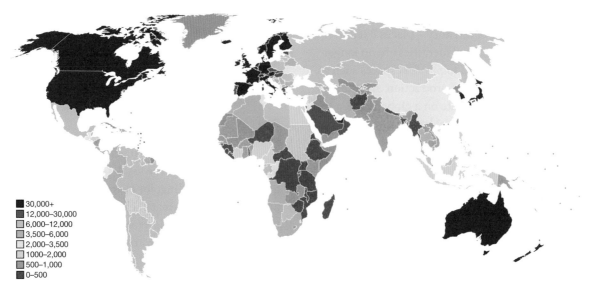

30,000+
12,000–30,000
6,000–12,000
3,500–6,000
2,000–3,500
1000–2,000
500–1,000
0–500

International GDP, 2007. Is the extent of economic globalisation overstated?

Source: IMF

Lima, Ohio to Lima, Peru'. Rugman (2001), however, argues that this type of economic globalisation 'does not, and has never, existed in terms of a single world market with free trade'.

Suggest one reason 'globalisation' does not exist on a global scale.

Political

Smith and Doyle claim that one of the main themes of 'full-on globalisation' is that nation states lose power and authority. There is 'a decline in the ability of national governments to direct and influence their economies'. This consequence of political globalisation stops national governments from controlling major areas of economic policy such as:

■ Employment – where nations experience rising or falling employment depending on how capital, labour and jobs move across national borders.
■ Taxation policies relating to businesses, especially transnational corporations. If taxation is too high, 'capital flight' occurs, with TNCs relocating to lower-tax nations. Alternatively, companies such as Amazon are registered in Luxembourg, a low-tax country, thereby avoiding paying higher taxes in countries such as the UK where they do substantial business. TNCs can also export profits, making it difficult for national governments to track what profit is being made and where.
■ Investment: there is increased competition and pressure on governments to provide environments and packages to attract corporate investment.

The idea that national economies are locked into a global financial system that limits the actions of governments represents a form of hyper-globalisation. It is essentially the idea that globalisation has created a worldwide political, economic and cultural web. Under hyper-globalisation, national governments are secondary players on the world stage, if they have a role at all. Ohmae (1995) argues that political globalisation marks the end of 'the modern nation-state itself'.

Veseth (1998) questions the claim that globalisation connects 'people and businesses without much attention to geography, government or regulation'. In a similar way, Gray (2002) is sceptical that globalisation involves 'the world becoming a true single market, in which

nation-states have withered away, supplanted by homeless multinational corporations'. He claims that new-right/neo-liberal theorists simply *want* this to be the case.

Although hyper-globalisation may be exaggerated, global economic developments undoubtedly have an impact on political interrelationships. Hirst and Thompson (1996), for example, suggest that nations are key to creating the stable political conditions under which trade and international development can continue. Shaw (1997) argues that nation states should not be seen as being 'in opposition' to globalisation, since 'globalisation does not undermine the state but involves the transformation of state forms'.

Suggest one reason for the possible disappearance of nation states.

Cultural

Cultural globalisation is frequently embodied in two apparently opposed tendencies: diversity (difference) and homogenisation (similarity). In terms of diversity, Lechner (2001) suggests that cultural interactions between societies can have different outcomes:

■ They can produce cultural hybrids based on the 'mixing of cultures in particular places and practices'. Some form of new and different cultural practice or behaviour develops from the meeting and mixing of different cultural traditions.
■ They may also produce contestations, whereby the 'spread of ideas and images provoke reactions and resistance' within and between different cultural groups. This is particularly relevant to religious cultural ideas that may express opposed notions of things such as gender and sexual equality.

Diversity may be diminished in two ways:

1 Coca-colonisation involves the idea that the global reach of TNCs such as Coca-Cola creates what Lechner calls a particular kind of 'consumerist culture in which standard commodities are promoted by global marketing campaigns to create similar lifestyles'. Coca-colonisation, therefore, refers to a form of cultural hegemony – one culture is effectively colonised by the cultural products and lifestyles of another.

2 McDonaldisation is a related process that represents the idea that contemporary corporate cultural products are standardised, homogenised and formulaic. When this idea is applied to cultural relationships and experiences, homogenisation occurs because global cultural products are designed:

- efficiently, using a limited range of themes to appeal to the widest number of consumers
- rationally, where all aspects of the production and consumption process are measured and evaluated to produce standard products in standard settings
- predictably, in the sense that global cultural products are designed to be undemanding and unthreatening.

Uncertainty

Beck (1992) argues that uncertainty is an inherent condition of late modernity. In situations where individuals face more choices in cultural consumption, there is always the risk of making the 'wrong choices'. The homogenisation of global products, however, quantifies and reduces risk in two ways:

1 Through standardised experiences – each time a product is consumed, the individual knows exactly what to expect.
2 Where millions, perhaps billions, of people are making exactly the same consumption choices, the 'comfort of the crowd' reassures consumers they have made the 'right' choices.

These two processes may appear contradictory. People increasingly see themselves as diverse individuals living out their chosen identities while simultaneously making very similar consumption choices from a relatively narrow range of homogenised products. Bryman (1999), however, suggests that diversity and homogenisation co-exist in the same cultural space. The contradiction is resolved in late postmodernity by the ability of TNCs to create consumer identities and brand loyalties that both homogenise cultural behaviours within and between societies and create the impression of tailored choices within homogenised cultural structures.

Disneyisation

Cultural life is increasingly expressed through the kind of manufactured experiences analogous to Disney World, a theme park that is safe and secure, within which different individuals have different consumption experiences. The disneyisation of cultural life involves things like:

- theming – the creation of 'themed consumption experiences' whereby people buy in to a general, standardised, lifestyle

- de-differentiation – where consumers are offered a range of related products that provide a seamless 'lifestyle experience'; the book that becomes the film that spawns the lunchbox packed with themed products
- merchandising – by consuming cultural products, people take 'themed lifestyles' into their homes and social groups
- cultural imperialism – a situation where a particular culture is the ideal to which all cultures should aspire; Western lifestyles, values, customs and traditions, for example, introduced into non-Western societies that damage or destroy traditional cultural lifestyles.

TEST YOURSELF

Identify and explain two features of the McDonaldisation of culture.

While global companies undoubtedly influence cultural development, it is important not to overemphasise this influence. McDonald's may have restaurants all over the world, but that does not necessarily mean that all cultures are converging.

Cultural production and reproduction do not operate along simple behaviourist lines – if people consume similar, standardised, cultural products they will not inevitably become identical consumers. Cultural development can be filtered and changed by the social contexts within which products are used by people in different situations.

Glocalisation

This idea can be expressed by glocalisation, a combination of 'globalisation' and 'localisation', in which Adamu (2003) argues, 'global events/processes interact with local events/processes'. In other words, the meaning and impact of global cultural products, ideas and behaviours are interpreted, adapted and used differently in different local settings. Malone (2002) suggests that glocal sub-cultures are a form of hybridity in contemporary societies, in which global styles are given a unique local interpretation by different cultural groups.

Hip-hop, for example, exists as a global youth culture based on a particular style and identity. However, the meaning of this style is interpreted differently by youth in different countries, depending on their cultural background and traditions. This produces glocalised youth sub-cultures that mix and match local cultural traditions in the context of a global youth style. These ideas suggest that globalisation creates tensions between two areas:

- the local or particular, characterised in terms of high levels of cultural diversity
- the global or universal, characterised in terms of homogeneity.

While the two can theoretically be separated, there are also places where they meet. Robertson (1992) expresses this in terms of how the local and the global interact: each *influences* and is *influenced by* the other.

Appadurai (1990) rejects the idea that cultural interrelationships flow 'from the core to the periphery', whereby globalised, homogeneous, cultural forms are picked up by individual cultures. Rather, these interrelationships should be seen in terms of a variety of 'scapes' – imagined worlds that cross territorial borders and are connected in a variety of ways:

- Ethnoscapes reflect how people of different cultures physically interact.
- Technoscapes reflect the interaction of different forms of technology and its cultural adaptations and uses.
- Finanscapes refer to the interplay of financial relationships and their effect on political and social cultures.
- Mediascapes involve the flow of information across different societies and cultures.
- Ideoscapes reflect how people interact in terms of the exchange of images and ideas.

In this way, Appadurai argues, local cultural concepts spread across national boundaries, both influencing and being influenced by the ideas and relationships they encounter.

ACTIVITY

Divide into three groups, each of which should design a poster to illustrate one of the following:

- *Coca-colonisation*
- *McDonaldisation*
- *Disneyisation.*

What is the common ground and the differences between these three themes?

The role of transnational organisations in national economic and cultural systems

This section examines the role played by two types of **transnational organisations** in relation to national economic, political and cultural systems: international agencies and transnational corporations.

KEY TERM

Transnational organisations: private or public organisations that operate on a global level across national borders.

International agencies

Although international agencies are too numerous and diverse to examine individually, we can look at their general role in national and global **development strategies** in terms of their broadly economic, political or cultural focus.

KEY TERM

Development strategies: plans, usually adopted and put into effect at government level, that suggest ways for underdeveloped and developing countries to become developed.

Economic agencies

The two most significant international agencies are:

1 The IMF, which currently (2013) has a global membership of 188 countries, each paying a subscription based on its relative economic size; the USA, for example, is the largest net contributor. In general terms, the IMF plays two main roles in the world economic system:

- It lends to members to address and correct socioeconomic problems. This includes loans to help states overcome economic problems and 'concessional loans to help fight poverty in developing countries'.
- It establishes crisis-prevention measures that involve providing advice, as well as funding, to encourage members to adopt 'sound economic policies'.

The IMF's main purpose, therefore, is to act as a transglobal agency that keeps track of the economic stability of member countries and offers advice, criticism, technical expertise and economic aid as and when required to fulfil its primary role. Officially, its main objective is to promote an orderly system of world trade, within which member nations can develop their economic capabilities. It therefore tries to promote the balanced development of global trade and the stability of world exchange rates.

2 The World Bank, which has the primary objectives of reducing poverty and improving living standards among its member states. To this end, the World Bank provides two main services:

- educational support, relating to economic concerns, such as debt management, repayment and relief and cultural concerns, such as health issues
- economic support, such as 'low-interest loans, interest-free credit and grants' to developing countries for education, health, infrastructure and communications development.

The World Bank HQ in Washington, D.C. Agents of development or Western hegemony?

TEST YOURSELF

Identify and explain two objectives of international economic agencies.

Political agencies

Although agencies like the IMF and the World Bank play an implicit political role in global affairs by providing economic advice and aid, a range of international agencies play a more explicit political role. The UN, for example, has a complex membership structure covering a range of institutions (the IMF is technically a 'specialized agency of the United Nations', although it maintains both distance and independence from the UN). These institutions include:

- political institutions, such as the General Assembly, a forum for debate; the Security Council, which focuses on issues relating to international peace and security; and the International Court of Justice
- economic institutions, focused on development issues, such as international trade, finance and sustainable development
- cultural institutions that relate to social issues associated with development in areas such as gender discrimination and health issues.

The UN's official aims include:

- ensuring international peace and security
- encouraging co-operation to resolve economic, political and cultural problems
- dispute resolution
- promotion of **human rights** and freedoms.

KEY TERM

Human rights: fundamental human freedoms to which everyone is entitled.

The World Trade Organization (WTO) is a further example of a major international political institution. It was established in 1995 with the primary aim of regulating world trade through:

- government-level negotiation of economic treaties
- international agreements
- international trading rules
- dispute resolution between trading partners.

Cultural agencies

A range of international agencies focus on various forms of social and cultural development, many of which have been established and funded through the UN. Examples here include:

- the Office on Drugs and Crime
- the International Research and Training Institute for the Advancement of Women
- the Children's Fund (UNICEF)
- the World Health Organization (WHO).

NGOs

Non-government organisations are sometimes characterised as civil society organisations (CSOs) to indicate that they function independently of the state. They differ from agencies such as the IMF, UN or WTO because, as Malena (1995) notes, they are private organisations. NGOs pursue activities such as:

- relieving suffering
- promoting the interests of the poor
- protecting the environment
- providing basic social services
- undertaking community development.

Shah (2005) argues that this general perception of NGOs covers a wide range of groups with different forms of funding, organisation and objectives. These include:

- corporate-funded think tanks
- community groups
- development and research organisations
- charities
- relief agencies.

Although a defining characteristic of NGOs is their economic and political independence from government, their diversity makes them difficult to classify. For example, some NGOs work openly with national governments, but others do not. Others may work *covertly* with or against national governments to promote certain economic and political aims (such as, Schuh (2005) suggests, the overthrow of the Iranian government).

Over the past 50 years, NGOs have increased rapidly in type and number. The World Bank estimates that there are more than 30,000 NGOs operating in developed countries. The United Nations puts this number at up to 50,000 NGOs operating in areas such as development, human rights, security and peace politics. Robbins (2005) suggests a number of reasons for this increase:

- New forms of communication, such as the internet, have made it easier to create international communities of like-minded individuals and organisations.
- Public awareness of development issues is greater now than in the past, with humanitarian and environmental issues receiving greater media attention.
- Ideological changes to how states view economic, political and cultural development have resulted in national governments channelling initiatives and assistance through NGOs, partly because of their ability

to respond rapidly to development problems. Many NGOs have established networks within developing countries that allow them to direct assistance to where it is most urgently needed.

A further reason for the rise in private, non-profitmaking NGOs is the ideological shift that has taken place at both government and individual levels in developed nations. There has been a move towards neo-liberal ideas about the relationship between aid and trade as development strategies. This has resulted in a move away from bilateral assistance, which is now seen as ineffective, economically destabilising and open to corruption, towards greater NGO involvement.

TEST YOURSELF

What types of activity are pursued by NGOs?

The role of international agencies

Having outlined some basic features of international **aid agencies**, we will now explore some aspects of their political and economic roles, which have recently become a matter for debate and dispute. In particular, people have questioned the role of such agencies within a general development strategy. We can illustrate this using the example of international debt.

 KEY TERM

Aid agencies: organisations that distribute aid.

Agencies such as the IMF and the World Bank have been criticised for trying to impose a particular, model of economic reform (*monetarism*) on developing countries as a condition of both aid and trade. WE can see this in the 'debt crisis' among developing nations which began in 1982, when Mexico announced that it was unable to meet its debt repayments.

The World Bank's response was the Structural Adjustment Programme (SAP), designed to bring developing economies into line with developed nations and, by so doing, stimulate economic recovery. The programme focused on two strategies:

1 powering economic growth through the private sector
2 encouraging foreign investment through high interest rates.

241

A condition of receiving aid was that developing countries were required to adopt a range of political and economic free-market measures. These included:

- deregulation of private industry and the ending of restrictions on foreign investment
- privatisation of state-owned industries and services
- currency devaluation that increased the costs of domestic production and goods
- cutting government expenditure on social spending in areas such as health, education and food subsidies
- lower corporate taxation
- export-led strategic growth that involved producing goods for foreign markets, to increase national income.

Hong (2000) argues that these measures caused huge economic and social changes in developing nations. Many countries abandoned crop diversity for domestic consumption in favour of producing cash crops, such as coffee and cotton, that could be sold in developed markets. While this offered several economic benefits for developed nations and TNCs, the overall result of the SAP strategy, according to Hong, was that developing nations suffered in a number of ways:

- Increased unemployment and poverty, as domestic industries were exposed to fierce competition from TNCs. State spending on social services was sharply reduced.
- Increasing government and private corruption. Hawley (2000), for example, argues that 'Western businesses pay huge amounts of money in bribes to win friends, influence and contracts, conservatively estimated to run to £50 billion a year or roughly the amount the UN believes is needed to eradicate global poverty'. Hanlon (2004) claims that corruption flourishes in developing countries as a direct result of the 'economic liberalisation policies required of Southern countries by Northern donors'.
- Deteriorating social conditions, including the 'collapse of both preventive and curative care due to the lack of medical equipment, supplies, poor working conditions and low pay of medical personnel'.
- Altered ecosystems that result from the environmental impact of enforced changes in land use. The introduction of monoculture has resulted in more intensive farming methods, the increased use of pesticides and herbicides and the introduction of genetically modified (GM) crops. Illegal logging in areas such as the Amazon Basin has also resulted in deforestation, land deterioration and increased carbon dioxide emissions from burning woodland.

- Social dislocation and unrest: Hanlon (2005) argues that 'the World Bank stresses the free market, small government, and fiscal austerity' that, in countries like Sierra Leone, have contributed to social dislocation and unrest. He argues that cuts to education budgets meant many young people received no schooling, leading to both social grievances and social exclusion, two factors that contributed to civil war during the 1990s.

Although initiatives such as the SAP have raised questions about the strategic role of international agencies, Dalmiya and Schultink (2003) argue that some international agencies, including the World Bank and WHO, have 'played a significant role in' raising nutritional standards and combating disease in developing countries.

The role of transnational corporations

TNCs play an important role in world trade. Raghavan (1996) estimates that they account for around one-third of total world economic output and control around 'two-thirds of the world economy'. Anderson and Cavanagh (2000) give an idea of the immense size and economic scope of TNCs when they note:

- In terms of revenue, of the 100 largest economies in the world, 51 are TNCs.
- The top 200 TNCs account for around 25% of the world's daily economic activity.
- Around 30% of world trade involves 'economic transactions among various units of the same corporation'.

Comparing nation states with TNCs, measured by national GDP and TNC revenues, US supermarket chain Wal-Mart ranks 35th in world economic terms. It has greater revenues than countries such as Portugal and Ireland (Table 7.14).

5 largest nations		5 largest TNCs		TNC larger than:
1	USA	35	Wal-Mart	Switzerland
2	China	36	BP	Portugal, Chile
3	Japan	37	Exxon Mobil	Ireland
4	Germany	39	Royal Dutch/Shell	Luxembourg
5	France	45	General Motors	Nicaragua

Table 7.14   Ranking nations and TNCs by income

Sources: TNCs: Fortune Magazine (2005); Nations: US Central Intelligence Unit (2005)

A further feature of contemporary TNCs is the extent of their global connections. Vitali et al. (2011), for example, mapped the 'architecture of the international ownership network' through ownership and control patterns among the world's largest TNCs. They found a relatively small number of financial institutions, mainly banks but also insurance and private hedge funds, at the centre of a global network of ownership and control.

Strategy: The strategic role of TNCs in the global marketplace has also attracted criticism. ActionAid (2005), for example, argues that the failure to regulate the behaviour of global food corporations has caused problems developing nations that also affect developed consumers:

- Abuse of market power – forcing down the prices paid to producers in developing countries.
- Profiteering – despite forcing down prices for producers of coffee, rice and tea, Western consumers do not pay lower retail prices.
- Marginalisation – producers who fail to comply with the economic terms laid down by corporations are 'forced out of the supply chain'; their produce remains unsold.
- Human rights and the environment – TNCs 'operate in a regulatory void' in developing nations that allows them to 'weaken labour, environmental and public health laws'. They do, however, 'behave more responsibly in countries with tighter regulation'.
- Corporate social responsibility – these are 'voluntary efforts by companies to improve their social and environmental performance', but such self-regulating efforts 'are ineffective, unworkable and rarely observed in developing countries'.
- Social harm – the poorest sections of the global economy find it difficult to seek redress for harms caused by the activities of TNCs. Weak national laws and the difficulties of applying international laws conspire to allow TNCs to largely escape sanction. An extreme example is the 1984 explosion at the then Union Carbide-owned pesticide factory in Bhopal India. This exposed around 500,000 people to toxic chemicals and led directly to around 2000 deaths. Twenty-five years later, eight ex-employees were given two-year prison sentences for their role in the disaster.

Madeley (2003) concludes that TNCs have 'used their money, size and power' to influence governments, particularly in the developing world. In 2009, for example, Royal Dutch Shell paid $15 million, without admitting

Bhopal, India, was the site of one of the world's worst industrial disasters in 1984

liability, to settle a lawsuit alleging that the company colluded with the Nigerian government to pay soldiers to silence critics of the company's operations. In the developing world, the newer global breed of internet-based companies, from Amazon to Google, have been accused of developing elaborate ways to minimise their tax liabilities. Griffiths and Bowers (2013), for example, found that Amazon paid little or no corporation tax on its profits from UK sales worth £4 billion.

Benefits: Despite the examples outlined above, TNCs do not always occupy a destructive position in the global economy. Aisbett (2003) argues that, although in the public consciousness 'benefit to transnational corporations implies loss to everyone else, particularly the most poor and marginalized groups', empirical data suggests that this is not the case. It is, for example, possible to note a range of benefits to developing countries deriving from TNC activities.

Trade and investment can generally be related to both economic growth and poverty reduction and, more specifically, as Contreras (1987) argues, to benefits such as:

- employment and income increases
- educational development resulting from TNCs needing local workers with particular knowledge and skills
- capital income that develops from 'rents, dividends and other capital income for shareholders'
- capital incomes also increase indirectly through the development of supplier and service industries linked to the primary economic activities of TNCs
- increased government income for infrastructure development, welfare, health and educational services, results from taxation on the economic activity stimulated by TNCs.

243

A range of technological developments flow from the presence of TNCs and their specific benefits, for Contreras, include:

- regional development, whereby economically isolated and underdeveloped regions can realise their productive capabilities
- industrial growth, as technological developments provide a 'short cut' to economic development
- technology transfer that gives increased access to the knowledge and skills possessed by TNCs.

Through TNCs, developing countries gain access to markets in developed nations for their domestic produce, and the technological benefits of TNC activity enable developing nations to compete successfully in such markets. This, in turn, brings both foreign exchange and investment. In terms of the overall development process, the presence of TNCs provides the 'industrial and technological spark' that modernisation and free-market theorists see as essential to escape from subsistence agriculture and poverty.

Aisbett points out that the economic benefits of international trade are not always shared equitably between TNCs and the countries in which they operate. However, she argues this is more a matter for national governments, international law and consumer behaviour in developed countries than an inevitable consequence of capitalist corporate behaviour. In general, therefore, Contreras argues, 'TNCs have had a decisive influence in the development of Africa, Latin America and Asia, particularly in those countries where rapid economic growth and industrialization have high priority and where sophisticated technology and massive capital investments are needed'.

Summary points

- **Indicators and classifications of development include:**
  - economic
  - social
  - Socioeconomic
- **There are three main models of development:**
  - modernisation
  - underdevelopment/ dependency
  - world systems.
- **Aid has various forms:**
  - non-repayable grants
  - repayable loans
  - technological and military help, advice and training
  - development finance.
- **Debates about 'trade as aid' framed around three main approaches:**
  - neo-liberal
  - interventionist
  - three-dimensional sustainable development.
- **Trends in population growth involve understanding:**
  - birth rates
  - death rates.
- **Global trends involve:**
  - primary drivers: industrialisation and globalisation
  - secondary drivers: employment and living standards, health and education.
- **Regional trends involve:**
  - developed nations – zero population growth
  - developing nations reducing birth rates
  - underdeveloped nations increasing birth rates.

- **Consequences of global population growth:**

  Pessimistic:
  - classical Malthusian model
  - neo-Malthusian models.

  Optimistic:
  - demographic transition
  - demographic regulation
  - Marxist models.
- **Demographic changes:**
  - migration patterns
  - employment patterns:
    - employment emigration
    - international labour mobility.
  - unemployment and 'wage poverty'
  - health
  - education.
- **Definitions of poverty:**
  - absolute
  - relative.
- **Cultural explanations:**
  - underclass theory
  - culture of dependency
  - culture of poverty
  - cycle of deprivation.
- **Structural explanations:**
  - labour-market theory
  - capitalism
  - risk
  - memberships theory
  - inter-generational transmission.
- **Globalisation across three forms:**
  - Economic globalisation
  - Political globalisation
  - Cultural globalisation.
- **Transnational organisations include:**
  - International agencies
  - Transnational corporations (TNCs).

Exam-style questions

1 a Explain why not all forms of aid are helpful for development. [9]

  b Assess the impact of transnational corporations on global development. [16]

2 a Explain the problems in defining the concept of 'development'. [9]

  b Assess the strengths and limitations of the dependency theory of development. [16]

3 a Explain the problems in defining the concept of poverty. [9]

  b Assess different explanations for development. [16]

4 a Explain the term 'globalisation'. [9]

  b Assess the strengths and limitations of different explanations of poverty. [16]

Total available marks 100

245

Chapter 8:
Media

Learning objectives

The objectives of this chapter involve understanding:

- national and global trends in media ownership and control

- Marxist and pluralist interpretations of the relative importance of media ownership and control

- Marxist and pluralist interpretations of the nature and role of the media, including concepts of mass society and mass culture

- economic, political and ideological factors affecting the selection and presentation of media content, including the concept of news values

- different perspectives on the relationship between the media and the state

- features, issues and processes surrounding the impact of new media on society

- modernist and postmodernist perspectives on the role of the media in the representation of social groups and ideas

- social patterns in listening, viewing and reading

- theories of direct, indirect and limited media effects and uses

- positive and negative media impacts in relation to behaviour, violence and deviance

- problems with researching media effects on audiences.

Introduction

This chapter looks at different aspects of the media, from how it is defined, through new and old media to an assessment of its social effects. We initially focus on questions of media ownership and control and how this helps us understand national and global media processes; this includes the relationship between the media and the state and the media's general role in society. This chapter also investigates media representation of social groups and how this relates to different theories of media effects.

Ownership and control of the media

Trends in the organisation and control of the media; ownership patterns

Defining the media

Before we examine trends in the organisation and control of the **media**, it is useful to explain and define the distinction between 'old' and 'new' forms of media.

KEY TERM

Media: channels of mass communication through which information is sent and received.

A medium is a 'channel of communication' – a way of sending and receiving information. When people read a newspaper, watch television or view a website, something is communicated in some way. Collectively, these channels represent media (the plural of medium).

The term 'media' usually refers to communication with large numbers of people. This is conventionally seen as 'one-to-many' communication: one person, such as the author of a newspaper article, simultaneously communicates to many people (the audience). Dutton et al. (1998) suggest that the media has a number of characteristics that set it apart from other types of communication, such as interpersonal communication that occurs on a one-to-one basis (for example, a telephone call). In the media, communication is:

- impersonal: the sender of the message does not know the receivers
- lacking in immediacy: the audience has no involvement with the production of a media message
- one-way: from the producer/creator to the consumer/audience
- physically and technologically distant: everyone receives the same intended message

- organised: it requires a vehicle, such as a television receiver, printed page or internet connection, which allows messages to be sent and received
- large-scale and simultaneous: the global audience for something like the football World Cup numbers hundreds of millions
- commodified: it comes at a price. You can watch the latest films if you can afford a television and a subscription to a satellite or cable company. The audience may also be the commodity that is bought and sold. For example, 'free-to-air' television programmes deliver a mass audience to advertisers.

These characteristics apply to 'old media', such as newspapers, magazines, books, television, radio and film. However, the situation is complicated and in some ways changed, by newer, computer-based technologies that do not fit easily into these categories. Mobile (cell) and smartphones or personal computers have the capacity for communication that is:

- one-to-one: such as email
- one-to-many: such as Facebook, Twitter or a blog
- many-to-many: what Shirky (2008) calls 'group conversations' that include things like peer-to-peer (P2P) networks that use software to link individual computers in a network to exchange information; this has diverse uses, from sharing work documents to downloading (illegal) copies of films, music and software.

This variety of ways of communicating is one of the defining characteristics of **new media**. However, one similarity between old and new media is the nature of ownership and control.

KEY TERM

New media: contemporary channels of communication characterised by their interactivity, individualisation and network capabilities.

247

How is new media different from old media?

Owners

Media owners can be broadly characterised as a group that falls into two areas:

- Private ownership refers to companies that are run for profit by individuals, families or shareholders. Rupert Murdoch, for example, owns a controlling interest in News Corporation, a global media company that publishes newspapers, books, films and magazines, and broadcasts satellite TV programmes.
- State ownership involves government controls that differ between societies. In China, for example, the government directly oversees the content of state-run television and tightly regulates access to the internet. In other societies, public broadcasters have greater autonomy (independence and freedom of action).

The significance of ownership in this context is that owners have the potential to decide what sort of information an audience receives. This reflects a form of **censorship** that can be both direct and indirect. Private owners may decide not to publish information critical of their company, whereas state-owned companies may be subject to political control over what they can broadcast or publish.

> **KEY TERM**
>
> **Censorship:** the deliberate suppression of communication or information.

Controllers: Controllers, such as the editor of a newspaper, manage a company on a daily basis. While they may be *shareholders* in the company – a notable trend in **media ownership**, especially at the higher levels of media management – they do not *own* the company for which they work.

> **KEY TERM**
>
> **Media ownership:** economic control of a media organisation.

Different sociological interpretations of ownership and control place different levels of significance on this distinction.

> **TEST YOURSELF**
>
> Identify three characteristics of old media.

Trends

To understand trends in ownership and control in a global context we can identify two processes common to all forms of media behaviour in modern industrial societies: concentration and conglomeration.

Concentration: This refers to how the media is increasingly owned by a relatively small number of large corporations and powerful individuals. Over the past 50 years, for example, the trend has been for fewer media owners controlling larger corporations.

The concentration of ownership is also part of a long-term global trend. Compaine (2004), for example, notes that the global media market is dominated by seven giant corporations, including Disney, News International and Bertelsmann. McLiesh et al.'s (2001) examination of media in 97 countries found that most large media firms are owned by private families. The concentration of ownership is significant in terms of product diversity – consumers are offered a limited range of similar media products. However, recent concerns about concentration have focused on the extent to which it affects *information diversity*.

The availability of a wide range of products means very little if they all say much the same thing. McChesney (2000), for example, argues that having lots of different media products simply gives the 'appearance of choice' because they still only communicate a limited range of ideas. While satellite and cable television offer hundreds of different channels, their content is largely homogeneous, cheaply made and repetitive.

Compaine (2001) disputes this interpretation: the global trend is not necessarily for increased concentration because media organisations are not static entities; they develop, grow, evolve and disappear.

The global media companies that were dominant in the 1980s were not necessarily dominant in the 2000s. Fifteen years ago, Amazon did not exist, but today it is

248

one of the world's largest media outlets. Social networking companies are also a good illustration here. Founded in 2003, Myspace was the most visited social networking site in the world until 2008, when it was overtaken by Facebook, a company that did not exist until 2004. By 2013, Facebook was one of the most successful internet sites, with around 1 billion users, profits of around $1 billion and a net worth of around $50 billion. In 2011, Myspace was sold for $35 million.

TEST YOURSELF

Define the term 'media concentration', using an example to illustrate your answer.

Conglomeration

Conglomeration is an ownership trend related to concentration. It involves the same company developing interests across different media through a process of diversification. One example of this type of **cross-media corporation** is Fininvest, the media company owned by the former Italian Prime Minister Silvio Berlusconi. It has a diverse range of interests that include television, book, newspaper and magazine publishing. In terms of new media, Amazon, the world's largest bookseller, has diversified its interests over the last few years into areas such as publishing, with the development of the Kindle range of digital book readers, and book review websites, with the acquisition of Goodreads in 2013.

KEY TERM

Cross-media corporation: private or public company that owns different types of media, such as a newspaper, television channel and film production studio.

ACTIVITY

In groups, choose a particular aspect of the media (such as newspapers, magazines and television) and use the internet to research media ownership in your society. All groups will then need to compare their findings across different media (e.g. newspapers and television) to see 'who owns what'.

What does your research tell you about media concentration and conglomeration in your society?

Different perspectives on the relationship between ownership and control of the media

This section examines two opposing views on the significance of trends in media organisation and control: Marxist and pluralist.

Marxism

According to traditional Marxism, capitalist society involves a distinction between two social classes: the proletariat (or subject class) and the bourgeoisie (or ruling class). The fact that the ruling class owns and controls ideological (or cultural) institutions gives it the power to decisively shape how people view the social world. In contemporary societies, the media is the most important and influential ideological institution. Whoever owns the media, therefore, exercises a great deal of power. In some ways this reflects a determinist approach: the media is seen as a powerful agency that can shape, and in some instances, fully decide people's general thoughts and behaviours.

The media is part of the political and ideological superstructure in capitalist society. Its role is to propagate values that support the *status quo*, shaping how people see the world through a range of legitimating ideas. These may include:

- support for capitalism
- rationalising and justifying social inequalities
- defending the concept of private property
- the private ownership of profits
- negatively labelling alternatives to capitalism.

The media is a tool or instrument used by a ruling class to teach an **ideology** that favours the interests of bourgeoisie. Milliband (1969) argues that this is possible because members of the ruling class share a common economic and cultural background, which is created and reinforced through educational and family networks.

KEY TERM

Ideology: system of related beliefs.

From this viewpoint, owners ultimately control a company, while managers are employed to oversee day-to-day operations. A newspaper editor may control the stories that appear and be responsible for hiring and firing employees for example, but the owner dictates the political opinions expressed in the paper, the type of audience it aims to reach and, most importantly, who

249

is or is not employed in managerial roles. Ownership and control, therefore, are part of a hierarchical system. Both are necessary features of capitalist corporations, but owners are always the dominant force in this relationship.

Owners and controllers use the media to manipulate how subject classes see the world to create the belief that societies work in the interests of all rather than the interests of a few. In this way the media creates a 'false consciousness': the lower classes co-operate with a ruling class in their own exploitation and against their own interests. In the UK, for example, following the global financial crisis in 2008, the media has characterised recovery in terms of 'austerity' and the need for 'everyone to work together' to make sacrifices to pay off the national debt. From this perspective, therefore, the ability to control the type and quality of information people receive means a ruling class controls and broadly determines how people think.

Evaluation: Traditional Marxist approaches reflect a conspiratorial approach to the relationship between a ruling class and the media, in which the media is a 'willing tool' in the hands of the elite. However, this is not always the case, as the recent (2011) phone-hacking scandal at News International showed. The media is also critical of many forms of capitalist behaviour, from 'greedy bankers' to environmental crimes.

The idea that a ruling class is a coherent body with members who all share the same interests has also been questioned, in particular by neo-Marxist approaches. If financial capitalists, such as bankers, and industrial capitalists, such as manufacturers, do not have much in common, they are unlikely to use the media to present a unified view of the world to the rest of society.

The usefulness of concepts like a dominant ideology and false consciousness have also been questioned. People in contemporary democratic societies have a wide range of media choices that offer access to different economic, political and ideological viewpoints. The development of new media makes it increasingly difficult to see how the flow of information can be tightly controlled by a ruling class. The traditional Marxist approach also tends to portray media consumers as passive recipients of whatever owners want to publish.

Neo-Marxism

The concept of class lies at the heart of neo-Marxist approaches to the relationship between ownership and control. However, Wright (1985) theorises class as a dynamic system of shifting social relationships, rather than as a static classification system. This suggests that conflict, divisions and contradictions occur *within* a ruling class as well as *between* this class and other classes. These conflicts may be:

- economic – between different types of capital, such as financial/banking and manufacturing
- political – some parts of the British bourgeoisie support the European Community, while others do not
- ideological – some parts of the ruling class advocate liberal, free-market capitalism with little or no state involvement in economic affairs, while others are more interventionist, believing that governments should intervene at various times to support and regulate industries.

Hegemony

This dynamic approach means that class associations can also accommodate ethnic and gender divisions. Individuals from some ethnic groups may be economically successful even if they do not see themselves as part of a (white) middle or upper class.

In addition, status groups such as professionals and intellectuals (the upper middle class) occupy what Poulantzas (1975) calls 'contradictory class positions'. These groups are neither wholly bourgeois nor wholly proletarian, and this is significant in understanding the relationship between media owners, controllers and audiences.

This approach, therefore, questions the idea that the behaviour of subject classes is directly manipulated through the media. For this to happen, a ruling class would need a level of cohesion that it simply does not have. The media is not without influence, but such influence is hegemonic not manipulative. The concept of **hegemony** is used to show how both owners and controllers in modern capitalist societies are locked into a mutually beneficial structural relationship based around economic profit:

- Owners must make profits if their business is to survive.
- Managers rely on profits for their jobs, salaries and lifestyles.

 KEY TERM

Hegemony: leadership with the consent (real or implied) of those who are led.

Do media owners and their employees share similar values?

Core values

According to this hegemonic view, owners and controllers have a common economic interest, expressed in terms of core values. For example, they both have a fundamental belief in capitalist economic systems. Although they necessarily share a common cause in promoting and preserving their core values through the media they do not always agree on the best way to promote and preserve such values.

Managers enjoy *relative autonomy* – the freedom to make certain decisions – because media corporations are too large and too complex to be easily controlled by an owner on a daily basis. Therefore, owners employ managers who can be trusted to reflect their views. Editors who insist on ignoring their employer's interests are likely to find themselves unemployed. As long as the output is legal, the key principle is profitability; some owners may not care too much about the behaviour and activities of their media managers as long as they make a good profit.

Hegemonic control suggests that beliefs are not simply imposed 'from above' by a ruling class. Strinati (1995), for example, argues that dominant groups maintain their position through the 'consent' of subordinate groups. This consent that may be actively manufactured through what Althusser (1971) calls *ideological state apparatuses* (ISAs) that involve **socialisation** processes, both personal and political, which are carried out by cultural institutions such as the media.

Socialisation: process in which people are taught and learn the various forms of behaviour consistent with their membership of a particular culture.

Evaluation: Criticism of neo-Marxist approaches focuses on the hegemonic significance of the media and the specific ideological role of cultural institutions in capitalist societies. The development of new global media forms limits the ability of national governments or private owners to control information as they may once have done. In the digital age, most populations are no longer restricted to information which they receive passively from the media. Not only can people 'search the globe' for information but, as Weinberger (2012) argues, 'For every fact on the internet, there is an equal and opposite fact'. These ideas question the effectiveness of the media's ideological role.

TEST YOURSELF

Identify and explain the key differences between traditional and neo-Marxist explanations of the relationship between media ownership and control.

251

Pluralism

An alternative approach, known as pluralism, stresses how social groups compete against one another in the economic marketplace as they pursue their own interests. Such competition may be:

- economic – different newspaper groups competing for readers
- ideological – different political groups competing to promote their views.

Media owners are potentially powerful players, because they can demand that their views are expressed. However, pluralist approaches argue that control of the media is increasingly in the hands of what Galbraith (1967) calls a 'technocratic managerial elite', who, however well remunerated, remain *employees* rather than employers. Many media organisations are owned by shareholders rather than individuals. Where no single shareholder has overall control of a company, directors and managers make all the important day-to-day business decisions.

Managerialism

Burnham (1941) called this change in control a managerial revolution based, in part, on commercial necessity – the needs of consumers. In a competitive world, the consumer exercises a huge (collective) influence over organisational behaviour. If consumers do not like what they are being offered, then an organisation must respond to consumers' demands or risk being driven out of business by other companies who are more willing to adapt. In this situation, the ideological content of media messages is less important than profit. And where media companies are forced to compete for customers, power really lies in the hands of consumers.

Globalisation has encouraged diversity and competition through what Davis and McAdam (2000) call a 'new economic shift'. Media corporations have become networks operating across national boundaries, with flexible organisational structures that allow them to respond to new technological developments. These organisations normally have shareholders, such as banks and pension funds, but they rarely have individual owners. Even an organisation such as Facebook, originally developed and owned by a very small group of employees, including the creator, Mark Zuckerberg, is now owned by a wide group of institutional and individual shareholders.

252

> **KEY TERM**
>
> **Globalisation:** various processes – economic, political and cultural – that occur on a worldwide basis.

Modern media conglomerates can therefore be seen as diverse organisations that operate in a wide range of different markets and cater for an equally wide range of consumer needs and demands. This economic situation results in many different types of publication, from print through broadcasting to digital media. A further boost to media diversity involves the rapid growth of cheap, widely available computer technology, from desktop computers to smartphones. These are built on a web-based distribution system (the internet) that has:

- reduced the costs of media production
- made entry into the media marketplace open to all
- given all producers access to a global audience.

> **TEST YOURSELF**
>
> Identify and explain two differences between Marxist and pluralist explanations of the relationship between media ownership and control.

Evaluation: Although pluralist arguments about the changing nature of media markets and organisations have some validity, especially in the context of new media and the rise of cheap, accessible, global distribution systems such as the internet, they have been criticised for several reasons.

Firstly, the separation of ownership and control in modern media conglomerates is overstated. At the senior levels of global corporations, 'managers' are 'employees' in name only. Murdock and Golding (1977), for example, argue that the separation of interests between owners and controllers is more apparent than real, since managers often own the companies they control. They think and act in much the same way as the individual media owners of the past.

Secondly, major shareholders still exert control over a business. Rupert Murdoch, for example, has a 35% share in News Corporation, the parent company of a range of subsidiary companies such as News International. This effectively gives Murdoch control. Curran (2000) acknowledges that the power of media owners 'is qualified and constrained' by a range of people and interests that include:

- consumers
- employees
- the suppliers of various forms of content
- regulators
- rival producers
- the wider cultural beliefs of a society.

Curran also argues that owners remain the most powerful actors in these organisations. They may not personally oversee the content of the media they own, but they are unlikely to employ managers who are opposed to their social and economic interests.

Thirdly, although the internet makes it more difficult for owners to control what their audience sees, reads and hears, old media may actually have far larger audiences than most new media. Logan (2010) notes that while there are around 175 million unique blogs on the internet, 'the average number of readers of any given blog is seven'. More significantly in this context, some forms of old media may also be trusted more as sources of information.

Are owners like Rupert Murdoch the most powerful actors in media organisations?

Finally, pluralists argue that media diversity guarantees consumer choice, but competition does not automatically mean media diversity. Economies of scale, for example, mean the majority of consumer demands can be satisfied by a few giant corporations wielding great economic, political and ideological power on a global scale. Nor does this depend whether ownership of these corporations is concentrated in the hands of a single individual or a large number of anonymous shareholders. The diversity of web-based media may also be overstated. Giant corporations such as Apple, through its iTunes store, and Amazon increasingly exert tight controls over what is published. Apple directly controls what may or may not be sold through its online store. If a song is deemed unacceptable it is excluded from sale. Individual song titles and lyrics are also strictly censored. As iTunes currently has a 66% share of the global download market, the ability to exclude products from sale gives Apple significant control of media content.

Pluralist and Marxist theories of the nature and role of the media

Traditional Marxism

Traditional Marxism sees the media as a significant ideological institution in capitalist society. An important dimension of the media's role is to shape how people think by controlling the nature, extent and type of information on which they make judgements. In this manipulative model, owners and controllers use the media as a tool to influence public opinion. They promote a particular ideological world view that explicitly favours the interests of a ruling class.

A second dimension to this role is the promotion and policing of the values of capitalist society. Marxists therefore see the media as an increasingly important

agency of social control, expressed through two significant processes:

- Those whose views reflect the interests of owners are given access to the media.
- Those with alternative or contradictory views are generally denied such access.

Ideas favourable to a ruling class are continually highlighted and promoted, while opposing views are ignored, misrepresented or marginalised. Oppositional ideas are represented in ways that suggest they are not to be taken seriously:

- The Glasgow Media Group (1976) showed how UK television news broadcasts portrayed owners positively and trade unions negatively during industrial actions in the 1980s.
- Hussain (2002) documents how, in Denmark, ethnic-minority groups suffered 'exclusion and marginalisation in the mainstream media' that used 'openly anti-immigrant and anti-Muslim' language.
- Petersen (2008) argues: 'Every major US newspaper and TV news show has a business section, but not a labor section. If the stock market drops, it's "Stop the presses". But if the infant mortality rate rises, it's questionable if it'll even make the papers. If you created a blueprint for an apparatus that erased critical thought, there's none more efficient than corporate media'.

These examples point to another manipulative process in which marginalised social groups, such as immigrants, minorities and the unemployed, are represented as the cause of social problems. This 'scapegoating' is designed to create divisions within and between groups and to deflect the blame for social problems away from the behaviour of the elite. The general role of the media, therefore, is to ensure that the views and interests of the elite are presented in ways that encourage people to accept social and economic inequality as 'normal and right'.

Mass society: The roots of this perspective are found in the Frankfurt School, which developed ideas about the role of the media in *totalitarian societies* (those ruled by a political dictatorship, such as Germany in the 1930s) based on the concept of a mass society. As Ross (1995) notes, this is a type of society in which 'the masses' are characterised by:

- geographic isolation – a lack of daily face-to-face contact

- social isolation – a lack of participation in larger groups or organisations and the failure to develop strong community ties
- limited social interaction – people increasingly see themselves as 'anonymous individuals' who are not part of a functioning social group, community or society.

Mass culture: Ross argues that where a society is characterised by 'demographically heterogeneous [mixed] but behaviourally homogenous [similar] groups', the media is used, by both individuals and powerful elites, to create a sense of community and culture. A mass society develops a mass culture. This is sometimes called 'popular' or 'low' culture to distinguish it from the **high culture** of the social elite. Mass culture joins together mass society because it provides the 'things in common', such as values and beliefs, that socially isolated individuals share. However, because mass culture is created through the media it can be manipulated to reflect the interests of a ruling class.

> **KEY TERM**
>
> **High culture:** the idea that some cultural products and practices are *superior* to others: 'the art, music and literature preferred by the well-educated elite'.

Does new media encourage or discourage social isolation?

A contemporary variation of this argument links behaviour in late postmodernity to mass communication channels such as the internet. Lang and Lang (2009), for example, note how the internet

involves communication processes that are both physically and socially distant. Instant communication can occur between people who are in different countries and who may know little about the person with whom they are communicating. They may not even know their real name. The features of a mass society can be exploited by powerful elites, from governments and political groups to public-relations specialists. In the past, it was difficult to directly influence a socially isolated mass of individuals in democratic societies. Now, Lang and Lang suggest that 'The internet, though open to many uses, has this potential', mainly because people 'at best, have a vague awareness of the numerous but nameless others attracted by the same object or media content, who adopt the same fashion, behave in a similar way, or move in a parallel direction'. This suggests that people may be open to various forms of **media manipulation** through their involvement in new media networks.

> **KEY TERM**
>
> **Media manipulation:** various ways in which the media attempts to influence and control how information is received and understood by an audience.

> **TEST YOURSELF**
>
> Suggest two features of mass society.

Neo-(Hegemonic) Marxism

From this perspective the role of the media reflects the complexity of class relationships and interests in contemporary societies. The media's ideological role is considered in terms of how it creates and sustains a broad political consensus around a set of core values, rather than how it manipulates people's behaviour directly. In this way, the media can reflect a variety of different opinions while simultaneously absorbing critical views that may threaten the stability of the social system.

Neo-Marxists do not believe that the media's ideological role is to provide a 'common culture for the masses'. They argue that concepts of mass society and mass culture are both unrealistic and over-simplified, because in contemporary societies the range of behavioural choices is too great to be simply and easily manipulated. The media's role, therefore, is considered in terms of how it helps to maintain the *status quo* by policing and protecting core social values.

A key idea here is that the media plays a crucial role in creating a consensus that allows people to be socialised into core values. People must be made to accept the values of their society or, if they try to reject them, be powerless to change them.

Manufacturing consensus: Traditionally, producing a media product for a mass audience was restricted by the cost of creating, marketing and distributing a newspaper, film or television programme. However, the development of new media has made some forms of access, such as blogging or self-publishing, easier and cheaper. This presents a problem for traditional Marxists, because it means that a much wider range of views can be heard. However, hegemonic Marxists argue that ruling elites can absorb, accommodate and even promote information diversity through 'hierarchies of trust' (that is, the faith people have in the truth of different forms of media).

Agendas: In this sense, therefore, the media holds certain beliefs about core values that are taken for granted. In so doing, the media sets the agenda for debate; some things are simply not up for discussion. For example, no major media corporation discusses economic organisation in anything other than capitalist terms.

While ensuring that certain core values are questioned, the media also steers public opinion in particular ways. Just as advertisers try to convince people to buy one product rather than another, so does the media through 'preferred readings'. This is something the writer of a newspaper article, for example, wants their audience to believe without noticing that their opinions are being influenced. One way this is achieved is through the use of headlines and subheading, which effectively tell the reader how they should interpret an article. Another way is to use captions to tell an audience what a picture means. At worst, this control is a form of propaganda.

Those who control the media have the power to disseminate one political viewpoint across an entire society

255

Pluralism

Pluralism covers a range of perspectives on the role of the media that can be loosely characterised by their rejection of Marxist interpretations. Pluralist perspectives share a number of general beliefs about the role of the media, although they are expressed in different ways and with different levels of emphasis.

One characteristic of these approaches is the significance they place on information diversity. Even where old-media forms are highly concentrated, pluralists believe that there is still a range of views available. Such diversity is enhanced through the development of new media, where relatively low start-up, production and distribution costs have created a proliferation of media outlets. In this respect, diversity is related to choice – not just in the range of different media and views, but also in terms of consumers.

Diversity and choice come together in the sense that it is media consumers, not producers, who are central to the relationship between the media and ideology. If a producer does not offer the things people want to read, watch or listen to, that company will go out of business. This 'discipline of the marketplace' – finding ways to give people what they want – is driven by the fact that owners compete to win market share and create profits. This, in turn, creates innovation and diversity. Owners and

KEY TERM

Propaganda: selective, partial and one-sided forms of communication designed to influence the attitudes of an audience towards a particular point of view.

controllers are continually looking for ways to improve their product:

- technologically, such as digital television, smartphones and digital books
- qualitatively, such as developing new types of programming or video gaming.

This drive for innovation gives audiences an important position in relation to the media. Media audiences are not *passive*, simply buying whatever owners provide, but *active*. They buy what they like and ignore the things that do not fit their lifestyles or beliefs. In this respect, new media simply increases the choice available to consumers on a global scale. There are, for example, websites that reflect most political and ideological opinions.

In this sense, pluralist perspectives reverse the traditional Marxist argument that audiences consume whatever owners decide to give them. Instead, media owners demand from their employees whatever consumers want. This places media controllers in a unique and potentially powerful position. Part of their job is to seek out and respond to consumer demand and if they do this successfully, all sections of society are satisfied. Owners and consumers each get what they want: profits for the former, entertainment and information for the latter.

Overall, therefore, the role of the media is to provide consumers with the information and services they demand. A diverse range of media exists and people can choose from different sources of information. This that applies to both old and new media; internet access, for example, means people can get information from both national and global sources. A variety of media reflecting a range of views also means that some sections will represent the interests of 'ordinary people' and the activities of the powerful can be scrutinised, exposed and criticised.

Suggest two ways in which 'pluralism reverses the Marxist argument' about the role of the media.

Different explanations of the processes of selection and presentation of media content

Explanations of the processes involved in the **selection and presentation of media content** relate to what Barrat (1992) calls the 'social context of media production'.

Write a caption for this picture that portrays the behaviour in:

a *a positive light*
b *a negative light.*

Media content is socially constructed because it involves the selection of some types of information for presentation in particular ways. We can explore in terms of economic, political and ideological factors.

 KEY TERM

Selection and presentation of media content: the various ways in which media content is chosen (selection) and given (presented) to an audience in order to influence their understanding of an issue, idea or group.

Economic factors

Production and distribution costs, especially for old media, influence factors such as news gathering. A national media company, for example, has more resources at its disposal than a local one. However, both companies use agencies such as the Press Association or Reuters, which collect and sell stories collected from a variety of sources to lower the cost of reporting. In terms of distribution networks, Peters (2001) argues that some companies, such as BSkyB in the UK, 'use their position as gatekeepers to distribute mainly information and programme services of their own media group, thus limiting free access'.

Production values relate to the *quality* of the product presented to an audience. The BBC, for example, routinely spends more on its content than small satellite TV stations. As a result, it produces more varied content with higher production values. Programming costs also vary between different forms of media and this can affect how content is selected and presented. Rewriting corporate press releases, for example, is much cheaper than investigative reporting. Similarly, two people sitting on a sofa chatting is less expensive than producing original TV drama.

The delivery of some physical media, such as newspapers, magazines and books, also places limits on content. Print media, for example, has space restrictions, with additional costs related to the production of extra pages that do not apply to new media such as websites. Technological costs are another factor that affects both production and distribution. A global media company can select programming from a wide range of sources. Individuals producing small websites or blogging about events in their local community do not have such a wide range of sources.

Competition between media can affect the selection and presentation of content in two main ways:

- *Intra-medium* competition involves companies working within the same medium capturing or losing different kinds of content.
- *Inter-media* competition involves content being tailored to the strengths of a particular medium. Music, for example, is packaged differently on radio than on websites, where a visual dimension can be added.

Most forms of privately owned media rely on advertising income in order to make a profit. As such, they are unlikely to behave in ways that upset their principal advertisers. Chomsky (1989), for example, documented how pressure from US advertisers resulted in articles and programmes being withdrawn or 'amended'. Similarly, Lee and Solomon (1990) point to examples of pressure by advertisers: 'In 1989, Domino's Pizza cancelled its advertising on *Saturday Night Live* [an American satirical TV programme] because of the show's alleged anti-Christian message'.

Political factors

While political factors in democratic societies may not have a direct influence on the selection and presentation of media content, many governments lay down basic rules governing acceptable and unacceptable content. China,

for example, operates strict censorship rules across a range of media and subjects; news outlets are banned from mentioning events such as the 1989 Tiananmen Square democracy protests, and web content unacceptable to the state is also blocked.

Democratic governments rarely use direct media censorship, except in 'national emergencies'. However, various forms of covert censorship often occur. Many governments, including the UK and the USA, do not allow state secrets to be published. More usually, media content is *regulated* through a variety of legal rules covering areas such as publishing, broadcasting and advertising.

Media content is also covered by legal restrictions on what can and cannot be published, relating to things such as:

- copyright – whether or not something like a book, song or film can be freely copied and distributed
- libel – what can be legally written about someone.

Ideological factors

In the previous section, we examined the role of the media through a Marxist/pluralist duality. These ideas provide a theoretical context for understanding ideological factors related to the selection and presentation of media content.

'News' is not simply something that waits to be discovered. What counts as news is socially constructed and determined – an event only becomes news when someone with the power to apply this label decides it is newsworthy. This, in turn, is determined by ideological rules that classify events in particular ways – as 'news' or 'not news', for example. These rules are guided by a set of organisational demands, or 'news values'.

News values

Chibnall (1977) defines these news values as 'the criteria of relevance which guide reporters' choice and construction of newsworthy stories, learnt through a process of informal professional socialisation'. Thus these values are determined by organisational needs that translate into the professional codes used by editors and journalists to guide their assessment of media content. In this respect, particular news values directly influence how and why certain types of information are selected and presented as news (Table 8.1).

TEST YOURSELF

Define the term 'news values', using two examples to support your definition.

News values	Meaning
Galtung and Holmboe Ruge (1973)	
Frequency	Visual media feature fast-moving stories with lots of action.
Size	Scale and importance; larger = more newsworthy.
Unambiguous	The easier an event is to simplify, the more likely it will be defined as news. Complex events reduced to simple, clear, issues ('good' and 'bad').
Meaningfulness	The closer the fit between an event and an audience's cultural background, the more newsworthy it will be.
Consonance	The ability to predict or want something to happen makes it news. If the predicted events do not happen, that is also news.
Continuity	Stories need a context, such as a past and a future.
Chibnall (1977)	
Immediacy	'News' is what is happening now.
Adventure	The more dramatic an event, the more likely it is to be news.
Personalisation	'Important people' (such as celebrities or politicians) are given more attention and prominence in different media. Stories also have more value if they have a 'human interest'.
Titillation	Sex sells some newspapers, magazines and TV programmes.
Convention	Events can be explained in ways that are familiar to an audience.
Structured access	Reporters and experts have more opportunity to define the meaning of an event. Hierarchies of credibility mean greater importance is given to some definers or news than others.
Novelty	Unusual or rare events are more newsworthy.
Lanson and Stephens (2003)	
Weight	An event's significance in relation to other, current, stories.
Controversy	Arguments and debates increase newsworthiness.
Usefulness	Does the story help people understand the meaning of something?
Educational value	Extent to which people are taught something.

Table 8.1 Selection of different news values

Theories

For pluralists, news values are evidence of consumer choice and diversity because they reflect the demands of the audience. For example, people who read the *Times of India* do not want pictures of topless women or trivial stories about minor American celebrities. This idea can be extended to all forms of media content. The news values of perezhilton.com, for example, reflect an audience demand for celebrity trivia.

For Marxists, news values are evidence of how audiences are shaped and manipulated – they learn to want whatever the media decides is newsworthy. From this perspective, news values are shaped by the ideological demands of owners. This can be linked to the argument that while owner intervention is subtle and indirect.

Owners offer 'guidance' and 'discussion' with senior editors on issues such as hiring journalists who reflect the owner's views.

News values, therefore, are linked to the political and economic beliefs of owners, and they broadly determine the overall political stance of a newspaper, magazine, TV channel or website. This, in turn, is linked to how media producers influence audience demands.

Agenda setting

In a media organisation, the editor is responsible for ensuring that the news agenda set by owners is followed. The editor is also responsible for making sure that journalists understand and conform to organisational news values. **Agenda setting** concerns decisions about what and what not to report. Where a media company relies on advertising for its profitability, agenda setting also includes keeping advertisers happy. In the UK the closure of the *News of the World* in 2011 was partly prompted by the catastrophic withdrawal of advertising it suffered after it was discovered that journalists from the newspaper had hacked the mobile phone of a murdered schoolgirl.

> ### KEY TERM
>
> **Agenda setting:** neo-Marxist concept that argues that decisions made by editors and owners about what and what not to report 'set the agenda' for how the general public receives and perceives news.

Legitimating values

While editors play an important **gate-keeping** role content selection does not end there. The role of journalists, for example, is not simply to gather and report the news. They interpret the meaning of an event for their audience. Hall (1980) argues that journalists offer a preferred reading, one aspect of which, Chibnall suggests, is to legitimate values: positive and negative ideas that provide cultural cues that 'tell' an audience how to interpret meanings. In this respect, positive/legitimate and negative/illegitimate values structure how an audience reads media content (Table 8.2).

> ### KEY TERM
>
> **Gate-keeping:** the ability to limit access to the media. An editor's gate-keeping role, for example, involves making decisions about what counts as 'news' as well as policing the news values of particular organisations.

Positive values	Negative values
Consensus	Conflict
Moderation	Extremism
Order	Disorder
Honesty	Corruption
Communication	Spin
Good	Evil
Democracy	Dictatorship

Table 8.2   Positive and negative legitimating values

Source: Chibnall (1977)

TEST YOURSELF

Briefly explain how journalists use legitimating values to tell an audience how to read a news story.

Discourse

Fiske (1987) defines a 'discourse' as a way of representing the world from a particular viewpoint. In other words, a discourse reflects the ideas, beliefs and values of specific, powerful groups. Discourse is generally used by postmodernists to show how the media creates a framework for audience interpretation. Making certain values appear legitimate for example, structures how an audience receives information and, by so doing, shapes how such information is understood. Part of the purpose of a news discourse is to define the concept of news. Once this occurs, further refinements take place, including defining the meaning of certain things such as 'good or evil'. The definition of meaning indicates to an audience how they are supposed to interpret something and, in some instances, determines their response to whatever is being presented as news.

An example here is Cohen's (1972) concept of **folk devils**, people who are believed to threaten the established moral order. While different societies produce different folk devils, examples include:

- the poor, constructed in ways that blame poverty on the individual
- welfare claimants who 'play the system' to support 'leisure lifestyles'
- immigrants who 'fail to integrate' into a dominant culture
- terrorists who threaten 'our way of life'.

> ### KEY TERM
>
> **Folk devils:** individuals and groups singled out for special attention and blame because they are seen to represent a challenge or threat to the existing moral order.

Folk devils are a way of creating a sense of social solidarity in a population by identifying people 'not like us'; they are 'outsiders' or 'the Other'. The selection and presentation of relatively powerless groups as folk devils in a news discourse is generally done in the context of a moral panic (see page 268).

ACTIVITY

Using a selection of newspapers, identify the news values they employ. Do different types of newspaper aimed at different audiences use different news values?

259

Debates about the relationship between the media and the state

Debates about the relationship between the state and the media occur between three main groups:

- Marxists, who see the media as either an instrument of the state or as an institution whose beliefs and interests are closely aligned to a ruling class and its control of state institutions.
- Pluralists, who generally argue that the media in most societies is relatively free from state control. The media enjoys a level of autonomy, particularly in capitalist democracies, that leaves it free to criticise the activities of the powerful or pursue ideas that go against the particular interests of governments and political parties.
- Postmodernists, who argue that the increasingly global nature of the media makes it largely immune from the control of nation states.

Marxism

Eriksen (2004) argues, that the state is not a 'neutral framework for struggle and compromise'. Rather, state power is directed towards promoting and maintaining values favourable to a ruling class. It pursues this objective in two main ways:

1 Through its 'monopoly of violence', the power of the state is used to maintain unequal class relationships, either directly for instrumental Marxists such as Milliband (1973), or indirectly for hegemonic Marxists such as Poulantzas (1975).
2 Through its ability to exert ideological control over a population. In this context, the media is, again directly or indirectly, an agency of state control. Althusser (1971), for example, sees the media as an **ideological state apparatus (ISA)**; the state attempts to directly assert the interests of a ruling class through an interlocking relationship between the political and economic members of this class. Milliband believes that this class shares a common cultural background and economic interest; hegemonic Marxists such as Poulantzas, on the other hand, suggest that the media enjoy a *relative autonomy* from ruling class control.

> ### KEY TERM
>
> **Ideological state apparatus (ISA):** Marxist concept that argues that institutions such as the media propagate values favourable to the interests of a ruling class in capitalist societies.

The media may advocate ideas and policies that go against the particular, short-term interests of a ruling class, but in the long term their behaviour is closely aligned with the economic and political interests of the bourgeois class of its owners and controllers. In this respect, the role of the media is one of 'policing capitalist values' to maintain and reproduce capitalism as an economic system. If this involves making concessions to the working class, such as a minimum wage or legal trade unions, they must be made in order to ensure the stability of capitalist society.

Glasberg (1989) sees this general position in terms of 'state capture', the idea that 'capitalists control key positions within the political structure to attain their goals and further their interests'. The media is only separated from the state by its specific functions. Owners and controllers recognise their common economic, political, and ideological interests as an integral part of the bourgeoisie. As such, they can be trusted to act in ways that reflect those interests. This ideological role, therefore, involves such things as promoting core values that:

- justify social inequality
- marginalise dissent
- marginalise alternatives to capitalism
- socialise exploited groups to accept their exploitation
- scapegoat 'minority groups' – both ethnic and class – as a way of setting one section of the working class against another.

Mechanisms: The ideological relationship between the media and the state is based on three types of selective media mechanisms:

- Negative selection mechanisms exclude anti-capitalist ideas and proposals, such as worker control of the economy. These are rarely given prominence or serious consideration in the media.
- Positive selection mechanisms promote ideas favourable to a capitalist class. A recent (2013) UK example is the promotion of government welfare reforms as part of an 'austerity drive' to repay national debt created by the global banking crisis.
- Disguising selection mechanisms maintains the illusion that the media is neutral by suggesting that it reflects all points of view and the interests of 'society as a whole'. Antagonism to industrial action, for example, is frequently couched in terms of 'preventing public disorder'. By hiding the former, which might appear

partial and unreasonable, in the latter (no reasonable person could be in favour of public disorder), the media message is effectively disguised.

How does the state influence media content?

In modern capitalist societies, therefore, the state is rarely required to exercise direct control of the media, because it can usually be trusted to 'do the right things'. Instead, the state establishes legal rules and regulations that both preserve relative media autonomy – making it appear to be independent of state control – and set the boundaries for media behaviour in case some sections decide to exercise that autonomy.

Pluralism

Pluralist approaches generally see the role of the state in capitalist societies as an 'honest broker' between various sectional interests. The state's role is to mediate between these interests – to balance the interests of a media based on ideas such as freedom of speech with the interests of those whose activities are reported. This involves the idea of a representative state – one that reflects the interests of different, competing groups, and in so doing, represents the interests of society as a whole.

The state is neutral in terms of how it relates to different groups. It does not, for example, necessarily favour one group, such as a business elite, over another, such as trade unions. What the state does, however, is act to resolve conflicts between these groups. The state, therefore, consists of a set of politically neutral institutions, such as a civil service and judiciary, that can be directed, but not directly controlled, by governments to modify the behaviour of sections of society such as the media. As Held (1989) puts it: 'The state becomes almost indistinguishable from the ebb and flow of bargaining and the competitive pressure of interests'.

The media's role is to co-ordinate social resources, through the institutions and machinery of government, to maintain order in three ways:

1   Politically – to ensure that where competing groups exist, the state sets out the conditions under which each can operate. For example, there are regulations governing fair competition and levels of media ownership. The objective, at least in capitalist democracies, is to ensure that all voices can be heard and interests represented. Where the media reflect a plurality and diversity of ideas and interests, the choice about which to consume is left to the individual.

2   Legally – to regulate potential conflicts. The state acts to balance the interests of a free media with the interests of businesses, groups and individuals through laws relating to things like copyright and libel. Disputes between different interest groups, such as a newspaper and an individual or group, can also be settled legally.

3   Socially – in the sense of maintaining the conditions under which different institutions, such as the media, can operate in an orderly way to fulfil their social functions, responsibilities and obligations.

More specifically, once the state has set and guaranteed certain behavioural boundaries, the media is free to act out its general role in pluralist societies. This role includes:

■   helping to maintain democratic ideas and institutions through criticism and assessment of different political parties and polices

■   checking the behaviour of political and economic elites by exposing things like corruption

■   maintaining a separation between economic ownership of the media and political control.

TEST YOURSELF

Suggest two differences between Marxist and pluralist explanations of the relationship between the media and the state.

New-right approaches

New-right approaches are similar to pluralist approaches. However, they take particular issue with the role of government in relation to media ownership. Government ownership is seen to work against the interests of consumers by distorting economic markets. Where public broadcasters are guaranteed funding from the taxpayer, they do not have to compete against private media corporations for viewers and revenue. From this perspective, government media ownership limits or removes competition at the expense of consumer choice.

The new right believes that processes such as media convergence, where different types of media organisation combine to create newer forms of media, should be encouraged. State regulation governing or preventing cross-media ownership stops companies developing these new technologies. Anything that hinders the working of economic markets is undesirable, because only free markets can deliver innovation and economic development. Although state regulation is generally something to be resisted, where some form of **media regulation** is required, this is normally expressed in two ways:

KEY TERM

Media regulation: the rules whereby governments attempt to control areas like media ownership and output.

- Self-regulation where, in terms of newspaper publishing, Meyer (2003) argues: 'Any infringement of self-regulation would not just erode the freedoms of the press, it would curtail the freedoms of the citizen, who will always depend on media uninhibited by both control by the state and deference to the establishment to protect their liberty.'

- Market discipline, which involves the idea that where consumers reject the ideological content of the media they will either not buy it or will seek out media that does fit their ideological requirements.

TEST YOURSELF

Suggest one way in which government ownership of the media may work against the interests of consumers.

Postmodernism

This approach represents a different view of the relationship between the state and the media, mainly because globalisation and the development of new globalised forms of media make any relationship problematic. McCluhan and Powers (1989) claim that

in a world which increasingly resembles a 'global village', the media cannot be subject to controls that restrict the free flow of ideas and information.

How is the world like a global village?

Where postmodernism differs from other perspectives is in the characterisation of information structures. Whereas modernism views information *hierarchically*, the flow is from producers at the top to consumers at the bottom, postmodernism sees it in terms of networks. Castells (1996) suggests that 'networks have become the dominant form of social organization'.

For this reason, power – in terms of control over the production and distribution of information – is no longer concentrated within *institutions*, such as the state or media, but within *social networks,* where it is both produced and consumed by the same people. Information, therefore, flows between different nodal points (people) within a network in ways that make it impossible to distinguish between producer and consumer. They are, increasingly, one and the same. This clearly makes state regulation difficult, if not impossible, on both a national and global scale.

Tuomi (2002) suggests that a significant feature of postmodern media is that content reflects interpretation; how different people in the network interpret information contributes to media development. The implication here is that we must not consider modernist concepts such as truth or falsity when thinking about the ideological role of the media and its relationship to the state, because all knowledge is ideological.

On a global scale, therefore, the media propagates, controls, organises, criticises, promotes and demotes (marginalises) a variety of competing narratives, all of which are true and all of which are false. In a situation where knowledge, as Sarup (1993) argues, is 'fragmented, partial and contingent' (relative to all other forms of knowledge or dependent on your particular viewpoint) information cannot be tightly controlled by the state.

Information can, however, be *managed*. Just as some forms of old media, operating within particular national boundaries, attempt to organise information in line with a range of political, economic and ideological discourses promoted by the state, the same is true of the state itself. The state's relationship with all forms of media becomes one of managing something – information and data – that cannot be safely and simply controlled as it perhaps once was.

ACTIVITY

'Some state regulation and censorship of the media is necessary to ensure the physical and moral safety of its citizens.' How might this statement be viewed from different perspectives?

The impact of the 'new media' on society

We can consider the impact of new media by looking at the features that make it 'new', the issues raised by new media forms and the implications of changing technologies on economic, political and cultural behaviour.

Features

As Socha and Eber-Schmid (2012) argue: 'Part of the difficulty in defining New Media is that there is an elusive quality to the idea of new.' Crosbie (2002) suggests that three features of new media make it qualitatively different from old media:

- New media cannot exist without the appropriate (computer) technology.
- Information can be personalised; individualised messages tailored to the particular needs of those receiving them can be simultaneously delivered to large numbers of people.
- Collective control means that each person in a network can share, shape and change the content of the information being exchanged.

As an example, Crosbie suggests 'Imagine visiting a newspaper website and seeing not just the bulletins and major stories you wouldn't have known about, but also the rest of that edition customized to your unique needs and interests. Rather than every reader seeing the same edition,

each reader sees an edition simultaneously individualized to their interests and generalized to their needs.'

New media can also be truly global in scope and reach. Older technologies like TV and film do of course have global features – the US and Indian film industries, for example, span the globe – but they are fundamentally local technologies. They are designed to be consumed by local audiences that just happen to be in different countries. In contrast, new media, such as websites and social networks, are global in intent. They enable global connections through the development of information networks based on the creation and exchange of information. A significant aspect of these global features is the ability to create and share text, images, videos and other content without being hindered by physical borders.

Essentially, new media has a different emphasis, one that breaks down the conventional 'old media' producer–consumer relationship and reinvents it in ways that blur the boundaries. In networks such as Facebook and Twitter, the consumer is the producer. New media thus has much higher levels of **interactivity** between consumers and in terms of how users relate to different forms of media technology.

 KEY TERM

Interactive media: media, such as video games, that allow the user to influence the direction and flow of debates, actions and outcomes.

Linearity

On one level, old media is a linear technology. Information, such as a film, song, newspaper/magazine article or television programme, has a start, middle and end and the consumer must follow this linear logic. New media, however, has the capacity to organise information differently, through a non-linear or nested logic – information placed inside other information. Hypertext, for example, allows information to be organised and explored in non-linear ways rather than, as Socha and Eber-Schmid argue, 'simply following a straight order'. This gives the user, rather than the producer, the potential to control how information is received and developed.

On another level, new media connects all kinds of information – text, images, sound and video – in many different ways across a global network. A key feature, therefore, is interconnectedness, not just of information but also of people. A good example of this is the development of Wikipedia, a free non-linear online encyclopaedia created by its users and which anyone can edit.

New media also empowers its users by encouraging creativity. With old media, creativity resides with the producer, such as a director or author, and flows in one direction only – from producers to consumers. New media changes this flow of information. Whether it is digital publishing or social networks such as Flckr or YouTube, the consumer is also the producer.

What are the advantages and disadvantages of linear/non-linear texts?

TEST YOURSELF

Identify and explain two features of new media.

Issues

The various features of new media raise a new set of issues for both producers and consumers. For example, the development of global computer networks has presented problems for media industries whose products are relatively easy to copy and distribute digitally. The development of peer-to-peer networks has led to the rise of global forms of intellectual property theft ('piracy'). Media conglomerates have responded to this in a range of ways:

- Legal prosecutions of individual offenders and attempts to shut down sites, such as Napster and Megaupload, from which consumers could download illegal copies of music, film and TV programmes.
- The development of new economic models. 'Freemium' models, for example, provide a free service, such as software or a game, but users then pay a premium

for 'added extras'. Popular Facebook games, such as Farmville, have successfully taken this approach.

A further issue is the unauthorised access to computers and networks ('hacking'). This involves:

- Governments: cyberwarfare, for example, is when governments engage in the politically motivated hacking of rival government computer networks for reasons that range from espionage to sabotage.
- Organisations: in 2010, the US government claimed that the cybertheft of copyrights and patents by China remained at 'unacceptable levels'.
- Individuals: viruses and malware designed to damage computers, extort money or steal information.

One of the main issues for consumers is personal privacy. Social media such as Facebook makes money through advertising, which can now be targeted to individuals through the sale of users' personal data to third parties. Users, therefore, exchange 'free' services for some loss of privacy. While corporations such as Facebook simply monitor how their network is used in terms of what an individual likes or dislikes, discusses or avoids in order to deliver adverts matched to these behaviours, Kosinski et al. (2013) have shown it is possible to accurately infer a wide range of personal information from an analysis of an individual's 'likes'. This includes information such as ethnicity, IQ, sexuality, substance use and political views.

In this respect, Socha and Eber-Schmid argue that new media is 'characterized by an astonishing and uncharted level of personal experience/exposure. Online companies and sites can track the content of personal emails and site visits in order to target advertisements on users'. There are also websites whose sole purpose is to compile and share personal data with web surfers. A further privacy issue is the rapid spread and persistence of online data. Once data is released into the wild of the web, whether in the shape of sites, blogs, tweets or tagged photos, it is difficult, often impossible, to erase or withdraw it.

While these ideas represent one form of surveillance, more explicit forms are facilitated by new media technology. The state, for example, may monitor its citizens to identify which websites they visit, who they email or who they talk to using voice over internet protocols (VoIP) such as Skype. Digital transmissions are relatively easy to intercept and read, especially if they are unencrypted. Surveillance targets, from environmental activists to political parties, may not realise that they are being monitored. Monitoring 'from above' (surveillance) is an issue, therefore. However, so is monitoring 'from below' (sousveillance) – a situation arising from the ability of smartphone and tablet technology to record and publish people's everyday behaviour.

A greater willingness and ability to share information online also leaves people open to forms of surveillance such as digital stalking and bullying. Neelamalar and Chitra's (2009) study of Indian college students and their use of social networks like Facebook does, however, suggest an 'awareness of the danger and risk involved in using these sites'. They interpret this as 'a positive indicator Indian youth are not only techno-savvy and socially active through social networking sites but they also possess social consciousness'.

Suggest one issue raised by new media that does not apply to old media.

Implications

The development of new media has led to a general debate about the impact that changing technologies have on economic, political and cultural life. This debate revolves around two opposing views: digital optimism and pessimism.

Digital optimism

From this viewpoint, the defining characteristic of new media is a form of *digital liberation* that Negroponte (1995) claims is based on four processes:

- decentralisation
- globalisation
- harmonisation
- empowerment.

These processes impact on society in a range of ways.

In economic terms, we see the development of new models of production, distribution and exchange, particularly 'free' or 'gifting' models, where the consumer pays nothing to use a medium. One significant new model is the development of open economic systems where software, for example, is developed collaboratively to take advantage of wide creative pools of talent. Tapscott and Williams (2008) call this 'Wikinomics', in acknowledgement of the pioneering collaborative efforts of Wikipedia.

Producers – especially large corporations – have to be more responsive to consumer demands because the ability to act as a global crowd, passing information swiftly from individual to individual, means corporate behaviour

is continually being monitored, evaluated and held to account. Surowiecki (2005) argues that digital technology assists crowd-sourcing. This process is based on 'the wisdom of crowds': if you ask enough people their opinion, a basic 'crowd truth' will emerge.

Politically, the global flow of information weakens the state's hold over individuals and ideas. Repressive state actions are much harder to disguise or keep secret when populations have access to instant forms of mass communication, such as Twitter. The internet also makes it harder for the state to censor or restrict the flow of information. This contributes to **political socialisation** because people have a greater understanding of the meaning of issues and events.

Political socialisation: the various social processes involved in the teaching and learning of political ideas and practices.

Culturally, behaviour can be both participatory *and* personalised. The global village combines collectivity with individuality; co-operation flourishes while people simultaneously maintain what Negroponte calls the 'Daily Me' – the personalisation of things like news and information focused on the specific interests of each individual. Personalisation contributes to participation by encouraging a diverse individuality that leads to the development of new ways of thinking and behaving. The fact that people can be anonymous on the web encourages both freedom of speech and whistle-blowing.

Digital pessimism

An alternative interpretation argues that the globalising processes on which new media depends are neither wholly beneficial nor unambiguous. While globalisation involves decentralising processes, for example, it also produces greater centralisation across economic, political and cultural behaviours.

In economic terms, 'free' business models are only free in the sense that their costs are hidden from the consumer. These costs include the following:

- Exploiting free labour – the news and opinion site *The Huffington Post*, for example, was built around the free labour provided by its blogging contributors; the site was sold by its owners for $300 million in 2011.

- Driving down quality – companies that cannot rely on cheap or free labour must either cut their costs, thereby potentially undermining quality, or go out of business.
- Privacy – new media that depends on free labour, such as social networking sites where consumers create content, make money by selling user data to advertisers.
- Copyright – some corporate social media sites lay claim to the copyright of user-generated content, such as photographs and videos, that can then be sold to advertisers.

New media ownership is sometimes likened to what Socha and Eber-Schmid call 'the growing pains of the American Wild West', where a diversity of companies compete for market share. However, the situation may really be similar to that of old media, where large corporations exert considerable control over the choices made by consumers. For example, owners of internet search engines, such as Google, use various techniques to discourage consumers from switching to other service providers. A further similarity between the behaviour of old and new media corporations involves two related processes:

- locking out competitors from markets
- locking in consumers to products.

An example of both is Amazon's development of an eBook reader (the Kindle) that gave the company control over who could publish eBooks for this product and how consumers could use the product (to buy eBooks from Amazon).

Conglomeration is a related process that mirrors the behaviour of old-media corporations. The highly concentrated ownership of new media allows global corporations to buy up competitors or emerging technologies. Schecter (2000) claims that this leads to a decrease in digital diversity in areas such as news production. As he argues: 'The internet is not very diverse, even though it appears to be. The concentration in ownership that is restructuring old media has led to conglomeration in news transmission and a narrowing of sourcing in new media. It is cheaper for Web sites to buy someone else's news than generate their own.' It is also 'cheaper' for global corporations to take and republish content generated by individual users with little or no prospect of recompense.

Politically, mass communication tools can be used by repressive regimes to restrict individual freedoms and enhance various forms of state surveillance. For example, GPS technology be used to track both the online and offline behaviour of users. The 'wisdom of crowds'

equation can be applied to the development of a 'hive mind', where individual dissent is not tolerated. In addition, the 'stupidity of crowds' is emphasised in terms of their being more prone to moral panics based on 'mob rule'.

ACTIVITY

Create a poster to demonstrate either digital optimism or digital pessimism. Present your poster to the class, debating the pros and cons of these two views.

Media representation and effects

The role of the media in the representation of social groups and ideas, with particular reference to class, gender, ethnicity and age

Modernism

A modernist context for understanding **media representation** is based on the belief that objects and ideas have an essential reality that can be identified and compared to representations of 'the real thing'. For example, there is a Taj Mahal in Uttar Pradesh, India and a Taj Mahal in Atlantic City, USA. The former is a religious shrine while the latter is a hotel. Despite being designed to mimic the architecture of the real Taj Mahal, the building in Atlantic City is clearly just a representation of the original that would not be mistaken for the real thing. Applying this logic to the media, something can be represented in one of two ways:

- accurately, by describing it as 'it really is', such as in a photograph
- inaccurately, through deliberate or accidental *misrepresentation*.

KEY TERM

Media representation: the various ways the media portray ideas, individuals and groups.

When examining modernist notions of media representations, it is important to assess the extent to which categories like class, age, gender and ethnicity are accurately or inaccurately represented.

Class

Media representations of social class take a range of forms, with different classes stereotypically represented in different ways. The working class, for example, is routinely represented through a relatively narrow and limited range of identities:

- historical, such as popular costume dramas that focus on servitude, poverty and criminality
- contemporary, where a similar range of themes recur, with working-class life represented through socially problematic behaviours such as crime, welfare dependency, unemployment, violence and sexual promiscuity.

Recurrent themes, from news reports, through documentaries to entertainment shows, represent the working classes as:

- dangerous – people to be feared because of their unpredictability
- problematic in terms of their involvement in illegal/ immoral behaviours
- dependent on both the state and the tolerance and generosity of the middle and upper classes.

Representations rarely portray the *ordinariness* of working-class life, preferring instead to focus on a narrow range of situations that are occasionally positive, such as professional sport, but more usually negative.

Middle-class representation is generally broader, ranging across professional employment and cultural associations such as music, fashion and art. Such representations help to link class associations with culture. Lower-class **popular culture** is represented as:

- manufactured
- artificial
- superficial
- disposable
- undemanding and culturally valueless.

KEY TERM

Mass/popular culture: the 'culture of the masses', as opposed to the high culture of a ruling elite, characterised as simple, worthless, mass-produced and disposable.

Middle- and upper-class cultural life is represented as a high cultural reflection and opposition of low culture:

- difficult
- demanding

- deep
- long-lasting
- culturally valuable.

A related dimension here is the marginalisation of working-class life. The Glasgow Media Group's study of television reporting of industrial disputes, for example, argued that the working classes had less direct access to the media and less control over how they were portrayed. If they were represented at all, it was usually in a negative way. Marginalisation can also be seen in the way that dramas and documentaries largely ignore or erase working-class life and contributions to historical movements. Instead, these programmes tend to focus on the actions of upper-class historical figures. For example, British history is largely represented in film, television, newspapers and books through the thoughts and actions of royalty and the aristocracy.

Contemporary forms of invisibility exclude working-class life through a focus on the interests, actions and activities of business leaders, middle- and upper-class politicians and philanthropists. Where the working classes feature in accounts of social and economic development, they are more likely to be cast as beneficiaries of middle-class help and advice or as subjects for discussion by middle-class 'experts' about working-class vices. In contrast, middle-class identities are often represented by virtues such as resourcefulness, productivity, culturation and helpfulness. These virtues are displayed in relation to the 'less fortunate', from teaching them how to discipline children to how to find work. Members of the working class are represented as subjects of middle-class power and control. They are portrayed as dysfunctional, dependent and socially problematic, while the middle class is purposeful, independent and socially supportive.

Aggregations: Stereotypes, or one-sided representations, of working-class life are aggregated – they are applied to the class as a whole. Ehrenreich, for example, argues that, for the media, to be 'working class' means being:

- inarticulate
- old-fashioned
- uneducated
- lazy
- incapable.

KEY TERM

Stereotype: the practice of assigning particular, one-sided, partial, characteristics to whole groups, regardless of their individual differences.

She suggests that these representations silence working-class voices, making them both literally and metaphorically dumb.

Higher-class aggregations are more positive, highlighting their virtues as a class. Problematic behaviour – greed, selfishness or criminality – is represented as indicative of individual human weaknesses rather than symbolic of a whole class. The 2008 global financial crisis, for example, is generally represented in terms of the actions of a few 'rogue bankers' rather than indicating fundamental and wide-reaching social problems caused by middle- and upper-class behaviour.

TEST YOURSELF

Suggest two ways in which working- and middle-class media representations differ.

Age

Youth: Ownership and control of national and global media is often characterised as middle-aged, middle-class, and male. This idea of power and control suggests that representations of young people are largely constructed through an 'adult gaze'. How this power is used, however, varies across time and space. Contemporary societies, in particular, demonstrate high levels of ambivalence about childhood and youth:

- On one level, children are represented in terms of their innocent and uncorrupted nature.
- On another, they are represented as unruly, lacking self-control and requiring adult discipline and guidance.

Both forms often feature in relation to youth and new technologies, including cinema, television and computers. In relation to the internet, for example, children's perceived innocence combined with (adult) technological fears results in children being seen as victims of their own lack of control and discipline, through exposure to a variety of ideas and experiences that they are not equipped to deal with. This can lead to **moral panics**. As Pearson (1983) demonstrates, moral panics about the behaviour of young people and technology have been a persistent feature of media representations over the past century, involving traits like:

- rebellion
- disrespect

- selfishness
- obsessions with self and sex.

KEY TERM

Moral panics: heightened sense of fear of behaviour seen as a threat or challenge to the moral order in society. 'Terrorism', for example, may be considered a contemporary form of moral panic in Western societies.

Aggregate or collective representations frequently represent male youth as delinquent and politically apathetic. Representations are also mixed, which reflects both changing social *mores* and youth as a fragmented category, with clear divisions across categories such as class and gender. Representations of young working-class males tend to be very different from those of young middle-class females.

A particularly dominant form of representation over the past 40 years has been the distinction between normal and abnormal youth. Normal youth are defined in opposition to various spectacular youth sub-cultures such as Mods and Rockers, Skinheads, Hippies and Punks, which enjoyed a short time in the media spotlight. Contemporary representations also focus on celebrations of youth. These might take the form of rebellion from adult rules and responsibilities, vibrant social change, or adults' perception of youth as a highly desirable physical state.

How is youth represented positively and negatively in the media?

Old age: As with youth, the elderly have traditionally been represented in a narrow range of roles, with a particular emphasis on social problems. Their problematic status has recently been constructed around how the burden of an ageing population affects the rest of society through the increasing costs of state pensions, hospital treatment and social care. Individually and collectively, their representation is also largely unsympathetic, based on images of:

- senility
- illness, both mental and physical
- unattractiveness.

Willis (1999), for example, notes how representations of older people are 'often crudely stereotyped in television drama', with fictional portrayals showing them as grumpy, interfering, lonely, stubborn, not interested in sex, silly (especially older women) and miserable.

A reverse form of gendered stereotyping also occurs when elderly men are used to add a sense of seriousness/ moral gravity, particularly in news coverage.

Although these images can still be seen in some parts of the media, in others, the changing nature of representation is reflected in more sympathetic portrayals that reflect the changing nature of media audiences. Willis notes that the elderly watch more television than other social groups and they increasingly demand programming that reflects their interests. Their lack of representation in areas like popular drama and film has also changed in response to wider social changes.

Changing representations of older women are particularly apparent. This group, traditionally portrayed as objects of pity, charity, social work and the medical profession, are increasingly represented as fashionable, active and *sexual* beings. While numbers alone do not guarantee positive representations, two further reasons make this more common:

- The elderly are an increasingly affluent population segment; the Institute for Fiscal Studies (2006) estimated that around 80% of wealth in the UK is held by those aged 50+ and the 'global grey pound' is attractive to the advertisers who fund large areas of the media.
- Television as an important mass medium is a relatively new phenomenon and, as the people who own, control and work in it grow older, their interests are reflected in new and different representations of the elderly.

TEST YOURSELF

Briefly explain what is meant by the 'adult gaze' and how it relates to representations of youth.

Gender

Gender stereotypes relating to masculinity and femininity generally focus on two areas: physical and emotional. While traditional representations tend to reinforce clear gender differences, contemporary representations occasionally display a greater gender convergence.

Physical representations of bodies were traditionally focused on women, but they are increasingly relevant to men. These representations are important in two ways:

- how they have changed – the greater frequency with which *male bodies* are represented, especially by advertisers, as sexually desirable for women and culturally desirable for men
- the way in which they have *not* changed: female bodies are still used to sell everything from cars to camping equipment, and men are still allowed a greater range of acceptable body shapes.

Body representation forms part of a wider set of ideas about beauty, attractiveness and how women in particular should look and behave. This is particularly relevant in unstated assumptions that female beauty is both heterosexual and largely for the benefit of what Mulvey (1975) calls 'the male gaze'. This reflects the idea that female lives are viewed, sometimes literally, through a masculine lens and controlled by male needs and desires. The male media gaze defines feminine identities in ways that are attractive to men. Where the media shapes social perceptions of femininity, it follows that there are important consequences if women are unable or unwilling to match these perceptions. One aspect of media-defined femininity that encapsulates age inequality is the association between attractiveness, desire and youth. Young women are portrayed as 'objects of desire', but elderly women are not.

Ferguson (1983) studied the influence of women's magazines on perceptions of femininity. She suggests that women's magazines socialise women into a 'cult of femininity' by focusing on such topics as beautification, child-rearing, housework and cooking. McRobbie (1981) carried out a similar study of magazines aimed at teenage girls. She found that these magazines rely on a formula of written stories, photo-stories and problem pages. The central message is that girls should focus on capturing and thinking about boys. The male is portrayed as dominant while the female is passive, adapting to the interests and needs of the male.

Grant et al. (2006) suggest that women face 'a double jeopardy of age and gender discrimination' that has a different impact on women of different ages. Younger women, for example, face a range of pressures – how to look, dress and behave, to conform to media notions of femininity. Older women must confront the problem that if women are defined by their sexuality, attractiveness and desirability, they suffer from a diminished identity once they lose these characteristics.

In the Western world, advertisements for food and household goods have often reflected perceptions of gender in society

Media representations often reflect broader assumptions about male and female behaviour. For example, women should be co-operative and submissive, and dominant females are often represented as figures of fun or (deviant) sexuality. Macdonald (2003) notes a particular category of female ('ladettes') that challenges these stereotypes and breaks down gender barriers. It does so through representations emphasising women's ability to behave in the same way as men. This suggests that gender representations are 'not static and woman are permitted to take on certain masculine behaviours in certain situations'. 'Abnormal representations' may, however, simply prove the general rule. Female sexuality, for example, is routinely used to sell consumer goods, employing an exaggerated form of (hetero)sexuality that combines the physical, such as thinness, and the emotional, such as patriarchal notions of 'availability'.

Gauntlett (2002) argues that there are increasingly positive aspects to media representations. He suggests, for example, that the media is 'within limits, a force for change'; traditional stereotypical representations of women have been replaced by 'feisty, successful "girl power" icons', while male representations have changed, from 'ideals of absolute toughness, stubborn

self-reliance and emotional silence' to a greater emphasis on emotions, the need for help and advice and 'the problems of masculinity'.

Ethnicity

One feature of ethnic representation in the Western media is the gradual disappearance of crude stereotypes and demeaning representations of 'black people'. While overt racism is no longer tolerated, Hall (1995) argues that it has been replaced by inferential racism – black ethnicities are represented in ways that stress their *cultural*, rather than *biological*, difference. Part of this representation involves their 'problematic nature': minority ethnicities are represented as the source, rather than victims, of social problems. This, in turn, reflects two forms of representation:

1 Over-representation, according to Klimkiewicz (1999), in areas such as news and fiction as perpetrators and victims; UK news reporting of Africa, for example, represents black ethnicities as:

   ■ victims of 'natural disasters' such as floods and famines
   ■ perpetrators of man-made disasters involving wars and corruption.

   In this context, ethnic minorities are mainly viewed through a white, middle-class and male gaze. In news reporting, this frequently represents whites as saviours, through things like government and public aid/charity.

2 Under-representation in areas such as advertising and drama. Sweney (2011) reports that 'Actors from black, Asian or other ethnic minorities appeared in just 5% of UK TV ads'. Sreberny (1999) argues that contemporary television representations involve 'two-dimensional characters, often negatively stereotyped'. Morris (2000) illustrates this through the experiences of Roma minorities – criticised for *not* fitting the stereotype of the 'true' Gypsy while simultaneously represented as 'dirty, thieving, parasitic and living outside the law'.

The white gaze: Carrington (2002) claims that the white gaze extends to apparently positive black images constructed around cultural spaces such as sport, fashion and music. He calls these representations of hyper-blackness which promote stereotypes of black bodies solely in terms of 'athleticism and animalism' (the idea these features of black excellence are 'natural').

A further aspect of the white gaze is the representation of ethnic minorities in terms of their 'Otherness' – how

'They' are different from 'Us'. This is usually constructed in terms of cultural difference as the cause of social problems. Gilroy (1990) refers to this as a new racism that focuses on cultural differences. Where scientifically discredited notions of race focused on biological differences such as skin colour, new racism is based on differences in language, religion and family life. 'Otherness' is also represented by threat:

- cultural threats that challenge a dominant, white, way of life through practices such as arranged and forced marriages or the notion of Shari'ah law, a legal system based on Islamic religious principles
- physical threats in terms of terrorism and criminality. Hall et al. (1978), for example, note moral panics about 'black muggers' in the 1970s and, more recently, the claim by the Metropolitan Police (2002) that mugging in London is 'predominantly a black crime'.

Postmodernism

Modernist approaches consider representations in terms of how and why they *misrepresent* particular groups. However, Baudrillard (1995) argues that representations cannot be assessed in terms of whether class or gender is accurately or inaccurately represented because how something is represented *is* its reality.

Modernist approaches suggest that the media represents something like 'ethnicity' in ways that distort its reality – 'the real' is compared to its media representation in order to distinguish it from the 'not real'. Baudrillard suggests that this approach is mistaken on two levels:

1 It assumes that things in the social world have a reality beyond how they are represented. In the physical world, for example, we can look at the original, authentic, Taj Mahal and compare it with the various ways it has been represented through inauthentic copies, such as the Taj Mahal hotel. Concepts such as class or ethnicity, however, have no 'authentic' reality because they are social constructs, the product of how they are initially described and represented. All the media does, therefore, is construct *representations of representations*.

2 'Reality' is experienced differently depending on who you are, where you are and your source of information. Every audience constructs its own version of reality, and everything represented in the media is experienced as multiple realities, all of which – and none of which – are *authentically real*. Everything is simply

a representation of something seen from different viewpoints. The reality of anything – class, age, gender, ethnicity – cannot be found in any single definitive account or experience.

Hyper-reality

Baudrillard uses the term **hyper-reality** to express how different narrative accounts interweave and conflict in a constantly changing pattern of representations built on representations. Eventually they form a 'reality' in themselves – something that is 'more real' than the reality it purports to describe. For example, if we change how a concept such as age is represented, we change its reality.

KEY TERM

Hyper-reality: postmodern concept that argues that the media creates realities that are 'more real' than the ones they purport to represent. Our 'knowledge' of the American Wild West, for example, is filtered through the lens of Hollywood film, just as our knowledge of Africa may be filtered through media images of famine, war, corruption and poverty.

TEST YOURSELF

Briefly explain the term 'hyper-reality'.

Each reality is constructed from the way in which individuals pick and choose different ideas to suit their own prejudices or beliefs. Baudrillard calls this process *simulacra* ('representations that refer to other representations') – simulations that are the reality they depict. To talk about media representations as distortions of a hidden or obscured 'reality' ('*deep structures*') misses the point. The media does not simply 'mediate the message' through representations; as McCluhan and Powers (1992) argue, 'they *are* the message'.

This idea is important in relation to the social construction of media content, because this content involves a representation of reality that Fiske calls the 'transparency fallacy'. This is a rejection of the idea that reporting of something like ethnicity offers a neutral 'window on the world' that describes an objective reality. The world represented through the media is always and inevitably a reconstructed reality. It is filtered through a media lens that is no more and no less objective than any other reality filter.

How is Disneyland an example of hyper-reality?

Power

Modernism considers power in the context of how institutions such as the media use it to impose representations of class, gender, age and ethnicity on the powerless. Postmodernists argue that power over the production and distribution of information is no longer concentrated within institutions, but within social networks. Essentially, this means that information is produced and consumed by the same people. Information flows between different points (nodes) within a network in such a way as to make it impossible to distinguish between producer and consumer. This idea challenges modernist notions of power that centre on class (Marxist) and gender (feminist), and which claim that misrepresentations flow from this centred control of information.

In postmodernity, there are many centres of information, each of which disseminates different representations. There are no dominant forms of representation because there are no dominant forms of media any more. What we have, in a media-saturated society built on information structures and networks, is a series of shifting representations of these categories. They are no more and no less real than whatever they represent.

ACTIVITY

Using a selection of newspapers, identify how they use stereotyped pictures and language to represent different classes, ages, genders or ethnicities.

Social patterns in listening, viewing and reading

How people use the media – listening, viewing and reading – is related to two particular social contexts:

- The nature of social development, considered in terms of what Baran and Davis (2011) call the strong association between media use and 'social and demographic variables like age, sex, social status and education'.
- Levels of technological development, considered in terms of the range and type of media and content available for consumption within any given population.

The relationship between these two forms of development is significant. In the past, the take-up of media, such as television, was closely related to factors such as income and social status. Television receivers were expensive and the new medium represented a form of conspicuous consumption that suggested a higher level of social status. Current technological take-up, in the shape of computers, smartphones and broadband internet access, is still linked to class, in that these can be expensive technologies so individuals must have a certain level of income to afford them. However, an arguably more significant development is the relationship between media use and age. Newer technologies, for example, have a much lower age profile than older technologies. OfCom (2008) found that 'under-45s tend to be more engaged with digital media'. Over the past century, there has been a change from vertical population splits based on class to horizontal splits based on age, gender and ethnicity.

TEST YOURSELF

Make a list of ways in which differences in technological development between societies help explain differences in their patterns of media use.

Digital convergence

In basic terms, activities such as listening, viewing and reading remain separate – people listen to music, watch television and read newspapers using different media. However, new technologies have forged a convergence between these activities because they allow different types of media to be consumed on the same device and at the same time.

Access measures	Indian	Pakistani	Black Caribbean	Black African	UK total
Multiple platform (TV, internet and mobile)	62	65	55	62	53
Digital TV ownership	83	89	81	82	82
Mobile phone	90	91	88	95	85
Internet use	76	72	64	69	62
Willingness to get internet	25	35	30	30	15

Table 8.3   UK adult media use by ethnic group

Source: OfCom (2008)

Are patterns of listening, viewing and reading converging with new media?

Listening

Despite being one of the oldest forms of media, audio (radio, hi-fi and new technologies such as MP3 players) remains popular all over the world (Table 8.4). While China ranks lowest for radio/hi-fi listening, it ranks highest for MP3 usage, which suggests that emerging nations may embrace newer technologies and bypass the older ones. The age profile for radio listening in the UK is skewed towards older listeners; those over 55, for example, listen to almost twice as much radio as those aged 15–24.

	Radio	Hi-Fi	MP3 player
Germany	76	22	32
USA	74	21	33
UK	69	30	36
China	44	18	49

Table 8.4   Percentage of adults who regularly consume audio

Source: OfCom (2012a)

A further point to note is the rise of online radio listening and the development of streaming radio services such as Spotify (with both free and premium services). Spotify currently averages around 2 million listeners per month, with a range of competitor services averaging between 0.25 and 1 million listeners.

If we consider the global market for something like radio, OfCom (2007) notes that among the BRIC nations (the emerging markets of Brazil, Russia, India and China) 'where access to television is not ubiquitous, the role of radio in society can be more akin to that of television in the West'. In India, for example, 'radio listening is growing rapidly and now enjoys a weekly reach of around 27%, a figure comparable to newspaper readership'. The most popular FM radio station in India, Akashvani, has around 68 million listeners per week, despite only being available to around 30% of the population.

Reading

In many countries there has been a significant long-term decline in the percentage of the adult population reading a daily newspaper. More specifically, there has been a decline across all sections of the newspaper market. One feature of this particular market is its horizontal splits, with marked readership divisions occurring in relation to:

- **Age:** The long-term age profile of newspaper readership in the UK is rising, with some, such as the *Telegraph*, having around 75% of their readership in the 50+ age group. A similar pattern emerges in US readership, with a gradually ageing newspaper profile.
- **Gender:** Slightly more men than women read a daily newspaper, although this hides a wide range of readership differences across different newspapers.
- **Ethnicity:** Newspaper readership in India, for example, is divided by language. The most popular newspaper, *Dainik Jagran*, has around 17 million readers and publishes in Hindi, *Malayala Manorama* (around 10 million readers) publishes in Malayalam, while the *Times of India* is the most popular English-language

newspaper (around 5 million readers). One complicating factor to note here is geographic location; accessibility to newspapers, radio and television is directly proportional to regional geography. In mountainous regions, for example, there is greater exposure to television and radio, and less to print media.

In terms of vertical splits, readership patterns broadly reflect three 'cultural divisions of taste' identified by Lynes (1949):

- Highbrow refers to 'superior and refined' tastes and represents the highest cultural forms to which a society should aspire.
- Middlebrow refers to the mediocre that aspires to be highbrow but which lacks originality, subtlety or depth.
- Lowbrow involves the brutal and worthless aspects of a culture that lack any pretence at sophistication, insight or refinement – cultural forms that are characteristic of 'the masses'.

While these categories were intended to be *satirical*, they fit quite well with class patterns in newspaper content and readership. Those at the lower end of the market attract far more working-class readers than those in the middle and top.

OfCom (2012b) notes that 'the general trend is falling engagement with print formats' as a whole, accompanied by a substantial increase in online newspapers. The *Mail*, for example, is the most visited newspaper site in the world, with around 50 million visitors each month. The next most visited are, in order, the *Chinese People's Daily*, the UK *Guardian* and the US *New York Times*.

Newspapers across the globe are also migrating from print to digital formats, through smartphone and tablet-based apps. This has resulted in a wider readership and people spending more time reading. As OfCom (2012b) suggests, 'the platforms are not necessarily substitutional, and indeed might be considered complementary'.

TEST YOURSELF

Suggest reasons for 'falling engagement with print media'.

Viewing

Television was and remains a hugely popular leisure activity in modern industrialised countries, with around 85% of adults watching in their free time. It is an equally popular medium for all age groups, although the elderly are the highest consumers. This is probably because a higher proportional of this age group are housebound, but it may also be because alternative forms of leisure are increasingly aimed at a younger, generally more affluent, audience.

More recently, the development of digital television has expanded the range and scope of services to include many more channels, high-definition channels, video-on-demand services, such as sporting events and films, and digital video recording.

Globally, this has resulted in both a changing television audience, drawing a greater proportion of younger viewers, and different levels of access to digital television, for which some country data follows:

- UK: 90%
- USA: 80%
- India: 25%
- China: 25%

This situation is likely to change in the near future, however. India, for example, is due to enact a digital changeover from analogue services in 2016.

While television remains a significant source of news for global populations, patterns of viewing differ markedly between developed and developing nations. Average daily consumption figures include:

- USA: 280 minutes
- UK: 225 minutes
- India: 138 minutes
- China: 158 minutes.

One significant change in television use in countries such as the UK and the USA, where the technology is well established, is the fragmentation of audiences. Apart from a small number of 'communal events', such as the football World Cup, families are less likely to watch television together. This is partly explained by the much lower cost of television sets, which means that many households now have more than one. However, it is also a result of greater programming diversity introduced by digital technologies.

This change in viewing, away from the communal and onto the individual, is reflected in niche programming introduced by the increased number of digital channels. Programmes targeting specific interests are now much more widely available. Bjur (2009) argues: 'In 1999 social viewing, watching together, accounted for

45%, and in 2008 it was down to 37%. We are becoming more and more individualistic in our TV choices. We can no longer speak of TV as a social adhesive, a unifying force'.

Over the course of seven days, keep a diary that lists your viewing, listening and reading and the medium you use for each. How might your pattern of media use be different from the same diary kept by someone of your age 50 years ago?

Different theories of the effects and uses of the media; hypodermic syringe; uses and gratification; cultural effects studies

In previous sections we have looked at how media content is selected and presented, and considered the role of the media in the representation of social groups. In addition to these factors, it is important to understand the ways in which audiences are affected by the media. If the media has no effect on people's ideas and behaviour, then how content is selected and presented is of little significance. In this section, therefore, we can examine a range of 'media effects' theories, based on categories of direct, indirect and limited effects.

 KEY TERM

Media effects: the various ways in which the media affects or influences people.

Direct effects

Models that argue that the media has a direct and tangible effect (usually a negative one) on behaviour are sometimes called media-centric. Older forms of this model suggest a relatively simple, direct and effective relationship between media and the audience.

Hypodermic

Hypodermic syringe or *magic bullet* models argue that media messages are like a drug injected into the audience's mind. This implies that messages are transmitted and received by an audience in ways that change or reinforce their ideas and behaviour. Media messages, therefore,

determine how audiences see and understand the world in a directly measurable causal fashion.

 KEY TERM

Hypodermic syringe: media-effects theory that argues that media messages are like a drug injected directly into the audience's mind in ways that change their behaviour.

The media (cause) transmits information and the audience reacts (effect) in a broadly predictable way that can be directly attributed to the message received. Audiences, therefore, are seen as passive receivers rather than active interpreters of media messages. This is based on the concept of mass society. Where people are socially isolated, they have few strong links to social networks, such as family, friends, work colleagues or wider communities, that can provide alternative sources of information and interpretation. Audiences are receptive to whatever the media transmits because their social isolation means they depend on it for information.

Cumulation theory is a variation of this basic idea that suggests that media effects are cumulative, rather than immediate. Prolonged exposure to violent films or games can result in both changed behaviour and desensitisation. The more someone is exposed to media violence, for example, the less likely they are to be moved, shocked or appalled by real violence.

275

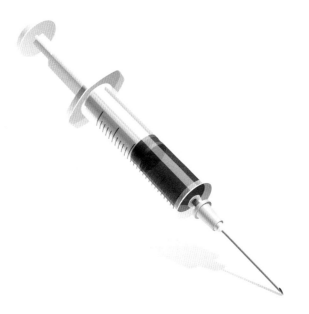

How are media messages directly injected into an audience?

Transmission

Transmission models developed by Shannon and Weaver (1949) suggest that the transmission process is split into two parts:

- the information source (such as a government announcement)
- the transmission source (such as a newspaper or television report of the announcement).

Media messages can have different sources: *direct* reporting might involve a newspaper printing a speech made by a government minister, while *indirect* reporting involves the speech being selectively quoted to support a particular story. The source of the message, in other words, will significantly affect how it is received. It is also possible for audiences to be indirectly affected by a media message through their interaction with people who are directly affected. These are people who pass on media messages through conversation with those who have not personally experienced them. This introduces concepts of noise and interference – anything that distracts from or interferes with the transmission of a message. The media can introduce noise through selective reporting, while audiences may receive the same message in different ways, both directly and indirectly. Transmission models are a more sophisticated explanation of media effects than their hypodermic counterparts because, although they suggest direct effects, these are mediated and modified through different channels and sources. This makes it more difficult to measure the exact effect of the media.

Gauntlett (1998), however, suggests that all transmission models have a basic flaw: they see audiences as uncritical individuals, easily influenced by whatever they read, see or hear. Gauntlett also suggests that the empirical evidence for direct media effects is weak, partly because most research takes place under artificial conditions, such as a laboratory. These do not adequately represent the real situations and contexts in which people use the media (an ecological fallacy):

- Bandura et al.'s (1961) 'Bobo doll' experiment is frequently cited as evidence that watching televised violence produces violence in children. One of the weaknesses of the study was that the children were 'rated for violence' by adult assessors, which raises questions about the objectivity of the research.

- Belson (1978) also claims that prolonged exposure to media violence produces violent behaviour in young males. Hagell and Newburn (1994), however, found a general lack of interest in television among young offenders.

The focus of direct-effects models has also changed in recent times. It has moved away from general audiences and towards the idea of *vulnerable audiences*, children in particular. The argument here is that their lack of social experience and tendency to copy behaviour makes children more susceptible to direct media effects (and copy-cat violence in particular) than adults. Evidence for direct effects tends to be *anecdotal* – the media claims, rather than proves, a relationship between, for example, violent behaviour and violent play. Gauntlett (1995) demonstrates how even very young children may be media literate – they have an understanding about the media and how it works. For example, most children can distinguish between fictional and factual representations of violence.

TEST YOURSELF

Suggest one way in which the media might directly affect people's behaviour.

Indirect effects

Cultural-effects models suggest that while effects are strong in the long term, they are slow, cumulative and operate through the media's ability to become part of an audience's cultural background. The more the media plays a valued role in everyday interaction, the greater the consumption, and the stronger the long-term influence.

KEY TERM

Cultural-effects model: neo-Marxist theory that argues that although media effects are strong in the long term, they are slow, cumulative and operate through the ability to become part of an audience's cultural background.

These models see the media as a cultural (or ideological) institution whose primary role is to promote and police cultural values. The media is an agent of social control the ideas that it propagates decisively influence people's behaviour. Newbold (1995), for example, argues that the media acts at the institutional (large group) level of society, not at the level of individual beliefs. It exercises social control through its actions as a socialising agency, advising and guiding audiences and, by so doing, exercising a hegemonic role.

Cultivation: Cultivation theory suggests that television, in particular, cultivates distinctive attitudes and orientations in its audience over time, rather than directly determining behaviour. People who watch a lot of television gradually take on board the beliefs and attitudes to which they are exposed. If crime is constantly portrayed on television, people become fearful of crime in ways that are out of all proportion to their risk of becoming a victim to it. For Chandler (1995), the media 'induces a general mindset' around particular areas of social life, such as crime, taking on a hegemonic role where some beliefs are encouraged and others discouraged. Attitudes and behaviour do not change overnight, however. Media effects are gradual, long term and built up through a range of techniques:

- the consistent promotion of particular ideas
- the marginalisation of dissenting views
- the repetition of ideas until they taken for granted (to the point that, for example, 'everyone knows' crime is increasing).

According to this perspective, the media leads people towards particular ideas and ways of thinking. As Gerbner et al. (1986) suggest: 'The continual repetition of patterns (myths, ideologies, "facts", relationships, etc.) serve to define the world and legitimize the social order'. **Audience reception** theory is an example of this type of model. It is based on the idea that media messages always have a range of possible meanings and interpretations. Some of these are intended by the sender (a newspaper owner or an author, for example) and others are read into the message by the audience. As Hall (1980) argues, even simple media texts, such as an advert, involve:

- encoding – the ideas the author wants an audience to grasp
- decoding – how an audience interprets or decodes the message, depending on factors such as their social background or the context in which the message is received.

KEY TERM

Audience reception: media-effects theory based on the idea that media messages always have a range of possible meanings and interpretations, some intended by the sender and others read into the message by the audience.

A receiving audience always has some choice about whether to accept or reject a message. Their receptiveness, however, depends on a range of personal and social factors. Hall suggests three main ways a media message is read by an audience: **hegemonic codes**, **negotiated codes** and **oppositional codes**. (**Professional codes** of presentation also package the message in a recognisably professional format.)

KEY TERMS

Hegemonic codes: the audience shares the assumptions and interpretations of the author and reads the message in the way it is intended.

Negotiated codes: although an audience broadly shares the author's views, they modify their interpretation in the light of their own particular feelings, beliefs or attitudes.

Oppositional codes: an audience is antagonistic towards the author and therefore rejects or attempts to challenge the message.

Professional codes: the values used by editors and journalists to guide their assessment of media content and presentation.

This basic set of responses is, however, complicated by three further media processes:

1. Agenda setting: McCombs and Shaw (1972) argue that the media identifies and selects the ideas people are encouraged to think about. It has the power to put certain issues 'up for discussion' while attempting to close down issues they do not want discussed.

2. Framing involves presenting ideas to audiences in ways that suggest how they *should* be interpreted. Audiences are primed to understand issues and ideas in terms of what Simon and Xenos (2000) call 'elite discourses': how media owners and controllers want their audiences to understand an issue. This may involve, for example, highlighting certain opinions while marginalising or ignoring others.

3. Myth making: Gerbner (1994) argues that the media has grown so powerful and pervasive in global societies that it creates *mythical realities* for audiences who immerse themselves in media content. The heavier an individual's media consumption, from watching television, reading newspapers, surfing the web or social networking, the more likely they are to be drawn into a 'fantasy world' of the media's creation, such as believing crime and violence are more prevalent than they actually are.

TEST YOURSELF

Suggest one way the media might indirectly affect people's behaviour.

Limited effects: Audio-centric or diffusion approaches focus on how audiences *use* the media to satisfy particular needs. These approaches suggest that the media has few, if any, measurable effects, an idea neatly summarised by Berelson et al.'s (1948) observation that 'some kinds of communication on some kinds of issues brought to the attention of some kinds of people under some kinds of conditions have some kinds of effects.' Diffusion theories focus on how media messages spread across an audience through a trickle-down effect. Although messages originate with media producers, they are received by an audience in two ways:

- directly, such as personally viewing a news broadcast
- indirectly, through interaction with those who directly received the message, other media sources reporting the original message and so forth.

In other words, an original message is continually relayed throughout an audience and, at each stage of the retelling, the message may be subtly changed or reinterpreted.

Two-step flow: Katz and Lazarfield (1955) suggest a **two-step flow model**, in which messages flow in two distinct steps:

1 From the media to opinion formers – people who directly receive a message, such as a news report, are interested enough to want to relay it to others and influential enough for them to take note of the message.

2 From opinion formers to people in their social network, those who receive the original message in a mediated form – edited, condensed, embellished – from people like family and friends (*primary groups*).

KEY TERM

Two-step flow model: normative model of media effects that argues that messages flow from the media to opinion formers, who then interpret such messages for people in their social network.

In this **normative model** of media effects, Katz and Lazarfield argue 'informal, interpersonal relations' are the key to understanding how mass audiences responded to media messages. Any behavioural changes result from how messages are interpreted, discussed and reinterpreted within primary groups, rather than from any direct media influence. This idea is supported by Shannon and Weaver's concept of noise; the original message easily becomes lost, over-simplified and misrepresented through social interactions. In this respect, Klapper (1960) concludes that mass communication 'does not serve as a necessary and sufficient cause of audience effects.' Rather, it functions in highly selective ways, in terms of:

- perception – people notice some messages but not others
- exposure – people choose media messages consistent with their beliefs
- expression – people listen to the opinions of people important to them
- retention – people remember things that fit with their beliefs and forget those that do not
- selection – some messages are never relayed.

 KEY TERM

Normative model: model of media effects that argues that the key to understanding how mass audiences respond to media messages is through a knowledge of how messages are filtered through informal, interpersonal relationships.

Reinforcement Theory is related to flow/diffusion models in that it focuses on the social context of media use. How the media affects people depends on the social groups to which they belong. Klapper, for example, argues that people's beliefs are related to their social groups (primary groups being the most significant). One important role of a secondary group such as the media was to reinforce, either positively or negatively, the beliefs already formed. This suggests a very limited type of 'media effect'.

Uses and gratifications: This model takes the separation between media and audience a step further by arguing that consumers pick and choose both media *and* messages; they use the media for a range of gratifications. McQuail et al. (1972) suggest four primary **uses and gratifications**:

- Entertainment – as a **diversion** from everyday life.
- Social solidarity – talking about a shared experience, such as seeing the same film or television programme or playing the same online game, serves an integrating function by making people feel they have things in common.

- Identity – to create or maintain a sense of 'who we are'. It is a resource, from reading lifestyle magazines to maintaining a Facebook presence, used to construct and maintain and project a sense of self.
- Surveillance – providing news and information about an increasingly complex world.

KEY TERMS

Uses and gratification: normative model of media effects that argues that consumers pick and choose both media *and* messages. The media are used by audiences to gratify their own particular uses and needs.

Diversion: break from everyday life, to relax, for mental stimulation and so forth.

Severin and Tankard suggest another use – companionship – when they found the heaviest media users were those who were lonely or socially isolated.

Overall, therefore, the uses and gratification model suggests the media is:

- powerless, in terms of its ability to directly influence or change behaviour
- neutral, in the sense of not having any direct effect on attitudes
- unimportant as far as researchers are concerned, since the object of study is the active *audience* rather than the media.

Although the idea of active audiences is important in understanding media effects, particularly as they relate to old media, its significance may be overstated in two respects:

- Stam (2000) claims that limited effects models 'essentialise the audience' by giving them an unwarranted and unsupported primary significance in terms of how media messages are interpreted.
- Diffusion models suggest the media has few, if any, effects, yet advertisers spend billions each year precisely because they believe the media has clear and direct effects that can be measured in terms of sales.

ACTIVITY

Divide into groups. Each group should produce a diagram to summarise the main features of one theory/explanation of how the media affects audiences. Groups can then comment on the effectiveness of each other's diagrams and suggest improvements.

Impact of the media on behaviour, violence, deviance amplification

Conventional analysis of the media's impact on behaviour tends to focus on its *negative* impact. This ranges from encouraging violence to creating a docile, manipulated audience. However, it also important to understand the positive effects that the media can have.

Negative impacts

There are three key ways to view negative media impacts:

- Across society as a whole, which involves noting some general economic, political and cultural negatives.
- Across social groups – as an example we can look at how the media contributes to moral panics.
- At the individual level, where we can look at the media as a causal or contributing factor to violent behaviour.

Societies

In economic terms, large media corporations divide up global markets and operate as oligarchies that:

- prevent entrance to media markets
- restrict competition
- limit consumer choice.

Lechner (2001) argues that this creates media homogenisation by developing a 'consumerist culture, in which standard commodities are promoted by global marketing campaigns to create similar lifestyles'.

Politically, one impact of new media in particular has been the extension of surveillance and a loss of personal privacy. Governments and private companies have exploited the capacity for information gathering afforded by new media to extend population surveillance. Mobile phone and satellite technology, for example, can be used both to track individuals and to monitor their contacts, while social networking sites collect, store and sell extensive personal information about users to advertisers.

Culturally, global media is encourages a cultural hegemony that colonises local cultures with the products and lifestyles of dominant cultures. One example of this is the global domination of the US film industry or the influence of brands such as Coca-Cola and Nike. On a more individual level, Kraeplin (2007) notes how 'popular teen magazines link appearance and consumerism'. Here, globalised media contributes to the development of a consumption culture in which the buying of goods and services, from mobile phones to social networks funded by advertising, is an end in itself.

These negative impacts are explained by traditional Marxists in terms of manipulation theories. These suggest that the media directly influences audience perceptions and beliefs. In a mass society characterised by social isolation and alienation, the media becomes a source of mass culture through the agency of what Adorno and Horkheimer (1944) term a 'culture industry'. Audiences are uniquely receptive to whatever the media transmits because there are few links to alternative sources of information. The media reflects other forms of industrial production in capitalist society by creating various elements of a popular culture, such as film, magazines, comics and newspapers. These are all consumed uncritically and passively by the masses. Through control of the culture industry, a ruling class controls the means of mental production, and populations, as Schor (1999) puts it, are 'manipulated into participating in a dumbed-down, artificial consumer culture, which yields few true human satisfactions'.

Deviance amplification

Wilkins (1964) developed the concept of **deviance amplification** to show how the development of crime and deviance involves a positive feedback loop:

- initial or primary deviance is identified and condemned by the media, which leads to …
- the deviant group becoming socially isolated and resentful. This behaviour leads, through a general media labelling process, to …
- an increased social reaction (including the development of a moral panic) by the media, politicians and formal control agencies; there is less toleration of the original deviant behaviour. This develops into …
- secondary deviation, involving an increased level of deviance. As a consequence …
- the reaction from the media, politicians and police increases, leading to new laws (the criminalisation of deviants) or increased police resources to deal with 'the problem'.

> ### KEY TERM
>
> **Deviance amplification:** theory of deviance that argues that a range of social reactions, particularly those orchestrated through the media in terms of moral panics, have the effect of creating more serious forms of crime.

In this way, each group, deviant and control, feeds off the actions of the other to create a 'spiral of deviance'. Moral panics created by the media are a crucial component of this.

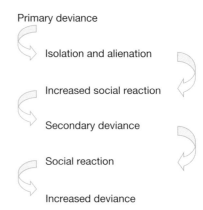

Primary deviance

Isolation and alienation

Increased social reaction

Secondary deviance

Social reaction

Increased deviance

Deviancy amplification spiral

Moral panics: Cohen (1972) defines a moral panic as a situation in which 'a condition, episode, person or groups of persons emerges to become defined as a threat to societal values and interests'. Although the media is central to the development of moral panics, their precise role is explained differently by different sociological approaches.

Interpretivist approaches see 'societal values' as emerging from day-to-day interactions and experiences – people construct the social world in terms of a range of ideas that are simply taken for granted. Goode and Ben-Yehuda (1994) argue that interpretivists see moral panics arising from 'anxiety in the grassroots of communities'. The role of the media in modern societies is to express public concerns. By representing groups that threaten social cohesion as 'deviant', the media focuses public concern and leads control agencies such as the police and courts taking action. According to this perspective, moral panics develop spontaneously out of a general public concern towards behaviour that threatens the that moral order. Cohen suggests that moral panics reinforce established moral values in two ways:

- by setting moral boundaries for acceptable behaviour
- by creating a sense of social and moral solidarity at a time of change and uncertainty.

This approach sees the media as a channel that amplifies, rather than creates, public concern. Media audiences are seen as 'active and critical' consumers rather than passive recipients of media representations. If an audience chooses to ignore media concerns, a deviancy amplification spiral does not occur. Hilgartner and Bosk

(1988) argue that responsibility for moral panics is also shifted away from the media because a range of social problems exist in any society at any given time. Any of these social problems may cause public concern and lead to moral panic. Those who 'work in various public arenas attempt to surf on the shifting waves of social problems'. Whether one form of behaviour or social group is targeted for action by the media depends on those occupying middle levels of power, such as police officers, politicians and civil servants, convincing media outlets that a problem exists – something they do to enhance their own power. Those who are seen to resolve a moral panic gain prominence.

Neo-Marxist approaches examine moral panics across two dimensions:

- How and why they are created by powerful groups.
- How they contribute to the maintenance of elite hegemony.

Neo-Marxists understand moral panics as political phenomena – the defence of a certain type of moral order defined by a ruling class but shared, to varying degrees, throughout society. Moral panics are an important way for a ruling class to exercise control, by focusing condemnation on a particular 'moral threat'. While moral panics are in some ways manufactured as **media sensationalism**, this does not mean they are necessarily deliberately created. At various times, capitalist societies offer up opportunities for moral panics and elites take advantage of these to criticise those who threaten both moral order and, by extension, ruling-class hegemony.

KEY TERM

Media sensationalism: process whereby the media attempt to increase the dramatic content of an issue or story.

For Hall et al., opportunities for moral panics occur at times of economic, political and ideological crises in capitalist society. Their function is to distract public attention from the real causes of such crises by generating panics around groups and behaviours that create easily identifiable scapegoats or 'folk devils'. These people are relatively powerless and can be subjected to physical control on a tide of 'public moral indignation'. This type of crisis is rare, however, and a more mundane explanation for moral panics is that they represent periodic attempts

to establish moral order by taking action against those who challenge it. In relation to deviancy amplification, for example, this operates on two levels:

- the surface reality of different types of deviance
- the deeper reality of promoting a particular kind of moral order.

These two levels are linked, of course, and expressed through the agency of the media. To protect and enhance the moral order, folk devils must be identified and blamed. Scapegoating performs two main functions:

- It distracts attention from 'real moral issues' (such as large-scale social inequalities).
- By allowing the full force of control agencies to be directed at moral deviants, the public is both co-opted and warned; behaviour that challenges the existing moral order will be met with force.

From this perspective, moral panics trigger increased surveillance and control of subject populations through both the media and other control agencies. In addition, such steps are taken with the consent and co-operation of those being controlled. Rather than being a cause of moral panics, deviancy amplification is actually a result of it. Where the object of moral panics is usually seen as deviants, for neo-Marxists, the real object of control is the population as a whole.

Why is the behaviour of young males frequently the object of media moral panics?

In this way, the media is responsible for creating moral panics, with the intention of controlling the behaviour of those who support action against deviants. Each panic results in greater levels of control, until a situation is reached where public surveillance and control is an integral part of everyday life in a way that is both welcomed and accepted in order to ensure 'public safety' – which, for neo-Marxists, means 'the interests of powerful elites'.

Livingstone and Hargrave (2006) suggest that the media plays a significant role in the development of moral panics. They note that contemporary concerns over 'teenage boys shooting classmates, fears of increasing xenophobia [hatred of 'foreigners'], rising levels of obesity or appalling murders with sexual elements are commonly linked back to the (mis)use of particular types of media content, be they delivered by film, television, the internet, advertising or even print'. There are, however, other causal links between the media and these negative effects:

■ Television – there is some evidence to suggest that 'under certain circumstances, television can negatively influence attitudes in some areas, including those which may affect society (through the creation of prejudice) and those which may affect the individual (by making them unduly fearful, for example)'.

■ Video – there is evidence that consumption of 'violent (non-consensual) pornography' results in 'more negative or aggressive attitudes and behaviours towards women as well as supporting the desire to watch more extreme content', although the evidence for the effect of viewing online pornography on children is limited.

■ Internet – while this is a wide-ranging form of media, there is some evidence that various forms of harm exist, from online bullying to 'the grooming of children by paedophiles'. Violent video games have also been linked to the development of violent behaviour in young and 'vulnerable' adults with 'particular personality disorders', although this, as we will see, is disputed.

Violence

The idea that exposure to violent media, from television and internet depictions of real-life violence to violent films and video games, contributes to or causes violent behaviour, especially among vulnerable groups, is a pervasive one across many cultures. However, evidence for this is not as clear-cut as some sections of the media suggest.

Theories: One of the most common connections between the media and violent behaviour is *imitation*. This explanation stems from social learning studies such as Bandura et al.'s 'Bobo doll' experiment. Different groups

of children witnessed an adult behaving violently. The play of each group was then observed and it was discovered that those children shown violent behaviour subsequently played violently. This leads to the idea that immature and vulnerable audiences simply imitate the behaviour they see. This explanation that recurs throughout various media from time to time:

■ In the USA, for example, two students, Eric Harris and Dylan Klebold, shot dead 12 of their fellow students at Columbine school in 1999. Their actions were subsequently explained in some parts of the media as a consequence of playing 'violent video games', *Doom*, in particular.

■ In the UK, the murder of three-year-old James Bulger in 1993 by two 10-year-old boys was attributed, by the judge at their trial, to a violent horror film called *Child's Play 3* rented by the father of one of the boys and which it was assumed they had watched. There was no evidence they had.

Cultivation theories, Chandler (1995) notes, involve the idea that 'heavy media consumption' cultivates attitudes that are 'more consistent' with the content being consumed than with the mundane reality of everyday life. Heavy consumers of violent films and television, or those who spend a lot of time playing violent, immersive, video games, develop a 'violent mindset'. These individuals see the world as a more violent place than it actually is, and this can induce violent real-world behaviour. Gerbner (1994) argues that powerful and pervasive media in global societies creates mythical realities for audiences, and heavy media consumers find it difficult to distinguish media myth from reality. They are drawn into a world where reality is distorted and violence is constantly presented as a glamorous solution to individual and social problems.

Social-developmental models reject the idea that there is a relatively simple one-way relationship between the media and violence (i.e. that media violence makes people more susceptible to real violence). Huesmann and Miller (1994), for example, argue that there is a more complex, reciprocal, relationship between the media and the audience. Early social development is influenced by 'cognitive scripts', ideas that people develop through childhood experiences, which tell them how to behave appropriately in certain situations. These scripts are influenced by many different factors, such as whether the individual was subject to violence and abuse during their formative years, or whether they were exposed to violent media. These 'learned scripts' subconsciously determine how people respond to real-world situations. Those whose cognitive scripts involve seeing violence as a way of dealing with problems, for example, are more likely to exhibit violent behaviour in certain situations, such as when they are placed under great stress or fear.

If this is true, it can be difficult to separate cause and effect in the relationship between the media and its audiences. **Discourse analysis**, for example, shows that, while many media discourses argue that 'violent people' consume violent media and then commit acts of violence because of the 'thrill' they get form it, an alternative interpretation is that for certain audiences, violent behaviour is something they are socially programmed to enjoy, whether it is real or imaginary. However, while the two are connected there is no way to tell which causes the other: do people play violent video games because they like violence or do these games make them violent?

KEY TERM

Discourse analysis: method of media analysis that examines how language shapes the way people think about something.

Desensitisation theories are based on the development of emotional responses to media violence. The more a person is exposed to media violence, both real and fantasy forms, the more likely they are to accept real-world violence. This occurs on an individual level, where the desensitised believe that violence is an appropriate response to certain situations. It also occurs on a more general cultural level – these people are more likely to accept violence as 'a way of life'.

TEST YOURSELF

Identify and explain two negative media impacts on behaviour.

Positive impacts

Most interest has focused on the negative impacts of media. However, there is also a range of positive impacts that should not be ignored:

1 Diversions involves the idea the media is used positively for a range of everyday purposes, such as relaxation or entertainment.
2 Education – media can be used for educational purposes, both consciously, for something like

information gathering, and subconsciously, where learning, in its widest sense, is embedded in entertainment such as video gaming.

3 Community – where different forms of media are embedded in everyday life, experience and discourse they are a significant basis for social interaction, such as talking about the latest events in a soap opera, discussing the news or arguing about who should be evicted from reality TV programmes. This shared knowledge helps to create a community of interest in the sense that people feel part of a social group on the basis of their common interests and preoccupations. Even in the virtual world of social networks or message boards, where people may not physically know each other, like-minded people can discuss the things they find important.

4 Identity consolidation – for some, the media is used for identity checking on two levels:

- Individual: where people create or maintain a sense of personal identity through the media they consume. This can involve things such as lifestyle magazines or creating and maintaining a sense of self through the consumption of cultural products such as literature and film.
- Social: the media can define particular forms of social identity, from class, through age and gender to ethnicity, by explaining the meaning of these categories and, in doing so, shaping ideas about individual, communal and national forms of identity.

5 Empowerment – post-feminists have argued that new media can be empowering for particular gender and age groups because it allows greater freedom of personal expression and identity creation. Butler (1990), for example, argues that, where gender scripts were once limited and restrictive, forcing men and women into a limited range of identities, they are now many and varied. Thanks to the media, people have much greater awareness of the different ways they can 'perform gender'. This is also true for perceptions of age-related behaviour. Haraway (1991) takes these ideas a step further with her concept of 'the cyborg'. As people increasingly interact in cyberspace, traditional notions of gender and biology become redundant. How people are connected in cyberspace is more significant than how they are connected in 'the real world' because interaction across computer networks can be *agendered*; gender, as with class, age and ethnicity, can be hidden or disguised.

283

6 Awareness – in a complex world, the media provides news and information that can be used to keep in touch with what is happening. A significant positive impact, therefore, is the creation of a greater global awareness of:

- Economic trends, such as the development of countries like China and India as important production centres.
- Political developments – events surrounding the 2011 Arab Spring, for example, were extensively reported through Twitter in the absence of more traditional media.
- Cultural exchanges involving a greater exposure to and understanding of cultural similarities and differences.

TEST YOURSELF

Identify and explain two positive media impacts on behaviour.

The media may also promote political changes by exposing people to new ideas that makes them question traditional ways of thinking and behaving. Increased media choice and diversity brings with it a willingness to question 'authority'. Lyotard argues that a defining feature of postmodernity is its 'incredulity towards **metanarratives**' such as religion, science or political philosophies, that claim to explain 'everything about something'. Such incredulity, he suggests, means the media is less likely to influence people's behaviour negatively.

KEY TERM

Metanarrative: a 'big story' that attempts to explain 'everything about something' or, in the case of religious and scientific metanarratives, 'everything about everything'.

The ability to make quick, easy and direct contact with like-minded individuals through new media networks also contributes to the general political process through greater participation and activism. New media also change the nature of political representation: the public can not only interact directly with elected politicians, through email and social networks, they can use it to pressurise politicians and parties to act in particular ways. New media open up greater opportunities for discussion and self-expression, giving groups a voice

who may not have had one in the past. This, in turn, has a significant impact on how we understand the deviance of political leaders or large-scale transnational corporations. For example, both are under increasing surveillance 'from below'.

ACTIVITY

Discussion
The negative impacts of the media outweigh their positive impacts.

Problems of researching the effects of the media on audiences

As we have seen researching media effects can be problematic. In this section, we consider this idea in more depth by looking at media definitions, methodology and audiences.

Definitions

In order to research something there must be a broad agreement about how it can be defined. Without such agreement, it is impossible, for example, to compare different explanations of media effects because they may be measuring different things. While there is a tendency to see 'the media' as a relatively simple, homogeneous, category, closer analysis reveals this is not the case. Contemporary forms of media are characterised more by their diversity than their similarity. Although we could define the media simply in terms of 'mass communication', this hides a range of differences in how and why the media communicates with an audience. These differences are important in assessing how we can measure the effects of the media. In this respect, media diversity relates to two main areas:

1 Different types of media, from newspapers, books and magazines, through television and film to video games and social networks. Research conducted in one medium may have little or no application to other forms of media.

2 Old and new forms of media. The point to consider here is whether consumption of old media, such as a newspaper, is similar to consumption of new media, such as a social network. A significant research problem, therefore, is the changing nature of the media. Both a film and a video game can draw the viewer into a world that only exists on screen, but a video game is interactive – the

audience's actions and choices change how the drama unfolds. This involves both a significant difference in the nature of the media and makes researching effects more difficult, because the distinction between producer and consumer – on which most effects theory rests – is decisively blurred.

So, old and new media do not necessarily affect audiences in similar ways. To put this in context, when researching crime, it is unlikely we would consider the motives for murder as similar to those for car theft. The same is true when studying media effects. The only thing watching a two-hour television drama and spending the same amount of time playing the online video game *World of Warcraft* may share is that they are both classified as 'mass media'.

A second area to note is how concepts like 'violence' are operationalised. This relates to two areas:

- The media portrays many different types of violence, from the real-life brutality of news broadcasts through fictional violence to cartoon violence.
- We cannot simply assume that an audience will interpret representations of violence in a particular way; different audiences may interpret meaning in very different ways depending on their social characteristics, such as class, age and gender, and the context in which the violence is seen.

A third area to note is the meaning of 'an effect'. Just as there is no general agreement about whether effects are direct or indirect, strong or weak, long term or short term, there is no agreement about what is or is not a 'media effect'. Is an effect something that produces a clear and immediate behavioural change in an audience, or one that produces a slow, cumulative change? The problem here is that finding a 'media effect' may owe more to how such effects are studied than to any real change in audience behaviour.

Suggest one way in which changes to the media might affect how it can be studied.

Methodology

If the media is difficult to define and effects difficult to operationalise, it follows that different methods may measure different things to give different results, depending on what the researcher is looking to test. One

set of problems here, for example, relates to whether effects can be measured:

- quantitatively, using something like **content analysis**
- qualitatively, using something like **semiotics**
- using a combination of the two.

KEY TERMS

Content analysis: research method used for the systematic analysis of media texts and communications.
Semiotics: the study of signs, codes and symbols used in communication processes.

A further methodological problem relates to the different meanings and interpretations of media content. For example, a researcher may interpret something in a different way to the audience. This can be a particular problem with new media, if the researcher is less familiar with it than the subjects of their study. Rose (2007) argues that a researcher requires a thorough understanding of their subject matter if they are to identify and understand the **symbolisation**, codes and conventions involved. A semiological analysis of the Indian film industry, for example, would be difficult for a researcher with little or no knowledge of this culture and genre. Alternatively, Livingstone and Hargrave argue that in relation to rap-music lyrics, 'different people do not interpret content in the same way'. For example, there is a difference between the interpretation of 'fans of a genre vs. those who only occasionally view' and this, they argue, makes it 'risky to draw conclusions about media effects'.

KEY TERM

Symbolisation: the idea of conveying meaning through symbols.

How a medium is researched also creates problems when measuring effects. Experiments are unusual situations and respondents may behave differently inside and outside a laboratory's controlled environment. Where research is carried out in a 'natural environment', such as in the home, it still may not be possible to anticipate all behavioural influences. Uncontrolled independent variables range from a simple awareness of being studied to the context in which media is set and consumed. Livingstone and Hargrave also suggest that the

285

consumption context affects how it is experienced and hence its possible effect. This relates to:

- physical consumption – whether this is shared or consumed alone
- mental consumption – how different audiences understand the context of the behaviour portrayed in something like a television programme, for example the extent to which they identify and empathise with those portrayed.

Livingstone and Hargrave believe that one of the problems with media research is that it 'demonstrate[s] short-term effects on attitudes and behaviours, among a particular research sample, such as college students, under particular conditions'. While these effects are real, they question the reliability and validity of generalising results that have been obtained from very specific groups under very specific conditions to large groups under different conditions.

In addition, it is difficult to know how research carried out in one society, such as India or the USA, can be applied to different societies that have different:

- cultures – where there may, for example, be different levels of tolerance to violent and sexually explicit content
- media regulations governing what can be shown in media such as television
- media content.

Research into the influence of the media on violent behaviour is full of methodological problems. Sociological research in this area has usually been conducted through field studies, using questionnaires, interviews and observation. Belson's (1978) study was based upon in-depth interviews with 1565 teenage boys in London. Boys with high television exposure were compared to those with low exposure. Belson drew the conclusion that those boys who had seen a lot of television had committed 49% more acts of violence than those with low exposure. However, Belson's work has been criticised for failing to distinguish adequately between high exposure to television in general and high exposure to violent television programmes in particular. Howitt (1992) has also pointed out that Belson's results actually show that there are three types of viewer: those with light, moderate and high exposure to television. Of these, it was actually those with a moderate level of exposure to violent television programmes who were more prone to commit violent acts.

It appears, therefore, that Belson's work can be interpreted in several different ways. This is a good example of both the methodological difficulties in studying the influence of the media and the difficulty of making direct links between TV violence and social behaviour.

TEST YOURSELF

Briefly explain one methodological problem with studying media effects.

Audiences

Postmodernists take a different theoretical approach by suggesting that conventional effects theories look for the wrong things in the wrong places in the wrong ways. In this respect, they question three major assumptions on which conventional 'media effects' theories are based:

- Undifferentiated mass audiences are now rare; audiences are increasingly fragmented by age, gender and ethnicity, as well as by more individualised categories such as cultural and technological competence. This makes it impossible to think about how 'the media' impact on behaviour.
- Media literacy: conventional effects research generally fails to credit audiences with any understanding of the media they consume, particularly the conventions employed by media producers. For postmodernists, contemporary media users have far higher levels of understanding and cultural competence than consumers in the past and this 'active audience' dimension makes conventional forms of effects research problematic.
- Producers and consumers: conventional effects research takes for granted the distinction between those who produce media and those who consume it. This means that research is designed to measure how one affects the other. This presents two main problems:
  - With various forms of new media in particular, from websites through blogs to social networks such as Facebook, Twitter and Instagram, consumers *are* producers. This makes it increasingly difficult to maintain the distinction on which much conventional media effects research rests.
  - Similarly, there is a tendency to assume a separation between 'the media' and 'the audience', such that the effect of the former on the latter can be quantified. Staiger (2000), however, argues that

audiences are increasingly *perverse spectators* – they use media in their own way and for their own means through activated meanings created by how they interact with media. This creates, in effect, an uncertainty principle: the meaning of a TV programme, for example, is created by how it is consumed, such that the meaning of a drama or news broadcast changes each time it is viewed by different individuals. It is therefore impossible to quantify a media effect in any meaningful or coherent way because, Staiger argues, any 'impact is changed each time it is identified'.

ACTIVITY

Think about how you would design a research activity into the effects of the media on social behaviour. How would this activity differ if it was conducted:

- *in one individual's home*
- *in a single town of 30,000 people*
- *in an entire country.*

How would the context affect what types of evidence you focused upon?

Summary points

Media ownership is split between:
- private ownership
- state ownership.

Two main perspectives on ownership and control are:
- Marxist
- pluralist.

Three main theories of the nature and role of the media are:
- instrumental Marxism
- neo-Marxism
- pluralism.

Theories of selection and presentation of media content are:
- pluralist:
  - consumer choice and diversity.
- Marxist:
  - agenda setting
  - legitimating values: positive and negative
  - gate-keeping.
- postmodern:
  - discourse
  - narratives.

Debates about the relationship between the media and the state:
- Marxism:
  - instrument of the state
  - delivers hegemonic social control
  - implements censorship and regulation.
- pluralist:
  - autonomy
  - supportive and critical of government.
- new right:
  - self-regulation
  - market discipline.
- postmodernism:
  - globalisation
  - information freedom.

New media
Issues:
- digital piracy

- new economic models of production and distribution
- hacking
- viruses
- personal and data privacy.

Theories and impacts of media effects:
Direct:
- hypodermic syringe/magic bullet model
- transmission models.

Indirect:
- cultivation theory
- audience reception theory.

Limited:
- two-step flow
- uses and gratifications.

Negative impacts:
- cultural hegemony
- mass culture
- deviancy amplification
- moral panics
- violence.

Positive impacts:
- diversions
- education
- community
- identity consolidation
- empowerment (post-feminism)
- promoting political awareness and change.

Problems of researching media effects:
Changing media:
- intra-medium diversity
- inter-medium diversity.

Methodological:
- content analysis
- semiotics
- experiments.

Changing audiences:
- mass media?
- mass audiences?
- producers or consumers?
- interchangeability of producer and consumer.

Exam-style questions

1. **a** Explain the factors that influence the content of the news. [9]

   b Assess the view that the media reflect the interests and values of all groups in society. [16]

2. **a** Explain the role of the media in creating moral panics. [9]

   b Assess sociological explanations for how television may influence the behaviour of audiences. [16]

3. **a** Explain how the media may serve the needs of the individual. [9]

   b Assess the view that the messages audiences receive from the media directly influence behaviour. [16]

4. **a** Explain how the media can be used to support the interests of the ruling class. [9]

   b Assess the view that the media acts as an agency of state ideological control. [16]

Total available marks 100

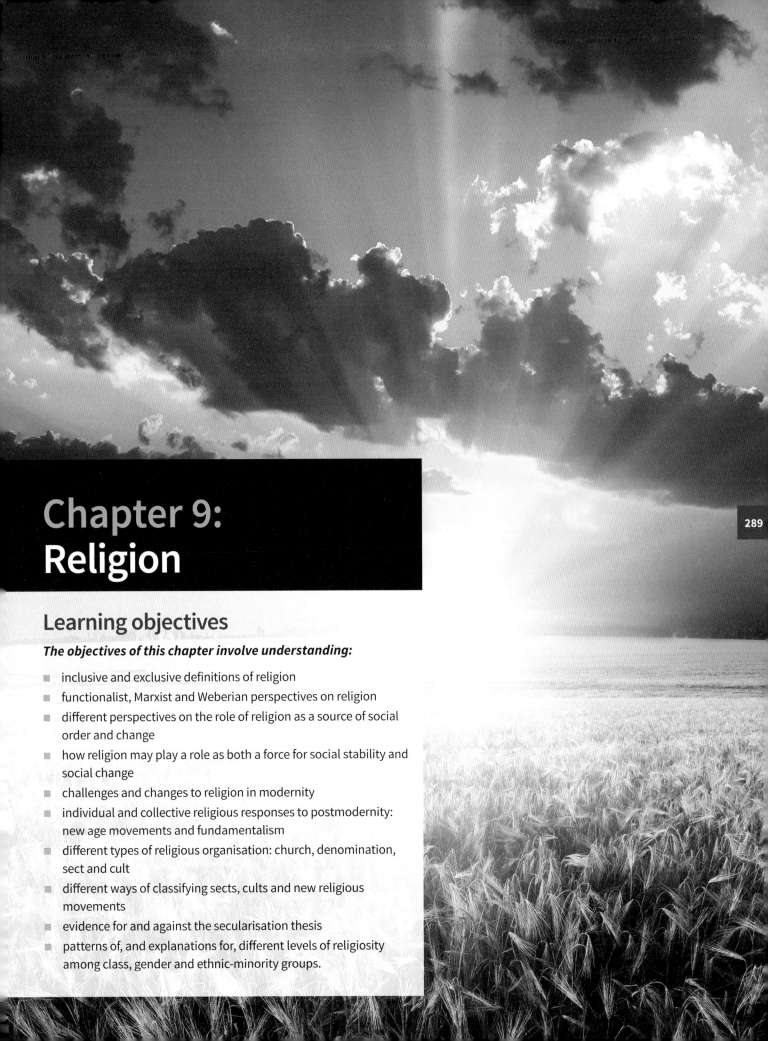

Chapter 9:
Religion

Learning objectives

The objectives of this chapter involve understanding:

- inclusive and exclusive definitions of religion
- functionalist, Marxist and Weberian perspectives on religion
- different perspectives on the role of religion as a source of social order and change
- how religion may play a role as both a force for social stability and social change
- challenges and changes to religion in modernity
- individual and collective religious responses to postmodernity: new age movements and fundamentalism
- different types of religious organisation: church, denomination, sect and cult
- different ways of classifying sects, cults and new religious movements
- evidence for and against the secularisation thesis
- patterns of, and explanations for, different levels of religiosity among class, gender and ethnic-minority groups.

Introduction

Although religious beliefs and behaviours are a feature of all known human societies, how these are expressed has been a matter of some debate in the context of different types of society: pre-modern, modern and late/postmodern. These categories form the general context for a chapter that explores a range of themes. These include how religion is defined, the implications of different definitions for our understanding of religious behaviour and the extent to which religion declines in power and influence over time. Further themes examine the role of religion in society, its role as a conservative social force/initiator of social change and the part played by religious beliefs and behaviours in the lives of different social groups. The chapter also looks at different types of religious organisation, from traditional forms in the shape of churches and denominations to newer forms expressed through new religious movements and new age movements.

Religion and social change

Sociological perspectives on religion

Before we begin our investigation into sociological perspectives on the role and purpose of religion, it is useful to understand how of religion is defined.

Defining religion

Religion can be usually defined in terms of three broad ideas:

1 A set of *beliefs* that includes a notion of 'god', or some kind of supernatural force or being that exists beyond our direct experience. There are many versions of these beliefs. Some forms are:

   - monotheistic – a belief in a single god, such as Christianity, Judaism and Islam
   - polytheistic – a belief in many gods, such as Hinduism and Paganism
   - non-theistic – no worship of gods. The North American Sioux, for example, understood the world in terms of *Waken*-Beings or Powers – the expression of anything 'incomprehensible'.

2 A set of *practices* involving such things as collective worship and prayer, which can be expanded to include ceremonies such as weddings or funerals and religious festivals. As with beliefs, religious practices vary. Some religions involve:

   - personal communication with God through prayer (Christianity)
   - communal worship, such as Christianity and Islam
   - exorcism, in which 'evil spiritual entities' are evicted from a person or place they 'possess', such as Roman Catholicism and Eastern Orthodox Churches

   - baptism for the dead, as practised by the Church of Jesus Christ of Latter-day Saints ('Mormons') – those who have died can be baptised by proxy; they are considered Mormons after their death, even though they may not have been Mormons in life.

Muslim worshippers surround the Kaaba in Mecca, Saudi Arabia. How do religious practices 'bring people together'?

3 Some form of *organisation* that allows practices and beliefs to be collectively expressed. This includes sacred places reserved for the expression of beliefs, such as a church, mosque or meeting hall, and people, such as vicars, priests and imams, employed by a religious organisation to take services or generally look after believers' well-being.

Diversity

These examples suggest that a notable characteristic of religion is its diversity. Rather than being a single (homogeneous) entity, religion is expressed in many ways across three dimensions:

- historical – in the same society over time
- contemporaneous – in the same society at the same time
- cross-cultural – between different societies.

In this respect, McGuire (2002) suggests that problems of definition arise because religion has a 'dual character' – it is both individual *and* social. On an individual level, different religions encompass different beliefs and practices and teach a variety of ways to 'be religious'. Some of these involve communal practices, such as attending religious ceremonies, others do not. It is possible, for example, to be a 'Christian' without ever setting foot inside a church. On a social level, religions perform certain functions for society:

- socialisation into a range of moral beliefs and values
- **social solidarity** – giving people a sense that they have things in common
- social control, both direct, such as Islamic codes defining what people may wear or eat, and indirect: moral values that provide a template for how the individual is expected to lead their life 'in accordance with God'.

KEY TERM

Social solidarity: belief in a society that its members have things, such as values, norms, beliefs and practices, in common.

Any definition of religion must avoid focusing too closely on one particular aspect of religious behaviour, such as beliefs, practices or organisational forms, in isolation from other aspects. As a large and complex phenomenon, religion needs to be defined and understood in terms of how its various parts relate to and influence one another. This has given rise to two distinctive approaches: inclusive and exclusive.

Inclusive

The inclusive approach sees religion in the broadest possible terms. Rather than trying to define religion by what it *is* – a precise set of beliefs and practices – this functional approach focuses on what religion *does* for the individual, for example providing answers to questions such as what happens after death, and for society. Durkheim (1912) claimed that religion fulfilled two necessary functions:

- Social solidarity: This relates to how religion creates a feeling of belonging to a particular group by providing individuals

with shared beliefs and values. It also acts as a source of personal and social identity, by specifying a moral code to follow, such as the Ten Commandments of Christianity.
- Social integration: This relates to the specific ways in which social solidarity is created, through mechanisms such as shared practices and experiences. This might include things like religious services and ceremonies.

The focus on function means the *content* of religious beliefs is unimportant – it does not matter who, what or how people worship. There is, for example, no difference between worshipping in a Christian church, a Muslim mosque in front of a totem, or at a personal shrine. Nor does it matter if people pray to one god, many gods or no gods at all. What is important is the fact that people act in specific, often collective ways, and that they hold certain types of belief that influence their behaviour. As Cline (2005) puts it: 'If your belief system plays some particular role either in your social life, in your society, or in your psychological life, then it is a religion; otherwise, it's something else.'

For inclusive approaches, therefore, the key to understanding religion is to see it as a belief system, or **ideology**, based on faith: the uncritical and unconditional acceptance of a particular set of ideas.

KEY TERM

Ideology: system of related beliefs.

An extension of this general approach is to focus on how people in different societies and at different times define a situation as religious. According to Blasi (1998), definitions develop through people's own behaviour, not because of an artificial standard created by sociologists to measure 'religious' behaviour. In this sense, religion and religious behaviour are whatever people claim them to be.

KEY TERM

Totemism: religious belief that an object, animal or plant is both sacred and has some form of supernatural power.

This inclusive approach has been criticised for seeing religion 'everywhere and nowhere'. For example, we can see 'religious-type' behaviour in everything from football to shopping to church attendance, yet we cannot identify precisely which aspects of that behaviour are uniquely religious. As a result, there is no way of knowing if societies are becoming less religious (secularisation) or more religious (resacrilisation).

292

Many religions, such as Christianity, have strong symbolic systems to make their faith 'visible'

Exclusive

The exclusive approach considers religion in a narrower way, in terms of things conventionally seen as religious:

- belief in a god or the supernatural
- behaviour such as prayer, collective worship and ceremonies.

This excludes 'quasi-religious' behaviour that might serve a similar function to religion but which is not actually religious in the strict sense of the term. Although it is necessarily based on faith, religion is not defined by that idea alone; religious beliefs are qualitatively different from other forms of belief. Exclusive approaches involve a substantive definition of religion focused on its content or substance: the beliefs, practices and organisations that are distinctively religious and that mark religious behaviour as substantively different from other, similar, behaviours.

Beckford (1980), for example, characterises exclusive approaches as 'restricting the term "religion" to phenomena displaying definite properties which do not occur together in other phenomena'. Religions, therefore, have essential characteristics:

- The sacred, something Maguire (2001) defines as 'that which is utterly and mysteriously precious in our experience' and which is frequently represented through objects.
- Moral codes with a sacred origin, such as the Ten Commandments, given to Moses by God in Christian religions, or Shari'ah in Islam.
- Communication with the supernatural, through mechanisms such as prayer.

Luckmann (1967) argues that religion is a unique belief system because it:

- explains the individual's place in the world
- provides a sense of moral and political order
- explains 'why we are here' and what happens after death.

Exclusive approaches, therefore, define religion as behaviour that is both special and different. In addition, substantive definitions make it possible to measure levels of religious behaviour in a society – to test, for example, whether society is becoming secularised or resacrilised.

Critics of this approach question whether religion really does have unique and exclusive features. These critics claim that exclusive approaches simply adopt a definition that fits neatly with conventional, mainstream world religions such as Christianity or Islam. From this perspective religion is defined as whatever these institutions say it is. This creates two problems:

- Such organisations have a vested interest in ensuring the product they are 'selling' (religious experience) is both unique and has limited competition.
- To identify the unique characteristics of religion, the definition is drawn so narrowly that it excludes behaviours not conventionally seen as religious, as well as behaviour that has some characteristics of mainstream religion but not others. Scientology, for example, makes no distinction between 'the **sacred**' and the '**profane**' and has no concept of 'god' as understood by conventional religions. It does, however, focus on ideas about spirituality that are religious in nature.

 KEY TERM

Sacred and profane: all societies make a distinction between the sacred, anything considered special or holy, and the profane, the everyday and ordinary.

TEST YOURSELF

Identify two features of an exclusive definition of religion.

Perspectives on religion

These different definitions of religion are reflected in a range of sociological perspectives: functionalist, Marxist and Weberian.

Functionalism: Traditional functionalism takes an inclusive approach. It focuses on understanding how religion functions to create, promote and maintain the cultural values that provide the moral basis for social order. Cultural institutions (including education and the media) create and maintain order and continuity by promoting and supporting a **collective conscience** – a set of shared beliefs, values and meanings that unify a population through an individual sense of 'collective personality'.

> **KEY TERM**
>
> **Collective conscience:** Durkheim considered this to be the expression of a society's 'collective will' that bears down on individuals, shaping their beliefs and behavioural choices.

Durkheim (1912) described this in the following way: 'There can be no society which does not feel the need of upholding and reaffirming at regular intervals the collective sentiments and the collective ideas which make its unity and personality. Now this moral remaking cannot be achieved except by the means of reunions, assemblies and meetings where the individuals, being closely united to one another, reaffirm in common their common sentiments.' Social integration is, therefore, an important function of religion, particularly in pre-modern, tribal societies. There, the development of social solidarity or 'moral togetherness' is based on practical religious mechanisms, such as collective ceremonies and services. In modern societies, religious practice may be important, but it progressively gives way to other forms of 'religious-type' practices (from sport to shopping) that serve a similar unifying function.

For Durkheim, therefore, the key to understanding religion is not its ideological *content* but its ideological *effect*: 'The power of society over the individual so transcends individual existence that people collectively give it sacred significance. By worshiping God people are worshiping the power of the collective over all, they are worshiping society.'

In this context, Alpert (1939) suggests that religion serves four major functions:

1 **Discipline**: a Sense of shared beliefs and values is created by following a set of religious moral rules and codes; these common values create and connect people to 'society'.

2 **Cohesion**: Religious ceremonies bring people together in situations where they put into practice their shared norms, values and experiences, thereby reinforcing social solidarity. Ceremonies such as marriages and funerals also involve symbols with shared meanings that. Ricoeur (1974) believes these are important because 'by expressing one meaning directly' (a wedding ring, for example, directly symbolises marriage), they 'express another indirectly' (such as a deep moral commitment to a partner). Haviland et al. (2005) illustrate this idea more generally by exploring the wider social significance of different religious **rituals** and rites:

   - Rituals such as marriages and funerals play a significant role in 'marking important life transitions'. In some forms of Judaism, for example, the *bar mitzvah*, for boys aged 13 and *bat mitzvah* for girls aged 12 symbolise a religious rite of passage: a ceremony marking the passing between life stages, such as childhood and adulthood.
   - Intensification rites function to 'mark group occasions' and involve the 'expression and affirmation of common values'. Religious ceremonies and festivals have an integration function – that of binding people through shared beliefs and practices.

Durkheim claimed that religious symbols reflect a significant distinction between 'the sacred' or special and 'the profane' or everyday, although their actual form was unimportant. They could be objects, such as a book or an animal, ceremonies, like a wedding, or places, such as the home of a prophet. Their function was simply to develop shared values – the fundamental things on which people could agree, thus drawing them together in a society.

> **KEY TERM**
>
> **Ritual:** constantly repeated aspects of religious belief and practice, usually involving some form of ceremony.

293

3 Vitalisation: Shared religious beliefs and experiences give life to shared values in ways that allow people to use the ideas, binding them together as sources of:

■ identity – people understand who they are through membership of religious groups

■ revitalisation – a common culture is transmitted from one generation to the next, thereby providing social continuities through religious traditions and customs, for examples.

4 Euphony (*harmony*): There are times of pain and crisis in life that require individual or collective efforts to re-establish harmony. Religion's euphonic function is expressed in the following:

■ Tension management – Parsons (1937) argues that the religious rituals surrounding death help manage this traumatic situation by providing a structure (the funeral) that permits certain forms of social action, such as public grieving. Farley (1990) also notes how religion provides important psychological support in times of personal crisis.

■ Meaning – in his study of the Trobriand Islanders, Malinowski (1926) noted how religion provided 'explanations for the inexplicable', such as what happens after death, and Thompson (1986) suggests that 'religion offers an explanation of the events for which other frameworks could not account'.

A Catholic nun holds a candle during a prayer service. What are the functions of ritual for any religion?

Neo-functionalism: Many of the ideas we have noted so far can be applied to contemporary cultures. However, neo-functionalists note a particular problem for many modern societies – notably Europe and parts of North America. This is the fact that the majority of the population are not particularly 'religious' – they do not participate in collective religious ceremonies and services other than events such as weddings and funerals. This does not necessarily invalidate traditional functionalist arguments about the function of religion (other forms of collective ceremony, such as sporting events or music festivals, may serve similar collective functions), it suggests a need to re-evaluate the specific functions of religion.

This involves exploring how these functions evolve in late/postmodern society, to focus, as Luhmann (1977) argues, on very specific areas, such as explaining 'that which is not currently known or understood'. This also involves a shift away from explaining religion as 'functional to whole societies' and towards defining its functions for *some* individuals and groups. This change of emphasis is based on the idea that postmodern societies are characterised by cultural diversity. As a consequence, the social significance of organised religion, Christianity in particular, has declined. Kung (1990), for example, argues that the functions of religion are now more closely related to questions of personal identity.

Gans (1971) claims that in culturally diverse societies 'few phenomena are functional or dysfunctional for society as a whole and most result in benefits to some groups and costs to others'. Membership of a religious organisation can, for example, confer benefits to individuals by defining who they are, promoting clear moral guidelines and satisfying psychological, social and spiritual needs. These, as Perry and Perry (1973) note, are 'particularly important in times of rapid social change, in which problems of identity are critical'.

Neo-functionalism also places much greater emphasis on the idea of dysfunctions – religion is not automatically and inevitably functional. In culturally diverse societies it can create conflict; some American Christian fundamentalist groups, for example, are violently opposed to abortion. As Bruce (1995) observes: 'Social scientists have long been aware of the role of religion as social cement; shared rituals and shared beliefs that bind people together. What is not so often noted is the idea religion often divides one group from another'.

The greater emphasis on small-scale functionality, therefore, is sometimes expressed in terms of religion as a mechanism for social change. Membership of a religious organisation may provide oppressed groups with the solidarity and sense of purpose they need to challenge unjust laws. The civil rights movement in the USA in the 1960s, for example, was organised and articulated through Christian church membership to challenge the unequal treatment of black Americans.

294

Criticisms of this general approach have focused on a range of problems. Methodologically, an important question is how to operationalise (test or measure) the concept of function. For example, how do we know whether something like religion is actually functional and, if it is, whether these functions outweigh any dysfunctions?

Functionalism focuses on what religion *does* for individuals and societies, so any form of collective behaviour can be considered a religion if it performs the required functions. This idea is theoretically convenient because it explains apparent contradictions or mutually exclusive observations through the concept of functional alternatives:

- If religious observance and practice is widespread in a society, this is evidence *for* the function of religion.
- If religious practices decline (Christian church attendance has fallen steeply in Europe over the past century, for example), the theory is saved by reference to functional alternatives that take over the role religion once performed.

TEST YOURSELF

Identify and explain any two functions of religion.

Marxism: This approach is based on the idea of conflict, and Marxists see the role of religion in capitalist societies as that of promoting a consensus that ultimately benefits a ruling class.

Traditional Marxism takes an exclusive approach to religion, focusing on the particular features that make it qualitatively different from other forms of belief and practice. More specifically, Marxists explore the role of religion in promoting consensus through its status as an ideology capable of explaining 'everything about everything'. From this perspective, religion shapes how people see the world, and its role is to represent that world in ways that reflect and support the existing social order.

Marx (1844) believed that religion was an oppressive social force that operated in hugely unequal capitalist societies, such as the UK, France and Germany in the 19th century. The role of religion was to make the vast majority of the population, who lived in abject poverty and misery, accept their situation. They should neither question nor challenge their relationship with a ruling class who kept the best things in life for themselves. In this respect, religion is theorised as a source of social control. Its ideological message was for everyone, rich and poor alike, to accept the world 'as it is'. At the same time, its purpose was to stifle conflict: to stop people questioning why so much poverty existed in a very rich society.

Religion was an efficient form of social control because if people believed in God this helped:

- uphold the status quo – the social world could be portrayed as 'god-given' and beyond the power of people to change
- legitimise economic exploitation – if God made the world, it was not the place of people to question why some were rich and most were poor
- justify poverty – poverty was portrayed as a virtue, something to be endured without complaint.

Marx called religion 'the opiate of the masses' because it 'dulled the pain of oppression' with its promise of eternal life (Christianity) or reincarnation into a higher social caste (Hinduism) for those who did their religious duty. He also suggested that it was a form of false consciousness. That is, by embracing 'illusory religious ideas' people fail to understand the real causes of their misery and oppression – capitalism and its system of economic exploitation.

A number of problems have been noted with regard to this general analysis:

- Turner (1983) argues that if we measure religious conviction in terms of things such as church attendance and membership of religious groups, the working classes have never been particularly religious.
- Contemporary societies also seem to be generally less religious. In many industrial societies religion plays a relatively minor public role. In many cases it is restricted to christenings, weddings and funerals.

Similarly, if religion functions to support the status quo and prevent social change, it can be difficult to explain its pivotal role in some secular conflicts:

- The Iranian Revolution in 1979 involved the overthrow of the (secular) regime of the Shah of Persia and the establishment of a theocratic (religion-based) democracy.
- **Liberation theology** – Boff and Boff (1987) note the involvement of Roman Catholic priests in revolutionary political movements in parts of South America from the 1960s onwards.
- The civil rights movement – in the USA, social change was promoted and supported by black religious organisations and leaders such as Martin Luther King.

KEY TERM

Liberation theology: political philosophy which argues that the church should use its power and resources to liberate the poor from their poverty.

Neo-Marxism: Neo-marxism embraces the concept of hegemony to explain the role of religion in contemporary society. This is partly because of social changes – modern industrial societies are generally more culturally diverse than in the past – and partly because of weaknesses in the idea of false consciousness.

For Gramsci (1934), hegemony involves the idea that beliefs about the world that benefit a ruling class are not simply imposed by religious organisations. Rather, ruling groups maintain their dominant position through the 'consent' of those lower down the social scale. This social scale itself is manufactured by cultural institutions such as religion, education and the media – what Althusser (1971) calls ideological state apparatuses. All, in their different ways, transmit messages supporting the status quo. One common message, for example, is that there are legitimate ways to express dissent, such as voting for a change of government. These forms of expression never directly challenge the economic status quo and the hegemony of the ruling class.

Hegemony makes it possible for religious ideas to be seen as influential in contemporary societies without necessarily having to show that the majority of people either believe or support them. Strinati (1995), for example, argues that the lower classes 'accept the ideas, values and leadership of the dominant group not because they are physically or mentally induced to do so, nor because they are ideologically indoctrinated'. In fact they accept those ideas because they are powerless to challenge or change them. In addition, Turner argues that neo-Marxists see religion less as a directly oppressive force on the working class and more as a source of cohesion for a ruling class. Shared religious beliefs and practices represent one way in which the various elements of a ruling class come to see themselves as a 'class apart' with common political, ideological and economic interests. Religion provides a set of moral guidelines for ruling-class behaviour, in relation to things such as marriage and the inheritance of property, that enable it to reproduce both itself and its domination of society.

Weberian approaches: Weberian approaches focus less on what religion *does* (its *functions* or *ideological* purpose) and more on what it *means* for:

- Individuals: this involves studying, for example, the motivations, behaviours and beliefs of those who classify themselves as religious.
- Society: this aspect looks at 'collective religious beliefs' existing in a particular society and how these influence the development of cultural identities, legal systems or, in Weber's (1905) case, a complete economic system (capitalism).

Weber wanted to understand why capitalism developed in some societies, such as England, but not others, even though they had reached similar levels of economic and technological development. He argued that it was a particular form of Protestant religion called Calvinism that provided the 'final push', allowing England to change, in the 16th century, from a relatively poor, agriculture-based, pre-modern society into a wealthy, modern, industrial society. It was Calvinism that provided the 'spirit of capitalism' – a powerful set of ideas, beliefs and practices that promoted a strong and lasting social transformation. The basis of this 'spirit' was predestination.

Calvinists believed that God would know, before individuals were born, if they were destined to achieve salvation. Nothing a person did in the course of their life could change this situation. However, because God would not allow sinners into heaven, the way to prove that you were destined for heaven would be, as Bental (2004) notes, to 'associate morality and Godliness with hard work, thriftiness, and the reinvestment of money'. In basic terms, those destined for salvation had to be:

- successful (throughout life)
- hard-working
- moral
- thrifty (careful about how you spent your money)
- modest.

Weber argued that these were just the kinds of attributes required to develop capitalism, an economic system built on the creation and reinvestment of profits to ensure long-term business success.

Weber's analysis of the relationship between religion and social change is an example of how meaning influences social action – a *belief* in predestination led to the development of specific behavioural norms. However, the argument that Calvinism and the **Protestant ethic** of hard work and constant reinvestment was a 'cause of capitalism' has been questioned:

- Tawney (1926) argued that capitalism came into being through technological developments that revolutionised how goods could be produced and distributed.
- Fanfani (2003) argued that capitalism developed in some areas of Europe where Calvinism was not a religious force.
- Viner (1978) claimed that where Calvinism was the *dominant* religion it acted as a conservative force that prevented economic development and change. Calvinist Scotland, for example, developed capitalism much later than Protestant England.

Protestant ethic: philosophy based on the idea of serving God through hard work, thrift and moral uprightness. Weber identified this as one of the main reasons for the development of capitalist ideas and practices.

These ideas point towards a general principle: while structural theory suggests that religion is a conservative social force, action theories generally argue that religion can be a force for change. In this respect, contemporary Weberian analyses look at how religion can be a focus for dissent, a channel through which discontent can be expressed:

- Liberation theology: Bruneau and Hewitt (1992), for example, argue that in Brazil the Catholic Church became a 'vehicle for working with the poor' as a way of promoting social and economic changes.
- The Arab Spring: in 2011, many Arab countries experienced pro-democracy protests on a huge scale. In Egypt, for example, religious organisations such as the Muslim Brotherhood played an important role in organising and channelling dissent before eventually being elected into government.

A political protestor in Egypt holds up both a Koran and a Christian cross. Can religion be a vehicle for social change?

Interactionism (neo-Weberian): Contemporary interactionist theories focus on the way in which collective religious beliefs provide a framework for understanding the world. Before the development of scientific explanations, religion in pre-modernity provided a way to explain events in a seemingly chaotic and threatening world. Religious and magical beliefs imposed a sense of meaning and order on a world threatened by death, disaster and disease, which could not be explained in any other way. This ability to 'explain the inexplicable', means that religion encourages certainty – there is nothing religion cannot explain.

This idea can be connected to religious fundamentalism as well as explanations for the role and persistence of religion in contemporary societies through culture mapping. Religious beliefs are part of the 'mental maps' that people use to navigate their way through increasingly complex cultural formations. Religion guides understanding by:

- explaining experiences
- interpreting their meaning and significance
- creating common cultural meanings.

Whether or not people are 'personally religious' is unimportant, because how they look at and understand the social world is shaped by religious beliefs, behaviours and practices that can be:

- strongly influential, in the sense that some groups live their lives in accordance with strict moral teachings derived from their religion
- weakly influential – while some groups may at times reference religious values, these groups have no strong allegiance to a particular religion.

The relationship between belief systems and cultural mapping is significant because it helps us how and why religious ideas persist and change historically. It also explains why some groups hold very strong religious beliefs while others have only a weak religious attachment – or none at all.

Through an inclusive approach, interactionist perspectives explore how religious ideologies provide an organising structure to peoples' lives. The specific content of religious beliefs is therefore of no real importance. All that matters is that religious ideas are believed because they plausibly explain something. When these explanations are no longer considered plausible, they are discarded and replaced with new explanations. Luckmann suggests that this 'plausibility test' explains why religious practice is so low in contemporary industrial societies even though levels of individual belief are relatively high. There are different areas of plausibility:

- The public – where religions compete with other belief systems, such as science, that may have greater plausibility in some areas.
- The private – the realm of individual beliefs. Questions of identity, what happens after death, etc., are reduced to personal concerns that religion may be able to explain.

One criticism of Weberian sociology in general is that it overplays the significance of action and underplays the importance of social structures in explaining religious behaviour. Wuthnow (1992), for example, argues that Weberian theory ignores questions of how and why social conditions influence our beliefs: 'When research finds religious friendships reinforce religious convictions, the question still remains why some people choose religious friends and others do not'. This suggests that religious beliefs and behaviours persist because they serve important and significant functions for both the individual and society.

More generally, one of the problems with an inclusive approach is that just about anything can be considered 'religious' if it seems to perform a particular role in supporting a belief system. This also applies to beliefs and behaviours that are only nominally religious. For example, new age religions, involving things like crystal healing and an emphasis on spirituality, have little or nothing in common with conventional religions such as Islam or Hinduism, apart from their general classification as 'religions'. In this respect, it is difficult to evaluate the influence of religious beliefs in contemporary societies when they are so vaguely defined.

298

TEST YOURSELF

What is meant by the following terms?

- polytheistic religion
- totemism
- collective conscience.

ACTIVITY

Although widespread expressions of grief and mourning are relatively rare, the death of an important national person, such as a monarch, president or celebrity, can provoke an outpouring of public grief.

Use Alpert's four functions of religion (discipline, cohesion, vitalisation and euphony) to write a brief analysis (around 100 words for each function) of how such public displays of national mourning are explained by functionalist approaches.

Religion and social change

In the previous section, we looked at arguments about the role of religion as either a conservative social force or a source of social change. This section develops these ideas

by looking at different perspectives on the relationship between religion and change.

Social stability

Traditional functionalism: Durkheim's argument that by worshipping God people 'are worshiping society' sums up traditional functionalist perceptions of religion as a conservative social force that promotes social solidarity. Durkheim argues that this is necessary because individuals will instinctively act in their own best interests, which is not conducive to social living. As a result, people must be encouraged to give up some aspects of their 'selfish side' – the desire to behave as they want, when they want – to society.

For Bental (2004), this involves creating 'a strong attachment to society' as a means of guiding individual behaviour. Durkheim expresses it in terms of the collective conscience: the 'will of society' experienced as an external force that controls individual behaviour. Bental argues that the collective conscience involves a range of 'collective presentations that hold society together', which are expressed through a variety of norms and values.

As a cultural institution, religion is an important source of collective norms and values. This is particularly true of tribal and pre-modern societies where other cultural institutions are absent. However, it is also true of modern societies where alternative cultural institutions have neither the power nor the authority to perform this role successfully. In this respect, religion promotes and maintains the collective conscience in three main ways:

- Through moral codes that apply to all and which cannot be realistically challenged because they are given by God – a power higher than the individual.
- Through participation in collective ceremonies society is given substance or 'made real'; through collective behaviour people develop a necessary sense of their relationship to and dependence on others.
- Participation in religious rituals, Bental suggests, 'brings about the psychological phenomenon of "collective effervescence"; an emotional high and feeling we are part of something bigger than ourselves'.

In this respect, religion can have a monopoly on cultural power and influence in some societies. However, in many modern, culturally diverse societies, traditional forms of religion no longer have a 'monopoly of faith' and cannot therefore integrate people into society as a whole. This has been called the 'problem of secularisation', and involves religious institutions losing their power and control over secular (non-religious) affairs. Bellah (1967) argues that such societies develop **civil religions** – a set of fundamental beliefs shared by the majority of people in a society.

This argument claims that societies cannot exist *as societies* without developing a communal sense of self. This means that the beliefs and values that define a society, by extension define the individuals within that society. If religion gradually loses its power to provide a collective conscience, other institutions develop to provide it. Civil religions can take many shapes and forms. They may incorporate traditional aspects of religion, such as a general belief in God, but equally they may be wholly secular. As Wimberley and Swatos (1998) note, civil religion involves 'an institutionalised collection of sacred beliefs'. These beliefs may be overtly religious, overtly secular or a combination of the two.

TEST YOURSELF

Suggest one way in which religion may contribute to the development of social solidarity.

Traditional Marxism: Although this general approach also sees religion as a broadly conservative social force, it does so for very different reasons. Religion is an integral part of the political and ideological superstructure in modern capitalist societies, and its role is to support and promote the economic base. For Balibar and Althusser (1970), for example, religion provides the ideological justification for things like social inequality that flow from a particular set of capitalist economic relationships. Religion is, therefore, an inherently conservative force that exists to support the economic status quo in two main ways:

- Oppressively, by imposing a set of 'god-given' values and beliefs. This role is generally played out in societies where religious leaders exercise wide-ranging political and economic power. In countries such as Iran, for example, the religious authorities' interpretation of Shari'ah (Islamic law)

places restrictions on various aspects of individual freedoms relating to things such as food and dress.

- Supportively, in the sense that there are times when capitalist societies undergo economic crises that threaten their stability. In such moments, religion channels social dissent and helps to preserve the status quo by either promoting limited but crucial forms of social change or by managing social transformations.

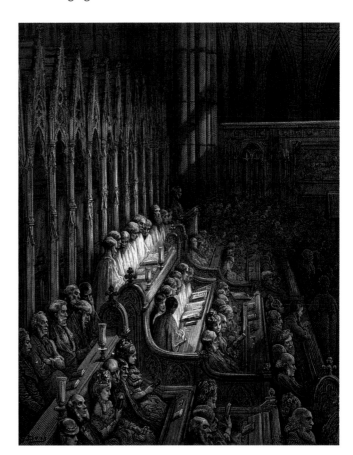

Westminster Abbey, London, c.1900. Christianity directly underpinned the values of capitalism during the 19th century in Britain

According to traditional Marxism, while religion plays an important role in managing social change, it does not *initiate* change. Social change is caused by economic conflicts between and within social classes; religious ideas play a significant role *only* in relation to the abilities of powerful economic classes to use such ideas as a rationale for change.

Azad (1995) applies a similar analysis to social transformations such as the Iranian Revolution (1979). The overthrow of the 'old order' – a tyrannical, secular dictatorship, supported by countries such as the UK and the USA – occurred through an alliance of 'progressive elements' among the working classes, such as intellectuals and students, and Islamic religious

299

organisations. Only *after* the Shah was deposed, Azad argues, did a power struggle for control emerge in which religious leaders proved stronger. In this example, the struggle for power was primarily political and ideological, because no major economic transformation took place in Iran: 'In 1979 the Iranian economy was a capitalist economy. Sixteen years later, despite many religious edicts, that is still its essence'.

> ## TEST YOURSELF
>
> Suggest one way in which religion may be used to justify social inequality.

Social change

In contrast to traditional functionalism and Marxism, some approaches argue that religion can initiate social change.

Neo-functionalism: Alexander (1995) draws on the work of Parsons (1951) to see societies in terms of functional sub-systems – groups of institutions carrying out different but interrelated functions. The cultural sub-system, for example, includes education, the media and religion and is related to sub-systems such as work, the family and the political process. However, the cultural sub-system has degree of autonomy from other parts of the system. This is because it involves institutions whose primary function is socialisation and the creation/propagation of cultural values. Under certain conditions, therefore, cultural institutions have the potential to promote change. Alexander suggests that this is because many religions contain theories of the past, present and future. They are not just concerned with questions of order and stability but also change. We can demonstrate this using the example of Jehovah's Witnesses, a Christian sect:

- Past: the world was created by Jehovah ('God'). 'The very existence of the intricately designed wonders in the universe surrounding us reasonably argues that a supremely intelligent and powerful Creator produced it all'.
- Present: we currently live in the 'time of the end' where 'Satan is the invisible ruler of the world'. Although the Earth will never be destroyed, people can die and, unless they are Witnesses, go to Hell.
- Future: while the 'Second Coming' of Christ will destroy everyone, 'True Believers' (Jehovah's Witnesses) will be resurrected to enjoy the Kingdom of Heaven ('paradise') on Earth.

This idea is characteristic of **millenarian movements**, which, Wessinger (2012) notes, expect 'an imminent transition to a collective salvation, earthly and/or heavenly'. Followers expect to be rewarded by God for their religious beliefs and behaviour. This may occur in one of two ways:

- Catastrophic millenarianism involves 'a cataclysmic destruction of the current order so that the "millennial kingdom" can be created'.
- Progressive millenarianism involves 'humans working under divine or superhuman guidance to create the millennial kingdom'.

> ## KEY TERM
>
> **Millenarian movements:** religious movements characterised by their belief that God will intervene to create some form of collective salvation, on Earth and/or in heaven for the chosen believers.

From this perspective, change can be:

- Transformative – some, such as Jehovah's Witnesses, aim to transform the world; followers of Islam aim to create societies based on Islamic Law (the Shari'ah).
- Transitional, such as changing religious attitudes to homosexuality or the ordination of female priests.

In this respect, neo-functionalists characterise modern societies as being in a state of moving equilibrium. They are constantly adjusting in order to maintain social stability. The development of education systems in modern societies is an example of this process. Formal schooling develops as a structural response to changes in the workplace, such as the need for a literate and numerate workforce. Religion is a cultural institution, so it is both subject to and an integral part of this process. While it may initiate small-scale social changes in order to restore balance to the system, the very nature of religion's structural role means it is more likely to inhibit than promote large-scale social transformations.

Neo-Marxism: More recent forms of Marxism have looked at the role of religion in terms of **cultural transitions**. Although the basic economic and political structure of society does not change, the relative positions of people and groups within a society do. More specifically, the role of religion is explored in terms of 'system maintenance'. There are times when capitalist societies undergo economic crises that threaten their stability. In such moments, the conservative role of religion acts as a channel for social dissent. This helps to preserve political and economic stability by promoting a limited, but crucial, level of change. Robinson (2001) identifies 'six conditions that shape the likelihood of religion becoming a force for social change':

1 A religious worldview shared by the oppressed class or group.
2 Religious teachings that challenge the beliefs and practices of the existing social order.
3 Clergy closely associated with oppressed groups.
4 A single religion shared by the oppressed groups.
5 Differences between the religion of the oppressed and the religion of the ruling class.
6 Channels of legitimate political dissent blocked or denied.

KEY TERM

Cultural transitions: neo-Marxist concept to express the idea of relatively small-scale changes in the lives and positions of people and groups within a society.

We can consider this view by using the example of the civil rights movement in the USA in the 1950s and 1960s. Black Americans were not only among the very poorest sections of society, they also had fewer civil rights than poor white people. The oppression of black minorities threatened the stability of US capitalism through civil unrest organised partly through the Baptist church, a minority religion that differed from the mainstream Protestantism of the ruling class.

For neo-Marxists, economic and political deprivation is the root cause of social change. However, for change to actually occur it needs a trigger; this is where ideological institutions such as religion may play a role. In December 1955, Rosa Parks, a black civil rights activist, refused to give up her seat on a bus to a white passenger. This action violated Alabama segregation laws, and Parks was arrested. Farley suggests that 'black churches were largely responsible for organising the massive bus boycott that followed. Parks had discussed her plans and their possible consequences with church leaders and civil rights organisations', including Dr Martin Luther King [a Baptist Minister] and the Southern Christian Leadership Conference. In this example, religion is a channel through which protest is organised and focused. Ultimately it led to major changes in the relative social positions of black and white Americans. However, it could also be argued that such change was essentially conservative; it left the unequal economic structures of US society unchanged.

Catholic Church support for the Polish Solidarity Movement in the 1980s is another example of religion's role in cultural transitions

There are also contemporary examples to support the idea that religion may play an important role in social change, as a channel through which dissent can be expressed. This includes the development of liberation theology in South American countries such as Brazil. Here, *some* Catholic priests formed political alliances with revolutionary groups to oppose government policies – against the wishes of the Catholic Church hierarchy. As Bruneau and Hewitt argue: 'For its proponents, the theology of liberation becomes the only way to understand the church and its mission; the church must be involved, it must opt for the poor, and it must use its resources to assist the poor in their liberation. Churches, for their part, become the privileged vehicle to work with the poor and promote their awareness, mobilization, and organization'. Although it is difficult to evaluate the success or otherwise of liberation theology in bringing about social change, its existence does suggest that religions may play a role in any multi-causal explanation of change.

Weberianism: Weber's analysis of social transformations points more directly to evidence that religion can initiate social change. Giddens (2006) states that 'Weber differs from Durkheim in concentrating on the connection between religion and social change, something to which Durkheim gave little attention. In contrast with Marx, Weber argues religion is not necessarily a conservative force; on the contrary, religiously inspired movements have often produced dramatic social transformations.' Weber was interested in developing a multi-causal analysis of social change that explored how economic, political and ideological factors could, at certain times and under certain conditions, combine to promote change. One important example he used was the transformation between feudal and capitalist

301

society and, in particular, the example of Britain as the first society to undergo this transformation.

The objective was to understand how and why capitalism developed in some societies but not others, even though they had similar levels of economic and technological development. For example, China and the Roman Empire once had advanced technologies for their time, yet both of them remained feudal societies. Weber suggested that religion, in the form of Calvinism, provided the 'final push' that allowed a society with a particular level of technological development to break through the barrier dividing pre-modern, agriculture-based, feudal societies from modern, industrial, capitalist societies. Calvinism Weber argued, provided the necessary 'spirit of capitalism' – a set of ideas and practices that promoted a strong and lasting social transformation. Religion was a source of social change because, in this instance, two things came together at the right moment:

- technological changes that provided opportunities to create wealth in a new and dynamic way
- a social group (Calvinists) with an ideology that allowed these opportunities to be exploited.

As Bental puts it: 'Calvinists associated morality and Godliness with hard work, thriftiness, and reinvestment of money. Given Western Europe and America served as home for these people, should we be surprised capitalism took off in the West?'

While Weber's analysis suggests that religion could, at the very least, contribute to social change, writers such as Tawney, Fanfani and Viner have disputed Weber's interpretation. They question the role of religion as an initiator of change, although their evidence is inconclusive. Marshall (1982), for example, disputes Viner's interpretation, especially in relation to Scotland. He argues that Calvinism provided an impetus for social change, but it was held back by factors such as the lack of capital available for investment. Similarly, Pierotti (2003) argues that we should not ignore or necessarily reject Weber's analysis: 'Something happened in the long sixteenth century that saw an explosion of capitalist economic activity, free thought, and religious rebellion. Whether the relationship among these is causal or coincidental will be grounds for conjecture for years to come'.

TEST YOURSELF

Briefly explain the difference between social transformations and cultural transitions.

Stability *and* change

Canin (2001) argues that it is a mistake to see religion and its relationship to change as *either* conservative *or* radical. Instead, he argues, it may play a *contradictory* role. His research into the Santo Domingo fiesta in Nicaragua suggests that in recent years, religious organisations have faced the dilemma of pursuing two roles:

- Conservative – the 'traditional paternalistic control of the faithful, focusing their attention away from poverty and suffering in this world and toward miracles and salvation in the next world'.
- Liberating – a role that developed, at times, out of peasant discontent. 'Beyond merely functioning as an "escape valve" for dissent against the status quo, the ritual rebellion of the Santo Domingo fiesta has exploded into actual rebellion at specific historical moments that have preserved a historically forged culture of rebellion. More than providing the sensation of liberation, rituals such as the fiesta provided the framework, if not the material conditions, for the transformation of the social order'.

Overall, therefore, the evidence suggests that religious organisations are intimately involved, at various times and in various contexts, in both the promotion of change and the maintenance of social order. As we have seen, the two processes may even occur within the same religious organisation.

ACTIVITY

In small groups, use the internet to research one of the following:

- *Brazil: liberation theology*
- *Nicaragua: before and after the Sandinista revolution*
- *The USA: civil rights movement*
- *Iran: the Islamic revolution*
- *Poland: Solidarity movement*
- *South Africa: Apartheid*
- *Egypt: Arab Spring.*

Discover as much as possible about the role of religious organisations and their involvement in the social change that occurred in each society. Report your findings to the class.

Religion and its links with modernity and postmodernity

Modernity

Modern societies have developed at different times and different rates – from Britain around the end of the 16th century to emerging nations such as Russia, China and India over the past 150 to 200 years. The significant idea to note is that modernity, whenever and wherever it occurs, results in three interrelated forms of developmental change:

- economic and industrial forms of production
- political and various forms of democracy
- cultural and new, powerful, belief systems centred around science.

While each of these has a different effect on the role and status of religious organisations, beliefs and practices, the perception of the relationship between modernity and religion remains one of challenge and a loss of power, control and influence. Examples of these challenges to the power and authority of religion include:

- Political developments that question the traditional basis of secular power and authority, such as the 'divine right of monarchs' to rule in feudal societies because their authority comes directly from God.
- Cultural developments, such as the emergence of scientific explanations about the origin and nature of the world, that weaken the power of religious explanations.

In this respect, the general relationship between modernity and religion can be expressed in terms of three main links. Each of these argues for a loss of religious influence over the individual and/or society: disappearance, decline, and retreat and reinvention.

Disappearance: This is the most extreme interpretation. It is associated with philosophers such as Comte (1830), who argued that in pre-modern societies, tradition, custom and religion were the main ways of explaining the world and the individual's position in society. Pre-modern societies lacked the scientific knowledge to understand natural phenomena such as crop failure or disease. Religious or magical explanations filled the gaps in people's knowledge, providing explanations for events that seemed explicable. Comte argued that as scientific knowledge developed, the need for religious explanations declined. Religion

was just a necessary stage in human development – one characterised by superstition and primitive theorising, which would gradually disappear as science provided real answers.

Decline: Wilson (1966) argues that an important feature of modernity is how religion is increasingly marginalised as a social force. While religion does not disappear entirely, he suggests that it retreats from the public to the private sphere and this results in a decline in religion's power and influence over people's perceptions of the world. This results from two main processes:

1 Modern religions have come under increasing ideological attack from scientific rationalism, which provides ways of explaining the natural and social worlds that are more plausible than religious explanations, such as:

- theories of evolution
- the 'big bang' theory of the creation of the universe.

The result of such challenges is a gradual retreat into mysticism and magic on the part of religious organisations that further loosens their influence on secular affairs.

303

Darwin's theory of evolution challenged religious explanations of human origins and intensified the clash between science and faith

2 The promise of modernity to create a more rational, understandable and equal set of social relationships has not come to pass and this has left large numbers of people feeling confused and betrayed. A variety of sects, cults and new religious movements have filled this ideological vacuum in increasingly cynical and exploitative ways. Wilson (1966) argues that they involve

the manipulation of psychologically fragile personalities who are promised the respect, status and material rewards denied to them in modern societies through 'divine intervention' and adherence to the teachings of influential leaders.

This fragmentation of religious beliefs, practices and organisations is evidence of religious decline rather than renewal. Wilson argues that newer religions appeal to 'the naive, the gullible, the oppressed' in ways that 'do not serve society. They are indeed almost irrelevant to it, since their sources of inspiration are exotic, esoteric, subjective and subterranean.' This means that religion has become increasingly marginalised and irrelevant in modern societies.

Retreat and reinvention: Neo-functionalists such as Luhmann (1977) and Bettinger (1996) argue that religion in late modernity is characterised by both a retreat from secular society and reinvention through a process of structural differentiation. While cultural institutions such as religion have lost many of the functions they performed in pre-modernity, they have become differentiated ('separated') and more *specialised* – tightly focused on the core functions they perform most effectively. Lambert (1999) agrees that modernity produces two processes:

1 Decline, evidenced by:

- fewer people overtly engaging in religious practices
- more people defining themselves as atheists or agnostics
- a general loss of secular political influence.

2 Adaptation and reinterpretation, whereby religions:

- adapt to their changed position in modernity
- reinterpret their role and function to carve out a new niche in different societies.

Lambert also argues that modernity produces two further effects:

- Conservative reactions that result in various forms of religious fundamentalism as people struggle to come to terms with the demands of change. This process involves a reinvention of religion as a political and ideological force in both single societies, such as the 'Religious Right' in the USA, and across the globe with the rise of Islamic fundamentalist movements.
- Innovation where religions adapt to the new and different challenges people face. A defining feature of religions is their ability to reinvent themselves for a variety of purposes.

Hervieu-Leger (1990) notes that the prevailing interpretation of the relationship between religion and modernity is that they are 'mutually exclusive'; modernity leads to the decline of religion. She argues that while this may have been a feature of early modernity, in late modernity the various forms of religious renewal 'are in harmony with modernity, especially in respect to the private and individualistic character of their beliefs and the fluidity of their organizational forms'. These ideas are discussed in more detail later, in relation to sects and cults.

TEST YOURSELF

Identify and briefly explain one possible link between modernity and religion.

Postmodernity

There is no single, definitive, modernist view of religion, and the same is true of postmodernism, which Grassie (1997) suggests 'represents a great range of viewpoints' that are frequently difficult to group into a coherent and unified perspective. Taylor (1987), for example, observes that postmodernist approaches to religion include arguments that:

- 'God is dead' and religion is disappearing
- we are witnessing a 'return of traditional faith' (resacrilisation)
- religion evolves and takes new forms.

It is difficult to reconcile these views under the banner of a postmodern perspective, but we can identify a range of general concepts that can be applied to religion in postmodernity.

Metanarrative: For postmodernists, knowledge about the world is organised around a series of competing metanarratives: all-encompassing stories that explain 'everything about something' or 'everything about everything'. Religious metanarratives represent a general framework around which individual beliefs, practices and experiences are orientated and ordered. They also involve a claim to exclusive truth – the narratives they promote are not simply true, they are the only form of truth.

For Lyotard (1979), postmodernity involves an 'incredulity toward metanarratives' – the idea that no single set of beliefs has or can sustain the claim to a monopoly of truth. This increasing scepticism about religious metanarratives suggests two things:

- a decline in the ability of religion to exert significant power and control over people's lives in the way it did in both pre- and early modernity
- a gradual retreat into 'local narratives' – small stories about people's personal situations and circumstances; while religion loses power and influence in secular society, it continues to influence individual identities.

Do religions in postmodernity have greater personal than social significance?

Jencks (1996) notes that postmodernity 'is a time of incessant choosing. It's an era when no orthodoxy can be adopted without self-consciousness and irony, because all traditions seem to have some validity.' The outcome of greater choice and more opportunities, meanings and behaviours, is that religious symbols lose much of their original meaning and power as they are adopted into the everyday (*profane*) world of fashion and display. Baudrillard (1998) explains that these symbols become simulacra: things that simulate the meaning of something that may once have had a real meaning. These simulations are not imitations; they are just as real as the things they simulate. Televised religious services, for example, give the appearance of participation in a real religious service. The two experiences are equally real but qualitatively different. For Baudrillard, religious simulacra give the appearance of religiosity, but they actually devalue the meaning and substance of religion. Religion, in this respect, no longer holds a central place in people's everyday life or identity. Instead, religious symbols and beliefs are merely *adornments* to someone's identity.

New forms of religious belief develop not as metanarrative but as part of individual narratives. These, as with the objects that accompany them, are 'picked up, worn for a time and then discarded' Religion in postmodernity, therefore, is reduced to a personal identity statement.

Contradictions: Postmodernism reflects and encourages a contradictory set of beliefs about the significance of religious ideas, practices and organisations in both the past and the present. At one and the same time there is religious:

- decline, as organised religions lose their ability to control and influence events in the secular world
- development, as religious beliefs and practices shift and change. This may reflect basic beliefs in 'supernatural phenomena', but these beliefs are not expressed in the form of organised religious services. In this respect, religions are constantly reinvented to reflect how people choose and discard different forms of personal identity.

McLeod (1997) suggests that one of the contradictory links between religion and postmodernity is that religion becomes:

- less important in terms of practice (for example, fewer people attend services)
- more important as a source of personal and social identity.

McLeod argues that globalising processes that cause people to lose faith in the power of metanarratives also cause people to see religions as representing order and certainty in an increasingly confusing world. This situation is reflected in ideas such as the privatisation and de-privatisation of religion. Although there are clear signs of a move towards **privatised forms of worship**, where religion is practised in the private rather than the public sphere, organised religion still survives. For example, some forms of Islam and Christianity show evidence of a contrary process, in which organised religion re-emerging as a significant aspect of public life.

305

KEY TERM

Privatised forms of worship: religion that is practised in the private rather than the public sphere.

TEST YOURSELF

Identify and briefly explain one possible link between postmodernity and religion.

New age movements (NAMs): Melton (2001) suggests 'the term **new age** refers to a wave of religious enthusiasm that emerged in the 1970s', which, for Cowan (2003), has two defining characteristics:

1 NAMs represent new ways of 'doing religion' and 'being religious', with the focus on finding solutions to individual and social problems through 'personal transformations'; the individual must change their life in some way. In this respect, Michael Brown (2004) notes that NAMs focused specifically on 'transformations of the self and society', including:

■ astrology
■ channelling (direct communication with spirits)
■ work with one's 'inner child'
■ 'a laundry list of unconventional healing techniques'.

Langone (1993) identifies four main 'streams' within NAMs (Table 9.1), involving different ways to 'transform the self' through personal lifestyle changes.

These categories may at times overlap – occult practices might involve beliefs about lifestyle changes – but one feature common to all NAMs is the belief that 'spiritual knowledge and power can be achieved through the discovery of the proper techniques'.

Stream	Transformation
Transformational training	Learning how to changing your personal life through a range of techniques and practices. For example, this might involve **asceticism** where one adopts a lifestyle based on strict self-discipline and austerity
Intellectualism	Personal transformations through the exploration of 'alternative beliefs'
Lifestyle	Changing society through behavioural changes, such as anti-globalisation or environment movements
Occult	Personal transformations achieved through beliefs and practices such as witchcraft and areas such as astrology, palmistry and crystal healing

Table 9.1   Transformational streams

Source: Langone (1993)

2 Spiritual consumption involves the idea that rather than being members or believers, people are consumers who 'shop for spirituality'. Cowan argues that this search for personal salvation is expressed through various individual preoccupations and concerns:

■ peace of mind
■ positive self-image
■ physical health
■ personal empowerment
■ enlightenment/insight.

This type of **religious consumerism** is, for Fraser (2005), one that 'offers a language for the divine that dispenses with all the off-putting paraphernalia of priests and church; it's about not believing in anything too specific, other than some nebulous sense of otherness or presence. It offers God without dogma'. Brown similarly suggests that NAM followers are 'less inclined to accept the personal compromises needed to maintain a stable group'. This gives NAMs the appearance of 'consumerist movements': loose collections of individuals engaging in **spiritual shopping**, whose most cohesive feature is the desire to buy into a particular belief system.

KEY TERMS

Asceticism: the practice of a strict self-discipline that uses abstinence and austerity for spiritual benefit.

Religious consumerism: the claim that in postmodern society religions behave more like business organisations, where customers are encouraged to buy into a range of different beliefs, practices and organisations.

Spiritual shopping: idea that in postmodernity religious consumers are more likely to 'shop around' for a faith or religion that suits their individual needs.

Sedgwick (2004) sees NAMs as a reflection of the individualistic tendencies of postmodern society; people 'want the feel-good factor, but not the cost of commitment. Putting it bluntly it is essentially selfish religion.'

Postmodern religion

NAMs represent a variety of beliefs and practices that are rarely, if ever, organised into a stable 'community of believers'. This fact highlights a postmodern perspective and fulfils a range of requirements for a postmodern religion.

For example, other than a general belief in personal transformation, NAMs have very few features in common. Their organisational diversity makes it difficult to identify or sustain a consistent worldview. In addition, people follow NAMs to find personal solutions to individual problems, and this individualistic nature makes it difficult to identify a new age metanarrative.

The choice on offer to these 'spiritual shoppers' encourages a 'pick-and-mix' approach to problem-solving. People choose the elements that appeal to them from different NAMs (for example, meditation, channelling or ear-candling) and mix them to create something new and personal. This consumer experience is one notable feature of new age religion. A person simply finds what they think is right for them, without questioning the rationality of the experience. Such consumers also discard various ideas when they no longer suit them.

Where a central tenet of modernity is rationality and various forms of objective testing and proof, a central condition of postmodernity is experience. As Cimino and Lattin argue: 'Whether soul-shaking experiences and religious conversions are the true action of the Holy Spirit, hypnotic trance states, or some other psychological trick makes little difference. They feel real. They inspire people to change their lives and commit themselves to another power, whether it's a higher power outside themselves or an inner voice crying out from the depths of their soul.'

This 'validation through personal experience' is a further reflection of postmodern uncertainties, just as organised religion was a reflection of pre-modern uncertainty. Langone, for example, argues that 'new age mysticism' appeals to a wide range of consumer groups, particularly those searching for 'meanings' that traditional religions have failed to supply.

TEST YOURSELF

Briefly explain the term 'spiritual shopping'.

Fundamentalism

Postmodernity is a time of constant change and uncertainty – economic, political and cultural reflected in notions of personal and social identity – and as such it embodies a range of contradictory processes. One reaction to experience identity confusion is to turn inwards in search for private forms of religious experience. Another response is to reverse this process, to reach outward, to deprivatised forms that seek to impose a sense of certainty on both believers and non-believers alike:

- NAMs represent a move towards privatised forms of religious belief – religion as something practised in the private rather than the public sphere.
- **Fundamentalism** represents an opposing process; religion is practised in the public sphere in ways that seek the 'remoralisation' of both self and society.

 KEY TERM

Fundamentalism: forms of belief and organisation that advocate a strict observance of the 'fundamental beliefs' of a religion.

For Bauman (1997), fundamentalism refers to forms of belief and organisation that advocate a strict observance of the 'fundamental beliefs' of a religion, whether of the Christian variety in the USA or the Islamic variety in Iran. Fundamentalist religions draw their strength from the ability to provide certainties in an uncertain world. This may be a belief in the Christian principles laid down in the Old Testament, such as an 'eye for an eye', or it may be the clear specification of how men and women should dress and behave in Islam.

Religious fundamentalism develops to remove risk in an uncertain world by removing the choices that create uncertainty. Fundamentalism is based on the idea that giving individuals clear moral guidelines, drawn from religious texts, removes both the fear and the consequences of taking risks. In this respect, Sahgal and Yuval-Davis (1992) suggest three common features of all fundamentalist religions:

1 They claim their version of religion 'to be the only true one'; all other forms are, therefore, heretical and must be opposed.
2 The movement feels threatened by alternative secular and religious views of the world. Christian fundamentalism, for example, sees both **atheism** (a lack of belief in God) and Islam as enemies.
3 They exercise control over both the individual and society across three main areas:

- ideological: what members believe
- internal: how members behave
- external: how everyone in society should behave.

KEY TERM

Atheism: belief that there is no deity or divine supernatural being.

Sahgal and Yuval-Davis see fundamentalist movements as 'basically political movements which have a religious imperative and seek in various ways to harness modern state and media powers to the service of their gospel'. In other words, we should see religious fundamentalism as a set of political ideas and practices that use religion as a vehicle to:

- halt 'undesirable' political and ideological changes
- change society in ways that suit the particular ideological beliefs of the movement.

Fundamentalist religions are, therefore, 'modern political movements use religion as a basis for their attempt to win or consolidate power and extend social control'. Giroux (2004), for example, sees Christian fundamentalism in the USA as closely aligned to the 'religious right'. This includes loose-knit groups such as the Moral Majority and, more recently (2010), the politically conservative Tea Party political movement. The Tea Party combines specific and selective forms of 'religious correctness' with attempts to legitimise a particular political ideology that is authoritarian, anti-democratic and intolerant of difference. It involves the teaching of creationism (a literal belief in the creation myth of the Christian bible) in schools, bans on sex education and the subordination of scientific ideas, such as evolution or global warming, to religious dogma.

Globalisation: Giroux explains the contemporary development of fundamentalist religious movements – Christian, Islamic and Buddhist – in terms of globalisation. Global economic and cultural processes expose people to different views and belief systems. This leads to notions of moral relativism – nothing is intrinsically good and nothing wholly bad. Without moral certainties, many people see the world as a more frightening and dangerous place, and they feel 'alone, vulnerable and largely unconnected with those around them'. In this situation, 'fundamentalism taps into very real individual and collective needs' by providing moral certainties 'given by God'.

Under these conditions, Berer and Ravindran (1996) argue that fundamentalist religions appeal to 'supreme authorities, moral codes or philosophies that cannot be questioned'. They exist to impose a sense of order and stability on a world that, to some, has become disorderly, unstable and confusing.

In postmodern societies, fundamentalist religions provide believers with a sense of identity and moral certainty expressed through a close-knit community of believers. This is what Castells (1997) calls a 'collective identity' based on a set of fundamental and unchanging moral certainties shared by believers and imposed on non-believers.

> **ACTIVITY**
>
> *Use the internet or other media to research the claim that some forms of religious belief and practice that are bound up with consumption have meaning in terms of fashion and lifestyle. In particular, look for examples of:*
>
> - *'religious lifestyle shopping'*
> - *religious symbols used as fashion items to adorn a particular lifestyle.*
>
> *How does the combination of religious beliefs and individual lifestyle choices reflect postmodern ideas about the role of religion in contemporary societies?*

Religious movements

Different religious movements and their power within society: cults, sects, denominations, churches and new religious movements

This section builds on some of the ideas we have examined in relation to the changing organisational structure and diversity of religions in modernity and postmodernity. In particular, it outlines both the organisational basis of modern religions and the differences *within* religions in terms of their general structure and purpose.

Church-type organisations

Churches are one of the most powerful forms of religious organisation, although their influence varies:

- Historically – in Europe, for example, the Christian church was:
  - ideologically powerful because of its control of knowledge
  - economically powerful through its ownership of land
  - politically powerful through its ability to align its interests with powerful and influential individuals and groups.

> **KEY TERM**
>
> **Church:** type of religious organisation characterised by its relative size, power and influence over religious and secular matters.

- Cross-culturally – in some societies, such as modern Iran, Islamic (religious organisations) are a powerful political, ideological and economic influence on secular matters, while in contemporary Britain, the church's economic, political and ideological power and influence has gradually declined.

Whatever levels of power churches have over societies, they all have important organisational features that differentiate them from other religious organisations. The first such feature is their size (Table 9.2): churches are very large, global organisations.

Religion	Millions
Christianity	2,100
Islam	1,600
Hinduism	900
Buddhism	450

Table 9.2   Major world religions by size

Source: adherenets.com (2005)

Size is undoubtedly important, but these figures should be considered broad estimates due to methodological problems:

- Reliability is relatively low. Different organisations count their followers in different ways and at different times, both in terms of who counts as 'a member' and how such counts are carried out, by whom and for what reason.
- Validity is also questionable. Such statistics do not differentiate between active members and who are counted as members simply because they were born in a country where a particular church is the official (state or established) religion.

A further distinguishing feature of church-type organisations is the way they exert power and influence. Bruce (1995) argues that formal religions have traditionally tried to dominate all areas of society, from how people dress to how they worship and the beliefs they hold. In pre- and early modernity, both Christianity and Islam had considerable political power, although the church's secular power and influence has generally declined in modernity. Notable exceptions, such as the power of Islam in countries like Iran or Saudi Arabia, merely reinforce this general rule. In late modernity, there was a gradual separation between church and state that resulted in churches turning away from attempts to influence the state, back to strictly religious matters. Bruce believes that 'the gradual distancing of the state churches from the

state allowed churches to rediscover the prophetic role of religion, but that freedom has been bought at the price of the government listening to them'.

Why might it be difficult to estimate the number of members of formal religions across the world?

Like other large, international organisations, churches have relatively formal, bureaucratic, structures, where power and control flow downwards. Roman Catholicism, for example, has a strong hierarchal structure, with the Pope at the top surrounded by cardinals, and lower levels of authority further down the organisation. These hierarchies of power may involve paid officials, such as priests, vicars or imams, organised by their different statuses. This structure means that churches are generally exclusive in terms of their ministry, since only certain individuals are authorised to tend to the religious needs of believers.

Churches once excluded relationships with other religious organisations, but this has changed in more recent times. Now churches often show toleration towards – and sometimes actively co-operate with – similar organisations. Most churches still oppose sects and cults, although a few do tolerate sects within their overall organisation. Staples (1998), for example, suggests that the Protestant church is characterised by 'substantial levels of internal pluriformity'. This means it is made up of different groups, with varying degrees of autonomy.

Churches may be exclusive at an organisational level, but one of their key features is their inclusiveness at an individual level. Churches will usually allow anyone to join. Islam, for example, simply requires a 'belief in God' for membership, while Christian membership is often assumed and acknowledged through ceremonies such as baptism and confirmation. Most churches have no membership tests or entry qualifications. This is a feature they share with denominations (see below) but not with sects and cults. Converts from a different religion are usually welcomed, if not always actively pursued. Unlike sects and cults, churches rarely have an overtly *proselytising role* – they do not actively try to convert people of different faiths to their own religious beliefs.

TEST YOURSELF

Identify and briefly explain three features of church-type organisations.

Social capital

A further dimension to inclusiveness relates to social capital – how people are connected to social networks and the implications these have for 'norms of reciprocity' (what people are willing to do for each other). Contemporary churches are able and willing to use what Putnam (2000) identifies as two dimensions of social capital:

1 Bridging capital relates to inclusiveness *and* notions of co-operation, trust and institutional effectiveness. Church-type organisations are more likely than sects and cults to use this type of social capital. Zmerli (2003) argues that this makes contemporary churches:

   - outward-looking: not just concerned with religious matters
   - heterogeneous: they tolerate a range of different beliefs and religious groups
   - reciprocal: they are willing to co-operate with and learn from other organisations, both secular and religious, within their particular network
   - ecumenical: they pursue varying levels of cross-church co-operation.

2 Bonding capital is more exclusive. It bonds particular group members, but it still sets an organisation apart from other organisations. Cult members, for example, form strong bonds with each other that set them apart from wider society, but the same is also true of church members; as Durkheim (1912) argued, social solidarity is an important function of religion.

Ideology

As large-scale cultural institutions, churches invariably make some contribution to the collective conscience in contemporary societies. As a result, they are more likely to understand the secular values of the society in which

they exist than organisations such as sects or cults. Historically, this meant churches frequently aligned themselves with the ruling powers in society by offering their political, economic and ideological support to the general social objectives of ruling groups. Because of this, churches are more integrated with the secular world than sects and cults, which often detach themselves from this association.

Denomination

Denominations are organised sub-divisions of a major religion. For example:

- Roman Catholicism and Protestantism are denominations of Christianity.
- Sunni and Shia are denominations of Islam.

KEY TERM

Denominations: organised sub-divisions of a major religion.

Hinduism is slightly different because it does not recognise a single definitive set of beliefs or practices. It involves many denominations built on the central idea of a 'universal soul'. In general, therefore, a denomination is a sub-group that forms within a religion.

Ideologically, denominations generally begin as a breakaway group within a church, formed through schisms (splits), which develop from:

- ideological differences, such as how religious beliefs should be interpreted
- political differences, such as how a church should be organised
- geographic isolation and separation from the main church that leads to differences in beliefs and practices.

Examples of schisms include:

- Christianity and the Catholic/Protestant division in 16th-century Europe.
- Islam and the Sunni/Shia split in the 7th century.

Denominations are usually less tightly formed groups than churches. They may, for example, unite a geographically and ideologically dispersed group of congregations, such as people who share similar beliefs and practices. In some ways, therefore, a denomination represents an administrative system that links and serves separate groups from religious organisations. This enables co-operation between the various elements of the denomination for activities such as missions and welfare efforts. Unlike churches, denominations rarely claim a monopoly of religious truth.

Like churches, denominations are inclusive – people may choose to join or may be born into an organisation if their parents are members. Denominations do not have membership tests. All they generally require is an implicit commitment to the organisation. Their authority structures also tend to be similar to those of church-type organisations.

There are variations in the organisation and distribution of power and control within and between denominations. For example, Baptist congregations have been allowed to develop different beliefs and practices within the overall structure of the organisation. Denominations normally have a professional clergy with responsibility for ministering to their members and they are generally more democratic than churches, sects or cults.

Are schisms important in the development of denominations?

Pluralism

This diversity is sometimes seen as indicative of **religious pluralism**. Different denominations compete for members, but most are tolerant of other forms of religious behaviour, both within and between religions. In contemporary societies, there is also a general tolerance for those who hold no religious beliefs (*atheists*). Bruce (1995) argues that this 'pluralist feature' represents a major difference between denominations and sects, even though sects often develop

 KEY TERM

Religious pluralism: idea that people in contemporary societies have a wide range of religious beliefs and organisations from which to choose, and that no religious organisation can claim a monopoly of belief and practice.

from denominations through **sectarian cycles** of dispute that lead to schisms.

 KEY TERM

Sectarian cycles: cycles of religious conflict that lead a discriminated group to split from the main religion to form their own denomination or sect.

Sects

Although sects and denominations share some general organisational features, Glock and Stark (1965) argue that **sects** normally develop around two forms of dissent:

1 Religious – including dissatisfaction (**disenchantment**) with the prevailing religious orthodoxy or a belief that the 'purity' of a religious organisation's ideals are compromised through contacts with secular authorities. This 'dissension explanation' is tied to what Niebuhr (1929) identified as the church–sect dynamic. As a religious organisation becomes established, it is forced to compromise with the secular order. A good example here is the Mormon Church in the USA. The church's founder, John Smith, originally advocated polygamous marriage for its members, but when this was banned by the church, some dissenters broke away from the main body of Mormonism to form polygamous sects.

2 Social – relating to feelings of individual deprivation, and Glock and Stark suggest that different types of deprivation lead people to form or join sects:

- economic – looking for monetary benefits from membership
- social – membership can provide status, prestige and power
- ethical – where the values of the individual are not compatible with those of the group or society in which they live, a sect provides a community of 'like-minded individuals'
- psychic – people 'searching for meaning and direction' in their lives find it in the sect's strict religious teachings.

 KEY TERMS

Sect: type of religious organisation characterised by a membership held together by collective feelings of deprivation. Charismatic leaders frequently offer innovative solutions to the religious and secular problems experienced by individual members.

Disenchantment: feeling of being let down by a religion or particular religious beliefs, practices and organisations; a weakening of faith.

Glock and Stark argue that deprivation is necessary for a sect to develop. However, it is not the only factor involved. Other contributing factors include:

- collective feelings of deprivation
- alternative channels for problem resolution being closed
- the emergence of leaders with 'innovative solutions' to the problems people face.

Wilson (1982) relates sect development to rapid social changes that disrupt traditional norms and create feelings of confusion and despair. Sects offer a 'solution' to these problems by giving people something 'solid and lasting' in which to believe. This results in a range of basic characteristics, including exclusiveness: sects offer their followers exclusive insight into religious and moral truths. They often claim special religious knowledge, such as the 'one true way to salvation', which is denied to non-members. For Scientology, this special knowledge is of oneself – how the problems of an individual's 'past lives' have created problems in their current life that need to be identified ('audited') and removed ('cleared'). In return, sects demand high levels of commitment and allegiance, and they punish those who break the rules.

Sects tend to be less formally organised than churches or denominations. There are no paid clergy, for example. Sects also place more emphasis on the role of leaders – many of whom claim divine authority. Individual behaviour is more highly regulated, and strict rules are often enforced by other members of the sect. This is possible because sects are comparatively small organisations, partly because of their exclusive membership. Belonging to a sect is usually a matter of choice rather than birth.

Entry to a sect often involves a probationary period followed by some form of testing before full membership is granted. Scientology, for example, initially invites people ('pre-clears') to join, but in order to remain a member, people must progress through a series of levels of knowledge.

TEST YOURSELF

Suggest two reasons for the development of sects.

Typologies

Although sects are more varied than churches or denominations, they can be classified by the needs of their members and by how those needs are satisfied. Yinger (1957) classifies sects (Table 9.3) in terms of how they

Type and example	'Problem' and its resolution
Acceptance: Christian Science	Members are largely middle class and life has been personally good. The 'key problems' they face are personal and philosophical, such as searching for 'the meaning of life'. Problem resolution involves individual and collective faith, self-help, and so forth.
Opposition or 'aggression': Branch Davidian (7th Day Adventists)	A radical reaction to problems of poverty and powerlessness, with membership drawn from the lower social classes. They both oppose secular society and adopt a generally antagonistic attitude towards it.
Avoidance: Exclusive Brethren	Members project their hopes onto the supernatural world and problems are addressed by appealing to a 'higher social order'. They avoid direct contact with secular society.

Table 9.3   Types of sect

Source: Yinger (1957)

see and react to the secular world. Marczewska-Rytko (2003) classifies sects as interest groups: goal-orientated organisations that offer incentives or benefits for members (see Table 9.4). Sect members weigh up the likely costs and benefits of membership:

- Benefits might involve feelings of superiority through access to 'hidden knowledge' or the feeling of belonging to a strong, supportive, moral community.
- Costs might include separation from former friends and family.

Such groups try to 'share' these benefits with society, sometimes benevolently, for example, Jehovah's Witnesses must give everyone the opportunity to be saved from damnation, and sometimes do so aggressively.

Cults

The religious experience in **cults** is highly individualistic, Price (1979), for example, argues that a deep-rooted, fundamental individualism is a necessary characteristic, and this varies with personal experiences and

 KEY TERM

Cult: loose-knit, individualistic, type of religious/spiritual organisation that collects around a set of common themes, beliefs or interests.

Type and example	Sect orientation
Reformative: Transcendental Meditation (TM)	The objective is to change people's spiritual awareness and, by so doing, 'reform the secular world'. The objective is to convert as many as possible to the sect's worldview.
Revolutionary: Aum Shinrikyo (Japan)	The objective is to change a condemned social order, usually by 'divine intervention' such as an apocalyptic, 'end-of-the-world'. While some, such as Jehovah's Witnesses are content to await Armageddon, others try to help things along; members of the *Aum Shinrikyo* sect released Sarin nerve gas in the Tokyo underground in 1995, killing 12 and injuring around 5,000.
Introvert: Scientology	This type looks inward to the spiritual well-being and welfare of members, who derive strength from feelings of moral superiority over the outside world. The focus is on personal development as members strive for spiritual enlightenment.
Manipulative: Neo-paganism	Focuses on the manipulation of things like the occult, through magical practices, for the benefit of practitioners.

Table 9.4   Sect orientations

Source: Marczewska-Rytko (2003)

interpretations. Cults differ from sects in that they lack a clearly defined exclusive belief system. The general lack of formal organisational structures, such as clerical hierarchies, meeting places and official records, makes it difficult to specify a minimum or maximum size for a cult. In addition, cult followers are more like consumers members. There is rarely any formal joining mechanism and those interested in a particular cult activity, such as Transcendental Meditation (TM), are encouraged to participate in the practices to varying degrees.

Cults are, therefore, broadly characterised by their diversity, both in terms of numbers and beliefs. Lewis (1998) identifies more than a thousand cults worldwide, encompassing a huge range of beliefs, behaviours and practices. This makes it difficult to identify their essential characteristics. As Hume (1996) notes: 'various scholars have attempted to give definitions of the term 'cult' but there has been little agreement to date'. We can, however, note several similarities in cults, including values that reject or modify those of mainstream society. For example:

■ Survivalist cults in North America reject society completely, and focus on cult members surviving an unspecified future conflict.

■ Cults offer alternatives to conventional values, such as using magic to find the perfect partner.

■ They also offer enhancements to conventional values, for example using TM to relieve the stresses, strains and pressures of everyday life.

Cults usually focus on individual rights and responsibilities, within a loose supporting framework of ideas over which there may be discussion and dispute. Cults also tend to

attract those looking for relatively short-term solutions to specific problems. For this reason, cults are inclusive – they rarely have any formal joining conditions and are less likely to have 'members' than practitioners who subscribe to particular beliefs and perform certain practices. Zimbardo (1997), for example, argues that 'cult methods of recruiting, indoctrinating and influencing their members' are similar to the socialising methods employed in any group or organisation. The attraction of cults is explained by the fact that 'cult leaders offer simple solutions to the increasingly complex problems we all face daily; the simple path to happiness, to success, to salvation by following their simple rules, simple group regimentation and simple total lifestyle'.

Transcendental meditation: psychological technique or cultish practice?

Where cults have a recognised authority structure – what Stark and Bainbridge call Movement cults – they generally conform to internal authority structures. Robbins and Anthony (1982) characterise these as follows:

- Authoritarian: Enroth's (1993) study of American Christian cults revealed situations where 'the leaders have justified the use of abusive authority in order to follow Jesus. They demand submission even if the leaders are sinful and un-Christlike'. Price also notes 'the beliefs of members of the Divine Light Mission derive from the dictates of their leader, indeed the knowledge they possess is his knowledge'.
- Centralised: authority is concentrated in a relatively small group at the top of the organisation or, as van Leen (2004) puts it: 'leader, or leadership, centred, usually by persons claiming some divine appointment or authority; while members are accountable to the leadership the leadership is not accountable to anyone else and often make significant decisions for members'.
- Communal: members are often isolated, both geographically and philosophically, from the secular world.
- Totalising: communal living and isolation are control mechanisms through which all aspects of the member's life can be regulated. Van Leen argues that control often extends to 'criticism of natural parents and family members' and the depiction of the cult as a 'family'.

TEST YOURSELF

Identify and briefly explain two features of cults.

New religious movements

Miller (1995) suggests that **new religious movements** (NRMs) do not represent a new religious category but a combination and repackaging of two old categories (sects and cults). However, Barker (1999) argues that the concept is justified because it both describes movements that developed in the mid 20th century and resolves the theoretical confusion over the similarities between sects and cults. Chryssides (2000) suggests that NRMs involve:

- answering fundamental questions about life and death
- rites of passage that mark 'key life events'
- life-coping strategies addressing 'problems of existence' rather than simply personal life issues, such as how to be more successful in business
- ethical codes that set out how life should be lived.

In other words, for a movement to be classified as an NRM it must be *substantively* rather than *functionally* religious.

NRMs have a range of characteristics. Many recruits are first-generation converts, and these 'early adopters'

KEY TERM

New religious movements (NRMs): an alternative way of classifying sects and cults that attempts to remove the stigma from these terms. NRM describes movements that developed in the mid 20th century and resolves the theoretical confusion surrounding the similarities between sects and cults.

tend to be highly committed and enthusiastic. Many of them will actively try to convert other people.

Recent (post-1970) NRMs attract more young, middle-class recruits than other religious organisations, partly because the young are more likely to be targeted for recruitment and partly because they are more open to new experiences. Young converts are attracted by the religious and personal certainties offered by NRMs. These groups promote a particular form of 'truth' that is less open to questioning by converts than the 'truths' promoted by churches and denominations.

This combination gives many NRMs the characteristics of a total institution – something Goffman (1961) defines as 'a place of residence and work where like-situated individuals, cut off from the wider society, lead an enclosed, formally administered life'. This has led some to argue that many NRMs use brainwashing techniques to recruit and keep members. Singer et al. (1996), for example, claim that NRMs 'have used tactics of coercive mind control to negatively impact an estimated 20 million victims [in America]. Worldwide figures are even greater'.

Why are some people attracted to total institutions?

Others, however, note that most people join NRMs voluntarily. Converts consciously choose to become part of a total institution because, Zimbardo suggests, such institutions offer qualities that many people feel are lacking in modern societies: 'Imagine being part of a group in which you will find instant friendship, a caring family, respect for your contributions, an identity, safety, security, simplicity, and an organized daily agenda. You will learn new skills, have a respected position, gain personal insight, improve your personality and intelligence. There is no crime or violence and your healthy lifestyle means there is no illness. Who would fall for such appeals? Most of us, if they were made by someone we trusted, in a setting that was familiar, and especially if we had unfulfilled needs'. Barker (1984) found these ideas reflected in her participant observation study of the Unification Church ('Moonies').

The nature of total institutions does, however, encourage converts to make a sharp distinction between the movement's members and non-members/unbelievers. This separation frequently leads to suspicion and antagonism between NRMs, secular society and other religious organisations. Antagonism towards non-members can, however, be an important way for an NRM to establish a clear identity and then to maintain it by demonising the competition.

Wallis explains the emergence of NRMs in terms of what Weber described as the process of **rationalisation** in modern industrial societies. Through rationalisation, life has become organised in terms of instrumental considerations: the concern for technical efficiency; maximisation of calculability and predictability; and subordination of nature to human purposes. Wallis suggests that the disenchantment that results from living in such a routine and predictable world leads many, particularly the young, to search for meaning to an otherwise pointless existence.

 KEY TERM

Rationalisation: in a religious context, ideas used by powerful groups to justify and explain their domination in society.

TEST YOURSELF

Suggest two ways in which NRMs are different from church-type organisations.

Typologies

Categorising NRMs can be difficult, but Wallis (1984) suggests they can be classified into three broad types, based on their orientation to and relationship with the 'outside world' (Table 9.5).

 KEY TERMS

World rejecting: type of sect whose members reject the secular world by collectively withdrawing from contact with that world.

World accommodating: type of sect that neither rejects nor promotes the secular world; the two simply co-exist.

World affirming: type of sect that offers to unlock the individual's 'hidden potential' in ways that will make them more successful in the secular world.

Type	Characteristics
World rejecting	This type is critical of the secular world and withdraws from contact with it, usually through communal living. Similar to Yinger's 'opposition sect', Smith (2005) notes how this type 'always find themselves in a confrontation with the "evil world" they despise and this normally ends with tears before bedtime in terms of the confrontation between their world and that of an increasingly secular society'. While confrontation occasionally ends in violence (76 Branch Davidian members died in a confrontation with American law-enforcement authorities at Waco, Texas, in 1993), rejection also occurs through mass suicide, as with the Heaven's Gate members in 1997.
World accommodating	Björkqvist's (1990) study of neo-Hinduism in India found this type 'draws a clear distinction between the spiritual and the worldly spheres', but neither rejects nor promotes the secular world; the two simply co-exist.
World affirming	Björkqvist suggests that this type is not 'conventionally religious'; they 'may have no ritual, no official ideology, perhaps no collective meetings whatsoever'. The key characteristic is the claim to 'unlock hidden potential, whether spiritual or mental, without the need to withdraw from or reject the world', with Scientology being a particular example.

Table 9.5   Types of NRM

Source: Wallis (1984)

More recently, Daschke and Ashcraft (2005) suggest a typology (Table 9.6) based on 'five interrelated pathways', each of which identifies the unique features of a range of NRMs.

Debates about secularisation

Secularisation refers to the ways in which religious influence has declined in contemporary societies. While this may seem a relatively straightforward idea to test – by comparing past levels of belief, behaviour and commitment (**religiosity**) with present ones – it is complicated by two problems. The first is

KEY TERMS

Secularisation: making changes to something so that it is not influenced by religion.

Religiosity: being religious, especially in terms of levels of belief, behaviour and commitment.

how 'religion' is defined; inclusive definitions are less likely to find evidence of decline because they include behaviours, such as NAMs, that are not categorised as 'religious' by exclusive definitions.

Second, the point at which comparisons are made is also significant. The further back in time we go, the more likely it is that we will find high levels of religious behaviour. Within this general debate there is no real agreement about at what point 'in the past' can be chosen for comparative purposes.

Religiosity

More specific questions about religiosity relate to the indicators used to measure the concept. McGuire (2002), for example, suggests that religion has a 'dual character' that involves measurement across two dimensions:

- Individual indicators, such as whether someone holds **religious beliefs** and whether these are orthodox (such as believing in a single all-powerful deity) or unorthodox (such as believing in witchcraft or, more vaguely 'spirituality').
- Social indicators that measure things like religious participation, such as attendance at religious services and membership.

KEY TERM

Religious beliefs: belief in a deity or supernatural power that may have some control over people's destiny.

Movement type	Characteristics
Perception	Involves a new way of looking at the 'problem of existence and understanding'. The focus and attraction is on philosophical questions such as 'the meaning of life'.
Identity	These overlap with perception movements, where they focus on self-identity, but are less likely to address philosophical questions. The focus is human potential: the development of new personal identities. They attract those who seek personal enlightenment through the mastery of certain techniques and practices designed to release their 'inner spirituality'.
Family	The focus here is on the social solidarity aspect of religious practice; they offer of a sense of community and well-being through the development of close, personal relationships with like-minded individuals. They involve those who want to explore 'alternative' ways of living and working, usually by distancing themselves from wider society.
Society	These focus group solidarity outwards rather than inwards. A major attraction is the possibility of changing society to align it more closely with the spiritual beliefs of the group. This involves transforming social institutions, such as work, school and family, through the application of a particular moral or ethical code or 'design for living'.
Earth	The goal here is world transformation in two main ways: planet transformation through an apocalyptic end to the Earth, through supernatural or human intervention, and the creation of a new 'golden age' and group transformation through transportation to a new world; hence their characterisation as 'exit-orientated' movements.

Table 9.6   NRM pathways

Source: Daschke and Ashcraft (2005)

In this respect, Cornwall et al. (1986) identify three broad dimensions of religiosity. Taken as a whole, these represent an overall level of religious commitment:

- knowing or the 'belief dimension'
- doing: an indicator of religious participation/membership
- feeling: a specific measure of commitment to both an individual's beliefs and any religious organisation with which they identify.

These issues have given rise to pro- and anti-secularisation arguments. We can consider these issues in terms of problems that influence the debate.

Belief (*knowing*): When measuring religiosity we have to take into account the fact that it is possible to:

- Believe without belonging: people can hold religious beliefs while showing little or no commitment to religious organisations or practices; they can believe in 'God' without collectively practising their belief or aligning that belief to any particular religious organisation.
- Belong without believing: this involves those who attend religious services without having any strongly developed sense of religious belief. Religious practice may have secular functions, with people attending services for reasons such as friendship, social status, custom or tradition.

Uncovering religious beliefs also presents reliability problems. For example, do 'religious beliefs' mean the same thing to everyone? One way around this problem is, as Hughes and Church (2010) note, to use a proxy indicator of belief, such as whether people believe in a 'higher being'. If they do, this indicates that they hold some form of religious belief. If they do not this suggests that they are unlikely to hold further beliefs that could be classified as religious.

While this type of indicator is useful for those who hold conventional religious beliefs, it is less helpful as a broad measure of unconventional beliefs. Many NRMs and NAMs, for example, define religiosity in terms of 'spirituality' – another concept that is difficult to define and measure reliably – and do not necessarily believe in a conventional god or higher being.

Participation (*doing*): The extent to which people participate in religious activities can be viewed in two basic ways:

1. Attendance at religious services/meetings, with participation data frequently supplied by religious organisations. Although such data is useful, it cannot simply be taken at face value because it hides methodological problems relating to its creation and meaning. More specifically, religious organisations frequently use different ways of defining and counting attendance.

   The lack of a standard way to count attendance means that it is difficult to track changes over time, even for the same organisation, and this makes estimates of changing religious attendance unreliable. An alternative way to estimate attendance is through social surveys. Asking people about their attendance is more reliable because questions can be standardised. It also has construct validity, because attendance figures measure what they claim to measure.

   However, the validity of the survey can be questioned:

   - Hadaway and Marler (1998) note that US opinion-poll data about religious attendance showed significant discrepancies between the numbers claiming to attend services and those who actually attended.
   - The National Secular Society (2010) noted that in the UK 'people tend to "over-claim" when asked about virtuous behaviour'; Hewitt (2010), for example, reports that around 1.3 million Catholics claimed to attend church services at least once a month, compared with a figure of around 850,000 calculated by Christian research.

2. Membership figures should be a more reliable and valid measure of participation because they count those who actually join a religious organisation. However, these figures are complicated by different interpretations of 'membership'. For some, membership of a religion is assumed or linked to ethnic identity. We must, therefore, distinguish between *active members* and those counted as 'members' on the basis of being born in a country where a particular church is the official religion. Understanding membership figures is further complicated for the following reasons:

   - Smaller religious organisations are more reluctant to reveal their membership numbers to 'outside researchers'.
   - Where organisations supply their own data, membership may be increased to create the impression that the organisation is larger than it actually is.
   - Some religious organisations do not hold services or enrol members. They may have clients – people who buy a particular course of teaching – and customers who purchase a particular product or service from time to time.

Commitment (feeling): Abrams et al. (1985) suggest that a more valid way to understand religiosity is to measure commitment – the extent to which people feel they belong

317

to a particular religion using a scale that measures and combines four main commitments:

- Disposition examines the philosophical dimension to religiosity through questions about spiritual ideas and experiences, such as whether people 'draw comfort from prayer'.
- Orthodox belief measures the extent to which people believe in ideas like god or the soul.
- Moral values examines how these are influenced by religious values and teachings.
- Institutional attachment examines the frequency with which people attend religious services, meetings and ceremonies.

Religious commitment and participation tend to go hand in hand

The Kendal project

A good example of the methods and problems associated with research into both religiosity and secularisation is provided by Heelas et al. (2004). Their study of the town of Kendal in the UK looked at both conventional and unconventional forms of religious behaviour:

- recording church attendance
- interviewing congregations
- observing and interviewing new age spiritual practitioners of things such as t'ai chi, reflexology and TM.

The objective was to build as full a picture as possible of 'religious activity', its continuities and changes, across a number of spiritual domains. This included:

- counting everyone who attended one of Kendal's 23 churches on a single Sunday
- counting everyone who participated in alternative forms of spiritual behaviour – a task made more difficult because this behaviour does not conform to regular weekly or monthly cycles.

While the Kendal project shows that it is possible to accurately measure various dimensions of religiosity across different kinds of spiritual behaviour, it also demonstrates some of the difficulties and limitations:

- A study of one small (28,000 people) town in one small area of one country took two years to complete.
- The study only looked at Christian churches (no other major religions were practised in the town).
- Defining 'alternative spiritualities' involves grouping a variety of practices, from Wicca through TM to yoga, that may have very different spiritual significance for their practitioners. For example, yoga or t'ai chi could be seen as a lifestyle, rather than a spiritual practice.

Kendal Parish Church. What does the Kendal project tell you about secularisation?

Operationalising secularisation

The various definitions and dimensions of religion come together in terms of how we can operationalise (*measure*) secularisation across three basic dimensions:

- Institutional: the role played by religious organisations in the general governance of society; its focus is on the power and influence wielded by these organisations.
- Practical: the extent to which people practise their beliefs through things such as attendance and membership.
- Ideological: the extent to which people hold religious beliefs that may involve no actual practice (Davie's (1994) concept of 'believing without belonging').

The question here is whether evidence of decline has to be found across all three dimensions, two out of three or just one for secularisation to be occurring. Bruce (2002), for example, argues that we can only really measure secularisation across two types of decline:

- Institutional – reflected in a reduced role for religious organisations in areas such as government and the economy.
- Organisational – reflected in a general questioning of religious ideas, explanations and practices.

Marshall (1994), however, argues that to understand secularisation we must take account of possible changes to the nature of religious belief. The focus should, therefore, be on the 'privatisation of belief' rather than the influence of organisations or public religious practice. This means measuring people's 'core beliefs' as expressed through:

- the importance of religion in any society
- how seriously people take it
- the number of people who take it seriously.

While beliefs are likely to be the most valid indicator of secularisation, the problem is not just objectively measuring these ideas but also the fact that there is little or no objective data from the past against which to compare them. As Hadden (1987) notes: 'Public opinion polling has only existed for about sixty years'. Keeping these methodological difficulties and qualifications in mind, we can outline a range of evidence for and against secularisation.

TEST YOURSELF

Identify and explain two problems involved in the study of secularisation.

Pro-secularisation

Pro-secularisation arguments are based on the claim that religion has declined in significance, at least in many parts of the developed world. There has been a progressive **disengagement**, from a past when religion dominated all aspects of political, economic and cultural life, to the present, where its influence is marginal. In this case, secularisation is due to modernisation and social change. Crockett and Voas (2004) argue that as societies modernise, 'the social significance of religion, and religious participation, declines' because:

- Ideas and organisations that once had a strong hold over people's lives are weakened in large-scale, complex, modern societies.
- People are exposed to knowledge, such as scientific explanations or different cultural beliefs, that challenge religious ideas and weaken their power.

- As people develop a more individualistic outlook in modernity their choices of behaviour and belief are reflected in religious pluralism; different forms of religious, quasi-religious and non-religious belief.

 KEY TERM

Disengagement: process by which people withdraw from religious involvement, in terms of beliefs and/or practices.

In this respect, **religious diversity** undermines the 'plausibility of any single religion', leading to a general decline in religious influence. Diversity means that religious organisations can no longer present a 'united ideological front' to the world. Their ability to impose religious discipline and sanctions, influence social and economic policies or challenge scientific ideas is seriously weakened. Hadden (2001) argues that we can best understand secularisation by thinking in terms of its impact on three main dimensions of behaviour:

- Cognitive dimensions focus on how information and beliefs are organised. People in postmodernity think very differently about the nature of God or the social and natural worlds from people in the past, with a decline in the plausibility of religious explanations.
- Institutional dimensions involve the idea that many of the functions once performed by religion have been taken over by secular institutions.
- Behavioural dimensions suggest that religious behaviour retreats from the public to the private sphere; it becomes a matter of 'personal faith'.

KEY TERM

Religious diversity: the existence of different forms of religious belief, practice and organisation in a society.

Evidence: Evidence for religious decline is divided into three areas:

1 Institutional decline involves ideas like:

- Privatised beliefs: religion is relegated to personal beliefs about 'god' or the supernatural that have little or no meaning outside personal crises, such as illness and ill health; people look to religious beliefs as a last resort when all else fails.
- Loss of practical functions: there are examples of this in many modern industrial societies, with governments

319

taking on many of the functions previously undertaken, partly or wholly, by religious organisations. For example, education and welfare are now more likely to be organised by public authorities rather than by the church.

Bruce (2001) suggests that further evidence includes the fact that over the past 100 years in the UK the number of full-time, professional clergy has declined by 25%, despite a rising population. Even relatively minor expressions of religious practice, such as baptisms, confirmations and weddings, are in decline: 'In the 19th century almost all weddings were religious ceremonies'. Now, it is believed to be about one in three.

2   Practical decline involves a fall in religious engagement: Dobbelaere and Jagodzinski (1995) argue for a long-term decline in attendance since the 19th century, with a particularly sharp decline since the 1950s. Only around 10% of the UK population are members of the main Christian church, with a much smaller percentage regularly attending other churches. NRMs are often cited as evidence of both religious transformation, as people express their religiosity in non-traditional ways, and a **religious revival** (*revitalisation*). Bruce (2001), however, argues that if NRMs were 'religious compensators' we should have seen 'some signs of vigorous growth'. This, he argues, has not happened.

3   Ideological: although 'believing without belonging' is often seen as evidence against secularisation, Bruce (2001) argues that there is strong evidence for a general decline in religious beliefs; it simply 'lags behind' the decline in religious practice.

KEY TERM

Religious revival: a contemporary growth in the popularity of different religions.

Wilson (1982) argues that an important individual dimension of secularisation is the extent to which people's understanding of the natural and social world has changed. As a society, for example, we have moved away from a magical (spells and charms) or religious (prayer) understanding to one based on secular, scientific, explanations. The things we once explained by reference to religion are now explained by science.

TEST YOURSELF

Explain two arguments in favour of secularisation.

Anti-secularisation

Anti-secularisation theorists have offered their own interpretations of the evidence discussed above. Martin (1978) claims that it is impossible to distinguish between the religious and the secular in a way that is accessible to academic study, because the belief systems combined under the name religion are so varied and diverse. Martin suggests that the concept of secularisation has become an intellectual tool that is used to attack religion. Stark (1999) argues that the influence of religious organisations and beliefs in the past has been overstated and the contribution made by religion to contemporary societies understated. Religious influence in modern societies is still strong. For example, it provides the rationale for moral codes that form the basis for political life. Religion also takes the lead in arguing for ethical practices to inform economic life. He also claims that there is a strong undercurrent of individual religious belief, even in secular societies.

From this perspective, religion has evolved and changed, rather than declined. People are less likely to follow religious practices because these served purposes that are either no longer needed or are performed by other institutions. Religious ceremonies and festivals, for example, served a recreational function in the past when there were few other sources of leisure; a festival was a day spent not working. Today, people are surrounded by leisure services, so religion no longer serves this function. This is evidence of evolution rather than secularisation.

Evidence: Berger (1999) argues that Western Europe may have seen declining congregations, but this is not the case in the USA where church attendance is rising, nor in emerging nations. The idea that secularisation (if indeed it is occurring) does not have worldwide causes is important because it questions the claim that secularisation is an inevitable feature of modernisation and social change. Kelley (1972) suggests that secularisation, where it has occurred, is related to particular forms of religious organisation – those that try to accommodate to the secular world – rather than religion itself. Religious practice declined only in organisations that were:

- image conscious – appealing to the widest range of people
- democratic in their internal affairs
- changed to accommodate particular audiences
- relativistic in terms of their teaching and morality.

In contrast, religious growth occurred in fundamentalist organisations that offered a set of basic ideas and principles that were:

- traditional
- autocratic
- patriarchal
- morally absolute.

This means that if a religious organisation evolves to become a consumer religion, it may actually lose members. It neither attracts those looking for something different in their spiritual life, nor does it keep those who are looking for the 'traditional' features of a religion.

Are new forms of religious belief and practice evidence for or against secularisation?

Shopping for religion

A different way of approaching the secularisation debate involves religious economy theory. Here, both Iannaccone (1994) and Stark and Finke (2000) argue that secularisation is too limited an explanation for developments in postmodern societies.

Religion should not be seen as a cultural institution, evaluated in terms of its success at propagating particular values in culturally homogeneous societies where established religions have little or no competition. Rather, religions should be seen as economic organisations. In culturally diverse societies where spiritual competition is fierce, religion should be studied as businesses.

In the past, major world religions established 'monopolies of belief' that not only discouraged competition but actively destroyed it. While this made established religions powerful, it also made them lazy; they took their customers for granted. Although this is not a problem when the secular order supports religious monopolies, if societies change and the established order is challenged, religious pluralism develops. Organisations must compete for 'customers' in the religious marketplace if they are to survive. This competition encourages:

- innovation – religious organisations find new ways to attract customers
- invigoration – organisations must listen and respond to what customers want, otherwise they will shop elsewhere
- reinvigoration – organisations continually reinvent both themselves and their services to 'keep ahead of the competition'.

Established religions are slow to change in the face of increased competition. As their congregations decline, they focus on retaining their monopoly position rather than finding ways to attract new adherents. On one level, therefore, anti-secularisation theorists concede that a form of secularisation occurs among established religions as they lose members, attendance at services declines and their influence over secular matters declines.

However, just because established religions secularise, this does not mean the decline of religion itself. Rather, religion evolves in new, dynamic, forms, such as NRMs and NAMs that compete for believers with established religions. Their success is measured in terms of their ability to offer alternative forms of religious beliefs and ways to express those beliefs.

The anti-secularisation argument, therefore, is that the nature and shape of religious organisations has changed. Rather than evidence of overall decline, this is merely evidence of different forms of belief and practice that are harder to quantify but which still count as religious forms.

Resacrilisation

Anti-secularisation theorists do not simply question secularisation. They argue that religious changes are evidence not of **desacrilisation** but of a resacrilisation of society – people are becoming *more* religious and spiritual.

- In the past, people had no choice but to 'be religious'. While this meant there were a lot of apparently religious people, we do not know very much about their actual religious commitment; did they attend church services because they were coerced into attending?
- People now choose their religion and by so doing they are actually showing greater commitment. Fewer, more committed, believers demonstrates resacrilisation.

 KEY TERM

Desacrilisation: process in which self and society become progressively less religious/spiritual.

321

Those who support the idea of resacrilisation argue that it explains things such as the growth of Christian and Islamic fundamentalist religious movements, as well as the fact that, in many countries around the world, religious beliefs and practices are, at worst, not declining, and, at best, flourishing. Against this, however:

- Crockett and Voas note that 'British religious markets have become more competitive' through the influence of various ethnic groups, but there has been little or no corresponding rise in overall religious practice or belief.
- Norris and Inglehart's (2004) research goes further to argue that in Europe, contrary to religious economy theories, countries with the closest links between church and state have the highest levels of practice.

Yip (2002) summarises the contradictory nature of a secularisation debate as one that sees religion 'in a constant state of transformation (and persistence)'. In other words, evidence for or against secularisation depends more on how religion and religiosity is defined than on any real sense of either decline or resacrilisation:

- Pro-secularisation theory takes a 'top-down' approach, with modern societies being prone to secularisation; institutions become secularised, then organisational practices and, eventually, individual beliefs – although this last one often appears optional.
- Anti-secularisation theory reverses this process, with individuals being prone to religion; religion is a cultural universal that serves a human need. While organisational and practical features may change, people remain essentially religious.

TEST YOURSELF

Explain and assess two arguments against secularisation.

Post-secularisation

The inconclusiveness of this particular debate has led some to argue that secularising processes do not involve a simple, linear movement from 'the religious' to 'the secular' and, as a consequence, the debate requires reframing. Rather than a simple pro/anti approach, something more subtle is required.

Phillips (2004) argues that secularisation should be reconceptualised around differentiation. Institutions once influenced or controlled by religious organisations and ideas become secularised, and a separation occurs between religious and non-religious institutions. The extent of secularising tendencies is, however, limited to institutions and practices.

Post-secularisation, therefore, argues that differentiation involves a separation between social structures and actions. This makes it possible to chart the secularisation of two dimensions of religiosity, institutions and practice, by leaving a third dimension, individual beliefs, out of the equation. In an institutionally secularised society, whether people hold religious-type beliefs is only significant if those beliefs inform social actions. In this respect, it is not important whether or not people say they believe in ideas such as 'god'. What is important is what they do, or fail to do, as a result of these beliefs.

- If religious beliefs are so strongly held that they become the basis for social action, such as active involvement in political parties advocating strict religious laws and observances, this must be addressed by secularisation theory.
- If religious beliefs are 'simply matters of personal preference' with little or no impact on social structures, they are irrelevant to any wider debate. As Tschannen (1991) suggests, the main object of study is the changing institutional position of religion; whether people personally believe religious ideas is conceptually unimportant.

This general position is summarised by Sommerville's (1998) argument that institutional differentiation is not something that 'leads to secularisation. It *is* secularisation'.

Participation

Putnam reworks the idea of 'believing without belonging' by arguing that social capital is the *social glue* binding people as a *society*. Cohen and Prusak (2001) suggest that this involves 'the trust, mutual understanding and shared values and behaviours that bind the members of human networks and communities and make cooperative action possible'.

Putnam argues that modern societies have seen a gradual withdrawal of public participation in all areas of society, from trade unions to political parties. This suggests that the secularisation of participation is part of a general cultural transition, not one restricted to religious organisations. As Davie (2002) suggests, a decline in religious participation is, therefore, part of a general 'process of withdrawal from the public sphere' in contemporary societies.

Wuthnow (2002), however, argues that while there has been some decline in the social capital of religion in the USA, this has not been to 'drastically low levels' and certainly not enough to fully explain changes in religious participation. While lower levels of social capital should result in a decline in religious participation, many religions in the USA have witnessed a recent revival.

TEST YOURSELF

Briefly explain the term 'post-secularisation'.

ACTIVITY

Divide into two groups (four if the class is large). Each group should develop ideas and evidence about one of the following:

1 *evidence for/indicators of a decline in significance of religion*
2 *evidence for/indicators of the continued significance of religion.*

Take it in turns to state and discuss the evidence you have identified to the rest of the class.

Once the discussion is complete, group the different ideas into three categories, those dealing with:

- *institutions*
- *practices*
- *beliefs.*

What conclusions can be drawn from the evidence about secularisation?

Sociological studies of the relationship between religious beliefs, organisations and social groups (including links to class, gender and ethnicity)

In previous sections, we touched on the relationship between religious beliefs, practices, organisations and social groups. In this section, we develop these ideas by looking at religiosity in the context of class, gender and ethnic groups (see for example Table 9.7).

Social class

Any understanding of the relationship between class and beliefs is complicated by two ideas:

- Definitions and measurements of class vary both historically and cross-culturally, which makes both longitudinal and comparative studies difficult.
- Measuring people's belief is similarly complicated, not least because, as Navone (2002) argues 'just because people say they are religious, does not make it so, no more than if they say they are intelligent or moral'.

Country	% of adults for whom religion is important
Senegal	97
Nigeria	92
India	92
Pakistan	91
South Africa	87
Kenya	85
Brazil	77
USA	59
Great Britain	33
Canada	30
Italy	27
Germany	21
Russia	14
Japan	12
France	11

Table 9.7   The personal importance of religion

Source: Pew Research Center (2002)

Keeping these limitations in mind, much of the data about the relationship between class and belief suggests that there are few differences in belief about the existence of 'god' or some form of supreme being, and in general religious concepts, such as heaven or life after death. This is unsurprising when we consider that traditional religions address major philosophical questions, such as what happens after death, that transcend narrow class interests.

Similarly, religious practice shows a closer correlation between class and areas such as attendance at services.

323

Regular attendees (weekly or monthly) are more likely to be middle or upper class, while those who never attend church, except for weddings and funerals, are more likely to be working class.

Explanations: The relationship between class and religiosity varies across different societies with different levels of economic development and professed beliefs. However, O'Beirne (2004) notes that 'respondents affiliated to particular faiths share certain socio-economic experiences and characteristics'. We can investigate this further by examining some possible explanations for the relationship between religious affiliation and social class.

In developed nations, religion was historically a source of status for both the upper and middle classes. Members of the upper class used their positions within powerful religious institutions such as the church to exert power over their society. Members of the middle class used church attendance as a measure of 'social respectability' and acceptance. These religious functions may no longer apply in industrial societies, but they could still do so in emergent and developing nations.

In developed societies, the decline in the significance of religion as a source of group identity (rather than individual identity), is important in terms of the uses of religion for things like social status and social control. When Colls (2005) talks about 'a post-industrial, post-colonial, post-masculine, post-Christian world of fluid identities', he argues that the 'religion and respectability' class markers of the past no longer have the power they once had. O'Beirne found little evidence of religious belief/practice forming a significant part of self-identity; only 20% of respondents considered religion 'an important part of their personal description'. Even then religion ranked far down the scale of significance after family, age, work and interests. If religion is no longer a source of class identity for Christians, it is according to O'Beirne, significant for some faith communities such as Muslims and Hindus. However, this broadly cuts across class boundaries; in a global context, religion is mainly a source of ethnic identity for all social classes.

With one major exception, O'Beirne's respondents with religious affiliations 'lived in places with low-to-moderate levels of area deprivation'. This suggests the changing nature of class relationships – they are not played out in relation to strong concepts of social inequality and deprivation. This also reflects the changing nature of established religions; they no longer represent a source of 'hope' for the most deprived.

The exception, however, is the Muslim faith, associated with 'the highest levels of area deprivation'. This suggests that, in the UK, Muslims largely inhabit the lowest social strata and that religious belief, practice and commitment are an integral part of 'Muslim life and identity'. They provide moral codes for a community and a mode of group/individual identity represented by a strong and vital religious organisation.

How is religion related to material and cultural deprivation?

Looking more generally at global trends, concepts of globalisation and postmodernity change the meaning of:

- Religion – as we have seen this now encompasses a diversity of meanings, from established churches through NRMs to NAMs
- Social class – it is both more difficult to measure this concept objectively while, subjectively, it appears to have both a looser individual meaning and less coherence as a collective concept.

In this respect, postmodern societies are different in terms of two kinds of relationship:

- Individually, people are less likely to define themselves in terms of class and, consequently, less likely to behave in ways that reflect their perception of class relationships. Petre (1999) notes that there has been a general withdrawal from all forms of public participation, political as well as religious, across developed nations.
- Institutionally, religious pluralism is a feature of contemporary societies in terms of the choices available to the 'religious consumer', both *between* religions such as Christianity and Islam and *within* religions, such as liberal or fundamentalist Christianity/Islam. If we include NRMs, the range of consumer choices is even greater.

In postmodernity, religious affiliation relates more to individual, personal identities rather than the collective, social identities of the past. The weakening of traditional class associations, along with increased consumer choice, explains why social class no longer correlates very closely with affiliation. As Bruce (2001) argues, the logic of this argument is that 'competitive free markets [in religion] are supposed to be better at meeting not only material but also spiritual needs'.

We can note a closer relationship between class and more marginal religious groupings. Stark and Bainbridge argue that cults draw their members from the higher social classes, whereas Kelly (1992) has suggested that NRMs are founded and populated by the educated middle classes. Adler's (1979) research has drawn attention to the fact that, in the USA, members of witch covens mainly come from the professional middle classes. Bader (2003) also notes that two thirds of those who claim to have been abducted by aliens previously held middle-class occupations.

NAMs add a further dimension to the relationship between class and religion in terms of the argument that they involve 'meaning without motivation'. Middle-class, disillusioned and middle-aged people turn to NAMS that promise to help them live more harmoniously or successfully in a world that seems to largely pass by these people. NAMs offer meaning to life without the need to break with routine or make personal sacrifices, but this is both a strength and weakness:

- If an individual feels their involvement produces benefits, they will consume more of what's on offer, by buying into 'new and deeper levels of enlightenment'.
- Most people will not experience a great life change, which encourages consumer disenchantment and a desire to move on to the next religious product.

In this respect, Bruce (1995) argues that the general attraction of NAMs to the middle classes is based on the idea that 'spiritual growth appeals mainly to those whose more pressing material needs have been satisfied. Unmarried mothers raising children on welfare tend to be too concerned with finding food, heat and light to be overly troubled by their inner lights and when they do look for release from their troubles they prefer the bright outer lights of bars and discotheques.'

TEST YOURSELF

Suggest one reason why the middle classes are more religious than the working classes.

Gender

Walter and Davie's (1998) observation that 'in western societies influenced by Christianity, women are more religious than men on virtually every measure' is a useful starting point for any examination of the relationship between gender and religiosity. O'Beirne (2004), for example, found that across the major UK religions:

- more women (83%) than men (74%) claimed some form of affiliation to a religious organisation such as a church or denomination
- this pattern was maintained across non-traditional religions such as spiritualism and Wicca (both nearly 70% female).

In the USA, the Pew Research Center (2009) found a similar distribution:

- 86% of women claimed a religious affiliation.
- 79% of men claimed a religious affiliation.

This pattern was maintained across a range of religious organisations, from established churches and denominations to NRMs and NAMs. Bader (2003), for example, suggests that NRMs and NAMs have more female than male adherents.

As with class, the reliability and validity of data about religious beliefs is often questionable. However, the data that exists suggests that women believe more strongly in things such as the existence of a god. Crockett and Voas found:

- 36% more British women than men believed in the certainty of a god's existence
- in the USA the difference was 15%.

Women are also more likely to pray by themselves and have higher believe more in concepts such as life after death and heaven.

Participation: In terms of participation, women generally have greater involvement in religious activities, such as attendance at services and clubs. Crockett and Voas suggest that this difference is even more pronounced among men and women aged between 21 and 40. O'Beirne found that Christian women were slightly more likely than men to participate 'in groups or clubs with a religious link'. Although the reverse was true for Muslims, this may reflect gender norms (Muslim women are not allowed to participate independently of men in religious activities), rather than any significant difference in religiosity.

This pattern of attendance and participation is not restricted to the UK and Western Europe. Among

Americans, the Pew Research Center (2009) found women were more likely to attend a church service, pray daily, say religion is important in their life and have a certain belief in a personal god.

While the evidence points to greater female involvement in religious belief and practice, Malmgreen (1987) notes that this is not necessarily reflected in religious organisations. Across the globe, religion 'has been a predominantly female sphere', but it is generally men who 'monopolized positions of authority'.

Are women more religious than men?

Explanations: Traditional feminist explanations for greater levels of female religiosity focus on the concept of gender socialisation. This examines how the behaviour of cultural groups is conditioned by the values and norms of different group members. In this respect, the idea that men and women develop different cultural identities has been used to explain gender differences in participation in ways related to **patriarchy**.

Christianity, Steggerda (1993) notes, promotes concepts of love and care that are more attractive to non-working women whose role is mainly one of childcare. They translate their general family role into religious behaviour. Levels of religiosity between working males and females are very similar.

Daly (1968) argues that patriarchal forms of religion have a certain attraction in terms of offering:

- order, where religious beliefs and institutions provide certainties in an increasingly 'senseless and confusing world'

- rules that clearly specify the limits of acceptable behaviour.

As long as both men and women 'understand, know and accept' their place in this moral order, religions also provide women with:

- shelter – a 'home and haven' in a male-dominated world
- safety in a threatening world
- belonging, in the sense of finding personal identity through group membership.

Daly (1973) argues that these benefits come at a price for women in terms of submission to patriarchal control. Religions are male-dominated, hierarchical institutions that 'serve the interests of sexist society'. This applies to traditional religions, such as Islam and Christianity, where women are rarely found in positions of power and influence (although the Church of England has allowed female priests since 1992). It also applies to NRMs, where men hold most of the powerful positions. Palmer (1994) argues that the type of women that NRMs attract are not seeking power and suggests 'women join to bring order to their lives'.

The argument here is that female involvement in religious organisations exchanges a sense of cultural identity and stability for patriarchy. Palmer suggests that this 'patriarchal order' can be seen in three basic organisational types:

- Complementary groups, where each gender has different spiritual qualities that, when combined (in marriage, for example), balance each other.
- Unity groups emphasise 'inner spirituality' as 'sexless', a belief that rests on recognising traditional forms of gender division in the non-spiritual world.
- Polarity groups emphasise essential, different and non-complementary qualities in men and women, with men seen as the superior sex.

The third group is more likely to characterise both Christian and non-Christian fundamentalist churches, sects and denominations that emphasise an exaggerated form of 'traditional' gender roles and relationships. For example, Bartkowski (2000) notes that the aim of the US-based 'Promise Keepers' sect is the 'rejuvenation of godly manhood' through an emphasis on 'traditional masculine roles' such as breadwinner and provider.

Other forms of feminism suggest that we can see female participation in religious organisations as 'challenging the institution from within'. Involvement should not be considered in terms of binary oppositions such as participation/non-participation or patriarchal/non-patriarchal. Rather, Winter et al. (1994) argue, we should look at how both men and women are involved in changing the nature of religious faith and practice through 'defecting in place'. This is the idea that various forms of feminist theology, such as critiques of patriarchal practices and images, are promoting changes within traditional religions in two ways:

- Spaces within religions, in the sense that women carve out areas of religious belief and activity that relate specifically to female interests and concerns.
- Ideologies supporting female authority within religious movements. Some forms of ecofeminism, for example, link themes such as environmentalist politics, spirituality and animal rights to what Spretnak (1982) terms concepts of 'pre-patriarchal myths and religions that had honoured women'. Neitz (1998), for example, notes how some NRMs are 'oriented primarily to female deities exploring how these female-affirming beliefs, symbols, and rituals may be empowering to women'.

While matriarchal/matrifocal religious movements are very small in number, of more immediate significance is a process Swatos (1998) calls the 'feminisation of religions'. This is the idea that religions in Western Europe and the USA are undergoing a 'fundamental orientational change' where 'feminine images of the nature of deity and the role of the clergy come to predominate. God is seen as loving and consoling rather than as authoritarian and judgemental'. Similarly, members of the clergy are seen as 'helping professionals' rather than as 'representatives of God's justice'.

Risk: A different perspective argues that sex-role socialisation fails to explain gender differences in religious/irreligious belief and behaviour. As Stark and Finke (2000) note, traditional explanations argue that women are more religious because they are:

- more involved in socialising children
- less involved in their careers
- more likely to join social groups.

Miller and Stark (2002), however, argue that there is little evidence to support the idea that 'gender differences in religiousness are a product of differential socialization'. Rather, drawing on evolutionary psychological ideas, Kanazawa and Still (2000) suggest that a lack of religious belief 'is an aspect of a general syndrome of short-sighted, risky behaviours'. Men are more likely to indulge in risky behaviour, such as not believing in a god, because of their biological evolution. Stark (2002) draws this conclusion on the basis that 'in every country and culture men were less religious than women'.

Lizardo and Collett (2005) reject the claim that gender differences in attitudes to risk explain male and female religiosity. As evidence, they point to the work of Hagan et al. (1988) in relation to power control theory. Although there are broad gender differences in risk taking, there are also differences within gender groups; some men engage in riskier behaviours than others.

This theory argues, therefore, that 'gender differences in risk preference are closely related to class based differences in the socialization of children, with women raised in patriarchal families more likely to be risk-averse than men raised in the same type of households and women raised in more egalitarian households'. Lizardo and Collett demonstrated the following:

- Women raised by highly educated mothers show lower religiosity than those raised by less educated mothers.
- A mother's education has little effect on men's chances of being irreligious.
- A father's education has little effect on gender differences in religiosity.

In other words, levels of gender religiosity are explained by class-based differences in socialisation. Contrary to Stark's (2002) argument about the lack of evidence for secular attitudes in modern societies, young people as a group appear to have converging gender attitudes to religion. This would not happen if religious belief was based on fundamental evolutionary gender differences.

TEST YOURSELF

Suggest one reason why women are more religious than men.

Ethnicity

On a global level, there are marked differences in religiosity across different nations. Emergent nations in Africa, Asia and South America have higher levels of religious belief and practice than developed nations such as the UK and Germany. This means that societies with very high levels of general religiosity – such as Nigeria, India and Pakistan – are statistically unlikely to show great ethnic differences. In order to understand the relationship between ethnicity and religion, therefore, we need to look at developed societies with much lower overall levels of religiosity to discover if some ethnic groups are 'more religious' than others. We can, in this respect, use the UK as an example of a developed nation with a low general level of religiosity.

327

Cook (2003) warned that 'collecting data on ethnicity is difficult because there is no consensus on what constitutes an ethnic group'. However, British society reflects a range of ethnicities and religious affiliations, considered not just in terms of different ethnic groups associating themselves with different religions, but also in terms of the diversity of affiliation within some ethnic groups. Indian ethnicities, for example, involve a mix of Hindu, Sikh, Muslim and Christian religious affiliations.

Identity: O'Beirne (2004) notes that religion is a relevant factor 'in a person's self-description, particularly for people from the Indian subcontinent'. This suggests that 'religion is important to migrant minority ethnic groups because it is integral to their cultural and ethnic identity'.

It is important to note that there are significant variations in affiliation and strength of belief based on gender and age across all ethnicities. Age, in particular, is significant when comparing the experiences of different generations within recent immigrant ethnicities. There are generational differences among minority groups in how young and old classify themselves:

- Older, first-generation, immigrants are more likely to identify with their country of origin.
- Younger, third-generation, individuals are more likely to classify themselves in terms of their country of birth.

Explanations: We can explore a range of explanations for the relationship between ethnicity and religiosity, starting with deprivation. In the UK, the highest levels of religious affiliation are found among Pakistani (92%) and Bangladeshi (92%) minorities. Berthoud (1998) has shown that these ethnic groups are among the very poorest in British society. This suggests a correlation between poverty/class and religiosity among some ethnic groups. While this correlation is interesting, deprivation of itself is not a sufficient explanation for higher levels of religiosity, measured in terms of both affiliation and practice.

Although Christians generally profess high levels of affiliation, this does not translate significantly into religious practice. As Crockett and Voas put it: 'All major ethnic minority populations are more religious than British-born whites'. Since high levels of deprivation exist among the white working class, the question here is why do some ethnic groups display higher levels of religiosity under similar economic circumstances?

The answer is linked to ideas and issues related not just to ethnicity but also to the experience of being an ethnic

minority. The key to understanding levels of ethnic group religiosity, both majority and minority, is found in two areas:

- inter-group relationships – how, for example, different minority groups relate to both other minorities and to the ethnic majority
- intra-group relationships – differences, for example, within ethnic-minority groups, such as class, gender and age, that relate to how these groups interact with the ethnic majority.

Identity: These different experiences, therefore, relate to questions of identity, considered in terms of both the self-perception of different ethnic groups and the various social factors that go into the 'constructive mix' of such identities. We can illustrate this idea by contrasting the experiences of the white British majority ethnic group in the UK, following a predominantly Christian faith, with those of the Pakistani minority following a predominantly Muslim faith.

The measured differences in religiosity between these two groups are conventionally explained in terms of a distinction between two types of 'believer':

- Nominal: where people are 'born into a religion', such as the Church of England and generally associate themselves with this religion without having much firm faith or commitment to it; they may, in this respect, be considered largely **agnostic** – neither believing nor disbelieving.
- Authentic: people who demonstrate their firmly held beliefs through various forms of practice and commitment. Pakistani Muslims generally fall into this category.

KEY TERM

Agnosticism: the belief that one cannot know that God exists and therefore neither believes nor disbelieves in a deity.

However, this raises the question of why nominal belief should be considered 'less authentic' than overtly practised beliefs:

- Private beliefs may be sincerely held without the need to have them continually and publicly reaffirmed.
- Public practice may be indicative of social processes, such as status considerations or cultural/peer pressures, rather than strict religious belief.

Suggest two reasons why religion might be an important source of identity for ethnic minorities.

Privatised religion

Bruce (1995) develops these ideas by arguing that in modern, secular societies a distinction arises between two spheres of behaviour and practice that involve different basic values and norms:

- The public sphere is governed by ideas of rationality, instrumentalism and, most importantly, universal values and norms: 'Supermarkets do not vary prices according to the religion, gender or age of the customer.' This sphere is that of the community, a space where people meet, greet and interact according to a set of shared ideas and beliefs.
- The private sphere is characterised by ideas of expression and affection. It represents a space where the individual is, to some extent, set apart from the communal, public sphere.

Using this distinction, Christianity has evolved to accommodate itself to changes. This is especially true of developments that have taken place in the public sphere, such as the rise of secular politics, the demands of economic globalisation and cultural and ethnic diversity. In so doing, Christianity has slowly retreated from the public sphere of religious practice into the private sphere of religious belief. While people still attend services, the church understands that, for the ethnic majority, the role and function of organised religion has changed. This group no longer needs religion to perform functions like:

- communality – bringing people physically together
- social solidarity – the idea that people have things in common binding them together
- identity – the idea that we become 'centred' or secure in the knowledge of 'who we are' through communal religious practices.

Although people still require these things, they are increasingly satisfied by other institutions and activities, from the media, through shopping, to sport. Thus, as the Christian church loses its public functions, attendance and practice also decline, but religion does not necessarily disappear from people's lives. In fact, Bruce argues that it has simply been 'reworked so as to confine it to the private sphere'. Davie (2001), however, argues that religious practice often remains important even in situations where religiosity has become confined to the private sphere. People still feel the need to make public affirmations, such as weddings and funerals, because these are important life events that require *both* private and public acknowledgement.

Bruce suggests that the situation is different for minority ethnicities. In the UK, these groups have moved from a situation in which 'their religion was dominant and all-pervasive to an environment in which they form a small, deviant minority, radically at odds with the world around them'. Recent immigrant groups especially find themselves in a society that is at best indifferent and at worst hostile. In such a situation, it is not surprising that Pakistani minorities, for example, look to familiar traditions, customs, values and norms.

These behaviours require affirmation and reaffirmation through communal gatherings that promote both social solidarity and a sense of ethnic identity. Religious practices are also a source of protection – a **cultural defence**, both physical and psychological, in a challenging world. Religions such as Islam, therefore, are articulated in the public sphere. As Davie (2001) notes: 'Islam is not a religion that lends itself to private expression.' This suggests that religions relate to a sense of belonging, not just in the literal sense of being part of a religion or organisation, but also of belonging to a specific, definable group, membership of which is affirmed through public practices.

KEY TERM

Cultural defence: process whereby religious ideas and practices are used by social groups as a source of physical and psychological protection in a hostile and challenging world.

For Bruce (1988), the rise of the New Christian Right in the southern states of the USA is another example of cultural defence, although he links it more with regionalism than with any notion of ethnicity. Bruce explains the appeal of the New Christian Right as a reaction of the southern states to the permissive era of the 1960s and 1970s, which seemed to threaten the more conservative values of the white majority in the deep south.

For ethnic-minority groups in particular, religiosity performs significant services and functions in terms of social identities. One function of religious organisations for many ethnic-minority groups is that of providing a sense of homogeneity, shared purpose, and cultural continuity and permanence.

The concept of identity implies both a sense of Self and, by definition, a sense of Other sustained both:

- internally, in terms of the particular beliefs and practices of the group
- externally, by contrasting these beliefs and practices with groups 'not like us'.

Further functions involve emotional involvement that gives someone a sense of well-being through membership of a particular group, such as a religion. For some minority groups, the emotional aspect of religious belief and practice is valued in an unfamiliar world. Finally, belonging to a coherent group that values a person's presence and contribution gives them a sense of power that gives them the strength to face the world. This is especially significant for politically and economically marginalised ethnic groups.

ACTIVITY

Discussion

Why are women more religious than men? Do you think that this is always the case?

Summary points

- **There are two basic definitions of religion:**
  - Exclusive
  - Inclusive.
- **Perspectives on religion include:**
  - functionalism – functional for society
  - Marxism
  - Weberian.
- **Social change in terms of religion includes:**
  - transformations
  - transitions.
- **Modernity and religion – focuses upon religion's:**
  - disappearance
  - decline
  - retreat and reinvention.
- **Postmodernity and religion – focuses upon religion's:**
  - resacrilisation
  - new age movements
  - fundamentalism.
- **Religious organisations include:**
  - church
  - denomination
  - sect
  - cult
  - new religious movements.
- **Pro-secularisation:**
  - declining power and influence
  - declining institutional influence.

- **Anti-secularisation:**
  - declining institutional influence and conventional practices
  - flourishing beliefs and unconventional practices.
- **Postmodernism:**
  - secularisation as metanarrative
  - competing narratives.
- **Participation in religion involves:**
  - social class:
    - middle and upper classes – greater:
      - involvement in traditional religions
      - institutional representation and practice.
    - younger middle classes:
      - greater involvement in NRMs and new age movements.
  - gender and religion – women:
    - are more religious
    - have lower representation in organisations
    - have higher religiosity in the context of:
      - patriarchy
      - risk
      - cultural identities.
  - ethnicity - explanations for religiosity:
    - material deprivation
    - cultural deprivation
    - identity.

Exam-style questions

1 **a** Explain the difficulties in assessing the extent of religious belief in a society. [9]

  b Assess the view that the influence of religion is declining in modern industrial societies. [16]

2 **a** Explain why some feminist theorists believe that religion is an instrument through which women are dominated and oppressed. [9]

  b Assess sociological explanations for the growth of new religious movements. [16]

3 **a** Explain the differences between types of religious organisation. [9]

  b Assess the claim that religion is always and everywhere a conservative social force. [16]

4 **a** Explain how religious beliefs and organisations relate to social class, gender or ethnicity. [9]

  b Assess the relationship between religion, modernity and postmodernity. [16]

Total available marks 100

331

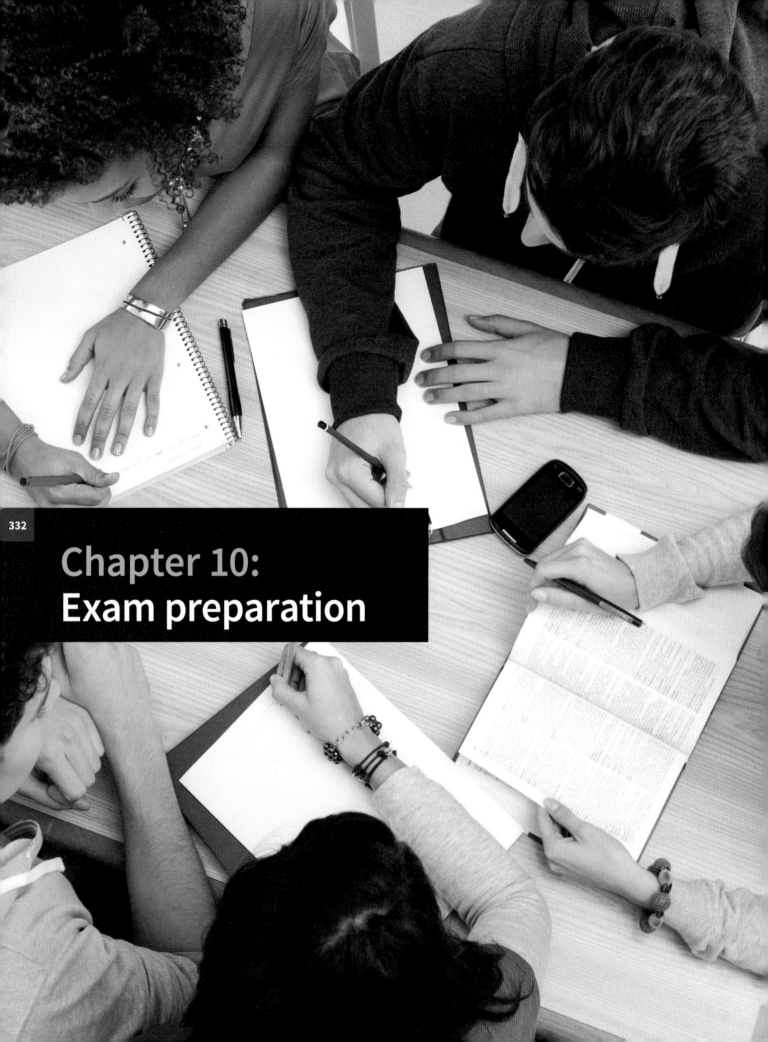

Chapter 10:
Exam preparation

Revision

The purpose of revision is to ensure that you can retrieve information when it is required. Revision should not be something you undertake in the last few days before examination, but needs to be an ongoing process throughout your course. The initial objective is to condense your notes into a revision-friendly format. One way of doing this is to transform large blocks of text into a more memorable form based on keywords/key ideas.

Notes	Keywords
Traditional Marxist approaches favour materialist explanations, with poverty and deprivation as the main source of differential achievement. Material deprivation, for example, involves a combination of things that give working class pupils a relative disadvantage in education.	**Material deprivation = Disadvantages for the working class.**

Keywords

Keywords help with memory recall; they help unlock your knowledge in two ways:

1 by condensing a large amount of information into a single word or short phrase that's easier to remember

2 by opening the door to a more extensive range of knowledge by linking to ideas you have stored but find difficult to recall.

When reviewing and condensing your notes, look for key-words that contain a great deal of related meaning, such as:

■ **S**ociological perspectives
■ **C**oncepts
■ **E**vidence
■ **N**ames
■ **T**heories.

The keyword 'Marxism', for example, should unlock a wide range of related knowledge that can be applied to a question.

Mnemonics

A mnemonic is a word or phrase formed by taking the first letters from a list, as in the example of SCENT above. Remembering a single word helps you remember key ideas to use in an exam. Mnemonics are a good recall technique because they condense large amounts of information.

Refreshing your memory

A second objective of revision is to recall the things you have learned; the more you 'refresh your memory' the easier it is to recall information. The best way to

do this is to keep revising throughout your course, to consolidate understanding by continually reviewing what you have learnt. This means taking the time to identify and record keywords, to help you condense your notes, and reviewing everything you have learnt on a particular day or week. Treating revision as a continuous process means:

■ integrating revision into your normal workload – doing 'a little and often' is easier and more productive than trying to cram everything into a few shorts days or weeks prior to an exam

■ reducing the risk that something like a minor illness will have a major disruptive impact on your exam revision

■ using the time between the end of your course and the start of the exam as a period of more intense consolidation.

Revision planning

1 Create a revision routine by setting aside time at the end of each week to review your learning and add to your keyword lists.

2 Revise for short periods of no more than one hour, then take a break.

3 Sleep properly during periods of intensive revision. The brain consolidates information when you sleep and this helps you remember what you have revised.

4 Revise actively; do not just do the same thing over and over again. For example, mix memory tests with things like question planning and answering.

Assessment

Assessment involves clear behavioural rules. Understanding these will help you reach your full potential. There are two key questions to consider, which are described below.

What is being tested?

A sociology examination is not simply a knowledge test; it also tests your ability to apply the things you know. This combination relates to three assessment objectives (AOs), each of which covers two skill domains.

Assessment objective	Skill domains
AO1	Knowledge and understanding
AO2	Interpretation and application
AO3	Analysis and evaluation

The following tables show how the assessment objectives from the Cambridge syllabus are broadly related to the

333

aims of the rest of the syllabus in terms of the evidence they require a student to demonstrate.

AO1: Knowledge and understanding

Syllabus aims

- knowledge and understanding of sociological concepts, theories, methods and research findings
- understanding sociological research methods.

Evidence

- offer definitions and explanations
- demonstrate appropriate knowledge
- demonstrate awareness of relevant sociological arguments, debates and issues
- discuss theoretical and practical considerations
- outline the findings from relevant sociological studies and research data.

Weighting

AS Level		A Level
Paper 1	Paper 2	Paper 3
40%	40%	30%

Knowledge involves the ability to do things such as provide clear definitions and use appropriate sociological ideas. Understanding means being able to locate practical and theoretical knowledge in a relevant sociological context. You must for example, use your knowledge to answer a particular question.

AO2: Interpretation and application

Syllabus aims

- an appreciation and understanding of diversity, continuity and change
- an understanding of the relationship between sociological findings and everyday life, including contemporary social, cultural and political issues.

Evidence

- interpret sociological material presented in different forms
- distinguish sociological knowledge from subjects such as biology and psychology
- apply concepts, theories and evidence to support arguments and conclusions.

Weighting

AS Level		A Level
Paper 1	Paper 2	Paper 3
30%	30%	30%

Interpretation broadly involves the ability to explain what something means, while application tests your ability to use different areas of knowledge develop and support the point being made in an answers. This could involve, for example, showing how a particular theory can be used to explain a specific type of behaviour.

AO3: Analysis and evaluation

Syllabus aims

- explore the links between sociological concepts, theories and research findings
- use sociological material appropriately to analyse relevant arguments and debates
- compare and contrast different theoretical positions.

Evidence

- evaluate the strengths and limitations of theories and methods
- analyse and assess evidence and arguments
- reach conclusions based on evidence and arguments
- recognise limitations and bias in evidence.

Weighting

AS Level		A Level
Paper 1	Paper 2	Paper 3
30%	30%	40%

Analysis involves making connections between concepts, theories and studies to draw conclusions based on the arguments and evidence you present. Evaluation involves thinking critically about arguments and evidence.

Weighting

The weighting given to each AO is important because it tells you how the marks are distributed in examination.

At AS Level, for every 10 marks awarded:

- 4 are for knowledge and understanding
- 3 are for interpretation and application
- 3 are for analysis and evaluation.

60% of the exam marks, therefore, are awarded for what you *do* with the information you use.

At A Level, for every 10 marks awarded:

- 3 are for knowledge and understanding
- 3 are for interpretation and application
- 4 are for analysis and evaluation.

In other words, 70% of the marks are awarded for what you *do* with the information you use.

Understanding assessment weighting

Understanding the assessment weighting for an examination is important to help you know how you should answer questions within the examination:

- Think about the question and what it is asking.
- Reflect on the skills you need to demonstrate.
- Select relevant knowledge.
- Apply knowledge to the question appropriately.

A common exam error, particularly when answering higher-mark extended questions, is to write pages of *descriptive* prose. While this may gain marks for knowledge and, to some extent understanding, it does not address the other skill domains. A key thing to remember here is that once you have all the available marks for, say, 'knowledge and understanding', you cannot gain any more marks for this AO. If you earned these marks by writing ten lines in an answer, you will not gain any more marks if you go on to write ten more pages filled with 'knowledge and understanding'.

How is it tested?

Exam questions are written to allow students to meet the requirements of assessment objectives. If you understand the skills each question demands, you can tailor your answer accordingly. You should, therefore, read each question carefully to look for clues about which skill domains are required.

AS Level

AS Level papers contain a mix of questions constructed with increasing levels of difficulty. This is signposted by different instructions:

a **What is meant by** the term basic and irreducible family functions? [2]

*The instruction here (and its variant '**Identify**') indicates this is a knowledge and understanding question. It tests your ability to identify relevant knowledge in order to demonstrate your understanding of the term 'basic and irreducible family functions'.*

b **Describe** two ways in which the existence of family structures may benefit capitalism. [4]

The instruction here says that while you need to identify relevant knowledge and understanding ('two ways') you must also interpret its significance and apply it to the question.

c **Explain** how the family may contribute to value consensus. [8]

This instruction requires knowledge interpreted correctly and applied relevantly to the question. It also requires conclusions to be drawn in response to the question.

d **Assess** the view that the family exists more to benefit society rather than individual family members. [11]

*The final type of instruction (and its variant '**explain and assess**') is the most demanding because you must use all of the skill domains in your answer. Evaluation, for example, is encouraged, because to 'assess' you must weigh up evidence 'for and against'; you have to produce an answer that gives equal weight to these arguments and then draw appropriate conclusions from the evidence.*

A Level

The A Level paper is built around two types of instruction, with a greater emphasis on AO3 assessment objectives:

a **Explain** why the educational performance of girls has improved compared with that of boys in many modern industrial societies in recent years. [9]

b **Assess** the view that the main factor influencing educational achievement is the social class background of the pupil. [16]

Instruction	Skills tested	You will be able to:
Identify / What is meant by	Knowledge Understanding	Correctly name something (*identify*) or show you understand what something means
Describe	As above *plus*: Interpretation Application	Give an accurate account of something in a way that captures its most important characteristics. Accurately convey a meaning or relationship
Explain	As above	Clarify something, such as a concept or theory, by identifying and describing its basic qualities and then show how and why these relate to something else
Assess	As above *plus* Analysis Evaluation	Weigh up the value of something, such as a concept, theory or study, by considering its strengths and weaknesses/uses and limitations. Draw conclusions about that value based on your assessment

The following table summarises the links between:

- the instructions given
- the skills they are designed to test
- what you need to do to fulfil these criteria.

We can illustrate the difference between these various instructions by thinking about how each one encourages you to approach a concept such as primary socialisation in different ways:

- **What is meant** by primary socialisation?
- **Describe** how the family is an agency of primary socialisation.
- **Explain** how the family is the main agency of primary socialisation.
- **Assess** the importance of the family group in the socialisation process.

Exam structure

Understanding the structure of your exam paper means you will know what to expect and how best to approach answering different types of questions.

AS Level: Papers 1 and 2

Although Paper 1 examines the Family and Paper 2 examines Theory and Methods, they have the same structure. Each is:

- 90 minutes
- worth 50% of the AS mark – together they are worth 50% of the total A Level
- based on three questions, two of which must be answered
- structured in the same way:
  - Question 1 is compulsory and consists of information to read followed by four questions of increasing difficulty worth 2, 4, 8 and 11 marks, respectively.
  - There is a choice between answering either question 2 or question 3; this is always an extended 25-mark question.

A Level: Paper 3

This paper covers Education, Media, Religion and Global Development. This paper is:

- 180 minutes
- worth 50% of the total A Level
- based on four options each consisting of two questions split into two parts worth 9 and 16 marks, respectively:
  - You must answer questions from three different options.

- You can only answer one question from each option.
- All questions involve extended answers.

Timing

Understanding the structure of an exam will also give you an idea of how long you might wish to spend on each question.

AS Level: Although you have 90 minutes to work through questions worth 50 marks, some of this time may be used to:

- read through the supplied data, understand and select questions: approximately **2 minutes**
- plan your answer to higher-mark questions: approximately **3 minutes**
- review, revise and correct your answers: approximately **10 minutes**.

If you choose to follow the timings suggested above, this would leave you with around 90 seconds per mark, which could be used as an approximate guide to how long you should spend on each question.

Marks	Minutes (approximate)
2	3
4	6
8	12
11	16–17
25	37–38

A Level: You have 180 minutes to work through questions worth 75 marks. From this you may wish to subtract:

- **5 minutes** to read all the questions carefully before you choose which to do
- **15 minutes** to plan answers to three higher-mark questions
- **10 minutes** to review, revise and correct your answers.

If you choose to follow the timings suggested above, this would leave you with around 2 minutes per mark, which could be used as an approximate guide to how long you should spend on each question:

- 9 marks = 18 minutes (approx)
- 16 marks = 32 minutes (approx)

Timing is important, because if you spend too long on small-mark questions you have less time to plan and answer higher-mark questions. You may miss marks because you have run out of time or have had to rush your answer to the extended questions.

Answering exam questions

You can bring together your knowledge of the assessment objectives and exam structure to think about how to

answer different types of question. Some examples of exam-style questions and suggested approaches to answering each question follow. Suggested timings are offered as a guide.

Example 1

The following example questions reflect the style of questions you can expect to encounter in the Cambridge AS Level papers (Paper 1 and Paper 2).

2 marks	What is meant by the term basic and irreducible functions?	3 minutes

You need to write a short, straightforward, statement that explains the term using relevant examples.

4 marks	Describe two ways in which the existence of family structures may benefit capitalism.	6 minutes

You need to:

- identify two ways and ensure that you include a brief explanation of how each way 'benefits capitalism'
- if you only write about one way, or you identify without explaining, you will not receive both available marks
- if you write about more than two ways you **do not** get extra marks.

8 marks	Explain how the family may contribute to value consensus.	12 minutes

Your explanation should cover at least two points in depth using relevant examples drawn from sociological research. Each point will score up to a maximum of 4 marks if it is:

- identified correctly and relevantly
- explained in relation to the question
- exampled to show how information is applied to the question.

11 marks	Assess the view that the family exists more to benefit society rather than individual family members.	16–17 minutes

To gain a high mark for this type of question you will:

- contrast two or more arguments
- provide basic accounts of the arguments for and against the statement, using knowledge, interpretation and application
- evaluate each of the arguments using relevant evidence
- draw conclusions based on the arguments you have assessed.

25 marks	'Marriage has less importance in modern industrial societies than it has in traditional societies.' Explain and assess this view.	37–38 minutes

To gain a high mark for this type of question you will:

- introduce your answer by defining the key terms in the question and explaining any assumptions used in the answer
- contrast two or more arguments
- provide detailed accounts of the arguments for and against the statement, using knowledge, interpretation and application
- evaluate each of the arguments using relevant evidence based on sociological research
- draw conclusions based on the arguments you have assessed
- provide an overall conclusion about the statement based on the evidence presented.

Example 2

The following example questions reflect the style of questions you can expect to encounter in the Cambridge A Level paper (Paper 3).

11 marks	Explain why the educational performance of girls has improved compared with that of boys in many modern industrial societies in recent years.	16–17 minutes

To gain a high mark for this type of question you will:

- focus clearly on modern industrial societies and the educational performance of boys and girls
- provide a detailed discussion of at least four factors that explain differences in educational performance
- develop each factor, using knowledge, interpretation and application
- draw conclusions about the question based on the arguments you have considered.

25 marks	Assess the view that the main factor influencing educational achievement is the social class background of the pupil.	37–38 minutes

To gain a high mark for this type of question you will:

- introduce your answer by defining the key terms in the question. Explain any assumptions you're going to use in the answer
- clearly and concisely explain why some argue class is the most important factor in educational achievement and contrast this with alternative arguments
- evaluate each of the arguments using relevant evidence that draws heavily on sociological research
- draw clearly reasoned conclusions based on the arguments you have assessed
- provide an overall conclusion based on the evidence you have presented.

Planning

Of all the different types of question that can be asked in examination, the extended 'assess' type is often the most difficult to answer because they:

- are wide-ranging rather than tightly focused
- involve the use of all the skill domains
- involve sustained, extended, arguments
- must include arguments for and against the question.

Given you are likely to be writing for nearly 40 minutes at A Level, it is important to plan your answer carefully to:

- avoid simple description
- avoid repetition and confusion
- cover all the assessment objectives
- answer the question asked.

In this respect, a plan is both vital and useful – and it needs to be:

- quick and easy
- evocative – one that 'jogs your memory'
- well structured
- easy to follow and reference as you write.

One way to do this is to use key words, a simple example of which is a 'for and against' table we can illustrate using the question:

'Assess the view that the main factor influencing educational achievement is the social class background of the pupil.'

Create a table labelled 'for' and 'against' and brainstorm any key ideas you could use in your answer.

For	Against
Material deprivation	IQ
Cultural deprivation	–
Cultural capital	–
Gender and achievement	Gender and achievement
Ethnicity and achievement	Ethnicity and achievement
Interrelationship – class	Interrelationship – gender and ethnicity
Correspondence theory	–
Teacher labelling	Teacher labelling

The key ideas can then be used as the basis for constructing an answer. This involves asking the kinds of questions implicit in the assessment objectives (what, why, how and where) to construct a paragraph focused on the question.

Skill domain	Ask yourself...
Knowledge	**What** is the key idea I am explaining?
Understanding	**How** does this knowledge relate to the question?
Interpretation	**Why** is this idea significant in the context of the question?
Application	**Where** is the evidence to support the idea?
Evaluation	**What** evidence can I use to criticise the idea?
Analysis	**What** conclusions can I draw about the idea from the material I have written in answer to the previous questions?

Try writing a paragraph on the key idea of 'material deprivation' using the 'ask yourself' questions in the table.

This type of simple plan gives a basic structure to follow in examination and it can be revised as you write; if you suddenly think of a key idea, just add it to your table to remind you to use it later.

A more detailed planning technique is to construct a spider diagram. While this takes longer to create, it helps you make important connections between the key ideas in your plan. For example, using 'material deprivation' as a key idea you could note:

■ different types of theory (class cultures, sub-cultures, situational constraints and investment theory)

■ evidence associated with each theory (situational constraints, for example, could be evidenced by Willis's 'Learning to Labour').

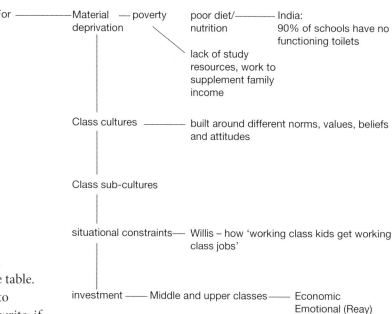

Try writing about 'material deprivation' based on a spider diagram you have created and the 'ask yourself' questions outlined earlier.

Errors

It is easy to make simple errors when you are under pressure. An awareness of common errors – and how to avoid them – can help you gain the marks your efforts deserve.

Not answering the question:

The student writes a great deal of information but they lose sight of what the question is asking.
Avoid by continually referring to the question throughout your answer.

Not answering a question according to the instructions:

Errors here include things like only giving one example when two are required or only giving one side of an argument when you have been asked to 'assess' a statement.
Avoid by reading the question carefully, identifying the instruction (identify, describe, explain, assess...) and making the mental connection with the assessment objectives.

Not using all the required skills in an answer:

For extended questions this often involves spending too much time describing something, rather than analysing and evaluating. Instead of simply referring to a study, for example, and explaining why it is significant in the context of the question, the student describes the study and its findings at great length.
Avoid by understanding how the instructions relate to assessment objectives. Practise writing well-structured answers to different types of questions.

Running out of time:

Students spend too much time on some questions and leave themselves too little time to complete the paper.
Avoid by understanding the relationship between the time and marks available. Look at the number of marks available for each question and time yourself strictly. Stop writing and move on to the next question once you have hit your time limit.

Exam check list

Do:

Practise answering questions under exam conditions.	The more you practise the better you become.
Sleep on it.	Memory functions best when activity, such as revision, is followed by sleep. During sleep the brain consolidates learning and retention.
Read each question carefully.	Be clear about what each question is asking and how you plan to answer it.
Answer all parts of a question.	If the question has two parts then each part will carry half the available marks.
Relate your effort to the marks available.	Do not waste time chasing one or two marks.
Spend time planning your answer to extended questions.	Structure your answer and use all the relevant assessment criteria.
Review your answers.	By taking a few minutes to read through your answers you can rectify mistakes of spelling, punctuation, grammar and content.
Present your answers clearly and neatly.	Only use black or blue ink. Punctuate properly and avoid abbreviations.

Don't:

Leave your revision to the last few days before the exam.	While all revision is useful, it is better to revise a little over a long period than a lot over a short space of time.
Revise all night before an exam.	Sleep is crucial to memory retention and you will not recall much of what you covered the night before. You will also be tired and this makes recall more difficult.
Revise on the morning before an exam.	Last-minute revision is not very productive. You are also less likely to retain learning that has not been consolidated by sleep. If you don't know it by the morning of the exam then a last-ditch effort is probably not going to change your performance.
Spend too long on small-mark questions.	If you spend too long chasing a small number of marks you risk running out of time to answer higher-mark questions, potentially losing more marks than you gained.
Choose the first question you read.	When there's a choice, read all questions carefully to understand what they require.
Answer a question that has not been set.	Make sure you constantly refer your answer back to the question.

Bibliography

Abbot, Pamela and Wallace, Claire (1996) *Feminist Perspectives*. Routledge.

Abrams, Dominic (2005) 'Ageism', Conference Paper: British Association for the Advancement of Science.

Abrams, Mark, Gerard, David and Timms, Noel (eds.) (1985) *Values and Social Change in Britain*. Macmillan.

Ackroyd, Stephen and Hughes, John (1992; first published 1981) *Data Collection in Context* (2nd edn). Longman.

ActionAid (2005) *Power Hungry: Six Reasons to Regulate Global Food Corporations*. ActionAid.

Adams, Scott and Marshall, Sheila (1996) 'A Developmental Social Psychology of Identity: Understanding the Person in Context', *Journal of Adolescence*, Vol. 19, No. 5: 429–42.

Adamu, Fatima (2003) 'Globalisation and Economic Glocalisation in Northern Nigeria', Development Studies Associations Annual conference Globalisation and Development.

Adler, Margot (1979) *Drawing Down the Moon*. Viking Press.

Adomaitiene, Ruta (1999) 'The Conceptualization of Sociology of Disability as a Part of Mainstreamed Sociology', *Education, Physical Training: Sport*, Vol. 2, No. 31.

Adorno, Theodor and Horkheimer, Max (1944) *Dialectic of Enlightenment*. Social Studies Association Inc.

Aisbett, Emma (2003) 'Globalization, Poverty and Inequality: Are the Criticisms Vague, Vested, or Valid?', NBER Pre-conference on Globalization, Poverty and Inequality, University of California at Berkeley.

Aldridge, Alan (2003) *Consumption*. Polity Press.

Aldridge, Stephen (2001) *Life Chances and Social Mobility: An Overview of the Evidence*. Prime Minister's Strategy Unit.

Aldridge, Stephen (2004) *Social Mobility: A Discussion Paper*. Performance and Innovation Unit, Cabinet Office.

Alexander, Jeffrey (1995) 'Modern, Anti, Post, Neo', *New Left Review*, No. 210, March/April.

Alpert, Harry (1939) *Emile Durkheim and His Sociology*. Columbia University Press.

Althusser, Louis (1970) 'Ideology and Ideological State Apparatuses (Notes towards an Investigation)', *La Pensée*.

Althusser, Louis (1971) 'Ideology and Ideological State Apparatuses', in Louis Althusser, *Lenin and Philosophy and Other Essays*. Monthly Review.

Althusser, Louis (1972) *Ideology and Ideological State Apparatuses*. David McKay.

Ambert, Anne-Marie (2003) *Same-Sex Couples and Same-Sex Parent Families: Relationships, Parenting, and Issues of Marriage*. Vanier Institute of the Family.

American Academy of Child and Adolescent Psychiatry (2011) *Grandparents Raising Grandchildren*. American Academy of Child and Adolescent Psychiatry Report No. 77.

Anderson, Benedict (1983) *Imagined Communities: Reflections on the Origin and Spread of Nationalism*. Verso.

Anderson, Michael (1989) 'New Insights into the History of the Family in Britain', Economic History Society: Recent Findings of Research in Economic and Social History (ReFresh), No. 9.

Anderson, Michael (1995; first published 1980) *Approaches to the History of the Western Family*. Cambridge University Press.

Anderson, Sarah and Cavanagh, John (2000) *The Rise of Global Corporate Power*. Corporate Watch.

Anshan, Li (2010) *China-Africa Medical Cooperation: Another Form of Humanitarian Aid*. Médecins Sans Frontières.

Appadurai, Arjun (1990) 'Disjuncture and Difference in the Global Cultural Economy', in Mike Featherstone (ed.), *Global Culture: Nationalism, Globalization and Modernity*. Sage.

Archard, David (2004) *Children: Rights and Childhood* (2nd edn). Routledge.

Archer, David (with Jeng, Yaikah) (2006) *Writing the Wrongs: International Benchmarks on Adult Literacy*. ActionAid International.

Aries, Philip (1962) *Centuries of Childhood*. Vintage Books.

Avramov, Dragana and Maskova, Miroslava (2003) 'Active Ageing in Europe', *Population Studies*, Vol. 1, No. 41, Council of Europe Publishing.

Aymer, Cathy and Okitikpi, Toyin (2001) *Young Black Men and the Connexions Service*. Department for Education and Skills.

Azad, Ali (1995) 'Imperialism and Struggle in Iran', *Workers' World*, March.

Babb, Penny, Butcher, Hayley, Church, Jenny and Zealey, Linda (2006) *Social Trends No. 36*. Office for National Statistics.

Bader, Christopher (2003) 'Supernatural Support Groups: Who Are the UFO Abductees and Ritual-Abuse Survivors?', *Journal for the Scientific Study of Religion*, Vol. 42, No. 4.

Badri, Belghis (1994) *The Concept of Sustainable Development*. United Nations Non-Governmental Liaison Service.

Bakewell, Oliver (1999) 'Can We Ever Rely on Refugee Statistics?', *Radical Statistics*, No. 72, www.radstats.org.uk/no072/article1.htm.

Balibar, Étienne and Althusser, Louis (1970) *Reading Capital*. New Left Books.

Ball, James, Milmo, Dan and Ferguson, Ben (2012) 'Half of UK's Young Black Males Are Unemployed', *The Guardian*, 9 March.

Ball, Stephen (1981) *Beachside Comprehensive*. Cambridge University Press.

Bamford, Caroline (1989) 'Gender and Education in Scotland: A Review of Research', *Research in Education*, No. 42.

Bandura, Albert, Ross, Dorothea and Ross, Sheila (1961) 'Transmission of Aggression Through Imitation of Aggressive Models', *Journal of Abnormal and Social Psychology*, Vol. 63: 575–82.

Bandura, Albert, Ross, Dorothea and Ross, Sheila (1963) 'Vicarious Reinforcement and Imitative Learning', *The Journal of Abnormal and Social Psychology*, Vol. 67, No. 6: 601–7.

Baran, Stanley and Davis, Dennis (2011) *Mass Communication Theory: Foundations, Ferment and Future*. Wadsworth.

Barbanti, Olympio (2004) 'Development and Conflict Theory', in Guy Burgess and Heidi Burgess (eds.), *Beyond Intractability*. Conflict Research Consortium, University of Colorado.

Barker, Eileen (1984) *The Making of a Moonie: Brainwashing or Choice?* Blackwell.

Barker, Eileen (1999) *New Religious Movements: A Practical Introduction*. HMSO.

Barnhart, Adam (1994) *Erving Goffman: The Presentation of Self in Everyday Life*. Trinity International University.

Barrat, David (1992) *Media Sociology*. Tavistock.

Barrett, Anne, Westerhof, Gerben and Steverink, Nardi (2003) 'Forever Young? A Comparison of Age Identities in the United States and Germany', *Research on Aging*, Vol. 25, No. 4.

Barrett, Ray (1999) 'Middle Schooling: a Challenge for Policy and Curriculum', *Education Horizons*, Vol. 5, No. 3.

Barro, Robert and Lee, Jong-Wha (1994) *Sources of Economic Growth*. Carnegie-Rochester Series on Public Policy, No. 40.

Bartkowski, John (2000) 'Breaking Walls, Raising Fences: Masculinity, Intimacy, and Accountability Among the Promise Keepers', *Sociology of Religion*, Vol. 61, No. 1.

Bates, Inge and Riseborough, George (eds.) (1993) *Youth and Inequality*. Open University Press.

Baudrillard, Jean (1995) *The Gulf War Did Not Take Place*. Oxford University Press.

Baudrillard, Jean (1998) 'Simulacra and Simulations', in Mark Poster (ed.), *Selected Writings*. Stanford University Press.

Bauer, Peter (1971) *Dissent on Development: Studies and Debates in Development Economics*. Weidenfeld & Nicolson.

Bauman, Zygmunt (1997) *Postmodernity and Its Discontents*. Polity Press.

Beaumont, Jen (2011) *Households and Families: Social Trends 41*. Office for National Statistics.

Bechhoffer, Frank and Paterson, Lindsay (2000) *Principles of Research Design in the Social Sciences*. Routledge.

Beck, Ulrich (1992) *Risk Society: Towards a New Modernity*. Sage.

Becker, Gary (1991) *Treatise on the Family*. Harvard University Press.

Becker, Gary, Landes, Elizabeth and Michael, Robert (1977) 'An economic analysis of marital instability', *Journal of Political Economy*, Vol. 85, No. 6.

Becker, Howard (1967) 'Whose Side Are We On?', *Social Problems*, Vol. 14, No. 3.

Beckford, James (1980) *Scientology, Social Science and the Definition of Religion*. Freedom Publishing.

Bell, Daniel (1999; first published 1973) *The Coming of Post-Industrial Society: A Venture in Social Forecasting*. Basic Books.

Bell, Norman and Vogel, Ezra (1968) *A Modern Introduction to the Family*. Free Press.

Bellah, Robert (1967) 'Civil Religion in America', *Daedalus: Journal of the American Academy of Arts and Sciences*, Vol. 96.

Belson, William (1978) *Television Violence and the Adolescent Boy*. Saxon House.

Bengston, Vern (2001) 'Beyond the Nuclear Family: The Increasing Importance of Multigencrational Bonds', *Journal of Marriage and the Family*, Vol. 63: 1–16.

Bental, Brian (2004) *Sociological Theory*. East Central University.

Benyon, John (2002) *Masculinities and Culture*. Open University Press.

Berelson, Bernard, Lazerfeld, Paul and Gaudet, Hazel (1944) *The People's Choice*. Duell, Sloan and Pearce.

Berer, Marge and Ravindran, Sundari (1996) *Fundamentalism, Women's Empowerment and Reproductive Rights*. Global Reproductive Health Forum.

Berger, Peter (1997) 'Four faces of global culture', *The National Interest*, No. 49.

Berger, Peter (ed.) (1999) *The Desecularization of the World*. Ethics and Public Policy Center, Washington.

Berger, Peter and Luckmann, Thomas (1967) *The Social Construction of Reality: A Treatise in the Sociology of Knowledge*. Anchor.

Bernstein, Basil (1971) 'On the Classification and Framing of Educational Knowledge', in M. F. D. Young (ed.), *Knowledge and Control*. Collier-Macmillan.

Beron, Kurt and Farkas, George (2001) 'Family Linguistic Culture and Social Reproduction: Verbal Skill from Parent to Child in the Preschool and School', Population Association of America conference paper.

Berthoud, Richard (1998) 'Incomes of Ethnic Minorities', in Institute for Social and Economic Research, *Low Income Dynamics*. Department for Work and Pensions (2002).

Best, Lesley (1992) 'Analysis of Sex-Roles in Pre-School Books', *Sociology Review*. Philip Allan.

Bettinger, Robert (1996) 'Neofunctionalism', in David Levinson and Melvin Ember (eds.), *The Encyclopedia of Cultural Anthropology*. Henry Holt.

Billikopf, Gregorio (1999) 'Cultural Differences? Or, are we really that different?', University of California http://nature.berkeley.edu/ucce50/ag-labor/7article/article01.htm.

Binet, Alfred (1916) *The Development of Intelligence in Children: The Binet–Simon Scale*. Williams and Wilkins.

Björkqvist, Kaj (1990) 'World-Rejection, World-Affirmation, and Goal Displacement: Some Aspects of Change in Three New Religious Movements of Hindu Origin', in Nils Holm (ed.), *Encounter with India: Studies in Neo-Hinduism*. Åbo Akademi University Press.

Bjur, Jakob (2009) *Transforming Audiences: Patterns of Individualization in Television Viewing*. University of Gothenburg.

Blackman, Shane (1995) *Youth: Positions and Oppositions – Style, Sexuality and Schooling*. Avebury.

Blair, Maud, Bhattacharyya, Gargi and Ison, Liz (2003) 'Minority Ethnic Attainment and Participation in Education and Training', DfES Research Paper.

Blake, Trevor (2004) *What is Systematic Ideology?*. George Walford.

Blasi, Anthony (1998) 'Definition of Religion', in William Swatos, Jr (ed.), *Encyclopedia of Religion and Society*. Hartford Institute for Religion Research.

Boaz, Annette and Ashby, Deborah (2003) *Fit for Purpose? Assessing Research Quality for Evidence Based Policy and Practice*. ESRC UK Centre for Evidence Based Policy and Practice: Working Paper 11.

Boff, Leonardo and Boff, Clodovis (1987) *Introducing Liberation Theology*. Pantheon Books.

Bogue, Donald (1969) *Principles of Demography*. John Wiley.

Bonke, Jens (1999) 'Children's Household Work: Is There a Difference Between Girls and Boys', IATUR Conference Paper, University of Essex.

Borrego, John (1995) 'Models of Integration, Models of Development in the Pacific', *Journal of World-Systems Research*, Vol. 1, No. 11.

Bourdieu, Pierre (1973) 'Cultural Reproduction and Social Reproduction', in Robert Brown (ed.), *Knowledge, Education and Cultural Change*, Papers in the Sociology of Education: Tavistock.

Bourdieu, Pierre (1984) *Distinction: A Social Critique of the Judgement of Taste*. Harvard University Press.

Bourdieu, Pierre (1986) 'The Forms of Capital', in John Richardson (ed.), *Handbook of Theory and Research for the Sociology of Education*. Greenwood Press.

Bowles, Herbert and Gintis, Samuel (1976) *Schooling in Capitalist America*. Routledge & Kegan Paul.

Bowles, Herbert and Gintis, Samuel (2002) 'Schooling In Capitalist America Revisited', *Sociology of Education*, Vol. 75, No. 1: 1–18.

Brannen, Julia (2003) 'The Age of Beanpole Families', *Sociology Review*, No. 13.

Brannen, Julia and Oakley, Ann (1994) *Adolescent Health and Parenting: Young People, Health and Family Life, 1989-1992*. Oxford University Press.

Braveman, Paula and Gruskin, Sofia (2003) *Poverty, Equity, Human Rights and Health*. Bulletin of the World Health Organization.

Breen, Richard (1997) 'Risk, Recommodification and the Future of the Service Class', *Sociology*, Vol. 31, No. 3.

Breen, Richard and Goldthorpe, John (1999) 'Class Inequality and Meritocracy: a Critique of Saunders and an Alternative Analysis', *British Journal of Sociology*, Vol. 50, No. 1.

Brewer, John (2000) *Ethnography*. Open University Press.

Brimi, Hunter (2005) 'The Influence of Cultural Capital on Twenty-First Century Secondary School Literature Curricula', *Electronic Journal of Sociology*.

British Medical Association (2005) *Improving Health, Fighting Poverty*. BMA.

343

Broad, Bob, Hayes, Ruth and Rushforth, Christine (2001) *Kith and Kin: Kinship Care for Vulnerable Young People*. Joseph Rowntree Foundation.

Brooks, Rachel (2006) 'The Middle Classes and Higher Education Choice', University of Surrey.

Brown, Donald (2000) 'Human Universals and Their Implications', in Neil Roughley (ed.), *Being Humans: Anthropological Universality and Particularity in Transdisciplinary Perspectives*. Walter de Gruyter.

Brown, Michael (2004) 'American Spirits: the Neopagan and New Age Movements Have Now Been Put Under the Microscope of Anthropology', *Natural History*, November.

Browne, Anthony (2006) *The Retreat of Reason: Political Correctness and the Corruption of Public Debate in Modern Britain*. Civitas.

Bruce, Steve (1995) *Religion in Modern Britain*. Oxford University Press.

Bruce, Steve (2001) 'Christianity in Britain, R.I.P.', *Sociology of Religion*, Summer.

Bruce, Steve (2002) *God is Dead: Secularization in the West*. Blackwell.

Bruce, Vicki and Young, Andy (1986) 'Understanding Face Recognition', *British Journal of Psychology*, Vol. 77.

Bruegal, Irene (1979) 'Women as a Reserve Army of Labour: A Note on Recent British Experience', *Feminist Review*, No. 3.

Brundtland Commission: World Commission on Environment and Development (1987) *Our Common Future*. Oxford University Press.

Bruneau, Thomas and Hewitt, William (1992) 'Catholicism and Political Action in Brazil: Limitations and Prospects', in Edward Cleary and Hannah Stewart-Gambino (eds.), *Conflict and Competition: The Latin American Church in a Changing Environment*. Lynne Rienner.

Brusdal, Ragnhild and Lavik, Randi (2005) 'Young Hedonist and Rational Grown Ups? a Closer Look At Consumer Identities in Norway', Paper presented at ESA Conference, National Institute for Consumer Research, Norway.

Bryman, Alan (1999) 'The Disneyisation of Society', *The Sociological Review*, Vol. 47, No. 1.

Bryman, Alan (2004) *The Disneyization of Society*. Sage.

Burden, Bob (2004) in Berliner, Wendy 'IQ: A Hundred?', *The Guardian*, 20 January.

Burnham, James (1941) *The Managerial Revolution*. John Day.

Butler, Judith (1990) *Gender Trouble*. Routledge.

Calvert, Susan and Calvert, Peter (1992) *Sociology Today*: Harvester Wheatsheaf.

Cameron, John and Cameron, Stuart (2006) *The Economic Benefits of Increased Literacy*. UNESCO.

Campbell, Lee (1996) 'Postmodernism and You: Science', Xenos Christian Fellowship, www.xenos.org/ministries/crossroads/dotsci.htm.

Canin, Eric (2001) *Minguito, Managua's Little Saint: Christian Base Communities and Popular Religion in Urban Nicaragua*. California State University.

Cano-Garcia, Francisco and Hughes, Elaine (2000) 'Learning and Thinking Styles: an Analysis of Their Interrelationship and Influence on Academic Achievement', *Educational Psychology*, No. 20.

Capitán, Antonio Luis Hidalgo and Lambie, George (1994) *A Background to Development Theory and some Practical Applications*. University of Huelva.

Caplan, Pat (2006) 'Is It Real Food? Who Benefits from Globalisation in Tanzania and India?', *Sociological Research Online*, Vol. 11, No. 4.

Capra, Fritjof (1983) *The Turning Point*. HarperCollins.

Carlin, Norah (2002) 'Family, Society and Popular Culture in Western Europe c. 1500-1700', Middlesex University.

Carrington, Ben (2002) '"Race", Representation and the Sporting Body', *Critical Urban Studies: Occasional Papers*, Centre for Urban and Community Research, Goldsmiths College, University of London, pp.1–37.

Carter, Greg (2001) *Analyzing Contemporary Social Issues* (2nd edn). Allyn & Bacon.

Carter, Rebecca and Wojtkiewicz, Roger (2000) 'Parental Involvement with Adolescents' Education: Do Daughters or Sons Get More Help?', *Adolescence*, Vol. 35, No. 137.

Castells, Manual (1996) *The Information Age: Economy, Society and Culture*, Vol. I: The Rise of the Network Society. Blackwell.

Castells, Manuel (1997) *The Information Age: Economy, Society and Culture*, Vol. II: The Power of Identity. Blackwell.

Catton, William (1982) *Overshoot: The Ecological Basis of Revolutionary Change*. University of Illinois Press.

Catts, Ralph and Ozga, Jenny (2005) 'What Is Social Capital and How Might It Be Used in Scotland's Schools?', *CES Briefing No. 36*. University of Edinburgh.

Cauffman, Elizabeth, Steinberg, Laurence and Piquero, Alex (2005) 'Psychological, Neuropsychological and Physiological Correlates of Serious Antisocial Behaviour in Adolescence: The Role of Self-Control', *Criminology*, Vol. 43, No. 1.

Center for Social Welfare Research (1999) *Ethnicity and Identity*. School of Social Work, University of Washington.

Chahal, Kusminder (2000) *Ethnic Diversity, Neighbourhoods and Housing*. Joseph Rowntree Foundation.

Chaliand, Gerard (1977) *Revolution in the Third World*. Viking.

Chamberlain, Jessica and Gill, Baljit (2005) *Focus on People and Migration: Fertility and Mortality*. Office for National Statistics.

Chambers, Deborah, Tincknell, Estella, Van Loon, Joost and Hudson, Nichola (2003) 'Begging for It: New Femininities, Social Agency and Moral Discourse in Contemporary Teenage and Men's Magazines', *Feminist Media Studies*, Vol. 3, No. 1.

Chandler, Daniel (1995) 'Cultivation Theory', University of Aberystwyth, www.aber.ac.uk/media/Documents/short/cultiv.html.

Chase-Dunn, Christopher and Grimes, Peter (1995) 'World-Systems Analysis', *Annual Review of Sociology*, Vol. 21.

Chibnall, Steve (1977) *Law-and-Order News: an Analysis of Crime-Reporting in the British Press*. Tavistock.

Chien, Robyn and Wallace, John (2004) 'The Use of Bernstein's Framework in Mapping School Culture and the Resultant Development of the Curriculum', AARE Conference.

Chitty, Clyde (2009) *Education Policy in Britain*. Palgrave Macmillan.

Chomsky, Noam (1989) *Necessary Illusions: Thought Control in Democratic Societies*. South End Press.

Chryssides, George (2000) 'Defining the New Spirituality', CESNUR Conference Paper, August.

Chua, Amy (2011) *Battle Hymn of the Tiger Mother*. Bloomsbury.

Cimino, Richard and Lattin, Don (2002) *Shopping for Faith: American Religion in the New Millennium*. Jossey-Bass.

Claire, Hilary (2004) 'Mapping 'race', class and gender: A summary of the report by David Gillborn and Heidi Mirza', in Hilary Claire (ed.), *GENDER in Education 3–19: A Fresh Approach*. Association of Teachers and Lecturers.

Clarke, Lynda and Berrington, Ann (1999) 'Socio-Demographic Predictors of Divorce. High Divorce Rates: the State of the Evidence on Reasons and Remedies', Lord Chancellor's Department, Research Paper 2/99.

Clemens, Michael, Kenny, Charles and Moss, Todd (2004) 'The Trouble with the MDGs: Confronting Expectations of Aid and Development Success', Working Paper 40, Economics Working Paper Archive.

Cline, Austin (2005) 'What Is Religion?', http://atheism.about.com/od/religiondefinition/a/types.htm.

Cohen, Don and Prusak, Larry (2001) *In Good Company. How Social Capital Makes Organizations Work*. Harvard Business School.

Cohen, Stanley (2002; first published 1972) *Folk Devils and Moral Panics: The Creation of the Mods and the Rockers*. Routledge.

Cohen, Stanley and Taylor, Laurie (1977) 'Talking About Prison Blues', in Colin Bell and Howard Newby (eds.), *Doing Sociological Research*. George Allen and Unwin.

Coleman, Kathryn, Jansson, Krista, Kaiza, Peter and Reed, Emma (2007) 'Homicides, Firearm Offences and Intimate Violence 2005/06 (Supplementary Volume 1 to Crime in England and Wales 2005/06)', Home Office Statistical Bulletin.

Collier, Paul and Dollar, David (2002) 'Aid, Allocation and Poverty Reduction', *European Economic Review*, Vol. 45, No. 1.

Colls, Robert (2005) 'When We Lived In Communities', in Robert Colls and Richard Rodger (eds.), *Cities of Ideas. Governance and Citizenship in Urban Britain 1800–2000*. Ashgate.

Compaine, Benjamin (2001) 'The Myths of Encroaching Global Media Ownership', *Open Democracy*, www.opendemocracy.net/media-globalmediaownership/article_87.jsp.

Compaine, Benjamin (2004): *The Media Monopoly Myth: How New Competition Is Expanding Our Sources of Information and Entertainment*. New Millennium Research Council.

Comte, Auguste (1830) *Course of Positive Philosophy*. Various.

Comte, Auguste (1853) *The Positive Philosophy*. Various.

Congressional Budget Office (1997) *The Role of Foreign Aid in Development*. Congress of the United States.

Connell, Robert (1995) *Masculinities*. University of California Press.

Connell Robert and Messerschmidt, James (2005) 'Hegemonic Masculinity: Rethinking the Concept', *Gender and Society Online*, Vol. 19.

Connell, Robert, Radican, Norm and Martin, Pip (1987) 'The Evolving Man', *New Internationalist*, No. 175.

Contreras, Arnoldo (1987) 'Transnational Corporations in the Forest-Based Sector of Developing Countries', *Unasylva*, Vol. 39, No. 157/158.

Conway, Stephen (1997) 'The Reproduction of Exclusion and Disadvantage: Symbolic Violence and Social Class Inequalities in "Parental Choice" of Secondary Education', *Sociological Research Online*, Vol. 2, No. 4.

Cook, Len (National Statistician) (2003) *Ethnic Group Statistics: A Guide for the Collection and Classification of Ethnicity Data*. Office for National Statistics.

345

Cooley, Charles Horton (1909) *Social Organization: A Study of the Larger Mind.* Charles Scribner.

Cooney, Patrick (1994) *The Only Non-Racist History of the USA.* The Vernon Johns Society.

Cooper, David (1972) *The Death of the Family.* Penguin.

Cornwall, Marie, Albrecht, Stan, Cunningham, Perry and Pitcher, Brian (1986) 'The Dimensions of Religiosity: A Conceptual Model with an Empirical Test', *Review of Religious Research*, No. 27.

Coser, Lewis (1977) *Masters of Sociological Thought: Ideas in Historical and Social Context* (2nd edn). Harcourt Brace.

Coury, Ralph (1997) 'Neo-Modernization Theory and Its Search for Enemies: The Role of the Arabs and Islam', *Left Curve*, No. 21.

Cowan, Douglas (2003) *Health as the Integrating Core of New Age.* Religious Movements Project.

Cowgill, Donald (1974) 'Aging and Modernization: A Revision of the Theory', in Jaber Gubrium (ed.), *Late Life: Communities and Environmental Policy.* Thomas.

Crespi, Isabella (2003) *Gender Socialization Within the Family: a Study on Adolescents and Their Parents in Great Britain.* Centre of Studies and Research on Family.

Crockett, Alasdair and Voas, David (2004) 'Generations of Decline: Religious Change in Twentieth-Century Britain', *Journal for the Scientific Study of Religion*, Vol. 45, No. 4: 567–84.

Crompton, Rosemary (2003) 'Class, Service Careers And Social Polarisation', *Stream 24: (Re) Investigating Class in Service and Consumer Society.* City University.

Crosbie, Vin (2002) *What Is New Media?* Digital Deliverance.

Crozier, Gill, Reay, Diane and Vincent, Carol (eds.) (2004) *Activating Participation: Parents and Teachers Working Towards Partnership.* Trentham Books.

Curran, James (2000) 'Global Media Concentration: Shifting the Argument', *Open Democracy*, www.opendemocracy.net/media-globalmediaownership/article_37.jsp.

Dahl, Stephan (2000) *Communications and Culture Transformation: Cultural Diversity, Globalization and Cultural Convergence.* ECE.

Dahrendorf, Ralf (1979) *Life Chances.* University of Chicago Press.

Dale, Angela (2002) 'Social Exclusion of Pakistani and Bangladeshi Women', *Sociological Research Online*, Vol. 7, No. 3.

Dale, Angela, Dex, Shirley and Lindley Joanne (2004) 'Ethnic Differences in Women's Demographic, Family Characteristics and Economic Activity Profiles, 1992–2002', *Labour Market Trends*, Vol. 112, No. 4: National Statistics Online.

Dallos, Sally, Dallos, Rudi and Foreman, Sally (1997) *Couples, Sex and Power: The Politics of Desire.* Open University Press.

Dalmiya, Nita and Schultink, Werner (2003) 'Combating Hidden Hunger: the Role of International Agencies', *Food and Nutrition Bulletin*, Vol. 24, No. 4.

Daly, Mary (1973) *Beyond God the Father.* Beacon Press.

Daly, Mary (1986; first published 1968) *The Church and the Second Sex.* Beacon Press.

Daschke, Dereck and Ashcraft, W. Michael (eds.) (2005) *New Religious Movements: A Documentary Reader.* NYU Press.

Davie, Grace (1994) *Religion in Britain Since 1945: Believing without Belonging.* Blackwell.

Davie, Grace (2001) 'From Obligation to Consumption: Patterns of Religion in Northern Europe', Seminar Paper on European Secularity in Berlin.

Davie, Grace (2002) 'Praying Alone? Church-going in Britain and the Putnam Thesis: A Reply to Steve Bruce', *Journal of Contemporary Religion*, Vol. 17, No. 3.

Davies, James, Sandstrom, Susanna, Shorrocks, Anthony and Wolff, Edward (2008) 'The World Distribution of Household Wealth', *Working Papers DP2008/03.* World Institute for Development Economic Research.

Davies, Lizzy (2012) 'Poundland Steps Back from Work Experience Scheme', *The Guardian*, 24 February.

Davis, Caroline (2000) 'The Culture of Publishing Website', Oxford Brookes University.

Davis, Gerald and McAdam, Doug (2000) 'Corporations, Classes and Social Movements After Managerialism', *Research in Organizational Behaviour*, Vol. 22.

Davis, Kingsley and Moore, Wilbert (1945) 'Some Principles of Stratification', *American Sociological Review*, Vol. 10 No. 2.

Davis, Nanette (1985) 'Becoming a Prostitute', in Henslin, James, *Down To Earth Sociology.* The Free Press.

Day, Ellen (1998) 'Know Consumers Through Qualitative Research', *Marketing News*, Vol. 32, No. 1: 14.

Dean, Hartley (2006) *Social Policy.* Polity Press.

Deary, Ian, Strand, Steve, Smith, Pauline and Fernandes, Cres (2007) 'Intelligence and Educational Achievement', *Intelligence*, Vol. 35, No. 1: 13–21.

Demack, Sean, Drew, David and Grimsley, Mike (1998) *Myths About Underachievement: Gender, Ethnic and Social Class. Differences in GCSE Results 1988–93.* British Educational Research Association.

Denzin, Norman (1970) *Sociological Methods: A Sourcebook*. Aldine.

Department of Economic and Social Affairs (2012) *Population Facts*. United Nations.

Desforges, Charles (2003) *The Impact of Parental Involvement, Parental Support and Family Education on Pupil Achievement and Adjustment: a Literature Review*. DfES Research Report 433.

DeVault Marjorie (1994) *Feeding the Family: The Social Organization of Caring as Gendered Work*. University of Chicago Press.

Devine, Fiona (1992) *Affluent Workers Revisited: Privatism and the Working Class*. Edinburgh University Press.

Dewey, John (1916) *Democracy and Education*. The Macmillan Company.

Diken, Bülent and Laustsen, Carsten Bagge (2004) *Sea, Sun, Sex…and Biopolitics*, Department of Sociology, Lancaster University, www.lancs.ac.uk/sociology/research/publications/papers/diken-laustsen-sea-sun-sex-biopolitics.pdf.

Ditton, Jason (1977) *Part-Time Crime: An Ethnography of Fiddling and Pilferage*. Macmillan.

Dobbelaere, Karel and Jagodzinski, Wolfgang (1995) 'Religious and Ethical Pluralism', in Jan van Deth and Elinor Scarbrough (eds.), *Beliefs in Government: the Impact of Values*. Oxford University Press.

Dodd, Tricia, Nicholas, Sian, Povey, David and Walker, Alison (2005) *Crime in England and Wales 2003/2004*. Office for National Statistics.

Douglas, James William Bruce (1964) *The Home and the School: A Study of Ability and Attainment in the Primary School*. Panther.

Dove, Adrian (1971) 'The "Chitling Test"', in Lewis Aiken Jr., *Psychological and Educational Testings*. Allyn & Bacon.

Dowd, James (1986) 'The Old Person as Stranger', in Victor Marshall (ed.), *Later Life: The Social Psychology of Aging*. Sage.

Downes, David and Rock, Paul (2003) *Understanding Deviance* (4th edn). Oxford University Press.

Draper, Stephen (2006) 'The Hawthorne, Pygmalion, Placebo and Other Effects of Expectation', University of Glasgow, www.psy.gla.ac.uk/~steve/hawth.html.

Duckworth, Angela and Seligman, Martin (2005) 'Self-Discipline Outdoes IQ in Predicting Academic Performance of Adolescents', *Psychological Science*, Vol. 16, No. 12: American Psychological Society.

Dugan, Máire (2003) 'Understanding Power', in Guy Burgess and Heidi Burgess (eds.), *Beyond Intractability*. Conflict Research Consortium, University of Colorado.

Duncombe, Jean and Marsden, Dennis (1993) 'Love and intimacy: The Gender Division of Emotion and "Emotion Work"', *Sociology*, Vol. 27.

Dunican, Enda (2005) 'A Framework for Evaluating Qualitative Research Methods in Computer Programming Education', in P. Romero, J. Good, E. Acosta Chaparro and S. Bryant (eds.). *Proceedings of the Psychology of Programming Interest Group*, 17, pp. 255–67.

Durkheim, Emile (1893) *The Division of Labour in Society*. Free Press (1964).

Durkheim, Emile (1895) *The Rules of Sociological Method*. Collier-Macmillan (1938: 8th edn).

Durkheim, Emile (1897) *Suicide: A Study in Sociology*. Free Press (1951).

Durkheim, Emile (1912) *Elementary Forms of the Religious Life*. The Free Press (1995).

Durlauf, Steven (2002) *Groups, Social Influences and Inequality: A Memberships Theory Perspective on Poverty Traps*. Santa Fe Institute Working Paper.

Dutton, Brian, O'Sullivan, Tim and Rayne, Phillip (1998) *Studying the Media*. Arnold.

Easterly, William, Levine, Ross and Roodman, David (2003) 'New Data, New Doubts: Revisiting Aid, Policies and Growth', Centre for Global Development, Working Paper 26.

Economist (2013) *The Big Mac Index*. The Economist Newspaper.

Eichler, Margrit (1980) *The Double Standard*. Croom Helm.

Eichner Maxine (2010) *The Supportive State: Families, Government, and America's Political Ideals*. Oxford University Press.

Eisenstadt, Shmuel (1968) *From Generation to Generation*. Free Press.

Eitzen, D. Stanley and Baca-Zinn, Maxine (2003) *Social Problems*. Allyn & Bacon.

Elkins, David (1992) 'Waaah, Why Kids Have a Lot to Cry About', *Psychology Today*, www.psychologytoday.com/articles/200910/waaah-why-kids-have-lot-cry-about.

Elkins, David (1998) *Schooling the Post-Modern Child*. Waldorf Education Research Institute.

Emerson, Robert and Pollner, Melvin (1988) 'The Dynamics of Inclusion and Distance in Fieldwork Relations' in R. M. Emerson (ed.), *Contemporary Field Research: A Collection of Readings*. Waveland Press.

Enroth, Ronald (1993) *Churches That Abuse*. Zondervan.

Epstein, Debbie, Elwood, Jannette, Hey, Valerie and Maw, Janet (eds.) (1998) *Failing Boys? Issues in Gender and Achievement*. Oxford University Press.

The Equal Opportunities Commission (2007) *The Gender Equality Duty and Schools: Guidance for Public Authorities in England*. Equal Opportunities Commission.

Eriksen, Stein Sundstøl (2004) *The State in Africa: Theoretical Perspectives and Empirical Cases*. Norwegian Institute of International Affairs.

Erlich, Paul (1968) *The Population Bomb*. Ballantine Books.

Evans, Sarah (2006) 'Young Women and the Pursuit of Status', UK Postgraduate Conference in Gender Studies e-paper no.16, University of Leeds.

Falkingham, Jane (2000) *A Profile of Poverty in Tajikistan*. Centre for Analysis of Social Exclusion.

Fallon, James (2006) 'Neuroanatomical Background to Understanding the Brain of the Young Psychopath', *Ohio State Journal of Criminal Law*, Vol. 3, No. 34.

Fanfani, Amintore (2003) *Catholicism, Protestantism, and Capitalism*. HIS Press.

Farley, John (1990) *Sociology*. Prentice Hall.

Farson, Richard (1974) *Birthrights*. Macmillan.

Favell, Adrian (2006) 'London as Eurocity: French Free Movers in the Economic Capital of Europe', in Adrian Favell and Michael Smith (eds.), *The Human Face of Global Mobility*. Transaction Publishers.

Ferraro, Vincent (1996) *Dependency Theory: An Introduction*. Mount Holyoke College.

Figueroa, Peter (1991) *Education and the Social Construction of Race*. Routledge.

Finch, Naomi (2003) *Welfare Policy and Employment in the Context of Family Change*. Social Policy Research Unit.

Finlay, Andrew (1999) '"Whatever You Say, Say Nothing": An Ethnographic Encounter in Northern Ireland and Its Sequel', *Sociological Research Online*, Vol. 4, No. 3.

Finn, Dan (1988) 'Education for Jobs: The Route to YTS', *Sociology Review*, Vol. 4, No. 1.

Fionda, Julia (ed.) (2002) *Legal Concepts of Childhood*. Hart Publishing.

Firestone, Shulamith (1970) *The Dialectic of Sex: The Case for Feminist Revolution*. William Morrow.

Firestone, William (1987) 'Meaning in Method: The Rhetoric of Quantitative and Qualitative Research', *Educational Researcher*, Vol. 16, No. 7.

Fisher, Glen (1997) *Mindsets: The Role of Culture and Perception in International Relations* (2nd edn). Intercultural Press.

Fiske, John (1987) *Television Culture: Popular Pleasures and Politics*. Methuen.

Fletcher, Ronald (1973) *The Family and Marriage in Britain*. Penguin.

Flynn, James (1987) 'Massive IQ gains in 14 Nations: What IQ Tests Really Measure', *Psychological Bulletin*, Vol. 101, No. 2: 171–91.

Fortier, Anne-Marie (2003) 'Making Home: Queer Migrations and Motions of Attachment', Department of Sociology, Lancaster University.

Fortune Magazine (2005) *Fortune Global 5000*. Time Inc.

Foster, Liam (2005) 'Gender, Pensions and the Life Course', adapted from paper presented at the Annual British Sociological Conference (2004).

Foster, Peter, Gomm, Roger and Hammersley, Martyn (1996) *Constructing Educational Inequality*. Falmer Press.

Foucault, Michel (1970) *The Order of Things: An Archaeology of the Human Sciences*. Pantheon.

Foucault, Michel (1977) *Discipline and Punish*. Penguin.

Foucault, Michel (1983) *Beyond Structuralism and Hermeneutics* (2nd edn). University of Chicago Press.

Francis, Becky (2000) *Boys, Girls and Achievement: Addressing the Classroom Issues*. Routledge.

Francis, Becky and Skelton, Christine (2005) *Reassessing Gender and Achievement*. Routledge.

Frank, Andre Gunder (1995) *The Abuses and Some Uses of World Systems Theory in Archaeology*. American Anthropological Association.

Fraser, Giles (2005) 'God's Been Mugged', *The Guardian*, 6 June.

Frieden, Betty (1963) *The Feminine Mystique*. Norton and Co.

Friedman, Milton (1962) *Capitalism and Freedom*. University of Chicago Press.

Froyum, Carissa (2005) *The Gendered Body as Resource: Practices of Masculinity & Femininity In an Inner City*. American Sociological Association.

Fuller, Margaret (1984) 'Black Girls in a London Comprehensive School', in Rosematy Deem (ed.), *Schooling for Women's Work*. Routledge & Kegan Paul.

Galbraith, John Kenneth (1967) *The New Industrial State*. Penguin (1983 edn).

Galtung, Johan and Holmboe Ruge, Mari (1973) 'Structuring and Selecting News', in Cohen and Young (eds.), *The Manufacture of News*. Constable.

Gans, Herbert (1971) 'The Uses of Poverty: The Poor Pay All', *Social Policy*, July/August.

Gans, Herbert (1974) *Popular Culture and High Culture*. Basic Books.

Gardner, Howard (1999) *Intelligence Reframed: Multiple intelligences for the 21st Century*. Basic Books.

Gardner, Howard (2003) *Multiple Intelligences After 20 Years*. American Educational Research Association.

Garfinkel, Harold (1967) *Studies in Ethnomethodology.* Prentice Hall.

Garforth, Lisa and Kerr, Anne (2010) 'Let's Get Organised: Practicing and Valuing Scientific Work Inside and Outside the Laboratory', *Sociological Research Online*, Vol. 15, No. 2.

Gauntlett, David (1995) *Moving Experiences: Understanding Television's Influences and Effects.* John Libbey.

Gauntlett, David (1998) '10 Things Wrong with the "Effects Model"', in Dickinson, Harindranath and Linné (eds.), *Approaches to Audiences: A Reader.* Arnold.

Gauntlett, David (2002) *Media, Gender and Identity: An Introduction.* Routledge.

Gazeley, Louise and Dunne, Máiréad (2005) *Addressing Working Class Underachievement.* Multiverse.

Gerbner, George (1994) 'Reclaiming Our Cultural Mythology, *IN CONTEXT*, No. 38.

Gerbner, George, Gross, L., Morgan, M. and Signorielli, N. (1986) 'Living with Television: The Dynamics of the Cultivation Process', in J. Bryant and K. D. Zilmann (eds.), *Perspectives on Media Effects.* Lawrence Erlbaum Associates.

Gershuny, Jonathan, Lader, Deborah and Short, Sandra (2006) *The Time Use Survey.* Office for National Statistics.

Gewirtz, Sharon (1998) 'Can All Schools Be Successful? An Exploration of the Determinants of School "Success"', *Oxford Review of Education*, Vol. 24, No. 4.

Ghose, Ajit (2000) 'Trade and International Labour Mobility', *International Labour Review*, Vol. 139, No. 3, International Labour Organization.

Gianoulis, Tina (2006) 'Disability Issues', in *An Encyclopedia of Gay, Lesbian, Bisexual, Transgender, and Queer Culture*', glbtq, Inc, www.glbtq.com/.

Gibbs, Anita (1997) 'Focus Groups', *Social Research Update*, Vol. 19, University of Surrey.

Giddens, Anthony (1984) *The Constitution of Society: Outline of the Theory of Structuration.* Polity Press.

Giddens, Anthony (1990) *The Consequences of Modernity.* Polity Press.

Giddens, Anthony (2001) *Sociology* (4th edn). Polity Press.

Giddens, Anthony (2006) *Sociology* (5th edn). Polity Press.

Gillborn, David (1992) 'Citizenship, "Race" and the Hidden Curriculum', *International Studies in Sociology of Education*, Vol. 2 No. 1.

Gillborn, David (2002) *Education and Institutional Racism.* Institute of Education.

Gillborn, David and Gipps, Caroline (1996) *Recent Research on the Achievements of Ethnic Minority Pupils.* HMSO Office for Standards in Education.

Gillborn, David and Mirza, Heidi (2000) *Educational Inequality: Mapping 'Race', Class and Gender: A Synthesis of Evidence.* Ofsted.

Gillis, John (1985) *For Better For Worse: British Marriages 1600 to the Present.* Oxford University Press.

Gilroy, Paul (1990) 'One Nation under a Groove: The Cultural Politics of "Race" and Racism in Britain', in Geoff Eley and Ronald Suny (eds.) 1996, *Becoming National: A Reader.* Oxford University Press.

Ginn, Jay and Arber, Sara (2002) 'Degrees of Freedom: Do Graduate Women escape the Motherhood Gap in Pensions?', *Sociological Research Online*, Vol. 7, No. 2.

Giroux, Henry (2004) 'The Passion of the Right: Religious Fundamentalism and the Growing Threat to Democracy', www.dissidentvoice.org.

Glasberg, Davita Silfen (1989) *The Power of Collective Purse Strings: The Effect of Bank Hegemony on Corporations and the State.* University of California Press.

Glaser, Barney and Strauss, Anselm (1967) *The Discovery of Grounded Theory: Strategies for Qualitative Research.* Aldine Publishing.

Glasgow Media Group (1976) *Bad News.* Routledge & Kegan Paul.

Global Campaign for Education (2004) *Learning to Survive: How Education for All Would Save Millions of Young People from HIV/AIDS.* Campaign for Education.

Glock, Charles and Stark, Rodney (1965) *Religion and Society in Tension.* Rand McNally.

Goffman, Erving (1959) *The Presentation of Self in Everyday Life.* Doubleday.

Goffman, Erving (1961) *Asylums: Essays on the Social Situation of Mental Patients and Other Inmates.* Doubleday Anchor.

Goldthorpe, John, Lockwood, David, Bechhofer, Frank and Platt, Jennifer (1968) *The Affluent Worker in the Class Structure.* Cambridge University Press.

Goleman, Daniel (1995) *Emotional Intelligence.* Bantam.

Gomm, Roger (1989) *The Uses of Kinship.* National Extension College.

Goode, Erich and Ben-Yehuda, Nachman (1994) 'Moral Panics: Culture, Politics, and Social Construction', *Annual Review of Sociology*, Vol. 20.

Goode, William (1963) *World Revolution and Family Patterns.* Free Press.

Goodman, Alissa and Gregg, Paul (eds.) (2010) *Poorer Children's Educational Attainment: How Important Are Attitudes and Behaviour?* Joseph Rowntree Foundation.

Gorard, Stephen, Rees, Gareth and Salisbury, Jane (2001) 'Investigating the Patterns of Differential Attainment of Boys and Girls At School', *British Educational Research Journal*, No. 27.

349

Gordon, Dave, Townsend, Peter, Nandy, Shailen, Pantazis Christina and Pemberton, Simon (2003) *Child Poverty in the Developing World*. Policy Press.

Gordon, Michael (1972) *The Nuclear Family in Crisis: The Search for an Alternative*. Harper and Row.

Gough, Kathleen (1959) 'The Nayars and the Definition of Marriage', *Journal of the Royal Anthropological Institute of Great Britain and Ireland*, Vol. 89: 23–34.

Gramsci, Antonio (1971; first published 1930–34) *Selections from the Prison Notebooks*, edited and translated by Quintin Hoare and Geoffrey Nowell Smith. Lawrence & Wishart.

Grant, Diane, Walker, Helen, Butler, Natasha, Meadows, Mark, Hogan Mike and Li, Drew (2006) *Gender Discrimination and Ageist Perceptions*. European Social Fund Objective 3 Research Report, Liverpool John Moores University.

Grassie, William (1997) 'Postmodernism: What One Needs to Know', *Journal of Religion and Science*, March.

Gray, John (2002) 'What Globalization Is Not', *Turkish Time*.

Greenhill, Romilly (2004) *Urban Poor are Neglected in World Bank Project*. ActionAid.

Gribben, Roland (2003) 'Dyson Production Moves To Malaysia', *Daily Telegraph*, 21 August.

Griffiths, Ian and Bowers, Simon (2013) 'Fresh Questions for Amazon Over Pittance It Pays in Tax', *The Guardian*, 16 May.

Grusky, David (1996) 'Theories of Stratification and Inequality', in David Grusky, James Baron and Donald Treiman (eds.), *Social Differentiation and Inequality*. Westview Press.

Hadaway, Kirk and Marler, Penny (1998) *Did You Really Go To Church This Week? Behind the Poll Data*. The Christian Century Foundation.

Hadden, Jeffrey (1987) 'Toward Desacralizing Secularization Theory', *Social Forces*, March.

Hadden, Jeffrey (2001) *Secularization and Modernization*. University of Virginia

Hagan, John, Simpson, John and Gillis, A. R. (1988) 'Feminist Scholarship, Relational and Instrumental Control, and a Power- Control Theory of Gender and Delinquency', *British Journal of Sociology*, Vol. 39, No. 3: 301–36.

Hagell, Ann and Newburn, Tim (1994) *Young Offenders and the Media: Viewing Habits and Preferences*. Policy Studies Institute.

Halbwachs, Maurice (1980) *On Collective Memory*. Harper and Row.

Hall, Granville Stanley (1904) *Adolescence*. Appleton.

Hall, Stuart (1980) 'Encoding/Decoding', in the Centre for Contemporary Cultural Studies (ed.), 1973/1980, *Culture, Media, Language: Working Papers in Cultural Studies*. Hutchinson.

Hall, Stuart (1995) 'The Whites of Their Eyes: Racist Ideologies and the Media', in Gail Dines and Jean Humez (eds.), *Gender, Race and Class in Media*. Sage.

Hall, Stuart, Crichter, Chas, Jefferson, Tony, Clarke, John and Roberts, Brian (1978) *Policing the Crisis: Mugging, the State and Law and Order*. Macmillan.

Hallam, Sue, Ireson, Judy and Hurley, Clare (2001) *Ability Grouping in the Secondary School: Practices and Consequences*. Institute of Education.

Hamid, Saima, Johansson, Eva and Rubenson, Birgitta (2010) 'Security Lies in Obedience - Voices of Young Women of a Slum in Pakistan', *BMC Public Health*, Vol. 10: 164.

Hanafin, Joan and Lynch, Anne (2002) 'Peripheral Voices: Parental Involvement, Social Class, and Educational Disadvantage', *British Journal of Sociology of Education*, Vol. 23, No. 1.

Hanlon, Joseph (2004) *How Northern Donors Promote Corruption: Tales From the New Mozambique*. The Corner House, Briefing No. 33.

Hanlon, Joseph (2005) *Reconstructing Peace*. Open University.

Haraway, Donna (1991) *Simians, Cyborgs and Women: the Reinvention of Nature*. Free Association Books.

Hardill, Irene (2003) *A Tale of Two Nations? Juggling Work and Home in the New Economy*. London School of Economics.

Hardin, Garrett (1968) 'The Tragedy of the Commons', *Science*, Vol. 162, No. 3859: 1243–48.

Hargreaves, David (1967) *Social Relations in a Secondary School*. Routledge.

Harris, Christopher (1983) 'The Family and Industrial Society', *Studies in Sociology*, No. 13.

Harris, Dave (2005a) 'Reading Guide to: Willis, P. (1977) 'Learning to Labour: How Working-Class Kids Get Working-Class Jobs', www.arasite.org/willisltol.html.

Harris, Dave (2005b) 'Reading Guide to Davis and Moore ', www.arasite.org.

Hartley, Ruth (1959) 'Sex-Role pressures and the Socialization of the Male Child', *Psychological Reports*, Vol. 5, No. 3: 457–68.

Harvey, David (1990) *The Condition of Postmodernity: An Enquiry into the Origins of Cultural Change*. Blackwell.

Harvey, Lee and MacDonald, Morag (1993) *Doing Sociology*. Macmillan.

Harwood, Jake (1997) 'Viewing Age: Lifespan Identity and Television Viewing Choices', *Journal of Broadcasting and Electronic Media*, Vol. 41, No. 2.

Haviland, William, Fedorak, Shirley, Crawford, Gary and Lee, Richard (2005) *Cultural Anthropology* (2nd edn). Nelson.

Hawley, Susan (2000) *Exporting Corruption: Privatisation, Multinationals and Bribery.* The Corner House, Briefing No. 19.

Heath, Sue (1997) *Preparation for Life? Vocationalism and the Equal Opportunities Challenge.* Ashgate.

Hecht, Tobias (1998) *At Home in the Street: Street Children of Northeast Brazil.* Cambridge University Press.

Heelas, Paul, Woodhead, Linda, Seel, Benjamin, Szerszynski, Bronislaw and Tusting, Karin (2004) *The Spiritual Revolution: Why Religion Is Giving Way to Spirituality.* Wiley-Blackwell.

Held, David (1989) *Political Theory and the Modern State.* Polity Press.

Henderson, Penny (1981) *A-Level Sociology.* NEC.

Hendrick, Henry (1990) 'Constructions and Reconstructions of British Childhood', in Alison James and Alan Prout (eds.), *Constructing and Reconstructing Childhood: Contemporary Issues in the Sociological Study of Chidhood.* Falmer.

Herndon Peter (2004) *Family Life Among the Ashanti of West Africa.* Yale-New Haven Teachers Institute.

Hervieu-Leger, Daniele (1990) 'Religion and Modernity in the French Context: For a New Approach to Secularization', *Sociological Analysis*, Vol. 51, No. 5.

Hewitt, Benita (2010) 'Church Attendance Has Bottomed Out', *The Guardian*, 11 September.

Hey, Valerie (1997) *The Company She Keeps: An Ethnography of Girls' Friendships.* Open University Press.

Heywood, Colin (2001) *A History of Childhood: Children and Childhood in the West from Medieval to Modern Times.* Polity Press.

Hilgartner, Stephen and Bosk, Charles (1988) 'The Rise and Fall of Social Problems: A Public Arenas Model', *American Journal of Sociology*, Vol. 94, No. 1: 53–78.

Hill, Dave and Cole, Mike (eds.) (2001) *Schooling and Equality: Fact, Concept and Policy.* Kogan Page.

Hillebrand, Randall (2003) *The Shakers / Oneida Community.* CCN.

Hills, John, Brewer, Mike, Jenkins, Stephen, Lister, Ruth, Lupton, Ruth, Machin, Stephen et al. (2010) *An Anatomy of Economic Inequality in the UK.* Centre for Analysis of Social Exclusion, LSE.

Hillyard, Mick and Miller, Vaughne (1998) 'Cuba and the Helms-Burton Act', Library Research Paper 98/114, House of Commons.

Hine, Thomas (2000) *The Rise and Fall of the American Teenager.* HarperCollins.

Hinsliff, Gaby (2002) '"Scared" White Teachers Fail Black Students', *The Observer*, 06/01/02.

Hirst, Paul and Thompson, Graham (1996) *Globalization in Question.* Polity Press.

Hobsbawm, Eric and Ranger, Terence (eds.) (1992) *The Invention of Tradition.* Cambridge University Press.

Hockey, Jenny and James, Allison (1993) *Growing Up and Growing Old: Ageing and Dependency in the Life Course.* Sage.

Hogenraad, Robert (2003) 'The Words That Predict the Outbreak of Wars', *Empirical Studies of the Arts*, Vol. 21, No. 1: 5–20.

Hollows, Joanne (2000) *Feminism, Femininity and Popular Culture.* Manchester University Press.

Home Office (1996) *Home Office Statistical Findings.* Office for National Statistics.

Hong, Evelyne (2000) *Globalisation and the Impact on Health.* Third World Network.

Horwitz, Steven (2005) 'The Functions of the Family in the Great Society', *Cambridge Journal of Economics*, Vol. 29, No. 5.

Howard, Dave (2010) 'Cameron Warns on Child Carer Cuts', *BBC News*, 14/11/10.

Howard, Marilyn and Garnham, Alison (2001) *Poverty: The Facts.* Child Poverty Action Group.

Huesmann, Rowell and Miller, Laurie (1994) 'Long Term Effects of Repeated Exposure to Media Violence in Childhood', in Rowell Huesmann (ed.), *Aggressive Behavior: Current Perspective.* Plenum Press.

Hughes, Kirsty, MacKintosh, Anne Marie, Hastings, Gerard, Wheeler, Colin, Watson, Jonathan and Inglis, James (1997) 'Young People, Alcohol, and Designer Drinks: Quantitative and Qualitative Study', *British Medical Journal*, Vol. 314: 414.

Hughes, Matthew (ed.) (2009) *Social Trends No. 39.* Palgrave Macmillan.

Hughes, Matthew and Church, Jenny (eds.) (2010) *Social Trends: No. 40.* Office for National Statistics / Palgrave Macmillan.

Hughes, Michael, Kroehler, Carolyn and Vander Zanden, James (2002) *Sociology: The Core* (6th edn). McGraw-Hill.

Hume, Lynne (1996) 'A Reappraisal of the Term "Cult" and Consideration of "Danger Markers" in Charismatic Religious Groups', *Colloquium*, Vol. 28, No. 1, University of Queensland.

Humphreys, Cathy and Thiara, Ravi (2002) *Routes to Safety: Protection Issues Facing Abused Women and Children and the Role of Outreach Services.* Women's Aid Federation of England.

351

Humphries, Laud (1970) *Tea Room Trade*. Duckworth.

Hussain, Mustafa (2002) *Mapping Minorities and their Media: The National Context – Denmark*. LSE.

Iannaccone, Laurence (1994) 'Why Strict Churches Are Strong', *American Journal of Sociology*, Vol. 99, No. 5.

Illich, Ivan (1973) *Deschooling Society*. Harmondsworth.

Independent Commission on International Development Issues (the Brandt Report) (1980) *North-South: A Programme for Survival*. Pan Books.

Institute for Fiscal Studies (2006) *Top 0.1% of GB Taxpayers, 2004/5*. IFS.

International Labour Office (2003) 'Working Out of Poverty: Views from Africa', Tenth African Regional Meeting.

International Labour Organization (2005) *Global Employment Trends*. ILO.

Jackson, Phillip (1968) *Life In Classrooms*. Holt, Rinehart and Winston.

Jagger, Gill and Wright, Caroline (1999) 'End of Century, End of Family? Shifting Discourses of Family Crisis', in Gill Jagger and Caroline Wright (eds.), *Changing Family Values*. Routledge.

James, Alison (1998) 'Imaging Children "At Home", "In the Family" and "at School"', in Nigel Rapport and Anthony Dawson (eds.), *Migrants of Identity: Perceptions of Home in a World of Movement*. Berg.

Janis, Irving (1982) *Groupthink: A Psychological Study of Policy Decisions and Fiascos*. Houghton Mifflin.

Jansson, Krista, Coleman, Kathryn, Kaiza, Peter and Reed, Emma (2007) *Homicides, Firearm Offences and Intimate Violence 2005/06* (Supplementary volume 1 to Crime in England and Wales 2005/06). Home Office Statistical Bulletin.

Jarvis, Sarah and Jenkins, Stephen (1997) 'Changing Places: Income Mobility and Poverty Dynamics', Working Paper 96-19, University of Essex.

Jencks, Charles (1996) *What Is Post-Modernism?* Academy Editions.

Jencks, Chris (1989) 'What is the Underclass–and is it Growing?', *Focus*, Vol. 12, No. 1.

Jenks, Chris (1996) *Childhood*. Routledge.

Jensen, Arthur (1973) *Educational Differences*. Taylor & Francis.

Jensen, Jesper Bo, Dahl, Anne-Marie, Baastrup, Kristine, Nielsen, Tine, Nielsen, Martin Riise and Urban, Line (2000) 'Consumers in the Future', *Members Report No. 4*, Copenhagen Institute for Futures Studies.

Jessop, Bob (2003) 'Governance and Meta-governance. On Reflexivity, Requisite Variety, and Requisite Irony', in Henrik Bang (ed.), *Governance as Social and Political Communication*. Manchester University Press.

Johnson, Hans and Tumanka, Simon (2004) *The Maasai*. Maasai Culture Foundation.

Jones, Susan and Myhill, Debra (2004) 'Seeing Things Differently: Teachers Constructions of Underachievement', *Gender and Education*, Vol. 16, No, 4.

Jones, William (2004) *Politics UK* (5th edn). Longman.

Joseph, Martin (1990) *Sociology For Everyone*. Polity Press.

Justino, Patricia (2001) *Social Security and Political Conflict in Developing Countries, with Special Reference to the South Indian State of Kerala*. School of Oriental and African Studies.

Kagan, Mary Dianne (1980) *Being Old in Bojacá: A Study of Aging in a Colombian Peasant Village*. Dissertation: University of California.

Kampmeier, Anke (2004) *Gender and Qualifications*. New Perspectives for Learning - Briefing Paper 45. The European Commission.

Kan, Man-yee (2001) 'Gender Asymmetry in the Division of Domestic Labour', British Household Panel Survey Research Conference, ISER.

Kanazawa, Satoshi and Still, Mary (2000) 'Why Men Commit Crimes (and Why They Desist)', *Sociological Theory*, Vol. 18, No. 3: 434–47.

Kaplan, Jack (1998) 'Does IQ Matter?', Commentary.

Katz, Cindi (2004) *Growing Up Global: Economic Restructuring and Children's Everyday Lives*. University of Minnesota Press.

Katz, Elihu and Lazarsfeld, Paul (1955) *Personal Influence*. The Free Press.

Katz-Gerro, Tally, Raz, Sharon and Yaish, Meir (2007) *Class, Status, and the Intergenerational Transmission of Musical Tastes in Israel*. University of Haifa.

Keddie, Nell (1971) 'Classroom Knowledge', in M. F. D. Young (ed.), *Knowledge and Control*. Collier-Macmillan.

Keesing, Roger (1976) *Cultural Anthropology. a Contemporary Perspective*. Holt Rinehart and Winston.

Kelley, Dean (1972) *Why Conservative Churches Are Growing. Consumer Versus Commitment Based Congregations*. Harper & Row.

Kelly, Aidan (1992) 'An Update on Neopagan Witchcraft in America', in James Lewis and Gordon Melton (eds.), *Perspectives on the New Age*. State University of New York Press.

Kelly, Liz and Regan, Linda (2003) *Rape: Still a Forgotten Issue*. Child and Women Abuse Studies Unit, London Metropolitan University.

Kerr, David, Lines, Anne, Blenkinsop, Sarah and Schagen, Ian(2002) *England's Results from the IEA International*

Citizenship Education Study: What Citizenship and Education Mean to 14-Year-Olds. DfES Publications.

Kessler, Matthew (2000) 'Sponsorship, Self-Perception and Small-business Performance', *American Association of Behavioral and Social Sciences*, Vol. 3.

Khosla, Romi, Hasan, Sikandar, Samuels, Jane and Mulyawan, Budhi (2002) *Removing Unfreedoms: Citizens as Agents of Change*. Department for International Development.

Kiemo, Karatu (2004) *Towards a Socio-Economic and Demographic Theory of Elderly Suicide: A Comparison of 49 Countries At Various Stages of Development*. University of Uppsala.

Kirkwood, Catherine (1993) *Leaving Abusive Partners*. Sage.

Kitchen, Erica (2006) 'The Negotiation of Gender and Athleticism by Women Athletes', unpublished thesis, Georgia State University.

Kitzinger, Jenny (1995) 'Introducing Focus Groups', *British Medical Journal*, Vol. 311: 299–302.

Klapper, Joseph (1960) *The Effects of Mass Communication*. The Free Press.

Klimkiewicz, Beata (1999) *Participation of Ethnic Minorities in the Public Sphere*. Jagiellonian University Press.

Knight, Peter (2001) 'A Briefing on Key Concepts Formative and Summative, Criterion and Norm-Referenced Assessment', *Assessment Series* No. 7, LTSN Generic Centre.

Kosinski, Michal, Stillwell, David and Graepel, Thore (2013) 'Private Traits and Attributes Are Predictable from Digital Records of Human Behavior', *PNAS*, March 2013.

Kraeplin, Camille (2007) 'Teenage Beauty & Fashion Magazines: Selling Sexuality and Consumerism to Our Kids?', Paper presented at the annual meeting of the Association for Education in Journalism and Mass Communication, The Renaissance, Washington, DC.

Kruger, Daniel (2003) 'Integrating quantitative and qualitative methods in community research', *The Community Psychologist*, No. 36, American Psychological Association Society for Community Research and Action.

Kung, Hans (1990) *Theology for the Third Millennium: An Ecumenical View*. Anchor.

Kvale, Steinar (1996) *Interviews: An Introduction to Qualitative Research Interviewing*. Sage Publications.

Lacey, Colin (1970) *Hightown Grammar: The School as a Social System*. Manchester University Press.

Laing, R. D. and Esterson, Aaron (1970) *Sanity, Madness and the Family: Families of Schizophrenics*. Pelican.

Laing, Stuart (2007) 'Walter Greenwood: Working Class Writer', in Ann Gray, Jan Campbell, Mark Erickson, Stuart Hanson and Helen Wood (eds.), *CCCS Selected Working Papers* Volume 2. Routledge.

Lambert, Yves (1999) 'Religion in Modernity as a New Axial Age: Secularization or New Religious Forms?', *Sociology of Religion*, Vol. 60, No. 3.

Lang, Kurt and Lang, Gladys (2009) 'Mass Society, Mass Culture, and Mass Communication: The Meaning of Mass', *International Journal of Communication*, Vol. 3.

Langone, Michael (1993) 'What Is New Age?', *Cult Observer*, Vol. 10, No. 1.

Lanson, Gerald and Stephens, Mitchell (2003) *Writing and Reporting The News*. Oxford University Press.

Lareau, Annette (2003) *Unequal Childhoods: Class, Race, and Family Life*. University of California Press.

Laslett, Peter (1965) *The World We Have Lost*. Methuen.

Laslett, Peter and Wall, Richard (eds.) (1972) *Household and Family in Past Time*. Cambridge University Press.

Lawler, Stephanie (2005) 'Disgusted Subjects: the Making of Middle-Class Identities', *The Sociological Review*, Vol. 53, No. 3: 429–26.

Leach, Edmund (1967) *A Runaway World*. Reith Lectures, BBC.

Lechner, Frank (2001) 'Globalisation Issues', The Globalisation Website, http://sociology.emory.edu/faculty/globalization/.

Lee, Martin and Solomon, Norman (1990) *Unreliable Sources: A Guide to Detecting Bias in News Media*. Kensington Publishing Corp.

Lees, Sue (1993) *Sugar And Spice: Sexuality and Adolescent Girl*. Harmondsworth.

Leinbach, Thomas (2005) *The Concept of Development: Definitions, Theories and Contemporary Perspectives*. University of Kentucky.

Lenski, Gerhard (1994) 'New Light on Old Issues: The Relevance of 'Really Existing Socialist Societies' for Stratification Theory,' in David Grusky (ed.), *Social Stratification: Class, Race, and Gender in Sociological Perspective*. Westview Press.

Lewis, James (ed.) (1998) *The Encyclopedia of Cults, Sects and New Religions*. Prometheus Books.

Lewis, Oscar (1959) *Five Families: Mexican Case Studies in the Culture of Poverty*. Basic Books.

Lewis, Oscar (1961) *The Children of Sanchez: The Autobiography of a Mexican Family*. Random House.

Light, Ivan (2013) 'Cultural Capital', in *New Dictionary of the History of Ideas*, Vol. V.

353

Lindauer, Margaret (2005) 'What to Ask and How to Answer: a Comparative Analysis of Methodologies and Philosophies of Summative Exhibit Evaluation', Virginia Commonwealth University.

Lips, Hilary (1993) *Sex & Gender: An Introduction* (2nd edn). Mayfield Publishing.

Litwak, Eugene (1960) 'Geographic Mobility and Extended Family Cohesion', *American Sociological Review*, Vol. 25: 385–94.

Livingstone, Sonia, Hargrave, Andrea Millwood (2006) 'Harmful to Children?: Drawing Conclusions from Empirical Research on Media Effects', LSE Research Online.

Lizardo, Omar and Collett, Jessica (2005) *Why Biology Is Not (Religious) Destiny: A Second Look at Gender Differences in Religiosity*. University of Arizona.

Lofland, John and Stark, Rodney (1965) 'Becoming a World-saver: A Theory of Conversion to a Deviant Perspective', *American Sociological Review*, Vol. 30, No. 6: 862–75.

Logan, Robert (2010) *Understanding New Media: Extending Marshall McLuhan*. Peter Lang.

Luckmann, Thomas (1967) *The Invisible Religion*. Macmillan.

Luhmann, Niklas (1977) *Funktion der Religion*. Suhrkamp.

Luhmann, Niklas (1997) 'Globalization or World Society?: How to Conceive of Modern Society', *International Review of Sociology*, Vol. 7, No. 1.

Lukes, Stephen (ed.) (1990) *Power*. New York University Press.

Lupton, Ruth (2004) *Do Poor Neighbourhoods Mean Poor Schools?* London School of Economics.

Luscher, Kurt (2000) 'Ambivalence: A Key Concept for the Study of Intergenerational Relations', in Sylvia Trnka *Family Issues Between Gender and Generations*. European Observatory on Family Matters.

Lynes, Russell (1949) 'Highbrow, Lowbrow, Middlebrow', *Harper's Magazine*.

Lyotard, Jean François (1979) *The Postmodern Condition*. Manchester University Press (1984).

Mac an Ghaill, Mairtin (1996) 'What about the Boys? Schooling, Class and Crisis Masculinity', *Sociological Review*, Vol. 44, No. 3.

Macdonald, Allyson and Jónsdóttir, Svanborg (2008) 'Regulation and Innovation: Stimulating Students' Creativity and Thinking Through Innovation Education in Ingunnarskóli', Nordic Symposium on Teacher Education.

Macdonald, Helen (2003) 'Magazine Advertising and Gender', *MediaEd*.

MacDonald, Robert and Marsh, Jane (2005) 'Disconnected Youth? Young People, the "Underclass" and Social Exclusion', in Robert MacDonald, *Disconnected Youth? Growing Up In Poor Britain*. Palgrave Macmillan.

Mack, Joanna and Lansley, Stewart (1984) *Poor Britain*. Allen and Unwin.

Mackenzie, Jeannie (1997) *It's a Man's Job…Class and Gender in School Work-Experience Programmes*. Scottish Council for Research in Education.

MacKeogh, Carol (2001) 'Taking Account of The Macro in the Micro-Politics of Family Viewing: Generational Strategies', *Sociological Research Online*, Vol. 6, No. 1.

Mackintosh, Nicholas (2002) *Genetics and Human Behaviour the Ethical Context*. Nuffield Council on Bioethics.

Madeley, John (2003) 'Transnational Corporations and Developing Countries: Big Business, Poor Peoples', *The Courier ACP-EU*, No. 196.

Magolda, Marcia (2004) *Making Their Own Way*. Stylus.

Maguire, Daniel (2001) *Sacred Choices: The Right to Contraception and Abortion in Ten World Religions*. Fortress Press.

Mahony, Pat (1985) *Schools for the Boys: Co-Education Reassessed*. Hutchinson.

Malena, Carmen (1995) *A Practical Guide to Operational Collaboration between The World Bank and Nongovernmental Organizations*. World Bank Operations Policy Department.

Malinowski, Bronislaw (1926) *Crime and Custom in Savage Society*. Routledge.

Malmgreen, Gail (1987) 'Domestic Discords: Women and the Family in East Cheshire Methodism, 1750–1830', in Jim Obelkevich, Lyndal Roper and Raphael Samuel (eds.), *Disciplines of Faith: Studies in Religion, Patriarchy and Politics*. Routledge & Kegan Paul.

Malone, Karen (2002) 'Hop Scotch Versus Hip Hop: Questions of Youth Culture, and Identity in a Postmodern World', Monash University.

Malthus, Thomas (1798) *An Essay on the Principle of Population*. Joseph Johnson.

Mann, Robin (2009) *Evolving Family Structures, Roles and Relationships in Light of Ethnic and Social Change*. Oxford Institute of Ageing.

Marczewska-Rytko, Maria (2003) 'Religious Communities as Interest Groups', Centre for Studies on New Religions (CESNUR) Conference Paper.

Mariaye, Hyleen (2008) *Mapping Educational Achievement*. Institute of Education.

Marshall, David (1994) 'Canadian Historians, Secularization and the Problem of the Nineteenth Century', *CCHA, Historical Studies*, Vol. 60.

Marshall, Gordon (1982) *In Search of the Spirit of Capitalism*. Columbia University Press.

Marshall, Gordon (1986) 'The Workplace Culture of a Licensed Restaurant', *Theory, Culture & Society*, Vol. 3, No. 1.

Marshall, Gordon (1998) 'Official Statistics', in *A Dictionary of Sociology*. Oxford University Press.

Marshall, Victor (1996) 'The Stage of Theory in Aging and the Social Sciences', in Robert Binstock and Linda George (eds.), *Handbook of Aging and the Social Sciences* (4th edn). Academic Press.

Marsland, David (1995) 'Which Sociology? A Consumer's Guide', *Sociological Notes*, No. 23, Libertarian Alliance.

Martin, Carol and Ruble, Diane (2004) 'Children's Search for Gender Cues: Cognitive Perspectives on Gender Development', *Current Directions in Psychological Science*, Vol. 13, No. 2: 67–70.

Martinson, Brian, Anderson, Melissa and de Vries, Raymond (2005) 'Scientists Behaving Badly', *Nature*, Vol. 435.

Marx, Karl (1844) *Contribution to the Critique of Hegel's 'Philosophy of Right'*. Deutsch-Französische Jahrbücher.

Marx, Karl (1867) *Capital*. Lawrence and Wishart (1977).

Matveev, Alexei (2002) 'The Advantages of Employing Quantitative and Qualitative Methods in Intercultural Research', in Irina Rozina (ed.), *Bulletin of Russian Communication Association 'Theory of Communication and Applied Communication'*, Issue 1.

Maxwell, Simon (1999) *The Meaning and Measurement of Poverty*. Overseas Development Institute.

Mayo, Elton (1933) *The Human Problems of an Industrial Civilization*. Macmillan.

Mazrui, Ali (1996) 'Perspective: The Muse of Modernity and the Quest for. Development', in Philip Altbach and Salah Hassan (eds.), *The Muse of Modernity: Essays on Culture as Development in Africa*. Africa World Press Inc.

McAllister, Fiona and Clarke, Lynda (1998) *A Study of Childlessness in Britain*. Joseph Rowntree Foundation.

McChesney, Robert (2000) *Rich Media, Poor Democracy: Communication Politics in Dubious Times*. New Press.

McCombs, Maxwell and Shaw, Donald (1972) 'The agenda-setting function of mass media', *Public Opinion Quarterly*, Vol. 36.

McCullough, Dick (1988) *Quantitative vs. Qualitative Marketing Research*, Position Paper, Macro Consulting Inc.

McFalls, Joseph (2003) *Population: A Lively Introduction* (4th edn). Population Reference Bureau.

McGuire, Meredith (2002) *Religion – The Social Context* (5th edn). Wadsworth.

McLeod, Hugh (1997) *Religion and the People of Western Europe 1789–1989*. Oxford University Press.

McLiesh, Caralee, Djankov, Simeon, Nenova, Tatiana and Shleifer, Andrei (2001) *Who Owns the Media?* National Bureau of Economic Research.

McMahon, Anthony (1999) *Taking Care of Men: Sexual Politics in the Public Mind*. Cambridge University Press.

McMichael, Philip (2004) *Development and Social Change*. Pine Forge Press.

McQuail, Dennis, Blumler, Jay and Brown, J. R. (1972) 'The Television Audience: a Revised Perspective', in McQuail (ed.), *Sociology of Mass Communication*. Longman.

McRobbie, Angela (1996) 'More!: New Sexualities in Girls' and Women's Magazines', in James Curran, David Morley and Valerie Walkerdine (eds.), *Cultural Studies and Communication*. Arnold.

McRobbie, Angela and Garber, Jenny (1976) 'Girls and Subculture', in Stuart Hall and Tony Jefferson (eds.), *Resistance Through Rituals: Youth Subcultures in Post-War Britain!*. Hutchinson.

Meadows, Donella (1999) 'The World's Top Five Consumers in Many Categories', *The Global Citizen*.

Meadows, Donella, Meadows, Dennis, Randers, Jørgen and Behrens William (1972) *The Limits to Growth*. Signet.

Meadows, Pamela (2003) 'Retirement Ages in the UK: a Review of the Literature', *Employment Relations Research Series* No. 18, Department for Trade and Industry.

Meins, Elizabeth, Fernyhough, Charles, Fradley, Emma, Gupta, Mani Das and Tuckey, Michelle (2002) 'Maternal Mind-Mindedness and Attachment Security as Predictors of Theory of Mind Understanding', *Child Development*, Vol. 73, No. 6.

Melton, Gordon (2001) *New Age Transformed*. Institute for the Study of American Religion.

Merton, Robert (1938) 'Social Structure and Anomie', *American Sociological Review*, Vol. 3, No. 5.

Merton, Robert (1942) 'The Normative Structure of Science', in Norman Storer, *The Sociology of Science*. University of Chicago Press (1973).

355

Merton, Robert K. (1957) *Social Theory and Social Structure*. Free Press of Glencoe.

Meyer, Sir Christopher (2003): Press Complaints Commission Speech to the Newspaper Society.

Milgram, Stanley (1974) *Obedience to Authority*. Harper and Row.

Miller, Alan and Stark, Rodney (2002) 'Gender and Religiousness: Can Socialization Explanations Be Saved?', *American Journal of Sociology*, Vol. 107.

Miller, Timothy (ed.) (1995) *America's Alternative Religions*. State University of New York Press.

Millett, Kate (1969) *Sexual Politics*. Granada Publishing.

Milliband, Ralph (1969) *The State in Capitalist Society*. Weidenfeld & Nicolson.

Mills, C. Wright (1959) *The Sociological Imagination*. Oxford University Press.

Mirza, Heidi (2001) 'Black Supplementary Schools: Spaces of Radical Blackness', in R. Majors (ed.), *Educating Our Black Children: New Directions and Radical Approaches*. Routledge.

Mirza, Heidi, Davidson, Julia, Powney, Janet, Wilson, Valerie, Hall, Stuart (2005) 'Race and Sex: Teachers' Views on Who Gets Ahead in Schools', *European Journal of Teacher Education*, Vol. 28, No. 3.

Misra, Joya (2000) *Cross-Cultural Perspectives on Family, Economy, and the State*. University of Massachusetts.

Mitchell, Barbara (2003) *Life Course Theory*. The Gale Group.

Modood, Tariq, Berthoud, Richard, Lakey, Jane, Nazroo, James, Smith, Patten, Virdee, Satnam and Beishon, Sharon (1997) *Ethnic Minorities in Britain: Diversity and Disadvantage - Fourth National Survey of Ethnic Minorities*. Policy Studies Institute.

Moore, Karen (2001) *Frameworks for Understanding the Intergenerational Transmission of Poverty and Wellbeing in Developing Countries*. Chronic Poverty Research Centre Working Paper 8.

Morgan, David (1997) *Focus Groups as Qualitative Research*. Sage.

Morgan, David. (2001) 'Family Sociology in from the Fringe: The Three "Economies" of Family Life', in Robert Burgess and Anne Murcott (eds.), *Developments in Sociology*. Prentice Hall.

Morley, David (1980) *The Nationwide Audience*. BFI.

Morris, Rachel (2000) 'Gypsies, Travellers and the Media: Press Regulation and Racism in the UK', *Communications Law*, Vol. 5, No. 6.

Morrison, Wayne (2000) 'China's Economic Conditions', Issue Brief for US Congress.

Mulvey, Laura (1975) 'Visual Pleasure and Narrative Cinema', *Screen*, Vol. 16, No. 3.

Murayama, Kou, Pekrun, Reinhard, Lichtenfeld, Stephanie and vom Hofe, Rudolf (2012) 'Predicting Long-Term Growth in Students' Mathematics Achievement: The Unique Contributions of Motivation and Cognitive Strategies', Child Development, Vol. 84, No. 4: 1475–90.

Murdock, George Peter (1945) 'The Common Denominator of Culture', in Ralph Linton (ed.), *The Science of Man in the World Crisis*. Columbia University Press.

Murdock, George Peter (1949) *Social Structure*. Macmillan.

Murdock, Graham and Golding, Peter (1977) 'Capitalism, Communication and Class Relations', in James Curran, Michael Gurevitch and Janet Woollacott (eds.), *Mass Communication and Society*. Arnold.

Murphy, Jim (1990) 'A Most Respectable Prejudice: Inequality in Educational Research and Policy', *British Journal of Sociology*, Vol. 41, No. 1.

Murphy, John (1988) 'Making Sense of Postmodern Sociology', *British Journal of Sociology*, Vol. 9, No. 4.

Murphy, Patricia and Elwood, Jannette (1998) 'Gendered Experiences, Choices and Achievement - Exploring the Links', *International Journal of Inclusive Education*, Vol. 1, No. 2.

Murray, Charles and Herrnstein, Richard (1994) *The Bell Curve*. Free Press.

Murray, Charles and Phillips, Melanie (2001) *The British Underclass 1990–2000*. Institute for the Study of Civil Society.

Murray, Janet (2013) 'The Heat Is on to Pass the 11-Plus', *The Guardian*, 18 March.

Mutran, Elizabeth and Burke, Peter (1979) 'Feeling "Useless", A Common Component of Young and Old Adult Identities', *Research on Aging*, Vol. 1, No. 2.

Nash, Robin (1972) 'Keeping In With Teacher', *New Society*.

National Commission of Inquiry into the Prevention of Child Abuse (1996). The Stationery Office.

National Secular Society (2010) 'Catholic Spin Doctors Try to Mislead Journalists Over Mass Attendances', www.secularism.org.uk.

Navone, John (2002) in James, Barry 'Religion plays a vital role for 6 in 10 Americans', *International Herald Tribune* 21 December.

Neale, Bren (2000) 'Theorising Family, Kinship and Social Change', Workshop Paper 6: Statistics and Theories for Understanding Social Change.

Neelamalar, M. and Chitra, P. (2009) 'New Media and Society: a Study on the Impact of Social Networking Sites on Indian Youth', *Estudos em Comunicacao*, No. 6.

Negroponte, Nicholas (1995) *Being Digital*. Alfred Knopf.

Neitz, Mary Jo (1998) 'Feminist Research and Theory', in William Swatos, Jr (ed.), *Encyclopedia of Religion and Society*. Hartford Institute for Religion Research.

Newbold, Christopher (1995) 'Approaches to Cultural Hegemony within Cultural Studies', in Boyd-Barrett and Newbold (eds.), *Approaches to Media, A Reader*. Arnold.

Newson, Lesley, Postmes, Tom, Lea, Stephen and Webley, Paul (2005) 'Why Are Modern Families Small? Toward an Evolutionary and Cultural Explanation for the Demographic Transition', *Personality and Social Psychology Review*, Vol. 9, No. 4: 360–75.

Nicholas, Sian, Kershaw, Chris and Walker, Alison (eds.) (2007) 'Crime in England and Wales 2006/07', *Home Office Statistical Bulletin*.

Nichols, Paul (1991) *Social Survey Methods*. Blackwell.

Niebuhr, Richard (1929) *The Social Sources of Denominationalism*. Holt.

Norman, Fiona, Turner, Sue, Granados-Johnson, Jackie, Schwarcz, Helen, Green, Helen and Harris, Jill (1988) 'Look, Jane, Look', in Martin Woodhead and Andrea McGrath (eds.), *Family, School and Society*. Oxford University Press.

Norris, Pippa and Inglehart, Ronald (2004) *Sacred and Secular: Religion and Politics Worldwide*. Cambridge University Press.

Oatey, Alison (1999) 'The Strengths and Limitations of Interviews as a Research Technique for Studying Television Viewers', University of Aberystwyth, www.aber.ac.uk/media/Students/aeo9702.html.

O'Beirne, Maria (2004) *Religion in England and Wales: Findings from the 2001 Home Office Citizenship Survey*. Home Office Research, Development and Statistics Directorate.

Oberg, Dianne (1999) 'Teaching the Research Process – for Discovery and Personal Growth', Conference Paper, 65th IFLA Council and General Conference, Thailand.

O'Brien, Mike and Briar, Celia (eds.)(1997) 'Beyond Poverty: Citizenship, Welfare and Well-Being in the 21st Century', Conference Proceedings, Peoples Centre, Auckland.

OECD (1995) *Development Cooperation 1994: Efforts and Policies of the Members of the Development Assistance Committee*. OECD Development Assistance Committee

OECD (2010) *Childlessness*. Organisation for Economic Co-operation and Development, Directorate of Employment, Labour and Social Affairs.

OECD (2013) *Economic, Environmental and Social Statistics*. OECD Factbook.

OfCom (2007) *Emerging Markets: Brazil, Russia, India and China*. OfCom.

OfCom (2008) *Media Literacy Audit: Media Literacy of UK Adults from Ethnic Minority Groups*. OfCom.

OfCom (2012a) *Proportion of Adults Who Regularly Consume Audio*. OfCom.

OfCom (2012b) *The Communications Market*. OfCom.

Offe, Johanna (2001) 'Smart Guys Plan for the Future!: Cultural Concepts of Time and the Prevention of AIDS in Africa', *Afrika Spectrum*, Vol. 36, No. 1: Institute of African Affairs, German Institute of Global and Area Studies.

Office for National Statistics *(2000 - 2010) Social Trends Nos. 30-41*. Office for National Statistics.

Ogundokun, M. and Adeyemo, D. (2010) 'Emotional Intelligence and Academic Achievement: The Moderating Influence of Age, Intrinsic and Extrinsic Motivations', *The African Symposium 127*, Vol. 10, No. 2.

Ohmae, Kenichi (1995) *Evolving Global Economy: Making Sense of the New World Order*. Harvard Business School Press.

O'Neill, Rebecca (2002) *The Fatherless Family*. CIVITAS – The Institute for the Study of Civil Society.

Ossorio, Pilar (2003) 'Interview with Pilar Ossorio', www.pbs.org.

Oswald, Andrew (2002) 'Homes, Sex and the Asymmetry Hypothesis', Warwick University.

Otsuka, Setsuo (2005) 'Cultural Influences on Academic Achievement in Fiji', in Peter Jeffery (ed.), *Proceedings of Australian Association for Research in Education Conference*.

Padfield, Pauline (1997) '"Skivers", "Saddos" and "Swots": Pupils' Perceptions of the Process of Labelling Those "in Trouble" At School', Scottish Educational Research Association Annual Conference paper.

Paechter, Carrie (1999) *Issues in the Study of Curriculum in the Context of Lifelong Learning*. Open University.

Page, Mike (2005) 'Shall We Call It Global Warming, Climate Variability or Human Climate Disruption? The Social Construction of Global Warming', Paper submitted to the Berlin Conference on The Human Dimensions of Global Environmental Change.

Pahl, Jan (2007) 'Power, Ideology and Resources Within Families: A Theoretical Context for Empirical Research on Sleep', *Sociological Research Online*, Vol. 12, Issue 5.

Pahl, Jan and Vogler, Carolyn (1994) 'Money, Power and Inequality Within Marriage', *Sociological Review*, Vol. 42, No. 2: 263–88.

357

Pain, Rachel, Williams, Sarah and Hudson, Barbara (2000) 'Auditing Fear of Crime on North Tyneside: A Qualitative Approach,' in George Mair and Roger Tarling (eds.), *British Criminology Conference: Selected Proceedings*. Volume 3.

Painter, Kate and Farrington, David (1997) 'Street Lighting and Crime: Diffusion of Benefits in Stoke-on-Trent Project', in Kate Painter and Nick Tilley *Crime Prevention Studies*, Volume 10. Lynne Rienner.

Palacios, Robert (2002) 'The Future of Global Ageing', *International Journal of Epidemiology*, Vol. 31, No. 4.

Palmer, Susan (1994) *Moon Sisters, Krishna Mothers, Rajneesh Lovers: Women's Roles in New Religions*. Syracuse University Press.

Parke, Jonathan and Griffiths, Mark (2002). Slot Machine Gamblers: Why Are They So Hard to Study?', *Journal of Gambling Issues*, Issue 6.

Parker, Howard (1974) *A View from the Boys: Sociology of Downtown Adolescents*. David and Charles.

Parsons, Talcott (1937) *The Structure of Social Action*. McGraw-Hill.

Parsons, Talcott (1951) *The Social System*. Routledge & Kegan Paul.

Parsons, Talcott (1959a) 'The School Class as a Social System', *Harvard Educational Review*, Vol. 29.

Parsons, Talcott (1959b) 'The Social Structure of the Family', in Ruth Anshen (ed.), *The Family: Its Functions and Destiny*. Harper.

Parsons, Talcott (1964) *Social Structure and Personality*. Free Press.

Parsons, Talcott and Bales, Robert (1956) *Family, Socialization and Interaction Process*. Routledge & Kegan Paul.

Pascall, Gillian (1997) *Social Policy: A New Feminist Analysis*. Routledge.

Pateman, Trevor (1991) 'Education and Social Theory', in William Outhwaite and Tom Bottomore (eds.), *The Blackwell Dictionary of Twentieth-Century Social Thought*. Blackwell.

Paterson, Lindsay and Iannelli, Cristina (2005) 'Does Education Promote Social Mobility?', CES Briefing No. 35.

Patrinos, Harry and Psacharapoulos, George (2002) *Returns to Investment in Education: A Further Update*. World Bank Policy Research Working Paper 2881.

Payne, Geoff, Williams, Malcolm and Chamberlain, Suzanne (2004) *Methodological Pluralism in British Sociology*. BSA Publications Ltd / SAGE Publications.

Pearce, Frank (with Steve Tombs) (1998) *Toxic Capitalism: Corporate Crime and the Chemical Industry*. Ashgate.

Pearson, Geoffrey (1983) *Hooligan: A History of Respectable Fears*. Macmillan.

Peele, Gillian (2004) *Governing the UK: British Politics in the 21st Century* (4th edn). Blackwell.

Perry, John and Perry, Erna (1973) *The Social Web*. Canfield Press.

Peters, Bettina (2001) *Corporate Media Trends in Europe*. CPBF.

Petersen, Kim (2008) 'Media Marginalization of 'Third ' Parties: Interview with Mickey Z', *Dissident Voice*.

Petre, Jonathon (1999) 'Christianity "in Crisis" as Pews Empty', *Sunday Telegraph*, 28 November.

Petty, Michael (2011) 'The IQ Myth', www.selfgrowth.com.

Pew Research Center (2002) *The Pew Global Attitudes Project*. Pew Research Center.

Pew Research Center (2009) *The Stronger Sex – Spiritually Speaking*. Pew Forum U.S. Religious Landscape Survey.

Pfohl, Stephen (1998) *Deviance and Social Control*. Boston College.

Phillips, Catherine (2003) 'How Do Consumers Express Their Identity Through the Choice of Products that They Buy?', *Working Paper Series 2003.17*, University of Bath.

Phillips, Rick (2004) 'Can Rising Rates of Church Participation Be a Consequence of Secularization?', *Sociology of Religion*, Summer.

Philo, Greg and Berry, Mike (2004) *Bad News from Israel*. Pluto Press.

Philo, Greg, Hewitt, John, Beharrell, Peter and Davis, Howard (1982) *Really Bad News*. Writers and Readers Publishing Cooperative.

Pierotti, Sandra (2003) *The Protestant Ethic and the Spirit of Capitalism: Criticisms of Weber's Thesis*. California State University.

Pilcher, Jane (1995) *Age and Generation in Modern Britain*. Oxford University Press.

Pilcher, Jane (1998) 'Gender Matters? Three Cohorts of Women Talking about Role Reversal', *Sociological Research Online*, Vol. 3, No.1.

Pimple, Kenneth (2002) 'Six domains of research ethics: A heuristic framework for the responsible conduct of research', *Science and Engineering Ethics*, Vol. 8.

Pincs, Maya (1997) 'The Civilizing of Genie', in Loretta Kasper (ed.), *Teaching English Through the Disciplines: Psychology*. Whittier.

Platten, Jon (1999) 'Raising Boys' Achievement', *Curriculum*, Vol. 20, No. 1.

Pleck, Joseph (1985) *Working Wives, Working Husbands*. Sage.

Plumb, Donovan (1995) 'Declining Opportunities: Adult Education, Culture, and Postmodernity', in M. Welton (ed.), *In Defense of the Lifeworld: Critical*

Perspectives on Adult Learning. State University of New York Press.

Podder, Ray and Bergvall, Jonas (2004) 'Global Brand Culture', www.brandchannel.com.

Polaski, Sandra (2004) 'Job Anxiety Is Real – and It's Global', Carnegie Endowment for International Peace.

Polkinghorne, Donald (1991) 'Narrative and Self-concept', *Journal of Narrative and Life History*, Vol. 1, Nos. 2 and 3: Lawrence Erlbaum Associates.

Pollack, Linda (1983) *Forgotten Children: Parent-Child Relations from 1500 to 1900*. Cambridge University Press.

Polsky, Ned (1971) *Hustlers, Beats and Others*. Harmondsworth.

Polyani, Michael (1958) *Personal Knowledge: Towards a Post Critical Philosophy*. Routledge.

Popenoe, David (1988) *Disturbing the Nest: Family Change and Decline in Modern Societies*. Aldine de Gruyer.

Popper, Karl (1934) *The Logic of Scientific Discovery*. Hutchinson (1968).

Postman, Neil (1994) *The Disappearance of Childhood*. Vintage/Random House.

Potter, James (2003) *The 11 Myths of Media Violence*. Sage.

Poulantzas, Nicos (1975) *Classes in Contemporary Capitalism*. New Left Books.

Poulantzas, Nicos (1978; first published 1974)) *Classes in Contemporary Capitalism*. Verso.

Powell, William (2002) 'Finding Closure', *Journal of Contemporary Human Services*, Vol. 83, No. 3.

Power, Anne, Willmott, Helen and Davidson, Rosemary (2011) *Family Futures: Childhood and Poverty in Urban Neighbourhoods*. Policy Press.

Power, Sally, Edwards, Tony, Whitty, Geoff and Wigfall, Valerie (2003) *Education and the Middle Class*. Oxford University Press.

Prandy, Ken and Lambert, Paul (2005) *Long-Run Changes in the Significance of Social Stratification in Britain*. Economic and Science Research Council.

Prelli, Lawrence (1989) 'The Rhetorical Construction of Scientific Ethos', in Herbert Simons (ed.), *Rhetoric in the Human Sciences*. Sage.

Price, Maeve (1979) 'The Divine Light Mission as a Social Organization', *Sociological Review*, Vol. 27.

Provenzo, Eugene (2002) *Teaching, Learning, and Schooling: A 21st Century Perspective*. Allyn & Bacon.

Putnam, Robert (2000) *Bowling Alone*. Simon & Schuster.

Raghavan, Chakravarthi (1996) 'TNCs Control Two-Thirds of World Economy', Third World Network Features.

Rake, Katherine (2009) *Family Trends*. Family and Parenting Institute.

Ramachandran, Vimala (2007) *Status of Basic Education in India: An Overview*. Azim Prenji University.

Ramos, Xavi (2003) 'Domestic Work Time and Gender Differentials in Great Britain 1992–1998', British Household Panel Survey conference, ISER.

Rampton, Ben (2002) 'Continuity and Change in Views of Society in Applied Linguistics', *Working Papers in Urban Language & Literacies* Paper 19.

Rapoport, Rhona and Rapoport, Robert (1969) 'The Dual-Career Family', *Human Relations*, Vol. 22, No. 1.

Ray, John (1987) 'A Participant Observation Study of Social Class Among Environmentalists', *Journal of Social Psychology*, Vol. 127, No. 1:99–100.

Reay, Diane (2000) 'A Useful Extension of Bourdieu's Conceptual Framework? Emotional Capital as a Way of Understanding Mothers' Involvement in Children's Schooling', *Sociological Review*, Vol. 48, No. 4.

Reay, Diane, Crozier, Gill and Vincent, Carol (eds.) (2004) *Activating Participation: Parents and Teachers Working Towards Partnership*. Trentham Books.

Redding, Gordon (1990) *The Spirit of Chinese Capitalism*. De Gruyter.

Regev, Motti (2003) 'Rockization: Diversity Within Similarity in World Popular Music', in Beck, Sznaider and Winter (eds.), *Global America? The Cultural Consequences of Globalization*. Liverpool University Press.

Riach, Kathleen (2007) 'Over the Hill or Under the Table? Organizing Age Identities At Work', Conference Paper, 25th Standing Conference on Organizational Symbolism.

Ricoeur, Paul (1974) *The Conflict of Interpretations*. Northwestern University Press.

Riley, Matilda (1994) 'Introduction: The Mismatch between People and Structures', in Matilda Riley (ed.), *Aging and Structural Lag: Society's Failure to Provide Meaningful Opportunities in Work, Family and Leisure*. John Wiley & Sons.

Ritzer, George (1996) *The McDonaldization of Society*. Pine Forge Press.

Robbins, Lionel (1963) *The Robbins Report*. HMSO.

Robbins, Richard (2005) *Global Problems and the Culture of Capitalism*. Allyn & Bacon.

Robbins, Thomas and Anthony, Dick (1982) 'Cults, Culture, and Community', in Florence Kaslow and Marvin Sussman (eds.), *Cults and the Family, Marriage & Family Review*, Vol. 4, No. 3: Haworth Press.

Robertson, Roland (1992) *Globalization*. Sage.

Robertson, Stephen (2001) *New Attitudes Towards Children*. University of Sydney Press.

359

Robinson, Leland (1987) 'When will revolutionary movements use religion?', in Thomas Robbins and Roland Robinson (eds.), *Church–State Relations: Tensions and Transitions*. Transaction Books.

Robinson, Leland (2001) 'When Will Revolutionary Movements Use Religion?', in Susanne Monahan, William Mirola and Michael Emerson (eds.), *Sociology of Religion: A Reader*. Prentice Hall.

Robinson, Phil (2006) 'Race and Theories of Masculinities', The European Men Profeminist Network.

Rooney, Cleo and Devis, Tim (2009) 'Recent Trends in Deaths from Homicide in England and Wales', *Health Statistics Quarterly* 03: Office for National Statistics.

Rose, Gillian (2007) *Visual Methodologies: An Introduction to the Interpretation of Visual Materials*. Sage.

Roseneil, Sasha (2006) 'On Not Living with a Partner: Unpicking Coupledom and Cohabitation', *Sociological Research Online*, Vol. 11, Issue 3.

Rosenfeld, Michael (2007) *The Age of Independence: Interracial Unions, Same-Sex Unions and the Changing American Family*. Harvard University Press.

Rosenhan, David (1973) 'On Being Sane in Insane Places', *Science*, Vol. 179: 250–58.

Rosenthal, Robert and Jacobson, Lenore (1968) *Pygmalion in the Classroom*. Holt, Rinehart and Winston.

Rosling, Hans (2013) in Provost, Claire 'The Man Who's Making Data Cool', *The Guardian*, 17 May.

Ross, Alistair (2001) 'Ethnic Minority Teachers in the Workforce', Supplementary Report 8, Teacher Supply and Retention Project , Teacher Training Agency.

Ross, Kristina (1995) 'Mass Culture', Mediahistory.com.

Rostow, Walter (1960) *The Stages of Economic Growth: A Non-Communist Manifesto*. Cambridge University Press.

Rowntree, Seebohm and Joseph (1901) *Poverty, A Study of Town Life*. Macmillan.

Rugman, Alan (2001) 'The Myth of Global Strategy', *Insights* (Academy of International Business newsletter), Vol. 1, No. 1.

Rugman, Alan and Hodgetts, Richard (2000) *International Business*. Pearson Education.

Runnymede Trust (1998) *Commission on the Future of Multi-Ethnic Britain*. Profile Books.

Ruspini, Elisabetta (2000) 'Engendering poverty research. How to go beyond the feminization of poverty', *Radical Statistics*, Vol. 75.

Sahgal, Gita and Yuval-Davis, Nira (1992) 'Introduction: Fundamentalism, Multiculturalism and Women in Britain', in Gita Sahgal and Nira Yuval-Davis (eds.), *Refusing Holy Orders: Women and Fundamentalism in Britain*. Virago.

Sappleton, Natalie, Dhar-Bhattacharjee, Sunrita, Takruri-Rizk, Haifa and Bezer, Rae (2006) 'WAVE-ing Goodbye to the Women? Explaining Gender Segregation in the Audio Video Industries', University of Salford.

Sarup, Madan (1993) *An Introductory Guide to Post-Structuralism and Postmodernism*. Harvester Wheatsheaf.

Saunders, Peter (1990) *Social Class and Stratification*. Routledge & Kegan Paul.

Saunders, Peter (1996) *Unequal But Fair? A Study of Class Barriers in Britain*. Civitas.

Saunders, Peter (2002) 'Reflections on the Meritocracy Debate in Britain: a Response to Richard Breen and John Goldthorpe', *British Journal of Sociology*, Vol. 53, No. 4.

Savage, Mike (2007) 'Changing Social Class Identities in Post-War Britain: Perspectives from Mass-Observation', *Sociological Research Online*, Vol. 12, No. 3.

Schauer, Terrie (2004) 'Masculinity Incarcerated: Insurrectionary Speech and Masculinities in Prison Fiction', *Journal for Crime, Conflict and the Media*, Vol. 1, No. 3.

Schecter, Danny (2000) 'Why The Latest News About Online News Ain't So Good', MediaChannel.org.

Scholte, Jan Aart (2000) *Globalization: A Critical Introduction*. Palgrave.

Schor, Juliet (1999) 'The New Politics of Consumption', *Boston Review*.

Schultz, Majken and Hatch, Mary Jo (1996) 'Living with Multiple Paradigms: the Case of Paradigm Interplay in Organizational Culture Studies', *Academy of Management Review*, Vol. 21, No, 2.

Schutz, Alfred (1962) *Collected Papers, Vol. 1: The Problem of Social Reality*. Martinus Nijhoff.

Schwandt, Thomas (2002) *Evaluation Practice Reconsidered*. Peter Lang.

Schwimmer, Brian (2003) *Defining Marriage*. University of Manitoba.

Scott, Jacqueline (2004) 'Gender Inequality in Production and Reproduction: A New Priority Research Network', University of Cambridge, GeNet Working Paper No. 1.

Seaton, Andrew (2004) 'On Creating a Kind of Person: New Paradigms, New Pedagogies…New People?', Conference Paper for 6th Australian Conference on Quality of Life, Melbourne.

Sedgwick, Colin (2004) 'Gimme That Organised Religion', *The Guardian*, 12 June.

Self, Abigail (2008) *Social Trends No. 38*. Office for National Statistics.

Self, Abigail and Zealey, Linda (eds.) (2007) *Social Trends No. 37*. Office for National Statistics.

Settersten, Richard (2006) 'Becoming Adult: Meanings and Markers for Young Americans', in Mary Waters, Patrick Carr, Maria Kefalas and Jennifer Holdaway (eds.), *Coming of Age in America*. University of California Press.

Severin, Werner and Tankard, James (2001) 'Uses of Mass Media', in Werner Severin and James Tankard, (eds.), *Communication Theories* (5th edn). Longman.

Sewell, Tony (2000) *Black Masculinities and Schooling: How Black Boys Survive Modern Schooling*. Trentham Books.

Sewell, Tony (2010) 'Master Class in Victimhood', *Prospect Magazine*.

Shah, Anup (2005) 'Non-governmental Organizations on Development Issues', *Global Issues*, www.globalissues.org/article/25/non-governmental-organizations-on-development-issues.

Shain, Farzana (2003) *The Schooling and Identity of Asian Girls*. Trentham Books.

Shannon, Claude and Weaver, Warren (1949) *The Mathematical Theory of Communication*. University of Illinois Press.

Shapiro, Thomas (2004) *The Hidden Cost of Being African American: How Wealth Perpetuates Inequality*. Oxford University Press.

Shaw, Martin (1997) 'The State of Globalization', *Review of International Political Economy*, Vol. 4, No. 3.

Sheller, Mimi and Urry, John (2004) *Tourism Mobilities: Places to Play, Places in Play*. Routledge.

Shepherd, Jessica and Rogers, Simon (2012) 'Church Schools Shun Poorest Pupils', *The Guardian*, 5 March.

Shirky, Clay (2008) *Here Comes Everybody: The Power of Organizing Without Organizations*. Penguin.

Short, Clare (2001) *Globalisation, Trade and Development in the Least Developed Countries*. Department for International Development.

Silva, Elizabeth and Edwards, Rosalind (2005) *Operationalizing Bourdieu on Capitals: A Discussion on 'The Construction of the Object'*. ESRC Research Methods Programme Working Paper No 7.

Simon, Adam and Xenos, Michael (2000) 'Media Framing and Effective Public Deliberation', Communicating Civic Engagement conference paper.

Singer, Margaret, Lalich, Janja and Lifton, Robert Jay (1996) *Cults in Our Midst*. Jossey Bass.

Sizer, Theodore (1984) *Horace's Compromise: The Dilemma of the American High School*. Houghton Mifflin.

Skelton, Alan (1997) 'Studying Hidden Curricula: Developing a Perspective in the Light of Postmodern Insights', *Curriculum Studies No. 5*.

Sklair, Leslie (1999) 'Competing Conceptions of Globalisation', *Journal of World-Systems Research*, Vol. 5, No. 2.

Skolnick, Arlene (1995) 'Nuclear Families', *The International Encyclopedia of Marriage and Family*, Vol. 1. Macmillan.

Smallwood, Steve and Wilson, Ben (eds.) (2007) *Focus on Families*. Palgrave Macmillan.

Smart, Carol and Stevens, Pippa (2000) *Cohabitation Breakdown*. Family Policy Studies Centre.

Smith, Caroline and Lloyd, Barbara (1978) 'Maternal Behavior and Perceived Sex of Infant: Revisited', *Child Development*, Vol. 49, No. 4: 1263–65.

Smith, Lisa and Haddad, Lawrence (2001) *Overcoming Child Malnutrition in Developing Countries: Past Achievements and Future Choices*. International Food Policy Research Institute.

Smith, Mark and Doyle, Michelle (2002) 'Globalization', *Encyclopedia of Informal Education*.

Smith, Pete (2005) *Sects and the City*. Chartist Publications.

Smithers, Rebecca (2012) 'Cost of Raising a Child Rises to £218,000', *The Guardian*, 26 January.

Socha, Bailey and Eber-Schmid, Barbara (2012) *What is New Media?* New Media Institute.

Solovey, Mark (2001) 'Project Camelot and the 1960s Epistemological Revolution: Rethinking the Politics–Patronage–Social Science Nexus', *Social Studies of Science*, Vol. 31, No. 2.

Sommerlad, Hilary and Sanderson, Peter (1997) 'The Legal Labour Market and the Training Needs of Women Returners in the United Kingdom', *Journal of Vocational Education and Training*, Vol. 49, No. 1.

Sommerville, John (1998) 'Secular Society/Religious Population: Our Tacit Rules for Using the Term "Secularization"', *Journal for the Scientific Study of Religion*, Vol. 37, No. 2.

Song, Miri (1999) *Helping Out: Children's Labor in Ethnic Businesses*. Temple University Press.

Song, Miri (2003) 'Introduction and Ethnic Identities: Choices and Constraints', in Miri Song, *Choosing Ethnic Identity*. Polity Press.

Sorokin, Pitirim (1956) *Fads and Foibles in Modern Sociology and Related Sciences*. Henry Regnery.

Spencer, Liz, Ritchie, Jane, Lewis, Jane and Dillon, Lucy (2003) *Quality in Qualitative Evaluation: A Framework for Assessing Research Evidence*. National Centre for Social Research.

361

Sporer, Zeljka (2000) *Controversies of Globalisation*. University of South Australia.

Spretnak, Charlene (1982) *The Politics of Women's Spirituality*. Anchor.

Sreberny, Annabelle (1999) *Include Me In: Rethinking Ethnicity on Television: Audience and Production Perspectives*. Broadcasting Standards Commission.

Stacey, Judith (1998) *Brave New Families: Stories of Domestic Upheaval in Late Twentieth-Century America*. University of California Press.

Stacey, Judith (2002) 'Fellow Families? Genres of Gay Male Intimacy and Kinship in a Global Metropolis', University of Southern California.

Staiger, Janet (2000) *Perverse Spectators: The Practices of Film Reception*. New York University Press.

Stam, Rob (2000) *Film Theory*. Blackwell.

Stanley, Geoffrey (2004) *Contemporary Social Problems*. Staffordshire University.

Stanworth, Michelle (1984) 'Women and Class Analysis: A Reply to John Goldthorpe', *Sociology*, Vol. 18, No. 2: 159–70.

Stanworth, Michelle (1987) 'Reproductive Technologies and the Deconstruction of Motherhood', in Michelle Stanworth (ed.), *Reproductive Technologies, Gender, Motherhood, and Medicine*. University of Minnesota Press.

Staples, Peter (1998) 'Protestantism, Protestants', in William Swatos, Jr (ed.), *Encyclopedia of Religion and Society*. Hartford Institute for Religion Research.

Stark, Rodney (1999) 'Secularization RIP', *Sociology of Religion*, Vol. 60, No. 3: 249–73.

Stark, Rodney (2002) 'Physiology and Faith: Addressing the 'Universal', Gender Difference in Religious Commitment', *Journal for the Scientific Study of Religion*, Vol. 41, No. 3.

Stark, Rodney and Bainbridge, William (1987) *A Theory of Religion*. Rutgers University Press.

Stark, Rodney and Finke, Roger (2000) *Acts of Faith: Explaining the Human Side of Religion*. University of California Press.

Steggerda, Moniek (1993) 'Religion and Social Positions of Women and Men', *Social Compass*, Vol. 40, No. 1: 65–73.

Stephens, Paul (2009) 'The Nature of Social Pedagogy: an Excursion in Norwegian Territory', *Child & Family Social Work*, Vol. 14, No. 3: 343–51.

Sternberg, Robert (1986) *Intelligence Applied: Understanding and Increasing Your Intellectual Skills*. Harcourt Brace.

Sternberg, Robert (1987) 'Intelligence', in Richard Gregory (ed.), *The Oxford Companion to the Mind*. Oxford University Press.

Stokes, Jane (2003) *How to do Media and Cultural Studies*. Sage.

Strinati, Dominic (1995) *An Introduction to Theories of Popular Culture*. Routledge.

Suematsu, Dyske (2004) 'Postmodern Family', http://dyske.com/paper/723.

Sullivan, Alice (2001) 'Cultural Capital, Cultural Knowledge and Ability', *Sociological Research Online* Vol. 12, No. 6: 1.

Sullivan, Oriel, Coltrane, Scott and Gurion, Ben (2008) 'Men's Changing Contribution to Housework and Child Care: A Discussion Paper on Changing Family Roles', Council on Contemporary Families.

Surowiecki, James (2005) *The Wisdom of Crowds: Why the Many Are Smarter Than the Few*. Abacus.

Swatos, William (1998) 'Religiosity', in William Swatos, Jr. (ed.), *Encyclopedia of Religion and Society*. Hartford Institute for Religion Research.

Sweney, Mark (2011) 'Only 5% of TV Ads Feature Ethnic Minorities', *The Guardian*, 21 April.

Swenson, Don (2004) *A Neo-Functionalist Synthesis of Theories in Family Sociology*. The Edwin Mellen Press.

Tapscott, Don and Williams, Anthony (2008) *Wikinomics*. Portfolio.

Tawney, R. H. (1926) *Religion and the Rise of Capitalism*. Harcourt Brace.

Taylor, Mark (1987) *Erring: A Postmodern Theology*. University of Chicago Press.

Taylor, Mark (2004) 'Generation NeXt Comes to College: Meeting the Postmodern Student', Arkansas State University, www.taylorprograms.com/images/Teaching_Gen_NeXt.pdf.

Taylor, Steve (2011) *Psychology and Sociology: What Can They Learn from Each Other?* ShortCutsTv Ltd.

Thio, Alex (1991) *Sociology: A Brief Introduction*. HarperCollins.

Thirlwall, Anthony (2002) *The Nature of Economic Growth: An Alternative Framework for Understanding the Performance of Nations*. Edward Elgar.

Thomas, Alan (2000) 'Meanings and Views of Development', in Tim Allen and Alan Thomas (eds.), *Poverty and Development into the 21st Century*. Oxford University Press.

Thompson, Grahame (2000) 'Economic Globalization?', in David Held (ed.), *A Globalizing World? Culture, Economics and Politics*. Routledge.

Thompson, John (2004) 'The Emergence of Contemporary North America', Duke University.

Tiffen, Rodney and Gittins, Ross (2004) *How Australia Compares*. Cambridge University Press.

362

Todero, Michael and Smith, Stephen (2005) *Economic Development* (9th edn). Addison-Wesley.

Tombs, Steve and Whyte, Dave (2003) 'Unmasking the Crimes of the Powerful', Conference Paper, Centre for Studies in Crime and Social Justice.

Townsend, Peter (1986) 'Ageism and Social Policy', in Chris Phillipson and Alan Walker (eds.), *Ageing and Social Policy*. Gower.

Townsend, Peter and Abel-Smith, Brian (1965) *The Poor and the Poorest: A New Analysis of the Ministry of Labour's Family Expenditure Surveys of 1953-4 and 1960*. Bell.

Troyna, Barry and Hatcher, Richard (1992) *Racism in Children's Lives: a Study of Mainly-White Primary Schools*. Routledge.

Tschannen, Olivier (1991) 'The Secularization Paradigm', *Journal for the Scientific Study of Religion*, Vol. 30.

Tumin, Melvin (1953) 'Some Principles of Stratification: A Critical Analysis', *American Sociological Review*, Vol. 18, No. 4: 387–94.

Tuomi, Ilkka (2002) *The Blog and the Public Sphere: Future Media and Emerging Research Topics*. European Joint Research Centre.

Turner, Bryan (1983) *Religion and Social Theory*. Humanities Press.

Turner, Bryan (1989) 'Ageing, Status Politics and Sociological Theory', *British Journal of Sociology*, Vol. 40, No. 4.

Turner, Ralph (1960) 'Sponsored and Contest Mobility and the School System', *American Sociological Review*, Vol. 25, No. 6.

UN Data (2012) *Net ODA as Percentage of OECD/DAC Donors GNI*. United Nations.

United Nations (2000) *National Sustainable Development Strategy*. UN Department of Economic and Social Affairs.

United Nations (2004) *World Population to 2300*. Department of Economic and Social Affairs/ Population Division.

United Nations (2008) *World Population Distribution by Region: World Population Prospects, The 2006 Revision*. Department of Economic and Social Affairs/ Population Division.

United Nations (2010a) *World Population Prospects*. UN.

United Nations (2010b) *Average Life Expectancy At Birth*. UN World Population Prospects.

United Nations (2012) *Millennium Development Goals Report*. Department of Economic and Social Affairs.

Urry, John (2001) *The Tourist Gaze*. Sage.

Urry, John (2002) *Global Complexity*. Polity Press.

US Agency for International Development (2005) 'Frequently Asked Questions', www.usaid.gov.

US Census Bureau (2013) *Population Pyramid Summary for India*. US Census Bureau.

US Central Intelligence Unit (2005) *The World Factbook*. CIA.

US Population Reference Bureau (2005) *Improving the Health of the World's Poorest People*. Population Reference Bureau.

US Population Reference Bureau (2006) *Human Population: Fundamentals of Growth: Three Patterns of Population Change*. Population Reference Bureau.

Usher, Robin and Edwards, Richard (1994) *Postmodernism and Education*. Routledge.

van IJzendoorn, Marinus (1997) 'Attachment, Emergent Morality, and Aggression: Toward a Developmental Socioemotional Model of Antisocial Behaviour', *International Journal of Behavioural Development*, Vol. 21, No. 4.

van Leen, Adrian (2004) *The Nature of Cults*. Concerned Christians Growth Ministries.

Venkatesh, Sudhir (2009) *Gang Leader for a Day*. Penguin.

Veseth, Michael (1998) *Selling Globalization: The Myth of the Global Economy*. Lynne Rienner.

Victor, Christina (1987) *Old Age in Modern Society: A Textbook of Social Gerontology*. Croom Helm.

Viner, Jacob (1978) *Religious Thought and Economic Society*. Duke University Press.

Virilio, Paul (2000) 'The Kosovo War Took Place in Orbital Space', *Ctheory*, Vol. 23, No. 3.

Vitali, Stefania, Glttfelder, James and Battiston, Stefano (2011) *The Network of Global Corporate Control*. Swiss Federal Institute of Technology.

von Hayek, Friedrich (1973) *Law, Legislation and Liberty: A New Statement of the Liberal Principles of Justice and Political Economy*, Vol. 1, Rules and Order. Routledge & Kegan Paul.

von Stokar, Thomas and Steinemann, Myriam (2004) *Sustainable Development: Definition and Constitutional Status in Switzerland*. Swiss Agency for Development and Cooperation.

Walker, Barbara (1996) *Understanding Boys' Sexual Health Education and Its Implications for Attitude Change*. Economic and Social Research Council.

Wallerstein, Immanuel (1974) 'The Rise and Future Demise of the World Capitalist System: Concepts for Comparative Analysis', *Comparative Studies in Society and History*, Vol. 16, No. 4.

Wallis, Roy (1977) *The Road to Total Freedom: A Sociological Analysis of Scientology*. Columbia University Press.

363

Wallis, Roy (1984) *The Elementary Forms of New Religious Life*. Routledge & Kegan Paul.

Walter, Tony and Davie, Grace (1998) 'The Religiosity of Women in the Modern West', *British Journal of Sociology*, Vol. 49, Issue No. 4.

Ward, Jenni (2008) 'Researching Drug Sellers: An "Experiential" Account from "The Field"', *Sociological Research Online*, Vol. 13, No. 1: 14.

Warrington, Molly and Younger, Michael (2000) 'The Other Side of the Gender Gap', *Gender and Education*, Vol. 12, No. 4.

Wearing, Stephen and Wearing, Betsy (2000) 'Smoking as a Fashion Accessory in the 90s: Conspicuous Consumption, Identity and Adolescent Women's Leisure Choices', *Leisure Studies*, Vol. 19, No. 1.

Weber, Max (1905) *The Protestant Ethic and the Spirit of Capitalism*. Routledge (2001).

Weber, Max (1922) *Economy and Society* (edited by Max Rheinstein). Simon and Schuster (1954).

Weber, Max (1978; first published 1922) *Economy and Society*, transl. Guenther Roth and Claus Wittich. University of California Press.

Wegge, Simone (1999) 'To Part or Not to Part: Emigration and Inheritance Institutions in Mid-19th Century Germany', *Explorations in Economic History*, Vol. 36, No. 1.

Weinberger, David (2012) *Too Big to Know*. Basic Books.

Wellard, Sarah (2011) *Doing It All? Grandparents, Childcare and Employment: An Analysis of British Social Attitudes Survey Data from 1998 and 2009*. Grandparents Plus.

Wessinger, Catherine (2012) 'Millenarian Movements', in Mark Juergensmeyer and Wade Clark Roof (eds.) *Encyclopedia of Global Religion*. Sage.

Westergaard, John and Resler, Henrietta (1976) *Class in Capitalist Society: A Study of Contemporary Britain*. Heinemann.

Westland, Naomi (2008) 'Meet the Supergrandparents', *The Times*, 26/08/08.

Westwood, Sally (1984) *All Day Every Day: Factory and Family in the Making of Women's Lives*. University of Illinois Press.

Whyte, William (1943) *Street Corner Society*. University of Chicago Press.

Wikstrom, Per-Olof (2010) *The Peterborough Adolescent Development Study*. University of Cambridge.

Wilkin, Anne, Kinder, Kay, White, Richard, Atkinson, Mary and Doherty, Paul (2002) *Towards the Development of Extended Schools*. National Foundation for Educational Research.

Wilkins, Leslie (1964) *Social Deviance*. Tavistock.

Wilkinson, Helen (1994) *No Turning Back: Generations and the Genderquake*. Demos.

Wilkinson, Richard and Pickett, Kate (2009) *The Spirit Level: Why More Equal Societies Almost Always Do Better*. Allen Lane.

Williams, Malcolm (2005) 'Situated Objectivity', *Journal for the Theory of Social Behaviour*, Vol. 35, Issue 1.

Willis, Evan (2011) *The Sociological Quest: An Introduction to the Study of Social Life* (5th edn). Allen and Unwin.

Willis, John (1999) 'Over 50 and Overlooked', *The Guardian*, 5 July.

Willis, Paul (1977) *Learning To Labour: How Working Class Kids Get Working Class Jobs*. Saxon House.

Willmott, Michael (2000) *Complicated Lives: Sophisticated Consumers, Intricate Lifestyles, Simple Solutions*. William Nelson.

Willmott, Peter (1988) 'Urban Kinship Past and Present', *Social Studies Review*, November 1988.

Willmott, Peter and Young, Michael (1973) *The Symmetrical Family*. Routledge.

Willott, Sara and Griffin, Christine (1996) 'Men, Masculinity and the Challenge of Long-Term Unemployment', in Mairtin Mac an Ghaill (ed.), *Understanding Masculinities*. Open University Press.

Wilson, Bryan (1966) *Religion in Secular Society*. Penguin.

Wilson, Bryan (1982) *Religion in Sociological Perspective*. Oxford University Press.

Wilson, Edward (1979) *On Human Nature*. Harvard University Press.

Wilson, Tom (2002) 'Alfred Schutz, Phenomenology and Research Methodology for Information Behaviour Research', Paper delivered to Fourth International Conference on Information Seeking in Context, Lisbon.

Wimberley, Ronald and Swatos, William (1998) 'Civil Religion', in William Swatos (ed.), *Encyclopedia of Religion and Society*. Hartford Institute for Religion Research.

Wimmer, Andreas (2008) 'The Making and Unmaking of Ethnic Boundaries: a Multilevel Process Theory', *American Journal of Sociology*, Vol. 113, No. 4: 970–1022.

Winston, Robert (2005) *Child of Our Time*. The Open University.

Winter, Therese, Lummis, Adair and Stokes, Allison (1994) *Defecting in Place: Women Claiming Responsibility for Their Own Spiritual Lives*. Crossroad.

Wojtczak, Helena (2009) *Women's Status in Mid-19th Century England*. Hastings Press.

Wolff, Edward (2012) 'The Asset Price Meltdown and the Wealth of the Middle Class', NBER Working Paper No. 18559, New York University.

Wolf-Light, Paul (1994) 'The Shadow of Iron John', *Men & Families*, No. 17.

Womack, Sarah (2006) 'Family Size Shrinking Due to Cost of Children', *Daily Telegraph*, 10 April.

Wood, Michael and Welch, Christine (2010) 'Are "Qualitative" and "Quantitative" Useful Terms for Describing Research?', *Methodological Innovations Online*, Vol. 5, No. 1.

Woods, Peter (1976) 'The Myth of Subject Choice', *British Journal of Sociology*, Vol. 27, No. 2.

World Bank (2005) *Urbanisation*. World Bank Publications.

World Bank (2013) *GNI per capita, PPP (current international $)*. World Bank Publications.

World Health Organization (2003) *World Health Report: Shaping the Future*. WHO.

World Health Organization (2012) *World Health Statistics*. Department of Health Statistics and Informatics, WHO.

Wortley, Richard (2011) *Psychological Criminology: An Integrative Approach*. Willan.

Wright, Cecile (1992) *Race Relations in the Primary School*. David Fulton Publishers.

Wright, Eric Ohlin (1985) *Classes*. Verso.

Wrong, Dennis (1961) 'The Oversocialized Conception of Man in Modern Sociology', *American Sociological Review*, Vol. 26, No. 2.

Wuthnow, Robert (1992) *Rediscovering the Sacred: Perspectives on Religion in Contemporary Society*. Eerdmans.

Wuthnow, Robert (2002) 'Religious Involvement and Status-Bridging Social Capital', *Journal for the Scientific Study of Religion*, Vol. 41, No. 4.

Yinger, J. Milton (1957) *Religion, Society and the Individual*. The Macmillan Company.

Yip, Andrew (2002) 'The Persistence of Faith Among Nonheterosexual Christians: Evidence for the Neosecularization Thesis of Religious Transformation', *Journal for the Scientific Study of Religion*, Vol. 41, No. 2.

Young, Jock (1981) 'Beyond the Consensual Paradigm: a Critique of Left Functionalism in Media Theory', in Stan Cohen and Jock Young (eds.), *The Manufacture of News: Deviance, Social. Problems and the Mass Media*. Constable.

Young, M. F. D. (ed.) (1971) *Knowledge and Control*. Collier-Macmillan.

Young, Michael (1999) 'Knowledge, Learning and the Curriculum of the Future', *British Educational Research Journal*, No. 25.

Yule, Valeria (1986) 'Why Are Parents So Tough on Children?', *New Society*, No. 27: 444–46.

Zaretsky, Eli (1976) *Capitalism, the Family, and Personal Life*. Pluto Press.

Zeitlin, Marian, Megawangi, Ratna, Kramer, Ellen, Colletta, Nancy, Babatunde E. D. and Garman, David (1995) *Strengthening the Family: Implications for International Development*. UNU Press Books.

Zhou, Peterson (1997) 'Influences in the Timing of Retirement: Age Norms, Perception of Age and Life Course Events', www.superdirector.com.

Zimbardo, Philip (1997) 'What Messages Are Behind Today's Cults?', *American Psychological Association Monitor*, May.

Zmerli, Sonja (2003) *Applying the Concepts of Bonding and Bridging Social Capital to Empirical Research*. European Consortium for Political Research.

Index

372

Acknowledgements

The author[s] and publishers acknowledge the following sources of copyright material and are grateful for the permissions granted. While every effort has been made, it has not always been possible to identify the sources of all the material used, or to trace all copyright holders. If any omissions are brought to our notice, we will be happy to include the appropriate acknowledgements on reprinting.

Cover; AKIllustration/Shutterstock; p1 Digital Vision / Thinkstock; p3 © Bettmann / CORBIS; p5 © Hill Street Studios / Blend Images/Corbis; p7 AlexRaths / Thinkstock; p10 Ryan McVay / Thinkstock; p13 Wavebreakmedia Ltd / Thinkstock; p15 AFP/ Getty Images; p17 Olga Chernetskaya / Thinkstock; p20 khalus / Thinkstock; p25 Creatas / Thinkstock; p28 Ingram Publishing / Thinkstock; p30 Digital Vision / Thinkstock; p31 Jtasphoto / Thinkstock; p33 © ZUMA Press, Inc / Alamy; p36 Fuse / Thinkstock; p37 David Sacks / Thinkstock; p38 Digital Vision / Thinkstock; p40 Monkey Business Images / Thinkstock; p42l Daniel Kaesler / Thinkstock; p42r James Thew / Thinkstock; p43 KPG_Payless / Shutterstock; p46 © Rick Friedman/Corbis; p48 kieferpix / Thinkstock; p52 © DANISH SIDDIQUI/Reuters/Corbis; p54 Noel Hendrickson / Thinkstock; p56 Asergieiev / Thinkstock; p57 DragonImages / Thinkstock; p58 Michael Mosall II / Thinkstock; p60 Zoonar RF / Thinkstock; p62 © Ted Soqui/Corbis; p64 © Myrleen Pearson / Alamy; p65 Alessandro Franceschi / Thinkstock; p67 © Tetra Images/Corbis; p69 Amit Somvanshi / Thinkstock; p70t Monkey Business Images / Thinkstock; p70b Mopic / Shutterstock; p71 Ammit / Thinkstock; p73 © Dinodia Photos / Alamy; p75tl Creatas / Thinkstock; p75tr Burke / Triolo Productions / Thinkstock; p75bl Oleg Kalina / Thinkstock; p75br snvv / Thinkstock; p78 Pictac / Thinkstock; p82 themorningstudio / Thinkstock; p83 Laurence Gough / Shutterstock; p84 Ozgur Guvenc / Shutterstock; p85 William Perugini / Shutterstock; p86 Dim Dimich / Shutterstock; p87 auremar / Shutterstock; p88 Purestock / Thinkstock; p91 Purestock / Thinkstock; p92t Moofer / Shutterstock; p92b audioscience / Shutterstock; p98 alexemanuel / Thinkstock; p101 Catherine Yeulet / Thinkstock; p103 Photos.com / Thinkstock; p107 pushlama / Thinkstock; p110 Fuse / Thinkstock; p112 Time & Life Pictures/Getty Images; p116 Fuse / Thinkstock; p119 Tim Graham/Getty Images; p120 Andy Dean / Thinkstock; p122 diego_cervo /

Thinkstock; p123 Dejan Ristovski / Thinkstock; p124 Photos.com / Thinkstock; p125 whitetag / Thinkstock; p127 moodboard / Thinkstock; p132 Stockbyte / Thinkstock; p133 Linda Yolanda / Thinkstock; p134 jarenwicklund / Thinkstock; p135 Monkey Business Images / Thinkstock; p136 John Mock / Getty Images; p137 Jack Hollingsworth / Thinkstock; p138 Michael Blann / Thinkstock; p140 Fuse / Thinkstock; p141 © epa european pressphoto agency b.v. / Alamy; p142 Pal Teravagimov / Shutterstock; p143 Adriaen van der Linde / Bridgeman Art Library / Getty Images; p146 triloks / Shutterstock; p148 © John Warburton-Lee Photography / Alamy; p152 Hill Street Studios / Harmik Nazarian / Thinkstock; p153 Neveshkin Nikolay / Shutterstock; p156r Gautier Willaume / Thinkstock; p156l Wavebreakmedia Ltd / Thinkstock; p158 ZouZou / Shutterstock; p160 karelnoppe / Shutterstock; p161 Jack Hollingsworth / Thinkstock; p166 Getty Images; p169 Siri Stafford / Thinkstock; p172 Digital Vision / Thinkstock; p174 olesiabilkei / Thinkstock; p178 Fuse / Thinkstock; p181 archideaphoto / Shutterstock; p184 Fuse / Thinkstock; p188 moodboard / Thinkstock; p191 © Robin Laurance / Alamy; p195 Daniel Villeneuve / Thinkstock; p198 Michal Galazka; p199 Sergey Peterman / Thinkstock; p203 Xavier MARCHANT / Thinkstock; p206 Rikard Stadler / Thinkstock; p210 ruskpp / Shutterstock; p216 Thomas La Mela / Shutterstock; p224 lightpoet / Shutterstock; p235 Laurent davoust / Thinkstock; p240 Bloomberg via Getty Images; p243 Time & Life Pictures/Getty Images; p246 scanrail / Thinkstock; p248 Artur Marciniec / Thinkstock; p251 Digital Vision / Thinkstock; p253 WireImage; p254 Purestock / Thinkstock; p255 Burke / Triolo Productions / Thinkstock; p256 Digital Vision / Thinkstock; p261 S.Borisov / Shutterstock; p262 Lalith_Herath / Thinkstock; p264 Silent47 / Thinkstock; p268 Ridofranz / Thinkstock; p270 Getty Images; p272 s_bukley / Shutterstock; p273 Artem Gorokhov / Thinkstock; p275 pialhovik / Thinkstock;

374

p281 krysgold / Thinkstock; p289 mycola / Thinkstock; p290 Zurijeta / Thinkstock; p292 Ingram Publishing / Thinkstock; p294 Ryan Rodrick Beiler / Shutterstock; p297 AFP/Getty Images; p299 Getty Images; p301 Getty Images; p303 pictore / Thinkstock; p305 robert van beets / Thinkstock; p309 Vladimir Melnik / Thinkstock; p311 Денис Ларкин / Thinkstock; p313 Poike / Thinkstock; p314 Tommy Andersson / Thinkstock; p318l Digital Vision / Thinkstock; p318r Kevin Eaves / Thinkstock; p321 jordan mitchell / Thinkstock; p324 Charles Liu / Thinstock; p326 Digital Vision / Thinkstock.

The publisher would like to thank the following people who assisted in reviewing this book: John Simmonds, Shammim Dulymamode and Dr Jyothi Padmanabhan Nambiar.

375